Colonial Settlers

of

Prince George's

County

Maryland

Compiled by
Elise Greenup Jourdan

HERITAGE BOOKS
2006

HERITAGE BOOKS

AN IMPRINT OF HERITAGE BOOKS, INC.

Books, CDs, and more—Worldwide

For our listing of thousands of titles see our website
at
www.HeritageBooks.com

Published 2006 by
HERITAGE BOOKS, INC.
Publishing Division
65 East Main Street
Westminster, Maryland 21157-5026

International Standard Book Number: 978-1-58549-000-8

FOREWORD

This volume contains the vital statistics and proof of relationships of people who were in Prince George's County during the Colonial period found in the land, court and church records of the county as well as the records of the Prerogative Court of Maryland.

Pertinent information in the land records regarding relationships, such as the name of a spouse or child, was included only when it could not be proven from another source. Therefore, although ownership of some plantations is identified, the researcher requiring more details regarding land, witnesses, etc., should check the land records.

The microfilmed church records copied over 100 years ago by Mrs. L. H. Harrison were checked against the *Prince George's County, Maryland, Index of Church Registers, 1686-1885*; volumes I & II, compiled by Helen W. Brown, and, for the most part, were found to be identical. Omissions were found in both sources and included for the Colonial period.

All of the family relationships found in Prince George's County wills are included, but not the witnesses or non-relatives noted in the wills. Some entries in *Maryland Calendar of Wills* do not show a county name. These were investigated and all wills relating to Prince George's County were included.

Vernon I. Skinner, Jr. has abstracted, and Family Line Publications has published, all of the inventories and most of the administrative accounts of the Prerogative Court of Maryland for the Colonial period. Only those records which Mr. Skinner has specified as belonging to Prince George's County are included in this volume.

Elise Greenup Jourdan
Knoxville, Tennesse
July 1998

SOURCES

AA   *Abstracts of the Administrative Accounts of the Prerogative Court of Maryland, 1718-1750,* Liber I-28, V. L. Skinner, Jr., Family Line Publications, Westminster, MD

ABB   *Abstracts of the Balance Books of the Prerogative Court of Maryland; 1751-1777;* Liber I, Debby Moxey; Liber 2 - 7, V. L. Skinner, Jr., Family Line Publications, Westminster, MD

CCR   *Abstracts of Chancery Court Records of Maryland, 1669-1782,* Debbie Hooper, Family Line Publications, Westminster, MD

GB   Prince George's Co. Guardian Bonds; 1708-1778 (Microfilm CR 34, 68)

I   *Abstracts of the Inventories of the Prerogative Court of Maryland,* Liber 1 - 126, V. L. Skinner, Jr., Family Line Publications, Westminster, MD

I&A   *Abstracts of the Inventories and Accounts of the Prerogative Court of Maryland,* Libers 1 - 39c, V. L. Skinner, Jr., Family Line Publications, Westminster, MD

ICR   *Prince George's County, Maryland, Index of Church Registers, 1686-1885;* volumes I & II; Prince George's County Historical Society, Family Line Publications, Westminster, MD

KGP   King George's Parish; established 1691; one of the 30 original parishes; also known as Piscataway or St. John's at Broad Creek. (Microfilm MSA M 1010 & M 947)

MCW   *Maryland Calendar of Wills,* 1635-1777, first 8 volumes by Jane Baldwin Cotton; last 8 volumes by F. Edward Wright, Family Line Publications, Westminster, Maryland.

PGCR   Prince George's County Court Records
Liber A - Court Records of Prince George's County, Maryland, 1696-1699; The American Historical Association, Washington, D. C. in collaboration with the Hall of Records Commission of the State of Maryland
Liber B 1699-1705 (Old Series) - (Microfilm CR 34, 707)
Liber G 1710-1713 (Old Series) - (Microfilm CR 34, 707)
Liber H thru MM 1715-1754 - (Microfilms CR 34, 708 - 718)
[Only records relating to orphans and guardian bonds used from this source.]

PGLR   *Prince George's County, Maryland, Land Records; 1696-1702* Prince George's County Genealogical Society; *1702-1743* Elise G. Jourdan, Family Line Publications, Westminster, MD

PGP   Prince George's Parish was created from Piscataway Parish in 1726 covering what is now the District of Columbia, Montgomery, Frederick, Washington, Garrett, Allegany and part of Carroll Counties; the parish church was Rock Creek Church which is now in St. Paul's Parish, District of Columbia (Microfilm MSA M 261)

QAP   Queen Anne Parish Register (St. Barnabas Church, Leeland); the original has been reassembled; vestry minutes cover from 1706 to 1773 [not included]; the back of the book contains sections of births and marriages; therefore "QAP b/1" means the first page of the birth section and "QAP m/1" means the 1st page of the marriage section. Some records as early as 1686 were transcribed from the Chapel of Ease in St. Paul's Parish prior to the formation of the first parish church in Queen Anne Parish. (Microfilm MSA SC - M 687)

EXPLANATIONS

This volume presents families in alphabetical order with allied family names cross referenced. Brackets, both ( ) and [ ] are used throughout the text to separate material for readability.

Because of the large volume of material included, several shortcuts and abbreviations were used to save space. Locations are designated as in [England] or [VA] or [CA], etc. Such location after a name means that person was residing in that country, state or county at the time the document was written.

In most cases family names are not repeated in the text after each child's name. In a list of children where a double name is given for the son, the second name is, of course, a middle name; whereas a double name given for a daughter indicates her married name with the exception of a rare, strictly feminine middle name.

ABBREVIATIONS

b.	born	f-i-l	father-in-law	Maryland Counties:	
bapt.	baptized	gd-i-l	granddau.-in-law	AA	Anne Arundel
b-i-l	brother-in-law	g/s	grandson	CA	Calvert
bs-i-l	brothers-in-law	gs/o	grandson of	CH	Charles
ch/o	children of	m-i-l	mother-in-law	PG	Prince George's
chr.	christened	m.	married	SM	St. Mary's
ct.	court	nok	next of kin		
d.	died	s-i-l	son-in-law		
d/o	daughter of	ss-i-l	sons-in-law		
d-i-l	dau.-in-law	s/o	son of		
ds-i-l	daus.-in-law	ss/o	sons of		
ds/o	daughters of	w/o	wife of		

AARON

Aaron, Moses, b. 10 Jun last; bound out; Aug 1747 (PGCR GG.90)

ABBESS

Abbess, Mary; 6 months old 30 Nov instant; bound out; Nov 1727 (PGCR N.613)

ABINGTON

Abington, John; m. 20 Oct 1715 Mary Hutchison; child: Anne, b. 10 Aug 1720 (KGP p. 269)

Abington, John; 8 Dec 1738; 15 Jun 1739; wife Mary; dau. Sarah; sons Bowles, John, Andrew; tracts *Huntington, St. Richard's Mannor, Vineyard, Addition to Vineyard, White Haven, Wetwork, Friendship, Spring Garden, The Addition to Spring Garden* (MCW VIII.31); extx. Mary Scott [w/o Dr. Andrew]; dau. Sarah Needham [w/o John]; 15 Sep 1743 (AA 19.469); 15 Mar 1744 (AA 21.150) 31 Mar 1747 (AA 23.167); 20 Jun 1747 (AA 24.101)

Abington, John; merchant; widow Mary Scott; 20 Aug 1746 (CCR MSA 8.237);

Abington, Bowles & John; Dr. Andrew Scott ordered to deliver to John Needham as guardian; Mar 1746 (PGCR DD.410)

ABLE

Able, William; wife Mary; child: Sarah, b. 9 Sep 1765 Lower Chapel (KGP p. 346)

ABRAHAM

Abrahams, Hugh; planter; 14 Aug 1712; 12 May 1713; wife Easter [Hester]; s-i-l John Beckett; ds-i-l Mary Rodrey, Eliza. Becraft; tract *Essenton* (MCW III.249); 13 Apr 1714 (I&A 35a.114)

ACTON

Acton, Aaron; age 4 years next August; bound out; Mar 1715 (PGCR G.719)

Acton, Henry; wife Ann [widow of Richard Gambra]; tract *Batterzee*; 14 Nov 1726 (PGLR M.99)

Acton, Henry; age ca 47; 1731 (PGLR Q.297)

Acton, Henry; 5 Dec 1742; 14 Jan 1742; wife Hannah; sons Henry, John; daus. Ann Dunning, Barbara MacFerson; granddau. Hannah Dunning (MCW VIII.197)

Acton, Henry; wife Esther; children: Nancy Smallwood, bapt. 19 Jan 1766 Lower Chapel; Mary Eleanor, b. 21 Apr 1772 Lower Chapel (KGP p. 352, 383)

ADAMS

Adams, Benjamin; age ca 53; 1733 (PGLR T.123)

Adams, Francis; age ca 8; 6 Jun 1735 (PGLR T.280)

Adams, James; wife Mary; children: Elizabeth, b. 1 Mar 1742; William, b. 11 Dec 1743; James, b. 2 Nov 1745; John, b. 22 Nov 1747; Mary, b. 4 Jun 1750 (KGP p. 296)

Adams, James; 22 Jul 1750; 17 Dec 1750; wife Mary; sons Williams, James; daus. Elizabeth, Mary; tract *Markett Overton* (MCW X.123-4); extx. Mary; 14 Feb 1750 (I 45.160); exs. John Dunn & Mary his wife; 11 Dec 1751 (ABB 1.20); extx. Mary Dun [w/o John]; 11 Dec 1751 (AA 31.256); 28 Aug 1753 (AA 35.55)

Adams, James; heir William Webster; 8 Jul 1751 (GB 170); heirs William, Elizabeth, John, Mary; 28 Aug 1753 (GB 184)

Adams, Ann; son Benjamin; 1753 (MCW XI.53)

Adams, Thomas; wife Anne; children: Mary Ann, b. 4 Oct 1759; Cassandra, b. 1 Jan 1763 (PGP p. 270, 280)

Adams, Benjamin; wife Sarah; child: Alexander, b. 18 Feb 1760 (PGP p. 281)

Adams [Adames], William; wife Jane; children: Charles; bapt. 23 Mar 1766 Broad Creek; James, bapt. 19 Jun 1768 Lower Chapel; Ann, b. 30 Jan 1771 Lower Chapel; Walter, b. 8 Apr 1775 Lower Chapel; [also children b. aft. 1776] (KGP p. 348, 369, 376, 381)

Adams, James; wife Susanna; children: Elisabeth Dement, b. 30 Dec 1771 Lower Chapel; Josias, b. 29 Oct 1774 Lower Chapel (KGP p. 376, 380)

ADAMSON

Adamson, John; wife Leesey; tract *Ninian Beall Chase*; 15 Jan 1731 (PGLR Q.422)

Adamson, John Baldwin; 22 Mar 1744 (I 30.358); children: Lucy, Basill, Jeremiah; 25 Jun 1746 (AA 22.209); heirs Thomas, Basil, Jeremiah; 25 Mar 1747 (GB 155)

ADDISON

Addison, Thomas, age ca 22, s/o Col. John Addison; m. 21 Apr 1701 Elizabeth Tasker, age 15 years, d/o Thomas Tasker, Esq.; d. 10 Feb 1706;

children: Rebeckah, b. Mon. 3 Jan 1703 @ 11 a.m.; Elinor, b. Weds. 20 Mar 1705 @ 9:30 a.m. (KGP p. 264)

Addison, John; wife Rebecca; tract *Strife*; 1 May 1701 (PGLR A.387)

Addison, John [dec'd]; widow Rebecca; son Thomas; 19 Jul 1707 (PGLR C.187)

Addison, John, Col.; 29 Apr 1709 (I&A 29.193)

Addison, Thomas, Col.; m/2 17 Jun 1709 Elinor Smith, age ca 19 years, 2nd d/o Col. Walter Smith of Patuxent River; children: Ann, b. Mon. 18 Feb 1711/12 @ 2 a.m.; John, b. Weds. 16 Sep 1713 @ 3 a.m.; Thomas, b. Thurs. 26 May 1715 @ 12 o'clock (KGP p. 264)

Addison, Thomas; age ca 45; 6 Oct 1724 (PGLR I.601)

Addison, Thomas, Col.; [s/o John]; wife Ann [d/o William Hutchison]; tract *Strife*; 17 Sep 1725 (PGLR I.681)

Addison, Rebecca; widow; 5 Nov 1724; 20 Aug 1726; son Thomas; dau. Barbara Brooke [w/o Thomas]; grandchildren: Lucy, Baker, Thomas Brooke (MCW V.229); 7 Nov 1726 (I 11.673)

Addison, Thomas; sons Thomas, Henry; 1726 will of James Haddock (MCW VI.188)

Addison, Thomas; 9 Apr 1722; 28 Jun 1727; ch/o wife Eleanor: sons John, Thomas, Henry, Anthony; dau. Ann; also daus. Rebecca Bowles, Eleanor Lowe; tracts *St. Elizabeth, Discontent, Barnobie, Canton, Force, Gleening, Locust Thicket, Maddox Folly, Ginsburough, Berry, Pasture, Prevention, The Union, Barwick upon Tweed, Brother's Joynt Interest, Nonesuch, North Britton, Chichester, Addition, Friendship, Whitehaven, Philip and Jacob, Batchelors Harbour, Swan Harbour, Strife, Addison's Choice* (MCW VI.29); widow Elinor; 10 Aug 1727 (I 12.295); admx. Elinor; 26 Mar 1728 (I 13.48); admx. Eleanor; heirs Ann, John, Thomas, Henry, Anthony; 8 Aug 1728 (AA 9.62); dau. Eleanor Smith [w/o Richard]; 5 Jul 1731 (AA 11.117)

Addison, John; wife Susannah; father Thomas; 8 Nov 1736 (PGLR T.421)

Addison, Thomas, Capt; in General Bragg's Regiment; 1746 (MCW IX.124)

Addison, Henry, Rev. [3rd s/o Thomas Addison, Esq.]; m. 1 Aug 1751 Rachel Dulany [d/o Daniel Dulany, Esq. of Annapolis; relict of Mr. William Knight of Cecil Co.]; children: Anthony, b. 25 Apr 1754 (St. Mark's Day); Daniel Dulany, b. 10 Oct 1756; Elinor, b. 8 Jul 1759 (KGP p. 317, 318)

Addison, Eleanor; 17 Dec 1759; 13 Feb 1761; sons John, Thomas, Henry; grandchildren: Addison & John Murdock, Eleanor Hall, Thomas, John, Henry, Eleanor, Ann & Anthony Addison, Daniel Dulany Addison, Eleanor Addison [d/o Henry], Catherine Sim, Mary & Ann Murdock; sister Elizabeth Ball [or Batt] (MCW XII.47-8); 1 Apr 1761 (I 79.234)

Addison, John, Col.; 8 Jan 1764; 16 Nov 1764; wife Susannah; children: Thomas, John Jr., Eleanor, Ann; tracts *St. Elizabeth, Discontent, Force, Cariton, Locust Thicket, Hart Park, Hunter's Kindness, Maddox Folly* (MCW XIII.66); 14 Jan 1765 (I 87.133)

Addison, Thomas; 4 Nov 1770; 11 Nov 1770; bro. Henry; tract *Brother's Joint Interest* (MCW XIV.169)

Addison, Susanna; widow; 1 May 1773; 9 Aug 1774; children: John, Anne, Thomas [wife Rebecca], Eleanor Boucher, Ann; grandchild Susanna Addison [d/o John]; d-i-l Elizabeth Addison (MCW XV.178-9)

Addison, Thomas; 22 Jun 1771; 14 Mar 1775; wife Rebecca; children: Walter, John, Thomas Grafton [b. aft. 22 Jun 1771], Mary Grafton; unborn child; uncle Thomas Addison; father Thomas; bro. Henry, John; sisters Eleanor Boucher, Ann Addison; tracts *St. Elizabeth, Discontent, Hart Park, Bew Plains, Locust Thickett, Admination, Canton, Force, Oxon Branch, Oxon Hill Manor, Gisborough Manour, Prevention, The Union, Berwick upon Tweed, Brothers Joint Interest, Nonesuch, North Britain, Gleanings* (MCW XVI.71); 16 Mar 1775 (I 123.188)

ADGATE

Adgate, Abel; m. 11 Jun 1734 Joneacre Cook; children: Elias, b. 12 Jan 1735; Henry, b. 13 Sep 173_ (QAP m/6; b/28, 29)

ADINGTON

Adington, Thos.; 11 Aug 1740 (I 25.123); heirs [?England]; 1 Jul 1741 (AA 18.233)

ADKEY

Attkey, Thomas; wife Kathrine; son Thomas, age ca 5; bound out; Nov 1710 (PGCR G.38)

Adkie [Adkey], Thomas; 12 Oct 1751; 23 May 1760; wife Mary; child Mary; cous. Thomas Adkie Sullivan (MCW XI.267); 23 Feb 1760 (I 73.56); 4 Jun 1760; wife Mary rejects will (MCW XII.231); 10 Jun 1761; ex. Thomas Adkey, Jr. (ABB 3.74); heirs Mary Swillivan, Adkey Swillivan; 25 Aug 1762 (GB 222)

Adkey, Joseph; 15 Jun 1762; admn. Joseph Windsor, s-i-l; legatees children of dec'd dau.: Benjamin, Joseph, Jacob, Jonathan, Ignatius & Elisabeth Windsor, Mary Sabray (ABB 3.144)

ADKINSON

Adkinson [Attkinson], John; admx. Anne; 26 Jun 1746 (AA 22.210); admx. Anne; 22 Jun 1747 (AA 23.286); widow Ann; heir [Lord Proprietary]; 23 Jun 1747 (GB 160); 24 Jul 1751 (I 48.233); heirs [England]; 28 Mar 1753 (AA 34.49)

ADNEY

Adney, Moses; extx. Alice Drusy [w/o Charles]; 9 Apr 1735 (AA 13.80)

ALDER

Aulder, George; d. 28 Aug 1737; m. 16 Dec 1729 Elizabeth Keech; children: James, b. 7 Oct 1730; Bowles, b. 5 Jan 1732; Ruth Hawkins, b. 24 Mar 1735; Mary Lindzy, b. 12 Oct 1737 (KGP p. 285, 286)

Alder [Aletor], George; admx. Elisabeth; 13 Apr 1738 (I 23.366); admx. Elisabeth Simson [w/o Joseph Green Simson]; 3 children [names unclear]; 5 Mar 1738 (AA 17.80); heirs James, Bowles & Ruth Hawkins Alder; 29 Nov 1739 (GB 107)

Alder [Allder], James; wife Elizabeth; children: George, b. 23 Dec 1755, rec'd rites of the Church 7 Mar 1756; Elizabeth Ketch, bapt. _ Sep 1763 at Lower Chapel; Ruth Hawkins, bapt. 25 May 1766 Broad Creek; Markas, b. 24 Apr 1768, bapt. 8 May 1768 Lower Chapel; Mary, b. 17 Jan 1775 Lower Chapel (KGP p. 312, 335, 347, 368, 380)

Allder, James; 7 Oct 1775; 29 Nov 1775; wife Elizabeth; children: George, Johannah, James, Latimer, Elizabeth, Keech [or Elizabeth Keech], Ruth Hawkins, Marcus, Mary (MCW XVI.79); extx. Elisabeth; 26 Feb 1776 (I 123.311)

ALDRIDGE

Aldridge, Thomas; wife Mary; children: Mary, b. 21 Dec 1728; William, b. 23 Nov 1730 (PGP p. 249)

Aldridge, John; 30 Nov 1750; 14 Mar 1750; wife Eliner; sons John, Jacob, Thomas; dau. Susannah Prather (MCW X.133)

Aldridge, Eleanor; 6 Jul 1760; 11 Feb 1761; sons John, Jacob, Thomas; granddau. Ann Prather; grandsons William & John Prather (MCW XII.48); 12 Mar 1761 (I 74.153); 28 Sep 1761; exs. John & Jacob Aldridge; children: John, Jacob, Thomas (ABB 3.108); heir Thomas Aldridge; 29 Jun 1763 (GB 227)

ALEXANDER

Alexander, Robert; 31 Apr 1733 (I 19.11)

ALLEN

Allen, Richard [dec'd]; dau. Sarah Webb [w/o Joseph]; Aug 1700 (PGLR C.10)

Allen, Thomas; admx. Martha; 16 May 1755 (I 61.78)

Allin, Reynold; wife Mary; child: Edward, b. 5 Oct 1761 (PGP p. 263)

Allen, John; wife Dorothy; children: William, bapt. May-Jul 1761; John, bapt. 22 Jan 1764 Broad Creek; Thomas, bapt. 14 Jun 1767 Broad Creek (KGP p. 323, 356, 361)

Allen, John [Allin, Allon]; wife Dority; child: Mary, b. 13 Jun 1774 Broad Creek (KGP p. 386)

Allen, Thomas; 3 Nov 1775; 29 Feb 1776; wife Sarah; dau. Mary Allen [living in Devonshire, England]; sister Elizabeth Allen [living in England] (MCW XVI.167-8)

ALLEY

Alley, Samuel; wife Sarah; child: Robert Wilder, b. 28 Oct 1773 Lower Chapel (KGP p. 379)

ALLINGHAM

Allingham, Ann; innholder; 24 Oct 1761; 13 Dec 1761; sons Stephen, Joseph, Benjamin; dau. Elizabeth; uncle Thomas Jopson (?); mother Ann Allcum (MCW XII.97)

ALLISON

Allison, John; wife Ellinor; children: Henry, b. 9 May 1712; Sarah, b. 11 Jun 1710 (QAP b/6)

Allison, John; "father" John Henry; tract *Allison's Adventure*; 26 Mar 1734 (PGLR T.95)

Allison, John; age ca 51; 19 Oct 1730 (CCR-MSA 5.452); age ca 55; 1734 (PGLR T.208)

Allison, Charles; wife Barbery; children: Elizabeth, b. 22 Sep 1743; Thomas, b. 17 Oct 1745; James, b. 30 Mar 1747; Charles, b. 4 Mar 1750/1; Priscillah, b. 1 May 1761 (PGP p. 256, 261)

Allison, John; wife Elisabeth; children: Joshua, b. 11 Feb 1760; Ruth, b. 11 Jan 1762 (PGP p. 262.281)

Allison, Benjamin; wife Mary; child: Burch, b. 24 Feb 1763 (PGP p. 269)

Allison, Richard; wife Sarah; child: Lilley, b. 2 Jul 1763 (PGP p. 268)

ALVIS

Alvis, Martin; [England]; 1 Dec 1731 (I 16.395); 28 Aug 1732 (AA 11.482)

ANDERSON

Anderson, Robert; wife Elizabeth; tract *New Castle* part of *Essington*; 8 Jul 1701 (PGLR A.402)

Anderson, Robert; planter; 1 Aug 1705 (I&A 25.220); 8 Sep 1708 (I&A 29.34)

Anderson, John; wife Elizabeth; father Robert [dec'd]; tracts *Cattaile Meddows, Essington*; 22 Dec 1705 (PGLR C.148a)

Anderson, Robert [dec'd]; widow Elizabeth; son Robert; 30 Apr 1706 (PGLR C.239)

Anderson, John; wife Eliza; children: Jane, b. 2 Aug 1706; Elizabeth, b. 19 Feb 1707/8; Frances, b. 14 Apr 1710; Rachel, b. 5 Feb 1711/2 (QAP b/4, 5)

Anderson, Cuthbert; wife Mary; children: Robert, b. 1 7ber1707; Sarah, 26 Jul 1716; Mary, b. 16 Jul 1719 (QAP b/6, 12, 15)

Anderson, Robert; wife Jane; child: Grissel, b. 7 Feb 1712/3 (QAP b/8)

Anderson, John [dec'd]; widow Elizabeth [now Elizabeth Bradley]; 8 Dec 1719 (CCR CL.551)

Anderson, William; s/o Jane Anderson; age 13 months; bound out; Jun 1720 (PGCR H.1015)

Anderson, Cuthbert; wife Mary; tract *Walker's Pasture*; 11 May 1728 (PGLR M.278)

Anderson, John; age ca 57; 1734 (PGLR T.124)

Anderson, Mary; age ca 2 years 5 Feb last; bound out; Mar 1750 (PGCR LL.134)

ANDREW

Andrew, Patrick; wife Ann Bigger [extx. of John, dec'd, CA]; tract *Backland*; 6 Apr 1722 (PGLR I.274)

Andrew, Patrick; to marry Sarah Perrie [widow], sis. of Marsham Waring; 15 Feb 1730 (PGLR Q.309)

Andrew, Patrick [CA]; wife Sarah Perrie, dec'd [widow of Maj. Samuel]; 9 Nov 1733 (PGLR T.14)

Andrew, Sarah; 3 Aug 1733; 29 Aug 1733; daus. Ann, Sarah and Mary Perrie; mother Sarah Haddock (MCW VII.32)

Andrew, Patrick; 28 May 1735 (I 21.450)

Andrews, John [AA]; wife Allice; tract *Maiden's Dowery*; 21 Aug 1738 (PGLR T.640)

Andrews, George; age ca 2 years Aug last; bound out: Nov 1747 (PGCR GG.281)

ARBUTHNOT

Arbuthnot, Hugh [London]; 29 Jul 1736 (AA 15.62, 216); 5 Aug 1737 (AA 14.281)

ARMSTRONG

Armstrong, William; 11 Nov 1712 (I&A 33b.195); 26 Mar 1713 (I&A 34.139); 3 Apr 1714 (I&A 35a.66)

Armstrong, [?Miles]; m. 8 Oct 1752 Mary Askins (KGP p. 293)

ARNOLD

Arnold, William; wife Ann; child: Elizabeth, b. 12 Mar 1765 (PGP p. 275)

Arnold, Christopher; wife Mary; child: William, b. 4 Aug 1765 Lower Chapel (KGP p. 345)

ARTHUR
Arthur [Arther], Alexander; 14 May 1717; 22 Feb 1717/8; wife Mary (MCW IV.141); 22 Feb 1717 (I&A 39c.93, 128)

ARTIS
Artis, Amealea; children: Sushanna Thorn, bapt. 9 Mar 1766 Broad Creek; Benjamin Thorn, bapt. 15 May 1768 Broad Creek (KGP p. 353, 363)

ARVIN
Arvin, Anthony; wife Ann; child: Mary Elinor, b. 12 Apr 1755 (KGP p. 308)

ASHBY
Ashby, Stephen; daus. Mary; age ca 6; Martha, age 3; bound out; Jul 1696 Ct. (PGCR A.11)

Ashbees, Stephen; runaway; child raised by Ruth Sansbury; Feb 1698/9 Ct. (PGCR A.384)

ASHFORD
Ashford, Michael [VA]; wife Ann; tracts *Haddock's Ash, Seaman's Delight*; 11 Sep 1711 (PGLR F.95)

ASKEY
Askey, Mary; 22 May 1761 (I 75.7)

Askey, Elizabeth; child: Lucey, bapt. 5 Jun 1768 Broad Creek (KGP p. 363)

ATCHISON
Atchison, William; 19 Apr 1698; 8 Sep 1699?; sons William, James; dau. Christian; tract *Bread and Cheese Hall* (MCW II.193); 26 Sep 1698? (I&A 18.53)

Atchison [Actchison], John Ninian; wife Constant; children: Constant (f), b. 1 May 1709; Ann, b. 23 Jun 1712; Elizabeth, b. 25 Apr 1715; John, b. 15 Feb 1721 (ICR; KGP)

Atchison, William [CH]; wife Ann; tract *Bread and Cheese*; 12 Jun 1724 (PGLR I.556)

Atcheson, James; age ca 44; 1731 (PGLR Q.373)

Atchison, John; 22 Feb 1744; 14 Mar 1744; wife Mary Anne; dau. Elizabeth McFall (MCW IX.15); extx. Mary Anne; 16 Apr 1746 (I 32.185); 14 Aug 1746 (AA 22.290)

Atchison, James, Sr.; 2 Dec 1750; 11 Apr 1752; wife Mary; children: James, Jr., tract *Atchison's Pasture* (MCW X.208)

Atcheson, John; wife Ann; child: Henry, bapt. 1 Mar 1752 (KGP p. 294)

ATHEY

Athey [Aithey], George; wife Sarah; tract *St. Johns*; 26 Jun 1697 (PGLR A.60a)

Athey, George, Sr.; son George, Jr.; 15 Sep 1707 (PGLR C.192a)

Athey, John; m. 4 Jun 1711 Margratt Lewis; children: John, b. 10 Nov 1712; Mary, b. 13 Dec 1714; Thomas, b. 14 Feb 1717; George, 8 Aug 1721 (KGP p. 279)

Athey, Sarah, age 57; 17 Feb 1723/4 (PGLR I.542)

Athey, George, age 23; s/o George; 17 Feb 1723 (PGLR I.542)

Athey, John; admx. Margret; 21 Feb 1729 (I 15.511); admx. Magaret Smoot; heirs John, Mary; 25 Mar 1734 (AA 12.215)

Athey, Thomas; wife Elizabeth; children: Sarah, b. 2 Sep 1742; Mary Fenley, b. 30 Oct 1744; Elizabeth, b. 2 Apr 1746 (KGP p. 301)

Athey, Thomas; 25 Sep 1750 bought right of pew in Broad Church per receipt of bro. the sd. Atthey (KGP p. 289)

Athey, George; wife Ann; child: Hezekel MckClash, bapt. 22 Oct 1752 (KGP p. 297)

Athey, Thomas; wife Sarah; child: Mary, bapt. 24 Sep 1752 (KGP p. 297)

Athey, Thomas; wife Judith; child: Mary, bapt. 11 Feb 1753 (KGP p. 298)

Athey, Walter; wife Sarah; child: Benjamin, b. 10 Jun 1753 (KGP p. 300)

Athey, Thomas; wife Edrie; child: Benjamin, b. 16 Jul 1754 (KGP p. 306)

Athey, Joseph; wife Elizabeth; child: Ann, b. 12 Oct 1754 (KGP p. 306)

Athey, Elijah; wife Mary; child: Elijah, b. 2 Jan 1755 (KGP p. 309)

Athey, Thomas; wife Eleanor; children: John Queen, b. 24 May 1756; Elenor, b. _ Sep 1762; Atherelday, bapt. 13 Oct 1765 Broad Creek (KGP p. 313, 328, 349)

Athey, Thomas; 1 Feb 1760; 25 Mar 1761; wife Sarah; daus. Mary, Sarah, Lucy (MCW XII.48); planter; extx. Sarah; 26 Aug 1761 (I 75.1); 24 Sep 1762; extx. Sarah Turner [w/o John]; 3 daus. [unnamed] (ABB 3.163); heirs Mary, Sarah, Lucy; 24 Aug 1763 (GB 229)

Athey, Hesekiah; child: Penalapy, bapt. 6 Dec 1761 (KGP p. 324)

Athey, Owen; wife Lewcey [Lusey]; children: Zeffaniah, bapt. 2 Jun 1765; Neamiah, bapt. 2 Jun 1765 Lower Chapel; Readey, bapt. 17 Apr 1768 Lower Chapel (KGP p. 350-1, 369)

Athey, Esekiah; wife Rebecca; child: Elizabeth, bapt. 23 Jun 1765 Lower Chapel (KGP p. 351)

Athey, Hesekiah; wife Rebecca; child: Olever, bapt. 8 May 1768 Lower Chapel (KGP p. 369)

Athey, Benjamin; wife Edith; child: Hanson Stone, b. 19 Feb 1775 Lower Chapel (KGP p. 381)

Athy, Elijah; wife Mary; 1777 (MCW XVI.187)

AUSTIN

Austin, John; admx. Elisabeth; 13 Dec 1751 (I 48.382)

Austin, Thomas; wife Martha; child: Violinda, b. 19 Jan 1753 (PGP p. 256)

Austin, John [dec'd]; widow Elizabeth; heirs John, James, Michael; 27 Mar 1754 (GB 192)

Auston, Thomas; m. Charity; child: Thomas, b. 30 Sep 1760 (PGP p. 259)

Auston, James; wife Sarah; child: Charity, b. 7 Jun 1761 (PGP p. 261)

Auston, John; m. Charity; child: Zachariah, b. 20 Jan 1763 (PGP p. 269)

AYERS

Ayres, Mark; 17 Nov 1722 (I 8.227); 13 Jul 1723 (AA 5.190)

Ayre, Patrick [dec'd]; widow Dinah; tract *Horse Race*; 29 Apr 1726 (PGLR M.2)

Aires, James; 23 Jul 1726 (I 11.670)

Ayre, James; age 5 on 1 Jun instant; bound out; Jun 1730 (PGCR P.402)

BADEN

Baden, John; age 17 years on 9 Dec past; Margaret, age 15 years on 31 Jul past; choose Thomas Baden as guardian; Aug 1750 (PGCR LL.199)

Baden, Thomas; widow Eleanor; heirs John, Thomas, Martha, Lettice; 25 Jun 1756 (GB 247)

Baden [Beaden], Robert; 9 Jan 1760 (I 70.229); 26 Jun 1761; admx. Ann Baden; children: John, Martha (ABB 3.73); heirs John, Martha; 31 Aug 1764 (GB 239); heir John; 26 Aug 1771 (GB 295)

Baden, Thomas; 3 Nov 1761; 23 Jun 1762; wife Eleanor; children: John, Thomas, Martha, Lettice; bro. John; tracts *The Gores, Hargrove, The Exchange, Sarum's Forrest* (MCW XII.143); extx. Elisabeth [?error]; 2 Sep 1762 (I 79.223); 29 Nov 1764; ex. Eleanor Baden; legatees John, Thomas, Martha & Letitia Baden (ABB 4.94)

BAGBY

Bagby, Samuel; 20 Oct 1710; 16 Oct 1711; bro. John; uncle Whittington (MCW III.212); 6 Oct 1712 (I&A 33b.80)

BAILEY

Baly, Richard; 20 Jan 1696 (I&A 16.38)

Bayley, William; 30 Dec 1701; 20 Jan 1701; wife Jane; son William; dau. Jane (MCW II.232); extx. Jane Beven [w/o Richard]; 11 Jun 1703 (I&A 24.16)

Bally, William; 22 Mar 1724/5; 26 Mar 1725; [no relations] (MCW VI.1)

Balyly, Henry; age 28; 26 Feb 1725/6 (PGLR I.730)

Baily, John; wife Arabella; child: Catherine, b. 13 Feb 1729/30 (PGP p. 249)

Bayly, Henry; m. 21 Jul [?ca 1747] Martha Harrel by Rev. Addison (KGP p. 295)

Baley, John; wife Jemima [Jemimy]; children: Robert, b. 26 Dec 1751; John, b. 24 Apr 1753; Mary, b. 27 Apr 1760; Basil, b. 26 Apr 1762; Martha, b. 25 Jan 1764 (PGP p. 254, 258, 264, 271)

BAKER

Baker, Nicholas; wife Ellinor; children: John, b. 16 Oct 1700; Nicholas, b. 23 9ber 1703, Agness, b. 29 7ber 1706 (QAP b/1, 2)

Baker, Nicholas; admx. Elinor; 28 Jan 1709 (I&A 31.64); admx. widow Elinor Beall [w/o John]; 24 Jul 1710 (I&A 32a.32)

Baker, Nicholas; wife Mary; son John; tract *Bradford's Rest*; 30 Oct 1738 (PGLR Y.10)

Baker, John; age 3 last day of Jan next; bound to James Conn to age 21; Nov 1752 (PGCR MM.331)

Baker, John; wife Judith [Jude]; children: Arabellah, b. 15 Feb 1761; Sussanah, b. 12 Jan 1763 (PGP p. 260. 268)

Baker, Samuel; wife Sarah; child: Priscilla, bapt. 26 May 1765 Upper Chapel (KGP p. 358)

BALDWIN

Baldwin, John; 1 May 1706 (I&A 25.283, 386)

Baldwin, James; m. 20 Jan 1714 Mary Tyler; children: John, b. 1 May 1717; Susanna, b. 31 Jan 1719; James, b. 15 Jan 1720/1 (QAP m/1; b/15, 16)

BALL

Ball Edward [dec'd]; widow Easter; Jul 1696 Ct. (PGCR A.8)

Ball, Michaell [CA]; widow Elizabeth; tract [unnamed]; 16 Oct 1697 (PGLR A.80); bro. Edward; Jun 1698 Ct. (PGCR A.318)

Ball, Edward; wife Priscilla; bro. Michael [dec'd]; tract *Balls Good Luck*; 23 Aug 1698 (PGLR A.127, 132)

Ball, Hillary; wife Ann; tract *Wheeler's Purchase*; 21 Nov 1706 (PGLR C.175a)

Ball, John; wife Ann; children: Henry, b. 4 7ber 1707; John, b. 6 Dec 1713 (QAP b/9)

Ball, Hillery; 10 Dec 1710; wife Ann; sons Richard, John; tracts *Brother's Delight, Sister's Delight* (MCW III.213); admx. Anne Scandlen [w/o Michell]; 24 May 1712 (I&A 33a.211)

Ball, John; wife Elenor; tract *Beall's Purchase*; 17 ___ 1711 (PGLR F.92)

Ball, John; m. 19 Feb 17[?45-7] Sarah Johnston by Rev. Henry Addison (KGP p. 291)

Ball, Thomas; tailor; 24 Apr 1749; [no relations]; tract *Token of Cove* [?*Love*] (MCW X.9)

Ball, Richard; wife Elinor; child: Henry, b. 25 May 1753 (KGP p. 300)

Ball, Hileary; wife Elizabeth; children: Lisey Ann, bapt. 12 Jun 1763 at Broad Creek; Meekey, bapt. 19 May 1765 Broad Creek; Rosemond, b. 15 Feb 1772 Broad Creek (KGP p. 337, 347, 378)

Ball, Humphrey; 24 Aug 1758 (I 64.442)

Ball, John, Jr.; 17 Jul 1767 (I 94.66)

Ball, Richard; wife Sarah; children: Elizabeth, b. 12 Apr 1772 Broad Creek; Levi, b. 22 Feb 1774 Broad Creek; Ratio, b. 28 Feb 1776 Broad Creek (KGP p. 378, 382, 385)

Ball, Richard; 27 Feb 1775; 16 Oct 1775; daus. Ann Barrett, Sarah Simpson; sons Hillery, Henry, Richard; grandchildren: Arnold, Henry, Edward, Richard & Cassey Burgess, Joseph Lowden, Barritt Lissey, Ann & Mary Elnour Barritt, Elenour Walker, Zachariah & Jesse Wheat,

Richard & Daniel Readey, Verlinder & Elizabeth Wheat (MCW XVI.80); 20 Jan 1776 (I 124.6); 2 Oct 1776; legatees Ann Barret, Elisabeth Walker, Sarah Simpson, Hilliary Ball, Richard Ready, Henry Ball, Zachariah Wheat, Jesse Wheat, Virlinda Wheat, Elisabeth Wheat (ABB 7.73)

BALLENGER
Ballenger, Francis; wife Judith; children: Elizabeth, b. 2 Jun 1701; John, b. 19 Apr 1703; William, b. 16 Apr 1705; Richard, b. 25 May 1706 (QAP b/2)
Ballenger, Josiah; wife Mary; tract *Josiah Beginning*; 27 Nov 1739 (PGLR Y.117)

BANISTER
Banister, Thomas [dec'd]; widow Elizabeth; Mar 1701 Ct. (PGCR B.97)

BANKS
Banks, John; wife Elizabeth; children: Jane, b. 21 7ber 1701; Elizabeth, b. 17 Jun 1704; John, b. 23 Oct 1707; Sarah, b. 15 Jun 1710; Samuel, b. 7 Jan 1712/3; Ann, b. 1 7ber 1715 (QAP b/7, 11)
Bankes, John; wife Mary; child: Rebeccah, bapt. 5 Aug 1764 Upper Chapel (KGP p. 341)

BAPTISTYLER
Baptistyler, John; wife Ann; tract *Farmer's Purchase* part of *The Dutchman's Imployment*; 6 May 1706 (PGLR C.162)

BARACLOUGH
Baraclough, Jeremiah; son Joseph; age ca 14; Mar 1700 Ct. (PGCR B.26)

BARBER
Barber, Luke; wife Rebecca; grandfather Luke Barber, Esq.; tract *Warbarton Manor*; 14 May 1728 (PGLR M.306)
Barber, John; wife Lucy; child: Rezin, b. 8 Sep 1765 (PGP p. 277)

BARKER
Barker, Richard; age ca 13; servant; Jun 1698 Ct. (PGCR A.317)
Barker, Samuel; m. 15 Nov 1715 Mary Balard; children: Nathaniel, b. 22 May 1718; Eliza., b. 14 Mar 1720; Samuel, b. 11 Nov 1721; Mary, b. 12 Apr 1724; Sarah, b. 3 Jan 1725; Eallenor, b. 24 Jan 1727 (KGP p. 263)
Barker, Charles; wife Christian; children: Martha, b. 1 Feb 1729; John, b. 15 Oct 1736?; Mary, b. 6 Aug 1736? (KGP p. 282)
Barker, Samuel; 13 Oct 1746; 12 Jun 1747; wife Mary; sons Nathaniel, Samuel, John Ballard, William; daus. Elizabeth Holly, Mary Davis,

Sarah Athey, Elenor, Ann (MCW IX.109-10); extx. Mary; 29 Sep 1747 (I 35.286); 22 Dec 1748 (AA 26.20)

Barker, Nathaniel; wife Susana; child: Susanna, bapt. 10 Dec 1752 (KGP p. 297)

Barker, John; wife Mary; child: Thomas, b. 17 Dec 1761 (KGP p. 324)

Barker, William; wife Ann; child: Nathaniel, bapt. 19 Jan 1766 Lower Chapel (KGP p. 352)

Barker, William; child: Chloe Tiller, b. 8 Dec 1771 Lower Chapel (KGP p. 376)

BARNARD

Barnard [Bernard], Thomas; extx. Sabina Wickam [w/o Nathaniell]; 12 May 1696 (I&A 13b.89); 7 May 1702 (I&A 21.353)

Barnard [Bernard], Luke; age ca 39 on 8 Mar 1724 (PGLR I.624); age ca 44 on 22 Sep 1730 (PGLR Q.159); age ca 55 on 26 Nov 1739 (PGLR Y.107)

Bernard, Luke; wife Jane; tract *St. Andrew's*; 4 Jul 1725 (PGLR I.658)

Barnard, Jeremiah; wife Mary; children: Thomas Mullikin, b. 5 Mar 1760; William Burton, b. 19 Jun 1764 (PGP p. 258, 273)

Barnard, James; wife Dorcas; child: Virlinder, b. 20 May 1764 (PGP p. 272)

Barnard, Luke; wife Susannah; child: Margrette, b. 26 Jan 1765 (PGP p. 273)

BARNES

Barnes, Godfrey; admx. widow Elisabeth Thomas; [with 1716] (I&A 37c.130)

Barnes, Henry; son Benjamin; dau. Anne; [will of friend Thomas Plunket]; 1716 (MCW IV.138)

Barns, Henry; admx. Elisa; 24 Jun 1727 (I 12.277); admx. Elisabeth; heirs Mary, Henry [eldest age ca 5]; 27 Jun 1728 (AA 9.19); widow Elizabeth; heirs Mary, Henry; 27 Nov 1728 (GB 43)

Barns, Henry, age ca 52, 1728 (PGLR M.343); age ca 54, 1730 (PGLR Q.68); age ca 57, 1733 (PGLR T.123)

Barns, Weaver; wife Elizabeth; child: John, b. 18 Feb 1733/4 (QAP b/27)

Barns, Matt., Capt.; age ca 64; 6 Jun 1735 (PGLR T.280)

Barnes, Henry; wife Elizabeth; children: Elizabeth, b. 26 Jan 1752; Ann Stacey, b. 20 Oct 1753; John, b. 2 Nov 1755; Henry, bapt. 7 Mar 1762; Greenberry, b. 14 Jul 1765 Broad Creek, Benedick, b. 24 Jul 1773 Broad Creek (KGP p. 294, 304, 311, 325, 349, 385)

Barnes, Richard; wife Mary; child: Henry, b. 18 Jan 1753 (KGP p. 300)

Barnes, James; _ Feb 1773 (I 112.96)

BARNETT

Barnett, Thomas [CA]; Sabina [widow]; dau. Mary Barnett; son Luke Barnett; regarding estate; 26 Dec 1694 (PGLR A.30)

Barnett, Thomas; extx. Sabina Wickam [w/o Nicholas]; 2 orphans [unnamed]; 4 Apr 1698 (I&A 16.71)

Barnett, Thomas [lately dec'd]; orphan children: Luke Barnett and Mary Miles; bound out; 26 Jul 1703 (PGCR B.251); heirs children: Luke Barnett, Mary Miles; 26 Jul 1708 (GB 1)

Barnet, Luke; wife Jane; children: Thomas, b. 8 Jan 1715; John, b. 23 Aug 1717; Jane, b. 16 May 1719; Mary, b. 8 Apr 1721 (QAP b/7, 17)

Barnett, Elisabeth; age ca 8 years; bound out; Nov 1720 (PGCR K.12)

BARRACLIFT

Barraclift, John; age ca 8 months; s/o Mary; bound out; Mar 1721 (PGCR K.82)

BARRETT

Bairat, John; age ca 22; servant; Jun 1699 Ct. (PGCR A.430)

Barratt, William; wife Mary; child: Elizabeth, b. 6 10ber 1704 (QAP b/2)

Barrat, John, Jr.; child: Honor, b. 14 Aug 1712 (QAP b/8)

Barratt, John; wife Ann; tract *Stony Purchase*; 14 Nov 1713 (PGLR F.316)

Barrett, John, Jr.; planter; 10 Feb 1717 (I&A 39c.91); 7 May 1717 (I&A 38a.36)

Barrett, Edward; son John; 24 Apr 1720 (PGLR I.12)

Barrett, John, Jr. [dec'd]; widow Christian Tannehill [w/o Ninian]; son Alexander; tract *Gleaning*; 22 Aug 1719 (PGLR F.242/828); son Alexander; 24 Apr 1720 (PGLR I.12)

Barrett [Barret], John; 3 May 1722; 6 Jun 1722; wife Anne (MCW V.106)

Barrett, Anne; 5 May 1722; 6 Jun 1722; no relations named (MCW V.106); 13 Jun 1722 (I 8.223); 24 Jun 1724 (AA 6.8)

Barret, Alexander; wife Elizabeth; tract *The Gleaning*; 23 Jul 1743 (PGLR Y.714)

Barret, Robert; wife Sarah; children: Henry, b. 8 Apr 1762; Elizabeth, b. 30 Aug 1764; bapt. 30 Oct 1764 at Broad Creek; Mary Ann, bapt. 3 May 1767 Broad Creek; Sarah, b. 12 Dec 1773 Broad Creek (KGP p. 328, 339, 359, 360, 385)

Barrett, Edward; age 3 years on 20 Jan next; bound out; Nov 1722 (PGCR K.650)

Barret [Barrot], Richard; wife Ann; children: Elizabeth Ann, b. 9 Jul 1763 at Broad Creek; Joseph Lowden, bapt. 14 Sep 1766 Broad Creek; Mary Eleanor, b. 14 Sep 1769 Broad Creek (KGP p. 338, 373)

BARROW

Barrow, Joseph; admx. Mary Wiggfield; 22 Dec 1761 (I 77.87)

BARRY

Barry, John [CH]; wife Elizabeth; tracts *Perrie's Purchase, Pagett's Rest*; 17 Mar 1737 (PGLR T.574)

BARTON

Barton, William; 19 Apr 1703; 6 Nov 1705; wife Sarah; daus. Katharine, Sarah; father William; ss-i-l Bazill Waring, Marsham Waring; cous. Elizabeth Smoote; sister Margaret Hungerford; tracts *The Exchange, Perrywood, The Addition, Barton's Hope, Hadlow, Barton's Hazard* (MVW III.62); [as Col. William]; 15 Apr 1706 (I&A 25.397)

Barton, William; wife Sarah [d/o Thomas Gantt]; 6 Aug 1720 (PGLR I.26)

Barton, [unnamed]; heirs Martha, John; 26 Jun 1766 (GB 244)

Bartin, Thomas; child: Violettia, bapt. Broad Creek; [with 1774] (KGP p. 385)

BASILL

Basill, Ralph [AA]; wife Rose; tract *Ralpho*; 22 Feb 1717 (PGLR F.86/634)

BASINBY

Basinby, Edward; m. 4 Sep 1720 Sarah Evans (QAP m/2)

BASMAN

Basman, Joseph; wife Mary; children: Ann, b. 25 7ber 1707; William, b. 27 Mar 1710 (QAP b/9)

BATEMAN

Bateman, Ishamel; wife Mary; children: John, b. 9 May 1705; Rebecca, b. 31 Jul 1707; Martha, b. 18 8ber 1709; Mary, b. 27 Feb 1711/2 (QAP b/2, 3, 4, 5)

Bateman, Joseph; wife Sarah; child: Joseph, bapt. 18 Jul 1762 (KGP p. 331)

Bateman, John; 8 Feb 1767; 3 Mar 1768; wife Sarah; half-bro. William Goe; sister Rebecca and [?her] son John Tilley (MCW XIV.31); extx. Sarah; 19 Aug 1768 (I 104.142); 2 Nov 1770; ex. Mrs. Sarah Bateman (ABB 5. 392); widow Sarah; heirs William Goe, Thomas Tilley; 29 Aug 1771 (GB 297)

BATSWIN

Batswin, James [dec'd] [AA]; daus. Susana, Mary; tract *Mother's Gift*; 17 Oct 1728; from John Batswin of Cecil Co. (PGLR M.337)

BATT

Batts, Humphrey; m. 6 Apr 1737 Mary Tyler; children: Elizabeth, b. 10 Oct 1730; Marghayward (f), b. 21 Apr 1733 (KGP p. 279)

Batt, Humphry, ship carpenter; d. 12 Dec 1756 ca 4 a.m.; bur. following Tues. ca 2 p.m. (KGP p. 317)

Batt, Humphrey; shipwright; 14 Nov 1756; 9 Feb 1757; wife Elizabeth; ss-i-l James Trueman Greenfield, Richard Barnes [wife Mary Hayward], Samuel Barnes [wife Sarah]; tracts *Wantwater, Hinson* (MCW XI.157); 6 Aug 1758 (ABB 2.94)

BATTSON

Battson, Edward [CA]; wife Amy; tract *Battson's Vineyard Rectified*; 13 Mar 1707 (PGLR C.204a)

BAXTER

Baxter, Francis; m. 9 Jun 1720 Susanna Ray; child: George, b. 25 9ber 1720 (QAP m/2; b/16)

Baxter, George; age 12 years 25 Nov instant; bound out; Nov 1732 (PGCR S.117)

BAYNE

Baynes, Christopher; m. Elizabeth Higham, widow of Calvert Co.; son Christopher; Jun 1697 Ct. (PGCR A.186)

Bayne, Ebsworth [CH]; wife Catherine; tract *Irving*; 9 Nov 1714 (PGLR F.418)

Beans [Beanes], Christopher; 11 Dec 1716; 24 Dec 1716; sons Charles, Christopher; 2 daus. [unnamed]; bro. William; b-i-l Jno. Boon; tracts *Beard's Landing, New Designe* (MCW IV.53); 8 Jan 1716 (I&A 38a.22); 4 Jul 1718 (AA 1.1)

Bayne, Walter; [s/o John, dec'd]; tract *Locust Thickett*; 9 Aug 1717 (PGLR F.11/538); age ca 50; 1732 (PGLR Q.476)

Bayne [Bane], Walter; 9 Jul 1754 (I 57.328, 329)

Beanes, William; wife Elizabeth; tract *Grove Hurst*; 27 Mar 1723 (PGLR I.425)

Baynes, Daniel; wife Mary; child: John, b. 23 Mar 1726 Popescastle near Cockemouth, Cumberland, England; beginning the year the first of Jan'y (KGP p. 288)

Beanes, Christopher; 29 Dec 1726 (I 11.780)

John Baynes; late of Popescastle near Cockermouth in City of Cumberland, England; m. 28 Aug 1749 Miss Mary Noble of Piscataway (KGP p. 289)

Beanes, Christopher; wife Frances; tract *Land Over*; 7 Mar 1729/30 (PGLR M.544)

Beanes, William; sons John, Colmore; 1732 (MCW VII.2)

Beanes, William; age ca 53; 24 Dec 1736 (PGLR Y.84); age ca 59; 1743 (PGLR Y.703)

Bean, Richard; son Thomas; tract *Thomas' Inheritance*; 20 Apr 1738 (PGLR T.577)

Bayne, Elizabeth; children: Richard Swan, b. 15 Feb 1747; Walter, b. 2 Sep 1750 (KGP p. 309)

Bayne [Baynes], Ebsworth; wife Susana; children: Ann, bapt. 19 Apr 1752; Elinor, b. 27 Sep 1754; Elizabeth, bapt. 18 Apr 1762; Hearcort, b. 23 Apr 1764 at Broad Creek; Sarah, b. 29 Jun 1766 Broad Creek (KGP p. 295, 307, 326, 339, 360)

Bayne, William; m. 4 Nov 1753 Mary Fenley, both of this parish; children: Walter Fenley, b. 1 Oct 1754; Elisabeth, b. 19 Sep 175_; Martha Hawkins, b. 5 Sep 1762; William Granderson, b. 30 Sep 1764 Broad Creek; William, b. 24 Dec 1768; Colmour, b. 22 Apr 1774 Broad Creek (KGP p. 303, 306, 332, 342, 386)

Bayne [Bean], George; wife Mary; children: Bayne [or ?], b. 12 Sep 1755; Elizabeth, b. 25 Feb 1762; Ammey, bapt. 8 May 1764 at Broad Creek [no mother's name listed]; George, b. 26 Dec 1767, bapt. 26 Jun 1768 Upper Chapel; Levi, b. 1775 Broad Creek (KGP p. 312, 327, 339, 370, 387)

Bayne, Thomas; wife Elizabeth; children: John Philips, b. 7 Sep 1756; Priscall, b. 24 Nov 1759 (KGP p. 314, 318)

Beayn, Wineford; child: Neamiah, bapt. 21 Feb 1762 (KGP p. 325)

Bean, Thomas; wife Elizabeth; child: Daniel Jenkins, bapt. 4 Jul 1762 (KGP p. 330)

Baynes, Charles; wife Jane; child: Samuel, b. 20 Jul 1762 (KGP p. 328)

Beanes, Colmore; merchant; 20 Oct 1762; 23 Nov 1762; sisters Elizabeth Marbury, Mary Sutton; nephew Colmore Beanes (MCW XII.158); 13 Dec 1763 (I 82.1)

Bayne, Christopher [Bayns, Baynes, Beane]; wife Jane; children: Mary, bapt. 24 Oct 1762; John, bapt. _ Mar 1765 Upper Chapel; Catharine, bapt. 12 Jul 1767 Upper Chapel; Nancy, b. 13 May 1774 Upper Chapel (KGP p. 328, 332, 350, 366, 391)

Beanes, Charles; 2 Apr 1764 (I 87.130)

Beans, William, gent.; 29 Jan 1763; 26 Mar 1765; wife Elizabeth; children: William Jr., Mary Sutton, Elizabeth Marbury, Colemore Beans [dec'd]; grandchildren: William, Mary & Elizabeth Sutton, Mary Towgood, William & John Beans (MCW XIII.65-6)

Bayne, Jane; child: Shallote (f), bapt. 1 Jan 1766 Broad Creek (KGP p. 353)

Beanes, Josiah; wife Prissilla; child: Margrett, b. 2 Feb 1766 (PGP p. 278)

Bayne, Josias; wife Ann; child: Sarah, b. 2 Nov 1771 Broad Creek (KGP p. 377)

Beanes, Elizabeth; gentlewoman; 10 Jul 1772; 24 Nov 1773; children: Mary Sutton, William Beanes, Elizabeth Hawkins Wheeler; grandchildren: Eleanor Beanes, Luke Marbury (MCW XV.124)

Bayne, Josias; wife Nancy; child: Elizabeth, b. 2 Jun 1773 Broad Creek (KGP p. 385)

Bayne, Jacob Miller; wife Jane; child: Elizabeth, b. 6 Dec 1773 Broad Creek (ICR; KGP p. 385)

Bayne, Samuel Hawkins; wife Ann; child: Henneretta, b. 11 Oct 1775 Broad Creek (KGP p. 382)

Bayne, William; wife Ann; child: Mary, b. 28 Apr 1776 Broad Creek (KGP p. 383)

BAZILL

Bazill, Sarah; child: Mary, b. 24 Jun 1718 (QAP b/14)

Bazill, John; wife Elizabeth; children: Elizabeth, b. 8 Nov 1753; John, b. 15 Apr 1756; Joseph, b. 28 Sep 1758; James, b. 28 Nov 1760; Mary, b. 11 Jun 1764; Ralph, b. 7 May 1767 (QAP b/38)

BEACH

Beach, John; wife Sarah; child: John, b. 31 Aug 173_ (QAP b/28)

BEALL

Beall, Ninian; age ca 70, May 1696 Ct. (PGCR I.8); age ca 84, 10 Aug 1710 (CCR PC.844); age ca 87, 6 Oct 1712 (CCR CL.42); age ca 88, was servant of Rd. Hall ca 48 yrs. ago, 13 Oct 1714 (CCR CL.54); age ca 90, 20 Mar 1715 (CCR CL.274)

Beall, Ninian; wife Ruth; children: Charles, Ninian Jr., Thomas, John, George, Hester Belt [w/o Joseph], Mary, Rachel; 10 Mar 1706 (PGLR C.185- 186a)

Beall (Bell), Thomas, carpenter; 1 Sep 1707; 3 Aug 1708; bros. John, George, Ninian (MCW III.116)

Beall, Ninian, Jr.; 10 Nov 1710; 6 Jan 1710/1; wife Elizabeth; son Samuel, dau. Mary; tracts The Beginning of Sam'l Beall [dwel. plant.], Collington, Beall's Mill, Addition to Baron Hall (MCW III.185); 12 Feb 1710 (I&A 32b.95); extx. Elisabeth; 9 Apr 1711 (I&A 32b.246); 18 Apr 1711 (I&A 32c.157); extx. Elisabeth Beall [w/o William]; 23 Jul 1712 (I&A 33b.17); 14 May 1715 (I&A 36b.230)

Beal, John; 24 Jul 1710 (I&A 31.409); 21 May 1711 (I&A 32c.154)

Beall, Ninian; granddau. Mary [d/o son Ninian]; deed of gift; 27 Aug 1711 (PGCR G.78)

Beall, Thomas; no children; ex. Wm. Beall who m. Elisabeth Beall [widow of Ninian]; 20 May 1712 (I&A 33a.179)

Beall, Charles; wife Mary; tract *Turkey Thickett*; 10 Jul 1713 (PGLR F.269)

Beall, Charles; age ca 43, 20 Dec 1715 (CCR CL.278); age 53, 21 Aug 1725 (PGLR I.676); age 53, 28 Aug 1726 (PGLR M.63); age ca 55, 1727-28 (PGLR M.269); age ca 56, 10 Jun 1728 (PGLR M.292); age ca 59, 19 Oct 1730 (CCR-MSA 5.451); age ca 59, 8 Jun 1732 (PGLR Y.327); age ca 60, 28 Sep 1733 (PGLR T.17); age ca 61, 1734 (PGLR T.208)

Beall, Ninian; 15 Jan 1717; 28 Feb 1717; sons George, Charles, Ninian; granddau. Mary [d/o Ninian, dec'd]; grandson Samuel; ss-i-l Andrew Hambleton, Joseph Belt; tracts *Rock of Dumbarton, Dunn Back, Bacon Hall, Mt. Calvert, Sams Beginning, Good Luck, The Recovery* (MCW IV.135-6); Ninian, Col.; 9 Sep 1718 (I 445); Ninian, Col.; 18 Jan 1719 (AA 2.491)

Beall, James; wife Mary; tract *Bear Garden Enlarged*; 27 Jun 1717 (PGLR F.25/549)

Beall, Alexander; dau. Ruth Jackson [w/o John]; tract *Jackson's Improvement*; 9 Nov 1719 (PGLR F.258/843)

Beall, William; wife Elizabeth; tract *Beall's Park*; 25 Jun 1719 (PGLR F.173/759)

Beall, Thomas; children: Elizabeth Dryden, William, Benjamin, Uphen Tanihill; 24 Jul 1719 (PGLR F.183-770-185/772)

Beal, Mathew; wife Hannah; child: Mary, b. 25 9ber 1721 (QAP b/17)

Beall, John; wife Virlinda; tract *Generosity*; 16 Nov 1722 (PGLR I.354)

Beall, Mathew [dec'd]; widow Hannah; d. 8 Apr 1723; "young" child [unnamed] with mother on 28 Nov 1722; now ward of court; living with Elizabeth Bradent (PGCR L.82)

Beall, James; planter; 21 Nov 1723; 10 Jul 1725; wife Sarah; sons John, Nathaniel, James, Robert, Joseph, Zepheniah; dau. Sarah; s-i-l Thomas Odell; bro. Alexander; cous. William & John Beall, Sr.; tracts *Rover's Content, Fiffe, Good Luck, Drumaldree, Easy Purchase, Addition to Easy Purchase, Lone Head, Lay Hill, Allisons Park, Cooper, Beall's Mannour* (MCW V.197); James, Sr.; widow Sarah; 23 Nov 1725 (I 11.213); James, Sr.; 1 Jun 1726 (I 11.702); 24 Feb 1727 (I 13.110); widow, 8 children [unnamed]; 13 Jul 1727 (AA 8.262); 10 Oct 1727 (I 12.187); 27 Feb 1728 (AA 9.287); heirs Robert, Joseph, Zephaniah; 26 Jun 1728 (GB 39); heirs Joseph, Robert; 24 Mar 1736 (GB 90, 91); 8 children [unnamed]; 18 Jun 1728 (AA 9.211)

Beall, Nathaniel; of competent age; choses William Beall, Sr. as guardian; Aug 1725 (PGCR L.486); [Ed. - Nathaniel was s/o James]

Beall, Charles; children: Ninian, Elinor, Joshua, Mary, Rachell; 30 Aug 1725 (PGLR I.685); [last child abstracted as Richard with no mention of Rachell]; 4 Oct 1726 [last child abstracted as Richard with no mention of Rachell] (PGLR M.64)

Beall, James [s/o James, dec'd]; age 15 on Jan next; choses mother Sarah Beall and cous. John Beall, Sr. as guardians; Nov 1725 (PGCR L.509)

Beall, John, Jr.; wife Elizabeth; sis. Margaret Odell; tract *Ball Christ*; 14 Feb 1725/6 (PGLR I.705, 707)

Beall, Sarah; [d/o James, dec'd]; age 13 next Apr; chooses mother, Sarah Beall, as guardian; Nov 1725 (PGCR L.509)

Beall, Ninian, Jr.; wife Catherine; tract *Beall's Point*; 22 Nov 1726 (PGLR M.126)

Beall, William, Jr.; wife Elizabeth; tract *Denmark*; 29 Mar 1727 (PGLR M.146)

Beall, John; wife Elizabeth [d/o John Fendall]; tract *Aliquahook*; 11 Apr 1728 (PGLR M.322)

Beall, James; kinsman John [s/o my uncle Robert]; tract *Friend's Gift*; 28 Nov 1728 (PGLR M.336)

Beale, John, Sr.; wife Virlinda; 12 Dec 1728 (PGLR M.349)

Beall, James; sons John [wife Elizabeth], Nathaniel; tracts *Easy Purchase, The Addition*; 2 May 1729 (PGLR M.426)

Beall, James; son John, Jr. [wife Elizabeth]; Sarah Odell [wife of Rignall]; tract *Beall's Manor*; 8 Jun 1730 (PGLR M.598)

Beall, Benjamin; 18 Mar 1729/30; 21 May 1730; father Thomas Beall; bros. Thomas, William, Ninian; sister Dryden (MCW VI.154); 22 May 1730 (I 15.495); 1 Oct 1730 (AA 10.454); 17 Jul 1733 (AA 11.713)

Beall, Thomas, Sr.; wife Elizabeth; son William, Jr.; tract *Loving Acquaintance*; 1 May 1730 (PGLR Q.57)

Beall, Samuel; wife Jane; tract *Collington*; 24 Jun 1730 (PGLR Q.53)

Beall, Thomas, Jr.; wife Tabitha; tract *Friend's Goodwill*; 25 Oct 1730 (PGLR Q.168)

Beall, Alexander, Sr.; wife Elizabeth; 28 Aug 1731 (PGLR Q.363)

Beall, Thomas; son William; 25 Oct 1732 (PGLR Q.541)

Beall, Alexander; son John; 1732 (MCW VII.85)

Beall, Josias; m. Millisent Bradly, b. 5 Jan 1733/4; d. 21 Apr 1772 @ 5:30 am, age 39 [d/o Robert and Ann Bradly]; children: John Bradly (1st son), b. Sun 23 Nov 1760 @ 5 am, bapt. 7 Dec 1760; Josias Fendall (2nd son), b. Tues 31 Aug 1762 @ 8:45 am, bapt. 12 Dec 1762; _____ (f), b. died 1 Jan 1764; James Alexander (3rd son), b. Thurs 9 May 1765, bapt. 2 Jan 1765; Robert Augustus (4th son), b. Weds 7 Jan 1767 @ 4-5 am, bapt. 11

Jan 1767; Ann Fendall, b. Sun 18 Dec 1768 @ 3-4 am, bapt. 25 Dec 1768;
Benjamin Bradly (5th son), b. 13 Apr 1771 @ 6:30 am, bapt. 14 Apr 1771
Broad Creek (KGP p. 343, 344)

Beall, James, Sr.; 3 May 1733; 29 Nov 1733; wife Mary; daus. Jane, Rachel;
sons Alexander, Robert, Archibald, James, Allen and Thomas; tracts
Labyrinth, Brother's Content, Prevention, Batchelor's Forest (MCW VII.45);
admx. Mary; 23 Mar 1733 (I 18.133); widow Mary; 9 Sep 1735 (AA 13.271)

Beall, William, Jr.; age ca 34; 9 Dec 1734 (PGLR T.236)

Beall, James [dec'd]; sons James [wife Sophiah], John, Jr.; tract *Good Luck*;
19 Mar 1735 (PGLR T.244)

Beall, Robert; age ca 19 on 29 Nov next; choses Thomas Odell as guardian;
Mar 1735 (PGCR V.350) [Ed. - Robert , s/o James]

Beall, Joseph; age ca 16; choses Thomas Odell as guardian; Aug 1735 (PGCR
V.542); [Ed. - Joseph, s/o Alexander]

Beale, Ninian, Col.; d. ca 18 yrs. ago; 2 Apr 1736 (CCR-MSA 6.159)

Beall, James [dec'd]; widow Sarah Haswell [w/o Dr. John]; sons Robert,
Joseph; tract *Layhill*; 21 Dec 1736 (PGLR T.436)

Beall, William, Jr.; s/o Thomas; 27 Feb 1738 (CCR JK#4.63)

Beall, Robert; wife Margery; 7 Apr 1739 (PGLR Y.20)

Beall, Robert; son James; tract *The Farm*; 21 Jul 1739 (PGLR Y.75)

Beall, William, Sr.; wife Elizabeth; tract *The Farm*; 21 Jul 1739 (PGLR Y.75)

Beal, Robert, Jr.; planter; St. George's Parish; 22 Apr 1740; 15 Jul 1740;
sister Sarah Odell [w/o Regnale]; bro. Joseph (MCW VIII.87); 18 Jun 1741 (I
29.15); 9 May 1744 (AA 20.164)

Beall, Charles, Capt.; 24 Mar 1739/40; 27 Nov 1740; wife Mary; sons
Charles, Ninian, Joshua; daus. Mary, Rachel; tracts *Bealls Adventure, The
Constitution, Picheltons Rent, Cold Cranfords Adventure, Danby, Dispute,
Charles and William, Magruders and Bealls Honesty, Gruble Thickett,
Charles and Benjamin* (MCW VIII.106); dau. Mary; 17 Dec 1740 (I 26.22);
widow Mary; 29 Nov 1742 (AA 19.209); extx. Mary; 28 Feb 1743 (AA 20.63);
ex. Mary; son Charles; 19 May 1743 (AA 19.398); extx. Mary; 9 May 1744
(AA 20.179); heirs Ninian, Mary, Rachel, Charles; gurdian Joshua Beall; 28
Jun 1744 (GB 133)

Beal, Nathaniel; wife Elizabeth; sons James, Roger; 1740 (MCW VIII.87)

Beall, James [dec'd]; son Alexander; tract *Chestnut Ridge*; 10 Jul 1741 (PGLR
Y.343)

Beall (Bell), John, gent.; 7 Apr 1742; 18 May 1742; wife Verlinda; sons
Samuel, Joshua, Basil, John, Clement; daus. Sarah Offutt [w/o James],
Rebecca Magruder [w/o Nathan], Lucy, Hannah, Verlinda; father

Alexander; bros. Charles [dec'd], William; tracts *Loan Head, Charles and William's, Benjamin,New Drumfries, Industry, Poplar Thicket, Chittans Addition, Black Esh, Three Friends Delight, Dispute* (MCW VIII.173); extx. Verlinda; 16 Mar 1742 (I 28.167)

Beall, Samuel, Jr.; wife Elinor; tract *Black Ash*; 4 May 1743 (PGLR Y.670)

Beall, Andrew; 24 Aug 1743 (I 28.173)

Beall, Alexander; 16 Jan 1743; 5 Sep 1744; sons William, Ninian, James [dec'd], John [dec'd]; bro. Robert; s-i-l John Jackson; tracts *Neighborhood, Largo, Menella's Quarter* (MCW VIII.273); 27 Nov 1744 (I 30.86)

Beall, John [s/o John, dec'd]; choses Samuell Beall, Jr. as guardian; Mar 1745 (PGCR DD.20)

Beall, Verlinder; 29 Mar 1745; sons Bazel, John, Clement, Josiah; daus. Lucy, Hannah, Verlinder; granddau. Verlinda [d/o Josiah] (MCW IX.22); extx. Virlinda [dec'd]; her exs. Josiah and Lucy Beall; 11 May 1747 (AA 23.279)

Beal, Lucy; 30 Apr 1748 (I 35.508)

Beall, Ninian; child: Thomas, b. 19 Nov 1753 (KGP p. 305)

Beall, John, Jr.; d. 28 Oct 1756 (KGP p. 317)

Beall, Patrick; m. 2 Mar 1756 Elinor Goddard; children: Elizabeth Brook, b. 23 Feb 1757; John Godson, b. 8 Aug 1759; Lucy, b. 31 Jul 1761, bapt. 6 Sep 1761; Levin, b. 22 Feb 1764; bapt. 20 May 1764 at Broad Creek; John, b. 9 Dec 1765 Broad Creek; Jane Bean, bapt. 17 Jul 1768 Broad Creek; Walter Evins, b. 26 Feb 1774 Broad Creek (KGP p. 312, 318, 323, 338, 353, 363, 385)

Beall, John; adm. Elisabeth; 14 Mar 1757 (I 63.38); 27 Sep 1757 (I 65.1); 28 Jan 1758; admx. Elizabeth, Josias (ABB 2.86)

Beall, Allen; wife Sarah; child: Rebecca, b. 18 Sep 1759 (PGP p. 257)

Beall, George; wife Anne [Anney]; children: Leaven Coventon, b. 7 Jun 1760; Erasmus, b. 28 Oct 1762; Elizabeth, b. 18 Jan 1765 (PGP p. 259, 267, 274)

Beall, William; wife Hanah; child: Williams, b. 19 Jun 1761 (PGP p. 262)

Beall, Benjamin; wife Sarah; child: Mary, bapt. 22 Nov 1761; Benjamin, bapt. 2 Nov 1766 Upper Chapel (KGP p. 323, 354)

Beall, John; wife Mary; child: Arey Ann, bapt. _ Oct 1762 (KGP p. 307)

Beall, Roger; wife Ruth; child: Elizabeth Brook, bapt. 29 Aug 1762; Ann, bapt. _ Mar 1765 Upper Chapel (ICR; KGP p. 358)

Beall, Allen; wife Ann; child: Thomas Allen, b. 12 Oct 1762 (PGP p. 263)

Beall, Charles; 19 May 1763; 10 Jun 1763; sisters Mary Beall, Rachel Greenfield; nephew Charles Beall [s/o Mary]; niece Amelia Beall (MCW XII.193); 14 Jun 1763 (I 89.314)

Beall, Richard; wife Elliner; child: Elizabeth, b. 4 Oct 1763 (PGP p. 271)

Beall, Thomas; wife Elizabeth; child: Martha, bapt. 14 Nov 1764 Upper Chapel or Broad Creek (KGP p. 342)

Beall, Thomas; wife Virlinder; child: Ellener, b. 27 Jan 1765 (PGP p. 274)

Beall, James; wife Anne; child: James, b. 24 Mar 1765 (PGP p. 275)

Beall, Ninian or Neamiah; wife Catharine; children: Catharine, bapt. 16 Jun 1765 Upper Chapel; Zedock, bapt. 15 Nov 1767 Upper Chapel (KGP p. 358, 366)

Beall, Richard; wife Rebecca; child: Richard, bapt. 18 Aug 1765 Upper Chapel (KGP p. 359)

Beall, Jeremiah; wife Sabrarina; child: Sabra, b. 5 Sep 1765 (PGP p. 277)

Beall, Robert; wife Jane; child: Zedock, bapt. 31 Aug 1766 Upper Chapel (KGP p. 355)

Beall, John Fendall; m. 27 Sep 17__; Mary Wilkinson; d. 8 Aug 1767; children: William Wilkinson, b. 5 Sep 1765; John Fendall, Jr., b. 12 Jan 1767 Broad Creek (KGP p. 361-2)

Beall, John, s/o Robert; 23 Dec 1761; 24 Jan 1767; wife Elizabeth; children: Robert, James, Minnon, John, Cosson, Shadrack, Francis, Sesson; dau. Morgere; granddau. Nase Wood; tracts *Addition of God Father's Gift, God Father's Gift, Elizabeth Choice, James Crammer, Mill Land, Chands, James and Mary, Plummers Jock, Was There Nothing* (MCW XIII.176); 17 Apr 1767 (I 91.316)

Beall, James; wife Elizabeth; child: Sarah, b. 29 Jun 1773 Broad Creek (KGP p. 385)

Beall, Benjamin; 4 Mar 1776; 4 Jun 1776; wife Sarah; children: Josias, [others unnamed] (MCW XVI.120); 1776 (I 122.199, 200); 5 Aug 1776; wife Sarah; son Josias; other children [unnamed] (ABB 7.58)

Beall, John Fendall; 8 May 1776 (I 123.414)

BEAMAN
Beaman, John; b. 29 Sep last; base born s/o Lidia; bound out; Mar 1708 (PGCR C.201)

BEAUMONT
Beaumont, Darby; age 3 on 1 Jun last; s/o Lidia; bound out; Nov 1713 (PGCR G.455)

Beaumont, Darby; age 6 on 1 Jul next; bound out; Mar 1716 (PGCR H.32)

BEATTY
Beatty, Susanna; children: Thomas, William, John, James, Agness, Martha [w/o James Middagh]; tract *Dulany's Lott*; 20 Mar 1739 (PGLR Y.148)

Beatty, Edward; mother Susanna; tract *Providence*; bro. Thomas; tract *Well Water Bottom*; 20 Nov 1740 (PGLR Y.240, 242)

Beaty [Beatty], James; farmer; 4 Nov 1742; 29 Jan 1742; bros. & sisters [unnamed] (MCW VIII.191); 15 Mar 1742 (I 28.56); 14 Jun 1743 (I 28.474)

Beatty, John; admx. Henrietta Barton [w/o Jacob]; 12 Mar 1747 (I 35.516)

BECK

Beck, James; m. 1 Apr 1733 Sarah Duvall; children: Samuel Duvall, b. 7 Jan 1733/4; James, b. 6 Oct 1735; Anthony, b. 25 Oct 1737; ____ (f), b. 6 Jan 173_; [Richar]d (m), b. 9 Aug 1742; Osborn, b. 17 Aug 1744; Sarah, b. 13 Feb 1745/6; John, b. 14 Feb 1749; Ruth Duvall, b. ____; William, b. 11 Mar 17__ (QAP m/6; b/27, 29, 31, 33, 34, 35)

Beck, James; m. 23 Jun 1761 Rebekah Walker (QAP m/7)

Beck, Osborn; m. 8 Sep 1763 Mary Welsh; child: ____, b. 1 Feb ____ (QAP m/7; b/39)

Beck, Samuel Duvall; m. 29 Mar 1767 Susanna Tyler (QAP m/7)

Beck, James; 25 Jan 1768; 14 Apr 1768; children: Samuel, James, Osborn, Richard, Anthony, William, Sarah, John, Ruth; tracts *Mitchell's Addition, Tyler's Pasture* (MCW XIV.30); 29 Nov 1768 (I 103.190, 192)

BECKETT

Beckett, Humphrey; son Humphrey; 1712 (MCW III.249)

Beckett, Humphrey; age ca 44; 8 Dec 1719 (CCR CL.550)

Beckett, Humphrey; wife Mary; children: Benjamin (twin), b. 18 10ber 1722; Humphrey (twin), b. 18 10ber 1722; ____ (f), b. __ ___ 172_; Joseph, b. 4 Apr 1729 (QAP b/18, 22, 23)

Beckett, John; m. 18 Nov 1723 Mary Nicholls (QAP m/3)

Becket, John; m. 17 Nov 1724 Ann Drayne; child: Richard, b. 31 Dec 1729 (QAP m/3; b/23)

Beckett, Humphry; age ca 63; 1736 (PGLR T.444)

BECKWITH

Beckwith, George; dau. Ann; 4 Nov 1727 (PGLR M.253)

Beckwith, Ann; granddau. Ann Boswell; 9 May 1730 (PGLR M.590)

Beckwith, Ann; son Basil; 24 Mar 1730 (PGLR Q.240)

Beckwith, Williams; [s/o Charles, dec'd]; 25 Nov 1732 (CCR-MSA 6.11)

Beckwith, George, age ca 29; 8 Dec 1735 (CCR-MSA 6.24); 9 Dec 1735 (CCR-MSA 6.25)

Beckwith, William; admx. Elisabeth; 24 Jul 1738 (I 24.296); widow Elisabeth; children: Lucy, Ann, Mary William; 26 Mar 1742 (AA 19.107); admx.

Elisabeth Butler [w/o Peter]; children: Lucy, Anne, Margrett, William; 15 Dec 1746 (AA 23.93)

Beckwith, Sarah; orphan; bound out to age 16; Jun 1748 (PGCR HH.165)

Beckwith, Sarah; age 13 last of Nov past; bound to Jonathan Burch; Mar 1751 (PGCR MM.17)

BECRAFT
Becraft, Peter; 14 Jun 1716 (I&A 38a.28); 17 Jul 1718 (AA 1.1)

Becraft, Rebecka; 14 Nov 1717 (I&A 39c.84); widow; 5 Jun 1719 (AA 2.57)

BEEDLE
Beedle, Mary; age ca 7 years; [d/o William, a servant]; Mar 1701 (PGCR B.99)

Beadle [Biddle], Mary; 12 Mar 1721 (I 6.157)

BEGORLY
Begorly, Benjamin; wife Elizabeth; children: Elliner, b. 20 Mar 1763; Thomas, b. 23 Apr 1765 (PGP p. 270, 275)

Beggorly, Henry; wife Elizabeth; child: Hezekiah Tyson, b. 28 Feb 1773 (PGP p. 279)

BEIN
Bein, Charles; extx. Mary; [with 1700] (I&A 20.188)

BELL
Bell, James; wife Sarah [d/o Sarah Pearce]; 16 Mar 1700 (PGLR A.361)

Bell, John; wife Ellinor; child: Ellinor, b. 25 9ber 1710 (QAP b/38)

Bell, James; wife Anne; children: John, b. 28 Jan 1729; James, b. 22 Mar 1732; Mary, b. 24 Jan 1738/9 (KGP p. 277, 286)

Bell, John; s-i-l Nicholas Baker; tract *Hazard*; 27 Aug 1730 (PGLR Q.87); s-i-l William John Jackson; tract *Bell's Tract*; 27 Aug 1730 (PGLR Q.89)

Bell, Samuel; s/o Ninian [dec'd]; [Sarah Magruder's will]; 1731 (MCW VII.114)

Bell, James; wife Ann; tract *Dickenson's Delight*; 25 Mar 1736 (PGLR T.377)

Bell, Andrew; 31 Jan 1742; 23 Mar 1742; [no relations] (MCW VIII.205)

Bell, John; admx. unclear; mentions Mrs. Virlinda, Josiah, Lucy Beall; 27 Aug [with 1746] (AA 23.33)

Bell, Ann; child: Stryphena, bapt. 3 May 1752 (KGP p. 296)

Bell, James; child: Rebeckah, bapt. 5 Dec 1762 (KGP p. 329)

BELLFOARD
Bellfoard, Robert; age ca 13; servant; Jun 1699 Ct. (PGCR A.424)

BELT

Belt, Elizabeth [AA] [widow of John]; 2nd son Joseph; tracts part of *Good Luck, Widows Purchase*; 12 Apr 1701 (PGLR A.368)

Belt, Joseph; wife Ester; children: John, b. 13 Mar 1707; Rachel, b. 13 Dec 1711 [m. Osborn Sprigg]; Joseph, b. 19 Dec 1717; Tobias, b. 20 Aug 1720; Mary, b. 24 Dec 1722; Jeremiah, b. 4 Mar 1724; James, b. 23 Jul 1726 or 7 (QAP b/20, 22)

Belt, John, b. 13 Mar 1707, s/o Col. Joseph Belt; m. 4 Mar 1727/8 Margaret Queen; children: Katherine, b. 18 Mar 1729; Sarah Haddock, b. 18 Mar 17___ (QAP m/5, b/24, 25)

Belt, Joseph; age ca 35; 20 Dec 1715 (CCR CL.277)

Belt, Jeremiah; wife Mary [d/o Ann Wight, widow]; 1 May 1725 (PGLR I.633)

Belt, Joseph; grandson Thomas Clagett; s-i-l Thomas Clagett, Jr.; Jun 1730 (PGLR Q.38)

Belt, Benjamin; age ca 50; 1734 (PGLR T.362)

Belt, Joseph, Col.; wife Margery; tract *Good Luck*; 26 Jun 1735 (PGLR T.300)

Belt, Joseph; age ca 18; s/o Benjamin; 1734 (PGLR T.362)

Belt, Benjamin; age ca 80; 1738 (PGLR T.635)

Belt, Joseph, Col.; dau. Mary Hall; [will of Grace Thompson]; 1739 (MCW VIII.189)

Belt, Benjamin; age ca 50; 17 Apr 1740 (PGLR Y.176)

Belt, Jeremiah; m. 21 Jun 1746 Mary Sprigg; children: Richard, b. 26 Dec 1747; Edward, b. 15 Mar 1749; John Sprigg, b. 18 Sep 1752; George, b. 1 Mar 1755; Thomas Sprigg, b. 19 Jul 1756; Mary, b. 18 Aug 1758; Fielding, b. 29 Mar 1761; Margery, b. 18 Jan 1764; Tobias, b. 21 Jun 1766 (QAP m/7; m/8)

Belt, Joseph, Col.; 15 Oc6 1750; 23 Nov 1768; wife Mary; son Jeremiah, Joseph; grandsons Richard, Edward; mentions Tobias & Joseph Sprigg Belt & his bro. Thomas; 1750 (MCW XIV.63)

Belt, Joseph, Jr.; 19 Apr 1759; 27 Aug 1761; wife Ann [sister of Edward Sprigg]; sons Thomas, Joseph, Charles, William (MCW XII.81)

Belt, Joseph; 14 Jun 1761; 14 Sep 1761; wife Margery; sons Humphry, John, Tobias, Jeremiah, Joseph Jr. [dec'd], Thomas, [? William]; daus. Rachel Sprigg, Mary Pindle, Margery Lyles; grandchildren: Joseph, Osborn & Thomas Sprigg [ss/o Rachel], Richard Belt [s/o Jeremiah], Charles, Elizabeth, Ann & Joseph [ch/o Thomas], William & Joseph [ss/o Joseph]; d-i-l Ann Belt [widow of Joseph, Jr.]; tracts *Chelsea Hohim, Good Luck, Addition to Good Luck, Chevy Chase, Seneca Hills, Friendship, Thompson's Lot* (MCW XII.79)

Belt, Joseph; 6 Aug 1761; 21 Sep 1761; wife Elizabeth; father John (MCW XII.97); Joseph, Jr.; 24 Sep 1761 (I 75.203); Joseph, 3rd; extx. Elisabeth; 12 Nov 1761 (I 75.215); Joseph, Col.; 13 Nov 1761 (I 75.193)

Belt, Jeremiah, Col.; 15 Oct 1750; 23 Nov 1768; wife Mary; tracts *Belt's Tomahawk, Belt's Pigpen, Breshers Neck, Orphans Gift* (MCW XIV.63); 3 Aug 1769 (I 108.281)

Belt, Guy; wife Kesander; child: b. 16 Jun 1762 (KGP p. 328)

Belt, Benjamin; 19 Jun 1772; 28 May 1773; children: Benjamin, Joseph, Sophia Beall, Anne Brashears, Elizabeth Waring, Hester Watkins; grandchildren: Benjamin & Stephen Belt [ss/o Benjamin] (MCW XV.29-30)

Belt, Jeremiah, Col.; 6 Jul 1773; widow [unnamed]; legatees Jeremiah, Tobias (ABB 6.232)

Belt, Benjamin; 11 Apr 1775; 29 Jun 1775; wife Ruth; sons Benjamin, Thomas, Middleton; daus. Elizabeth Nixon, Easter, Rachell; tracts *Belts Poor Chance, Godfather's Gift, Norway, Belts Range, Belts Meddow, Belts Chance* (MCW XVI.72); 4 Sep 1775 (I 123.238)

Belt, Joseph; wife Margery; son Joseph, Jr.; tract *Cobreth's Lott*; 27 Oct 1741 (PGLR Y.399)

Belt, Middleton; 25 Feb 1745; 21 May 1746; father Benjamin; bro. Basil Brashear; nephew Middleton Brashear [s/o Basil] (MCW IX.72)

Belt, Thomas; wife Prisila; children: Ruth, bapt. 19 Dec 1762; Ester, bapt. 19 Dec 1762 (KGP p. 329)

Belt, Marsham; wife Elizabeth; _____ (f), b. 6 Jan 1764; Thomas, b. 15 Jun 1765; Marsham, b. __ Jul 1767 (QAP b/38, 39)

Belt, Tobias; wife Mary; son Levin; dau. Lucy; 1767; Belt, Joseph; wife Anne; son Charles; dau. Margery; 1767; will of Eliza. Evans (MCW XIV.11)

BENCE

Bence [Bounce], Michael; 30 Jan 1774; 23 Mar 1774; wife Barbara; children: George, Barbara, Elizabeth, Adam, Gabriel (MCW XV.137); 2 Jun 1774 (I 118.179; 121.321, 326)

BENFIELD

Benfield, Abraham; m. 15 Apr 1737 Mary _____ (QAP m/7)

BENJAMIN

Benjamin, Abraham; wife Ann; child: Rachel, b. 16 Feb 1764 (PGP p. 272)

BENNETT

Bennet, John; wife Ann; children: John, b. 10 8ber 1703; Thomas, b. 25 Dec 1705 (QAP b/12)

Bennett, Thomas; orphan; age 14 on 25 April next; bound out; Mar 1708 (PGCR C.209a)

Bennett, John [dec'd]; wife Ann [dec'd]; children: Ann [age 10], John [age 14 next Oct], Sarah [age 6 next Aug], Thomas [age 12 on 25 Dec next]; bound to Thomas Bennett and wife Mary; Mar 1717 (PGCR H.181)

Bennett, Thomas; age ca 44; 8 Dec 1719 (CCR CL.551)

BENSON

Benson, William [CH]; wife Catherine; tract *Ward's Wheel*; 18 Mar 1708 (PGLR C.243)

Benson, Edward; sadler; 11 Jun 1713 (I&A 34.84)

BENTLY

Bently, Thomas; admx. Elisabeth; 28 Jul 1763 (I 82.149)

BENTON

Benton, Joseph; [s/o Joseph & Anne]; age 2 years on 15 Oct next; bound out; Aug 1727 (PGCR N.489)

Benton, Jon.; wife Elizabeth; child: Mordica, b. 27 ___ 1762 (PGP p. 264)

Benton, Joseph; wife Elizabeth; children: Benjamin Smith, b. 7 Sep 1759; Erasmus, b. 18 Apr 1766 (PGP p. 278, 280)

BERKLEY

Berkley, Henry; wife Elizabeth; children: William, b. 5 Jul 1772 Broad Creek; George, b. 4 Jul 1775 Upper Chapel (KGP p. 378, 391)

BERNHOLD

Bernhold, Jeremiah; wife Elizabeth; child: Mary, b. 25 Apr 1754 (PGP p. 256)

BERRY

Berry, Benjamin; ordered to sit in stocks for 1 hr. for swearing in court; Oct 1696 Ct. (PGCR A.52)

Berry, Benjamin; wife Mary; tract *Berry Lott* part of *St. Andrews*; 22 Jun 1700 (PGLR A.230)

Berry, Elinor; age 7-1/2 years; bound out; Jun 1717 (PGCR H.241)

Berry, Benjamin; 7 Nov 1719; 10 Feb 1719; wife Mary; sons Benjamin, Jeremiah; daus. Mary, Verlinda; s-i-l Richard Keene; tracts *Thompson's Choice, Long Lane, The Chance, Charles and Benjamin, The Levell, Evan's*

Range (MCW IV.223); extx. Mary; widow, 2 sons & 2 daus. [unnamed]; [undated; with 1720] (AA 3.283)

Berry, Benjamin; wife Eleanor; tract *Moor's Fields*; 5 Jun 1729 (PGLR M.457)

Berry, Samuel; children: Joseph, b. 7 Aug 1751; Samuel, b. 2 Jan 1753; Benjamin, b. 21 Feb 1756; Mary Ann, b. 7 May 1758 (KGP p. 321)

Berry, Bassil; wife Jemima; child: Elizabeth, bapt. 10 Apr 1768 Upper Chapel (KGP p. 370)

Berry, Jeremiah; 2 Apr 1769; 3 May 1769; wife Mary; children: Jeremiah, Benjamin, William, Zachariah, Elisha, Mary, Amelia, Richard; tracts *Marlborough Plains, Charles and Benjamin, Rover's Content, Alias Good Luck, Good Will, Hanson Branch* (MCW XIV.85); 5 Sep 1769 (I 102.238)

Berry, Benjamin; planter; 6 Apr 1777; 1 May 1777; wife [unnamed]; sister Lucy Berry; bro. John Berry (MCW XVI.187-8)

BETTEYS
Betteys, Joseph; admx. Mary Kennedy [w/o Joseph]; 29 Mar 1768 (I 100.24)

BEUSEY
Beausey, Charles; admx. Mary; 25 Oct 1734 (I 20.68)

Beusey [Bousey], Sarah; 25 Aug 1745; 15 Oct 1745; children: Edward, Samuel, John; ss-i-l Joseph Richardson, Griffith Davis; grandchildren: Anne Davis [d/o Griffith], Mary Ray (MCW IX.48); 24 Dec 1745 (I 32.66)

BEVAN
Beaven, Charles; 20 Jun 1698; 21 Jun 1699; wife Mary; sons Richard, Charles; daus. Sarah, Margaret, Eliza., Catherine; tract *Her Grove, Hickory Thickit* (MCW II.182); 2 Sep 1699 (I&A 19-1/2b.1); widow Mary; heirs children: Charles, Elizabeth, Katherine Beaven; 5 Aug 1708 (GB 2)

Beaven, Charles; extx. Mary; Jun 1703 (PGCR B.239); Charles, Elizabeth, Kathrine, Mary, Richard Marsham Bevan; indebted to Charles, Elisabeth & Kathrine, orphan children of Charles Beven [lately dec'd]; Aug 1703 (PGCR B.250)

Beavan, Mary; 28 Apr 1712; 13 Jun 1713; [no relations] (MCW III.240); 22 Aug 1713 (I&A 34.238); 24 Aug 1713 (I&A 35b.17)

Biven, William; m. 10 Feb 1725/6 Ann Brushier (QAP m/4)

Bevan, Charles; age ca 42; Mar 1728 (PGLR M.293)

Bevan, Richard; age 53; 9 Jul 1731 (PGLR Q.521)

Bevan, Richard, Sr.; 27 Feb 1738/9; 21 May 1739; sons Charles, Richard, Blanford, Bazel, Henry; tract *Hare Grove* (MCW VIII.28); 25 Jul 1739 (I 24.189);

adms. Charles, Richard, Blanford, Basil & Henry Bevan; 27 Aug 1740 (AA 18.44)

Beavin, Henry; 22 Nov 1748 (I 27.410); children: John, Ann, Jane; 9 Jun 1750 (AA 28.241); heirs John, Ann, Jane; 23 Aug 1752 (GB 179)

Beaven, Charles, Sr.; 11 Jun 1761; 16 Dec 1761; wife Rebecca; children: Charles, Richard, Edward (MCW XII.101); extx. Rebecca Boone; 29 Mar 1762 (I 77.88); 27 Dec 1762; extx. Rebecca Beavin; children [unnamed] (ABB 4.112)

BIGGER

Bigger, Walter; [s/o John] [CA]; bros. John, James; tract *Too Good*; 28 Apr 1697 (PGLR A.68a)

Bigger, James, Capt.; son John apprenticed to Thomas Beall, Jr.; 12 Dec 1704 (PGLR C.121b)

Bigger, James; 4 May 1705; 1 Oct 1711; wife Eliza; son John; daus. Margarett, Mary; bro. John Bigger; tracts *Beale's Chance, Backland* (MCW III.229); James, Capt.; 21 Feb 1706 (I&A 25.388); admx. Elisabeth Beanes [w/o William]; 22 Nov 1708 (I&A 29.31)

Bigger, John, Col. [dec'd] [CA]; widow Ann; her son [?s-i-l] William Head [wife Ann]; tract *Beal's Chance*; 23 Jun 1715 (PGLR F.453)

Biggor, James; 9 May 1739; 28 Aug 1739; wife Elizabeth (MCW VIII.44)

BIGGS

Biggs, Robert [dec'd]; Sep 1696 Ct. (PGCR A.40)

Biggs, George [CH]; wife Mary; tract *Beale*; 25 Jul 1741 (PGLR Y.355)

Biggs, Henry; wife Mary; children: Henry, bapt. 12 Dec 1762; Samuel, bapt. 25 Dec 1765 Broad Creek (KGP p. 329, 350)

Biggs, George; 22 Apr 1772; 30 Dec 1776; wife Mary; children: Mary, Anne, Priscilla, Catharine, Elizabeth Davies; grandchildren: Sarah, Michael, Oden & Mary Price Davies [ch/o Elizabeth]; tract *Beale* (MCW XVI.186)

BILLINGER

Billinger, Francis [CA], wife Ellinor; lease of *Warmister*; 24 Dec 1695 (PGLR A.4)

BILLINGSLY

Billingsly; George [VA & CA]; sis. Elizabeth Jordan [w/o Thomas], Margaret, grandmother Agnes Billingsly; tract *Billingsly's Point*; 21 Dec 1681 (PGLR F.129)

Billingsly, George; sis. Margaret Burgh, Elizabeth Jordan, Mourning; tract
  Billingsley Point; 22 Apr 1725 (PGLR I.627)

BIRD
Bird, Francis; m. 5 Nov 1724 Jane Littleton; d. 14 Apr 1733; children: John,
  b. 9 Oct 1727; Thomas, b. 24 Dec 1729; Francis (m), b. 21 Feb 1731 (KGP p.
  278, 279)
Bird, Robert; 27 Sep 1731 (I 16.310); 24 Nov 1731 (AA 11.252)
Bird, Benjamin; wife Elizabeth; children: Cassandra, b. 3 Oct 1760;
  Thomas Allison, b. 10 Apr 1762 (PGP p. 259, 263)

BIRDWHISTLE
Birdwhistle, Thomas; age 2 on 22 Mar next; also Ann Ray; age 6 on 28
  Mar next; John Birdwhistle to make satisfaction if he is father of sd.
  children; bound out; Nov 1728 (PGCR O.331)

BIRMINGHAM
Birmingham, Alice; infant; d/o Eliza; Nov 1721 (PGCR K.421)

BISHOPP
Bishopp, Theophilus; "now wife" Mary; 14 Apr 1722 (PGLR I.258)

BLACK
Black, William; 28 Feb 1743 (I 28.505)

BLACKBURN
Blackburn, Edward; wife Lucy; child: Lucy, b. 19 10ber 1722 (QAP b/17)
Blackburn, Lucy; infant; bound out; Aug 1723 (PGCR L.132)

BLACKLOCK
Blacklock, Thomas; m. 15 ___ 1738 Charity Lanham (KGP p. 286)
Blalock, Thomas, Sr.; son Thomas, Jr.; tract *Dixson's Park*; 21 Jan 1742 (PGLR
  Y.589)
Blacklock, Richard; wife Mary; child: Richard, b. 6 Nov 1773 Broad Creek
  (KGP p. 385)

BLACKMORE
Blackmore, Samuell; wife Abirell [Abirillah]; children: Elisabeth, b. 15
  Apr 1762; James, b. 27 Feb 1764 (PGP p. 264, 271)
Blackmore, Thadeus; wife Mary; child: Lloyd Beall, bapt. 23 Feb 1766
  Lower Chapel (KGP p. 346)

BLACKWOOD

Blackwood, William; wife Elenor; child: bapt. _ Mar 1765 Upper Chapel
(KGP p. 358)

BLADEN

Bladen, Joseph; 1 Jan 1760 (I 69.328); 4 Jul 1761; admn. William Bladen (ABB
3.109); heirs Luke Church, William Usher, Stephen Rutter; 25 Jul 1764 (GB
237)

BLAKE

Blake, Archibald; b. 22 Apr 1721; s/o Anne Catherine; bound out; Nov
1727 (PGCR N.611)

Blake, John; age ca 6 years; bound out; Nov 1742 (PGCR AA.192)

Blake, William; 29 Nov 1744 (AA 21.61)

BLANCKLEY

Blanckley [Blankly], John; 29 Nov 1709 (I&A 30.439); 25 Sep 1710 (I&A 32a.33)

BLANEY

Blaney, Thomas [dec'd]; children: John, age 1 in Jan last; Elizabeth, age 4
on 2 Oct next; bound out; Jun 1711 Ct. (PGCR G.69)

BLANFORD

Blanford, Thomas; 18 Nov 1695; 28 Apr 1698; wife Tabitha; 5 children:
Thomas, Jean, Eliza., Grace, Martha (MCW II.141)

Blanforde, Tabitha; 20 Jan 1700 (I&A 20.175); 9 Jul 1702 (I&A 23.69)

Blanford, Eliza; 27 Jun 1709; 9 Apr 1710; sister Martha Lamar; bros.
Richard & Thomas Beven (MCW III.1167); [with 1710] (I&A 31.139)

Blanford, Thomas; age ca 53; 9 Jul 1731 (PGLR Q.522)

Blanford, Thomas; planter; 17 Jun 1749; 7 Aug 1749; wife Sarah; children:
Charles, John, Mary Edelen, Sarah Clackson, Tabitha Mitchell,
Margaret Hagan, Martha Clackson; grandson Philip Edelen; tracts
Ruden Shanking Point, Hirkley Thickett, Brook Chance, Timberland,
Shrusbury Plains, Widow's Trouble (MCW X.36)

Blanford, John; 9 Mar 1770; 17 Apr 1770; wife Eleanor; children: James,
John, Thomas, Richard, Joseph, Monica Hagan, Sarah Coomes, Elizabeth
Mary Green, Eleanor, Mary Ann, Henrietta, Susannah; tracts Timberley,
Brook Chance (MCW XIV.158); 14 Jul 1770 (I 104.277); 13 Aug 1771; widow
[unnamed]; legatees James, John, Thomas, Richard, Joseph, Eleanor,
Mary, Ann, Henrietta Maria & Susannah Blanford, Monica Hagan,
Sarah Cormas, Elisabeth Mary Green (ABB 6.88)

BLANDIGAN

Blandigan, David; servant; age ca 13; Nov 1698 (PGCR A.355)

BLEW

Blew, Richard; 23 Jun 1771 (I 105.296)

BLIZARD

Blizard, Giles [dec'd] [CH]; daus. Susannah, Anne; tract *Bleu Plaine, St. James, Cain's Purchase, Athelborough*; 19 May 1713 (PGLR F.241)

Blizard, Giles [dec'd]; widow Mary Smallwood [widow of James, dec'd]; dau. Ann Frazier [w/o John]; granddau. Mary Frazier; tract *Beauplaine*; 18 Apr 1715 (PGLR F.440)

BLONB

Blonb?, James; age ca 20; servant; Jun 1712 Ct. (PGCR G.211)

BLOYCE

Bloyce, William; wife Sarah; child: Sarah, b. 18 Nov 1762 (PGP p. 267)

BLUE

Blue, Richard; 27 Aug 1772 (I 114.74)

BLUMFIELD

Blumfield, Isaac; 27 Dec 1748 (I 44.194)

BOLTON

Bolton, James; age 13 on 17 Apr next; Nov 1714 (PGCR G.692)

Boulton, Henry; m. 6 Nov 1728 Susanna Mobborly (QAP m/5)

Bolton, James; wife Susanna; children: Thomas, bapt. 14 Jan 1753; James, b. 27 Dec 1754 (KGP p. 297, 307)

BOND

Bond, James; vagrant; apprenticed to sea; Jun 1748 (PGCR HH.185)

BONE

Bone, John; age ca 12; servant; Jun 1698 Ct. (PGCR A.320)

BONEFANT

Bonefont, James; wife Pricilla; tract *Manchester*; 30 Apr 1722 (PGLR I.295)

Bonefant, James; admx. Priscilla; 1 Aug 1740 (I 25.123); admx. Priscilla; children: James, Joan, Luke, Matthew, Samuel, Anne, Grigory [minor]; 6 Jul 1741 (AA 18.294)

Bonnifcent, James; wife Mary; child: Martha, b. 8 Sep 1753 (KGP p. 305)

BONIFIELD

Bonifield, Grigsby; wife Sarah; child: Martha, b. 20 Apr 1760   (PGP p. 258)

Bonifield, James; wife Joanna; child: Keziah, b. 26 Jul 1772 Broad Creek
(KGP p. 378)

Bonifield, Samuel; wife Sarah; childewn: Samuel, b. 1 Apr 1772 Upper
Chapel; John, b. 9 Dec 1774 Upper Chapel (KGP p. 390, 391)

BONNER

Bonner, Henry; 1 Oct 1702; 21 Oct 1702; wife Eliza.; tracts *Bonner's Camp*,
Bonnie's Interest; both in Baltimore Co. (MCW III.13)

Bonner, James; age 15 months; bound out; Jun 1720 (PGCR H.1015)

BOOG

Boog, James; merchant [Falkirk, Scotland] [dec'd]; nephew James
[Scotland]; 26 Aug 1701 (PGLR C.144)

BOONE

Boone John; age ca 52, 4 Apr 1732 (PGLR Q.573); age ca 57, 6 Aug 1735 (PGLR
T.359); age ca 58, 24 Dec 1736 (PGLR Y.84)

Boone, John, Jr.; age ca 55; 19 Mar 1733/4 (PGLR T.152)

Boone, John, Sr.; wife Elizabeth; son Henry; 22 Mar 1742/3 (PGLR Y.661)

Boon, James; admx. Mary; 1 Oct 1751 (I 48.375); 28 Nov 1753; admx. Mary;
children: Eleanor & Henrietta Boone (ABB 1.87); admx. Mary; 2 children:
Eleanor, Henerita [ages 7 & 3]; 28 Nov 1753 (AA 35.327); widow Mary;
heirs Charles, Henrietta; 25 Jun 1754 (GB 194)

Boone, Francis; 26 Jun 1775 (I 123.123)

BOOTH

Booth Robert; m. Sarah Filmoore; children: John, b. 2 Sep 1718; Jane, b. 18
Feb 1720 (KGP p. 262)

Boothe, John; age 11 years next Oct; bound out; Jun 1729 (PGCR P.2)

BOOZEMAN

Boozeman, Ann; age 4 on 25 Sep next; d/o Joseph; bound out; Aug 1714
(PGCR G.632)

Boozeman, William; age 4 on 27 Mar last; s/o Joseph; bound out; Aug
1714 (PGCR G.632)

BORDLEY

Bordley, Thomas [dec'd] [SM]; wife Ariana; tract *Collington*; 17 Jun 1727 (PGLR M.185)

BOSWELL

Boswell, James, Dr.; 4 May 1743 (I 27.438)

Bosell, John; 2 Jun 1751 (I 47.42)

Boswell, Anne; alias Phillips; 1751 (MCW X.185, 254)

Boswell, James; wife Prissilla; child: Elizabeth, bapt. 19 Jun 1768 Lower Chapel (KGP p. 369)

Boswell, John; 7 Jan 1753; rep. Elizabeth Boswell [age 4 yrs.] (ABB 1.59, 63); widow [unnamed]; child Elisabeth [age 4]; 7 Jan 1753 (AA 33.291)

Boswell, Mathew; wife Catharine; child: Elizabeth, bapt. 17 Nov 1765 Lower Chapel; John, b. _ Dec 1767, bapt. 24 Jan 1768 Lower Chapel (KGP p. 351, 368)

Boswell, Richard; wife Mildred; child: Bartin, b. 7 May 1774 Lower Chapel (KGP p. 379)

Boswell, John B.; wife Rebeccah; child: Horatio, b. [with 1775] Lower Chapel (KGP p. 380)

Boswell, John; wife Elizabeth; child: Ann, b. 16 Nov 1750; went to live in house of Josias Beall of this parish 12 Jan 1774; continued there until 29 Aug 1781 when she d. ca 8:30 pm; her children b. in the house of Josias Beall: David Fendall Beall, b. 23 Jul 1775; Anna Beall, b. 13 Feb 1777; Ann Elizabeth, b. 2 May 1781 (KGP p. 336)

BOTELER

Boteler, Edward [CA]; wife Ann; tract *Bealls Benevolence*; 28 Feb 1699 (PGLR A.396)

Boteler, Edward; niece Ales Buttlor [d/o Henry]; June 1703 (PGCR B.239)

Boteler, Henry; 7 Aug 1713; 5 Sep 1713; wife Catherine; sons Charles, Henry, Thomas, Edward; daus. Alice, Catherine; f-i-l George Lingam, dec'd; tracts *Renches Adventure, London Derry, Harry's Lott, Buttington, Appledore, Lingam's Adventure* (MCW III.253); extx. Catherine; 26 Sep 1715 (I&A 36c.32); extx. Katherine Normansell [w/o Richard]; 23 Nov 1722 (AA 6.83); Nov 1725; orphans Alice, Catherine, Charles, Edward, Henry & Thomas (PGCR L.550); heirs: Alice, Charles, Henry, Catharine, Thomas, Edward; 23 Nov 1726 (GB 23)

Boteler, Henry [dec'd]; son Charles; tract *Beall's Pleasure*; 16 Jul 1714 (PGLR F.378)

Boteler, Catherine [widow]; nephew Lingan Wilson; children: Charles, Henry, Thomas, Edward, Alice, Catherine; remarriage to Richard Normansell; 27 Jul 1726 (PGLR M.51)

Boteler, Thomas; s/o Henry [dec'd]; age ca 17 years; choses guardian; Jun 1727 (PGCR N.351)

Botler, Catherine; 26 ___ 1728 (I 14.6)

Boteler, Charles; wife Sophia; tract *Londonderry*; 5 Oct 1736 (PGLR T.412)

Boteler, Charles; age ca 34; 1737 (PGLR T.509)

BOULGER

Boulger, Thomas; wife Elizabeth; tract *Good Luck*; 9 Jan 1729 (PGLR M.527)

BOURN

Bourn, Ambrose; wife Elizabeth [widow of Richard Robson]; 25 Jan 1720 (PGLR I.97)

BOURNEVEETH

Bourneveeth, Jacob; wife Sarah; servants; Nov 1696 Ct. (PGCR A.84)

BOWEN

Bowen, Robert; admx. Sarah Tanyhill [w/o John]; 11 Apr 1711 (I&A 34.155)

Bowing, John; wife Elizabeth [d/o John Dorsett, dec'd]; tract *Greenwood*; 1 Mar 1721 (PGLR I.173)

Boyn, John [dec'd] [CH]; dau. Ann Dent [w/o Thomas]; tract *Locust Thickett*; 4 Dec 1724 (PGLR I.606)

Bowen (Browen, Bowin), John; planter; 15 Sep 1725; 5 Feb 1725/6; daus. Anne, Kessiah, Elizabeth, Sarah, Felessety; son John; sister Elizabeth Bowen [w/o Nathaniell]; bro. Thomas Dossett; tracts *Pye's Hard Shift, Twifoott* (MCW V.212); 14 Feb 1725 (I 11.671); heirs John [age ca 20], Elisabeth, Sarah, Anne & Filicity Bowin; 30 Oct 1727 (AA 8.446); heirs Elizabeth, John, Anne, Felicity and Casiah; 26 Jun 1728 (GB 38)

Bowen, John; 26 Nov 1735; aunt Ann Harris; sisters Kesiah, Sarah, Ann; cous. Joseph and Amy Harris (MCW VII.156); _ May 1736 (I 21.399)

BOWERS

Bowes, Richard; admx. Jane; 21 Dec 1771 (I 105.297); 7 Jun 1775 (I 123.239)

BOWES

Bowers, Geiles; age ca 7; orphan of Francis Bowers; bound out; Jan 1703 Ct. (PGCR B.289)

BOWIE

Bowie, John; age ca 41; 28 Feb 1731 (PGLR Q.431)

Bowie, John; dau. Eleanor Brook; 4 Nov 1732 (PGLR Q.560)

Bowe, John; m. 18 Dec 1735 Elizh. Pottinger (QAP m/6)

Bowee, William; wife Ann; children: ____ (f), b. 13 Oct 1738; ____(?), b. 22 Jul 173_; ____ (m), b. 17 Apr 174_ (QAP b/32 - page torn)

Bowie, John; wife Mary; son James; tract *Craycroft's Right*; 26 Nov 1741 (PGLR Y.410)

Bowie, John; wife Mary; tracts *Brook Ridge, Locust Thickett*; 11 Dec 1742 (PGLR Y.565)

Bowie, James; 28 Aug ____; 28 Sep 1744; daus. Lucy, Martha, Elinor; bro. Thomas; tract *Craycrofts Right* (MCW VIII.281); 18 Dec 1744 (I 30.250); 22 Aug 1748 (AA 25.109)

Bowie, Thomas; guardian to orphans of James Bowie: Eleanor, Lucy, Martha; Nov 1747 (PGCR GG.292)

Bowie, John, Jr.; 29 Nov 1752; 5 Feb 1753; wife Elizabeth; dau. Mary Magruder; sons Allen, James, John; unborn child; tracts *Hermitage, Pine Thicket, Enlarged, Allen and James, Railey's Discovery, Brockhall* (MCW X.245); extx. Elisabeth; 1753 (I 54.133); extx. Elisabeth; 26 Aug 1754 (I 57.330)

Bowie, William, Jr.; admx. Rachel; 9 Apr 1753 (I 54.132); admx. Rachel; 26 Aug 1754 (I 57.329)

Bowie, Thomas; 3 May 1758; 12 May 1758; wife Hannah; son Daniel; daus. Elizabeth Lawson Bowie, Barbara; bro. G. Scott (MCW XI.203); extx. Hannah; 26 Jun 1758 (I 66.205); 10 May 1761; extx. Hannah [w/o Joseph]; children: Elisabeth Lawson, Barbara, Daniel (ABB 3.81); 10 Oct 1762; extx. Hannah [w/o Joseph]; children: Daniel, Elisabeth, Barbary (ABB 3.164); heirs Daniel, Elizabeth, Barbara; 25 Jul 1764 (GB 236); heir Daniel; 29 Nov 1775 (GB 288)

Bowie, John; 4 Mar 1759; 25 Apr 1759; sons Allen, William; dau. Mary Beanes; grandsons Benjamin Brooke, Nicholas, Wiseman; granddaus. Eleanor & Margaret Claggett; s-i-l Edward Claggett; tracts *Brook Field, Croim* (MCW XI.238-9); 1 Jun 1759 (I 74.329)

Bowie, Allen; children: Priscills Duckett, Ann Blizaro Bowie; 1776 (MCW XVI.186-7)

Bowie, Daniel; 26 Aug 1776; 3 May 1777; sisters Elizabeth Belt, Barbara Hall, Little Sprigg; aunt Eleanor Skinner; ?bro. Philip Sprigg (MCW XVI.187)

BOWLER

Bowler, Joseph; wife Sarah; child: Silas, b. 7 Jan 1763 at Lower Chapel (KGP p. 334)

BOWLES

Bowles, James [SM]; wife Rebecca; tract *The Gores*; 31 Jan 1723 (PGLR I.517)

Bowles, Tobias [dec'd]; daus. Mary [widow of John Underdown], Jane Carr [w/o James], Margaret Primrose [w/o Henry Alexander]; son James [wife Rebecca who m/2 George Plater]; 15 Dec 1729 (PGLR M.553)

Bowles, Tobias; son James; 18 Aug 1730 (CCR-MSA 5.321)

Bowles, Mary; son John; 1759 (MCW XII.231)

BOWLING

Bowling, John [CA]; wife Mary; tract *The Exchange*; 24 May 1700 (PGLR A.317)

Bowling [Bowleing], John [CH]; wife Mary; tract *The Indian Field*; 24 Jul 1704 (PGLR C.121a)

Bowling, Thomas; wife Mary; tract *Strife*; 9 Sep 1740 (PGLR Y.211)

Bowling, Bazil; 15 Jul 1768; 16 Jan 1770; bro. William Langworth & sister Elizabeth Bowling; tract *Strife* (MCW XIV.158)

Bowling, Thomas; 14 Jun 1775 (I 123.234)

BOWMAN

Bowman, Absolon; age 11 years on 25 Mar next; orphan formerly in Anne Arundel Co.; Nov 1706 (PGCR C.95a)

Bowman, Charles; wife Elizabeth; tracts *Beall's Pleasure, Laxston's Delight, Widow's Purchase*; 25 Aug 1742 (PGLR Y.525)

BOX

Box, Thomas; 8 Feb 1707/8; daus. Sarah, Dinah; tracts *The Houserace [Horserace], Smithfield* (MCW III.150); 20 May 1708 (I&A 28.253); exs. Thomas Hines & wife Jane; 7 May 1714 (I&A 35a.342); 4 Dec 1714 (I&A 36a.149); 7 Jun 1715 (I&A 36b.182); 4 Oct 1717 (I&A 39c.126)

BOYCE

Boyce, Roger [CA]; wife Mary; tract *Brooke Court*; 28 Feb 1711 (PGLR F.168)

BOYD

Boyd, John; innholder; 5 Oct 1704; 9 Jul 1705; wife Mary; sons Charles, John, Abraham, Isaac; dau. Mary Bateman [w/o Ishamell], Martha; tract *Amphill Grange* (MCW III.60); 19 Jul 1705 (I&A 26.75, 109)

Boyd, John; wife Ellinor; children: Benjamin, b. 13 Jan 1706; John, b. 25 7ber 1709; Abraham, b. 5 Jun 1713; William, b. 19 Apr 1716; Ellinor, b. 27 Jun 1720 (QAP b/7, 14)

Boyd, Charles; wife Elizabeth; children: Mary, b. 17 Aug 1707; Frances (f), b. 16 Feb 1714/5; Martha, b. 29 Feb 1716 (QAP b/9. 10, 12)

Boyd, Mary; 16 Sep 1721; 4 Dec 1722; husband John [dec'd]; sons Charles, John, Abraham, Isaac; dau. Martha Wills [Wells] [w/o Thomas]; Mary Bateman [Batterman]; grandson John Bateman [s/o Mary] (MCW V.123); 20 Dec 1722 (I 8.98); 3 bros. & 2 sis; 23 Dec 1723 (AA 5.411); 15 Aug 1724 (AA 6.90); 21 Jun 1725 (AA 7.28)

Boyd, Frances; wife Barbara; tracts *Brooke Ridge, Beane's Landing*; 20 Nov 1728 (PGLR M.371)

Boyd, Abraham; m. 8 Nov 1728 Deborah Walley; child: Margaret, b. 23 7ber 1730 (QAP m/5; b/24)

Boyd, Benjamin; m. 30 Oct 1733 Elizabeth Harwood; children: Thomas, b. 14 Sep 1734; Abraham, b. __ May 17__; Ellinor, b. ____; Peggy, b. ____; Sarah, b. ____ (QAP m/6; b/28, 30, 33)

Boyd, John; m. 8 May 1734 Susan Baldwin (QAP m/6)

Boyd, Abraham; admx. Deborough; 20 Sep 1737 (I 23.172); admx. Deborah Wayman [w/o Leonard]; 22 May 1744 (AA 20.219); heir Margarett; 30 Aug 1744 (GB 136)

Boyd, John; son John, Jr.; tract *Boyd's Delay*; 27 Jun 1738 (PGLR T.595)

Boyd, John, Sr.; age ca 63; 1742 (PGLR Y.654)

Boyd, Benjamin; 6 May 1752 (I 95.220)

Boyde, Thomas; m. 24 Mar 1757 Charity Duckett; d/o Richard Duckett, b. 28 Dec 1757 (QAP m/7; b/37)

Boyd, Benjamin; m. 27 Feb 1758 Elinor Williams (QAP m/7)

Boyd, Benjamin; planter; 12 Apr 1762; 22 Apr 1762; sons Thomas, Abraham; daus. Eleanor Whatkins, Sarah, Peggy; tract *Sway and Frys Choice* (MCW XII.118)

Boyd, Abraham; wife Barbra; child: Ann, b. 11 Oct 1764 (PGP p. 274)

BOYLE

Boyle, John; m. 8 May 1734 Susan Baldwin (QAP m/6)

BRADCUT

Bradcut, Richard; wife Sarah; children: Elizabeth, b. 3 7ber 1704; Joanna, b. 1 May 1708; Richard, b. 29 Jul 1709; Sarah, b. 18 9ber 1711; Susanna, b. 31 Aug 1713 (QAP b/5, 8, 9)

Bradcutt, Richard; m. 24 Feb 1715 Eliza. Cook (QAP m/1)

Bradcut, Richard; wife Sarah; children: Charles, b. 19 Oct 1735; Richard, b. 18 May 1738 (QAP b/31)

BRADFORD

Bradfoard, ____; [s/o William Bradford]; age 4 last Mar; bound out by mother Rebecca Shaw; Jun 1700 (PGCR B.53)

Bradford, John; son John; 25 Mar 1711 (PGLR F.106)

Bradford, John; wife Joyce; child: William, b. 14 Sep 1713 (KGP p. 260)

Bradford, John; planter; 26 Mar 1726; 11 May 1726; wife Joyce; son John; uncle John Smith; father John Bradford; sister Mary Jones; nephews Evan & John Jones [ss/o Mary]; "bro." Thomas Gant; tracts *Tannyard, The Farme, Will's Good Will, Joseph's Good Luck, Essex Lodge, Dunbar, Anglice, Burbidg, Plain Dealing, Substraction, Addition to Charley Forrest, Scotch Ordinary, Batchelors Hall, Generosity, Island of Walnut Trees, Fair Isle, Concord, Progressive, Sinicar, Sugarlands, Hygam, Discovery, Jacob, Argile Cowell and Lorn, Bradford's Rest, Haddock Hills, Seaman's Delight, Cuckolds Delight, As Good as Any, Fletchalls Chance* (MCW V.216); ex. Joyce; 2 Aug 1727 (I 12.162); exs. Joyce, John; 11 Nov 1727 (AA 8.420); widow Joyce; 21 May 1729 (AA 9.362); widow Joyce; 18 Sep 1731 (AA 11.173)

Bradford, John [dec'd]; widow Sarah Hillyard [now w/o Benjamin]; sons John, Thomas; tracts *Abr___ Choice, Senecar, Long Acre*; 20 Jul 1734 (PGLR T.213)

Bradford, John; mariner; 29 Jan 1770; 14 Nov 1770; sister Elinor Lancaster [w/o Richard] (MCW XIV.150); John, Capt.; 1770 (I 105.264)

Bradford, John; wife Ann; tract *Cuckhold's Delight*; 9 May 1730 (PGLR Q.24)

Bradford, Joyce; widow; dau. Margaret Tylor [w/o Michael]; 18 Oct 1731 (PGLR Q.382)

BRADLEY

Bradley, Sarah; both parents dec'd; age 5 next March; bound out; Jun 1711 Ct. (PGCR G.69a)

Bradley, Robert; wife Ann; tract *Mt. Calvert Manor*; 6 Aug 1737 (PGLR T.500)

Bradley, Robert; 7 Jun 1769; 1 Dec 1772; children: Millicent Beall [granddau. of Clement Hill], Elianor Tyler, Mary Bradley, Sarah Holyday [w/o Dr. Leonard]; s-i-l Robert Tyler; grandchildren: Sarah & Ann Bradley Hollyday [ds/o Sarah]; tracts *Addition to Mooresfield, Four Hills, Berry's Fortune, Bacon Hill, Beginning Moor Craft, Moores Little Worth* (MCW XV.4)

BRADOCK

Bradock, Henry; wife Margrett; children: Thomas, b. 4 Apr 1758; Ann, b. 25 May 1761 (PGP p. 262)

BRADY
Brady, Hugh; age ca 19; servant; Jun 1698 Ct. (PGCR A.316)

BRAINWOOD
Brainwood [Bramewood], Benjamin; Quaker; 4 Mar 1702/3; 6 Jul 1703; mother Mary Brainwood; bro. Joseph Brainwood (MCW III.11); 9 Jul 1705 (I&A 25.129)

BRAMELL
Bramell, James; wife Mary; children: Mary, b. 29 Jul 1709; James, b. 9 Mar 1711 (KGP p. 265)

Bramill, James; wife Mary; dau. Mary Piles [w/o James]; tract *Addition to The Golden Rod*; 29 Jun 1726 (PGLR M.20)

Bramell, James; sawyer; 8 Mar 1727; 27 Mar 1728; wife Mary; son James; dau. Rebecca; tracts *The Refuse, Addition to the Golden Rod* (MCW VI.60)

Bramel (Bramile), James; 16 Mar 1734; 29 Apr 1735; mother Mary; tracts *Golden Rod, The Refuse* (MCW VII.135)

Bramwell, Zachariah; wife Parthenea; child: Margaret, b. 15 Aug 1773 Lower Chapel (KGP p. 384)

BRANDT
Brandt, Richard; wife Margaret; child: Randal, b. 6 Jan 1773 Lower Chapel (KGP p. 384)

BRASHEAR
Brushier, Benjamin; wife Mary; children: Thomas, b. 11 Sep 1690; Ann, b. 4 Jan 1692; Mary, b. 17 Nov 1695; Benjamin, b. 23 May 1698; Elizabeth, b. 30 Mar 1701 [m. Samuel Brushier, Jr.]; John, b. 19 Feb 1703; William, b. 15 Mar 1706/7; Elinor, b. 31 Jun 1710 (QAP b/1, 3, 5)

Brushier, Samuel, Sr.; wife Ann; children: William Jones, b. 28 Jan 1694/5; Samuel, b. 12 Feb 1696/7; Elizabeth, b. 27 Jul 1699; John, b. 21 8ber 1702; Robert, b. 19 Feb 1704/5; Ann, b. 4 Jan 1707; Basil, b. 18 Mar 1713/4; Otho, b. 28 9ber 1716; Mary, b. 10 Jun 1720 (QAP b/2, 3, 10, 12, 15)

Brushier, Robert; wife Mary; children: Thomas, b. 10 8ber 1706; Priscilla, b. 4 Mar 1712; Leonard, b. 26 8ber 1714; Elizabeth, b. 27 Mar 1721; Samuel, b. 13 8ber 1723; Rachel, b. 19 Aug 1726 (QAP b/2, 20)

Brashier, Robert; 4 Aug 1710; 17 May 1712; sons Robert, Samuel (MCW III.225); Robert, Sr.; [with 1712] (I&A 33b.80); 10 Dec 1712 (I&A 33b.215)

Brushier, Thomas; m. 11 7ber 1711 Ann Venman (QAP m/1)

Brushier, Samuel, Jr.; m. 17 Dec 1717 Eliza. Brushier [d/o Benj., Sr.]; children: Samuel, b. 5 Dec 1718; John, b. 15 Jan 1722/3; Maurice, b. 15 Jan 1724/5 (QAP m/2; b/14, 18, 19)

Brushier, Benjamin, Jr.; m. 24 Jan 1720/1 Rebecca Walker; children: Mary, b. 28 8ber 1723; Thomas, b. 15 10ber 1725; Benjamin, b. 6 Jul 1728; Mary, b. 5 Apr 1731; Rebecca, b. 27 Jul 1733 (QAP m/2; b/18, 19, 21, 24, 27)

Breshers, Samuel, Sr.; wife Elizabeth; tract *Breshear's Porcorson*; 27 Nov 1723 (PGLR I.519)

Brushier, John; m. 13 Aug 1723 Ruth Walker; children: Ann, b. 21 Aug 1724; Isaac, b. 27 Aug 1726; Ruth, b. 7 Aug 1728; Basil, b. 20 Oct 1732 (QAP m/3; b/23, 26)

Brushier, John, Jr.; wife Mary; children: Rachel, b. 22 Jun 1728; Mary, b. 5 Nov 1729 (QAP b/23)

Brushier, Thomas; m. 1 Feb 1728/9 Ann Hyatt (QAP m/5)

Brasseur, Benjamin, Sr.; wife Mary; son Benjamin, Jr. [wife Rebecca]; 21 Mar 1723/4; tract *Cuckold's Delight* (PGLR I.524)

Brashears, Samuel; age ca 51, 2 Oct 1724 (PGLR I.596); age ca 56, 20 Jun 1729 (PGLR M.438)

Brashier, Thomas; extx. Ann Bivan [w/o William]; 3 Feb 1725 (I 11.359)

Brashear, Samuel, Sr.; wife Ann; sons Robert [tract *Bresher's Meadow*]; son Samuel, Jr. [tract *Bresher's Industry*]; son John [tract *Breshear's Neck*]; 11 Oct 1726 (PGLR M.75, 77, 79)

Brashears, Benjamin, Sr.; age ca 60; 20 Jun 1729 (PGLR M.438); age ca 64, 22 Sep 1730 (PGLR Q.158)

Brashears, Samuel, Jr.; wife Elizth.; children: Mary, b. 20 Nov 1720; Benjamin, b. 19 Sep 1727; Ann, b. 20 Sep 1729; Jeremiah, b. 15 Nov 1731; Nasie (m), b. ____; Otho (m), b. _____ (QAP b/31, 32)

Brashears, John, Sr.; wife Ruth; children: John, b. __ Sep ____; Rachel, b. 25 Dec ____; Rebeckah, b. 19 Mar ____ [with 1730s] (QAP m/32)

Brasshere, John; wife Ruth; tract *Good Luck*; 1 May 1732 (PGLR Q.449)

Brasshere, Robert; wife Charity; tract *Goodwill*; 1 May 1732 (PGLR Q.452)

Brasheir, Robert; age ca 48; 1734 (PGLR T.362)

Brasheirs, Benjamin; age ca 37; 1734 (PGLR T.362)

Brashers, Samuel, Sr.; age ca 60; 1734 (PGLR T.202); age ca 61, 9 Dec 1734 (PGLR T.236)

Brashier, Benjamin; age ca 73; 1734 (PGLR T.362); age ca 80, 26 Nov 1739 (PGLR Y.107)

Brasher, William; m. 11 Jun 1734 Priscilla Prather; children: William, b. 5 Mar 173_; William, b. 14 Mar 1734; Rezin, b. 6 Nov 1736; Martha, b. 10 May 174_ (QAP m/6; b/31,32)

Brashears, Otho; m. 6 Jan 1736 Mary Holmes; child: Clara, b. 14 Feb 1737 (QAP m/7; b/32)

Brashears, John; wife Ruth; child: Samuel, b. 20 Sep 1739 (QAP m/32)

Brashear, Samuel; age ca 66; 17 Apr 1740 (PGLR Y.176)

Brasshear, Samuel; 1 Jun 1740; 27 Aug 1740; sons Samuel, John, Robert, William, Basill, Otho; cous. Benjamin Brasshear; tracts *Orphan Gift, St. Andrews, Thorpland, Hog's Harbor* (MCW VIII.98); 8 Sep 1740 (I 25.21); 15 Jun 1742 (AA 19.52)

Brashear, Otho; wife Mary; tract *Hog Harbor*; 1 Dec 1742 (PGLR Y.576)

Brashears, Benjamin; 23 Mar 1742 (I 27.358); 23 Jun 1742 (I 27.22); Benjamin, Jr.; 15 Aug 1743 (AA 19.449); heirs Thomas, Benjamin, Mary, Rebecca, Elizabeth Waymake, Charles; 5 Dec 1744 (GB 138); rec'd from this estate: Thomas, Maurice, 1 Jan 1746, Benjamin, Jr. & William, Nov 1749; Ezkiel [wife Rebecca], 17 Aug 1752; Elizabeth, 12 Sep 1761; Wamack, 18 Nov 1762; Charles Brashear [wife Rebecca], 19 Nov 1763 (GB 231)

Brashear, John, Sr.; wife Ruth; tract *Brashears Neck*; 29 Mar 1743 (PGLR Y.649)

Brashears, Samuel; _ Mar 1743 (I 28.394)

Brashers, Samuel; wife Elizabeth; children: Elizabeth, b. __ J__ ____; Turner, b. 18 May 174_ (QAP b/32)

Brashears, Samuel; wife Rachel; children: Barton, b. ____; Elizabeth, b. ____; Rachel, b. ____; ____ (f); ____ (f); F____ (m); ____ (?), b. __ Dec ____; ____ (m), b. 2 Mar ____; ____ (m), b. __ Ap_ ____ [with 1760s] (QAP b/39)

Brashears, Morris; wife Mary; child: Thomas, b. 2 Mar 1766 Upper Chapel (KGP p. 354)

Brashears, Benjamin; wife Rebecca; child: Ann, bapt. 2 Aug 1767 Upper Chapel (KGP p. 366)

Brashears, Morris; child: Samuel, bapt. 6 Nov 1768 Upper Chapel (KGP p. 372)

Beshears, John Pottenger; wife Ann; children: John Walker, b. 5 Dec 1772 Broad Creek; Anthony, b. 7 Feb 1775 Broad Creek (KGP p. 378, 386)

Brashears, Samuel; 15 Jan 1772; 1 Nov 1773; children: Samuel, Mary, John Morris, Benjamin, Ann, Jeremiah, Otho, Joseph & Elizabeth Brashears, Ruth Brown; tracts *Hayharbour, Brashears Industry* (MCW XV.123)

Brashear, Elizabeth; 27 May 1774; 6 Feb 1775; 12 children: Joseph, Ann, Samuel, Mary, John, Morris, Nacey, Benjamin, Jeremiah, Otho & Elizabeth Brashear, Ruth Brown (MCW XVI.59)

Brashears, Benjamin; wife Rebeckah; child: Elizabeth, b. __ Jun or Jan ____ [with 1730s] (QAP b/30)

BRAWNER

Brawner, John; m. 8 Jan 1716 Mary Dunning [or Downing]; children: Elizabeth, b. 30 Nov 1717; William, b. 16 Sep 1719; Mary, b. 19 Oct 1721 (KGP p. 262, 281)

Brawner [Broner], William; child: Henry, b. 16 Dec 1717 (KGP p. 280)

Broner, William; mother Mary Ellitt; bro. John Broner; 25 Feb 1720 (I 4.253); heir Henry; 27 Jun 1720 (GB 8); orphan [unnamed]; 25 Jul 1720 (AA 3.85)

Brawner, Henry; m. 2 Jan 1726/7 Elizabeth Barton (KGP p. 269)

Brawner, John; admx. Mary; 23 Apr 1741 (I 29.435); admx. Mary; 14 Oct 1745 (AA 22.50)

BRAYE

Braye, James; widow [unnamed]; 10 Apr 1699 (I&A 20.141)

BRENT

Brent, George [VA]; children: Henry, Mary, Martha; tracts *Pitchcroft, Rich Leavell, Pikemoke*; 3 Oct 1701 (PGLR C.16a)

Brent, James; planter; 20 Apr 1718 (I 1.447); 21 Oct 1718 (AA 1.297)

BREWSTER

Brewster, John; m. 26 Jun 1716 Jane Banister; children: John, b. 9 Jul 1716; Mary, b. 21 Jul 1718 (QAP m/1; b/1, 14)

BRIDGES

Bridges, Thomas; 21 Dec 1700 (I&A 20.138)

Bridges, Anne; 10 Mar 1703 (I&A 3.113); [with 1706] (I&A 25.408); 21 May 1708 (I&A 28.120)

BRIGHTWELL

Brightwell, Richard; 21 Aug 1698; 29 Aug 1698; eld. son Richard; 5 children [unnamed]; 2 daus., 3 sons; tracts *Blackwell, Mattawoman* (MCW II.162); 5 Sep 1699 (I&A 19-1/2b.1)

Brightwell, Richard; children: Richard, John, Elizabeth Kennett [w/o Jasper]; tract *Sugar Land*; 14 Feb 1718 (PGLR F.178/765)

Brightwell, Richard; wife Mary; tract *Spinham*; bro. Peter; 26 Nov 1725 (PGLR I.727)

Brightwell, Peter; age ca 46; 1737 (PGLR T.504); age ca 47; 1738 (PGLR T.607); age ca 53; 24 Aug 1741 (PGLR Y.360)

Brightwell, Richard; age ca 51; 1738 (PGLR T.607)

Brightwell, Peter; 27 Nov 1747; 23 Dec 1747; wife Ann; daus. Elizabeth, Catharine, s-i-l Joseph Cage; tract *Nest Egg* (MCW IX.138); extx. Ann; 1748 (I 37.43); extx. Anne [widow]; 26 Jun 1749 (AA 27.35); extx. Ann; children: [under age] Susanna, John; remainder of age gone from their parents; 29 Aug 1749 (AA 27.188); widow Ann; heir Elizabeth, Tabitha, Catherine, Mary, Lucy, Martha, Susannah, John; 28 Aug 1750 (GB 167)

Brightwell, John; 9 Mar 1766; 24 Nov 1774; children: John, Catherine Oden, Thomas Coleman, Urslee Morton, Pracilla Orme, Elioner Baden; grandchild Leonard Letchworth; mentions Verlindo Oden [d/o Elias] (MCW XVI.48)

Brightwell, Richard, Sr.; 9 Nov 1767; 29 Mar 1775; children: Richard, John Lawson, Elizabeth, Rebeckah Orme; tracts *Masonscon, The Addition, Retaliation* (MCW XVI.40)

Brightwell, Thomas; admx. Virlinda; 21 Dec 1775 (I 122.371)

BRISCOE

Briscoe, John; wife Ann; children: Trumon, b. 15 May 1758; Ann, b. 27 Jul 1760; Elliner, b. 2 Feb 1763; Mary Bonifield, b. 8 Sep 1765 (PGP p. 259, 268, 278)

Briscoe, Garrod; wife Ruth; child: Ann, b. 5 Feb 1760 (PGP p. 281)

BRITT

Britt, George; son Henry; 1708 (MCW III.144)

Britt, George; age ca 43; 1730 (PGLR M.567); 26 Apr 1735 (PGLR T.253)

BROADWRY

Broadwry, Alice; 16 Dec 1738 (I 24.254)

BROCKE

Brocke, Edward; 5 Mar 1712; 19 Jun 1714; dau. Mary Offett [w/o William]; granddau. Mary Nicholls; grandsons Mathew & Brock Mogbee, John, Edward, William, James & Thomas Offett [ss/o William]; tract *Brock Hall* (MCW IV.17); 29 Jun 1714 (I&A 36a.110); exs. William Nichalls & wife Mary; 23 Sep 1715 (I&A 36c.40); adms. William Nicholls & wife Mary; 25 Oct 1716 (I&A 37c.123)

Brocke, Edward [dec'd]; grandson Matthew Mockboy; tract *Brock Hall*; 30 Jan 1716 (PGLR F.581)

BRODEY

Brodey, Alexander; 12 Sep 1738; [no relations] (MCW VII.258)

BROGDON

Brogdon, William; wife Sarah; also [?mother] Elizabeth [widow]; tracts *Scott's Lott, Hugh's Labour, Riley's Folly*; 31 Mar 1739 (PGLR Y.63)

Brogdon, William, Rev.; wife El____; child: Elizabeth, b. 3 May 1753 (QAP b/36)

BROMFIELD

Bromfield, Peter; m. 28 Dec 1718 Barbara Bennet; m. 5 Jul 1731 Jane Tucker; child: John, b. 24 Jul 1722 or 3 (QAP m/2, 5; b/18)

Bromfield, Peter; m. 5 Jul 1731 Jane Tucker (QAP m/5)

Bromfield, John; orphan; age ca 13 years; bound out; Mar 1733 (PGCR S.246)

Bromfield, Peter; blacksmith; 7 Jul 1733 (I 17.360)

BROOKE

Brooke, Robert; 1664 granted 1,000 acres *Brooke Ridge* in Calvert Co.; 30 Sep 1667 Robert assigned tract to bro. Charles Brooke (PGLR T.519)

Brooks, Thomas; sons Thomas, Robert; tract *Brookfield, Wedge*; 25 Oct 1676 (PGLR A.83, 86)

Brooke, Baker [CA] [s/o Baker]; wife Katherine; tract *Brooke Wood*; 14 Feb 1694 (PGLR C.200a)

Brooke, Thomas; wife Barbara; tract *Reparration*; 4 Jan 1699 (PGLR A.209)

Brooke, Thomas; wife Rebeckah; dau. Sarah; tract *Dann*; 14 Jun 1704 (PGLR C.98); bro. Clement; tract *Dann*; 28 Sep 1704 (PGLR C.118)

Brooke, Robert; wife Grace; tract part of *Friendship*; 12 Jul 1706 (PGLR C.169)

Brooke, Roger [CA]; sons Roger [wife Elizabeth], James; dau. Ann Dawkins [now w/o James Mackall]; tract *Brookes Reserve*; 31 Mar 1709 (PGLR C.258)

Brooke, Basil; 27 Feb 1710/1; 30 May 1711; bros. Roger, John (MCW III.206); 4 May 1711 (I&A 33a.107)

Brooke, Thomas, Jr.; wife Lucy; 10 Apr 1713 (PGLR F.311)

Brooke, Richard; wife Ann; tract *Brook Hill*; 22 Jul 1713 (PGLR F.303)

Brooke, Edward; exs. William Nichalls & wife Mary; 22 Dec 1714 (I&A 36a.190)

Brook, John [CA]; wife Sarah; tract *Rencher's Adventure*; 22 Jun 1715 (PGLR F.457)

Brooke, Roger; 2 Dec 1717 (I 1.414)

Brooke, Roger; Deed of Gift; 4 Jun 1718; wife [?Elizabeth]; sons Robert, Bazel, James, Peter, Sam; daus. Betty, Dolley, Mary and Anne, Cassandra, "my 2 twins"; tracts *Brougdon, Ryly's Lott*; deed of gift filed by Elizabeth Brooke, admnx. of Roger Brooke (MCW V.240); 15 Apr 1719 (I 3.277); admx. Elisabeth; widow, 3 sons & 6 daus. [unnamed]; 18 Aug 1721 (AA 3.509); heirs James, Elizabeth, Dorothy, Mary, Anne, Roger, Cassandra, Priscilla, Basal; 20 Jun 1722 (GB 15)

Brooke, Thomas, Jr.; wife Lucy; tract *Heart's Delight*; 22 Nov 1721 (PGLR I.197)

Brooke, Richard; heirs Richard, Baker; 30 Mar 172_ (GB 31)

Brooke, James; wife Deborah; tract *Hazzard*; 23 Feb 1726 (PGLR M.130)

Brooke, Walter; [s/o Thomas, Gent.]; age ca 19; chooses his father as guardian; Aug 1726 (PGCR N.8)

Brooke, Francis; wife Deborah; tract *Brooke Refuse*; 23 Feb 1726 (PGLR M.121)

Brooke, Benjamin; admx. Eleanor Brooke; [A. Contee m. sister of Benjamin]; 28 Oct 1727 (I 13.30); admx. Eleanor; heir Benjamin [son, age 1 mo.]; 26 Mar 1728 (AA 9.138); widow Eleanor; heir Benjamin; 27 Aug 1728 (GB 40, 43)

Brooke, Robert; bro. Charles; sisters Ann Beane [w/o Christopher]; Elizabeth Smith [w/o Richard; their eldest son Richard]; 25 Aug 1737 (PGLR T.519)

Brooke, Clement; wife Jane; son Clement, Jr.; tract *Brookefield*; 7 Jan 1730 (PGLR Q.196)

Brooke, Thomas; 16 Nov 1730; 25 Jan 1730/1; wife [unnamed]; sons Thomas, Baker, Thomas [s/o present wife]; daus. Lucy, Elenor Sewall [w/o Charles]; ss-i-l Dr. Patrick Sim, Thomas Gantt, Alexander Contee, John Howard; grandsons Benjamin, Walter & Richard [ss/o 1st Thomas], Thomas Tasker [s/o Elizabeth]; tracts *Prospect, Vineyard, Delabrooke Mannour, Quantico, Brooke Chance, The Wedge, Cross Cloth, Brookfield* (MCW VI.175) 24 Apr 1731 (I 16.304); widow Barbara; sons Baker, Thomas; 25 Jun 1731 (PGLR Q.299)

Brooke, Thomas; son Benjamin; grandson Benjamin; 30 Jan 1730 (PGLR Q.208)

Brooke, Thomas; wife Barbara [d/o Rebecca Addison, widow, dec'd]; children: Lucy, Baker, Thomas; 6 Nov 1730 (PGLR Q.122)

Brooke, Clement, Jr., gent.; mariner; 31 Aug 1731; 28 Nov 1732; d. on voyage to London; wife Mary; dau. Rachel; father Clement Brooke (MCW VI.231); Capt. Clement; admx. Mary; _ Oct 1732 (I 17.357, 488); extx. Mary; heir Rachel [infant]; 22 Jun 1733 (AA 12.148); heir Rachel; 29 Apr 1735 (GB 69)

Brooke, Thomas; age ca 47, 2 Jun 1732 (PGLR Q.523); age ca 53, 24 Dec 1736 (PGLR Y.84)

Brooke, James; wife Barbara; tract *Widow's Troubles*; 29 Jun 1732 (PGLR Q.497)

Brooke, Thomas [dec'd]; eld. son Thomas; ss-i-l John Howard, Alexander Contee; 1 Nov 1735 (PGLR T.251)

Brooke, Thomas; wife Mary; 20 Dec 1735 (PGLR T.344)

Brooke, Thomas; sons Ignatius [England], Clement; 21 Mar 1736 (PGLR T.533)

Brooke, Thomas; 19 Jul 1736 (AA 15.36, 112)

Brooke, Walter; 31 Jan 1740; 19 Jun 1741; wife Mary Ashcom; sons Thomas, Isaac; granddau. Sarah & 3 others [unnamed] [ds/o Thomas] (MCW VIII.135); extx. Mary; 7 Sep 1741 (I 26.475); ex. Mary Ashcom Brook; children: Lucy, Thomas, Martha, Anne, Sarah; 19 Oct 1745 (AA 22.166); widow Mary; heirs Thomas Waring, Thomas Brooke, Martha, Ann & Sarah Brooke; 8 Jun 1747 (GB 158)

Brookes, Robert; admx. Margaret; 1 May 1740 (I 25.181); admx. Margrett; 27 Nov 1741 (AA 18.409)

Brooke, Leonard; _ Jun 1735; 4 May 1736; wife Ann; sons Leonard, Richard, Oswald, Baker; daus. Ann, Katherine, Jane, Mary, Henrietta (MCW VII.174); admx. Ann; 5 Jun 1736 (I 21.497); extx. Anne; children: Ann, Baker, Catherine, James, Leonard, Mary, Henerita & Richard Brooke; 30 Aug 1744 (AA 20.451); widow Ann; heirs Baker, Oswald, Leonard, Richard, Anne, Catherine, Jane, Mary, Henrietta; 23 Jul 1745 (GB 144)

Brooke, Clement; planter; 2 Aug 1734; 30 Jun 1737; wife Jane; sons, Henry, Joseph, Nicholas, Charles, William (MCW VII.222); extx. Jane; 15 Dec 1737 (I 23.156)

Brooke, Clement; age ca 59; 4 May 1736 (CCR-MSA 5.800)

Brook, Henry; age ca 37; 16 Feb 1741 (CCR JK#4.423)

Brooke, Thomas; 7 Dec 1738; 29 Mar 1745; wife Lucy; son Waller; tracts *Content, Brooks Content, Brookefield, Addition to Brookefield* (MCW IX.22); extx. Lucy; 8 May 1745 (I 32.182)

Brooke, Thomas [dec'd]; widow Lucy; son Thomas; 21 Jan 1745 (CCR MSA 8.257)

Brooke, Benjamin; chooses John Bowie as guardian; Mar 1746 (PGCR DD.406)

Brooke, Barbara; widow; 24 Feb 1748/9; 26 Jun 1754; dau. Lucy Hodgkin; son Thomas; granddaus. Mary Beall, Barbara Contee; grandsons Thomas Brooke Hodgkin, Benjamin Brooke, Benjamin Hodgkin, Alexander Contee Hodgkin; s-i-l Thomas Hodgkin (MCW XI.40)

Brooke, Henry; 25 Sep 1751; 26 Oct 1751; wife Margaret; sons Henry, Clement, John, Nicholas; daus. Jane, Mary, Ann, Rachel, Susanna (MCW X.193); extx. Margaret; 21 Apr 1752 (I 51.23); 10 Aug 1761; extx. Margaret Brooke; children: Jane, Mary, Ann, Rachel, Susannah, Clement, John,

Nicholas (ABB 3.83); 28 Jun 1762; extx. Margaret Brooke; children: Henry, James, Mary, Ann, Rachel, Susannah, John, Nicholas (ABB 3.163); widow Margaret; heirs Henry, Clement, Jane, Mary, Ann, Rachel, Nicholas, Susanna; _ Dec 1764 (GB 241)

Brooke, Thomas; age ca 34; 12 Dec 1751 (CCR MSA 8.1114)

Brooke, Isaac; 27 Jan 1757 (I 65.8); 30 Mar 1758 (I 65.492)

Brooke, Jane; 20 Jan 1761; 20 Feb 1761; husband, dec'd [unnamed]; sons Joseph & Charles Brooke; daus. Eleanor Harrison, Susanna Hoxter, Elizabeth Carroll (MCW XII.49); 3 Mar 1761 (I 75.211)

Brooke, Benjamin; planter; extx. Mary; 1 Jul 1765 (I 90.138); admx. Mary; 10 Feb 1767 (ABB 5.18); widow Mary; heirs Eleanor, Barbara; 30 Jun 1768 (GB 258)

Brooke, Joseph; 14 Jan 1767; 24 Mar 1767; cous. William Cooke [s/o John] (MCW XIII.176)

Brooke, Thomas; 16 Jul 1768; 5 Aug 1768; bro. Baker; father Thomas; nephew Joseph Walter Sim; tract *Prospect* (MCW XIV.59); admx. Elisabeth; nok Mary Bell, Lucy Wheeler; 25 Apr 1768 (I 95.340); heir Isaac; 31 Mar 1769 (GB 271)

Brooke, Charles; 11 Oct 1768; 7 Nov 1768; nephews Nicholas [s/o Margaret] & Henry Brooke; niece Ann Wade [d/o Margaret Brooke]; sister Eleanor Harrison (MCW XIV.65); 21 Dec 1768 (I 100.4); 7 Jul 1770; 5 children: Nicholas, Mary, Rachel Boarman, Susanna, Margaret [Wade]; grandchild Ann Wade (ABB 6.6)

Brooke, Anne; 15 Dec 1769; 2 Jul 1770; sons Baker, Richard; daus. Anne, Cathrine, Jane, Mary; grandsons Walter, Leonard [s/o Richard], John Leonard Brooke; Richard Oswald Brooke [s/o Richard]; granddaus. Ann Darnall Brooke, Easter, Anne [d/o Richard] (MCW XIV.159); Walter & Oswald; minors; 27 Nov 1775 (GB 326)

Brooke, Lucy; 25 Nov 1769; 30 Nov 1770; children: Robert, Richard, Clement, Rachel, Rebeccah, Elizabeth, Lucy Estep; grandson Brook Beall; tracts *Brookefield, The Vineyard* (MCW XIV.151)

Brooks, Eleanor; 20 Dec 1772 (I 121.329)

Brooke, Eleanor; 15 Jul 1776; 2 Nov 1777; mother Mary Brooke; father Benjamin Brooke; sister Barbara Brooke; tracts *Brooke Reserve, Brook Point* (MCW XVI.168)

BROTHERS

Brothers, Nathaniel [CA]; wife Mary; tract *Beginning*; 21 Jun 1697 (PGLR A.110)

BROUER

Brouer, John; wife Mary; tract *Hunter's Kindness*; 26 Aug 1736 (PGLR T.400)

BROWNE

Browne, Jane; servant; bastard son Christopher; "not gott in this county"; bound out; Jun 1697 Ct. (PGCR A.164)

Brown, Joseph; wife Ann; children: Sarah, b. 10 Feb 1701; Mary, b. 29 Jan 1702/3; Joseph, b. 29 9ber 1704; Ellinor, b. 12 Aug 1707; Thomas, b. 15 May 1709; John, b. 12 Nov 1711; Lucy, b. 13 Jun 1713; Ursula, b. 28 10ber 1713/4; Elizabeth, b. 2 7ber 1715 (QAP b/8, 11, 13)

Browne, Thomas; 6 Jan 1703/4; 25 Jan 1703/4; wife Sarah; eld. son Thomas; young. son Benjamin (MCW III.29); [with 1703] (I&A 5.355)

Brown, John, Sr.; wife Mary; tract *Warmister*; 31 Jan 1706 (PGLR C.207)

Brown, John; wife Dorcas; children: Mary, b. 27 Oct 1707; Sarah, b. 14 Jan 1710 (QAP b/6)

Brown, John; 9 Feb 1714; 28 Apr 1716; sons Francis, Jacob; dau. Mary Phippard; grandsons. John, William Pippard; granddau. Ursilla (MCW IV.67); 14 May 1716 (I&A 37a.47)

Brown, Mathew; 1 Nov 1715 (I&A 36c.229)

Brown, John; child: Mary, b. 3 Nov 1715 (QAP m/11)

Brown, Benjamin; age 8 month this date; s/o Mary; bound out; Nov 1716 (PGCR H.141)

Brown, Mark; m. 8 9ber 1716 Susanna Fowler; children: Mark, b. 10 Aug 1717; Alice, b. 2 10ber 1718; Mark, b. 29 May 1721; Frances, b. 27 9ber 1723 (QAP m/1; b/13, 14, 17, 18)

Brown, John; wife Margaret; child: Margaret, b. 8 Apr 1717 (QAP b/12)

Brown, John; 24 Jan 1718 (I 1.457)

Brown, Edward; 25 Mar 1719 (AA 1.370)

Brown, Proctor; bound out; Nov 1720 (PGCR K.11)

Brown, Alice; age 2 on 24 Jan last; bound out; Aug 1723 (PGCR L.132)

Brown, John; wife Mary; child: John, b. 21 Jan 1723/4 (QAP b/18)

Brown, Joseph; age ca 56; 20 May 1725 (PGLR I.675)

Brown, Samuel; b. 10 Jul 1712; bound out; Nov 1726 (PGCR N.105)

Brown, John; age 14-1/2; choses guardian; Nov 1725 (PGCR L.511)

Brown, John; 22 Dec 1726 (I 11.908); heirs [Scotland]; 12 Sep 1727 (AA 8.378); 22 Jun 1728 (AA 9.13); heir dau.; 25 Jun 1728 (GB 36)

Brown, Joseph, Jr.; m. 17 Aug 1727 Rebecca Simmons (QAP m/4)

Brown, John; wife Mary; child: James, b. 8 Oct 1727 (PGP p. 247-8)

Brown, Joseph; age ca 64; 18 Mar 1728/9 (PGLR M.481)

Brown, John; age ca 65; 1730 (PGLR Q.23)

Brown, John; m. 24 Apr 1732 Elizabeth Harper; child: Elizabeth, b. 28 Jan 1738 (QAP m/5; b/31)

Brown, Robert; m. 11 10ber 1732 Elizabeth Swan (QAP m/6)

Brown, Thomas; m. 20 Feb 1731/2 Anne Brushier; children: Basil, b. 25 Oct 1732; Nasy (m), b. 24 Jul 1734; Mary, b. 4 Apr 1736; Anne, b. 10 Mar 1739 (QAP m/5; b/8, 27, 28, 31, 32)

Brown, Joseph; age ca 73; 1734 (PGLR T.362)

Brown, Mary; orphan for 3 years; niece of Thomas Hill who has posession of her 90 acres of land; Mar 1735 (PGCR V.294)

Brown, Hannah; age ca 60; 1738 (PGLR T.607)

Brown, Henry; b. 24 Mar last past; bound out; Nov 1739 (PGCR X.501)

Brown, Joseph; age ca 33; 5 Jun 1740 (PGLR Y.185)

Brown, Joseph; 12 Sep 1738; 1 Sep 1740; wife Anne; son John (MCW VIII.99); admx. Anne; 23 Oct 1740 (I 26.98); widow Ann; 6 Aug 1741 (AA 18.258)

Brown, Virlindar; widow; 23 Apr 1741; 11 Jan 1741; granddaus. Priscalla & Virlindar Taylor; son Samuel Taylar; d-i-l Mary Taylor (MCW VIII.160)

Brown, Mark; age ca 57; 1742 (PGLR Y.654)

Brown, John; 25 Jun 1744 (AA 20.249)

Brown, John; 4 Mar 1750 (I 47.43)

Brown, Robert; 17 Aug 1750 (I 43.496)

Brown, Peter; wife Mary; children: John, b. 19 Nov 1754; Elizabeth, b. 11 Mar 1757; Ann, b. 5 Oct 1760 (PGP p. 256, 259)

Brown, John; wife Elizabeth; child: Elizabeth, b. 11 Mar 1757 (PGP p. 281)

Brown, William; wife Ruth; child: Ruth, b. 4 May 1760 (PGP p. 258)

Brown, William; wife Paticence; child: Aligia, b. 8 Jun 1760 (PGP p. 258)

Brown, John; wife Elenor; child: Lusey, bapt. 22 Nov 1761 (KGP p. 323)

Brown, Elisha; wife Margaret; children: Amelia, b. 16 Nov 1769 Broad Creek; William, b. 5 Jan 1772 Upper Chapel (KGP p. 373, 388)

Brown, Mark; 14 Jan 1771; legatees: children of Alice Duvall & Frances Sappington; Mark Brown Sappington [s/o Frances], Frances Hardesty (ABB 7.22)

BROWNNEN

Brownnen, Benjamin; wife Ann; child: Mary, b. 28 Sep 1761 (PGP p. 264)

Brownnen, William; wife Ruth; child: Elizabeth, b. 19 Aug 1762 (PGP p. 267)

BRUMLEY

Brumley, Nicholas; widow [unnamed m. John Wyet of Calvert Co.]; 15 Jun 1738 (I 24.94)

Brumley, Nicholas; 19 Oct 1744 (AA 20.531)

BRUNT

Brunt, James; wife Dosias; child: James, b. 11 7ber 1717 (QAP b/13)

BRYAN

Bryan, Tho.; s/o Terence; age 5 on 1 Sep next; bound out; Aug 1721 (PGCR K.372)

Bryan, Terence; dau. Elisabeth; Nov 1721 (PGCR K.419)

Bryan, Philip; age 16 on 1 Feb next; bound out; Apr 1738 (PGCR X.109)

Bryan, Derby; s-i-l Michael Dowden; 6 Jul 1740 (PGLR Y.190)

Bryan, Turrence; age ca 66; 1743 (PGLR Y.657)

Bryan [Broyan], William; m. 4 May 1750 Diana Gutteridge by Rev. Henry Addison; children: Thomas, bapt. 25 Aug 1751; Elizabeth, b. 23 May 1755; Richard, b. 6 Sep 1757; Sarah Ann, bapt. 12 Jun 1761; Rebeccah, bapt. 6 May 1764 Broad Creek; Phillop, bapt. 22 Mar 1767 Lower Chapel; Rachel, b. 5 Feb 1772 (KGP p. 289, 294, 308, 320, 322, 357, 360, 367, 389)

Bryan, Henry Richard; m. 30 Jan 1757 Rachel Lanham (KGP p. 317)

Bryan, George; wife Ann; children: Richard, b. 8 Jun 1773 Broad Creek; John, b. 19 Feb 1775 Broad Creek; others b. after 1776 (KGP p. 385, 386)

BUCK

Buck, Edward; age ca 18; fellon; Nov 1703 Ct. (PGCR B.262a)

BUCKLEY

Buckley, Miahael; age ca 10; bound out; Mar 1745 (PGCR DD.20)

BULL

Bull, Hillery; 1711 (I&A 33a.113)

BULLMAN

Bulman, John; wife Ann; child: Johanna, b. 27 Oct 1730 (PGP p. 249)

Bulman, John; wife Ann; children: John, b. 25 Aug 1733; Alice, b. 7 Aug 1735 (QAP b/27, 31)

BUNELL

Bunell, Francis; age ca 46; 8 Jun 1725 (PGLR I.647)

BUNT
Bunt, John; age ca 46; 23 Feb 1724 (PGLR I.624)

BUNYAN
Bunyan, Arthur; 18 Jan 1730 (I 16.134)

BURCH
Burch [Birch], John; planter; 12 Apr 1720; 12 Nov 1720; wife Eliza.; son Francis; dau. Easter Holly Ann (MCW V.28); 3 Dec 1720 (I 4.329); exs. James Reid & wife Elizabeth; widow, I son & 1 dau.; 2 Nov 1721 (AA 4.42)

Birch, Francis; m. 20 Jul 1720 Alie Orvin; child: John, b. 18 Oct 1721 (KGP p. 269)

Birch, Francis, age 30; 17 Feb 1723/4 (PGLR I.542); age ca 35; 1730 (PGLR M.558)

Burch, Thomas; wife Margaret; son Thomas, Jr.; tract *Bradford's Rest*; 30 Oct 1738 (PGLR Y.7)

Birch, John; wife Mary; children: James, bapt. 22 Oct 1752; Mary Elinor, b. 14 May 1754 (KGP p. 297, 306)

Birch, Jonathan; wife Elizabeth; child: Margaret, b. 26 May 1757 (KGP p. 314)

Burch, Edward; 26 Apr 1761; 22 Jun 1761; wife Stacy; sons Edward, Jestinian; daus. Ann, Mary, Stacy, Vineford, Edward; tracts *Burches Adventure, Discovery, Friends Advise, Content, Dickenson Parke, Weavers Prospect* (MCW XII.73); extx. Anastatia; 4 May 1761 (I 74.340); 31 Mar 1762 (I 78.318); 1765; ex. Annastatia McDonald [w/o Alexander]; widow Stacy; children: Ann, Mary, Stacy, Winifred, Edward, Justinian (ABB 4.89); heirs, Ann, Mary, Stacy, Veneford, Edward, Jestinian; 29 Aug 1767 (GB 255)

Burch, John; wife Mary ; child: Mary, bapt. 5 Feb 1764 at Upper Chapel (KGP p. 340)

Burch, Jonathan, Jr.; m. 15 Jan 1764 Ann Newton; children: Mary, b. 23 Dec 1764 Upper Chapel; Joseph Newton, b. 22 Oct 1766 Upper Chapel (KGP p. 366-7)

Burch, Thomas; wife Ann; child: Elizabeth, b. 2 Sep 1773 Broad Creek (KGP p. 385)

Burch, [unnamed]; heirs Edward, Jesse; 24 Mar 1774 (GB 319)

Burch, Olipher; wife Verlinder; child: Colmore, b. 19 Feb 1775 Broad Creek (KGP p. 386)

Burch, Leonard; wife Monaca; child: Ann, b. 3 Nov 1775 Lower Chapel (KGP p. 381)

BURGESS
Burgis, Margery; servant; had mulatto bastard child by Cezar; Jan 1696/7 (PGCR A.116; C.149))

Burges, George [AA], gent.; wife Katherine; tract *Burges Delight*; 18 Oct 1697 (PGLR A.140)

Burgess, James; wife Jane; son James; 24 Jul 1730; tract *His Lordship's Kindness* (PGLR Q.73)

Burgis, Charles; "son & dau." Meredith Davis & Usley his wife; tract *Westfalia*; 6 Oct 1730 (PGLR Q.173)

Burgess, James; age ca 60; 6 Aug 1735 (PGLR T.359)

Burgess, Charles; 14 Dec 1739; 3 May 1740; sons Charles [dec'd], Richard; dau. Elizabeth Offutt; d-i-l Martha [widow of Charles] (MCW VIII.75); [as Charles, Jr.]; admx. Martha; 16 Aug 1740 (I 25.177); heir Basil; 25 Aug 1741 (GB 120); admx. Martha Talbott [w/o Richard]; 6 Dec 1748 (AA 25.213)

Burgess, Charles; wife Martha; child: Basil, b. 20 Dec [with 1740s] (QAP b/34)

Burgess, Ann; guardian appointed; Nov 1748 (PGCR KK.36)

Burges, Basil; guardian appointed; Nov 1748 (PGCR KK.34)

Burgess, Ursula; guardian appointed; Nov 1748 (PGCR KK.35)

Burgess, James; wife Ann; children: Henry, b. 13 Aug 1755; Edward, b. 20 Jan 1757 (KGP p. 311, 314)

Burges, Basil; m. 8 Feb 1759 Anna [or Ann] Smith; children: Elizabeth, b. 16 Dec 1762; Charles, b. 18 Dec 1765; William Frederick Augustus, b. 15 Jan 1765/6 (QAP m/7; b/39)

Burges (Burgys), William; wife Mary; children: Josias, b. 27 Mar 1760; Elias, b. 4 Sep 1762; Milley (f), b. 7 Dec 1764 (PGP p. 258, 267, 273)

Burgess [Burgis], James; admx. Ann; 13 Nov 1760 (I 70.238); 5 Apr 1762; admx. Ann Burgess; children: Arnold, Henry, Casandria, Edward, Richard (ABB 3.117)

Burgess, Ed.; m. Margrett; child: Sarah, b. 16 Oct 1761 (PGP p. 263)

Burgess, Thomas; widow Ann; heirs Arnold, Henry, Cassandra, Edward, Rachel; 30 Nov 1762 (GB 223)

Burges, Arnold; 7 Jul 1770; 14 Dec 1770; wife Martha; children: Lidia Tennely, Martha Dove, Mary, Sarah, Milicent, Eleanor, Rachel, William (MCW XIV.173)

Burgess, Thomas; wife Sarah; child: Ann, b. 3 Jun 1772 Broad Creek (KGP p. 378)

BURKE

Burke, John; age ca 14 servant; Jun 1698 Ct. (PGCR A.317)

Burk, Hannah; b. ca Christmas last; bound out; Jun 1711 Ct. (PGCR G.69a)

Burk, Vlick; wife Eliza.; children: Thomas, b. 4 9ber 1712; Margaret, b. 10 9ber 1720 (QAP b/39)

Burke, John; 2 Jan 1717; 2 May 1718; wife Mary; tract *Good Luck* (MCW IV.162); [with 1718] (I 1.11); extx. Mary Burk [w/o Grove Tomlin]; 9 Dec 1719 (AA 2.489)

Burk, Benjamin; wife Margret; child: Vileta, bapt. 7 Feb 1762 (KGP p. 324)

BURLEY

Burley, Jonas; m. 30 8ber 1729 Elizabeth Reaves (QAP m/5)

BURKLEY

Burkley, Henry; wife Elizabeth; child: George, b. 4 Jul 1775 Upper Chapel (KGP p. 392)

BURNEE

Burnee, Williams; age 10 mos. on the 30th this inst.; bastard child of Elizabeth Burnee; bound out to James Conn; Mar 1753 (PGCR MM.376)

BURNES

Burnes, Godfry; 26 May 1715 (I&A 36b.236)

Burnes, David; wife Ann; tract *Hensly*; 28 Nov 1741 (PGLR Y.417)

Burnes [Burns], James; wife Jemina; children: David, b. 14 Feb 1745/6; Thomas, b. 27 Aug 1747*; John, b. 24 Aug 1749*; James, b. 19 Aug 1751*; Anne, b. 23 May 1753*; William, b. 3 Jul 1755*; Barton, b. 12 Aug 1757*; Margrett, b. 20 Nov 1759; Elisabeth, b. 2 Aug 1761; Frederick, b. 3 Sep 1763 (PGP p. 256, 262, 264, 269, 271, 280) [Note: * beside a name indicates that no parents are identified in the record, but dates & page numbers suggest they are all of the same family.]

Burnes, David; 5 Oct 1737; 28 Oct 1762; wife Ann; child James; s-i-l John Fleming; tract *The Hensley* (MCW XII.158)

BURNHAM

Burnham, Gabriel [NC]; wife Mary; tract *The Pasture*; 24 Oct 1721 (PGLR I.202)

BURRELL

Burrel, Francis; wife Jane; children: Elizabeth, b. 11 Sep 1707; Peter, b. 8 Sep 1710; Rebecca, b. 7 Mar 1712; Henarita, b. 11 Dec 1717; Christian, b. 20 Jan 1719; Jane, b. 26 Jul 1721 (KGP p. 280) [p. 285 lists Elizabeth, Peter, Rebecca and Heneritta with same day and month; no year; as children of Alexander and Ellinor; this is probably a transcription error as the parents of the family following are "Alix'der & Elenor"]

Burrell, Alexander, Mr.; m. 19 Aug 1759 Miss Elenor Dent; children: Elizabeth Dent, b. 17 Dec 1759; Daniel, b. 17 Oct 1761; Alexander Hawkins, b. 2 Nov 1763; George, b. 5 May 1765, bapt. 2 Jun 1765; John, b. 20 Jun 1766; Elenor, b. 1 Sep 1768 at Upper Chapel (KGP p. 285, 325, 334)

BURRIS

Burres, John; dau. Elizabeth Burres; 1698 (MCW II.162)

Burris [Burrus], Charles; wife Elizabeth; children: Elliner, b. 25 Mar 1760; Thomas, b. __ Dec 1762; Charles, b. 30 Mar 1766 (PGP p. 269, 278, 281)

Burris [Burrus], Henry; wife Mary; children: Mathew, b. 21 May 1762; Basil, b. 9 Mar 1765 (PGP p. 264, 276)

BURROUGHS

Burrows, William; wife Mary; children: Ann, b. 3 Feb 1700; Mary, b. 10 Jan 1707 (QAP b/5)

Burrows [Borrows]; James; m. 25 Jul 1718 Mary Brown; children: James, b. 9 8ber 1723; Mary, b. 8 8ber 1726 (QAP m/2; b/18, 20)

Burrough, Sarah; child: James, b. 17 Feb 1727/8 (QAP b/28)

Burroughs, James; age 9 mos.; bound out; Aug 1728 (PGCR O.334b)

Burroughs, James; age 12 years on 9 Dec next; bound out by mother Mary Burroughs; Nov 1734 (PGCR V.213)

BURTON

Burton, Thomas; 17 Jan 1722 (I 8.226); 19 Jul 1723 (AA 5.188)

Burton, Mary; 4 years old 25 Mar last; bound out; Aug 1731 (PGCR R.220)

Burton, William; wife Elizabeth; b. 7 Mar 1753 (PGP p. 254)

Burton, James; wife Katherine; child: Lucy, b. 6 Nov 1774 Lower Chapel (KGP p. 380)

BUSBY

Busby, Thomas; wife Margaret; tract *Ward's Pasture*; 15 Nov 1715 (PGLR F.485)

BUSEY

Busey, Henry; age 11 on 15 Jul next; bound out by mother Ann Ewens; 13 May 1697; rejected; "parents live in Calvert Co. & his f-i-l not willing"; Jun 1697 (PGCR A.189)

Bursie, George; wife Elizabeth; child: Ann, b. 22 Jan 1705 (QAP b/2)

Bussey, Hezekiah; [with 1714] (I&A 36b.190, 198)

Busey, Paul; wife Sarah; tract *Charles Hills*; 15 Sep 1714 (PGLR F.398)

Busey, Paul; planter; 24 Sep 1718; 1 Nov 1718; wife Sarah; 6 sons Paul, John, Charles, Samuel, Edward, Joshua; bro. Charles; tract *Charles Hill Land, Touloon* (MCW IV.194); [as Paul, Sr.]; 2 Feb 1718 (I 2.83); 4 Dec 1719 (AA 2.489); Sarah; widow, 6 sons & 4 daus. [unnamed]; 18 Aug 1721 (AA 3.514); 15 Oct 1723 (AA 5.412); heirs Paul, John, Charles, Sarah, Benjamin, Allan (f), Susannah, Samuel, Edmund, Joshua, Ann; 29 Mar 1724 (GB 18)

Bussee, Samuel; wife Hannah; tract *Taylor's Marsh*; 3 Apr 1725 (PGLR Q.546)

Bussey, George; age ca 54; 20 May 1725 (PGLR I.675)

Bussey, Hezekiah; age 48; 26 Feb 1725/6 (PGLR I.730)

Busey, Paul; 29 May 1731; 23 Jun 1731; mother [unnamed]; bro. John; sister Sarah (MCW VI.189); 7 Jul 1731 (I 16.252)

Busey, Sarah; 3 Jun 1743 (AA 25.94)

Busey, Charles; admx. Mary Jones [w/o Charles]; no heirs; 26 Nov 1735 (AA 14.79)

Bussey, Hezekiah; age ca 11; bound out; Mar 1750 (PGCR LL.134)

BUSTIAN

Bustian, William; wife Dosias [widow of James Brunt]; her dau. Mary Brunt; 28 Sep 1724 (PGLR M.192)

BUTLER

Butler, James; wife Joyce; child: Thomas, b. 14 Jun 1707 (KGP p. 260)

Butler, James; admx. Joyce [relict]; 21 Oct 1709 (I&A 30.205); 9 Oct 1710 (I&A 32a.78); admx. John Bradford & wife Joyce; 18 Apr 1713 (I&A 34.176); 15 Feb 1717 (I&A 39c.105); James [dec'd]; widow Joice [m/2 John Bradford, dec'd]; son Thomas; 24 Feb 1735/6 (CCR-MSA 6.167)

Butler, Rupert; m. 3 Jul 1711 Ann Harris (QAP m/1)

Butler, Margarett [SM]; heir of Robert Carvill [dec'd] [SM]; tract *Catton*; 21 May 1719 (PGLR F.163/745)

Butler, Thomas; m. 27 Oct 1722 Elizabeth Chew (PGP p. 229)

Butler, Thomas; age ca 18; choses guardian; Jun 1726 (PGCR L.636)

Butler, Charles; wife Sophia; tract *Fendall's Spring*; 14 Feb 1729 (PGLR M.542)

Butler, Rupert; 26 Mar 1734 (I 17.722); [heirs ?England]; 29 Mar 1735 (AA 14.219); 28 Apr 1735 (AA 13.83); 22 Mar 1736 (AA 15.334); 28 Mar 1738 (GB 97)

Butler, Thomas; wife Elizabeth; tract *The Hermitage*; 14 Dec 1737 (PGLR T.554)

Butler, Henry; 27 Jun 1739 (I 29.14)

Butler, Thomas; age ca 41; 31 Oct 1748 (CCR MSA 8.741)

Butler, John; children: Henry, bapt. 18 Apr 1762 [mother not named]; Violinda, b. 16 Sep 1764; bapt. 30 Oct 1764 at Broad Creek [mother Mary Ann]; Lewin Smith, bapt. 18 Jan 1767 Broad Creek [mother Mary] (KGP p. 327, 339, 360)

BUTT

Butt, Richard; wife Mary; children: Richard, b. 11 9ber 1703; Thomas, b. 29 10ber 1705; Diana, b. 5 Feb 1707/8; Mary, b. 2 Mar 1709/10; Samuel, b. 10 8ber 1712; Nicholas, b. 20 8ber 1714 (QAP b/7, 11)

Butt, Richard; 28 Apr 1715; wife [unnamed]; sons Richard, Thomas, Samuell, Nicholas; daus. Dinah, Mary (MCW IV.27); extx. Mary; 10 Aug 1715 (I&A 36b.231, 234); extx. widow Mary Medcalfe [w/o John]; 9 Apr 1716 (I&A 36c.169); ex. Mary Medcalfe [widow]; w/o John Medcalfe; 21 Aug 1718 (AA 1.188)

Butt, Samuel; m. 1 Aug 1734 Elizh. Swearingen (QAP m/6)

Butt, Richard; wife Rachel; children: Benjamin, b. 5 Nov 174_; Rachel, b. 28 Jul 1741 (QAP b/33,35)

Butt, Richard; 28 Nov 1744 (I 30.84)

Butt, Thomas; admx. Sophia Baldwin [late Butt]; 13 Dec 1757 (I 65.36)

Butt, Samuel; wife Racheale; child: Zacha (m), b. 10 Jul 1759 (PGP p. 257)

Butt, Aaron; wife Rachel; child: Barbary, b. 10 Oct 1760 (QAP b/39)

Butt, Samuel; wife Elizabeth; child: Azel (m), b. 10 Feb 1761 (PGP p. 260)

Butt, Samuel, Jr.; planter; 17 Jan 1765 (I 91.305?)

BYCRAFT

Bycraft, Peter; wife Rebecca; children: Margaret, b. 6 8ber 1702; Rebecca, b. 16 Aug 1705; Peter, b. 10 May 1707; Benjamin, b. 16 7ber 1710; George, b. 28 10ber 1713; Mary, b. 11 Mar 1716 (QAP b/8, 9, 11)

BYON

Byon, James; 15 Jun 1772; admx. Sarah (ABB 6.152)

BYRON

Byron, William; wife Dianna; child: Rachel, b. 5 Feb 1772 Upper Chapel (KGP p. 389)

CABINET

Cabinet, William Sherly; 20 May 1763 (I 81.363)

CADDICK

Caddick, Elizabeth [age 2-1/2], Margaret [age 4-1/2]; ds/o Sarah Caddick; bound out; Mar 1707 (PGCR C.127)

CADE

Cade, John; 5 Dec 1726 (I 11768); 17 Oct 1727 (AA 8.388); admx. Elisabeth Owen [w/o Thomas]; 2 children [unnamed]; 26 Oct 1732 (AA 11. 514, 645); son John, Jr.; 11 Jan 1728 (PGLR M.352); heirs Robert, Elizabeth; 29 Mar 1734 (GB 64)

CAHILL

Cahill, Richard; wife Catherine; child: Ann, b. 26 Jan 1765 (PGP p. 274)

CAIN

Cain, Jeremiah; age ca 2 years; orphan; bound out; Nov 1747 (PGCR GG.281)

Cane, Jeremiah; wife Mary; child: Mary Fletcher, bapt. 17 May 1752 (KGP p. 296)

CAINOUR

Cainour, John; 28 Aug 1731 (AA 11.178)

CALLENDER

Callender, William; m. 26 Jan 1724/5 Mary Mitchell (QAP m/4)

CALVERT

Calvert, William; [SM]; son Charles; 15 Jan 1703 (PGLR C.81a)

Calvert, Charles, Gov.; m. 21 Nov 1722 Rebecca Gerrard [d/o John Gerrard, dec'd, and Eliza. his wife] (QAP m/2)

Calvert, Maria; age ca 8; mulatto; d/o Heneretta Maria Calvert; bound to William Cummings; 20 Oct 1732 (PGLR Q.552)

Calvert, Joshua; 14 Feb 1734 (I 21.500); ?heir [England]; 28 Mar 1739 (AA 17.155)

CALVIN

Calvin, John; age 16 on 7th instant; choses guardian; Nov 1735 (PGCR V.620)

Calvin, William; m. 1 Aug 1754 Sarah Ray (PGP p. 255)

CAMBDEN

Cambden, John; m. 28 Dec 1718 Ester Wood; children: Henry, b. 14 Apr 1720; John, b. 30 Jun 1721 (QAP m/2; b/15, 17)

Cambden, John; m. 8 8ber 1724 Katherine Hall (QAP m/3)

Cambden, John; wife Catherine; 1 Mar 1725 (PGLR I.718)

Camden, Richard; [motherless boy; s/o John Camden, runaway]; age 14 on 31 Mar instant; bound out; Mar 1738 (PGCR W.652)

CAMMELL

Cammell, Ann; age ca 18; servant; Jun 1706 (PGCR C.61)

Cammell, John; age 3 yrs. 30 Apr last; mother runaway; bound out; Jun 1710 (PGCR D.318a)

CAMPBELL

Cambell, Joseph; s/o Catherine Cambell; bound out; Jun 1716 (PGCR H.85)

Campbell, Leonard; age 3 years 1 Jun inst; bound out; Jun 1726 (PGCR L.637)

Capbell, William; wife Ann; child: Alexander 20 Jul 1761 (PGP p. 261)

Campbell, Alexander; 30 Apr 1776; 24 Aug 1776; child John; grandchildren: Catherine & Arthur Campbell; d-i-l Christian Sasser [d/o John] (MCW XVI.138)

CANDLE

Candle, David; widow Elisabeth; ss-i-l Ambrose Cook, James Lee; bro. Richard; 16 Oct 1744 (AA 20.529)

CANN

Cann, James; age 2 years on 14 Oct last; mulatto child of Margaret; Jun 1707 (PGCR C.149)

CANVEN

Canven, Michaell; age ca 20; Jun 1702 (PGCR B.162)

CARLETON

Carleton, Arden; 4 Feb 1716 (I&A 37a.173)

CARLISLE

Carlisle, David; wife Jane; child: David, b. 5 Mar 1762 (PGP p. 263)

CARMACK

Carmack, Cornelius; *Manokesey*; planter; 13 May 1746; 14 Nov 1749; wife Guein; sons William, John; daus. Marey Boren, Elizabeth Evens, Mary Richards, Cathrine Richards (MCW X.55)

CARNES
Carnes, Thomas; wife Margrate; children: Josiah, b. 6 Jan 1760; Benjamin Nicholls, b. 18 Mar 1763 (PGP p. 258, 270)

CARRICK
Carrick, John, Jr.; wife Mary; children: Elizabeth, b. 16 Oct 1764; Henry, b. 19 Dec 1765; Francis, b. 21 Mar 1767; _____ (m), b. 23 Dec 1768; William, b. 19 May 1771 (QAP m/8)

CARROLL
Carroll, William; servant; age ca 18; Aug 1698 (PGCR A.332)

Carroll, Charles [AA]; wife Mary; tract *Enfield Chase*; 1 Jan 1708 (PGLR C.246)

Carroll, Charles [AA]; son Charles; 28 Jan 1724 (PGLR I.637)

Carroll, James; age ca 48; 27 Jun 1727 (PGLR M.220)

Carroll, Charles; wife Dorothy; 16 Mar 1732 (PGLR Q.637)

Carroll, Daniel; *Duddington*; 12 Apr 1734; 11 May 1734; wife Ann; son Charles; daus. Eleanor, Mary; sister Mary; bro. Charles; tract *Duddington Mannor* (MCW VII.74)

Carroll, Daniell, gent.; 10 Jul 1745; 22 May 1751; wife Eleanore; sons Daniel, John; dau. Ann; tracts *Town Quarter, Joseph Park, Partnership, John and Ann, Mistake* (MCW X.152-3); merchant; extx. Elleoner; 10 Jun 1751 (I 54.174)

Caroll, Patrick; wife Elizabeth; child: Patrick, bapt. 26 May 1765 Upper Chapel (KGP p. 358)

Caroll, William; wife Elenor; child: James, bapt. 24 May 1768 Lower Chapel (KGP p. 369)

Carroll, Charles, Jr.; *Duddington Manor*; 12 Mar 1768; 23 Mar 1773; wife Mary; children: Daniel, Henry Hill, Charles; f-i-l Henry Hill and his son Henry Hill; tracts *Duddington Manor, Duddington Pasture, New Troy, Clinmerelia, Captain Oulstons Garrison, Eli OCarroll, Litterlona, Girls Portion, Clouin Course, Aix la Chappelle, Iron Works* (MCW XV.95-6); admx. Mary; 17 May 1773 (I 115.1); extx. Mary; 22 Sep 1774 (I 119.111, 115)

CARTEEL
Carteel, Edward; extx. Cassandre; 10 Apr 1773 (I 114.44)

CARTER
Carter, William, Sr.; age ca 74; 26 Jun 1734 (PGLR T.124)
Carter, Michael; wife Hanah; child: Rebecca, b. 13 Sep 1758 (PGP p. 257)

CARTLEDGE

Cartledge, Edmond; 24 May 1740 (I 27.267)

CARTWRIGHT

Cartwright [Carthwright], John; wife Sarah; children: Mathew (?twin), b. 20 Feb 1754; Susanna (?twin), b. 20 Feb 1754; Hezekiah, b. 11 Oct 1761 (PGP p. 256, 263)

CASE

Case, Thomas; wife Sarah; child: Ann, b. 11 Jul 1761 (PGP p. 2652)

CASH

Cash, John; wife Mary; children: Mary Harr [w/o William]; Dauson:, b. 11 Aug 1712; John, b. 22 Aug 1714; Ruth, b. 5 Oct 1717; Rachel, b. 1 Jul 1720; Ann, b. 28 Apr 1722; Caleb, b. 10 Jul 1723 (QAP b/8, 10, 13, 17, 19)

Cash, John; 7 Oct 1726 (I 11.669); admx. Mary; 6 Jun 1727 (I 12.280); heirs Dawson, John, Ruth, Rachael, Caleb, Margrett, Mary; 28 Mar 1728 (GB 35); extx. Mary Trequair [late Mary Cash w/o Alexander]; 3 Jun 1730 (AA 10.305)

Cash, Caleb; wife Ellinor; children: Caleb, b. 15 ___ 1760; Dawson, b. 8 Mar 1765 (PGP p. 258, 275)

CASTEEL

Casteel, Edmond; wife Johanna; tract *Castell*; 25 Apr 1719 (PGLR F.142/714)

Casteel, Edmond, Sr.; son Edmond, Jr.; tract *Casteel*; Dec 1742 (PGLR Y.575)

Casteel, Edmund; wife Rebecca; child: Cassindra, b. 8 Jan 1753 (KGP p. 300)

Casteel, John; wife Rebeccah; child: Henry, bapt. 25 Aug 1765 Lower Chapel (KGP p. 351)

Casstell, Edmond; 11 Apr 1772; 24 Mar 1773; wife Rebeccah; children: Shadrack, Mechack, Abednego, Francis, Lucy Athy, Kezia Mitchal, Susanah Scace, Sarah Medley, Cassander, Charity; tracts *Cassteel, Edmonds Frolick Enlarged* (MCW XV.96)

Casteel, Mesheck; wife Katherine; child: Rebeccah, b. 18 Nov 1772 Lower Chapel (KGP p. 384)

CASTER

Caster [Castor], William; tailor; 10 Sep 1726; 11 Oct 1726; [no relations] (MCW V.232); 6 Jan 1726 (I 11.772); 11 Oct 1727 (AA 8.410)

CATON

Caton, Charles; wife Jemima; children: John, b. 7 Dec 1758; Jessey (m), b. 20 Apr 1762 (KGP p. 321, 327)

Caton, Stephen [Steven]; wife Eleanor; children: James, b. 29 Jan 1773 Broad Creek; Elizabeth, b. 28 Aug 1775 Broad Creek (KGP p. 378, 387)

CATTELEFF
Catteleff, Robert; 24 Jul 1741 (I 26.364)

CAVENOUGH
Cavenough, William Shirley; soldier in 44th Regiment; 14 Mar 1759; 21 Feb 1763; sister Monaca Hilton [w/o James] (MCW XII.181)

CAVY
Cavy [Cavey], Robert; wife Eliza.; children: Henry, b. 10 Mar 1714; Mary, b. 28 Mar 1720 (QAP b/10, 15)

CECIL
Cecill, Joshua; wife Mary; twin sons: Henry, b. 4 Nov 1696 @ 12:30 a.m.; Isaack, b. @ 1:30 a.m.; Jun 1698 Ct. (PGCR A.318)

Sesell, William; bound out children at request of wife on her death bed: John, age 7 on 24 Dec last; Phillip, age 5 on 28 day this inst.; Susan, age 2 on 3 Jan last (PGCR A.146)

Cecill, Phillip; wife Elizabeth; children: Susanna, b. 15 Mar 1712; Mary, b. 2 Jul 1716 (QAP b/14)

Cisell [Cicell], Donkin; children: William, b. 27 Sep 1715; Daniell, b. 27 Feb 1717 (KGP p. 274)

Cecell, Joshua; 5 Jun 1717 (I&A 37b.238)

Cecill, John; m. 1718 Elizabeth Sallars (QAP m/2)

Cecil, Isaac; wife Elizabeth; 3 Apr 1721 (PGLR I.81)

Cecil, Joshua; son Isaac; 1 Aug 1726/7 (PGLR M.267)

Cissell, Philip; planter; admx. Elisabeth; 9 Mar 1733 (I 17.720); admx. Elisabeth; children: Philip, John, William, Joshua, Elisabeth, Mary; 30 Apr 1735 (AA 13.87)

Cecil, John; 14 Jan 1757; 28 Jan 1759; wife Elizabeth; child: Zephaniah (MCW XI.231); extx. Elisabeth; 5 Feb 1759 (I 67.107)

Sissill [Sissle], Phillip; wife Elizabeth; children: Verlinda Thomas, b. 27 Oct 1764 Broad Creek; Zefaniah, b. 25 Jan 1763 at Upper Chapel; Samuel, b. 24 Dec 1773 Upper Chapel; Zachariah, b. 28 Jan 1776 Broad Creek (KGP p. 332, 342, 382, 390)

Siscill, Zephaniah; child: Elizabeth Solars, bapt. 26 May 1765 Upper Chapel (KGP p. 358)

CHAFFEE

Chaffee, Richard; 10 Mar 1697/8; 25 Aug 1698; daus. Mary, Margery; wife Ann (MCW II.193); 8 Jun 1700 (I&A 20.182); 5 Jul 1701 (I&A 21.142)

CHAMBERLAIN

Chamberlain, Henry; wife Mary; child: James, b. 1 7ber 1712 (QAP b/8)
Chamberlain, Mary Magdalane; age 11 next Christmas Day; bound to Edward Willett; Aug 1751 (PGLR MM.108)

CHAMBERS

Chambers, James; 28 Jun 1717 (I&A 38a.33); planter; 5 Oct 1717 (I&A 37n.195)
Chambers, Joseph; 9 Sep 1742 (I 27.264); 29 Mar 1744 (I 28.505); 28 Jun 1744 (AA 20.331)
Chambers, William; wife Ann; child: John, b. 5 Feb 1763 (PGP p. 268)
Chambers, Edwn.; wife Elizabeth; child: Amos, b. 10 Apr 1763 (PGP p. 270)

CHAPLAIN

Chapline, William; wife Elizabeth; children: Joseph, b. 5 7ber 1707; William, b. 25 Oct 1709; Mary, b. 17 7ber 1712; Anna, b. 2 10ber 1714; Moses, b. 11 Jun 1717; Elizabeth, b. 14 Nov 1722; William, b. 17 Apr 1726 (QAP b/7. 10. 14. 26)
Chaplain, John; m. 19 Sep 1758 Rebekah Cheny; children: _____ (m); _____ (f); William, b. 16 Oct 17__ (QAP m/7; b/38, 46)

CHAPPLE

Chappell, Newman; wife Mary; child: Henry, b. 7 Jan 1709 (QAP b/12)
Chapple, Henry; wife ___thin; child: George, b. 5 Sep 1760 (PGP p. 259)
Chaple, John; wife Virlinder; child: William, b. 2 Sep 1772 (PGP p. 278)

CHAPMAN

Chapman, John; wife Alice; child: James, b. 5 Jan 1702 (QAP b/2)
Chapman, John; 7 Jan 1702 (I&A 22.148); widow Alice Lashly; 16 Nov 1703 (I&A 3.99)
Chapman, John; wife Elizabeth; child: John, b. 3 Jan 1716 (QAP b/12)
Chapman, James; wife Mary; tract *Fortune*; 28 Jan 1726 (PGLR M.110)
Chapman, James; m. 29 9ber 1723 Mary Miles; child: Mary, b. 21 May 1726 (QAP m/3; b/19)
Chapman, Thomas; present wife Ann; sons Thomas, William; 8 Jun 1742 (PGLR Y.512)

CHARLES

Charles, Richard; 9 Jul 1698 (I&A 16.98)

CHARLETT
Charlett, Richard; 28 Jun 1698 (I&A 16.67; 18.172)

CHARLTON
Charlton, John, gent.; 29 Mar 1748; 21 Apr 1748; wife [unnamed]; sons John, Thomas; bro. Arthur; bs-i-l Thomas and Henry Charlton (MCW IX.148)

CHARTERS
Chartes, Thomas; wife Elizabeth; son Thomas; tract *His Lordship's Kindness*; 25 Mar 1725 (PGLR I.656)

Charter, Thomas; wife Elizabeth; child: Thomas, b. 24 Jul 1723 (KGP p. 281) [
Page 281 in the Harrison copy of KGP has a very ambiguous entry which appears as follows:
Elizabeth, dau. of Robt. Johnson and Elizabeth his wife, born 23 Mar 1709
Joseph & Benjamin, born 5 Dec 1715
Francis, son to Elizabeth, born 19 Feb 1718
Thomas Lockar her last husband died 1722
Thomas, son of Thomas Charter and Eliza. his wife born 24 Jul 1723

Charters, Thomas; admx. Elisabeth; 28 Nov 1752 (I 54.144); admx. Elisabeth; 21 Sep 1753 (AA 35.168, 320); admx. Elizabeth Charters; 19 Sep 1755 (ABB 2.3); widow Elizabeth; heirs [surviving]; 23 Nov 1757 (GB 207)

CHATTERSEA
Chattersea, Thomas; 10 Jul 1761 (I 74.328)

CHEENY
Cheeney [Cheyney], Richard, Sr. [AA]; wife Mary; tract *Cheeney's Beginning*; 8 Mar 1702 (PGLR C.49a)

Cheany [Cheeny], Charles; wife Mary; children: Charles, b. 13 Jan 1722/3; Dorcas, b. 15 Feb 1725; Ezekial, b. 25 May 1727; Jeremiah, b. 16 Jan 1731/2; Mary, b. __ ___ 17__ (QAP b/18, 21, 23, 24, 25)

Cheney, Charles; age ca 50; 17 Jul 1724 (PGLR I.580)

Cheany, Greenbury; wife Elizh.; child: Rebeckah, b. 11 Mar 173_ (QAP b/28)

Cheany, Samuel; wife Ann; child: Mary, b. 2 Apr 1735 (QAP b/29)

Cheeny, Charles, Sr.; son Charles, Jr.; tract *Cheeney's Delight*; 2 Nov 1723 (PGLR I.523)

CHESHIRE
Cheshire, William [SM]; wife Ann; tract *Brightwell's Range*; 26 Jun 1716 (PGLR F.545)

Cheshere [Chisheir], Burch [Birch]; wife Jane; children: Elisabeth, b. 3 Dec 1761; Salley, b. 25 Apr 1766 (PGP p. 262, 278)

CHESSMAN
Chessman; William [dec'd] [England]; widow Alice; 9 Feb 1741 (PGLR Y.533)

CHEW

Chew, Joseph; wife Mary; tract *Chew's Meadow*; 14 Dec 1720 (PGLR I.14 Dec 1720)

Chew, Joseph; age ca 40; 1730 (PGLR Q.13)

Chew, Joseph, Jr.; minor; choses Joseph, his father, as guardian; Nov 1733 (PGCR S.473)

CHIDLEY

Chidley, Richard; admx. Sarah Clay [w/o Henry Thomas]; 2 Sep 1740 (I 27.43); widow Sarah Clay [w/o Henry Thomas]; 11 Aug 1742 (AA 19.111)

CHILD

Child, John; wife Sarah; child: Elizabeth, b. 11 Feb 1711/2 (QAP b/7)

Child [Childs], John; m. 31 Dec 1730 Elizabeth Dumolin; children: John D'Million, b. 25 Nov 1732; Ann, b. 13 Jan 1733 (QAP m/5; b/25, 30)

Child, John; 10 Apr 1750; 27 Jun 1750; wife Elizabeth; sons Henry, Gabrial; daus. Elizabeth Wess, Ann, Cassandra; tracts *Newfoundland, Orphan's Gift* (MCW X.97); extx. Elisabeth; 24 Sep 1750 (I 47.288)

CHIPMAN

Chipman, John; admx. Alice Lashly [w/o John]; 15 Sep 1704 (I&A 25.150)

CHITTAM

Chittam, John; wife Ann; tract *Exchange*; 23 Jan 1698 (PGLR A.182)

Chittam, John; [with 1708] (I&A 28.257)

Chittam, John; wife Mary; tract *Weymouth*; 8 Sep 1711 (PGLR F.107)

Chittam, John; f-i-l Larance Morgan; tract *Black Ash*; 3 Sep 1713 (PGLR F.319)

Chittam, John; sons John, Philip; tract *Goose Ponds*; 1 Jul 1732 (PGLR Q.507)

Chittam, Thomas; Bladensburgh; 7 Aug 1768; 8 Aug 1768; [no relations] (MCW XIV.59); 27 Aug 1768 (I 106.168)

Chittem, John; 24 Nov 1707; 1 Mar 1707/8; wife Anne; grandson John Thomson [s/o William] dau. Grace Ramsey; son John (MCW III.105)

CHRISTMAS

Christmas, Charles; m. 9 Feb 1742 Barbary Welsh by Rev. Addison; children: Zachariah, bapt. 9 Feb 1752; Millinder, b. 26 Feb 1756 (KGP p. 290, 294, 312)

CHURCH

Church, Waitstill Singleton; 24 Jan 1776; 6 Mar 1776; sister Sarah Church; son Jonathan Montgomery Church; tract *Addition to Quebeck* (MCW XVI.168); 27 May 1776 (I 123.380, 404; 124.10)

CLADIUS

Cladius, Frederick; wife Phillis; tract *Long Looked For*; 6 Jan 1718 (PGLR F.151/727)

CLAGETT

Clegett, Thomas [CA]; gent.; wife Sarah; tract [unnamed]; 18 Aug 1702 (PGLR C.6a)

Clagett, Thomas; wife Mary; tract *Moore's Littleworth*; 27 Aug 1712 (PGLR F.202)

Clegett, Richard; wife Deborah; 10 Apr 1713 (PGLR F.279); son Edward; tract *Green Land*; 18 Nov 1732 (PGLR Q.557)

Clagett, Thomas, Capt.; age ca 49; 1 Mar 1728 (PGLR M.293)

Clagett, Thomas, Capt.; 26 Jan 1732; 27 Mar 1733; wife Mary; sons Richard, John, Charles, Thomas; daus. Elizabeth Prather, Sarah, Martha, Margaret, Ann; tracts *Huntington, Clagett's Purchase, Strife* (MCW VII.18); admx. Mary; 27 Jun 1733 (I 17.277), Capt.; admx. Mary; 27 Aug 1734 (I 20.64); extx. Mary; heirs Martha, Ann; rest [unnamed] of age; 30 Sep 1734 (AA 12.640)

Clagett, Thomas; son Richard [London]; tract *Huntington*; 9 Mar 1736 (PGLR T.512)

Clagett, Thomas; planter; 5 Aug 1737; 23 Nov 1737; wife Ann; son Henry; daus. Mary, Ann Fogg, Sarah, Lucy (MCW VII.230); extx. Ann; 16 Jan 1737 (I 23.174); extx. Anne; heirs Mary, Henry, Ann Hogg, Sarah, Posthumus [b. after father's death]; 1 Dec 1739 (AA 17.455); widow Ann; heirs Mary Clagett, Anne Fogg, Henry, Sarah; 25 Aug 1741 (GB 119)

Clagett, Sarah; 23 Aug 1737; 30 Sep 1737; sister Martha; father Thomas; mother Mary (MCW VII.221)

Clagett, Mary; son Charles; 3 Nov 1737 (PGLR T.542)

Clagett, John; m. 30 Jul 1739 Sarah ____; children: Thomas, b. 12 Feb 1740/1; Mary, b. 9 Oct 1742; Alexander, b. 2 Sep 1744 (?); Hezekiah, b. 27 Oct 1744 (?); Richard, b. 27 Jun 1746; William, b. 25 Jul 1748; David, b. 23 Jan 1749/50; Nathaniel, b. 27 Mar 1751; John, Jr., b. 23 Oct 1752; Horatio, b. 10 Aug 1756; Walter, b. 12 Nov 1763 (PGP p. 229, 254, 255, 256, 270)

Clagett, Richard; age ca 62; 1743 (PGLR Y.703)

Clagett, Thomas; wife Ann; child: John, b. 7 Dec 1744 (PGP p. 251)

Clagett, Richard; 27 Oct 1752; 7 Dec 1752; sons Edward, Samuel, Richard; daus. Mary Berry [w/o Jeremiah], Elinor Eversfield; grandson Richard Berry [s/o Jeremiah]; tracts *Greenland, Croome* (MCW X.243); 4 Jan 1753 (I 53.142); admx. Lucy; 12 Jul 1753 (I 56.31); admx. Lucy [widow]; 28 Aug 1754 (AA 36.388); 28 Aug 1754; admx. Lucy Clegett (ABB 1.118); widow Lucy; heirs

Martha, Deborah, Richard Keene, Edward, Margaret, Isaac; 27 Aug 1755 (GB 198)

Claggett, Mary; 29 Oct 1759; 30 Mar 1759; child Martha (MCW XI.231)

Clagett, Charles; wife Mary; child: Thomas, b. 1 Mar 1761 (PGP p. 260)

Clegitt, Richard; m. Ann Hutchinson; children: John, 13 Feb 1763 at Lower Chapel; George Parker, bapt. 16 Dec 1764 Upper Chapel (KGP p. 335, 355)

Clagett, Sabrit; 4 Dec 1766; 26 Mar 1767; sisters Ann, Sarah, Mary, Martha (MCW XIII.175)

Clagitt, Thomas, s/o John & Sarah of Frederick Co.; m. 11 Oct 1768 Mary Meek Magruder [d/o Enock and Meek Magruder]; children: Judson Magruder, b. 29 Aug 1769; Mary Meek, b. 24 Feb 1771 Broad Creek (KGP p. 374)

Clagett, John; 11 Oct 1768; 29 Mar 1769; children: Ann, Sarah, Martha (MCW XIV.94); extx. Ann; 22 May 1769 (I 101.238); 24 Jun 1771; extx. Ann Clagett; 3 daus. Ann, Sarah, Martha (ABB 6.38); widow Ann; heirs Sarah, Martha; 26 Mar 1772 (GB 301)

Clagget, Lucy; 11 Nov 1774 (I 120.175); 16 Oct 1775 (I 123.200)

Clagett, Jeen; [sis. of Peter Young]; her children: James, Margret, Sarah, Paty Clagett; 1775 (MCW XVI.167)

CLANCY

Clancy, Elizabeth; widow; dau. Elizabeth; 21 Jun 1742 (PGLR Y.516)

CLARKE

Clarke, John [wife Elizabeth]; Robert Clarke; Benjamin Clarke [wife Judith], Francis Clarke; tract *Clarkes Purchase*; 24 Feb 1699 (PGLR A.237)

Clarke, William; wife Ruth; son William; tract *Roziars Gift* part of *Admirothona*; 27 May 1700 (PGLR A.290)

Clark, William, Dr.; [with 1702] (I&A 21.395)

Clarke, Richard [AA]; wife Elizabeth; tract part of *Roper's Range*; 6 Jul 1703 (PGLR C.109)

Clarke, Robert; 11 Feb 1704 (I&A 25.146)

Clarke, Abraham; wife Elizabeth; tract [unnamed]; 27 Jun 1704 (PGLR C.102a)

Clarke, John [CH]; bro. Thomas; tract *Clarke's Inheritance*; 2 Jan 1706 (PGLR C.178)

Clarke, Thomas; wife Elizabeth; child: Elizabeth, b. 11 Feb 1711/2 (QAP b/6)

Clarke, Henry; wife Sarah [d/o Benjamin Parrott of Talbot Co.]; tract *Collington*; 1 Aug 1711 (PGLR F.31)

Clarke, Abraham [CA]; son Abraham; tract *Essington*; [undated, with 1712] (PGLR F.194)

Clark, Daniel; wife Margrett; children: Jefferson, b. 5 Apr 1716; Mary, b. 10 Jan 1723; James, b. 26 Feb 1725; William, b. 26 Jan 1728 (KGP p. 271)

Clarke, Thomas; 19 Jun 1719 (I 2.217); admx. Elisabeth Trunker; 27 May 1721 (AA 3.409)

Clarke, Neall; age ca 56; 17 May 1720 (CCR CL.612); age ca 60; s-i-l Samuel Farmer; 25 Jul 1724 (PGLR I.590); age ca 63; 1 Jul 1726 (PGLR M.32)

Clark, William; wife Ann; children: Joshua, b. 3 9ber 1720; Samuel, b. 1 Aug 1722; Gabriel, b. 8 7ber 1724; Elizabeth, b. 31 10ber 1726; Mary, b. 20 Sep 1729; Ann, b. 23 Dec 1731; Daniel, b. 14 Feb 1733 (QAP b/16, 18, 19, 20, 23, 25, 27, 30)

Clark, Abraham; 29 Feb 1723 (I 10.149); 23 Mar 1724 (AA 6.290)

Clarke, Richard; wife Ann; tract Clark's Purchase; 15 May 1723 (PGLR I.482)

Clarke, Richard; age 27; 24 Mar 1725 (PGLR I.715)

Clark, Mary [VA]; widow of Benjamin, dec'd; dau. Susannah, age 5; tract Bowdell's Choice; 9 Mar 1726 (PGLR M.41)

Clark, John; age ca 3; and Mary, b. 19 Mar 1725; ch/o Alexander & Rachel [both dec'd]; bound out; Jun 1727 (PGCR N.347, 354)

Clark, Abraham; wife Margaret; children: Mary, b. 28 Oct 1727; Elizabeth, b. 1728; Benjamin, b. 25 Mar 1730; Abraham, b. 8 Dec 1731; Margret, b. 6 Jan 1733; John Russel, b. 26 Jul 1735; Henry, b. 30 Dec 1737 (QAP b/22, 23, 25, 28, 29, 31)

Clarke, Daniel [dec'd]; sons Thomas, William, Richard; tract Clark's Fancy; 19 Sep 1733 (PGLR T.232)

Clarke, Thomas [dec'd]; son Thomas, age ca 15; 30 Sep 1734 (PGLR T.190)

Clarke, Robert; age ca 50; 24 Nov 1740 (PGLR Y.236)

Clark, Joshua; wife Mary; children: Caleb, b. ____; Elizabeth, b. 7 Jan 1743; Joshua, b. 6 Apr 174_; Mary, b. 7 Dec ____; Mareen, b. 11 Aug 174_; Samuel, b. 21 Au 174_; ____ Thomas, b. __ Aug ____ (QAP b/33, 34, 35, 36)

Clark, Gabriel; wife Rebecah; children: Ann, b. 20 Aug 17__; Priscilla, b. 24 Sep ____ [with 1740s] (QAP b/34)

Clark, Samuel; wife Sophia; children: George, b. __ Jul ____; William, b. 24 Sep 17__ [with 1740s] (QAP b/34)

Clark, Benjamin; wife Mary; children: Thomas, bapt. 23 Jun 1751; Chloe, b. 6 Jun 1753 (KGP p. 294, 300)

Clark, William; 23 May 1752; 28 Nov 1753; wife Ann; sons: Gabriel, Joshua, Samuel, Daniel; daus. Elizabeth Haraman, Mary, Ann; tracts Clark's Fancy, Ijams Choice (MCW X.287)

Clark, Thomas; admx. Ailce; 1 Oct 1756 (I 62.101)

Clark, William; wife Ann; child: Elisabeth, 17 Jun 1762 (PGP p. 167)

Clark, Ann; 19 Aug 1761; 22 Sep 1768; [no relations] (MCW XIV.94)

Clark, Hannah; child: Grace, b. 22 May 1764, bapt. 17 Jun 1764 at Broad Creek (KGP p. 339, 356)

Clark, Thomas; 14 Oct 1765; 24 Jun 1765; children: Elizabeth Sprigg, Charles, Priscilla Beall; grandchildren: John Clark Sprigg, Elizabeth & Ann Parker; tracts *Mawburn Plains, Marlborough, Good Luck, Craig Might, Groom's Lot* (MCW XIII.119); admx. Martha [widow]; 1 Sep 1766 (I 98.13)

Clark, Charles; 26 Jan 1767; 24 Apr 1767; wife Martha; sons Thomas, David (MCW XIII.176-7); extx. Martha [widow]; 7 Aug 1767 (I 98.1)

Clarke, Daniel; wife Margaret; child: Daniel, b. 23 Sep 1773 (QAP b/46)

CLARKSON

Clarkson, William; 20 Jul 1703; 27 Sep 1703; wife Ruth; dau. Eliza.; son William; bro. Notley Rozer; d-i-l Martin Gale; tracts *Stonyhill* or *Athey's Folly* (MCW III.34); extx. Ruth Guttrick; 14 Mar 1704 (I&A 25.145); 23 May 1704 (I&A 3.575); heir child: William; 4 May 1708 (GB 3)

Clarkson, William, m. 22 Nov 1713 Elizabeth Hagian; children: Thomas, b. 14 Sep 1714; William, b. 10 Feb 1716, Mary, b. 18 Oct 1717; Eliza., b. 5 Oct 1719; Edward, b. 6 Oct 1721 (KGP p. 262, 263)

Clarkson, William; admx. Eliza; 4 Nov 1736 (I 22.160); heirs that are under age: William, Mary, Elisabeth, Edward, Ruth, Joseph, Ann, Notley, Henry; 30 Feb 1737 (AA 16.184); heirs: William, Mary, Elizabeth, Edward, Ruth, Joseph, Anne, Notley, Henry; 27 Jun 1739 (GB 102)

CLARVO

Clarvo, Francis; planter; 29 Dec 1721; 21 Jan 1721/2; wife Bridget; son John; dau. Patt Howell [w/o John]; daus. Francis Dickison, Ann Jenkins [w/o Enoch] grandson Francis Jenkins (MCW V.79); 27 Jan 1721 (I 7.153); 8 Jan 1722 (AA 5.1744); daus. Frances Dickenson & wife of John Howell; 10 Mar 1724 (AA 6.278)

Clarvo, John; 28 Feb 1733/4; 21 Mar 1733/4; wife Elizabeth; sons Francis, John, Henry; dau. Bridget; mother Bridget Clarvo; b-i-l John Howell; tracts *Maiden Bradley, London Pleasure, The Addition, Market Overton* (MCW VII.70); extx. Elisabeth Downing [w/o Nicholas]; 3 Aug 1734 (I 20.60); heirs Francis, John, Henry; 23 Mar 1735 (GB 76); extx. Elisabeth Downing [w/o Nicholas]; children: Francis, John, Henry; 14 Apr 1735 (AA 13.82); ss-i-l John Dickason, Edward Person; 7 Jan 1735 (AA 14.140, 170); extx. Elisabeth Downing [w/o Nicholas]; _ Oct 1735 (I 21.217); admx. Elisabeth Downing [w/o Nicholas]; 15 Jul 1736 (I 21.400); heir Henry; 24 Aug 1748 (GB 164)

Clarvo, Francis [dec'd]; wife Bridgett; 25 Nov 1734 (PGLR T.199)

Clarvo, Henry; chooses guardian; Aug 1748 (PGCR HH.337)

Clarvo, Bridget; 14 Mar 1752; 15 Mar 1754; daus. Martha Lanham, Ann
   Phillips; grandsons Henry & Francis Claroe; granddau. Elizabeth
   Phillips (MCW XI.17); _ 15 1754 (I 60.144); 11 Feb 1755; ex. Henry Clarvoe
   (ABB 1.128)

Clarvo, Frances; admx. Sarah; 28 Apr 1756 (I 63.7)

Clarvoe, Henry; 16 Sep 1760; 24 Nov 1760; cous. Elizabeth and Martha
   Clarvoe; tract Markett Overton (MCW XII.10-11); admx. Sarah; 27 Jan 1761 (I
   74.159)

CLARY

Clary, Daniell; wife Elener; child: Linney (f), b. 14 Jul 1761 (PGP p. 261)

Clary, William Devern; wife Ann; child: Vachel, b. 22 Mar 1765 (PGP p. 276)

Clary, William; m. Sarah [?Sweringen]; children: Elisha, b. 19 Nov 1757;
   John Sweringen, b. 23 Jul 1759; Ann, b. 25 Nov 1761; Mary, b. 29 Jan
   1764 (PGP p. 273)

CLAYTON

Clayton, Thomas; age ca 7; bound out; Mar 1746 (PGCR FF.385)

CLELAND

Cleland, Thomas; wife Jane; children: Elizabeth, b. 26 Oct 1739;
   Cassandra, b. 25 Oct 1741; Ann, b. 3 Jan 1743; Mary, b. 18 May 1746;
   Sarah, b. 10 Aug 1748; Susanna, b. 26 Jan 1749; Philip, b. 10 Feb 1750
   (PGP p. 254)

CLEMENS

Clemens, John; age ca 49; 1728 (PGLR M.343); age ca 53; 11 Sep 1733 (PGLR
   T.123)

Clemens, Edward; age ca 54; 6 Jun 1735 (PGLR T.280)

Clements, John; wife Mary; children: Henry, bapt. 8 Dec 1751; Ralph
   Fisher, b. 14 Nov 1753 (KGP p. 294, 301)

Clements, William; 23 Apr 1754; 6 Aug 1754; wife Francis; sons
   Nehemiah, Ignatius, Edward, John, George; tract Green's Forrest (MCW
   XI.40); 23 Oct 1754 (I 60.145)

Clements, William; wife Ann; child: John, b. 7 Mar 1753 (KGP p. 305)

Clemons, John; wife Mary; child: Elener Ann, bapt. 10 Jul 1768 Lower
   Chapel (KGP p. 371)

CLIFFORD

Clifford, Abigall; servant; had two bastard children: Edward Riston & ____; Jan 1696/7 Ct. (PGCR A.116, 170)

Clifford, John; age 5 mos.; base born child of Abigaile Clifford; Oct 1699 (PGCR A.474)

Clifford, Elisabeth; age 4 years; base born child of Abigaile Clifford; Jun 1701 (PGCR B.111)

Clifford, Rachill; child: Reason (m), bapt. 6 Jun 1763 at Upper Chapel (KGP p. 333)

CLINTON

Clinton, Christopher; wife Mary; dau. Eleanor; tract *The Hermitage*; 1 Oct 1728 (PGLR M.369)

CLOYD

Cloyd, Robert; age ca 50; 1731 (PGLR Q.372)

Cloyd, Robert; extx. Elisabeth Bolton [w/o James]; 29 Jun 1745 (I 31.41); only child Elisabeth Bolton [w/o James]; 12 Sep 1745 (AA 22.49)

CLUBB

Club, John; age ca 57; 20 Apr 1719 (CCR CL.548)

Clubb, Phillip; wife Jane; children: Samuell, b. 5 Apr 1761; Ann, b. 21 Mar 1766 (PGP p. 260, 278)

CLUCKSON

Cluckson, William; extx. Ruth Goodrick [w/o Edmund]; 23 Jan 1706 (I&A 26.147)

CLYDE

Clyde, Robert; wife Christian; d. 17 Feb 1718; children: Robert, b. 31 Aug 1710, d. 10 Aug 1715; John, b. 1 Aug 1713, 14 Sep 1715; Elizabeth, b. 2 Jan 1717 (KGP p. 274)

Clyde, Robert; age ca 56; 19 Oct 1730 (CCR-MSA 5.459)

Clyd, Robert; carpenter; 21 Jan 1734; 14 Mar 1736/7; dau. Elizabeth; tract *Clyd* (MCW VII.206)

COATS

Coats, Robert; m. 25 Nov 1734 Mary ____ (QAP m/6)

Coats, Michael; wife Amey; child: Jesse (m), b. 29 Mar 1753 (KGP p. 305)

COBB

Cobbs, John; merchant; 11 Jun 1705 (I&A 3.680); 13 Apr 1708 (I&A 28.109)

Cobb, Michael; 22 Aug 1763 (I 83.165)

CODY

Cody, James; wife Mary; children: Hellen, b. 8 7ber 1716; Mary, b. 24 Mar 1717; Katherine, b. 24 Mar 1719 (QAP b/13. 16)

COE

Coe, John; wife Mary; child: Richard, b. 7 Dec 1753 (KGP p. 304)

Coe, John; admx. Mary; 20 Jul 1763 (I 82.146); 12 Sep 1765; admx. Mary (ABB 4.140); widow Mary Coe; heirs: Samuel, Cassandra, Elijah, Milbern, Mansilsa?, Richard, Keziah, William, Mary Ann, Ann; 25 Mar 1767 (GB 250)

Coe, Samuel; wife Phebe; child: John, b. 11 Sep 1775 Lower Chapel (KGP p. 381)

COFFEE

Coffee, John; m. Rebecca; children: Mary, b. 2 Sep 1724; James, b. 18 Nov 1727; Phillip, b. 14 Apr 1730 (PGP p. 249)

Coffee, John; s-i-l Ambrose Cooke; 21 Sep 1728 (PGLR M.328)

COFFER

Coffer, Thomas; wife Mary; 1716 (MCW IV 138)

Coffer, John [CH]; wife Elizabeth; sons John, Francis [VA]; tract *Nonesuch*; 10 Nov 1719 (PGLR F.273/856)

Coaffer, John, Jr.; age ca 34; 1728 (PGLR M.344)

Coaffer, John; age ca 62; 1728 (PGLR M.343)

COGHILL

Cloghell (Cloghele), William; 1 Aug 1702; 31 Aug 1702; wife Christian; son James, William, David; tract *Athey's Folly* (MCW II.252); 14 Sep 1702 (I&A 22.85)

Coghill, James; wife Amy; tract *Littleworth*; 13 Mar 1704 (PGLR C.155)

Cogwill, William; dau. Mary; 1724/5 (MCW VI.1)

Coghill, William; 24 Apr 1729; 4 Jun 1729; wife Ann; son Smallwood; daus. Mary, Lidia; tract *Athys Folly* (MCW VI.111); admx. Ann; 2 Sep 1729 (I 15.85); widow Ann [dec'd]; children: Smallwood, Mary, Lydia; 19 May 1731 (AA 11.106)

Coghil, Ann; children: Smallwood, Mary, Lydia; 19 May 1731 (AA 11.108)

Coghill, Smallwood; 23 Jul 1759; 27 Aug 1759; wife Keziah; cous. Isaac Smallwood Middleton; tract *Garner's Meadows Resurveyed* (MCW XII.233-4); extx. Kesiah; 31 Oct 1759 (I 69.330); 26 Jun 1761; extx. Keziah Coghill; cous.

Isaac Smallwood Middleton (ABB 3.74); widow Keziah; heir ?Isaac Smallwood Middleton; 24 Aug 1762 (GB 220)

COHAGAN

Cohagan, Jeremiah; wife Susanna; child: Anne, b. 27 Feb 1772 Upper Chapel (KGP p. 389)

COLBRON

Colbron, Francis; wife Deborah; child: Joseph, b. 14 Mar 1707/8 (QAP b/4)

Colbron, Joseph; m. 21 Dec 1710 Mary Stone (QAP m/1)

Colbron, Joseph; age 5 years; bound out by father Francis; Aug 1713 (PGCR G.385)

COLE

Cole. Edward, Jr.; age ca 23; 19 Feb 1741 (CCR JK#4.428)

Cole, Joseph; wife Rachel; child: Thomas, bapt. 4 Aug 1751 (KGP p. 294)

Cole, Joseph; wife Rachel; child: Sarah, bapt. 12 Jun 1768 Upper Chapel (KGP p. 370)

COLEMAN

Colemore, Thomas [London]; wife Anne [widow of Isaac Miller]; 18 Aug 1718 (PGLR Q.148)

Coleman, Thomas; age ca 65; 13 Sep 1729 (PGLR M.520)

Coleman, Joseph, Sr., Dr.; 31 Aug 1738; 27 Mar 1739; sons Thomas, Mordicai, Joseph; dau. Elizabeth, Lillias, Margaret (MCW VIII.30); 9 Aug 1739 (I 24.297), Dr.; 10 Jul 1742 (AA 19.58).; [with 1742] (I 26.564)

Coleman, Mordecai; 20 Mar 1740; bro. Joseph (MCW IX.4); 28 Aug 1747 (I 35.315)

Coleman, Thomas, Dr.; wife Joyce; tract Aaron; 30 Jan 1741 (PGLR Y.439)

Colemore, James; 23 Jun 1768 (I 96.336)

COLEY

Coley, Robert; wife Margaret; children: James, b. 4 Apr 1756; Horatio, b. 1773 Lower Chapel (KGP p. 313, 384)

Coeley, Letis; child: James, bapt. 1 Jun 1766 Broad Creek (KGP p. 353)

COLLARD

Collard, Samuel; m. 31 Oct 1762 Agnus Ochterloney, both of this parish (KGP p. 319)

COLLIER

Collier, Francis [CA]; wife Sarah; part of Cold Spring Manor; 25 Nov 1705 (PGLR C.146)

Collier, Francis, Sr.; age ca 65; 10 Aug 1710 (CCR PC.844)

Collyer, Charles; 21 May 1718 (AA 1.4)

Colyer [Collier], Francis; 8 Jul 1724 (AA 6.23); heir Francis; 20 Mar 1724 (GB 19)

Collier, Francis; s/o Charles [dec'd]; grandson of Francis [dec'd]; uncle Francis [dec'd]; tract Cold Spring Manor; 11 May 1741 (PGLR Y.282)

Collier, William; wife Mary; child: William, b. Sep 17__ (QAP b/29)

Colyar, William; planter; 8 Aug 1749; son William, Richard; dau. Mary; grandson Richard; tracts Elder's Delite, Dann, Stubb Hill (MCW X.46-7)

Collier [alias Calvin], William; m. 5 Aug 1754 Sarah Ray; child: Sarah, b. 18 Feb 1762 (PGP p. 229, 262)

COLLINS

Collings, Morgan; age ca 19; servant; Aug 1698 Ct. (PGCR A.333)

Collins, William; wife Ann; tracts Mansfield, The Farme, Collins Comfort; 19 Sep 1698 (PGLR A.148); gs/o George Collins; tract Collins Comfort; 26 Aug 1700 (PGLR A.311)

Collins, William [dec'd] [VA]; sons William, Moulton; tract Quick Sale; 12 Apr 1704 (PGLR C.101)

Collins, Morgan; wife Grace; child: Mary, b. 12 9ber 1724 (QAP b/10)

Collens, Arthur; widow Elisabeth; 7 Mar 1725 (I 11.773); 2 Oct 1727 (AA 8.381)

Collins, Thomas; wife Margratt; children: Richard, b. 26 May 173_; Sarah, b. 13 Oct 173_ (KGP p. 285)

Collins, John (Jon.); wife Mary; children: Hezekiah, b. 23 Mar 1762; Casandra, b. 27 Mar 1765 (PGP p. 263, 275)

COLLIS

Collis, Thomas; wife Theadore; children: Hephzibah (f), b. 3 Aug 1762; Mary, bapt. 4 Dec 1763 at Lower Chapel (KGP p. 328, 335)

Collis, Thomas; wife Dorathey; children: Rodey, bapt. 25 Aug 1765 Lower Chapel; George Thomas, bapt. 24 Jan 1768 Lower Chapel (KGP p. 351, 368)

Collis, Thomas; wife Theodasha; children: Hezekiah, b. 19 May 1772 Lower Chapel; Equila Johnson, b. 8 May 1774 Lower Chapel (KGP p. 379, 380)

Collis, John; wife Martha; children: James Thomas, b. 1 Aug 1772 Lower Chapel; Anne and John, b. 6 Feb 1775 Lower Chapel (KGP p. 380, 383)

COLMORE

Colmore, James; 11 Sep 1770; [no relations] (ABB 6.24)

COMBS

Combs, Enoch; wife Sarah; grandson Thomas Odell [wife Margaret]; 20 Dec 1725 (PGLR I.699)

Combs, Sarah; widow; 15 Dec 1736 (I 22.159)

Combes [Combs], Enoch; 8 Mar 1726 (I 11.783); 23 May 1728 (AA 9.162)

Cooms, Sarah; son John Poores; 2 Jan 1727/8 (PGLR M.252)

Coomes, Sarah; dau. Sarah Haswell; grandchildren: James, Jr., Robert, Joseph & Zepheniah Beall; 22 May 1730 (PGLR Q.109)

COMMEL

Commel, Daniel; age ca 60; 29 Jun 1736 (PGLR T.400)

COMPTON

Compton, John; wife Mary; children: Elizabeth, b. 27 Nov 1725; Mary, b. 22 Feb 1727 (KGP p. 278)

Compton, Ignatius; admx. Dorothea; 25 Nov 1773 (I 117.421)

CONDAL

Condal, David; m. 30 Dec 1733 Elizh. Warner (QAP m/6)

Condle, David; admx. Elisabeth; 24 Mar 1744 (I 29.142)

CONDON

Condon, David; wife Ellenor; tract *Cernabby Manor*; 27 Oct 1722 (PGLR I.405)

Condon, David; wife Elizabeth [widow of Francis Pearson]; tract *Collington*; 27 Aug 1734 (PGLR T.174)

Condon, Richard; admx. Cathrine; children [unnamed; 5 of age; 2 minors]; 27 Apr 1749 (AA 26.41)

Condon, Elisabeth; 30 Mar 1758 (I 65.192)

Condon, David; wife Frances; child: Richard, b. 12 Sep 1762 (PGP p. 267)

CONLEY

Conley [Congley], William; wife Ann; tract *The Gore*; 11 May 1708 (PGLR C.209)

Connelly, Daniell; adms. Richard Dalton & wife Mary; 5 Jul 1708 (I&A 28.157)

Conley, Robert; wife Mary; child: Jeremiah, bapt. 30 Aug 1767 Lower Chapel (KGP p. 367-8)

CONN

Conn, Hugh; Descenting Minister; 4 Mar 1748; 26 Aug 1752; 8 children; sons Hugh, James, John, George, Samuel, Joseph; daus. Ann, Elizabeth; tracts *Joseph Park, Hudson's Range, William and Ann, White Taskington*

(MCW X.234); 28 Nov 1752 (I 52.28); 4 May 1753 (I 54.261);; 28 Aug 1753 (AA 35.51) 27 Nov 1754; ex. James Conn; children: Jane, John, George, Samuel, Ann, Joseph & Elizabeth Conn (ABB 1.121)

Conn, Samuel; 5 Jun 1765; 10 Aug 1765; bro. Joseph (MCW XIII.93); [as ship carpenter]; 27 Sep 1765 (I 90.143, 144); 1 Jul 1766; ex. Jesse Conn (ABB 4.165)

Conn, George, Sr; being advanced in years; 10 Jul 1772; 26 Oct 1774; children: William, Hugh, George, Beatrix Rutter, Martha Pearce, Mary Veitch, Pennellopy Fenly; grandchild.: George Fenly, Priscilla Jenkins; tracts Barbados, Scotland (MCW XVI.7)

CONNELL
Connell, Daniell; 1705 (I&A 3.684)

CONNER
Conner (Coner), Richard, Sr., Piscataway Hundred; planter; 12 Dec 1721; 9 Mar 1721; wife Mary; sons Richard, Thomas; daus. Ann Hill, Mary Atcheson, Sarah Simson, Eliza. Stevens (MCW V.92); 25 Aug 1723 (AA 6.3); 19 Oct 1724 (AA 6.171)

Carnour, John; 26 Jun 1731 (I 16.253)

Conner, Thomas; wife Sarah; tract Rose Common; 27 Mar 1739 (PGLR T.713)

Conner, James; wife Ann; children: Margret, b. 19 Feb 1763 at Upper Chapel; Thomas, b. 2 Sep 1765 Lower Chapel; Richard, b. _ Dec 1769 Broad Creek (KGP p. 333, 345, 346, 373)

Conner, Owen; wife Charity; child: Ann, b. 30 Nov 1775 (ICR)

CONTEE
Contee, John; d. 3 Aug 1708; [s/o Francis Hopkins & Peter Contee]; m. ca Jun 1704 to Mary [late wife of Capt. Wm. Rogers of Annapolis]; John's sister m. William Arnold; 13 Sep 1725 (CCR CL.1057-1063)

Contee, Alexander; wife Jane; son John, b. 19 Feb 1723; Alexander, b. 6 Jun 1725 (PGLR I.682)

Contee, Peter; wife Francis Hopkins [widow of Capt. William]; sons John, Alexander; nephew John; 13 Sep 1725 (CCR CL.1057-1063)

Contee, Alexander; age ca 44; 25 Feb 1735 (CCR-MSA 6.155)

Conte, Robert; extx. Mary Marsham [w/o Phillip]; 15 Jan 1737 (I 23.171)

Contee, Alexander; clerk; 24 Jul 1739; 5 Jan 1740; sons John, Peter, Thomas, Theodore, Alexander; daus. Jane, Grace, Cathrine; tracts Rogers Refuge, Baltimore County, Wartinton, Elftonhills, Buck Range (MCW VIII.131); extx. Jeane; 30 Apr 1741 (I 26.56); extx. Jane; 10 May 1744 (AA 10.192); widow

Jane; heirs John, Peter, Thomas, Theodore, Aleander, Grace, Katherine; 29 Aug 1744 (GB 134)

Contee, Theodore; wife Elizabeth; 1762 (MCWXII.119)

COODY

Coody, James; wife Mary; children: Edmund, b. 7 Apr 1724; Margaret, 4 Jun 1725 (QAP b/20)

COOK

Cook, Edward; wife Sarah; children: George, b. 17 Jun 1702; William, b. 7 Jul 1706; Sarah, b. 30 Mar 1710; Edward, b. 11 7ber 1713; John, b. 29 7ber 1717 (QAP b/5, 10, 13)

Cook, William; m. 12 Aug 1712 Eliza. Anderson; children: Joneacre (f), b. 12 May 1713; Rebecca, b. 13 Feb 1714/5 (QAP m/1; b/6, 10)

Cooke, Jeremiah; s/o Thomas; bound out; Jun 1716 (PGCR H.85)

Cooke, Robert; wife Mary; 22 Feb 1717 (PGLR F.31/556)

Cook, George; m. 31 Jan 1726/7 Elizabeth Reynolds; children: George, b. 8 Feb 1728/9; Sarah, b. 18 Apr 173_ (QAP m/4; b/22, 28)

Cook, Edward; wife Sarah [d/o George Cope, dec'd]; tract Cope's Hill; 30 Dec 1729 (PGLR M.531)

Cook [Cooke], William; admx. Mary; 4 Sep 1729 (I 15.266); 1 Jan 1730 (I 17.66); admx. Mary; children 2 sons, 3 daus. [unnamed]; 6 Jan 1730 (AA 10.590); widow Mary Reiley; heirs Elizabeth, Robert Dove, Anne, Alice; 24 Jun 1735 (AA 13.266); heirs Elizabeth, Robert Dove, Ann, Alice; 24 Aug 1736 (GB 79)

Cook, William [dec'd]; widow Mary; [d/o Robert Dove]; son John Johnson; tract Penny's Choyce; 21 Aug 1730 (PGLR Q.94)

Cook, William; wife Mary; children: Sarah, b. 14 Oct 1731; William, b. 6 Oct 1734 (QAP b/25, 28)

Cooke, John; wife Sophia; tract Brook Grove, Reparation; 14 Jun 1742 (PGLR Y.496)

Cook, John; wife Rachel; children: Zedekiah, b. 17 Mar 1754; John, b. 7 Sep 1756; Mary, b. 20 Feb 1757; Sarah, b. 17 Jan 1763; Basil, b. 25 Sep 1764; Ruth, b. 22 Mar 1766 (PGP p. 256, 270, 272, 278)

Cook, Edward; admx. Mary; 2 Sep 1761 (I 77.85); 3 Aug 1762; admx. Mary Cooke; 8 children [unnamed] (ABB 3.144); widow Mary; heirs Joseph, Benjamin, Lewis, Jonathan, Sarah, Rebecca, Jeremiah; 25 Mar 1763 (GB 224)

Cook, Joseph; wife Martha; children: Moses Beasley, b. 25 Jan 1763 at Upper Chapel; Joseph, bapt. 7 Jul 1765 Upper Chapel (KGP p. 333, 358)

Cook, George, wife Sarah; child: Elizabeth, bapt. 1 Dec 1765 Lower Chapel (KGP p. 346)

Cook, Benjamin; wife Martha; child: Thomas, bapt. 20 Jul 1766 Upper Chapel (KGP p. 364)

Cook, Robert Dove; 12 Jan 1767; 26 Jun 1767; wife Mary; children: William, Jonathan [wife Mary], Mary, Sarah, Richard, Benjamin, Rebecca, John, Robert (MCW XIV.11); 21 Aug 1767 (I 95.12)

COOPER

Coopper, William; dec'd; Sep 1696 Ct. (PGCR A.39)

Cooper, William; 3 Jun 1697 (I&A 15.97, 279)

Cooper, Margaret; age ca 17; servant; Mar 1713 (PGCR G.292)

Cooper, William; wife Mary Ann; children: Leonard, b. 15 Jan 1740/50 (?); Ann, b. 20 May 1752 (PGP p. 253)

Cooper, John; [?England]; 12 Jul 1744 (I 29.309); 27 Mar 1745 (AA 21.217)

COOTS

Coots, Alexander; wife Elizabeth; child: Charles, b. 19 Oct 1712 (KGP p. 260)

Coutt, Robert; wife Mary; tract *Cabidge*; 26 Aug 1726 (PGLR M.104

Coot, Mary; 6 Nov 1730; 25 Nov 1730; husband Robert; former husband John Cozen, dec'd; tract *Lundee* (MCW VI.170)

Coots, Robert; m. 25 Nov 1734 Mary _____ (QAP m/6)

Coots, Robert; planter; 28 Jul 1737; 23 Nov 1737; wife Mary; former wife Mary [dec'd]; son Randolph; dau. Sarah Hay; grandson Robert Hay; tract *Lundee* (MCW VII.229); widow Mary Marshment [w/o Phillip]; 29 Nov 1738 (AA 17.12)

COPE

Coop, Nicholas; age ca 70; 13 Jan 1714 (CCR CL.107)

Coape [Cope], George; planter; 5 Aug 1727; 12 Jul 1728; dau. Sarah Cooke; granddau. Rachell Hill; grand-s-i-l William Barnshee [b-i-l to Rachel Hill]; grandson William Cook (MCW VI.65)

Cope [Coape], George [dec'd]; granddau. Rachell Hill; tract *Cope's Hill*; 30 Dec 1729 (PGLR M.531)

COPELAND

Copeland, Samuel; 27 Nov 1699; 7 Jan 1699; wife Margaret; son Samuel; dau. Hannah; unborn child; tract *Coxes Hays* (MCW II.192); extx. Margarett Sherdemitt [w/o John]; 14 Oct 1700 (I&A 20.190); children: Samuel, Joseph, Hannah; tract *Dunbar*; 27 Oct 1701 (PGLR A.414)

Copeland, Samuel; 27 Jan 1726; 23 Feb 1726/7; wife Barbary; only dau. Cathrine (MCW VI.22); admx. Barbara; 22 May 1727 (I 12.120); admx. Barbra; heirs Catherine, Samuel [eldest ca age 4]; 26 Jun 1728 (AA 9.18); admx. Barbara; 28 Aug 1728 (I 13.206); widow Barbara; heirs Catherine, Samuel; 26 Nov 1728 (GB 41)

Copland, John; m. 10 Nov 1726 Mary Fowler; child: Sarah, b. 12 Apr 1727 (QAP m/4; b/20)

COSDEN

Cosden, Alphonso [CA], wife Elizabeth; tract *Lower Growrey*; 1 May 1719 (PGLR F.188/775)

COSTER

Coster, Robert; wife Elizabeth; child: Robert, b. 10 Mar 1732 (QAP b/25)

Coster, John; wife Sarah; child: Alice, b. 14 Oct 1749 (KGP p. 290)

COTTON

Cotton, William [dec'd]; widow Elizabeth; children: Mary James, William James, Anne James, John Cotton; 25 Nov 1729 (PGLR M.512)

Cotton [Cotten], William; admx. Elisabeth; 25 Nov 1729; admx. Elisabeth Rowe [w/o William]; 14 Jul 1730 (AA 10.360)

COUDLE

Coudle, David; 30 Dec 1743; 16 Jan 1743/4; wife Elizabeth; bro. Richard; ch/o bro. Richard: William, David, Mary, Anne, Elizabeth, Eleanor, Stacy (MCW VIII.243)

COUGHLANE

Coughlane, John; age ca 17; servant; Jun 1698 Ct. (PGCR A.320)

COUZEN

Couzen, John; 16 Apr 1712 (I&A 33a.190)

Cozens, John [dec'd]; widow Mary; tract *William and Elizabeth*; 22 Aug 1713 (PGLR F.327)

Cussens, George; 19 Dec 1711; 22 Mar 1711/2; wife Mary; tract *Linde* (MCW III.222); 30 Jul 1712 (I&A 33b.29); 14 Aug 1713 (I&A 34.149)

COVER

Cover, John; wife Elizabeth; child: Mary, b. 6 Aug 1758 (QAP b/37)

COVILL

Covill, Jonathan; wife Mary; children: Mary, b. 5 May 1710; Susanna, b. 31 Aug 1712; Jeremiah, b. 6 May 1714; Josias, b. 28 Jul 1717; Sarah, b. 25 Jul 1720; Leah, b. 11 10ber 1723; Jacob, 30 9ber 1727 (QAP b/6, 10, 13, 16, 21)

COVINGTON

Covington, Levin; 27 Jan 1724; 24 Nov 1725; wife Margery; son Leonard; dau. Elizabeth; tracts *Hollydays Choice* (MCW v.212); extx. Margery; 10 Oct 1726 (I 11.623); admx. Margery; 25 Oct 1727 (AA 8.439); widow Margery; heirs Leonard, Elizabeth; 6 Jun 1728 (GB 37); widow Margery; 26 Aug 1730 (AA 10.451);

Covington, Leonard; admx. Priscilla; 24 Mar 1742 (I 27.360); admx. Pricilla; children: Rebecca, Levin; 8 Nov 1744 (AA 20.533); heirs Rebecca, Leonard; 26 Jun 1745 (GB 141)

COWIE

Cowie, William; mariner; admx. Ann; 10 Sep 1770 (I 106.161)

COWLEY

Cowley, Robert; wife Margret; child: Jeane, bapt. 2 Jun 1765 Lower Chapel (KGP p. 351)

COX

Cox, Henry [CA]; s/o Henry; tract *Battson's Vineyard Rectified*; 13 Mar 1707 (PGLR C.204a)

Cox, Henry [CA]; wife Sarah; tract *Good Luck*; 27 Sep 1711 (PGLR F.143)

Cox, John; wife Ann; children: Jeremiah, b. 12 8ber 1712; John, b. 1 May 1714 (QAP b/6,9)

Cox, Henry [CA]; sons Henry, John; 3 Dec 1725 (PGLR I.722)

Cox, John; chooses Abraham Cox as guardian; Aug 1748 (PGCR HH.341)

Cox, William; 20 Oct 1748 (I 40.187); children: William, Henry, Abraham, James Cox & Elisabeth Downs; 26 Apr 1751 (AA 30.32)

Cox, John; wife Mary; child: Ann, bapt. 12 Jun 1761 (KGP p. 322)

Cox, Jacob; wife Prisillah; child: Priscilla, b. 22 May 1763 (PGP p. 270)

Cox, John; admx. Sarah; [with 1772] (I 110.217, 222, 235); heir John Cox; 26 Aug 1773 (GB 312)

Cox, Richard; wife Mary Ann; children: Charles Burn, b. 14 Mar 1772 Lower Chapel; Hugh Thomas, b. 2 Nov 1773 Lower Chapel (KGP p. 379, 383)

Cox, Abraham; wife Mary; children: Jesse (m), b. 21 Feb 1773 Lower Chapel; Zachariah, b. 26 Sep 1774 Lower Chapel (KGP p. 380, 384)

COXEN

Coxen, Zachariah wife Elizabeth; child: George, b. 31 Mar 1776 Broad Creek (KGP p. 382)

Coxon, Ann; child: John, b. 10 Jul 1755 (KGP p. 313)

Coxon, Josias; wife Margaret; child: Ann, bapt. 9 Dec 1764 Broad Creek (KGP p. 342)

CRABB

Crabb, Ralph; m. 22 Aug 1716 Priscilla Sprigg [d/o Col. Thomas]; children: Sarah, b. 20 Oct 1717; Thomas, b. 21 Apr 1719; Margaret, b. 13 Aug 1720; Henry Wright, b. 16 Jan 1722/3; Ralph, b. 29 9ber 1724; Ellinor, b. 20 7ber 1726; Jeremiah, b. __ Oct 1728; John, b. 15 Jun 1731 (QAP m/2; b/17, 18, 19, 20, 21, 24)

Crabb, Ralph; wife Priscilla; tract *Two Brothers*; 28 Jun 1726 (PGLR M.10, 11)

Crabb, Ralph; 14 Dec 1733; 8 Mar 1733/4; wife Priscilla; daus. Sarah, Margaret, Eleanor; sons Thomas, Henry Right, Ralph, Jeremiah, John; unborn child; bro. Edward; tracts *Dear Park, Valentines Garden, Boleing Green, Essington* (MCW VII.66); widow Priscilla; 13 May 1735 (AA 13.65); dau. Sarah Magruder [widow of Robert]; 22 Aug 1737 (AA 14.358); widow Priscilla; heirs Thomas, Margaret, Henry Wright, Ralph, Eleanor, Jeremiah, John, Edward; 31 Mar 1738 (GB 98)

Crabb, Priscilla; 16 Mar 1763 (I 81.360)

CRADOCK

Cradock, Richard; wife Elizabeth; children: Ann, b. 7 Aug 1750; Mary, b. 26 Jan 1753; Charles, b. 14 Feb 1762; William, b. 2 Aug 1764 (PGP p. 254, 264, 272)

CRAIG

Craigg [Craige], Thomas, Dr.; 1 Aug 1738 (I 25.33); 23 Aug 1740 (I 25.82); 15 Jul 1741 (AA 18.235)

CRAMPHIN

Crampham, Henry; wife Mary; son John; tract *Colchester*; 6 Dec 1722 (PGLR I.324); son Thomas; tracts *Blackash, New Dumfries*; 1 Sep 1735 (PGLR T.311); son Henry, Jr.; tract *Mother's Goodwill*; 6 Nov 1735 (PGLR T.331)

Cramphin [Champin], Henry C.; 4 Jul 1741; 27 Nov 1746; wife Mary; sons John, Henry, Thomas, Bazil; grandsons Denman & Mary [ch/o John] (MCW IX.91); extx. Mary; 12 Jun 1748 (AA 25.97)

Craphin, Thomas; wife Elizabeth; child: Richard Pottinger, b. 29 Jun 1760 (PGP p. 258)

Cramphin, Thomas; wife Mary; children: Thomas, b. 26 Jan 1740; Ruth, b. 30 Aug 1742 (PGP p. 256)

Cramphin, Basil; admx. Mary; 15 Oct 1748 (I 37.235); admx. Mary; 26 Jun 1751 (AA 30.121)

CRANFORD
Cranford, James [dec'd] [SM]; son John; 14 Jan 1722/3 (PGLR I.429)

Cranford, John; 14 Jan 1722/3; 26 Jan 1724/5; father James [dec'd]; bro. James (MCW V.189)

CRAVEN
Craven, Michael; wife Ann; children: Mary, b. 29 Oct 1723; Rebecca, b. 22 May 1725; Sarah, b. 11 Oct 1729 (PGP p. 249)

CRAWFORD
Crawford, Susannah; age 11 years on 15 Jul last; Nov 1722 (PGCR K.650)

Crawford, James; m. 26 Dec 1723 Mary Anderson; children: Adam, b. 8 Aug 1724; Mary, b. 27 Jul 1726; Nathaniel, b. 31 Aug 1728; Elizabeth, b. 5 Aug 1730; Adam, b. 8 Aug 1731?; Eleanor, b. 22 Oct 1731?; James, b. 1 Oct 1732 (QAP m/3; b/19, 25, 26, 29)

Crauford, David; admx. Mary; 25 Jul 1749 (I 41.180); admx. Mary [widow]; 3 children: Mary, Martha, David; 31 Oct 1751 (AA 31.126); widow Mary; orphan David; 25 Jun 1752 (GB 178)

Crafford, Nathaniel; wife Rachel; children: Thomas Beall, b. 21 Jul 1760; Alexander Beall, b. 7 Oct 1762 (PGP p. 258, 267)

Crawford, Joseph; wife Mary; child: Mary, bapt. 19 Feb 1764 at Upper Chapel (KGP p. 340)

Crawford, James; wife Ann; child: Andrew, bapt. 1 Apr 1764 Upper Chapel (KGP p. 341)

Crawford, Thomas; wife Rachell; child: Alexander, bapt. 24 Jun 1764 Upper Chapel; [2nd entry: Alexander, bapt. 14 Jul 1764 Broad Creek]; Levy, b. 19 Aug 1772 Upper Chapel (KGP p. 341, 342, 389)

Crawford, Adam; wife Elizabeth; child: James, bapt. 13 Sep 1767 Upper Chapel (KGP p. 366)

Crawford, Thomas; child: Zachariah, bapt. 8 Jun 1766 Lower Chapel (KGP p. 346)

Crawford, Thomas; wife Rachel; child: (KGP p. 389)

CRAYCROFT
Cracraaft, John; 10 Mar 1697 (I&A 16.50)

Craycroft, Ignatius; 9 Aug 1704; 23 Sep 1707; wife Sophia; sons John, Ignatius, Henry, Charles; daus. Ann, Sophia, Elizabeth, Susannah; tracts *Gailwiths, Little Addition, The Hatchett, Truman's Place, Nutwell's Branches, The Denial* (MCW III.113); 2 Dec 1710 (I&A 32a.75); 22 Oct 1711 (I&A 32c.171); 29 Sep 1712 (I&A 33b.73); 22 Aug 1715 (I&A 36b.257); 14 Aug 1717 (I&A 39b.38); extx. Jane [d-i-l; widow of John]; sons Ignatius, John [dec'd]; 20 Jun 1731 (AA 11.120)

Craycroft, Ignatius; dau. Sophia [dec'd] [w/o Charles Diggs]; 26 Aug 1707 (PGLR C.191)

Creycroft, John; s/o Ignatius [dec'd]; chooses guardian; Mar 1709 (PGCR D.149)

Craycroft, Jane; 29 Nov 1738 (I 23.435); [extx. of John]; mentions 2 daus. of Ignatius Craycroft, dec'd: w/o Ignatius Doyne, w/o Edward Clements; 29 Sep 1741 (AA 18.309)

Craycroft, John; [with 1722] (I 7.299); extx. Jane; 22 Nov 1734 (AA 12.647)

Craycroff, Clement; admx. Elisabeth; 13 Sep 1743 (I 28.363)

CROAMY

Croamy, James; age ca 12; servant; Jun 1710 (PGCR D.316)

CROFT

Croft, James; child: John Anderson, bapt. 22 Dec 1765 Lower Chapel (KGP p. 346)

CROLEY

Croley, John; 31 Oct 1748; 7 Jun 1749; wife Miriam; dau. Elizabeth Snowden (MCW X.22)

CROOK

Crooke, John; admx. Anne; 20 Aug 1747 (I 35.284); John; admx. Anne; 7 Oct 1747 (AA 24.155)

CROSS

Cross, Ann Joyes; orphan b. last of Apr 1701; bound out; Sep 1701 (PGCR B.137)

Cross, George; wife Eliza.; children: George, b. 29 May 1706; Thomas, b. 30 9ber 1711; Sarah, b. 16 8ber 1716; Margaret, b. 16 Apr 1718 (QAP b/13)

Cross, Robert; wife Jane; children: Ann, b. 11 Jan 1731; John, b. 9 Jan 1732/3; Catharine, b. 27 Mar 173_; Robert, b. 1 Oct 1736 (QAP b/26, 28, 30)

Cross, Robert; age 10 mos.; s/o Margaret; Nov 1744 (PGCR CC.585)

Cross, John, wife Elizh.; child: _____ (m/f?), b. 8 Nov 1759 (QAP b/37)

Cross, Jeremiah; wife Ann; children: Sarah, b. 18 Dec 1763; Jacob, b. 28 Apr 1765; Jeremiah, b. 8 Jan 1765? (QAP b/38)

Cross, Richard; wife Ann; child: Richard, bapt. 2 Nov 1766 Upper Chapel (KGP p. 354)

Cross, William; wife Mary; child: _____ (f), b. __ Nov ____; [with 1760s] (QAP b/39)

CROW

Crow, James; 4 Jan 1776; 27 Mar 1776; wife Mary; children: James, Thomas, John & Anne Crow, Sarah Aldridge, Mary Rawlins, Elizabeth Aldridge, Lucy Owings, Martha Cheney; tracts *Samuels Forrest, The Addition to Samuels Forrest, Farmers Chance* (MCW XVI.131)

CUGNET

Cugnet [Cugnett], John Peter [Jean Pier]; 20 Aug 1769; 18 Sep 1769; cousins: Jacob Mayer, Abraham Dettie, Adam Laroy, John Jacob LeRoy (MCW XIV.101); 11 Oct 1769 (I 104.270)

CULLUM

Cullum, Francis; wife Susannah; child: Abigal, b. 8 Jan 1765 (PGP p. 274)

Cullin, Charles; age 3 on 16 Feb last; s/o Elisabeth; bound out; Mar 1715 (PGCR G.720)

Cullin, Charles; age 6; s/o Dennis and Elisabeth; bound out; Mar 1718 (PGCR H.798)

CULVER

Culver, Henry; planter; 27 Feb 1729; 26 Mar 1730; wife Catherine; sons Henry, William; daus. Mary, Sarah, Margaret, Monica, Catherine Culver, Elinor Brooke; tracts *The Addition to Culver's Chance, Littleworth, Woodbridge, Pitchcroft* (MCW VI.155); admx. Cathrine; 3 Oct 1730 (I 16.13); widow Catherine; son Henry; 30 Aug 1731 (AA 11.164); children: Sarah, Margaret, Monica, Ann, Elinor; 2 Sep 1734 (AA 12.396); widow Catherine; heirs William, Mary, Sarah, Margaret, Monica, Catherine, Eleanor; 27 Aug 1735 (GB 71)

Culver, Henry; 20 Feb 1741/2; 11 May 1742; wife [unnamed]; sons Henry, Thomas; daus. Drusilla, Ann, Rebecca, Elizabeth, Cassandra; m-i-l Catherine _____; tract *Batchelor's Forrest* (MCW VIII.169); extx. Frances; 10 Jan 1742 (I 29.17)

Culver, Catherine; widow; 6 Oct 1762; 20 Dec 1762; daus. Margaret Pierce, Elizabeth Truman, Monaci Culver, Eleanor Dorsett, Catherine Miles;

grandchildren: Eleanor, Henry Culver, Mary Miles [ch/o Catherine], Mary King (MCW XII.181)

CUMBERBATCH
Cumberbatch, John; wife Rebecca; Sep 1716 (PGLR F.549)

CUMBERLAND
Cumberland, John; wife Mary; children: William, b. 11 Nov 1711; John, b. 22 Nov 1713; James, b. 28 Feb 1721 (KGP p. 274, 275)

Cumberland, John; planter; 24 Mar 1722/3; 30 Apr 1723; sons William, John, James (MCW V.130); 13 Nov [1723] (I 9.222); 30 Nov 1723 (AA 5.293); 29 Sep 1727 (AA 8.379)

Cumberland, John; bound out; Jun 1726 (PGCR L.652)

Cumberland, James; bound out; Nov 1726 (PGCR N.108)

Cumberland, William; age 16 next Nov; bound out; Mar 1725 (PGCR L.558)

CUMMING
Cumming, William; wife Elizabeth; tract Accord; 8 Oct 1733 (PGLR T.1)

CUNNINGHAM
Cunningham, Daniel [CA]; nephew John Cunningham [England]; tract Mt. Calvert Manor; 22 Jun 1705 (PGLR C.134)

CURRENT
Current, Hugh; wife Ann; children: Tabither, b. 17 Feb 1760; John, b. 2 Aug 1762; Lydia, b. 23 Nov 1764 (PGP p. 262, 274, 281)

CUSICK
Cusick [Keusick], James; admx. Sarah; 9 May 1761 (I 75.8)

D'CREGOE

Decragoe, William; wife Elizabeth; children: ____(f), b. 23 Feb 1723; Sarah, b. 12 Jul 1726; Mary, b. 26 Jul 1730 (KGP p. 283; ICR)

D'Cregoe, William; wife Elizabeth; tract *Stone's Delight*; 29 Apr 1724 (PGLR I.546)

D'WITT

D'witt, John; wife Rose; son Robert; 29 Jul 1730 (PGLR Q.113)

DAINTREY

Daintrey, Richard; m. 23 Nov 1727 Elizabeth Mason (QAP m/4)

DALTON

Dalton, John; age 9 on 1 Jan last; orphan; bound out; Mar 1744 (PGCR CC.270)

DANIEL

Daniel, William; age ca 19; Mar 1700 Ct. (PGCR B.30a)

Daniel, Michael; admx. Elisabeth; 2 Feb 1725 (I 11.223); widow Elisabeth [dec'd]; 24 May 1727 (AA 8.238); extx. Elisabeth [dec'd]; 25 Jun 1728 (AA 9.16)

Daniel, Elizabeth; 17 Jan 1725; 11 Feb 1726/7; [no relationships] (MCW VI.11); 27 Feb 1726 (I 12.27)

DANIELSON

Daniellson, Elinor; fined for having bastard child by John Green; June 1703 (PGCR B.233a)

Danielson, Daniel; wife Elizabeth; child: Ann, b. 13 May 1704 (QAP b/1)

Danielson, Daniel; age ca 67; Feb 1717 (PGLR I.594)

Danielson, Daniel; 1726 (I 11.771); 30 Sep 1727 (AA 8.380)

DANNISON

Dannisone, Daniel, Jr. & Sr. [CA]; naturalized 26 Jan 1696 (PGLR A.31)

DANSON

Danson, Elizabeth; brought into Province 8 yrs. ago; Mar 1702 (PGCR B.152a)

DARBY

Darby, Josias; wife Henrietta; children: George, b. 12 Jun 1726; Rebecca, b. 12 Feb 1727/8; Joseph, b. 1 Apr 1730 (QAP b/25)

Darby, Benjamin; wife Elisabeth; child: Henneretter Maria, b. 19 Jan 1763 (PGP p. 269)

DARNALL

Darnall, Henry, Col.; wife Elinor; tracts *Timberly, Generals Guift*; 17 Nov 1698 (PGLR A.291, 292)

Darnall, Henry, Col.; d. ca 1711 (CCR-MSA 6.159)

Darnall, John; extx. Mary; 10 Jan 1728 (I 13.365)

Darnall, Henry; wife Ann; tract *His Lordship's Kindness*; 2 Apr 1728 (PGLR M.313)

Darnall, Henry; son Henry, Jr.; tract *The Addition*; 24 May 1729 (PGLR M.424)

Darnall, Henry; age ca 37; s/o Henry; 24 May 1740 (CCR JK#4.331)

Darnall, Henry of *Portland Manor* [AA]; wife Elizabeth; tract *Henrietta Maria*; 1 Apr 1741 (PGLR Y.262)

Darnall, Thomas; child: Samuel, bapt. 13 Feb 1763 at Upper Chapel (KGP p. 332)

Darnall, Henry; wife Elizabeth; her cousin Richard Bennett; 6 Sep 1763 (CCR MSA 10.218)

Darnall, Thomas; wife Susannah; child: Elizabeth Thomas, bapt. 30 Oct 1764 Broad Creek (KGP p. 357)

DARSEY

Dasey, John; wife Elizabeth; child: Joseph, bapt. 19 Feb 1764 at Upper Chapel (KGP p. 340)

Darsey, John; wife Elizabeth; child: John, b. 15 Jun 1766 Upper Chapel (KGP p. 365)

DAVIS

Davice, Thomas [CA]; wife Honnor; tract *Warmister*; son Thomas Davis; 24 Dec 1695 (PGLR A.4)

Davis, John; wife Elizabeth; tract Mt. *Calvert Manor*; 27 Sep 1698 (PGLR A.165)

Davis, Nicholas; wife Elinor; tract *Compass Hills*; 29 Aug 1704 (PGLR C.117)

Davis, Foulk; wife Katherine; children: Ann, b. 25 Apr 1709; David, b. 25 8ber 1714 (QAP b/10)

Davis, David; 4 Sep 1709 (I&A 30.219); Mary [widow]; 14 Nov 1710 (I&A 32a.79); admx. Mary; 25 Jul 1711 (I&A 32c.45); son David; 26 Aug 1712 (PGLR F.206)

Davis, Gregory; wife Margaret; children: George, age 8 on 9 Aug next; John, age 5 on 4 Oct next; bound out; Mar 1713 (PGCR G.291)

Davies, John, Sr. [SM]; wife Ann; tract *Remainder of Truman's Choice*; 5 Mar 1719 (PGLR F.291/871)

Davis, Nicholas; sons John, Nicholas; 20 Jun 1719 (I 2.139); 20 Jun 1719 (AA 2.58)

Davis, Thomas; m. 18 Aug 1719 Elizabeth Ryder; child: Thomas, b. 18 Jun 1719 (QAP m/2; b/15)

Davis, Griffith; wife Eleanor; tract *Duvall's Range*; 13 Jul 1721 (PGLR I.130)

Davis, Griffith; dau. Elizabeth; [with 1722] (PGLR I.347)

Davis, Charles; wife Jane; tract *Brotherhood*; 9 Jul 1727 (PGLR M.223)

Davis, Meredith; wife Usley; tract *New Park*; 10 Jan 1729 (PGLR M.529)

Davis, Nick; age ca 40; 1732 (PGLR Q.522)

Davis, Charles; son John; tract *Three Beall's Manor*; 12 Jan 1734 (PGLR T.221)

Davis, William; wife Mary; children: Vachel, b. 22 Apr 1734?; Mareen, b. 6 Jun 1734? (QAP b/28, 30)

Davis, Samuel; wife Deborah; children: Nathan, b. 17 Jul 1734; Samuel, b. 30 Jan 1735 (QAP b/30)

Davis, Nicholas; son David; tract *The Forrest*; 20 Mar 1734/5 (PGLR T.365)

Davis, John; age ca 51; 1738 (PGLR T.604)

Davis, Clammon; wife Mary; tract *Swearingen's Pasture*; 16 Apr 1741 (PGLR Y.306)

Davis, John; wife Mary; dau. Mary; tract *Brightwell's Hunting Quarter*; 2 Feb 1742 (PGLR Y.600)

Davis, Thomas; wife Margaret; son Thomas; tract *Brightwell's Hunting Quarter*; 2 Feb 1742 (PGLR Y.594)

Davis, Meredith; sons Charles, Meredith; tract *Josiah*; 16 Apr 1742 (PGLR Y.520)

Davis, Walter; admx. Anne; 20 Aug 1743 (I 37.41)

Davis, Thomas; s/o William; age ca 42; 1743 (PGLR Y.705)

Davis, John; age ca 59; bro. Allen; 7 May 1747 (CCR MSA 8.295)

Davis, Jonathan [CH]; age ca 73; immigrant; 8 May 1747 (CCR MSA 8.298)

Davis [Daviss], Clemontious; wife Mary; children: Clemontious, b. 17 Aug 1747; Blanford, b. 17 Jan 1749/50; Ruth, b. 26 Aug 1753; Martha, b. 24 Sep 1758; Vachel, b. 17 Jan 1761; Thomas Lemar, b. 2 Feb 1763 (PGP p. 260, 269, 280)

Davis, Meredith; 5 Sep 1751; 26 Sep 1751; wife Ann; sons Charles, Meredith; tracts *West Failure, Bails Benevolence, Good Luck, Josiah, New Park, Meredith Hunting Quarter, Meredith, Friends Good Will, Lost Breaches* (MCW X.178-9); 23 Feb 1754 (AA 36.88); 9 Jul 1754 (I 57.360; 58.7, 10); 12 Aug 1754 (AA 36.419)

Davis, John; wife Barbary; child: Jesse (m), bapt. 1 Dec 1751 (KGP p. 294)

Davis, Walter; 27 Aug 1752; admx. Ann Davis (ABB 1.60, 62); admx. Ann; 27 Aug 1752 (AA 33.150)

Daviss, John; 28 Mar 1755 (I 59.50)

Davis, John; planter; 31 May 1752; 12 Dec 1760; wife Catherine; sons John, William, James, Nicholas; daus. Elinor, Katherine, Sophonia; tracts *Davis's Range, Forrest* (MCW XI1.21)

Davis, Richard; wife Charity; children: Aaron, bapt. 22 Oct 1752; Sarah, b. 25 Dec 1754 (KGP p. 297; 307)

Davis, Charles; child: Charles Burgess, b. 27 May 1753 (KGP p. 305)

Davis, Henry; wife Susanna; children: Sarah, b. 15 Apr 1755; Jonathan, b. 11 Feb 1758; Nicholas, bapt. _ Aug 1763 at Broad Creek (KGP p. 311, 320, 337)

Davis, Samuel; 26 Mar 1756 (I 60.713)

Davis, Charles; wife Lidey; child: John Van Swearingon, b. 7 Aug 1759 (PGP p. 257)

Davis, Meredith; [with 1764] (I 86.67)

Davis, Robert; wife Deborah; child: William, b. 14 Sep 1764, bapt. 30 Oct 1764 Broad Creek (KGP p. 357)

Daviss, Lodowick; wife Ellinor; child: Lodowick, b. 3 Feb 1764 (PGP p. 272)

Daviss, Thomas; wife Elliner; child: Lamack, b. 17 Apr 1764 (PGP p. 272)

Davis, William; wife Ann; child: Ann, b. 23 Nov 1764 (PGP p. 273)

Davis, William; wife Sarah; child: William, bapt. 12 Oct 1766 Upper Chapel (KGP p. 354)

Davis, Samuel; wife Ann; child: Mary Etherton, b. 25 Nov 1775 Upper Chapel (KGP p. 392)

DAVISON

Davison, John; age ca 54; 17 Jan 1743 (CCR MSA 8.45)

Daverson, Humphrey; 6 Jul 1745 (I 31.375)

Davison, John; 5 Jul 1746 (I 32.294); admx. Elisabeth; 29 Jul 1748 (AA 25.106)

Davison, Henry; wife Martha; child: Ann, b. 26 Jul 1761, bapt. 4 Oct 1761 (KGP p. 323)

Davinson, John; wife Elizabeth; child: Lancelot, bapt. 15 May 1768 Broad Creek (KGP p. 363)

DAWS

Daws, Benjamin; 12 Mar [with 1764] (I 82.320)

DAWSON

Dawson, Edward; wife Mary; tract *Ware* part of *Major's Lott*; 9 Apr 1703 (PGLR C.63a)

Dawson, Elizabeth; son Abraham; 1708 (MCW 111.144)

Dawson, Edward, Jr.; m. 24 Jan 1720/1 Margaret Allum; children: James, b. 3 Mar 1721/2; Mary, b. 27 Feb 1723/4; Edward, b. 4 Mar 1726; John, b. 4

Apr 1728; Edward, b. 19 Jun 1730; Margaret, b. 19 Jul 1732 (QAP m/2; b/17, 18, 22, 26)

Dawson, Nicholas; admx. Mary; 12 Jul 1727 (I 12.285); widow Mary; children [unnamed]; 28 Mar 1729 (AA 9332); admx. Mary; heirs John, Thomas, William, Benony, Nichlas [eldest age ca 22]; 22 Aug 1728 (AA 9.64); admx. Mary; 23 Jun 1729 (AA 9.453);

Dawson [Darson], Edward, Sr.; age ca 81; 26 Jun 1728 (PGLR M.290)

Dawson [Dorson], Edward, Jr.; age ca 45; 26 Jun 1728 (PGLR M.290)

Dawson, Edward, Sr.; planter; 15 Dec 1729; 28 Jun 1732; wife Mary; son Edward; grandson John Cash [s/o John, dec'd], Edward Perry [s/o John]; granddau. Mary Harr [w/o William]; tract Mill-land (MCW VI.224); admx. Mary; son Edward; 28 Aug 1732 (I 16.628); extx. Mary; son Edward; 26 Nov 1734 (AA 12.666)

Dawson, Edward; age ca 45; 6 Feb 1732/3 (PGLR T.285)

Dawson, Edward; wife Margaret; tract Mill Land; 10 Apr 1734 (PGLR T.109)

Dawson, Mary; widow; 14 Dec 1734; 24 Jan 1734/5; sons John, Thomas, William, George, Nicholas; father Robert Doyn; tracts Saturday Work, Constant Friendship, Spring Banks, Selgo (MCW VII.125); 9 Feb 1734 (I 21.44); heirs [under age] George, Nicholas; 9 Apr 1736 (AA 14.221); 30 Aug 1736 (AA 15.186)

Dawson, John; wife Martha Ann [d/o Francis Marbury, dec'd]; tract Mistake; 23 Jun 1737 (PGLR T.466)

Dawson, Nicholas; wife Sarah; children: George, b. 10 Mar 1750; Richard Edelen, b. 10 Jan 1750/1 (KGP p. 290)

Dawson, John; wife Ann; child: John, rec'd rites of the church 12 Jul 1752 (KGP p. 297)

Dawson, Thomas; wife Elizabeth; child: Nicholas Lowe, bapt. 5 Nov 1752 (KGP p. 297)

Dawson, Thomas; wife Mary; children: William Fitchitt, b. 27 Nov 1761; Ann, bapt. _ Oct 1763 at Broad Creek; John Edwards, b. 11 Jul 1765 Broad Creek (KGP p. 324, 338, 349)

Dawson, George; wife Elliner; child: Elisah (f), b. 28 Feb 1762 (PGP p. 263)

Dawson, Lewrance; child: Elizabeth, bapt. 4 Jul 1762 (KGP p. 331)

Dawson, John; admx. Martha Ann; 23 Apr 1764 (I 84.204)

Dawson, Danes; 18 Sep 1773 (I 114.49)

Dawson, George; wife Martha; child: John, b. _ Feb 1775 Lower Chapel (KGP p. 380)

Dawson, Sarah; widow; 25 Jun 1775; 24 Aug 1775; children William, Robert, John, Peregrine & Sarah Dawson, Mary Thomas; grandchild Elizabeth Thomas [d/o Joseph Thomas] (MCW XVI.138)

DAY

Day, Matthew; approver Jeane Day; 13 Feb 1717 (AA 1.7, 2.55)

Day, Leonard; wife Catherine; children: Edward, b. 13 Oct 1728; Mary, b. 20 Apr 1730; Jane, b. 13 Jun 1732, Sarah, b. 1 Aug 1734; Elinor, b. 1 May 1736; Leonard, b. 20 Jan 1737; Diana, b. 17 Jun 1740; Catherine, b. 4 May 1742; John Armstrong, b. 5 Nov 1744 (KGP p. 310, 311)

Day, Edward; wife Elinor; children: Mathew, b. 8 Jun 1751, bapt. 23 Jun 1751; Zacharias, b. 13 Mar 1755; Ballard, bapt. 12 Jun 1761 (KGP p. 294, 300, 322)

Day, Mathew; wife Ann; children: Hesekiah, b. 31 Mar 1762; Sushanna, bapt. 19 Jan 1766 Lower Chapel (KGP p. 331, 352)

Day, William; wife Mary; children: Elizabeth, b. 6 Apr 1762; Truman, b. 14 Feb 1764 Lower Chapel; Drussillow, bapt. 14 Jun 1767 Broad Creek; William, b. 25 Jul 1768 Broad Creek (KGP p. 327, 345, 361, 363-4)

Day, Lenard; wife Tabitha; child: Sushannah, b. 27 Feb 1763 at Lower Chapel (KGP p. 335)

Day, Mathew; wife Ann; child: Luke, bapt. 4 Jul 1767 Broad Creek (KGP p. 361)

Day, Matthew; wife Ann; children: Clement Sanders, b. 9 Sep 1772 Broad Creek; William, b. 8 Feb 1775 Lower Chapel (KGP p. 380, 382)

DEAKINS

Deakins, John; wife Mary; tracts *Seaman's Delight, As Good as Any*; 16 Oct 1709 (PGLR F.9)

Deacons, John; age 57; 1732 (PGLR Q.468)

Deakins, John; age ca 62; 11 May 1733 (PGLR T.25)

Deakins, John; planter; 9 Aug 1743; 20 Mar 1744; wife Priscilla; sons Leonard, William, Richard, John, Joseph; daus. Elizabeth Hooker, Ann Taneyhill, Mary Lucas (MCW VIII.260); admx. Priscilla; 20 Apr 1744 (I 29.304); extx. Priscilla; legatees, William, Elisabeth Hooker, Mary Lueve, Anne Tanyhill, Leonard; 3 May 1745 (AA 21.286); widow Priscilla; heirs Richard, John, Joseph; 26 Mar 1746 (GB 150)

Deakins, Richard; age 15 on 26 May last; choses Wm. Deakins as guardian; Jun 1751 (PGCR MM.66)

Deakins, John; age 13 on 21 Nov last; ct. appoints Wm. Deakins guardian; Jun 1751 (PGCR MM.67)

DEALE

Deale, Hannah; 1 Oct 1743 (I 28.234); 25 May 1747 (AA 23.283); 11 Jul 1748 (AA 25.102)

DELONE
Delone, Mary; orphan; custody of John Green; Mar 1700 Ct. (PGCR B.30a)

DELOZEAR
Deloser, Edward; wife Ann; children: Asey (m), b. 16 Apr 1762; Roadey, bapt. 13 Oct 1765 Broad Creek (KGP p. 327, 349)

Delozear, Daniel; child: Thomas, b. 2 Jun 1724 (KGP p. 280)

Delozer, Daniel; wife Mary; 1721 (PGCR K.421)

DEMALL
Demall, John; wife Mary; tract Greenfield; 26 Mar 1700 (PGLR A.211)

Demall, John; age ca 62; 8 Dec 1719 (CCR CL.550); age ca 70; 24 Mar 1726 (PGLR M.221)

Demall, John; 8 Apr 1725; 28 Jun 1727; wife Mary; cous. Robert Pottenger (MCW VI.36); admx. Mary; 29 Nov 1727 (I12.530); widow Mary; family [unnamed]; 10 Jan 1728 (AA 9.240)

Demall, Mary; age ca 61; 6 Feb 1732/3 (PGLR T.285)

Demall, John; s-i-l of James Williams; 9 Dec 1734 (PGLR T.236)

Demall, Mary; 12 Aug 1742 (AA 19.89); 22 Nov 1744 (AA 20.523); 5 Sep 1745 (AA 21.409)

DEMENT
Dement, John; wife Sarah; children: Charles, b. 29 May 1744; Susanna, b. 19 Dec 1746; George, b. 5 Nov 1749; William, b. 23 Apr 1752, bapt. 26 Apr 1752 (KGP p. 291-2, 295)

Demant [Dimand], Charles; wife Sarah; children: John, bapt. 13 Apr 1766 Lower Chapel; Mary, bapt. 10 Jul 1768 Lower Chapel; Zilla, b. 5 Jul 1771 Lower Chapel; Charles, b. 5 Sep 1773 Lower Chapel (KGP p. 352, 371, 376, 384)

Dement, John; admx. Mary; 8 Feb 1775 (I 121.333)

DEMILIANE
Dirmillion, Giles; age ca 45; 1730 (PGLR M.558)

Demiliane, Ann; Queen Ann Parish; 13 Oct 1730; 5 Feb 1730; daus. Elizabeth, Ann (MCW VI.174); 6 Oct 1731 (I 16.301)

Dumoloin, Ann; dau. [w/o John Childs]; 29 Nov 1732 (PGLR Q.569)

Demiliane, Ann; 20 Aug 1746 (AA 22.285); 23 May 1747 (AA 23.233)

Demiliane, Ann; extx. John Child & wife Elisabeth; 12 Jun 1733 (AA 11.701)

DENES
Denes, William; m. 30 Dec 1733 Sarah Bennet (QAP m/6)

Dennes, Ignatius; wife Lucresy; child: John, b. 8 Dec 1774 Broad Creek (KGP p. 386)

DENIOSIA
Deniosia, Edward; age 11 years 13 Jan next; gs/o Mary Miles; Nov 1734 (PGCR V.225)

DENNOW
Denonghow, Barthoolomew; age ca 15; servant; Jun 1698 Ct. (PGCR A.317)
Dennow, William; admx. Elisabeth; 22 Jun 1756 (I 61.251)

DENT
Dent, William [CH]; wife Elizabeth; son Peter; tract *Friendship*; 26 Nov 1696 (PGLR A23)
Dent, William; son Thomas; grandson Peter; tract *White Haven*; 24 Feb 1715 (PGLR F.522)
Dent, Thomas [CH]; wife Anne; ttact *Whitehaven*; 5 Mar 1717 (PGLR F.68/608)
Dent, Thomas [CH]; age ca 39; 13 Sep 1725 (CCR CL.1057-1063)
Dent, Peter; wife Mary; children: Elizabeth, b. 23 Apr 1727; Peter, b. 10 Jan 1728; William, 8 Aug 1730 (KGP p. 278)
Dent, George [CH]; wife Anne; tract *Dent's Levell*; 22 Apr 1728 (PGLR M.311)
Dent, Peter; m. 6 May 1753 Mary Elinor Hawkins; child: William, b. 4 Mar 1756 (KGP p. 303, 312)
Dent, Peter, Sr.; 5 Oct 1757; 23 Nov 1757; wife Mary; sons Peter, William, Thomas, Walter, Richard; daus. Elizabeth, Mary Beall, Lucy Hardy, Ann, Eleanor, Barbara; tracts *Witchaven, The Barrens* (MCW XI.182); 14 Mar 1758 (I 65.195)r; widow Mary; heirs Elizabeth, Ann, Barbara, Thomas, Walter, Richard; 26 Mar 1760 (GB 214)
Dent, William; wife Virlinder; child: Peter, b. 16 Mar 1761 (PGP p. 262)
Dent, Peter; wife Ann; children: Theadosha, bapt. 12 Jun 1761; Mary Elenor, bapt. 27 Feb 1763 at Lower Chapel; Joseph, bapt. 16 Dec 1764 Upper Chapel; Martha, bapt. 28 Sep 1766 Lower Chapel; William, b. 4 Feb 1773 Broad Creek (KGP p. 322, 334, 355, 367, 370)
Dent, John; wife Sarah; child: Thomas Marshall, b. 22 Oct 1761 (KGP p. 324)
Dent, Walter; wife Elizabeth; children: Walter, b. 7 Jan 1765 Lower Chapel; Chloe Hanson, bapt. 25 May 1766 Broad Creek (KGP p. 348, 350)

DENUNE
Denune, William; m. 24 10ber 1728 Elizabeth Duvall; [d/o Maren Duvall at Western Branch]; children: Elizabeth, b. 18 7ber 1729; Alexander, b. 28 Jan 1730; Jane, b. 30 Jul 1732; _____ (f), b. 10 Mar 173_; Martha, b. 26

Dec 1736; Ann, b. 26 Dec 1737; Susannah, b. 18 Jun 1739; Jacob Henry, b. 24 Nov 174_; Catherine, b. 8 May 1743; [Willi]am, b. 14 Jan 1744; Elizabeth, b. 10 Apr 1745; Mary, b. 3 Mar 17__ (QAP m/5; b/23, 24, 26, 28, 30, 32, 33, 34, 35)

Denune, William, Dr.; wife Elizabeth; 1751 (MCW X.183); extx. Elisabeth; [with 1756] (I 62.95)

Denune, Elisabeth; 28 Sep 1760 (I 94.192)

DEVANNS

Devanns, Michael; 5 Sep 1773 (I 114.287)

DEVENPORT

Devenport, Abraham; wife Mary; children: Catharine, b. 4 Aug 1765 Lower Chapel; Nancey, bapt. _ Aug 1767 Upper Chapel (KGP p. 345, 366)

Devenport, Stephen; wife Verlinder; child: Samuel Stone, b. 29 Oct 1774 Lower Chapel (KGP p. 380)

DEVEROW

Deveron, William; 9 Apr 1733; 11 Oct 1733; wife Eleanor; daus. Eleanor Clary, Mary Clary; ss-i-l John Clary, Daniel Clary (MCW VII.45); _ Nov 1733 (I 17.532); extx. Eleanor; 3 Dec 1737 (AA 14.517)

Deavern, Eleanor; widow; granddau. Ruth Clary; 23 Mr 1741 (PGLR Y.453)

Deverow, Eleanor; 12 Dec 1743; 19 Nov 1744; dau. Eleanor Clary; s-i-l Daniel Clary; granddaus. Mary, Ruth; grandson. William Clary (MCW IX.3)

DEVERSON

Deverson, Humphry; 24 Nov 1746 (AA 23.91)

DEW

Dew, Ninian; had child, age ca 3, with Mary Davis; Nov 1697 Ct. (PGCR A.260)

Dew, Richard; wife Ann; child: John, b. 20 Oct 1757 (PGP p. 275)

DEWITT

Dewitt, John; age ca 62; 1 Mar 1731 (PGLR Q.604)

Dewitt, John, Jr.; wife Mary; son John; 4 Sep 1732 (PGLR Q.539)

DHOLOHUNDEE

Dholohundee, John; age ca 18; servant; Nov 1698 (PGCR A.355)

DICK

Dick, Henry; admx. Margaret; 22 Apr 1741 (I 27.359); widow Margarett; 23 Mar 1742 (AA 19.362)

Dick, Margaret; 17 Oct 1749; 24 Nov 1756; dau. Elizabeth Scott [w/o George]; grandsons John, George; granddaus. Elizabeth and Margaret Scott; niece Ann Skinner (MCW XI.149)

Dick, _____ (m); age 3 months; s/o Priscilla Gray [alias Mulatto Priscilla]; bound out; Mar 1730 (PGCR R.5)

DICKESON

Dickeson, Thomas; 11 Dec 1713; 18 Jan 1724/5; wife Elizabeth; sons Thomas, Henry, John; daus. Mary Lenham, Elizabeth; tracts *Foxes Hole, Dickeson's Lott, Dickeson's Delight* (MCW V.183); 27 Feb 1724 (I 10.336); 25 Aug 1725 (AA 7.140)

Dickison, Thomas; dau. Mary Lanham; tract *Dickison's Lott, Fox's Hole*; 2 Nov 1717 (PGLR F.19/545)

Dickinson, Henry; m. Sushana Saratt; child: John, b. 11 Feb 1720/1 (KGP p. 266)

Dickison, John; wife Frances; tract *Dickison's Park*; 16 May 1721 (PGLR I.178)

Dickinson, John; wife Francis; tract *Dickinson Folly*; 22 Nov 1726 (PGLR M.101)

Dickinson, John; cousin Thomas Lannam [s/o John, Jr.]; tract *Chance*; 10 Sep 1728 (PGLR M.326)

Dickson, George; age ca 48; 19 Oct 1730 (CCR-MSA 5.467); 17 Aug 1732 (PGLR Q.528)

Dickason, Henry; nephew Thomas Hunter [s/o Elizabeth sis. of Henry]; Thomas' bros. Jeremiah & Uriah Virgin; 6 Dec 1732 (PGLR Q.605)

Dickason, John; cous. Daniel Jenkins [s/o Enoch]; tract *Dickason's*; 26 Jun 1733; nephew John; tract *Dickason's*; 26 Jun 1733 (PGLR Q.655, 656)

Dickieson, Thomas [dec'd]; son Thomas; grandson Thomas; tracts *Foxes Hole, Dickieson's Lott*; 17 Mar 1738 (PGLR T.699)

Dickinson, John; 5 Nov 1742; 28 Aug 1744; bro. Henry; sisters Mary and Elizabeth; nephews Uriah Virgin, Garrett Dickinson [s/o Henry], Jeremiah Virgin; tracts *Dickinson's Delight, John and James Choice* (MCW VIII.280)

Dickeson, Henry; age ca 54; 1743 (PGLR Y.701)

Dickeson, John, Sr.; age ca 66; 1743 (PGLR Y.701)

Dickson, George; 4 May 1752 (AA 32.207)

Dickerson, Sirratt; wife Hanah; child: Nathan, b. 9 Jun 1763 (PGP p. 270)

DIGGES

Digges, Edward; 10 Apr 1714; 19 Apr 1714; bros. Charles, William, John & Dudley Digges; mother Eliza.; sisters Mary Digges, Mary Neale & ____ Darnall; "bros." Notley Rozer, Robert Brooke, Henry Darnall, Anthony Neale, Benjamin Hall; nephews Henry & Edward Neale, Francis Hall [s/o Benjamin]; niece Mary Wharton [d/o Mary Neale], Elizabeth Rozer; cous. Charles Pye; tracts *Barbadoes, Bengiah, Elizabeth's Delight; Cedar Neck, Digges Point, Denby, Bangiah Manor, Brandferd* (MCW IV.9); 30 Apr 1716 (I&A 36c.140)

Digges, Charles; wife Susannah; 21 Jul 1720 (PGLR F.285/865)

Digges, Edward [dec'd]; bros. Charles, William, John; sister Mary; 8 Feb 1727 (CCR-MSA 5.294-318)

Digges, William; wife Eleanor; tracts *Hackthorn Heath, Sewall's Addition*; 9 Feb 1735 (PGLR T.352)

Digges, Edward [dec'd]; bro. John; sister Mary; niece Mary Wharton; f-i-l Henry Darnall, dec'd [AA]; tract *Kingston*; 26 Sep 1735 (PGLR T.321)

Digges, William; bros. Edward [dec'd], John; 28 Jun 1736 (PGLR T.381)

Digges, Charles; dau. Mary to marry Clement Hill; 28 Dec 1737 (PGLR T.559)

Digges, William; son Edward; 10 Sep 1738 (PGLR Y.208)

Diggs (Digges), William, gent.; 1 Aug 1739; 20 Aug 1740; wife Elinor; sons Edward, Ignatius, Nicholas, Francis, Thomas; dau. Mary; tracts *Mellwood Park, Essex, Free School Farm, Cole Brigade, Crawcrofts Purchase, Hatchel, Little Addition, Aquascott Alias, Brook Court, Pyans Grove* (MCW VIII.98); 20 Apr 1741 (I 26.83); [with 1744] (I 29.210); legatee Edward; 6 Jul 1744 (AA 20.270)

Diggs, Elenor; 11 Sep 1740; 26 Nov 1740; sons Edward, Ignatius, Nicholas; dau. Mary; granddau. Elenor (MCW VIII.118)

Diggs, Charles; 28 Jan 1742; 28 May 1744; daus. Anne, Mary Hill; son William; grandson Charles & Thomas [ss/o William]; sister Anne Darnall; tracts *Partnership, Addition to Partnership, Warberton Manor, Frankland* (MCW VIII.268)

Digges, William; age ca 31; 1743 (PGLR Y.657)

Digges, William; sons Ignatius, Nicholas; 17 Jan 1743 (CCR MSA 8.45)

Digges, Nicholas, gent.; 9 Mar 1749/50; 27 Jun 1750; dau. Eleanor; bros. Edward, Ignatius; niece Eleanor Digges [d/o bro. Edward], Henrietta Waring (MCW X.97-8); 24 Sep 1750 (I 47.148)

Digges, Charles; 18 Aug 1761; 19 Apr 1769; father William (MCW XIV.87); 4 Jul 1769 (I 101.203, 204)

Digges, William, Esq.; son George; 1770 (MCW XIV.150)

DIMPSY
Dimpsy, John; age ca 52; 1730 (PGLR M.568)

DIXON
Dixon, George; m. 22 Jan 1708 Mary Petty; both of this parish; children: Anne, b. 14 Apr 1710; Mary, b. 15 Nov 1713; Martha, b. 17 Jun 1716; Sarah, b. 8 Mar 1718/9; Elizabeth, b. 10 Jul 1721 (KGP p. 273, 274)

Dixon, Henry; wife Sabina; children: Morrice, b. 20 Dec 1731; Mary, b. 30 May 1734 (QAP b/26, 28)

Dixon [Dickson], George; 18 Jul 1751 (I 47.161)

Dixon, George; wife Sarah; children: George, bapt. 24 May 1752; Elenor, bapt. 2 Jun 1765 Lower Chapel (KGP p. 296, 351)

Dixon, George, Jr.; wife Mildred; child: Edward, b. 14 Sep 1772 Lower Chapel (KGP p. 383)

DOCWRA
Docura, John; s/o Thomas; 22 Feb 1724 (CCR-MSA 4.49)

Docwra [Doucza], John, gent.; wife Salome; 1725 (MCW V.220)

Docwar, John; 14 Oct 1736; 25 Aug 1738; wife Solome; tract *Collington* (MCW VII.258)

Docwra, John [dec'd]; widow Solome; 19 Oct 1742 (PGLR Y.537)

DONELLSON
Donellson, Daniel; 17 Jan 1712 (I&A 33b.157)

DONNELL
Donnell, David; age ca 14; servant; Sep 1701 (PGCR B.137)

Donnell, Thomas; age ca 9 yrs; servant; June 1701 (PGCR B.108)

DORITY
Dority, Robert; wife Mary; child: Mary, b. 22 Mar 1773 (KGP p. 389)

DORSETT
Dossett [Dorsett], John; 9 May 1711; wife Ann; sons, Thomas, John; daus. Frances Hoy, Eliza Bowling, Ann Dossett, Sarah Dossett, Mary Dossett; tracts *The Orchard, The Farm, Twiner, Little Worth, Largoe* (MCW III.204); extx. Ann; 16 May 1711 (I&A 32b.183); 8 Aug 1711 (I&A 32c.23)

Dorset, John; planter; 22 Feb 1717; 18 Jun 1718; nephews Thomas Webster, John Bowers; sisters Ann and Mary [Dorset] and Eliza. Bowers, b-i-l John Bowers; mother [unnamed] (MCW IV.163); 25 Jun 1718 (I 1.5)

Dorsett, Mary; [d/o John Dorsett, dec'd]; tract *Greenwood*; 1 Mar 1721 (PGLR I.173)

Dorset, Ann; 14 Jan 1721; 5 Jun 1721; daus. Eliza. Boen, Mary, Sarah Winser [Winsher], Ann Harrison; son Thomas; grandsons Dorsey & James Hoey, John Beon, Jr. (MCW V.57); 15 Nov 1722 (AA 5.65); dau. Mary Buchannan [w/o Thomas], Sarah Winsor [w/o Thomas], Elisabeth Bowen [w/o John]; 24 Jan 1723 (AA 5.316)

Dowset, Francis; wife Jane; children: Rachel, b. 30 Dec 1724; ____(m), b. 18 Aug 1726; Henry, b. 14 Jun 1728; Ann, b. 2 Aug 1730; Jane, b. 10 Dec 1732 (QAP b/27)

Dorsett, Thomas, Sr.; 20 Nov 1761; 13 Jan 1762; wife Mary; sons Thomas, William Newman; daus. Eleanor Marlow, Sibby Noble, Mary Wright, Eliza Dorsett; tracts *Stephen's Hope*, *Norwick*, *Good Luck* (MCW XI1.102); [as planter]; 5 Apr 1762 (I 77.80) ; 7 Jun 1762 (I 78.328)

DOTTS

Dotts, Barton [Baston]; 17 Feb 1773 (I 114.41); 12 Feb 1774 (I 114.294)

Dotts, Boston; child: Mary, b. 3 Sep 1773 Broad Creek (KGP p. 385)

DOUGLASS

Douglass, John [dec'd] [CH]; son John; grandson Benjamin; tract *Cold Spring Manor*; 27 Mar 1714 (PGLR F.366)

Douglass, John [dec'd] [CH]; sons Charles, Joseph; grandson Benjamin; tract *Cold Spring Manor*; [undated, with 1714] (PGLR F.385)

Douglas, John [CH]; son John; grandson Benjamin; tract *Cold Spring Manor*; 11 May 1741 (PGLR Y.282)

Douglass, Benjamin; m. 16 Feb 1775 Ann Middleton; child: Samuel Middleton, b. 30 Apr 1776 Lower Chapel (KGP p. 377)

DOULEY

Douley, Henry; wife Mary; child: Jonathan, b. 7 Apr 1761 (PGP p. 260)

DOVE

Dove, Samuel; wife Martha; child: Mary Elenor, b. 16 Jun 1770 Broad Creek (KGP p. 374)

DOWDEN

Dowden, John; wife Ester; children: Thomas, b. 2 Jan 1712/3; Elizabeth, b. 29 Aug 1716 (QAP b/8, 12)

Dowden, Thomas; wife Mary; child: Clementious, b. 21 Mar 1763 (PGP p. 269)

DOWELL

Dowell, Hannel; wife Susannah; child: Major, bapt. 23 Jun 1751 (KGP p. 294)

DOWNES

Downs, William; 2 Apr 1720 (I 3.271)

Downs [Downes], William; admx. Mary Gordon [w/o Robert]; widow, 4 sons & 3 daus [unnamed]; 18 Aug 1721 (AA 3.512); heirs Sarah, William, Henry, Elizabeth, Benjamin, Mary, John; 25 Jun 1722 (GB 14); Henry; minor; tract *Friend's Advice*; *Burches Venture*; 19 Jul 1774 (GB 322)

Downs, John; 15 Oct 1725 (AA 7.108)

Downs, Isaac; wife Elizh._; child: Katherine Goldsmith, b. 10 Jun 1733 (QAP b/27)

Down, Abraham; heirs [none known]; 3 Dec 1740 (AA 18.138)

Downs, William; wife Ann; child: James Gordon, bapt. 28 Apr 1751 (KGP p. 293)

Downes, Henry; admx. Mary; 10 Oct 1747 (I 35.295); 23 Nov 1751; admx. Mary Clark [w/o Benjamin]; children Henry, Benjamin & John Downes (ABB 1.10); admx. Mary Clark [w/o Benjamin]; children [eldest ca 10 yrs.] Henry, Benjamin, John; 23 Nov 1751 (AA 31.163)

Downs, John; wife Elizabeth; child: Catherine, bapt. 1 Mar 1752 (KGP p. 294)

Downes [Downs], Benjamin; wife Mary; children: Lucy, bapt. 24 May 1752; Ann, b. 20 Jul 1755 (KGP p. 296, 311)

Downes, William; wife Rebeccah; child: John, b. 3 Dec 1765 Lower Chapel (KGP p. 352)

Downes, William; wife Elizabeth; children: Rebecca, bapt. 13 Nov 1768 Lower Chapel; Josias, b. 14 Dec 1771 Lower Chapel; Theophilus, b. 27 Jul 1774 Lower Chapel (KGP p. 371-2, 380, 383)

Downs, William; wife Heneritta; children: Katherine, b. 7 Feb 1773 Lower Chapel; Daniel, b. 12 Feb 1775 Lower Chapel (KGP p. 380, 384)

Downs, Eleanor; child: Latitia, b. 1 Mar 1776 Lower Chapel (KGP p. 381)

DOWNING

Downing, Terrence; wife Eleanor; tract *Beall's Levell*; 11 Jul 1730 (PGLR Q.55)

Downing, Terence; wife Eleanor [widow of William Gover, dec'd]; tract *Beall's Levell*; 17 Jun 1734 (PGLR T.138)

Downing, James; 14 Jun 1747; 12 May 1748; wife Ann; sons James, Henry, John, Nathaniel; tract *Doublin* (MCW IX.158); extx. Anne; 13 Jul 1748 (I 37.46); extx. Ann; children: Hanah Gray, Elisabeth Peckerson, James, Ann Wynn, Margery, Mary, Henry, Elinor, Phebie, Nathaniel, Barbary, Benjamin; 16 Jul 1750 (AA 28.244)

Downing, Terrence; age ca 14 mos. Oct next; bound out; Aug 1747 (PGCR GG.96)

Downing, Terrence; age 18 on 1 Oct next; mother and father dec'd; also Uncle James Downing; bound to James Wallace; Mar 1751 (PGCR MM.6)

Downing, James; wife Susanna; children [?twins]: James & John, b. 16 Feb 1756 (KGP p. 312)

Downing, Joseph, wife Jemima; child: Leticia, b. 1 Mar 1773 (PGP p. 279)

Downing, Henry; wife Sarah; child: Elizabeth Keech, b. 2 Apr 1775 Lower Chapel (KGP p. 380)

DOYAL

Doyal, John; wife Amealea; child: ____ (m), bapt. 24 Jul 1763 at Broad Creek (KGP p. 338)

DOYNE

Doyne, Robert [CH]; children: Wharton, William, Sarah, Verlinda Taylor [w/o Samuell], Elinor, Mary; tract *Carrick Fergus*; 20 Nov 1705 (PGLR C.172a)

Doyne, Robert [CH]; daus. Sarah, Virlinda, Mary Dawson [w/o Nicholas]; 22 Sep 1708 (PGLR C.224)

DRANE

Drain, Elizabeth, age ca 66; 6 Feb 1732/3 (PGLR T.285)

Drane, Anthony; 28 Mar 1719; 27 Mar 1723; wife Elizabeth; sons Thomas, Anthony, James (MCW V.152); extx. Elisabeth; 20 Sep 1723 (I 9.5); admx. Elisabeth; 5 May 1724 (AA 6.89)

Drane, Elizabeth; children James, Rachel, Thomas; granddau. Rebekah Drane; 3 Aug 1734 (PGLR T.195)

Drane, James; wife Elizabeth; children: Elizabeth, b. ____; Thomas, b. ____; Anthony, b. ____; James, b. __ Aug ____; ____ (m), b. 15 Oct 1756; ____(m/f?), b. 14 Jul ____ (QAP b/33, 36, 37, 38)

Drane, Thomas; 9 Oct 1771; admn. Mrs. Susannah Drane; 9 children [unnamed] (ABB 6.274); admx. Susannah; 2 Feb 1772 (I 112.50)

DRURY

Drury, Charles; 27 Aug 1740; 3 Oct 1740; wife Alice; son Charles; daus. Sarah, Ester Selby, Mary Dart, Sophia Boteler [w/o Charles]; grandson Edward Boteler; tracts *Essex Land, Drury's Adventure* (MCW VIII.105); admx. Alice; 23 Nov 1740 (I 25.297); extx. Alice; 3 Mar 1741 (I 26.177). Alice; 9 Sep 1741 (AA 18.299)

Drury, Charles; age ca 60; 24 Dec 1736 (PGLR Y.84)

DRYDEN

Dryden, Henry; 8 Dec 1700 (I&A 20.197)

Drydin, Elizabeth; daus. Elinor, Elizabeth; tract *Elizabeth & Thomas*; 15 Nov 1723 (PGLR I.527)

DUCK

Duck, John; age ca 8; servant; Jun 1702 (PGCR B.162)

DUCKER

Ducker, William; m. 21 Aug 1721 Mary Field; children: John, b. 23 Sep 1722 [see Christ Church, Queen Caroline Parish, Anne Arundel Co. for children of John and wife Cassandra]; Mary, b. 26 7ber 1723; William, b. 5 Jul 1725; Sarah, b. 2 Jul 1727; Nathaniel, b. 5 May 1729; Abraham, b. 17 Feb 1731/2; Ann, b. 20 Sep 1734 (QAP m/2; b/18, 19, 20, 22, 25, 28)

Ducker, William; wife Mary; tract *Jacob's Hope*; 22 Jan 1729 (PGLR M.536)

Ducker, William; 28 Fe 1749 (I 42.201)

DUCKETT

Duckett, Richard; m. 26 Jan 1698/9 All Hallow's Parish, Anne Arundel Co. to Charity Jacob; [d/o John and Ann Jacob]; children: Mary, b. 27 Oct 1699 [b. 21 Feb 1699; bapt. 26 Jul 1700 All Hallow's Parish, Anne Arundel Co.]; Elizabeth, b. 28 Dec 1700; [m. 9 Sep 1723 All Hallow's Parish, Anne Arundel Co. to Oliver Wallis]; Charity, b. 26 Mar 1703; Richard, b. 27 Feb 1704/5 [b. 21 Feb 1704; bapt. 8 Jul 1705 All Hallow's Parish, Anne Arundel Co.]; John, b. 31 Oct 1706 [bapt. 13 Apr 1707 All Hallow's Parish, Anne Arundel Co.]; Ann, b. 18 Mar 1710/1; Susanna, b. 30 8ber 1712; Jacob, b. 11 9ber 1714; Martha [twin], b. 14 8ber 1716; Rachel [twin], b. 14 8ber 1716; Sarah, b. 30 Jul 1718 (QAP b/4, 5, 8, 10, 12, 14)

Duckett, Richard, Jr.; m. 13 9ber 1729 Mary Nutwell; children: Richard, b. 12 Apr 1732; [John, Jr.] (m), b. 17 Mar 1733 (QAP m/5; b/25, 28)

Duckett, Richard; m. 2 Jun 1735 Elizabeth Williams; children: Martha, b. 17 Mar 1736 [m. Rignal Odell]; Elenor, b. 25 Dec 1737; Elizabeth, b. 20 Jan 1741; Charity, b. 10 Jun 174_; [m. Thomas Boyde]; Thomas, b. 26 Mar 1744; [Ann], b. 11 Sep 174_; [Rachel] William[s] (f), b. 2 May 1748; [Isaac], b. 23 Oct 1751; _____, b. 12 Jun 1753; [Rig]nal, b. 4 Mar 1755; [Elean]er, b. 19 Oct 1758; [Bar]uth, b. __ Dec 17__ (QAP m/6; b/31, 32, 33, 37)

Duckett, Richard; wife Martha; children: Martha, b. 29 Jun 17__; Mary, b. 6 Jan 1756; Jane, b. 7 Oct 1761; Lucy, b. 24 Oct 176_; Thomas Waring, b. 9

Oct 176_; Elizabeth, b. 12 Jul 1767; Anne, b. 5 Jun 1770; Basil, b. 26 Mar 1779 (QAP b/36, 46)

Duckett, John, Jr.; m. 9 Aug 1758 Ann Raitt; [d/o John and Ann] (QAP m/7)

Duckitt, Richard; wife Martha; child: Thomas Warren, bapt. 22 Dec 1765 Lower Chapel (KGP p. 346)

Duckett, Thomas; child by wife Priscilla Bowie: Ann Fraser Duckett; 1776 (MCW XVI.186)

DUEL

Duel, William; wife Elinor; child: Elinor, b. 8 Mar 1755 (KGP p. 308)

DUGG

Dugg, James; age ca 20; servant; Jun 1712 Ct. (PGCR G.211)

DULANY

Dulany, Daniel; wife Rebecca; tract Stoke; 17 Jan 1718 (PGLR F.132/700)

Dulany, Daniel; wife Sarah [dec'd]; tracts Long Acre, Sinacer Landing; 13 Jul 1736 (PGLR T.430)

Dulany, Daniel [AA]; wife Henrietta Maria; tract Dulany Lott; 28 Sep 1739 (PGLR Y.95)

Dulaney, Samuel; wife Ann; child: Walter, bapt. 23 Oct 1763 at Upper Chapel (KGP p. 334)

DUMALL

Dumall, Mary; 30 Jul 1740 (I 30.72)

DUNCAN

Duncon, John; [with 1696] (I&A 14.3)

Duncan, John; 12 Jul 1762; admx. William Dunkin (ABB 3.136); heirs Margaret, Rachel, Margaret Duncan and Mary Tucker; 25 Jul 1764 (GB 236)

DUNHUE

Dunhue, Mary; servant; swore Godfrey Barnes got her with child; Jun 1699 Ct. (PGCR A.424)

Dunhue, Mary [alias Mary Gregory]; age ca 3; bound out; Jun 1702 (PGCR B.163)

DUNN

Dunn, Hugh Smith; wife Alse; child: Elizabeth, b. 17 Jun 1764 (PGP p. 274)

Dunn, Catharine; child: William, bapt. 21 Dec 1766 Broad Creek (KGP p. 360)

DUNNING

Dunnins, Terrniss [Terrins, Turrin]; 29 Mar 1712; 13 Aug 1712; wife Eliza.; sons James, Terrins, Nathaniel (MCW III.228); extx. Elisabeth; 2 Mar 1712 (I&A 34.144); extx. Elisabeth Mason [w/o Phillip]; 1 Jan 1713 (I&A 35a.6)

Dunning, Jerome; extx. Elisabeth; 13 Nov 1712 (I&A 33b.213)

Dunning, James; m. 24 Jan 1720 Anne Acton; child: Hannah, b. 13 Jan 1721 (KGP p. 275)

Duning, James; wife Sarah; child: Henry Acton, b. 26 Nov 1766 Broad Creek (KGP p. 348)

DURHAM

Durham; Richard [England]; wife Alice; tract Moores Plaines; 28 Sep 1698 (PGLR A.200)

Durham, Francis; 1 Feb 1711 (I&A 33a.65); 6 Mar 1712 (I&A 33a.116)

DUTY

Duty, Mathew; wife Martha; tract Dickeson's New Design; 22 Mar 1738 (PGLR T.571)

DUVALL

Duvall, Mareen; wife Francis; tract part of Vale of Benjamin; 13 Aug 1701 (PGLR A.398)

Duvall, Mareen, Jr.; wife Elizabeth; Maren, b. 14 9ber 1702; Susanna, b. 12 Sep 1704; Elizabeth, b. 20 Jul 1706; Samuel, b. 27 9ber 1707; Ann, b. 8 May 1709; Benjamin, 4 Apr 1711; John, b. 20 Feb 1712/3; Jacob, b. 19 Apr 1715; Mary, b. 22 Mar 1717; Lewis, b. 3 10ber 1721; Gabriel, b. 13 7ber 1724 (QAP b/5, 9, 10, 15, 17, 19)

Duvall, Benjamin; age 18 years; chooses guardian; Jun 1704 (PGCR B.300)

Duvall, Samuel; wife Eliza; children: Ruth, b. 31 Jul 1703; Ester, b. 4 Oct 1705; Sarah, b. 28 Aug 1708 (QAP b/4)

Duvall, Mareen, the younger; wife Sarah; children: Mary, b. 2 9ber 1711; Mareen, Jr. & Samuel [twins], b. 22 Jun 1714; Benjamin, b. 30 7ber 1717; Elizabeth, b. 24 Aug 1720 (QAP b/5, 6, 10, 16)

Duvall, Benjamin; wife Sophia; children: Susanna, b. 16 10ber 1714; Sophia, b. 18 Mar 1716; Benjamin, b. 29 May 1719; Charles, b. 20 Jul 1729 (QAP b/14, 15, 23)

Duvall, Mareen; son Mareen; grandson Mareen, Jr.; tract Middle Plantation, Duvall's Range, Wilson's Plaine, Morly's Lot, Morly's Grove; 23 Jan 1720 (PGLR I.89)

Duvall, Lewis; m. 26 Nov 1722 Ellinor Farmer; [d/o Samuel Farmer] (QAP m/2)

Duvall, Lewis [AA]; wife Martha; tract *Martha's Choice*; 27 Nov 1723 (PGLR I.561)

Duvall, Samuel; wife Elizabeth; child: James, b. 3 Mar 1723/4 (QAP b/26)

Duvall, Mareen, Jr.; age ca 38; 10 Jun 1725 (PGLR I.649)

Duvall, Mareen, Jr. [at ye (Great) Marsh]; wife Ruth; children: Ruth, b. 25 9ber 1725; Elizabeth, b. 31 Mar 1726; Maren Howard, b. 23 10ber 1728; Cornelius, b. 23 Feb 1731; Sarah, b. 1 Oct 1732; Joseph, b. 16 Jan 1733; Henry, b. 7 Feb 1733/4; Priscilla, b. 11 Feb 1737; Alexander, b. 10 Jul 1739; Margaret, b. 9 Feb 1740; Ephraim, b. 12 Jul 1742; Zachariah, b. 10 Feb 1743; [En]os, b. __ Dec ____ (QAP b/19, 20, 21, 24, 26, 27, 29, 31, 33, 37)

Duvall, Mareen; of the Great Marsh; age 46; 4 Oct 1726 (PGLR M.216)

Duvall, Samuel; age ca 58; ca 4 Oct 1726 (PGLR M.216)

Duvall, Mareen; age ca 65; 4 Oct 1726 (PGLR M.215)

Duvall, Samuel; m. 16 May 1732 Elizabeth Mulliken; children: James, b. __ May 17__; Charity, b. ____; Elisha, b. 18 Jan 1737; Elizabeth, b. 15 ____ 1738; ____ (f), b. 31 Jan 17__; Samuel, b. 2 Jul 174_; Jesse (m), b. ____; Gabriel, b. 2 Oct ____; Jacob, b. 13 May 174__; Jeremiah, b. 24 Aug 1741 (QAP m/5; b/30, 31, 32, 34, 35)

Duvall, Samuel, Sr.; dau Sarah Beck [w/o James]; grandchildren: James, Samuel Duvall Beck; 23 Jun 1736 (PGLR T.379)

Duvall, Mareen; son & heir of Mareen, Sr. & wife Frances; tract *Vale of Benjamin*; 15 Apr 1738 (PGLR T.584)

Duvall, John; wife Ann; children: Elizabeth, b. 28 Aug 1739; Marsh Mareene, b. 17 Apr 1741; Susannah, b. 19 Mar 1743; John, b. 22 Feb 1745 (QAP b/33)

Duvall, Martha; 2 May 1739; 22 Nov 1739; cousins Mary Whitehead, Ann Carrick, Elizabeth Denune; sister Ann Way of SC (MCW VIII.51); cousins Mary Whitehead, Ann Carrick, Elisabeth Denune; Ann Way [sister in SC] 11 May 1744 (AA 20.194)

Duvall, Mary; 20 Jan 1739; 26 Jun 1740; cousins Ann Pottonger [w/o Robert, dec'd], Brock & Edward Mockbee (MCW VIII.95)

Duvall, Samuel, Sr.; planter; 11 Jan 1741; 24 Mar 1741; daus. Elizabeth Tyler, Susannah Falconar, Esther West, Sarah Beck, Lucy Forrest [w/o William], Rachel Butts; granddau. Elizabeth Forrest; grandsons Samuel Dewall Beck [s/o James], Samuel Tyler, Edward Tyler; ss-i-l William Forrest, James Beck (MCW VIII.162); 29 Mar 1742 (I 27.27); 19 Jul 1742 (I 27.358); daus. Susannah Falconer [w/o Alexander], Easter West [w/o William], Elisabeth Tyler, Lucy Forrest [w/o William], Rachel Butts [w/o Richard]; 19 Apr 1744 (AA 20.117)

Duval, Mareen; extx. Elisabeth; 17 Jun 1741 (I 26.315); widow Elisabeth; legatee Samuel; children: Benjamin, John, Ann Carrick [w/o John], Susannah Fowler [w/o William], Elisabeth Denune [w/o William], Jacob, Lewis, Mareen, Mary Clark [w/o Joshua]; 11 Oct 1744 (AA 20.440)

Devall, Margaret [wife of Joseph]; transported for 14 years; 8 Apr 1742 (PGLR Y.562)

Duvall, Samuel; wife Eleanor; tract *Duvall's Hunting Quarter*; 18 Jan 1743 (PGLR Y.681)

Duvall, Jacob [SM]; wife Margaret; 7 Jun 1743 (PGLR Y.692)

Duvall, William; m. 20 Oct 1745 Precilla Truitt; child: Sophia, b. 8 Jun 1755 (PGP p. 229, 256)

Duvall, Benjamin; wife Susannah; children: Delilah, b. ____; Gabriel, b. ____; Sarah, b. ____; Benjamin & Susannah (twins), b. 5 Nov 174_; Edward, b. ____; Elizabeth, b. 14 Dec 174_ (QAP b/34, 35, 36)

Duvall, Mareen; wife Martha; children: Ann, b. 25 Jan 174_; Lewis, b. __ J__ 174_ (QAP b/35)

Duvall, Mareen; heirs Leah, Jamima & Priscilla Soper; 27 Nov 1746 (GB 152)

Devalle, William; wife Precilla; children: Samuel, b. 24 Dec 1748; William, b. 3 Apr 1750; Pruite, b. 22 Nov 1752 (PGP p. 256)

Duvall, Elisah; admx. Wilhelmina; 1 Nov 1760 (I 73.50)

Duvall, Mareen; admx. Ruth; 25 Nov 1761 (I 76.304)

Duvall, Lewis; wife Anne; child: Bettsey, b. 12 Oct 1763 (PGP p. 268)

Duvall, Mareen; wife Sarah; children: William Mareen, b. 18 Oct 1763; Mareen, b. 9 Nov 1765 (PGP p. 273, 278)

Duvall, Acquilla; wife Elizabeth; child: Nelley, b. 25 Oct 1764 (PGP p. 276)

Duvall, Benjamin; wife Mary; children: John, b. 21 Jul 17__; Martha, b. __ Jun ____; Thomas, b. 15 Aug 17__ (QAP b/36)

Duvall, James; wife Sarah; children: Ruth, b. __ Feb ___; Samuel, b. ____; ____ (f), b. ____ (QAP 36, 38)

Duvall, Joseph; wife Susannah; children: David, b. 24 Nov ____; Mary Stewart, b. ____; Susanna, b. 14 Nov 176_; Joseph, b. 28 Jun 1763; Henry Howard, b. __ Sep ____; Elizabeth, b. 27 Sep 1773 (QAP b/36, 39, 46)

Devall, Benjamin; wife Ann; children: Clarke Skinner, b. 16 May 1766 Broad Creek; Maereen, bapt. 27 Sep 1767 Broad Creek; Nancey Skinner, b. 12 Aug 1768 Broad Creek (KGP p. 359, 361, 364)

Devaul, Lewis; wife Jemima; child: Nancy, b. 27 Oct 1772 Broad Creek (KGP p. 383)

Duvall, Samuel; 25 Jun 1773; 20 Nov 1775; wife Elizabeth; children: James, Charity Macdougall, Elizabeth Glover, Samuel, Jacob, Jeremiah, Jesse, Gabriel, Margaret Denune, Elisha; grandson Benjamin [s/o Elisha]; tracts *Pleasant Grove, Welches Chance* (MCW XVI.79); 24 Feb 1776 (I 123.405, 406, 407)

DYAR

Dyer, Patrick; m. 12 Oct 1702 Comfort Barnes; children: Eliza., b. 22 Jan 1711; Rebecca, b. 12 Mar 1714; Thomas, b. 12 Dec 1715; James, b. 4 Oct 1717; Edward, b. 29 Dec 1719 (KGP p. 263); 16 Oct 1724 (AA 6.172)

Dyer, Patrick; children: William, age 6 on 18 of this inst.; Penelope, age 8 on 24 Feb next; Nov 1711 Ct. (PGCR G.124)

Dyer, Santelo; m. 7 Nov 1723 Margaret Ryley (QAP m/3)

Dier, Santelo; [no heirs in Md.]; 10 Apr 1732 (I 16.501)

Dyar, William, Jr.; admx. Mary; 21 Apr 1753 (I 54.62); 2 Jun 1755; admx. Mary Dyer; children: Annestatia & Penelope Dyer; [eld. dau. ca 4 yrs old] (ABB 1.133); widow Mary; heirs Penelope, Annecliatus; 28 Jun 1758 (GB 211); widow Mary; heirs Elizabeth, James, Mary, Thomas, Penelope, Edward; 29 Mar 1758 (GB 208)

Dyar, William; admx. Susannah; 5 Mar 1754 (I 58.137); 21 Mar 1755; admx. Susannah Dyer; children: Elizabeth, James, William, Mary, Thomas, Penelope, Rebeccah, Edward, Susannah & John Dyer [last 5 minors] (ABB 1.128)

Dyer, Thomas; wife Sarah; children: Thomas, bapt. 30 Jan 1763 at Lower Chapel [no mother's name]; Elizabeth, bapt. 2 Jun 1765 Lower Chapel; Sushanna, bapt. 2 Oct 1768 Lower Chapel (KGP p. 334, 351, 371)

Dyer, Thomas; 19 Jan 1768; 25 Aug 1768; children: Edward, Thomas, Francis Clement, Henry Edelin, George, Walter, Giles Green, Jeremiah, Elizabeth; tracts *Edelin's Hogpen Enlarged, Edelin's Rest* (MCW XIV.58); ex. Henrietta; 8 Nov 1768 (I 100.1); 28 Nov 1769; exs. Henrietta Dyer, Thomas Clement Dyer; children: Edward, Elisabeth, others [unnamed] (ABB 5.229); 29 Nov 1775 (GB 286)

Dyer [Dyar], Thomas; wife Sarah; children: James, b. 15 Aug 1773 Lower Chapel; Philip Gibbs, b. 16 Feb 1776 Lower Chapel (KGP p. 381, 384)

Dier, James; wife Ann; child: John, b. 19 Aug 1764 (PGP p. 272)

DYATT

Dyatt, Elizabeth; d/o Anne Dyatt [dec'd]; bound out; Nov 1745 (PGCR DD.265)

EADS

Eates, Robert; wife Ann; child: Francis (m), bapt. 23 Jun 1751 (KGP p. 294)

Eads [Eades], Robert; wife Mary; children: Rebecca, b. 18 Feb 1756; Mathew Lodg[e], b. 28 ___ 1758; Edward Jones, b. 15 Sep 1759; Charles, b. 14 Jul 1760; Robert &William (twins), b. 7 Aug 1762; Thomas, b. 25 Dec 1764 (PGP p. 258, 267, 277)

EARL

Earl, Elisabeth; child: Charlote King, b. 4 Jul 1769 Broad Creek (KGP p. 373)

EARLY

Early, Benjamin; wife Katherine; child: Benjamin, b. 8 Dec 1771 Upper Chapel (KGP p. 389)

EASTWOOD

Eastwood, Benjamin; 15 May 1763; 22 Nov 1763; wife Elizabeth; 6 children; sons John, Bazil, Benjamin; daus. Elizabeth, Sarah, Mary (MCW XII.211); planter; extx. Elisabeth; 28 Mar 1764 (I 83.166)

EDELEN

Edelen, Christopher; age 18; chose bro. Thomas as his guardian; Mar 1701 (PGCR B.94)

Edelen, Edward; wife Elizabeth; children: Sarah, b. 18 Feb 1705; James, b. 14 Apr 1710 (KGP p. 277)

Edelen, Christopher; m. 1707 Jane Jones; children: Elizabeth, b. 10 Oct 1708; Anne, b. 1 Sep 1710; John, b. 16 Dec 1712; Richard, b. 4 Aug 1715; Jane, b. 12 Dec 1718; Benjamin, b. 5 Dec 1720 (KGP p. 276)

Edelen, Richard [CH]; wife Sarah; tract *Thomas' Choice*; 10 Jul 1713 (PGLR F.350)

Edelen, Thomas, s/o Richard Edelen; m. 9 Feb 1719 Mary Blanford; child: Thomas, b. 12 Nov 1720 (KGP p. 268)

Edelin, Thomas; age ca 56; 1728 (PGLR M.346); Thomas, Sr.; age ca 57; 1730 (PGLR M.558)

Edelin, Edward; age ca 54; 19 Oct 1730 (CCR-MSA 5.462); age ca 67; 1743 (PGLR Y.657)

Edelen, Christopher; age ca 50; bros. Richard, Thomas, Edward; 1732 (PGLR Q.485)

Edelen, Richard, Sr.; wife Anne; son Thomas, Jr.; tract *Appledore*; 23 Apr 1739 (PGLR Y.27)

Edelen, Thomas; 4 Jul 1749?; 1 Jun 1749; wife Comfort; bros. Richard, Edward, Christopher; s-i-l Thomas Dyar; d-i-l Elizabeth Green; gd-i-l Sarah Saunders; cous. Francis Simm; tracts *Edlenton, Edlen's Addition,*

Egerton's Mannor, Stone Hill, Edlen's Thickett, Edlen's Hogpen (MCW X.39);
Thomas, Sr.; 22 Nov 1749 (I 41.378); heir Susannah; 24 Mar 1757 (GB 203)

Edelen, John; wife Sarah; child: Mary, bapt. 3 May 1752 (KGP p. 296)

Edelen, Thomas; planter; 13 Aug 1751; 1 Dec 1752; wife [unnamed]; sons
Thomas, Christopher, Charles; tracts *Apple Door, Rome* (MCW X.242-3); extx.
Mary; 25 Jan 1754 (I 58.140)

Edelen, Mary; 11 Nov 1754 (I 58.343?)

Edelin, Edward; 2 Feb 1755; 30 Mar 1756; dau. Sarah Pye; son James;
grandsons Walter Pye, Samuel, Henry; granddaus. Catherine & Sarah
Queen, Catherine, Edward, Elizabeth, Mary & Catherine Solome
Edelin, Margaret Pye; bro. Christopher; tracts *Pinner, Dublin, Thomas
Chance* (MCW XI.125-6)

Edelen, Comfort; widow; 10 May 1760; 22 Sep 1760; sons Edward Dyar,
Thomas Dyar, William Dyar [dec'd]; daus. Penelope Howard, Elizabeth
Green, Rebecca Sanders, grandchildren Thomas & Ann Dyer [ch/o
Edward], Thomas Edelen Green [s/o James Green], Elizabeth Dyar [d/o
Thomas]; great-grandchild Ann Spalding [d/o Bazil] (MCW XII.11); widow;
6 Oct 1760 (I 72.49); heir Thomas Dyar; 22 Dec 1763 (GB 234)

Edelin, Thomas; 10 Sep 1762; admn. Thomas Edlin; children [unnamed]
(ABB 3.163)

Edelen, James; 7 Mar 1768; 28 Jun 1768; widow Solome; children: Edward,
Joseph, Samuel, James, Elizabeth, Mary, Catherine, Salome, Margaret,
Sarah; bro. James; tracts *Edelin's Enlargement, Little Ease, Little Worth,
Friendship, Two Johns, Lyonstrole, Smallwoods Meadows, Apple Dore, Rome*
(MCW XIV.59); 21 Nov 1768 (I 10-0.8); 4 Jan 1770; widow [unnamed]; children
Edward, Joseph, Samuel, James, Elisabeth, Mary, Catharine, Solome,
Margaret, Sarah (ABB 5.391) Joseph, age ca 12; tracts *Friendship, Two Johns,
Lyons Hole*; 17 Aug 1775 (GB 284); James, age ca 4; tracts *Apple Doore,
Roome*; 28 Aug 1775 (GB 285)

Edelen, Christopher, Sr.; 22 Sep 1770; 19 Dec 1771; wife Jane; children:
Christopher, Ann Garner, John, Richard, Elizabeth Wheeler, Catherine;
grandson James Edelen; tract *Mayor's Choice* (MCW XIV.202); 17 Mar 1772 (I
109.170)

EDEN

Eden, Thomas; wife Esther; child: Mary, b. 14 May 1775 Broad Creek (KGP
p. 387)

EDGAR

Edgar, Richard; wife Joanna; twin daus. Sarah & Elizabeth; 28 Oct 1706; filed Mar 1710 (PGCR D.276)

Edgar, Richard; [with 1718] (I 2.228); widow Johannah; heirs Sarah, Elizabeth; 28 Jun 1720 (GB 12); widow Johanna; 1 son & 4 daus. [unnamed]; 26 Aug 1720 (AA 3.212)

Edgar, Johanna; 3 Mar 1730/1; son John; daus. Johanna Barnes, Margerett, Sarah Eilbeck, Elizabeth Wade (MCW VI.180); 26 Jul 1731 (I 16.237); widow; legatees Johnana Barns, Margarett Edgar, Sarah Eilbeck [w/o William], Elizabeth Wade; 7 Apr 1736 (AA 14.220)

Edgar, John; 10 Nov 1736; 22 Nov 1736; sisters Margaret Tyler, Joanne Milsteed, Sarah Eilbeck; b-i-l William Eilbeck; nephew John Wade; niece Sarah Edgar Wade; tracts *Market Overton, Dent's Levells, The Adventure, Wheeler's Purchase, Long Acre, The Horse Pen* (MCW VII.202); 6 Apr 1737 (I 22.266); 29 Dec 1737 (AA 16.62); heirs John Wade, Sarah Edgar Wade; 26 Nov 1740 (GB 114)

EDGE

Edge, James; 31 Jan 1718 (AA 1.388); 25 Apr 1718 (AA 1.8)

EDGELY

Edgely [Edgley], Thomas; 17 Jun 1735 (I 21.269); 15 Jun 1736 (AA 14.262)
Edgley, John; 1728 (I 14.6)

EDMONDSON

Edmunson, Robert [dec'd]; Archibald Edmunson, admn.; Aug 1698 Ct. (PGCR A.334]

Edmondson, Thomas; merchant; 17 Oct 1698 (I&A 17.146)

Edmonston, Archibald, Capt.; age ca 60; 19 Mar 1728/9 (PGLR M.479); age ca 60 odd; 31 May 1731 (PGLR Q.608)

Edmondston, Archibald; wife Jane; son Archibald; 18 Jun 1728/9 (PGLR M.383); wife Jane; s-i-l William Smith; tract *Edmondston's Pasture*; 25 Mar 1730 (PGLR M.563); wife Jane; dau. Ruth Orme [w/o John]; tract *Leith*; 25 Mar 1730 (PGLR M.564); age ca 60; 1734 (PGLR T.202)

Edmundson, James; wife Mary; 4 Sep 1733 (PGLR Q.683)

Edmonston [Edmondson], Archibald; 13 Mar 1734; 28 Jun 1734; wife Jane; sons James, Archibald, Ninian, Thomas; daus. Mary Beall, Ellenor Offutt, Ruth Orme, Martha Allen; granddau. Jane Allen [w/o Thomas]; tracts *Dunkell, Dear Park, Bare Garden, The Goar, Addition to the Goar, Cool Spring Level* (MCW VII.96); 11 Sep 1734 (I 20.70); extx. Jane; 16 Aug 1735

(I 21.127); widow Jane; children: James Edmonston, Mary Beall, Elinor Offutt, Ruth Orme, Archibald Edmonston, Martha Allen; 10 Nov 1735 (AA 14.23); widow Jane; heirs Thomas Allen, Jane Allen, Thomas Edmonston; 25 Aug 1736 (GB 84)

Edmonston, James; age ca 36; 9 Dec 1734 (PGLR T.236)

Edmonston, Ninian; 28 Sep 1734 (I 20.61); 2 Sep 1735 (AA 13.270); 2 Jun 1737 (AA 15.328); heirs Jane Edmonston, Mary Catterall, James Smith's 9 children, Eleanor Offutt, Archibald Edmonston, Ruth Orme, Martha Allen, Thomas Edmonston; 30 Jun 1737 (GB 94)

Edmonston, Archibald; f-i-l James Williams; 17 Apr 1740 (PGLR Y.176)

Edmonston, James; wife Mary; 11 Jul 1741 (PGLR Y.332)

Edmonston, Thomas; wife Elizabeth; children: William, b. 17 Dec 1742; Maxemelian, b. 29 Mar 1744; Thomas, b. 25 Dec 1746; Ann, b. 1 Feb 1748/9 (PGP p. 252)

Edmonson, Jane; 1 Jun 1748 (I 36.21)

Edmondston, James; 23 Jan 1750; 10 Oct 1753; sons Archibald, Ninian, James; daus. Margery, Jane, Mary, Sarah, Rachel; tracts *Brothers Content, Hermitage, Prevention, Labrinth, Barren Ridge, Batchelor's Forrest, Diamond, Daily, Accord, Pile's Delight, Preston's Marsh, Yarrows, Long Green, Silent Grove, Cool Spring Mannour, Westerne Field, Lubserland, Amsterdam, Land of Ease, George, George's Delight, Discovery, Piler's Hall* (MCW X.286-7); extx. Mary Turner [w/o Samuel]; 11 Jan 1754 (I 58.269)

EDWARDS

Edwards, Richard [CA], wife Hannah; tract *Fendalls Spring*; 7 Sep 1695 (PGLR A.7); wife Hannah [widow of John Potts]; tracts *Mount Pleasant, Good Luck*; 2 Nov 1697 (PGLR A.133)

Edwards, John; wife [unnamed]; 8 Sep 1699 (PGLR A.185)

Edwards, John; age ca 14; Aug 1702 (PGCR B.168)

EELE

Eele, _____ (m); s/o Mary; age 11 weeks on 27 of this instant; bound out to John Breshears [s/o Samuel]; Nov 1726 (PGCR N.106)

EGAN

Egan [Eggan], Charles; 21 Feb 1721; 29 Mar 172_; wife Elinor; m-i-l [unnamed] (MCW V.90); Charles, Dr.; nok Elinor; 23 Apr 1722 (I 7.226); 1 Jul 1723 (AA 4.293)

Egan, Elinor; 21 Sep 1722; 21 Dec 1722; mother Mary Moore of Longford, Ireland; father William Moore; bro. Christopher Moore; husband

Charles Egan [dec'd]; dau. Anne White [dec'd] (MCW V.121); 23 Dec 1722 (I 8.225); 20 Jun 1724 (AA 6.1)

EGERTON

Egerton, Charles [SM]; wife Mary; tract [unnamed]; 15 Jan 1703 (PGLR C.81a); sons John, Thomas, Randolph, James; 10 Nov 1715 (PGLR F.535)

Egerton, Thomas [now of Somerset Co.]; age ca 50; s/o Charles of St. Mary's Co., [dec'd]; wife Elizabeth; no children; 30 Aug 1731 (PGLR Q.376)

Egerton, William; s/o James; 25 May 1743 (PGLR Y.685)

EGLON

Eglon, John; wife Ellinor; child: William, b. 31 Aug 1720 (QAP b/16)

ELBOROUGH

Elborough, John; age ca 29; 1730 (PGLR M.567)

Ellborough, John; 16 Jul 1742 (I 27.53)

ELDER

Elder, William; wife Elizabeth; tract Good Will; 23 Mar 1710 (PGLR F.60)

Elder, William; admx. Elisabeth; 16 Jul 1715 (I&A 36c.42)

Elder, William; wife Ann; tract Goodwill; 7 Jan 1736 (PGLR T.560)

Elder, Thomas; wife Hannah [d/o Rebecca Riley]; dau. Rebecca; tract Dan; 15 Jul 1743 (PGLR Y.699)

ELLINGSWORTH

Ellingsworth, Israell; [?relations VA]; 24 Jan 1734 (I 24 Jan 1734); heirs ?VA; 27 Aug 1735 (AA 13.275)

ELLIOTT

Ellet, Daniell; wife Elizabeth; Jan 1696/7 Ct. (PGCR A.139)

Ellott, Walter; 2 Mar 1702; 14 Nov 1703; wife [unnamed] (MCW III.30)

Ellett [Elliott], Daniell; [with 1703] (I&A 24.241); widow Elisabeth Thompson [w/o William]; 9 Feb 1707 (I&A 28.2)

Elliot, William; 1713 (I&A 34.42)

Elliot, Mary; 14 Nov 1727; 5 Mar 1727/8; sons Edward & John Broner; grandsons Edward, William, Thomas & John Broner [ss/o Edward]; Elizabeth & Abigall Broner [ds/o Edward]; Henry Broner [s/o William, dec'd]; tract Hunter's Kindness (MCW VI.56); 21 May 1728 (I 12.144)

Elliot, William; 2 Aug 1727; 19 Aug 1727; wife Mary (MCW VI.36); extx. [unnamed] dec'd prior to admn.; 21 Nov 1727 (I 13.29); extx. Mary [dec'd]; 27 Aug 1728 (AA 9.67)

ELLIS

Ellis, Christopher; wife Mary; children: Elizabeth, b. 15 Jun 1689; Agniss, b. 29 Aug 1697; Christopher, b. 29 Jun 1698 (QAP b/1)

Elles, John; 10 Apr 1714 (I&A 36a.155)

Ellis, Owen; dau. Ann; 1714 (MCW IV.67)

Ellis, Christopher; wife Elizabeth; children: James, b. 11 Jan 1723/4; John, b. 24 Mar 1726 (QAP b/18, 20)

Ellis, Owen; age ca 54; 1734 (PGLR T.124); age ca 55; 1734 (PGLR T.155)

Ellise, Owen; 4 Sep 1743; 14 Aug 1745; wife Mary; sons John, Johnathan, Owen Jr.; daus. Elizabeth, Mary, Jane (MCW IX.41)

Elliss, Robert; wife Mary; child: Jane, bapt. 19 Jul 1752 (KGP p. 297)

Ellis, Owen; 8 Nov 1764 (I 86.184)

Ellis, Jonathan; 12 Apr 1766; 20 Aug 1766; wife Elizabeth; children: John, Benjamin, Owen, Elijah, William, Leonard (MCW XIII.130); 15 Nov 1766 (I 89.304); 24 Nov 1767; extx. Elisabeth Ellis; sons William, Elijah (ABB 5.64); admx. Elizabeth; 24 Aug 1768 (GB 263)

ELLRIDGE

Ellridge, Abraham; 15 Feb 1734 (I 20.259)

ELLURBURTON

Ellurburton, Elizabeth, b. 3 Jan 1730/1; [no parents listed] (QAP b/24)

ELSON

Ellson, Anne; son John age ca 7 on 19 Jul last; bound out; Sep 1702 (PGCR B.193)

Elson, William; wife Anne; son Nicholas; age 11 on 2 Apr next; bound out; Mar 1712 Ct. (PGCR G.174)

Elson, Edward; dau. Elizabeth; son John; 29 Dec 1721 (PGLR I.227, 228)

Elson, John; m. 1 Feb 1728/9 Joanna Bradcutt; children: Sarah, b. 15 Dec 1729; John, b. 8 Oct 1732; William, b. 4 Sep 1734 (QAP m/5; b/23, 26, 28)

Elson, John; admx. Johannah; 11 Jun 1750 (I 43.493); admx. Johannah; 5 children [under age] John, William, Richard, Rachel, Archibald; 23 Oct 1750 (AA 28.350); widow Johannah; heirs John, William, Richard, Rachel, Archibald; 29 Aug 1751 (GB 171)

Elson, William; 27 Apr 1772; admx. Sarah Elson (ABB 6.116); widow Sarah; 28 Aug 1772 (GB 305)

Elson, Joanna; midwife; 23 Jul 1774; 27 Nov 1774; children: Archabald, Richard, Rachel Davis, Mary Elson [w/o Richard]; tract *Turkey Flight*

Enlarged (MCW XVI.9); 9 Feb 1775 (I 121.335); 29 Dec 1775; children Richard, Archibald, Rachel (ABB 7.49)

ELTINGE

Eltinge, Abraham; heir Rosloffs; 24 Aug 1736 (GB 81)

Eltinge, Abraham; son Roeloff; tract *New Esopus*; 25 Jul 1737 (PGLR T.493)

EMERSON

Emerson, Thomas; 26 Sep 1715 (I&A 36c.38)

Emerson, John; wife Mary; child: Lucy, b. 8 Mar 1754 (KGP p. 305)

Emerson, Elizabeth; child: Penalopey, bapt. 28 Mar 1762 (KGP p. 325)

Emerson, John; wife Penalopy [Penelope]; children: James, bapt. 11 Oct 1763 at Lower Chapel; William, bapt. 3 Mar 1765 Lower Chapel; John, bapt. 21 Aug 1768 Lower Chapel; Henry, b. 1 Feb 1774 Lower Chapel (KGP p. 335, 350. 371, 379)

Emerson, George; wife Mary; children: Mary, b. 18 Feb 1772 Lower Chapel; John, b. 22 Jan 1774 Lower Chapel; Richard, b. 28 Feb 1776 Lower Chapel (KGP p. 379, 381, 383)

ENSOR

Ensor, Joseph; 2 Apr 1740 (I 26.53); heirs [none known]; 23 Jun 1741 (AA 18.232); [undated with 1742] (AA 19.109); heirs [unnamed]; 1 Jul 1743 (GB 128)

ERICKSON

Erickson, Gunder [Middlesex, England]; mentions Mary Erickson; 23 Nov 1720 (PGLR M.495)

Erickson, Gunder; 7 Mar 1728/9; 22 Aug 1729; wife Mary; dau. Martha; tracts *Erickson's Hazard*; *Norway, Gunder's Delight* (MCW VI.128); widow [unnamed]; _ Aug 1729 (I 15.644)

Erickson, Gunder [dec'd]; widow Mary [also called Elizabeth] [m/2 John Smith]; 6 Dec 1738 (CCR JK#4.89)

ESTHER

Esther, Charles; wife Mary; child: Margaret, b. 28 May 1773 Upper Chapel (KGP p. 390)

EVANS

Evens, Ann [CA]; son Henry Busey; age 11 on 15 Jul next; Jun 1697 Ct. (PGCR A.188)

Evans, Elizabeth; children: Elisabeth & Samuel [over age 14]; Richard [under age 14]; choose guardian; Nov 1714 (PGCR G.691)

Evans, David; wife Ann; children: Eleanor, b. 5 10ber 1714; John, b. 21 Aug 1717; Arden (m), b. 15 Mar 1720/1 (QAP b/13, 16)

Evans, Walter; age ca 23; 20 Dec 1715 (CCR CL.278)

Evans, Thomas; 21 Apr 1716 (I&A 36c.194); 23 Sep 1717 (I&A 37b.195)

Evans, Samuel; wife Sarah; children: Mary, b. 30 8ber 1718; Sarah, b. 5 Apr 1725; Priscilla, b. 26 10ber 1726; John, b. 2 Nov 1728; Edward, b. 26 Mar 1734 (QAP b/14, 19, 20, 21, 27)

Evans, Phill; wife Anne; child: Thomas, b. 4 Dec 1721 (KGP p. 277)

Evans, John; wife 1 Jan 1722/3 Martha Evans, d/o John Evans (QAP m/3)

Evans, Thomas; wife Mary; tract Bread & Cheese; 2 Jul 1724 (PGLR I.572)

Evans, Walter; age ca 78; 20 May 1725 (PGLR I.675); age ca 81; 9 Oct 1728 (PGLR M.401); age ca 80; 15 Jul 1729 (PGLR M.487); age ca 85; 17 Aug 1730 (PGLR Q.163)

Evans, Thomas; age ca 52; 7 Nov 1726 (PGLR M.152)

Evans, Thomas; age ca 44; 1 May 1729 (PGLR M.443)

Evans, Walter; planter; 18 Jan 1730/1; 22 Jun 1731; sons Thomas, Walter, Butler, Philip; daus. Elizabeth Locker, Elinor Harbut; grandsons Charles [s/o Walter], Walter Locker [s/o Elizabeth], Philip & Thomas [ss/o Philip]; granddaus. Elizabeth [d/o Thomas], Elizabeth & Ann [ds/o Philip]; tracts Dunghill, Stony Hill, Littleworth (MCW VI.189) legatees Thomas, Butler, Elinor, Phillip [acct.], Elisabeth [d/o acct.], Phillip [s/o acct.]; 14 Mar 1733 (AA 12.188); heirs Philip, Elizabeth; 29 Nov 1734 (GB 65)

Evans, John; age ca 53; 1731 (PGLR Q.237)

Evans, Walter; 24 Aug 1731 (I 16.250); 29 Mar 1732 (I 16.469); 18 Sep 1732 (AA 11.476)

Evans, Harding; age 14 on 14 Mar instant; bound out; Mar 1735 (PGCR V.292)

Evans, Butler; wife Dorothy; tract The Dunghill; 30 Oct 1737 (PGLR T.539)

Evans, Philip; wife Ann; tract Stony Hill; 14 Oct 1738 (PGLR T.654)

Evans, John; age 14 on 6 May last; bound out; Jun 1743 (PGCR AA.676)

Evans, John; 24 Feb 1740 (I 26.25); admn. son John; 25 Jun 1744 (AA 30.447)

Evans, Philip, Jr.; wife Mary; children: Mary, b. 16 Jan 1752; John, b. 21 Nov 1753; Cassindra, b. 23 Sep 1755 (KGP p. 290, 305, 312)

Evans, Seth; admx. Margaret; 5 May 1754 (I 57.230)

Evans (Evens), James; wife Johannah_; children: Margrett, b. 1 May 1756; John, b. 15 May 1757; Mary; b. 8 Jul 1758; Mary, b. 8 Jul 1766 (PGP p. 257, 271, 280)

Evans, Zachariah; wife Elizabeth; children: Jean, bapt. 14 Mar 1762; Alexander, bapt. 5 Feb 1764 at Upper Chapel (KGP p. 325, 340)

Evans, Phillop; wife Mary; children: Walter, bapt. 29 Aug 1762; Phillop, b. 26 Aug 1764 Upper Chapel (KGP p. 332, 358)

Evans, John; 9 Mar 1763; 11 Dec 1766; wife Eleanor; step-son Philip Williams; tracts *Cool Spring Mannor* (MCW XIII.130)

Evans, Jeremiah; 10 Oct 1766 (I 91.312)

Evans, Jane; 8 Dec 1766; 12 Dec 1766; children: Sarah [b. 30 Nov 1754], Lucia Wilson [b. 8 Feb 1757, w/o Larkin]; grandchild Lucretia Wilson (MCW XIII.131)

Evans, Elizabeth; 18 Apr 1767; 8 Jun 1767; bro. Walter Evans (MCW XIV.11)

Evons [Evins], Samuel; wife Ann; child: Jeremiah, bapt. 10 Apr 1768 Upper Chapel; Denison, b. 15 Jan 1775 Upper Chapel (KGP p. 370, 391)

Evans, Phillip; 8 Jul 1773; _ Nov 1773; wife Mary; children: Phillip, Jesse, other children [unnamed] (MCW XV.125); 23 Mar 1774 (I 114.289); 19 Nov 1774 (I 121.369)

Evans, [unnamed]; heir Seth Evans; 28 Mar 1771 (GB 294)

Evins, Henry; wife Elizabeth; child: Mary, b. 26 Aug 1772 Lower Chapel (KGP p. 383)

Evins, John; wife Elizabeth; child: John, b. 13 Nov 1775 Upper Chapel (KGP p. 392)

EVERSFIELD

Eversfield, John, Rev.; infant grandson John Eversfield [s/o John Eversfield]; 5 Aug 1731 (PGLR Q.319, 320); son John [grandson of Richard Clagett]; tract *Eversfield's Map of Italy*; 27 Sep 1734 (PGLR T.181)

Eversfield, John; son John; 27 Nov 1733 (PGLR Q.706); wife Eleanor; dau. Eleanor; tract *Brookefield*; 22 Jun 1737 (PGLR T.483); son Edward; tract *Sewall's Addition*; 28 Nov 1739 (PGLR Y.111); children: John Jr., Eleanor Jr., Mary; 27 Nov 1740 (PGLR Y.245)

Eversfield, Matthew; children by his wife Susannah Fraser Bowie: John, Verlinda Fraser Eversfield; 1776 (MCW XVI.186)

Eversfield, John, Jr., Rev.; 8 Aug 1767 (I 95.16)

Eversfield, William; 19 Apr 1769; 29 Jun 1769; wife Eleanor; children: John Mathew, William Marshall, Mary White & Jane Harbert Eversfield; tract *Brookefield* (MCW XIV.101); extx. Eleanor; 19 Aug 1769 (I 102.27); 16 Sep 1770; extx. Eleanor Eversfield; 4 children: John Mathews, William Marshall, Mary White & Jane Hubbard Eversfield; 16 Sep 1770 (ABB 6.40); heir William Eversfield; 24 Mar 1773 (GB 310)

EVES

Eves, John; wife Elizabeth; child: Ann, b. 30 Sep 1774 Broad Creek (KGP p. 386)

EWING
Ewing, Samuel; wife Hannah; tract *Dewealls Range*; 27 Nov 1742 (PGLR Y.574)

EYRE
Eyre, Thomas; wife Jane [d/o John Severne]; tract *Mt. Pleasant*; 23 Nov 1697
(PGLR A.72)

FALBY

Falby, Esther; age 3 years on 29 Apr next; d/o Honoria Falby; bound out; Nov 1724 (PGCR L.376)

FALCONER

Falkner [Fulkner], Martin; 25 Jun 1698 (I&A 16.107); 3 Jul 1705 (I&A 25.133)

Falconer, Alexander; m. 9 Feb 1719 Susanna Duvall; children: Alexander, b. 11 Feb 1719/20; John, b. 13 Aug 1721; Gilbert, b. 15 Jan 1722/3; Margaret, b. 20 Aug 1724; David, b. 22 Apr 1726; Ellinor, b. 26 Nov 1727; Jane, b. 31 Jul 1729; Lucy, b. 15 Jan 1730/1; Samuel, b. 25 Oct 1732; Sarah, b. 7 Jan 1735; Rachel, b. 25 Apr 1737 (QAP m/2; b/15, 18, 19, 23, 28, 31)

Falconer, John; orphan; age 14 years on 25 Feb next; William; orphan; age 6 years next April; bound out; Nov 1729 (PGCR P.250)

Falconer, Gilbert; wife Margery; child: Elenor, b. 17 Jul 1765 (QAP b/38)

FARGUSON

Furguson, Hugh; age ca 24; Jun 1697 Ct. (PGCR A.164)

Forginson, John; admx. Katherine; 8 Feb 1715 (I&A 36c.228, 276)

Ferguson, John; m. 29 Nov 1715 Mary Williams (QAP m/2)

Fargison, Dankin [Dunkin]; wife Catherine; children: Mary, b. 25 Aug 1732; Thomas, b. 16 Jun 1735; Elizabeth, b. 3 May 173_ (KGP p. 281, 282)

Farguson, John; 2 Nov 1734 (I 20.383)

Ferguson, Mary; children: Daniel, Mary; 20 Jul 1738 (PGLR T.627)

Fergason [Ferguson], Dunkin; admx. Cathrine; 28 Nov 1751 (I 48.177); admx. Catharine; 14 Jul 1753 (I 56.26); admx. Catherine; 14 Jul 1753 (AA 34.249)

Farginson, John; wife Bathshabey; children: Susannah, bapt. 19 Dec 1762; Vialinda, bapt. 10 Aug 1766 Upper Chapel (KGP p. 329, 355)

Forgison, John; wife Elliner; child: Mordicae, b. 20 Apr 1765 (PGP p. 273)

FARMER

Farmer, Samuel; wife Elizabeth; tract *Farmer's Marsh*; 6 May 1706 (PGLR C.160a)

Farmer, Mary; orphan; age 8 on 5 Mar last; bound out; d/o William, dec'd; Nov 1709 (PGCR D.249)

Farmer, John; age ca 13 in Aug next; bound out; s/o William, dec'd; Nov 1711 Ct. (PGCR G.124)

Farmer, Samuel; age 12 on 1 Dec next; s/o William; Jun 1716 (PGCR H.84)

Farmer, Samuel; wife Sarah; children: Mary, b. 27 Feb 1718/9; Priscilla, b. 30 Jun 1724 (QAP b/15, 18)

Farmer, William; wife Elizabeth; children: Mary, b. 15 Aug 1723; William, b. 10 Jul 1726; Rachel, b. 10 Feb 1728 (QAP b/26)

Farmer, George; age 30; 26 Feb 1725/6 (PGLR I.730)

FARQUAR

Farquar, Allan; ex. William [Quaker]; payment to Ann [in Pennsylvania money], Susanna [alias Susanna Wilson]; 25 May 1743 (AA 19.398)

Farquar, Allan; wife Catherine; son William; tract *Dulany Lott*; 28 Sep 1739 (PGLR Y.95)

Farquer [Forker, Forquer], Allan [Allen]; Quaker; of *Manackus*; miller; 30 Nov 1738; 20 Dec 1738; wife Catren; 2 sons [unnamed] (MCW VIII.4); 2 Apr 1742 (AA 18.523)

Fraquear, Alexander; m. __ Dec 1727 Mary Cash (QAP m/4)

FARRELL

Farrell, Kennedy; wife Isabel; son Thomas; tract *Bradford's Rest*; 30 Oct 1739 (PGLR Y.11)

Farrell, Richard; wife Elizabeth; tract *Farrell's Hope*; 1741 (PGLR Y.381)

Ferril, Daniel; wife Ruth; child: Rebecca, b. 16 Jun 1755 (KGP p. 311)

Farrel, Richard; 16 Nov 1760 (I 70.229)

FARTHING

Farthing, William Maria [SM]; wife Ann; tract *Mary Ann's Choice*; 3 Nov 1719 (PGLR F.264/848)

FEE

Fee, Thomas; m. 6 Oct 1733 Margaret Hook (PGP p. 229)

Fee, William; wife Margrett; she d. 13 May 1760 (PGP p. 285)

FENDALL

Fendall, John [CH]; wife Elizabeth; tract *Berry*; 12 Aug 1707 (PGLR C.199a)

FENIX

Fenix, Edward; wife Mary; Jun 1699 Ct. (PGCR A.424)

FENLEY

Fenaly [Finly], Charles; m. 11 Apr 1711 Elizabeth Harris; children: Ann, b. 17 Oct 1715; Sarah, b. 27 Feb 1717; Elizabeth, b. 26 May 1720; Charles, b. 4 Jan 1722; John, b. 1 Jun 1725; James, b. 15 Apr 1728; William, b. 21 Oct 1730; Mary, b. 22 Nov 1733; Richard, b. 14 Aug 1736; Isaac, b. 23 Mar 1738/9 (KGP p. 283, 290)

Finly [Fenley, Finley], Samuel; 15 Mar 1738 (I 23.187); 24 Jun 1738 (I 24.95); heirs [none known]; 24 Aug 1739 (AA 17.318); 23 Jun 1741 (AA 18.232)

Fenley, Charles; wife Martha; children: Walter, b. 22 Mar 1751; Elizabeth, b. 6 May 1753; Charles Bayne, b. 22 Sep 1755; Ann, b. 25 May 1757; Martha Bayne, b. 25 Mar 1759; William, b. 24 Oct 1761; John Bayne, b. 28 Jan 1764 at Broad Creek; Martha Hawkins, b. 19 Mar 1766 Broad Creek; Thomas, b. 8 Feb 1768, bapt. 3 Apr 1768 Broad Creek; James, b. 14 Apr 1770; Mary, b. 9 Sep 1775 (KGP p. 300, 311, 321, 322, 353, 356, 362)

Fenley, John; wife Ann; child: Virlinda, b. 14 Sep 1754 (KGP p. 306)

Fenley, John; wife Nancy; child: Mary, b. 4 May 1757 (KGP p. 314)

Fendly, Richard; wife Penellipa; child: George Charter, b. 12 Sep 1760 (PGP p. 259)

Fenley, William; wife Mary; children: Sarah, bapt. 9 Sep 1764 Broad Creek; James, bapt. 26 Jan 1766 Broad Creek; Elizabeth, bapt. 5 Jun 1768 Broad Creek (KGP p. 352, 363, 357)

Findley [Fendley]; planter; admx. Mary; 4 Jan 1771 (I 106.162)

Fendley, Charles; wife Mary; child: Mary, b. 1 Sep 1775 Broad Creek (KGP p. 387)

FENNELL

Fennell [Fenniel], Stephen; wife Elliner; children: Elisabeth, b. 7 Feb 1763; Elliner, b. 9 Jun 1765 (PGP p. 269, 277)

FENWICK

Fenwick, Edward; wife Dinah; tract Cuckold's Point; 27 Nov 1711 (PGLR F.132)

Fenwick, Mary & Sarah; minors; tracts St. Anthony, St. Dorothy; 24 Aug 1771 (GB 296)

FIDEY

Fidey, John; admx. Elisabeth Stump; 13 Aug 1728 (I 13.194)

Fidee, John; 25 Aug 1729 (AA 9.455)

FIELDS

Fields, John; wife Isabelah; child: John, b. 26 Oct 1765 (PGP p. 273)

FIGGET

Figget, Thomas; wife Margaret; child: Margaret, b. 2 Nov 1751; bapt. 26 Apr 1752 (KGP p. 292)

Figget, Thomas; wife Mary; child: Mary, b. 7 Jul 1753 (KGP p. 301)

Figgett, Thomas; wife Catherine; child: Charles, b. 5 Jun 1755 (KGP p. 308)

FINCH

Finch, Guy [CA]; wife Rebecca; tract *Woodbridge*; 19 Mar 1696 (PGLR A.43)

Finch, Thomas; heirs Thomas, Charles; 27 Jun 1720 (GB 9); widow Mary Finch [w/o Thomas Davis]; 2 sons [unnamed]; 26 Aug 1720 (AA 3.211)

Finch, William, Jr., Capt.; admx. Priscilla; 15 Nov 1742 (I 27.270) admx. Precilla Brown [?Bowie] [w/o Allen]; 16 Oct 1744 (AA 20.530); widow Priscilla Bowie [w/o Allen]; 19 Jun 1747 (AA 23.283)

Finch, William; son William; granddau. Phoebe; 14 Aug 1742 (PGLR Y.539)

FISH

Fish, Robert; wife Priscilla; child: James, b. 30 Aug 1772 Upper Chapel (KGP p. 389)

FISHER

Fisher, William, Dr.; [with 1720] (I 3.336)

Fisher, Ralph; wife Jane; child: Mary Anne, b. 2 Oct 1726 (KGP p. 263)

FITCH

Fitch, Henry; wife Mary; child: William, b. 19 9ber 1709 (QAP b/5)

FITCHELL

Fitchell, Elizabeth; infant d/o Margaret; bound out; Aug 1730 (PGCR P.453)

FITZPATRICK

Fitspatrick, Richard; 27 Sep 1712 (I&A 33b.202); 22 Mar 1714 (I&A 35a.324)

FITZGERALD

Fitzgerald, Gerard; wife Mary; children: Margaret, b. 27 Aug 1722; Mary, b. 13 7ber 1725; Sarah, b. 11 Apr 1727; Gerrard, b. 2 Jun 1730; Edward, b. 19 Nov 1731 (QAP b/19, 22, 24, 25)

Fitzgerald, Garret; wife Elizabeth; child: Elizabeth, b. 18 Sep 1733 (QAP b/29)

Fitzgerald, Garret; wife Sarah; child: Sarah Mills, b. 11 Nov 1736 (QAP b/31)

Fitzgarald, Rd. [?Edward]; wife Jane; children: Catherine (?twin), b. 23 Oct 1761; Leonard (?twin), b. 23 Oct 1761 (PGP p. 263)

Fitsgarrel, William; wife Elizabeth; child: Sarah, b. 4 Oct 1763 at Upper Chapel (KGP p. 333)

Fitzgerald, Edward; wife Jane; child: Elizabeth, b. 8 Mar 1764 (PGP p. 274)

FLANN

Flann, Francis; age ca 18 mos.; bound out; Nov 1720 (PGCR K.8)

FLATFOOT
Flatfoot, Sarah; age ca 12; d/o John; bound out; Nov 1745 (PGCR DD.277)

FLEMAN
Fleman, William; age 4 on 3 Oct next; bound out to William Mordent & Anne his wife; Jun 1718 (PGCR H.670)

FLETCHALL
Fletchall, Thomas; wife Ann; tract *Clagett's Purchase*; 20 Jan 1714 (PGLR F.426)

Fletchell, Thomas; planter; 17 Jul 1717; 2 Aug 1717; wife Anne; son Thomas, dau. Elizabeth; tracts *Widows Mite, Lancaster, Containing* (MCW IV.110); extx. Anne [widow]; 9 Nov 1717 (I&A 37b.104); extx. Ann Renshaw [w/o William]; [undated with 1718] (AA 1.2, 8); extx. Ann Renshaw [w/o William]; 10 Dec 1725 (AA 7.198)

Fletchall, Thomas [dec'd]; son Thomas [wife Elizabeth]; tract *Widow's Mite*; 4 Mar 1722 (PGLR I.391)

Fletchell, Thomas; 30 Dec 1740 (AA 19.317)

Fletchall, Thomas; wife Mary; children: James, b. 23 Dec 1748; Thomas, b. 3 Dec 1751 (PGP p. 253)

FLETCHER
Fletcher, George; m. 23 9ber 1727 Elizabeth Stamp (QAP m/4)

Fletcher, Sarah; [d/o of Hannah Jefferies]; age ca 5 on 1 May last; Jun 1732 (PGCR R.522)

Fletcher, John; wife Sarah; child: Elizabeth King, bapt. 23 Oct 1763 at Upper Chapel (KGP p. 334)

FLINT
Flint, John; m. 26 Dec 1721 by Rev. John Frazer to Elizabeth ____; children: John, b. 6 Oct 1727; Elizabeth, b. 2 Jun 1729; Thomas, b. 8 Jul 1731; James, b. 6 Oct 1735 [d. 25 Jan 1756]; Margaret, b. 10 Nov 1737; Joshua, b. 20 Feb 1740; William, b. 21 Feb 1742? [d. 31 Mar 1747]; Hannah, b. 19 Jul 1742?; (PGP p. 229, 247-8, 250, 251, 255, 285)

Flint, John; age ca 38; 1730 (PGLR Q.14); age ca 40; 11 May 1733 (PGLR T.25); age ca 40; 16 Jul 1734 (PGLR T.154)

Flint, John; 28 Sep 1759 (I 67.403)

Flint, Thomas; wife Rebecca; child: Sarah, b. 22 Apr 1764 (PGP p.271)

FLOWER
Flower, William; m. 10 Dec 1732 Mary Brace (QAP m/6)

FLOOD

Flood, Jane [age 10 last Aug] and Margarett [age 2-1/2 this court]; bound out; Nov 1715 (PGCR H.6)

FLOYD

Floyd, David; admx. Mary Gatterige [w/o Henry]; 24 Jul 1697 (I&A 15.281)

FORBES

Forbes, John [SM]; wife Dryden; [?widow of ___ Jowles]; tract *Colonel's Brigade*; 29 Mar 1736 (PGLR T.459)

Forbes, George; heir Mary Gordon; 27 Nov 1741 (GB 122); heir Mary Gordon; 28 Nov 1745 (GB 147)

FORD

Ford, Abraham; 5 Mar 1708; 18 Jun 1709; wife Christian; s-i-l Thomas Pickrall; tract *Lunster* (MCW III.144); extx. Christian; 18 Jul 1709 (I&A 29.424)

Ford, James [AA]; s/o Thomas; sons John [wife Anne], James [wife Mary]; 1 Jul 1720 (PGLR I.280)

Ford, James; carpenter; admx. Mary Butt; 12 Apr 1728 (I 13.33)

Ford, John; son James; 25 Jun 1729 (PGLR M.447)

Ford, Thomas; age ca 67; 25 Apr 1735 (PGLR T.253)

Foord, Allison; m. 27 Mar 1760 Winnifred Wheeler (KGP p. 319)

Ford [Foord], John; wife Ann; children: Joseph, b. 15 Feb 1761; William, b. 5 Apr 1763; John, b. 12 May 1765 (PGP p. 260, 268, 273)

Ford, John; wife Mary; child: Robert, bapt. 2 Dec 1761 (KGP p. 324)

Ford, William; wife Susanna; children: Mary, b. 27 Oct 1763, bapt. 11 Mar 1764 Lower Chapel; Joseph, bapt. 19 Jun 1768 Lower Chapel; Edward Brook, b. 20 Feb 1774 Lower Chapel (KGP p. 344, 369, 379)

Ford, Alison [Allerson]; wife Hepshabeth [Hepsibah]; children: John Beall, b. 5 Feb 1767 Lower Chapel; George Noble, b. 2 Mar 1772 Lower Chapel (KGP p. 367, 383)

Ford, Allanson; 8 Jan 1774; 25 Jan 1775; wife Hephzicah; sons Charles Allanson, Edward, Josias Beall, Benjamin, John Beall, George Noble; bro. Charles Allanson Ford; dau. Elizabeth Fendall Fry Ford; unborn child (MCW XVI.48-9)

FORREST

Forrest, John, wife Elizabeth; tract *The Forrest*; 16 Dec 1696 (PGLR A.9)

Forrest, Elizabeth; widow; daus. Ellinor, age ca 12 on 2 Jan next; Lucy, age 8 on 23 Dec next; William; age 4 on 14 Jan last; Jun 1698 Ct. (PGCR A.317)

Forrest, John; [s/o Elizabeth Perry]; age ca 4 on Jan last; bound out; Jun 1700 (PGCR B.53)

Forrest, William; m. 1 Jul 1735 Lucy Duvall; children: Rachel, b. 16 Oct 1735; Elizabeth, b. 12 Oct 1737; Lucy, b. __ F__ ____ (QAP m/6; b/29, 31, 34)

FORRESTER

Forrester, James; wife Elinor; child: Mary, b. 4 Apr 1755 (KGP p. 308)

FOSSETT

Fossett, John; "a dumb lad"; age 3 years on 29 Nov ____; s/o Jane Fossett; Nov 1727 (PGCR N.612)

Fossett, John; m. 19 Nov 1723 Jane Fletcher (QAP m/3)

Fossett, Thomas; age 4 at end of Mar last; s/o John; bound out; Jun 1739 (PGCR X.344)

FOSTER

Foster, John [England & Boston of Mass. Bay Colony]; wife Lydia; tract *Hackthorne Heath*; 10 Feb 1674; [recorded 1736] (PGLR T.387-391)

Foster, John; m. 15 Feb 1709 Elizabeth Green; children: John, b. 24 Jan 1709; Richard, b. 14 Aug 1710; Thomas, b. 4 Feb 1711/2; Hugh, b. 7 Jul 1715; Richard, b. 4 Jul 1717 (QAP m/1; b/6, 14)

Foster, John; 16 Aug 1719 (I 3.150); admx. Elisabeth Swan [w/o John]; 4 children [unnamed]; 15 Feb 1720 (AA 284-6)

Foster, Thomas; m. 25 Nov 1735 Sarah Cross (QAP m/6)

Foster, John; 1 May 1740 (I 27.267); 28 Jun 1744 (AA 20.332)

Foster, Thomas; 15 Jan 1750 (I 48.487); 18 Jun 1752; admx. Sarah; children: Thomas, John, Basil, Benjamin, Ruth, Sarah, Richard Foster (ABB 1.40); admx. Sarah [widow]; 7 children: Thomas, John, Basil, Benjamin, Ruth, Sarah, Richard; 18 Jun 1752 (AA 32.271); heirs Thomas, John, Basil, Benjamin, Ruth, Sarah, Richard; 28 Nov 1753 (GB 189)

Foster, John; wife Mary; child: Margaret, bapt. 12 May 1751 (KGP p. 293)

Foster, Thomas; 10 Nov 1760 (I 73.49)

Foster, Basil; wife Priscilla; child, Richard Lewis, b. 16 Sep 1770 (QAP m/8)

FOUT

Fout, Jacob; wife Mary; tract *Rocky Creek*; 24 Jun 1740 (PGLR Y.181, 182)

FOWLER

Fowler, Thomas; wife Susanna; children: Elizabeth, b. 14 Jun 1697; William, b. 16 Feb 1699; Thomas, b. 11 Sep 1700; Susannah, b. 22 Mar 1702; John, b. 12 Sep 1703; Benjamin, b. 30 May 1705; Samuel, b. 19 Oct

1706; Mary, b. 3 Apr 1708; Richard, b. 6 8ber 1709; Jeremiah, b. 12 May 1711; Ann, b. 14 Jun 1713; Benony, b. 15 9ber 1714 (QAP b/3, 4, 9, 11); admx. Susannah [widow]; 22 Feb 1715 (I&A 36c.229, 270); Susannah [widow]; 8 Jun 1715 (I&A 36b.197); admx. Susanna; 25 Sep 1716 (I&A 37c.122); extx. widow Susanna Browne [w/o Marke]; 16 Mar 1717 (I&A 38a.104)

Fowler, William; m. 25 Aug 1724 Susanna Duvall; children: Elizabeth, b. 17 9ber 1725; Susanna, b. 25 Jan 1726/7; Thomas, b. 24 Feb 1728/9; Maren, b. 20 Jan 1731/2; Benjamin, b. 16 Dec 1733 (QAP m/3; b/19, 20, 21, 25, 28)

Fowler, John; orphan; 7 weeks old on 29 Nov instant; Nov 1725 (PGCR L.511)

Fowler, William; wife Elizabeth; child: William, b. 9 Apr 1730 (QAP b/24)

Fowler, Benoni; m. 24 Sep 1734 Kezia Isaac (QAP m/6)

Fowler, Benoni; wife Keziah; cous. Jonathan Simmons [wife Elizabeth]; tract *Batchelor's Hope*; 23 Mar 1736 (PGLR T.443)

Fowler, Jeremiah; wife Drusilla; tract *Spradax Forrest*; 16 Apr 1741 (PGLR Y.297)

Fowler, William; age ca 44; 1742 (PGLR Y.654)

Fowler, Abraham; age 6 on 25 Mar last; bound out to John Orme, Jr. at Mount Calvert to age 21; Jun 1753 (PGCR MM415)

Fowler, William; 29 Mar 1769 (I 100.26)

FRADY

Frady, James; age ca 13; servant; Jun 1698 Ct. (PGCR A.316)

FRAILE

Fraile, David; age ca 55; 11 May 1733 (PGLR T.25)

FRANCES

Frances, Jon.; wife Phebee; child: Frances, b. 12 Jan 1763 (PGP p. 263)

FRANCEWAY

Franceway, Norwood; wife Elizabeth [d/o Thomas Miles]; tract *Stony Stratford*; 22 Jan 1734 (PGLR T.218)

Franceway, Norwood; wife Elizabeth; son Joseph; tract *Girl's Portion*; 28 Nov 1739 (PGLR Y.138)

FRANCH

Franck, Henry; wife Elizabeth; tract *Rencher's Adventure*; 26 Aug 1718 (PGLR F.90/641)

Franch [French], Henry; 12 Feb 17127/8; 12 Apr 1729; son William; daus. Elizabeth, Mary (MCW VI.98); 9 May 1729 (I 15.87); 21 Oct 1730 (AA 10.471);

[with 1732] (I 16.580); 17 Oct 1732 (AA 11.486); heirs William Franch, Elizabeth Palmer, Mary Franch; 28 Mar 1733 (GB 60)

FRANKLIN

Franklin, John; age ca 59; 1730 (PGLR Q.67); age ca 64; 26 Apr 1735 (PGLR T.253)

FRASER

Frazer, John; age ca 50; 13 Sep 1725 (CCR CL.1057-1063)

Fraser, Daniel; wife Barbra; children: Daniel, b. 14 Aug 1723; Elizabeth, b. 11 Jul 1728; William, b. 15 Jun 1731 (KGP p. 281)

Frazer, John; wife Anne; children: George, John, Susannah, Ann, Virlinda; tract St. James; 29 Dec 1732 (PGLR Q.621)

Frazier, Alexander; wife Sarah; tract Wests Choice; 22 Mar 1735/6 (PGLR T.394)

Fraser, John; s-i-l William Magruder; 8 May 1738 (PGLR Q.643)

Fraser [Frazer], John, Jr.; 7 Nov 1738 (I 24.11); 1 Dec 1739 (AA 17.458)

Frazer, Peter; admx. Mary; 12 Jun 1740 (I 26.173)

Frasier, John; rector, King George's Parish; 15 Jan 1742; 25 Nov 1742; wife Ann; sons George, John [dec'd]; daus. Mary Magruder, Susannah Hawkins, Ann, Verlinda (MCW VIII.197); extx. Anne; 4 May 1744 (I 30.77); extx. widow Ann; 2 Nov 1744 (AA 20. 532)

Fraser, Daniel; wife Elizabeth; child: William Lanham, bapt. 28 Jun 1752 (KGP p. 296)

Fraser, Hannah; child: Henry, bapt. 24 Dec 1752 (KGP p. 297)

Fraser, Alexander; wife Susanna; child: Henry, b. 1 Nov 1755 (KGP p. 320)

Fraser, John; wife Jane; child: William, b. 9 May 1759 (KGP p. 319); [see John Luke]

Frazier, Alexander; 13 Feb 1760; 29 Aug 1764; wife Sarah; son James; daus. Martha, Anne; tract Lunder (MCW XIII.52)

Fraser, John; wife Agnus; children: Ann, b. 26 Mar 1762; Rebeccah, b. 2 Jan 1764; bapt. 5 Aug 1764 Upper Chapel (KGP p. 330, 341)

Fraser, Alexander; child: Patrick Dyer, bapt. 5 Dec 1762 (KGP p. 328)

Frazer, George; 2 Dec 1764; 14 Feb 1765; mother Ann; sisters Virlinda Frazer, Ann Bowe [w/o Allen], Susannah Hawkins [w/o John]; niece Susannah Frazer Bowe [d/o Allen]; nephews George Frazer Hawkins [s/o John], John Bowe [s/o Allen] and tracts Bayplain James Taken, St. James, Wade's Adventures, Fox Hall (MCW XIII.66); 3 May 1766 (I 89.317)

Fraser, Daniel; wife Elizabeth; child: Simon Alexander, bapt. 3 Nov 1765 Broad Creek (KGP p. 349)

Fraser, Ann; widow; 1 Jun 1769; 25 Nov 1773; children: Ann Bowie [w/o Allen], Mary Magruder [w/o William], Virlinda Fraser (MCW XV.123)

Fraser, James; 27 Oct 1774; 1 Nov 1774; wife Anne (MCW XVI.8); 3 Nov 1774 (I 123.230)

Frazer, Robert; wife Eleanor; child: James Riley, b. 13 Nov 1775 Upper Chapel (KGP p. 392)

Frazer, Henry; wife Verlinder; child: James Luin, b. 12 Feb 1776 Broad Creek; [other children b. after 1776] (KGP p. 382)

Fraser, Verlinda; 26 Aug 1776; 22 Aug 1777; sister Ann Bowie [w/o Allen]; nephew John Fraser Bowie [s/o Allen]; tract St. James (MCW XVI.186-7)

FRAYLE

Frayle, David; age ca 53; 1730 (PGLR Q.12)

FREDERICK

Federick, Thomas; 7 May 1709; 1 Aug 1709; wife Mary; tract Strife (MCW III.145); 12 Nov 1709 (I&A 30.207)

FREE

Free, John; admx. Eleanor; 4 Mar 1769 (I 100.22)

Free, John; widow Eleanor; heirs Elizabeth, Charles, John, Alice, Mary; 28 Aug 1772 (GB 306)

FREEMAN

Freeman, John [AA]; wife Mary; 27 Feb 1713 (PGLR F.387)

Freeman, Daniell; 26 Aug 1739 (I 24.189); sons Samuel, Edmund; 22 Feb 1742 (AA 19.312); heirs James, Edmund; 28 Mar 1744 (GB 130)

Freeman, Ann; 28 Nov 1760 (I 70.231)

Freeman, Henry; admx. Ann; 2 Dec 1757 (I 65.2)

FRY

Fry, Joseph & Elisabeth; 1 Oct 1696 (I&A 14.57)

Fry, David; [no descendants]; heir Edward Fry; tracts Sway and Frys Choice; 30 Nov 1699 (PGLR A.205)

Fry, James; wife Susana; children: Thomas, b. 13 Oct 1739; Rachel, b. _ ___ 1741; Joseph, b. 27 Jan 1746; Mary, b. 24 Jun 1749; George, b. 27 Oct 1751; Benjamin, b. 15 Dec 1753; Bethsheby, bapt. 19 Dec 1762 (KGP p. 293, 304, 329)

Fry, Thomas; wife Elizabeth; child: James, b. 20 Oct 1746 (KGP p. 293)

Fry, Joseph; wife Elizabeth; children: Thomas Lewis, b. 1 Jun 1746; Leonard Trueman, b. 1 Jun 1749; Ann, b. 11 Oct 1752; [children reg. 23 Oct 1757] (KGP p. 317)

Fry, Thomas; m. by 8 Sep 1754 Elizabeth Bayne when the births of her children were registered (KGP p. 309)

Fry [Froy], Thomas; wife Elizabeth; children: Ann, b. 20 Sep 1762; Elenor, b. 12 Sep 1764 Broad Creek (KGP p. 328, 342)

Fry, Ann; child: Sabrah, b. 19 Jan 1772 Broad Creek (KGP p. 377)

Fry, James; 22 Aug 1772 (I 109.374); 6 Feb 1775; admn. James Fry (ABB 7.5)

Fry, Thomas; child: Elizabeth, b. 3 Sep 1773 Broad Creek (KGP p. 385)

FRYBANK

Frybank, George; wife Mary; child: Nelley, b. 18 Jul 1763 at Upper Chapel (KGP p. 334)

FRYER

Fryer, John; wife Mary; child: Phebee, b. 18 Apr 1761 (PGP p. 274)

FULKES

Fulkes, Baultus; m. Sarah; child: William, b. 12 Jan 1763 (PGP p. 270)

FULKNER

Fulkner, Martin; 3 Jul 1705 (I&A 25.133)

FULLER

Fuller, Daniel; wife Elizabeth; children: Mary, b. 18 Jul 1736; John, b. 18 Jan 1739; Susanna, b. 19 Apr 1741 (PGP p. 251)

Fuller, Robert; wife Susan; child: Ann, b. 27 Sep 1754 (KGP p. 311)

Fuller, William; wife Elisabeth; child: James, b. 1 Aug 1770 Lower Chapel (KGP p. 376)

GAIMES

Gaimes [Games], James; Mary [widow, dec'd]; children: Mary [age 3], dau. [unnamed, age 7, by another wife]; 5 Aug 1751 (AA 31.76); admx. Isabel; 5 Aug 1751 (I 47.163)

GALE

Gale, John; 8 Jan 1711 (I&A 33b.5); 30 May 1711 (I&A 32b.182)

Gale [Gaile], Benjamin; 20 Mar 1724 (I 10.91); 8 May 1725 (AA 6.325)

GALWITH

Galwith, John; wife Jane; tract *Acquascat*; 22 Oct 1696 (PGLR A.44)

GAMBLIN

Gambling, James; St. Paul's Parish; 23 Jul 1698; 27 Aug 1698; wife Eliza.; daus. Mary, Eliza.; tract *The Pasture* (MCW II.150); 20 Nov 1698 (I&A 17.135)

Gamblin, James [dec'd]; extx. Elizabeth; Jun 1703 (PGCR B.239)

Gamblin [Gambling], James [lately dec'd]; orphans Mary, Elisabeth; Aug 1703 (PGCR B.250)

Gamblin, Elisabeth; age 11 years; chose b-i-l Gabb'll Burnam, Jr. as guardian; Jan 1706 (PGCR C.110a)

Gamblin, James [dec'd]; dau. Elizabeth Gamblin of North Carolina; 28 Aug 1718 (PGLR F.94/647)

GAMBRA

Gambra [Gambray], Richard; 7 Aug 1702; 8 Jun 1703; wife [unnamed]; son Richard; dau. Mary; tract *Battersea* (MCW III.13); inv.; adms. Henry Acton and wife Ann; 12 Oct [with 1703] (I&A 3.72); admx. Anne Acton [w/o Henry]; 10 Nov 1707 (I&A 27.262); heirs Richard, Mary; 13 Mar 1710 (GB 4)

Gambra, Richard [CH]; s/o Richard; wife Elizabeth; tract *Batezee*; 15 Nov 1726 (PGLR M.88)

GANTT

Gant, Thomas; extx. Ann Wight [w/o John]; 19 Mar 1699 (I&A 18.186)

Gant, Eliza.; 14 Nov 1717; 9 Mar 1718; mother Anne White (MCW IV.196)

Gant [Gantt], John; wife Margret; children: Margret, b. 11 Jul 1761, bapt. 25 Oct 1761; Henry Wright, bapt. 23 Oct 1763 at Upper Chapel (KGP p. 323, 334)

Gant, Thomas III; wife Susanah; children: John Makall, b. 14 May 1762; Mary, b. 13 Sep 1765 Lower Chapel; Richard, b. 2 Aug 1767 Upper Chapel (KGP p. 330, 345, 366)

Gantt, Margery; [w/o Thomas]; 16 Jan 1763; 29 Aug 1764; grandson Levin Covington; granddaus. Rebecca Mackall, Elizabeth Hawkins [w/o John Stone], Rebecca Letchworth; nephews Leonard & Clement Holliday; nieces Elizabeth Simms, Mary Waring; great-niece Margery Waring [d/o Mary] (MCW XIII.53)

Gantt, Thomas; 19 Feb 1765; 29 Aug 1765; sons Thomas, Edward, George, Fielder; grandchildren: Elizabeth Denwood, Edward Gantt [s/o Thomas]; tracts *Sylvanus Grove* (MCW XIII.85-6)

GARDINER

Gardiner, Luke, Sr. [SM]; wife Elizabeth; children: Theodotia, Luke, Jr.; tract *Good Luck*; 24 Aug 1703; [confusing wording] (PGLR C.67)

Gardiner, John [SM]; wife Susanna; tract *Warberton Manor*; 16 Nov 1705 (PGLR C.150a)

Gardiner, Luke; wife Ann; tract *Darberton* [?*Warberton*] *Manor*; 3 Apr 1706 (PGLR C.163)

Gardner, Luke; age ca 31; 20 Oct 1711 (CCR PC.766)

Gardner, James; innholder; 27 Sep 1717; 10 Oct 1719; wife Mary (MCW IV.214); 16 Oct 1719 (I 3.180)

Gardner, Ignatius; wife Ann; tract *Gardner's Meadow*; 29 Mar 1732 (PGLR Q.426)

Gardiner, John; age ca 80; 26 Apr 1735 (PGLR T.253)

Gardiner, Benjamin; wife Ellinor; tract *Mount Pleasant*; Mar 1739 (PGLR Y.173)

Gardiner, Michael; admx. Livia; 4 May 1765 (I 87.312)

GARRELL

Garrell, Richard; dau. Hannah Jones; Sep 1698 Ct. (PGCR A.343)

Garell, Richard; wife Elisabeth; child: Mary, b. 11 Jul 1761, bapt. 6 Sep 1761 (KGP p. 323)

GARINGE

Garing, Henry; wife Catherine; child: Jeremiah, b. ____ (QAP b/36)

GARLICK

Garlick, John; 24 Mar [?1761] (I 73.63)

GARNER

Garner, James; 5 Oct 1720 (AA 3.208); 19 Apr 1721 (AA 3.420)

GARRETT

Garrette, John; wife Elizabeth; child: b. 9 Mary 1760 (PGP p. 258)

Garrett [Garrott], Middleton; wife Barbra; children: Elliner, b. 12 May 1763; Elimelick (m), b. ____ (PGP p. 268, 274)

GARTH

Garth, John; wife Mary; tract Long Acre; 15 Aug 1723 (PGLR I.576)

GASKIN

Gaskin, William; 29 Apr 1711; 16 Jun 1711; wife Margaret (MCW III.205); extx. Margaret; 3 Aug 1711 (I&A 32c.148); extx. Margaret Dick [w/o Henry]; 3 Jun 1712 (I&A 33a.233)

Gaskin, Margaret; son John; tract Green Clift; 3 Nov 1711 (PGLR F.176)

Gaskin, John [AA]; wife Mary; tract Green's Clift; 20 Jul 1730 (PGLR Q.58)

GATHER

Gather, Alexander; m. 23 8ber 1729 Sarah Wells (QAP m/5)

GATRELL

Gatrell, Francis [AA]; wife Mary; tract John & Thomas; 23 Jun 1725 (PGLR I.654)

Gattrell, Francis; wife Caty; child: Elliner, b. 9 Jun 1765 (PGP p. 276)

GATTON

Gatten; Thomas; wife Elizabeth; tract Hickory Plaines; 1 May 1714 (PGLR F.364)

Gatton, Thomas, Sr.; sons Thomas, Joseph, Richard; 10 May 1727 (PGLR M.157)

Gatton, James; wife Elizabeth; children: Susannah, b. __ Sep 1759; Elizabeth, b. 6 ___ 1765 (PGP p. 274, 280)

Gatton, Richard; wife Mary; child: Mary, b. 16 Jun 1764 (PGP p. 272)

Gatton, Azariah; wife Elizabeth; children: Nancy, b. _ Nov 1771 Upper Chapel; Annjelene, b. 11 Mar 1774 Upper Chapel; Sally Ann, b. 5 Mar 1776 Broad Creek (KGP p. 383, 389, 390)

Gatton, Thomas; 23 Sep 1772; 24 Nov 1772; wife Elizabeth; children: Mary Bean, Lurainia Howard, Azariah, James, Notley; grandchildren: Villinder [d/o Benjamin], Thomas Bean, Jesse Philips (MCW XV.96)

Gatton, Elizabeth; widow; 7 Nov 1774; 6 Feb 1775; daus. Mary Bean, Lurania Howard; sons Notley, Azariah; granddau. Elizabeth Bean; s-i-l George Bean (MCW XVI.41); 21 Nov 1775 (I 123.228)

GENT

Gent, John; 6 Feb 1715 (I&A 36c.164)

GENTLE

Gentle, George; wife Elizabeth; tract part of *Hogpen*; 28 Apr 1714 (PGLR F.352)

Gentle, George, age ca 58; 1738 (PGLR T.604)

Gentle, George; 23 Nov 1743; 5 Dec 1743; sons George, Stephen; daus. Ann Robenson [w/o Charles], Dinah More; tract *Hogpen* (MCW VIII.243); 18 Feb 1743 (I 28.384); 10 Dec 1744 (AA 21.63)

Gentle, Stephen; wife Mary; children: Stephen, b. 17 Mar 1755, Thomas, b. 9 Apr 1757 (KGP p. 308, 320)

Gentle, Stephen; wife Sarah; child: John, b. 24 Jul 1761 (PGP p. 261)

GEORGE

George, John; age ca 64; 1734 (PGLR T.124)

GERMAN

German, Stephen; wife Ellenor; children: Sarah, b. 6 Feb 1704; Ellenor, b. 17 Oct 1710; Stephen, b. __ Apr 1714; John, b. 16 Jan 1715; Ruth, b. 29 Oct 1721 (KGP p. 280)

German [Jerman], Stephen; age 60-70; 1730 (PGLR M.561) & (CCR-MSA 5.466)

GERRARD

Gerrard, John; wife Elizabeth; child: Rebecca, b. 9 8ber 1706 (QAP b/2)

Gerrard, John; merchant; 20 Jun 1715 (I&A 37c.1); admx. Elisabeth; 14 Mar 1717 (I&A 39c.92); admx. Elisabeth; 8 Apr 1717 (I&A 38a.122)

Gerard, John [dec'd]; widow Elizabeth; dau. Rebecca; part of *Cold Spring Manor*; 20 Apr 1717 (PGLR F.606)

GIBBONS

Gibbins, Thomas; wife Elizabeth; tract *Smith's Green*; 15 Jul 1704 (PGLR C.112)

Gibbens, Thomas; 16 Apr 1711; 5 May 1711; sons George, Turnor, Thomas; dau. Christian; tracts *Barton Hope, Brookefield* (MCW III.209); admx. Elisabeth; 28 May 1711 (I&A 32b.185)

Gibbons, Thomas; age ca 27; 1738 (PGLR T.604); age ca 28; 1738 (PGLR T.604)

Gibbons, George; 2 Oct 1765; 25 Jun 1766; wife Ann; children: John, Arthur, Walter, Thomas; tracts *Burningham, Hickory Ford* (MCW XIII.119-20)

GIBBS

Gibbs, Henry; age ca 14; servant; Sep 1698 Ct. (PGCR A.343)

Gibbs, James; wife Mary; children: Philip [b. 9 Feb 1707]; James [b. 23 Feb 1709]; Mary Ann [b. 13 Jul 1712]; Mary [b. 3 Jan 1714]; Andrew [b. 12 Feb 1717]; Jane [b. 31 Aug 1720]; Mar 1724 (PGCR L.413)

Gibbs, James; 19 Jun 1725 (I 11.27); 21 Dec 1726 (AA 8.166)

Gibbs, Philip; age 20 years 9 Feb next; chooses guardian; Aug 1727 (PGCR B,496)

Gibbs, Jannett; poor helpless orphan infant; bound out; Nov 1728 (PGCR O.331)

Gibbs, Philip; sisters Elisabeth Webster, Miriam Gibbs; 3 Nov 1732 (I 16.620); 22 Sep 1733 (AA 12.57); heirs William, John, Mary, Andrew, Jane; 26 Mar 1735 (GB 68)

Gibbs, James; wife Ann; children: William, b. 17 Oct 1737; Elizabeth, b. 2 Apr 1740; Charles, b. 7 Oct 1742; Mary, b. 16 Mar 1744/5; Violinda, b. 2 Aug 1747; James Lewin, b. 9 Apr 1750; John Harris, b. 20 Jun 1753; Ann, b. 26 Sep 1756 (KGP p. 295, 300)

Gibbs, Andrew; children: Charity, b. 16 Jan 1741; James, b. 31 Dec 1743 (KGP p. 295)

Gibbs, James; 6 Feb 1763; wife Ann; sons William, Charles, James Levin, John Harris; daus. Elizabeth Williams, Mary Mudd, Violender, Ann; tracts *Phillips Folley, Stoney Hill* (MCW XIII.14); extx. Ann; 24 May 1764 (I 87.131); 28 May 1765; admx. Ann (ABB 4.102, 103); widow Ann; heirs William, Charles, Elizabeth, Mary, Virlinda, James, Levin, John Harris, Ann; 27 Aug 1766 (GB 245)

Gibbs, William; m. 17 Oct 1765 Ann Jenkins; child: Elisabeth, b. 17 Sep 1766 Broad Creek (KGP p. 357, 359)

Gibbs, Charles; wife Jane; child: Betsy Ann, b. 8 May 1774 Broad Creek (KGP p. 385)

Gibbs, Ann; 20 Oct 1776; 22 Oct 1776; sons James & John H. Gibbs (MCW XVI.188)

GIBSON

Gibson, James; wife Mary; tract *Beall's Chance*; 9 Nov 1722 (PGLR I.348)

Gibson, John; 7 Sep 1727 (I 12.283); 9 Apr 1728 (I 12.194); heir dau. [unnamed]; 30 Jul 1728 (AA 9.218); heir Saphiah [sophia] [age ca 6]; 27 Aug 1728 (AA 9.66)

Gibson [Gilson], William; wife Elizabeth; children: William, b. 20 Mar 1761; James, b. 13 Jul 1764 (PGP p. 261, 273)

Gibson, John; carpenter; 17 Sep 1762 (I 79.226)

Gibson, James; 13 Aug 1776; 15 Sep 1776; children: Ann Keadle, Elizabeth Keadle [w/o William]; grandchildren: John, Gibson & William Keadle; also Mary & Eleanor Keadle [ds/o William]; tracts *Beales Chance, Goodluck* (MCW XVI.166)

GILBERT

Gilbert, Francis; wife Mary Ann; child: Elizabeth, b. 17 Jun 1765, bapt. 14 Jul 1765 Lower Chapel (KGP p. 351)

Gilbert, Gilbert; wife Margery; child: Martha, b. 4 Feb 1766 (QAP b/38)

Gilbert, William; wife Dorathy; dau. Elizabeth; bound out; Aug 1711 Ct. (PGCR G.78)

GILBURN

Gilburn, William; wife Dorothea; child: Margaret, b. 16 Aug 1708 (QAP b/4)

Gilborn [Gilburne], William; wife Dorothy; children bound out: Sarah [age 10 on 10 Jun last past]; Aug 1710 (PGCR G.25); Elisabeth [age 6 yrs and 4 months]; Aug 1711 (PGCR G.78)

GILLUM

Gillum, Thomas; wife Mary; child: Elisabeth, b. ____ (PGP p. 267)

GILPIN

Gilpin, Edward; wife Ann; children: Benjamin, bapt. 6 May 1764 Broad Creek; Charity, b. 31 Jul 1773 Broad Creek (KGP p. 356, 385)

Gilpin, Jane; child: James, bapt. 24 Aug 1766 Broad Creek (KGP p. 359)

GIRTON

Girting, Thomas; wife Elizabeth; child: Leonard, bapt. 4 Feb 1753 (KGP p. 298)

Girton, Jas.; wife Eliz.; child: Rachael, b. 28 Feb 1762 (PGP p. 263)

Girton, Notley; m. 27 Mar 1768 Mary Tewill Upper Chapel (KGP p. 369)

GITTINGS

Gibings, Thomas; extx. Elisabeth Davies [w/o Nicholas, Jr.]; 19 Jul 1712 (I&A 33b.9)

Gittings, Phillip, Jr.; wife Eliza.; child: Philip, b. 1715 (QAP b/11)

Gittings, Philip; 8 Dec 1720; 25 Jan 1720; wife Ann; son John (MCW V.23); 27 Feb 1721 (I 4.331); ex. Anne; 19 Jun 1724 (AA 6.29)

Gittings, Philip; wife Elizabeth; tract Mt. Arrat Enlarged; 30 Apr 1722 (PGLR I.277)

Gittings, Phillip; 8 May 1727 (I 12.130); heirs Phillip, Mary, Ann, Allen [eldest age ca 12]; 26 Mar 1728 (AA 9.205)

Gittings, Thomas; age ca 29; bro. Philip [dec'd]; 9 Oct 1728 (PGLR M.401)

Gittins, Elizabeth; 15 Jan 1740/1; 20 Feb 1740; daus. Eleanor, Mary, Ann; son Philip; grandson Thomas (MCW VIII.173)

Giddons, John; wife Valender; child: Jasper, bapt. 4 Aug 1751 (KGP p. 294)

Getting, Ann; 10 Jun 1760 (I 70.236)

Gittins, Benjamin; wife Ann; children: Amealea, b. 27 Dec 1761; Vialinda, b. 9 Dec 1763, bapt. 29 Jan 1764 at Upper Chapel; Elizabeth, bapt. 1 Dec 1765 Lower Chapel (KGP p. 324, 340, 346)

Gittins, Jeremiah; wife Jane; children: Verlinder, b. 1 Oct 1761; Colmore, bapt. 19 Feb 1764 at Upper Chapel (KGP p. 324, 340)

Gidins, Thomas; wife Mary; child: John, bapt. 28 Mar 1762 (KGP p. 325)

Gittings, Thomas; wife Elizabeth; child: Elizabeth, bapt. 14 Oct 1764 Lower Chapel (KGP p. 345)

Gittings, Ann; child: Jemima, b. 15 Dec 1764 (PGP p. 278)

Gittins, Thomas; wife Mary; child: Thomas, bapt. 17 Apr 1768 Lower Chapel (KGP p. 369)

GIZBITZKY
Gizbitzky, Bartholomew; German born; 18 Jan 1754 (I 58.142); foreigner; 28 Mar 1754 (AA 36.289)

GLADSTONE
Gladstone, James [dec'd]; widow Joyce; dau. Mary; tract *The Ridge*; 7 Nov 1732 (PGLR Q.589)

Gladstone, James; age ca 39; 8 Dec 1719 (CCR CL.551)

Gladstone, James; wife Joice; children: Elizabeth, b. 10 May 1706; Thomas, b. 19 Dec 1707; Joyce, b. 5 Feb 1709/10; James, b. 29 10ber 1711; John, b. 2 Apr 1714 (QAP b/4, 9)

GLAIZE
Glaize, John; wife Charity; child: Elinor, b. 21 Sep 1753 (KGP p. 305)

Glaze, Patrick; wife Esther; child: Gidiah, b. 2 Mar 1762 (PGP p. 264)

GLASSFORD
Glassford, Hugh; 18 Jan 1767 (I 91.306)

GLASSOE
Glassoe, Richard; 6 Oct 1712 (I&A 33b.78)

GLOVER
Glover, Eleanor; heir; 25 Aug 1709 (GB 5)

Glover, William; adms. Thomas Stump & wife Elisabeth; 13 Mar 1717 (I&A 39a.56)

GODDART
Goddard, John; age 13 years Oct last; bound out; Mar 1717 (PGCR H.182)

Godard [Goddart], John; admx. Jane; 17 Sep 1765 (I 90.137); 14 Jun 1766; admx. Mrs. Jane Goddart (ABB 4.165); heir Eleanor Beall; 24 Nov 1767 (GB 253)

Goodart, Jane; 16 Dec 1768; 20 Feb 1769; children: Penelope Hatton Jones; s-i-l Patrick Beall; grandchildren: Elizabeth Brooke & Jane Bayne Beall (MCW XIV.95)

GODFRY

Godfry, Joshua; wife Jane; child: Sarah, b. 28 May 1727 (QAP b/26)

GOE

Goe, William; m. 27 Jan 1725 Mary Bateman; children: Margaret, b. 19 Aug 1727; William, b. 4 Aug 1729 (QAP m/4; b/20, 23)

Goe, William; m. 1754 Dorcas Turner; children: Phillip, b. 24 Mar 1767; Eleanor, b. 12 Sep 1768; Henry Bateman, b. 14 Jun 1770; Turner, b. 22 Jan 1772 (QAP m/7; b/46)

Goe, William; 3 Mar 1762; 25 Aug 1762; son William; dau. Margaret Hutton; grandchildren: Elizabeth, Mary, Margaret & John Goe, Mary Hutton (MCW XII.144); 24 Jan 1763; legatees grandchildren: Elisabeth Goe, Mary Hatton, Mary Goe, John Goe; residue to William Goe, Margaret Hatton (ABB 4.1)

GOFF

Goff, Bartholomew; wife Johannah [extx. of Thomas Hide, dec'd]; Oct 1699 Ct. (PGCR A.477)

GOLD

Gold, Joseph; m. 22 Dec 1715 Margaret Danielson (QAP m/2)

Gold, John; m. 28 Apr 1723 Elizabeth Nush (QAP m/3)

Gold, Joseph; wife Margaret; tract *Joseph and Margaret's Rest*; 7 Oct 1739 (PGLR Y.129)

GOLOP

Golop, John; wife Susannah; child: Richard, bapt. 20 May 1764 Upper Chapel (KGP p. 341)

GOODMAN

Goodman, John; m. 4 9ber 1714 Leah Davis; children: Rachel, b. 10 May 1715; John, b. 28 Mar 1717 (QAP m/1; b/10, 12)

Goodman, Humphrey; wife Kizia; child: Jeremiah, b. 11 Jun 1763 (PGP p. 269)

Goodman, Samuel; wife Elliner; child: Humphrey, b. 20 Dec 1763 (PGP p. 269)

Goodman, John; wife Jemima; child: Anna, b. 4 Feb 1772 Broad Creek (KGP p. 377)

GOODRICK

Goodrick, Edmond; Piscataway Parish; 10 Sep 1710; 2 Nov 1712; wife Ruth; bro. Geo. Goodrick; sisters Mary Sims, Julian Price; son Wm. Clarkson, daus. Marton Pearce, Eliza. Sims (MCW III.234); 22 Mar 1713 (I&A 35a.345)

Goodrick, Francis [CH]; wife Mary; tract Oxmontown; 21 Aug 1742 (PGLR Y.529)

GOODWIN

Goodwin, Edward; m. 30 Jun 1735 Sarah Beach; children: John, b. 9 Aug 1735; Sarah, b. 8 Nov 1737; Elizabeth, b. 14 Sep 1739; Gabriel (twin), b. 10 Mar 1743; Margret (twin), b. 10 Mar 1743; Mary, b. __ Feb ____ (QAP m/6; b/31, 32, 33, 35)

Goodwin, John; wife Tabitha; children: Ann, b. ____; Sarah, b. ____; Elizabeth, b. 28 Feb 1758 (QAP b/36, 37)

GOOSEY

Goosey, Jonathan; wife Martha; Aug 1699 Ct. (PGCR A.454)

GORDON

Gordon, Peter; age ca 13; servant; Jun 1710 (PGCR D.318)

Gorden, George; age ca 15; servant; Aug 1712 (PGCR G.245)

Gordan, Robert; wife Mary; children: ____ (m), b. 28 Dec 1721; ?Robert (m), b. 6 Jan 1723; Rebecca, b. 15 Feb 1725 (ICR; KGP p. 271)

Gordon, James; wife Elizabeth; dau. Rebecca; sons John, Thomas; tract part of Crawford's Adventure; 3 Oct 1734 (PGLR T.190, 191)

Gordon, George; age ca 45; 29 Oct 1745 (CCR MSA 8.63)

Gordon, James; wife Sarah; child: Elinor, bapt. 26 May 1751 (KGP p. 293)

Gordon, Charles; m. 9 Feb 1752 Elizabeth Flint; children: Ann, b. 29 Oct 1752; Levin, b. 4 Jul 1755 (PGP p. 251, 253, 256)

Gordon, Robert; wife Rebecca; child: Mary, b. 19 Aug 1757 (KGP p. 320)

Gordon, George; 10 May 1764; 25 Sep 1766; wife Christian; children: Mary Belt [w/o Capt. Tobias], John [in East India Service]; cous. George & Cuthbert Gordon of Leath; bro. Thomas of North Brittain; grandchildren: George Forbes & Charles Evans Hamilton, Horatio, Joshua, Lucy & Dryden Belt, Hannah West; wife's dau. Hannah West [w/o Stephen]; wife's niece Elizabeth Simpson of Edenborough (MCW XIII.129)

Gordon, Robert; wife Sarah; child: Latitia, b. 3 Feb 1775 Lower Chapel (KGP p. 380)

GORE

Goar, James; wife Mary; child: James, b. 7 Nov 1707 (QAP b/3)

Gore, James; widow Mary; 19 Jun 1717 (I&A 37b.100, 101)

GOSLING

Gosling, John [VA]; wife Mary [widow of John Nelson & Edward Rockwood, both dec'd]; tract *Gilliard*; 4 Oct 1719 (PGLR F.260/844)

Gosling, Robert; age 15 on 4 Nov instant; bound out; Nov 1731 (PGCR R.278)

GOULDSTONE

Gouldstone, Thomas; 16 Jun 1716 (I&A 37a.49, 91)

GOVER

Gover, Epharim; wife Mary; tract *Dear Bought*; 19 Sep 1724 (PGLR I.613)

Gover, John; m. 15 Dec 1757 Elizabeth Duvall (QAP m/7)

GOWIN

Gowin, Charles; age 4 years; bound out; Mar 1750 (PGCR LL.135)

GRAHAM

Graham, Mary; age 3 on 10 Nov next; d/o Elizabeth; bound out; Aug 1724 (PGCR L.334)

Graham, Sarah; age 2 mos; d/o Catherine; bound out; Jun 1740 (PGCR X.661)

GRANT

Grant, James; wife Elizabeth; tract *Grant's Delight*; 6 Feb 1738 (PGLR T.704)

GRAVES

Graves, James; 22 Jul 1711 (I&A 32c.60); 27 Aug 1711 (I&A 32c.156)

Graves, William; dau. Elizabeth; 2 Jan 1727/8 (PGLR M.252)

Graves, William; admx. Ann; 11 Apr 1729 (I 14.5); admx. Ann Thorne [w/o John]; heirs Elisabeth, William [eldest age ca 7]; 12 Oct 1730 (AA 10.473)

Graves, Thomas; wife Elizabeth; children: Humphrey, b. 14 Feb 1763; Joshua, b. _____ (PGP p. 271, 275)

Graves, Luis; wife Elenor; child: Benjamin, b. 9 Feb 1770 Broad Creek (KGP p. 374)

Graves, John; wife Sarah; child: Elisabeth, b. 24 Feb 1770 Broad Creek (KGP p. 374)

Graves, John Copher; wife Sarah; child: John Downs, b. 24 Feb 1773 Lower Chapel (KGP p. 384)

GRAY

Gray, John; 2 Jun 1705 (I&A 3.602)

Grey, William, 20 Jun 1718 (I 1.447); 9 Aug 1718 (AA 192)

Gray, William; wife Sarah; children: John, b. 26 Dec 1724; Ellinor, b. 5 Nov 1728 (QAP b/22)

Gray, John; wife Susannah; [will of Mary Henderson]; 1762 (MCWXII.102)

Gray, William Walsh; [s/o Robert]; Martha Walsh [widow, grandmother of William]; 22 Dec 1742 (PGLR Y.617

Gray, Robert; admx. Jayne White [w/o Richard]; 20 Jul 1748 (I 39.63); 12 Jun 1749 (AA 26.112); child: William Welch Gray; 28 Aug 1750 (AA 28.351); heir William Welsh Gray; 27 Nov 1751 (GB 172)

Gray, Richard; wife Mary; child: Mary Anney, bapt. 19 Jan 1766 Lower Chapel (KGP p. 352)

GREAR

Greer, Joseph [CA]; wife Sarah; tract [unnamed]; 30 May 1696 (PGLR A.58)

Greares, Benjamin; bro. Josep; 30 Sep 1696 (I&A 14.56)

Grear, Joseph; 8 Aug 1715; 14 Dec 1715; wife [unnamed]; 6 sons Joseph, Benja., James, Henry, Annanias, John; 2 daus. [unnamed] (MCW IV.41)

Grear, Ananias; 27 Oct 1760; 25 Mar 1761; wife Margaret; children: Hezekiah, James, Elizabeth, Benjamin, Ananias, William Johnson (MCW XII.48); [as blacksmith]; extx. Margaret; 24 Aug 1761 (I 74.326); 26 Mar 1767; extx. Margret; dist. to Hezekiah, James, Elisabeth, Benjamin, Annanias, William Johnson (ABB 5.18); widow Margaret; heirs James, Elizabeth, Benjamin, Annamas, William Johnson; 23 Mar 1768 (GB 257)

Grear, Henry; planter; 1 Sep 1767; 24 Nov 1767; wife Mary; children: Sarah Brightwell, Jane Parker, Priscilla Wheaten, Brightwell Grear; grandchildren: Jonathan, Catherine, Susan, Jane, Nathaniel & Mary Wheatan [ch/o Priscilla] (MCW XIV.11-2); 4 Dec 1767 (I 97.121)

GREEN

Greene, Thomas; [s/o Leonard]; chooses guardian; Nov 1696 Ct. (PGCR A.61)

Greene, Charles [England]; wife Elizabeth [d/o James Truman]; tract *Indian Creeke with Addition*; 17 Sep 1697 (PGLR A.97)

Green, Eliabeth; orphan; [d/o John]; age 13 months; Jun 1703 (PGCR B.249)

Green, Elizabeth; child: Elizabeth, b. 28 Mar 1704 (QAP b/6)

Green, John; wife [unnamed, dec'd]; [with 1704] (I&A 3.168, 169)

Green, Hugh; orphan; [s/o John, dec'd]; age 6 Oct next; bound out; Jun 1707 (PGCR C.149)

Green, Philip; wife Sarah; children: Sarah, b. 23 Apr 1712; John, b. 23 Aug 1714; Elizabeth, b. 1 10ber 1716; Ann, b. 16 Feb 1717; Comfort, b. 20 Apr 1720 (QAP b/6, 14, 15)

Green, Charles [England]; wife Elizabeth Truman; [undated, with 1713] (PGLR F.253)

Green, Thomas; m. 10 Aug 1716 Elizabeth Walker; both of this parish; children: Sarah, b. 6 Nov 1717; William, b. 15 Feb 1719 (KGP p. 274, 276, 277)

Green, Hugh; m. 18 Jul 1717 Susanna Holland; Mary, b. 23 Feb 1717; Indey (f), b. 11 Jul 1720; Hugh, b. 13 Apr 1724 (QAP m/1; b/13, 19)

Green, Philip; m. 7 Nov 1723 Eliza. Burrows; children: Mary, b. 14 Apr 1724; Elijah, b. 15 Aug 1732 (QAP m/3; b/19, 26)

Green, John; 1 Mar 1724 (I 11.222); 16 Feb 1725 (AA 7.273)

Greene, James; m. 26 Jul 1727 Elizabeth Dyar; children: Catherine, b. 16 Feb 1729; Mary, b. 30 Mar 1732; Elizabeth, b. 7 May 1734; Charity, b. 5 Oct 1736; James, b. 14 Oct 1738; Rebacca, b. 4 Apr 1741; Thomas Edelen, b. 9 Mar 1745/6 (KGP p. 286, 287)

Green, James, Sr.; 14 Feb 1727/8; 17 Feb 1734; wife Charity; dau. Mary Bowlin, Elizabeth Thompson, Ann, Eleanor, Charity, Jane, Sarah, Margaret; sons James, William, Roger; tracts *Strife, Air, Cowpen* (MCW VII.125); admx. Charity; 6 Mar 1734 (I 20.381); extx. Charity; orphans Jean, Sarah, Margarett; 23 May 1736 (AA 14.259); widow Charity; heirs James, Sarah, Margaret; 25 Aug 1736 (GB 82)

Green, John; 8 Jun 1730 (I 15.520); 11 Mar 1730 (AA 10.643)

Greene, James; age ca 73; 1730 (PGLR M.558)

Green, William; 8 Dec 1740 (I 26.27); 18 Jul 1743 (AA 19526); 30 Apr 1744 (AA 20.240); 30 Jun 1744 (AA 20.335); heirs Ruth, Margaret, William, Mary; 30 Nov 1744 (GB 139); 26 Mar 1745 (AA 21.212)

Green, Charity; 1 Dec 1748; 25 Oct 1754; son James Green; daus. Charity Gilpin, Jane, Margaret, Mary Bowling, Elizabeth Thompson, Ann Sympson; grandson James Thomson (MCW XI.54-5)

Green, Francis; admx. Elisabeth; 22 Apr 1772 (I 110.238); 19 Sep 1774; admx. Mrs. Elisabeth Green (ABB 6.267)

Green, Jacob; age ca 40; 27 Oct 1773 (CCR MSA 13.98)

Greene, James; planter; 15 Nov 1774; 23 Aug 1776; wife Eleanor; children: John, Thomas Edelen, Basil [not son of Eleanor]; tract *Strife* (MCW XVI.139); 21 Nov 1776 (I 124.3); 6 May 1777; widow [unnamed]; 9 children [unnamed] (ABB 7.70)

Green, Elizabeth; widow; 17 Apr 1777; 8 May 1777; b-i-l Marmaduke Simmes (MCW XVI.186)

GREENDELL

Greendell, William; age ca 18; servant; Jun 1698 Ct. (PGCR A.317)

GREENFIELD

Greenfield, Thomas; wife Martha; tracts *Quick Saile, Archers Pasture*; 21 Mar 1697 (PGLR A.101)

Greenfield; Thomas; age ca 64; 9 Apr 1713 (CCR PC.877)

Greenfield, Thomas; planter; 17 Aug 1715; 7 Nov 1715; wife Martha; sons Thomas Truman, Truman, James & Micajah Greenfield; daus. Jone Greenfield, Martha Waring, Eliza. Parker, Ann Wight; ss-i-l Gabriel Parker, John Wight, Basil Waring; kinsmen Benjamin Gale [s/o Jno. Gale, dec'd], James Hollyday; cous. Leonard Holliday; niece Mrs. Margery Covington; tracts *Archer's Pasture, Pheasant Tree, Retalliation, Pheasant Hills, Juxta Stadium Aureolum, Golden Race, Mills Town, Stokebardolph, Truman's Acquaintance, Anchovia Hills, Gledling Point, Billingsley's Point, Trent Neck, Pascuum, Nutwell's Adventure, Taylor's Coast* (MCW IV.39-40); [as Thomas, Col.]; 10 Apr 1716 (I&A 36c.222, 290; 37a.113); 2 Oct 1716 (I&A 37c.5, 128; 38a.42); 3 Jun 1719 (AA 2.60)

Greenfield, Thomas Truman; age ca 47; 13 Sep 1729 (PGLR M.520)

Greenfield, James, Capt.; age ca 46; 7 Jul 1731 (PGLR Q.525)

Greenfield, James; wife Eleanor; children: Sarah, Eleanor, Thomas; 9 Aug 1731 (PGLR Q.412)

Greenfield, James; dau. Elizabeth Skinner [w/o Henry]; 9 Dec 1731 (PGLR Q.433)

Greenfield, Thomas Truman, Col.; age ca 49; 7 Jul 1732 (PGLR Q.526)

Greenfield, James; 21 Nov 1733; 26 Mar 1734; daus. Mary Brooke, Elizabeth Skinner, Sarah, Eliner; tracts *Pheasants Hills, Truman's Hills, Beal's Gift* (MCW VII.71); admx. Eleanor; 28 Sep 1734 (I 20.418); admx. Elianor; 27 Sep 1734 (I 20.39); widow Eleanor; 11 Jun 1735 (AA 13.129); widow Elianor; 14 Aug 1736 (AA 15.98); James. Capt.; admx. Eleanor Gordon [w/o George]; 30 Nov 1739 (AA 17.454); heirs Sarah, Eleanor, Thomas Smith, Walter; 23 Aug 1742 (GB 124)

Greenfield, Martha; widow; 20 Feb 1737/8; 27 Mar 1739; son Thomas Truman Greenfield; daus. Ann Wightt, Martha Waring, Jone Hawkins [w/o Henry]; grandsons Thomas Truman Greenfield, Thomas Greenfield [s/o Truman], Isle of Wight, Walter Truman Greenfield, George Parker, Francis Waring, Garratt Truman Greenfield; granddaus. Innocense & Ann Wight, Sabina Truman Greenfield, Sarah, Elizabeth, Martha Hawkins, Mary Taylor; great-granddau. Verlinder Taylor [d/o Mary], Martha Burgis [d/o Martha Waring]; niece Margery Gantt; nephew Leonard Hollyday; tracts *The Golden Race, Dunnbar* (MCW VIII.30); 17 Apr 1739 (I 24.192); 28 Aug 1745 (AA 22.45)

Greenfield, Thomas, Col.; age ca 50; 24 Aug 1741 (PGLR Y.360)
Greenfield, James Truman; admx. Elisabeth; 21 Aug 1760 (I 75.198, 202); 26 Nov 1768; admx. Elisabeth Brook; children: Ann, Mary, William, Sarah, Susannah Eve (ABB 5.139); ?widow Elizabeth Brooke; heirs Ann Trueman Greenfield, Mary Greenfield, William Trueman Greenfield, Sarah Greenfield, Susannah Eve Greenfield; 28 Mar 1771 (GB 292)

GREENIFF
Greeniff, James; 13 Mar 1704 (I&A 3.390)

GREENUP
Greenup, William; wife Mary; children: Mary, b. 18 Aug 1701; John, b. 2 8ber 1707 (QAP b/2,3)
Greenup [Greenhap], William; 6 Mar 1712 (I&A 34.147); 6 Mar 1712 (I&A 35a.66); 28 Aug 1712 (I&A 33b.201)
Greenup, John; wife Ann; dau. Mary; 29 Apr 1731 (PGLR Q.258)
Greenup, John; wife Ann; mother Mary Johnston [Ed. - widow of William Greenup, Thomas Harris & Allen Lock; wife of Thomas Johnston]; tract *Beall's Pleasure*; 24 Jun 1736 (PGLR T.380)

GREENWELL
Greenwell, James; wife Martha; child: Thomas Biscour, bapt. 19 Apr 1767 Upper Chapel (KGP p. 365)

GREENWOOD
Greenwood, Samuel; wife Mary; children: Samuel, b. 12 Apr 1732; William b. 13 Sep 1733 (QAP b/25, 27)

GREGREY
Gregrey, Richard; wife Violetta; children: Ann, bapt. 25 Dec 1765 Broad Creek; Sushanna, bapt. 24 May 1768 Lower Chapel (KGP p. 350, 368)
Grigory, Richard; child: Sarah, b. 25 Aug 1773 Lower Chapel (KGP p. 384)

GRIFFIN
Griffen, Richard; age 11 on 22 Dec next; bound out; Jun 1750 (PGCR LL.176)
Griffen, Thomas; age 14 on 14 Jan next; bound out; Jun 1750 (PGCR LL.176)
Griffin, George; wife Mary; child: Mary, b. 7 Oct 1763 at Broad Creek (KGP p. 338)
Griffin, Martha; child: Sarah Walton, bapt. 14 Sep 1766 Broad Creek (KGP p. 359)
Griffin, James; wife Sarah; child: William, bapt. 21 Dec 1766 Broad Creek (KGP p. 348)

Griffin, James; wife Sarah Ann; child: Sarah Ann, bapt. 23 Oct 1768 Lower Chapel (KGP p. 372)

Grifin, Patty; child: William S., b. 23 Mar 1771 Lower Chapel (KGP p. 377)

Griffis, Thomas; wife Eleanor; child: Anne, b. 14 Jan 1776 Lower Chapel (KGP p. 381)

GRIFFITH

Griffith, Samuel; wife Elizabeth; tract Cold Spring Manor; 1 Aug 1699 (PGLR A.169)

GRIMES

Grimes, Susanah; servant; had bastard child John Browne Grimes; Jan 1696/7 Ct. (PGCR A.116, 170); servant; had bastard child; Feb 1698/9 (PGCR A.384)

Grimes, Thomas; wife Ann; Nov 1696 Ct. (PGCR p. 78)

Grimes, Thomas; 15 Oct 1712 (I&A 33b.61); admx. Anne; 12 Sep 1713 (I&A 35b.25)

Grimes, Edward; wife Martha; child: Elizabeth, b. 18 9ber 1721 (QAP b/17)

Grimes, Elizabeth; bastard child Rachel; bound out; Mar 1732 (PGCR R.402)

Grimes, Philip; orphan age ca 3 years; bound out; Nov 1743 (PGCR CC.156)

Grimes, John; age ca 7 on 25th instant; bound out; Mar 1744 (PGCR CC.275)

Grimes, Ann; age ca 6 weeks; d/o Catherine; bound out; Mar 1745 (PGCR DD.278)

Grimes, George; wife Catherine; child: Charles, b. 31 Aug 1757 (KGP p. 320)

Grimes, Thomas; 5 Apr 1758 (I 66.212)

GRIMMET

Grimmet, Robert; wife Eliza.; child: Margaret, b. 1 May 1720 (QAP b/15)

GRIMSON

Grimson, John; wife Jane; child: Benjamin, bapt. 3 May 1752 (KGP p. 296)

GRINDALL

Grindal, John; 27 Aug 1760; 28 Nov 1760; wife Catherine; sons William, John; other children [unnamed] (MCW XII.10); extx. Catharine; 25 Mar 1761 (I 73.64); 24 Jun 1762; ex. Catharina Grindall; legatees child of dec'd & wife's children [unnamed] (ABB 3.143); widow Catherine; heirs William, John, Rebecca, Josiah, Barker, Joseph Stone; 24 Mar 1763 (GB 225)

GRIPAH

Gripah, Zachariah; admx. Hannah; 2 Nov 1711 (I&A 33a.24); admx. Hanah; 13 Aug 1712 (I&A 33b.30)

GROOME

Groome, William [s/o William, dec'd]; wife Mary; bro. Richard; tract *Mount Calvert*; 24 Jul 169[7] (PGLR A.65, 91)

Groome, Richard [England]; tailor; age 26; wife Susan; mother ?Margaret; 10 Nov 1697 (PGLR A.132)

Groome, Richard; wife Ann; tract *Essex Lodge*; 7 May 1698 (PGLR A.108)

Groome, William of Charlestown; innholder; father William [dec'd], mother Mary; bro. Richard; tract *Mt. Calvert*; 9 Oct 1698 (PGLR A.137, 154)

Groome, Amy; 30 Jan 1743/4; 13 Feb 1743/4; husb. Richard [dec'd]; daus. Sarah, Lurainer (MCW VIII.244); 28 Feb 1743 (I 28.502); 11 Aug 1744 (I 30.82); dau. Sarah; 28 Nov 1744 (AA 21.59); children: w/o James Harvey, w/o Thomas Selby, w/o John Selby, Larana Hamilton, w/o George Jewel, w/o John Ormes; 20 May 1746 (AA 22.168)

Groome, Richard; planter; 25 Apr 1734; 27 Sep 1734; wife Amy; sons William, Samuel; daus. Sibell Orme, Elener Hearwe, Rebecca, Sarah, Amy, Lurane (MCW VII.113); planter; admx. Amey; 19 Nov 1734 (I 20.420); extx. Amy; 26 Nov 1736 (AA 15.260)

Groome, Richard; son William; [dau.] Cibby Orme [w/o John]; tract *Mt. Calvert Manor*; 10 Mar 1732; (PGLR Q.615, 617)

Groome, Richard; wife Amy; dau. Amy Jewell [w/o George]; 20 Apr 1740 (PGLR Y.175)

Grooms, Richard; 17 Dec 1774 (I 121.332)

GROVER

Grover, Jacob; wife Priselah; child: Catherine, b. 10 Jul 1765 (PGP p. 275)

GURRICK

Gurrrick, Edmund; 12 Jan 1712 (I&A 34.165)

GUTTRIDGE

Guttereg, Henry; 21 Dec 1711; 22 Jan 1711; daus. Ann Wheeler, Eliza. Guttereg (MCW III.215); exs. John Jones and wife Ann; 3 Nov 1712 (I&A 33b.178); extx. Ann Jones [w/o John]; 4 Jul 1713 (I&A 34.67); exs. John Jones & wife Ann; 23 Aug 1715 (I&A 36c.39); dau. Elisabeth; exs. John Jones and his wife Anne; 2 Jun 1719 (AA 2.59)

Gutteridge, Richard; wife Elizabeth; children: Mary, b. 14 Nov 1715; Elizabeth, b. 2 9ber 1717; Sarah, b. 6 8ber 1719; Johanna, b. 8 8ber 1723; Martha, b. 23 Mar 1726/7; Diana, b. 2 [or 3] Feb 1730; Rebeckah, b. 2 Nov 1733 (QAP b/11, 13, 15, 18, 20, 24, 27)

GUY

Guy, Jeremiah; wife Jane; child: Jeremiah, b. 8 Jun 1704 (QAP b/4)

Guy, Jeremiah; age ca 9 years in this instant Jun; bound out; Jun 1713 (PGCR G.348)

Guy, Charles; wife Elizabeth; child: Margret, bapt. 28 Mar 1762 (KGP p. 325)

Guy, William; wife Elizabeth; children: Letishia, bapt. 20 May 1764 Upper Chapel; John White, bapt. 28 Sep 1766 Lower Chapel (KGP p. 341, 367)

Guy, John; wife Cloe; children: William, bapt. 11 Feb 1765 Lower Chapel; Ann, bapt. 30 Aug 1767 Lower Chapel (KGP p. 350, 367)

Guy, William, Jr.; wife Elizabeth; child: William, b. 3 Jun 1774 Lower Chapel (KGP p. 379)

GUYTHER

Guyther, Sarah, Mrs.; now w/o John Bullen; 31 Oct 1748 (CCR MSA 8.744)

GWIN

Gwin, Edward; wife Ester; children: Elizabeth, b. 11 Aug 1729; Sarah, b. 9 Oct 1732 (QAP b/23, 26)

HADDOCK

Haddick, Benjamin; 24 Feb 1702; 4 Jun 1703; wife Eliza. in London (MCW III.14); [with 1703] (I&A 3.100)

Haddock, James, gent.; 16 Sep 1726; 2 May 1731; wife Sarah; son Marsham Waring; grandson James Haddock Waring; sisters Elizabeth Gibson, Sarah Newland, Mary Reynolds; nephew John Gibson; tracts *Weston* (MCW VI.188); extx. Sarah; 13 Aug 1731 (I 16.227); extx. Sarah; 12 Jun 1732 (I 16.444); extx. Sarah; 12 Jun 1732 (I 16.444); widow Sarah; 5 Jul 1732 (AA 11.424)

HAGAN

Hagen, John; age ca 17; servant; Jun 1698 Ct. (PGCR A.316)

Hagan, Ignatius; wife Rebecca [d/o Maj. John Lowe, dec'd, of St. Mary's]; tract *Garden*; 13 Aug 1720 (PGLR I.42)

HAGERTY

Hagerty, John; wife Sarah; children: Paul, bapt. 23 Feb 1752; George, b. 17 Jun 1754 (KGP p. 294, 306)

HAIR

Hair, William; wife Margrette; child: Linder, b. 25 Mar 1761 (PGP p. 260)

HALES

Hales, John; wife Jane; children: Thomas, b. 26 Feb 1728/9; John, b. 29 Dec 1730; Luke, b. 9 June 1733 (KGP p. 282)

HALINERD

Halinerd, James; wife Elizabeth; tract *Pines*; 29 Apr 1721 (PGLR I.77)

HALL

Hall, Joshua; wife Margaret; *Plumers Pleasure*; 24 Nov 1696 (PGLR A.24)

Hall, Joshua; 12 Jun 1711 (I&A 32b.181)

Hall, Margaret; age 14 on 23 Jan next; bound out; Jun 1717 (PGCR H.240)

Hall, Robert, gent.; 4 Dec 1719; 17 Dec 1719; wife Elizabeth (MCW IV.220); 2 Apr 1720 (I 3.287); 24 Jul 1721 (AA 3.515)

Hall, Benjamin; 4 Sep 1720; 29 Mar 1721; wife Mary; son Francis; nephews Richard, Elisha [ss/o Elisha]; nephew Joseph [s/o Joseph]; b-i-l Henry Darnall (MCW V.45); [with 1721] (I 7.74); extx. Mary Witham [w/o Dr. Henry]; 5 May 1722 (AA 4.180); widow Mary Witham [w/o Dr. Henry]; 20 May 1729 (PGLR M.449)

Hall, Katherine; child: Elizabeth, b. 12 Jul 1721 (QAP b/17)

Hall, Henry; m. 25 7ber 1723 Martha Bateman; children: Mary, b. 31 Jan 1724/5; Henry, b. 26 May 1727; John, b. 24 Nov 1729; Benjamin, b. 25 Jul 1732 (QAP m/3; b/19, 20, 23, 26)

Hall, Henry; heirs John, Magdalen; 8 Nov 1725 (GB 22); [Ed. - of AA]

Hall, Francis; wife Dorothy; 20 May 1729 (PGLR M.449)

Hall, Benjamin; m. 9 Dec 1731 Sophia Welsh; child: John, b. 30 Nov 1732 (QAP m/5; b/26)

Hall, James; 9 Oct 1733; [no relations] (MCW VII.45); 25 Oct 1733 (I 17.506); heirs none; 27 Sep 1734 (AA 12.627)

Hall, Henry; m. Elizabeth Lansdale [possibly 1734] (QAP m/6)

Hall, Joseph; m. 30 Apr 1735 Mary Tippin (QAP m/6)

Hall, Edward; 4 Dec 1741; 11 Jan 1741; wife Mary; dau. Ann; unborn child; tract *Parrot's Thicket* (MCW VIII.154); extx. Mary; 10 Jan 1742 (I 27.281); extx. Mary; 13 May 1742 (I 26.537); widow Mary; 18 May 1743 (AA 19.380); extx. Mary Sprigg [w/o Col. Edward]; 17 May 1745 (AA 21.244); extx. Mary Sprigg [w/o Col. Edward]; 13 Apr 1750 (AA 28.21)

Hall, William; planter; 24 Dec 1742 (I 27.26); 24 Mar 1742 (AA 19.364)

Hall, William; wife Sarah; child: William, bapt. 23 Aug 1752 (KGP p. 297)

Hall, Thomas; widow Mary; heir William Wheate; [Hall also spelled as Wall]; 30 Mar 1758 (GB 209)

Hall, Benjamin; ex. Sophiah; 2 Nov 1760 (I 76.100, 107)

Hall, Isaac; wife Ruth; 1761 (MCWXII.102)

Hall, John; child: James, bapt. 5 Dec 1762 (KGP p. 329)

Hall, Robert Clarke; wife Elizabeth; child: Verlinder, bapt. 12 Dec 1762 (KGP p. 329)

Hall, Francis; wife Dorothy; her cousin Richard Bennett; 6 Sep 1763 (CCR MSA 10.218)

Hall, Edward; m. 14 Jun 1764 Martha Odell; children: ____ (m), b. ____; ____ (f), b. 4 Jan 1767 (QAP m/7; b/38, 39)

Hall, John; wife Elizabeth; children: Francis Mattox, b. 17 Dec 1771 Broad Creek; Thomas, b. 29 Jul 1774 Broad Creek (KGP p. 377, 386)

Hall, William; wife. Nancy; child: Elizabeth, b. 3 May 1774 Upper Chapel (KGP p. 390)

Hall, William; admx. Ann; 15 Jul 1775 (I 123.124)

Hall, William; wife Ann; children: ____ (m), b. ____; Elizabeth, b. __ May ____; Rachel, b. __ May ____ (QAP b/39)

HALLAM

Hallam, John; wife Mary; tract *St. Andrew's*; 8 Aug 1733 (PGLR Q.678)

Hallum, John; 11 May 1711 (I&A 32b.184); widow Mary Holmeard [w/o James]; 8 Aug 1711 (I&A 32c.31)

HALLEY

Halley, Elizabeth; widow; 26 Jan 1763; 24 Aug 1773; dau. Elizabeth; s-i-l Robert Gordon (MCW XV.97); 14 Sep 1773 (I 117.319)

Halley, Esther; 22 Sep 1761 (I 76.302)

Halley, James Burch; wife Margaret; child: James Burch, b. 29 Aug 1772 Lower Chapel (KGP p. 383)

Halley, John; wife Elizabeth; children: Samuel, b. 23 Mar 1772 Lower Chapel; Aimy, b. 2 Jan 1774; Nathaniel, b. 9 Feb 1776 Lower Chapel Lower Chapel (KGP p. 379. 381, 383)

Halley, William; m. Bathsheba [Shaba] ____; children: Eleanor, b. 21 Mar 1774 Lower Chapel; Samuel, b. 8 Nov 1775 Lower Chapel (KGP p. 379, 381)

Hally, Nathaniel; wife Mary; children: William, b. 19 Jan 1747; Mary Elinor, b. 23 Nov 1752; Elizbeth, b. 12 Aug 1755 (KGP p. 314)

Hally, Thomas; 21 Feb 1769; 17 May 1769; wife Elizabeth; children: John, Samuel, James Burch, Bethsheba, Elizabeth, Sarah Gordon (MCW XIV.94)

HALLING

Halling, William; 15 Feb 1709 (I&A 30.438)

HALLSEY

Hallsey, John; wife Ann; children: Elizabeth, b. 11 Sep 1740; Ann, b. 27 May 1742; Ruth, b. 11 Oct 1745; John, b. 28 Jul 1748 (PGP p. 251, 252)

Halsey, John; wife Anne; 1741/2 (MCW VIII.234)

HALSET

Halset, John; wife Precious; child: William, b. 22 Oct 1762 (PGP p. 267)

HAMBLY

Hambly, John; 21 Oct 1734 (I 20.345); 14 Jul 1735 (I 21.45)

HAMILTON

Hambleton [Hamelton], Gavin; 30 Dec 1698; only son Andrew; 3 daus. [unnamed]; wife [unnamed] (MCW II.168); [with 1698] (I&A 18.54)

Hamilton, Andrew; m/1 Mary ____; children: Garven, b. 4 Nov 1701; Mary, b. 24 Nov 1705; m/2 Mary ____; child: Thomas, b. 21 May 1710 (KGP p. 259)

Hambleton, Andrew; wife Mary; tract *Attwood's Purchase*; 23 Mar 1703 (PGLR C.57a)

Hamilton, Andro; wife Mary; tract *Wheeler's Hope*; 28 Nov 1710 (PGLR F.44)

Hamilton, Andrew; 23 Oct 1718; 24 Jun 1719; wife Mary; unborn child (MCW IV.211); 22 Aug 1719 (I 3.202); 21 Nov 1720 (AA 3.150); 18 Jan 1720 (AA 3.214)

Hambleton, John; 21 Jul 1719 (I 2.214)

Hamilton, James; 18 May 1748 (I 35.529)

Hamilton, George; admx. Mary; 14 Feb 1752 (I 49.49)

Hamilton, Andrew; m. 5 Jan 1750/1 Mary ____; children: Anne, b. 9 Aug 1752; George, b. 7 Aug 1754 (PGP p. 229, 255; KGP p. 306)

Hamilton, Thomas; wife Ann; children: Samuel, bapt. 15 Mar 1752; Andrew, b. 16 Mar 1754 (KGP p. 295, 305)

Hamilton, William; admx. Martha; 26 Feb 1760 (I 69.312); admx. Martha; 24 Jun 1761 (I 75.10)

Hamelton, Andrew; wife Mary; children: Andrew, b. 7 Mar 1763 at Upper Chapel; Elizabeth, bapt. 16 Jun 1765; Walter, bapt. 13 Sep 1767 Upper Chapel Upper Chapel; Jane Evins, b. 24 Jun 1772 Upper Chapel (KGP p. 333, 358, 366, 389)

Hamilton, William; wife Ruth; child: Jemimah, b. 19 Apr 1774 Upper Chapel (KGP p. 390)

HAMPTON
Hampton, Steven; wife Margaret; tract *Rattle Snake Denn*; 14 Aug 1742 (PGLR Y.521)

HANAN
Hanan, Thomas; wife Mary; child: Elizabeth, b. 20 Jul 1755 (KGP p. 311)

HANBY
Hanby, John; 2 daus. [unnamed]; 1 Aug 1735 (AA 13.268)

HANCE
Hance, Francis; 3 Apr 1764; 26 Jul 1764; wife Sarah (MCW XIII.31)

HANCHETT
Hanchett [Hunchett], Edward; 1 Dec 1739 (I 25.94)
Hanchett, Edward; 12 Aug 1742 (AA 19.88)

HANDLY
Handly, Daniel; 5 Mar 1715 (I&A 36c.294)

HANKES
Hankes, William; wife Sarah; child: Fleetwood, b. 19 Jan 1764 (PGP p. 276)

HANN

Hann [Henn], John; 12 Mar 1747; 15 Apr 1748; wife Sarah; son John; daus. Hannah, Elizabeth, Catharine, Sarah (MCW IX.142-3)

HANNAN

Hannan, John; wife Grace; children: John, b. 3 Dec 1763, bapt. 4 Mar 1764 Broad Creek; Walter Warren, bapt. 22 Jan 1766 Broad Creek (KGP p. 353, 356)

HANSON

Hanson, Randolph [CH]; wife Barbara; tracts *Hansontown, Charley*; 18 Nov 1696 (PGLR A.19)

Hanson, John; wife Elizabeth; child: Sarah, bapt. 11 Feb 1753 (KGP p. 298)

HARBEN

Harben, William; wife Alice; children: John, b. 20 Aug 1711; Margaret, b. 20 Apr 1713; Johanna, b. 30 Mar 1716; William, b. 30 May 1718 (QAP b/11, 14)

Harbin, William; wife Alice; children: John, b. 20 Aug 1711; Margaret, b. 20 Apr 1713; Johanna, b. 17 Apr 1715; William, Jr., b. 20 Jun 1717; Elisabeth, b. 5 Jun 1720; Elisha, b. 5 Jun 1722 (PGP p. 247-8)

Harbin [Harben], William; yeoman; 25 Mar 1733; 14 May 1733; wife Mary; sons John, William, Elisha, James, Joshua, Edward & William Harben; tract *The Gleaning* (MCW VII.18); heirs John, Margaret, William, Elisha, James, Joshua, Ann, Edward; 23 Mar 1735 (GB 75)

Harbin, Edward; wife Lidia; child: Virlinder, b. 23 Sep 1763 (PGP p. 271)

Harbin, John; wife Elizabeth; child: William, b. 18 Apr 1763 (PGP p. 270)

Harbin, Joshua; m. 1 Mar 1753 Elizabeth Ray; child: John, b. 22 Jan 1765 (PGP p. 229, 278)

Harbin, William; wife Mary; children: Joshua, b. 29 Dec 1726; James, b. 29 Dec 1727 (PGP p. 247-8)

HARBERT

Harbert, James; admx. Elenor; 24 Mar 1741 (I 26.496); widow Hannah Pretchel [w/o William]; 4 children: William, Alice, Ann & Leonard Harbert; 25 Jun 1744 (AA 20.448); heirs William, Dulick, Ann, Lenny; 25 Nov 1745 (GB 145)

Harbert, William; age 18 on 18 Mar next; chooses Alexander Harbert as guardian; Jun 1742 (PGCR AA.3)

HARDESTY

Hardesty, Francis; wife Elseh; child: Francis, b. 26 Dec 1734 (QAP b/28)

HARDICK

Hardick, Sarah; age ca 11; servant; Jun 1701 (PGCR B.113a)

HARDING

Hardin, Thomas; one year old; bound out Jun 1710 (PGCR D.318)

Harding, John; wife Elizabeth; children: Charles, b. 26 9ber 1711; Elizabeth, b. 28 8ber 1713; Mary, b. 8 7ber 1715; John, b. 29 Apr 1718 (QAP b/5, 9. 11, 13)

Harding, John; wife Eliza.; children: John, b. 29 Apr 1718; Edward Solluck, b. 20 Jun 1720; Lewis, b. 20 Apr 1722; Lucy, b. 14 Oct 1724; Elias, b. 4 Jul 1728; Grove, b. 1 Sep 1729 (PGP p. 247-8)

Harding, Charles; wife Elliner; children: Vachel, b. 7 Feb 1763; Benjamin, b. 23 Jan 1765 (PGP p. 269, 273)

HARDY

Hardie, George; m. 4 Oct 1719 Elizabeth Drayen [?Drane]; children: William, b. 8 Aug 1720 [d. 11 Aug 1720]; William, b. 7 Apr 1722; George, b. 7 Mar 1723; Elizabeth, b. 27 Dec 1726; ____ (f), b. 27 Feb 1729; ____ (m), b. 23 Jul 1732 (KGP p. 262, 283)

Hardie, William; children: George, b. 2 Jan 1717; William, b. 9 Feb 1720; Henry, b. __ Apr 1722; Mary Ann, b. 27 Jun 1727 (KGP p. 282)

Hardy [Harding, Hardee], Isaac; wife Mary; tract Hardy's Purchase; 26 Jun 1728 (PGLR M.296)

Hardy, William; wife Ann; son George; 24 Jul 1730; tract His Lordship's Kindness (PGLR Q.75)

Hardee, John; wife Barbary; tract Brotherhood; 28 Aug 1731 (PGLR Q.336)

Hardy, Robert; wife Mary; tract Three Brothers; 20 Mar 1739 (PGLR Y.157)

Hardey, William; planter; 8 Aug 1740; 16 Aug 1740; sons George, Benjamin, Solomon, William, Henry; daus. Rachel, Elizabeth, Mary Ann; bro. George (MCW VIII.96); 24 Nov 1740 (I 27.272); 21 Mar 1742 (AA 19.361)

Hardey, George; m. 11 Feb 1753 Miss Lucy Dent; children: Ann, b. 9 Dec 1753; Thomas, b. 11 Aug 1755; Mary, b. 2 Nov 1757; George Dent, b. 15 Mar 1762; Elizabeth Burrell, b. 2 Apr 1764, bapt. 8 Apr 1764; Richard, b. Nov, bapt. 17 Nov 1765; Harrey, b. 22 Jul 1768; bapt. 7 Aug 1768; Letta, b. 23 Jun 1770 Broad Creek (KGP p. 316, 374)

Hardy, Ignatious; wife Rebecca; children: Baptist, b. 16 Jul 1753; Elizabeth, b. 17 Oct 1755; John, b. 28 Apr 1759; Susanah, b. _ ___ 1762; Jessey, b. ____; Rebecca, b. ____; Ammey, b. ____ (KGP p. 300, 313, 320)

Hardy, George, Jr.; wife Lucy; child: Ann, b. 5 Nov 1753; had rites of the church 22 Sep 1754 (KGP p. 306)

Hardy, John; wife Ann; child: John, b. 12 Nov 1753 (PGP p. 256)

Hardy, George; 18 Sep 1757; 13 Feb 1758; wife Elizabeth; sons George, Henry; daus. Elizabeth Hardy Wilcoxon, Mary Wade; grandsons George Hardy [s/o William, dec'd], Benedict Hardy; niece Elizabeth Hardy; nephew Solomon Hardy (MCW XI.198)

Hardy [Hardey], William; admx. Elisabeth, Jr.; 26 Jun 1758 (I 64.439); 5 Oct 1761; admx. Elisabeth Hardy; children [6 unnamed] (ABB 3.109); widow Elizabeth; heirs Virlinda, Anthony, Benedict, Mary, George, Elizabeth Ann; 15 Aug 1762 (GB 234); heirs Virlinda, Anthony, Benedict, Mary, George, Elizabeth Ann; 26 Dec 1763 (GB 233); heirs Benedict, George; 27 Aug 1766 (GB 246)

Hardy, John; wife Amey; child: George, b. 6 Sep 1760 (PGP p. 259)

Hardey, Ignatious; wife Elizabeth; child: Susanah, bapt. 11 Apr 1762 (KGP p. 326)

Hardey, Thomas; wife Daina; child: Thomas, bapt. 19 Dec 1762 (KGP p. 329)

Hardey, John; wife Mary; children: Levoy, b. 24 Mar 1763 at Upper Chapel; Elizabeth, bapt. 13 May 1764; Noah, bapt. 6 Nov 1768 Upper Chapel; Rebeccah, b. 16 Feb 1772 Upper Chapel; Ann, b. 12 Jan 1775 Upper Chapel (KGP p. 332, 372, 389, 391)

Hardie, John; wife Anna; child: Anna, b. 6 Mar 1763 (PGP p. 270)

Hardy, John; wife Mary; children: Elizabeth, bapt. 13 May 1764 Broad Creek; Jonathan, bapt. 31 Aug 1766 Upper Chapel (KGP p. 354-5, 357)

Hardy, George, Jr.; 13 Mar 1772; 25 Jul 1772; wife Lucy; bro. Thomas Dent & Henry Hardy; children: Thomas Dent Hardy, George, Clara, Mary, Elizabeth, Littey; tracts *Pittsburgh, Friends Hazard, Gantry, Boarmans Manor* (MCW XIV.227-8); 3 Jul 1772 (I 112.134); 24 Mar 1773 (I 112.100, 104); 18 Apr 1774; widow [unnamed]; children [unnamed] (ABB 6.315, 335); heirs Elizabeth, George; 27 Mar 1776 (GB 333); heir George; 27 Aug 1776 (GB 337)

Hardy, William; wife Marian; child: George, b. 1 Oct 1772 (PGP p. 278)

Hardey, Thomas; wife Susanna; children: Mary, b. 8 Jan 1773 Broad Creek; Rebecca, bapt. 30 Oct 1774 Upper Chapel (KGP p. 378, 391)

Hardy, Henry; 24 May 1773 (I 112.102)

Hardey, Ignatius; wife Elizabeth; child: Rachel, b. 26 Sep 1773 Upper Chapel (KGP p. 390)

Hardey, Baptist; wife Rachel; children: Henry, b. 16 Oct 1774 Broad Creek; Sarah, b. 5 Apr 1776 Broad Creek (KGP p. 382, 386)

HARE

Hare, William; wife Margritt; children: John Smith, b. 23 Apr 1763; Mary, b. 24 Mar 1766 (PGP p. 268, 278)

HARGEST

Hargest, Hollyday; admx. Sarah Hooke [otherwise Sarah Hargest]; 22 Jul 1727 (I 12.281); dau. Elisabeth; 21 Jan 1728 (AA 9.254); heir Elizabeth; 24 Jun 1729 (GB 46)

HARLENS

Harlens, James; admx. John Burch & wife [unnamed]; 29 Aug 1711 (I&A 32c.148); adms. John Burch & wife Elisabeth; 23 Jun 1713 (I&A 35b.24)

HARN

Harn, Charles; wife Mary; children: Lucy Davis, bapt. 29 Aug 1762; Sharlotta, bapt. 12 Jul 1767 Upper Chapel (KGP p. 332, 366)

HARPER

Harper, Nathaniel; wife Jane; children: John, b. 27 7ber 1711; Jane, b. 28 Feb 1713; Elizabeth, b. 11 9ber 1714, Francis, b. 11 9ber 1719; Elinor, b. 22 Dec 1721 (QAP b/15, 16)

Harper, Francis; wife Mary; child: William, b. 14 Dec 1761 (PGP p. 267)

Harper, William; wife Zella; child: Elizabeth, bapt. 29 Nov 1767 Broad Creek (KGP p. 361)

HARR

Harr, William; m. 7 Feb 1726/7 Mary Cash, d/o John (QAP m/4)

HARRILL

Harrill, William; admx. Elisabeth; 20 Aug 1740 (I 125.286); admx. Elisabeth; 17 Feb 1740 (AA 18.139)

HARRIS

Harris, Jane; servant woman; had bastard mulatto child; Nov 1697 Ct. (PGCR A.262)

Harris, Caleb; son Caleb; Nov 1711 Ct. (PGCR G.166)

Harris, William; wife Anne [d/o John Dorsett, dec'd]; tract *Greenwood*; 1 Mar 1721 (PGLR I.173)

Harris, Thomas (Jr.); wife Sarah; children: Thomas, b. 17 Dec 1726; Mary, b. 20 Jul 1728 (PGP p. 247-8, 249)

Harris, Thomas; planter; 24 Jan 1726/7; 29 Mar 1727; wife Mary; [step-son] John Greenup (MCW VI.17); admx. Mary Harris; 20 Apr 1727 (I 12.125)

Harris, Thomas, Sr.; planter; 26 Apr 1728; 25 Jun 1728; wife Rachel; sons Samuel, Benjamin (MCW VI.66); admx. Rachell; son Thomas [no other of age]; 2 Aug 1728 (I 13.209); widow Rachel; heirs Thomas, Rachel, Jamima, Rebecca, Ruth, Benjamin, Sarah, Samuel; 25 Jun 1729 (GB 48)

Harris, William; 12 Apr 1730; 23 Jun 1730; wife Ann; sons Joseph, William; dau. Amy; s-i-l [step-son] Thomas Webster (MCW VI.163); admx. Ann; 1 Jul 1730 (I 16.16, 155); admx. Ann; children: Amy, William, Joseph; 24 Mar 1731 (AA 10.692); admx. Ann; children: Ann, William, Joseph; 17 May 1731 (AA 11.104); widow Anne; heirs Amy, William, Joseph; 29 May 1732 (GB 58)

Harris, Thomas; age ca 46; 14 Jun 1745 (CCR JK#4.595)

Harris, Ann [Anne]; 22 Apr 1751; 26 Jun 1751; sons William, Joseph (MCW X.158); 26 Jun 1751 (I 47.291); 27 Nov 1751 (AA 31.253); 27 Nov 1751; exs. William & Joseph Harris (ABB 1.20)

Harris, Benjamin; wife Sarah Ann; children: Hepshabeth (f), b. 2 Jul 1762; Sarah, bapt. 15 Jan 1764; Mildared, bapt. 19 Jan 1766 Lower Chapel; John Alexander, b. 4 Dec 1767, bapt. 24 Jan 1768 Lower Chapel; Benjamin, b. _ Oct 1769 Upper Chapel; Elizabeth, b. 4 Aug 1773 Lower Chapel; Hezekiah, b. 21 Jan 1776 Lower Chapel (KGP p. 331, 344, 352, 368, 372, 381, 384)

Harris, James; wife Eady; child: Basill, b. 27 Mar 1763 at Lower Chapel (KGP p. 335)

Harris, Joseph; 13 Aug 1766 (I 89.305)

Harris, William; wife Susana; children: George Stone, b. 25 Feb 1773 Lower Chapel; James, b. 2 Dec 1775 Lower Chapel (KGP p. 381, 384)

Harris, John; wife Winefred; child: Robert, b. 16 Aug 1774 Lower Chapel (KGP p. 380)

Harris, James, planter; 25 Jun 1775; 23 Aug 1775; wife Edy; children: Josias, Edy, James, Basil, William, John, Elizabeth; grandson Bartin Harris [s/o William] (MCW XVI.73); 30 Aug 1775 (I 123.231); 12 Aug 1776; widow [unnamed]; children: Josias, Eddy, James, Basil (ABB 7.53)

Harris, John, Sr.; 2 Sep 1775; 21 Dec 1776; children: Benjamin, James [dec'd], Lydia Steal, John; d-i-l Edy Harris [widow of James];

grandchildren: Ann Owen, Elizabeth Wilson, Mary Burch, Eleanor
Wedding & Sarah Robey [ch/o son John], John Harris Robey, William
Harris; tract *The Ridge* (MCW XVI.168)

HARRISON

Harrison, Joseph [CH]; wife Mary; tract *Berry*; 12 Aug 1707 (PGLR C.199a)

Harrison, Robert; extrx. Anne [widow]; 28 May 1711 (I&A 32c.152)

Harison, Richard [CA]; wife Elizabeth; tract *The Partnership*; 27 Oct 1712
(PGLR F.224)

Harrison, William; wife Mary; child: Eli, b. 8 Sep 1762 (PGP p. 270)

Harrison, Josiah; wife Elizabeth; child: Henry, b. 30 Mar 1763 (PGP p. 270)

Harrison, Benjamin; wife Alse; child: Josiah Bucy, b. 15 Dec 1764 (PGP p. 273)

HARTLEY

Hartley, ____; wife Susan; child: Elizabeth, b. 30 Jul 1720 (QAP b/27)

HARVEY

Harvy [Harvie], Thomas; 21 Jul 1719 (I 2.218); 5 Sep 1720 (AA 3.208)

Harvey, John; wife Rachell; tract *Dear Bought*; 14 Aug 1730 (PGLR Q.83)

Harvey, Thomas; age ca 16; chooses guardian; Nov 1739 (PGCR X.496)

Harvy, Thomas; wife Elinor; child: Henry, b. 1 Oct 1755 (KGP p. 312)

Harvy, William; wife Mary; child: Elizabeth, b. 9 Feb 1755 (KGP p. 307)

Harvey, John; planter; 6 Feb 1764; 29 Mar 1764; wife Rachel (MCW XIII.14);
extx. Rachel; 28 May 1764 (I 84.159)

Harvey, Samuel; wife Elizabeth; children: Sarah, b. 6 Jun 1764 at Broad
Creek; Samuel, bapt. 19 Apr 1767 Upper Chapel (KGP p. 365)

Harvey, Richard; wife Elizabeth; Richard, b. 2 Oct 1764 (PGP p. 272)

Harvey, James; wife Mary Ann; children: George, b. 29 Jan 1773 Broad
Creek; Elizabeth, b. 25 Dec 1774 Broad Creek (KGP p. 378, 86)

HARVIN

Harvin, William; wife Stacy; child: Sarah, bapt. 10 Dec 1752 (KGP p. 297)

Harvin, Antoney; wife Ann; child: Edward, b. 22 May 1764 Upper Chapel
or Broad Creek (KGP p. 342)

HARWELL

Harwell, John, Dr.; _ Mar 1752 (I 49.42)

HARWOOD

Harwood, Samuell; 21 Jun 1704 (I&A 3.507)

Harwood, Thomas; wife Sarah; children: Elizabeth, b. 24 May 1719; Thomas, b. 28 8ber 1720; Richard, b. 8 9ber 1722; John, b. 10 7ber 1724; Thomas, b. 8 10ber 1726; John, b. 31 Jan 1728/9; Mary, b. 23 Jan 173_; Jeremiah, b. 23 Dec 1732 (QAP b/15, 16, 17 19, 21, 24, 26)

Harwood, Maj. Thomas, Sr.; 25 Jan 1760; 27 Sep 1770; wife Sarah; children: Benjamin, Richard, Thomas, Mary Watkins, Sarah; grandson Thomas Harwood [s/o Thomas], Richard Watkins [s/o Mary]; tract *Basonthrop Hall* (MCW XIV.158)

HASTINGS
Hastings, John; age ca 21; servant; Mar 1713 (PGCR G.292)

HASWELL
Haswell, John, surgeon; 12 Nov 1746; 11 Apr 1750; wife Sarah; tracts *The Brotherhood, The William and Mary Increased* (MCW X.87); extx. Sarah; 31 May 1750 (I 48.226); extx. Sarah; 18 May 1752 (AA 32.362)

Haswel, William; m. Rebecca; children: Sarah, bapt. 1 Dec 1751; Samson, b. 2 Dec 1753; Benoni, b. 27 May 1759 (KGP p. 294, 304, 321)

Haswell, Sarah; 22 May 1755; 28 Nov 1761; sons Joseph Beall, John Beall, Nathaniel, James; daus. Margarett, Sarah; granddaus. Charity [d/o James], Margarett [d/o John]; grandson. John [s/o John]; great-grandchildren: James & Sarah Williams (MCW XII.97); son Nathaniel Beall; grandson James Odell; 12 Oct 1762 (I 79.229)

HATHEY
Hathey, Benjamin; wife Eadey; child: Barbery, bapt. 2 Oct 1768 Lower Chapel (KGP p. 371)

HATTON
Hatton, William; 26 Dec 1711; 4 Aug 1712; wife Mary; dau. Penelope Middleton; son Joseph; grandchildren: Hatton & Mary Middleton; tracts *Thompson's Rest, Rich Hill* (MCW III.228); widow Mary; 21 Aug 1712 (I&A 33b.205); mentions Mrs. Mary Hatton; 17 Aug 1713 (I&A 35b.26); 10 Sep 1715 (I&A 36c.30)

Hatton, Joseph, s/o William Hatton, d. 2 Aug 1713; m. 17 Oct 1710 Lucy Marbury, d/o Francis Marbury; children: Mary, b. 19 Apr 1713; Mary, b. 25 Dec 1715; William, b. 13 Apr 1718; Joseph, b. 3 Jun 1721; Nathaniel, b. 3 Mar 1723; Richard, b. 2 Aug 1726; Elizabeth Penalipy, b. 16 ___ 172_; John, b. 9 Aug 173_ (KGP p. 259, 271, 274, 284)

Hatton, Mary; 6 Sep 1730; 13 Oct 1731; son Joseph; dau. Penelope Middleton; g/s Thomas & Hatton Middleton; granddaus. Sarah, Elizabeth, Elenar & Susana Middleton; great-granddaus. Penelope Hatton Middleton; sister Sarah Copping; cous. Abraham Alloy (MCW VI.198); grandson Thomas Middleton; granddau. Mary Hatton; 7 Feb 1731 (I 16.391); underage heirs Sarah, Elisabeth, Eleanor & Susanna Middleton; legatees Thomas, Jr. & Hatton Middleton; Barbary Frazer [w/o Daniel]; 8 Dec 1732 (AA 11.565; 12.23); heirs Sarah, Elizabeth, Eleanor & Susannah Middleton; 25 Mar 1735 (GB 66)

Hatton, Joseph; 1 Dec 1737; 14 Nov 1747; wife Lucy; father William; mother Mary; Penelope; daus. Mary, Elizabeth; Joseph, Nathaniel, Richard, Joshua (MCW IX.123); extx. Lucy; 25 Feb 1747 (I 35.494); extx. Lucy [widow]; children: Joseph, Mary, Nathaniel, Elisabeth, Richard, John [under age]; 1 Mar 1748 (AA 26.27)

Hatton, Joseph; age ca 52; 1743 (PGLR Y.657)

Hatton, Joseph; wife Mary; children: Cordele Meeks (f), bapt. 12 Jul 1752; Henry, b. 6 Feb 1755; Josiah, b. 1 Jul 1757 (KGP p. 297, 307, 320)

HAVIGAL

Havigal, Nathaniel; wife Sarah; child: Mary, b. 23 Feb 1756 (KGP p. 312)

HAWK

Hawk, William; child: Ann, b. ___ (QAP b/33)

HAWKER

Hawker, Ambros Cook; wife Lidie; children: Prisillah, b. 20 Jun 1760; Darcus, b. 10 Feb 1762 (PGP p. 259, 263)

HAWKINS

Hawkins, John; wife Elizabeth; tract *Thomases Chance*; 20 Jan 1699 (PGLR A.194)

Hawkins, John; 7 Jul 1705 (I&A 3.701); 26 Mar 1707(I&A 27.88, 136)

Hawkins, John; wife Elizabeth; child: John, b. 15 Aug 1713 (KGP p. 261), m. 17 Feb 1731 Susannah Fraser; children: Giles Bliszard, b. 27 Nov 1732; John Stone, b. 18 Jul 1734; Ann Fraser, b. 3 Oct 1736; d. 30 Jun 1738 (KGP p. 261)

Hawkins, James; age 14 on 7 Mar last past; Jun 1715 (PGCR G.764)

Hawkins, William; wife Mary [dec'd d/o Thomas Middleton]; son Thomas; tract *Long Point*; 26 Mar 1729 (PGLR M.399)

Hawkins, John, Sr.; wife Elizabeth; son John, Jr.; tracts *Hawkins Lott, Something*; 15 Apr 1733 (PGLR T.118)

Hawkins, John, Jr.; 23 Jan 1757; 28 Jun 1757; wife Priscilla; daus. Elizabeth Lawrence Hawkins, Susannah Fraser Hawkins; sons Alexander Thomas, John Stone, George Fraser; children-in-law [?step-children] Rebecca Mackall, Levin Covington; parents John & Elizabeth Hawkins; tracts *Contention, Bealls and Magruders Honesty, Never Fear, By Chance, Forest Needwood, Hawkins Plains, Hawkins Merry Peep A Day, Hazard, John and Priscilla, Hawkins Clover Bottom, Duke's Delight* (MCW XI.174); extx. Pricilla; 13 Dec 1758 (I 67.101)

Hawkins, John; 26 Jan 1758; 12 Sep 1772; wife Elizabeth; grandsons John Stone Hawkins, George Fraser Hawkins, Alexander Thomas Hawkins; granddaus. Elizabeth Lawrence Hawkins, Susanna Fraser Hawkins (MCW XIV.240)

Hawkins, John; wife Rebeccah; children: Elizabeth, b. 18 Apr 1774 Lower Chapel; Susanna, b. 21 Jan 1776 Lower Chapel (KGP p. 379, 381)

Hawkins, William; m. 13 May ____ Sarah Noble; children: Noble, b. 28 ___ 17__; d. 4 Mar 1750; James, b. 25 Oct ____; Mary Ellenor, b. 17 N__ 1730 (KGP p. 284)

Hawkins, William; planter; ____ 1745; 9 Nov 1751; sons Noble, James, John, William, Thomas, Samuel; dau. Mary Eleanor; bro. John Hawkins, Sr.; tracts *Stone's Delight, Comptons Treatment, DeCregoes Lott* (MCW X.185); 2 Jan 1752 (I 48.231); admn. James 22 Nov 1752 (ABB 1.59); admn. James Hawkins; children: Thomas [of age], John [age 14], William [age 12], Samuel [age 10]; 22 Nov 1752 (ABB 1.63); 20 Aug 1753; admn. James Hawkins; children: Mary, Eleanor, John & William Hawkins (ABB 1.87); children: Mary, Eleanor, John, William; 20 Aug 1753 (AA 35.54); children: Thomas, James, Mary, Elianor [all of age]; John [age 14], William [age 12], Samuel [age 10]; 22 Nov 1752 (AA 33.285); heirs John & William Hawkins, Peter Dent, Jr.; 30 Aug 1753 (GB 187)

Hawkins, John Stone; 25 Nov 1763; 21 Jan 1764; child Susanna Priscilla; father John, Jr.; bros. George Fraser Hawkins, Alexander Thomas Hawkins; sisters Elizabeth Lawrence Hawkins, Susanna Fraser Hawkins; uncle George Fraser; tracts *Grandfather's Gift, Hawkins* (MCW XIII.13); 19 Mar 1764 (I 83.158, 159); 20 Aug 1764 (I 84.343, 344); 14 Feb 1765 (I 86.181); heirs Susanna Priscilla, Elizabeth; 26 Mar 1767 (GB 251); heirs, Susannah, Elizabeth; 28 Mar 1771 (GB 293); Susanna Priscilla & Elizabeth Ann; minors; guardian Allen Bowie; tract *Hawkins Lott*; 25 Mar 1772 (GB 304)

Hawkins, Elizabeth; 26 Apr 1772; 16 Nov 1772; grandchildren: John Stone [dec'd], George Frasier, Alexander Thomas & Elizabeth Lawrence

Hawkins, Susannah Frasier Raley; great-grandchildren: John Trueman Hawkins & daus. [unnamed] of John Stone Hawkins (MCW XV.4-5); 12 Dec 1772 (I 121.368)

Hawkins, John Stone; child: Susanna Priscilla Hawkins; 1776 (MCW XVI.186)

HAWLIN

Hawlin, William; sister Hester Thacker [w/o Samuell]; 2 children: William [admn.], Hester Thacker [w/o Samuel]; 16 Jul 1711 (I&A 32c.152)

HAYMOND

Haymond, John; m. 22 Aug 1723 Margaret Calder; children: Mary, b. 16 Jun 1724; Hannah, 21 Mar 1726/7; Nicholas, b. 4 Jan 1729 (QAP m/3; b. 18, 20, 23)

Haymond, John; wife Margareat; children: Ann, b. 25 Sep 173_; Calder, b. 15 May 1733; William, b. 4 Jan 1739 (PGP p. 253)

Haymond, Caldar; wife Ellener [Elline]; children: Thomas Owen, b. 24 Aug 1761; Sabra, b. 21 Dec 1765 (PGP p. 261, 277)

Haymond, William; wife Cassandra; children: William, b. 14 May 1764; John, b. 7 Dec 1765 (PGP p. 271, 277)

HAYS

Hay, Charles; 14 May 1693 (I&A 16.105)

Hays, Charles; admx. Mary Johnson [w/o Thomas]; 28 Nov 1699 (I&A 19. 1/2b.5); admx. Thomas Johnson & wife Mary; 27 Jan 1701 (I&A 21.336)

Hay, John; wife Sarah; child: Robert, b. 5 9ber 1725 (QAP b/19)

Hay, Robert; age 9 on 15 Nov last; bound out; Jun 1735 (PGCR V.401)

Hays, Thomas; bros. & sis. [unnamed]; 30 Aug 1744 (AA 20.450)

Hays [?Huys], Nathaniel; 21 Aug 1746 (I 35.122); heirs [siblings] Charles, Jeremiah & William Hays, Mary Bursey; 24 Jun 1747 (AA 23.340)

Heays, Thomas; wife Eadey; child: Elizabeth, bapt. 31 May 1767 Upper Chapel (KGP p. 365)

Hays, Thomas; wife Edith; child: Verlinder, b. 12 Jan 1773 Upper Chapel (KGP p. 389)

HAYWARD

Hayward, William [AA]; wife Mary; tract *Lundee*; 28 Mar 1739 (PGLR T.716)

HEAD

Head, William; wife Ann; children: Ann, b. 4 9ber 1711; Katherine, b. 14 Jan 1712/3; John, b. 21 May 1714; Charity, b. 14 Jun 1717 (QAP b/5, 8, 10, 13)

Head, William; 14 Jun 1718; 5 Jun 1719; wife Ann; son Bigger; daus. Mary, Ann, Katherine, Charity; unborn child; tracts *William and Ann, Red House* (MCW IV.207); 15 Aug 1719 (I 2.230); extx. Ann; 16 Nov 1719 (AA 2.485)

Head, Bigger; heir of Kendall Head; tract *Beall's Chance*; 9 Nov 1722 (PGLR I.348)

Head, Bigger; wife Martha; tract *Brook Grove*; 6 May 1724 (PGLR I.548)

HEARBEN

Hearben, John; wife Ann; bro. William [wife Elizabeth]; tract *Gleaning*; 27 Jun 1739 (PGLR Y.47)

HEARNE

Hearne, Elizabeth; age ca 3 last Mar; d/o Grace; bound out; Sep 1704 (PGCR B.329)

HEDERICK

Hederick, Robert; wife Mary; children: Anthony, bapt. 1 Dec 1751; Ellinder, b. 8 Mar 1756; Thomas & Robert, b. 9 Jun 1758; Virlinder, b. Jan 1761; Cloea, b. 18 Feb 1763; Sushannah, bapt. 9 Sep 1764 at Broad Creek; Mary, b. 26 Sep 1765 Broad Creek; Peache, bapt. 3 Apr 1768 Broad Creek (KGP p. 294, 312, 318, 319, 330, 339, 349, 362); [Mary's last name written as Kedrick by Mrs. Harrison]

HEDGES

Hedges, Joseph; *Manaquicy*; 6 Sep 1732; 29 Nov 1732; wife [unnamed]; sons Solomon, Charles, Joshua, Jonas, Joseph, Samuel; daus. Ruth, Cathren, Dorcas; tract *Manaquicy* (MCW VI.236); 17 Feb 1732 (I 17.67)

Hedges, Solomon [VA]; wife Rebecka; tract *Hedg"s Delight*; 8 May 1740 (PGLR Y.170)

Hedges, William, farmer; 11 Aug 1742; 29 Jan 1742; wife Ann; son Joseph; 2 daus. [unnamed]; unborn child (MCW VIII.191); admx. widow Ann Julian [w/o Stephen]; 6 Mar 1743 (I 30.210); 23 Nov 1747 (I 35.316); admx. Ann Julian [w/o Stephen]; 12 Jun 1747 (AA 23.339)

Hedges, Andrew; 13 Mar 1747; 2 May 1748; wife Mary; sons Thomas, Andrew; bros. Peter, Joseph (MCW IX.149); 7 May 1748 (I 35.518)

HEGER

Heger, Catherine; sons George, Vallentine, Jacob; 27 Aug 1740 (PGLR Y.200)

HELLEM

Hellem, John; wife Katharine; child: Sarah, b. 28 Jul 1774 Upper Chapel (KGP p. 391)

HELLON

Hellon, Simon; age ca 13; Nov 1703 Ct. (PGCR B.262a)

HENDERSON

Henderson, Jacob; wife Mary [widow of Henry Ridgely, Sr.]; tract *Catton*; 21 May 1719 (PGLR F.163/745)

Henderson, Jacob; age ca 58; 1742 (PGLR Y.654); age ca 60; 29 May 1745 (CCR JK#4.592)

Henderson, Jacob; Rector of Queen Anne Parish; 4 Aug 1751; 26 Oct 1751; wife Mary; wife's nephew Robert Tyler [s/o Robert]; wife's niece Mary Tyler [d/o Robert]; sister Mary Thompson [w/o Thomas]; mother ____ Harrison [w/o John] and their children in Ireland; tracts *Duckett's Hope, Jacob's Addition, Ridge* (MCW X.185); 19 Nov 1752 (I 56.19); extx. Mary; 30 Nov 1753 (AA 35.323)

Henderson, Mary; widow of Rev. Jacob Henderson; 2 Oct 1761; 18 Feb 1762; ds-i-l Mary Whitehead, Susannah Lamar, Pricilla Wickham; ?grandson Robert Tyler [s/o Robert, dec'd]; nephew Daniel Stanton [s/o bro. Daniel] (MCW XII.102); 20 Feb 1762 (I 80.309); 20 Apr 1765 (I 87.132); 28 May 1765; ds-i-l Mary Whitehead, Susannah Lamar, Piscilla Wickham; grandson Robert Tyler [s/o Robert dec'd]; nephew Daniel Stanton [s/o bro. Daniel] (ABB 4.97)

Henderson, Richard of Bladensburgh, Prince George's Co., merchant, 3rd s/o Rev. Mr. Richard Henderson, minister of the Parish of Blantyre, Lanerk Shire in Scotland, and Janet Cleland; m. 19 Nov 1761 Sarah Brice, 2nd d/o John Brice of Annapolis; children: Richard, b. 1 Nov 1762; Sarah, b. 15 May 1764; Janet, b. 2 Sep 1765; Ariana, b. 20 Dec 1766 Upper Chapel (KGP p. 355-6)

HENEBERRY

Heneberry, Edward; age ca 46; 19 Mar 1728/9 (PGLR M.478)

HENLEY

Henley, Denis; age 19 months; bound out 'to learn the Art of a Lawyer'; Jun 1715 (PGCR G.764)

Henley, Elizabeth; age 7 on 'Twelfe Day last'; d/o Daniel Henley; mother Mary Cole; bound out; Mar 1716 (PGCR H.33)

Henly, Mary; bound out; Nov 1720 (PGCR K.11)

HENN

Henn, John; _ Apr 1748 (I 36.241, 247)

HENNIS

Hennis, David; wife Alice; children: Mary, b. 2 9ber 1698; Martha, b. 27 Jul 1704; Ann b. 1 Jul 1707; Samuel, b. 16 Mar 1710; Martha, b. 16 Jun 1713 (QAP b/1,2,3,11,12)

Hennis, David; wife Mary; child: David, b. 27 Sep 1701 (QAP b/1)

Hennis, David; wife Sarah; child: David, b. 14 Feb 1728/9 (QAP b/22)

Hennis, David; 1 May 1740 (I 27.268); _ May 1740 (I 30.76); planter; 16 Nov 1744 (AA 20534)

HENRIETTA

Henrietta; age ca 10 months; parents unknown; bound to John Peacock and wife Mary; Nov 1747 (PGCR GG.268)

HENRY

Henry, John; age ca 60; 20 Mar 1715 (CCR CL.273)

Henry, John; age ca 76; 8 Feb 1725 (PGLR M.63)

Henry, John; d-i-l Alice Indose; 1726 (MCW V.232)

Henry, John; age 13 years next Nov; bound out; Mar 1728 (PGCR O.16)

Henry, Moses; age ca 6 years on 27 Mar instant; s/o James Henry; bound out; Mar 1728 (PGCR O.331)

Henery, John; wife Isabelle; 13 May 1729 (PGLR M.429)

Henry, John; 7 Apr 1739; 26 Jun 1739; wife Isable; daus. Eleanar Ellison, Christian Tawnihill, Barbary Hardin; granddau. Jemima Lewces (MCW VIII.42); extx. Isabel; 6 Jul 1739 (I 24.291); extx. Isabell; 17 Aug 1742 (AA 19.87)

Henry, John; wife Martha; child: Priscilla, bapt. 19 Apr 1767 Upper Chapel (KGP p. 365)

HENSON

Henson, William; children: Samuel, Mary, Elianor; 15 Sep 1750 (AA 29.1); 6 Jun 1753 (AA 34.133)

HENWOOD

Henwood, Mary; children: John, b. 29 May 1712; Ruth, b. 23 Aug 1714 and 31 Aug1714; Sarah, b. 18 Dec 1719 (QAP b/12, 16)

Henwood, John; age 3 years on 29 May last past; s/o Mary; bound out; Aug 1715 (PGCR G.786)

HEPBURN

Hepburn, Patrick; to marry Elizabeth Holdsworth [relict of Samuel] [CA]; 15 Oct 1711 (PGLR F.147)

Hepburn, Patrick; admx. Elisabeth; 23 May 1728 (I 13.325); widow Elisabeth [also widow of Samuel Holdsworth of Calvert Co.]; 20 Feb 1729 (AA 10.190); [as Dr. Patrick]; widow Elisabeth; 17 Nov 1730 (AA 10.583)

Hepburn, Hepburn, Elizabeth; relict of Patrick Hepburn; 4 Feb 1734; 30 May 1735; dau. Elizabeth Beall; granddau. Mary Wilson, Elizabeth Scott; d-i-l Margaret Dick; ss-i-l John Hepburn, ?George Scott; great-grandson Lingan Wilson [s/o Lingan] (MCW VII.136)

Hepburn, John, Jr.; 30 Mar 1774; 1 Jun 1774; wife Henrietta Maria; bro. Samuel Chew Hepburn; father John; child John (MCW XV.177); 29 Aug 1774 (I 118.256; 119.102, 112); 4 Sep 1773?; 11 Sep 1775 (I 123.236, 237); heir John; 14 Dec 1775 (GB 332)

Hepburn, John; 6 Mar 1775; 20 Sep 1775; son Samuel Chew Hepburn; dau. Ann Leeke; grandson John Hepburn tracts *John and Mary's Chance, Upper Marlborough, Weymouth, Collington, Lumberland, Maidens Dowry, Grey Eagles, Hanover, Hermitage* (MCW XVI.77-8); 28 Dec 1775 (I 122.279, 299)

HERBERT

Herbert, William [CH]; wife Mary; tract *Gods Guift*; 22 May 1696 (PGLR A.372)

Herbert, Alexander; wife Mary [widow of Giles Blizard]; granddau. Mary Fraser; tract *Athellborough*; 21 Jul 1722 (PGLR I.326)

Herbert, James; wife Eleanor; tract *Dunghill*; 10 Aug1724 (PGLR I.577)

Herbert, Alexander; age ca 52; 1730 (PGLR M.556); age ca 60; 25 Sep 1733 (PGLR T.17)

Herbert, Mr. Alexander; d. 11 Sep 1754 (KGP p. 309)

Herbert, Alexander; 13 Apr 1753; 24 Oct 1754; grandsons Herbert, William, Alexander & James Wallace; granddau. Elinor Hopkins [w/o John]; tracts *Exchange, The New Exchange Enlarged* (MCW XI.54); 20 Jan 1755 (I 60.140)

HERDMAN

Herdman, Margaret; age ca 16; servant; Mar 1713 (PGCR G.292)

HESSILIUS

Hessilius, Gustavus; wife Lydia; child: Elizabeth, b. 8 Jun 1724 (QAP b/18)

HESTER

Hester, William; m. 24 10ber 1728 Zipporah Duvall, d/o Maren Duvall; child: Mary, b. 20 Sep 1729 (QAP m/5; b/23)

HEYSTEHEART

Heysteheart, Anna Catherina [age 6 this 28 Mar 1723], John Jacob [age 12 on 25 Nov last] and John Lodewick [age 8 on 14 Feb last]; Mar 1723 (PGCR A.343)

HICKS

Hicks, Nathaniel; adm. John Queen; wife Margrett [extx. of Henry Robince]; 3 Jan 1712 (I&A 33b.176)

HIGDON

Higdon, Benjamin; wife Ann; children: Elenor Downing, bapt. 3 Mar 1765 Broad Creek; Benjamin Downing, b. 8 Oct 1775 Lower Chapel (KGP p. 346, 381)

HIGGINBOTHAM

Higginbotham, Charles; Capt.; wife Margaret; tract *Dutch Folly*; 27 Mar 1740 (PGLR Y.144)

HIGGINS

Higgins, John; wife Sarah; children: Ann, b. 20 Jun 1729; James, b. 17 Nov 1733 (QAP b/23, 27)

Higgins, James; wife Susanah; children: Sarah, b. 29 Aug 1761; Ann, b. 1 Jul 1764 (PGP p. 262, 274)

Higgins, William; admx. Susannah; 1 Jun 1775 (I 123.171); 22 Jul 1776; admx. Mrs. Susanna Higgins; only child [unnamed] (ABB 7.53)

HILL

Hill, Eliabeth; son Richard, age 8 in Sep next; Jun 1697 Ct. (PGCR A.162)

Hill, Thomas; extx. Hannah Goff [w/o Thomas]; 29 May 1699 (I&A 19-1/2b.4)

Hill, John; wife Mary [lately Mary Wallis, widow]; Oct 1699 Ct. (PGCR A.495)

Hill, William; wife Sarah [admx. of William Willson, dec'd]; Mar 1701 (PGCR B.95a)

Hill, Thomas; 15 Dec 1701 (I&A 21.386)

Hill, Clement; wife Anne; tract *Swaringen* formerly *Hill's Choice*; 28 Mar 1705 (PGLR C.129a)

Hill, Jonathan; wife Elizabeth; child: Elizabeth, b. 18 May 1705 (QAP b/2)

Hill, William; 30 Dec 1710; 19 Jan 1710; wife Susannah; 4 children [unnamed]; wife's son John Page; s-i-l [?John] Wilson (MCW III.189); admx. Susannah [widow]; 7 Jul 1711 (I&A 32b.180); extx. Susannah; 23 Aug 1711 (I&A 32c.154)

Hill, Elizabeth [age 12 on 6 Jan next] and Mary [age ca 4]; orphans of William and Sarah Hill; bound out; Mar 1711 (PGCR G.43)

Hill, John; 7 Mar 1711 (I&A 33a.114); 3 Apr 1711 (I&A 32b.179)

Hill, Clement; son Clement, Jr.; 8 Jul 1720 (PGLR M.497)

Hill, Clement; dau. Ann; 1722 (MCW V.106)

Hill, James; m. 22 Oct 1723; Eliza. Clark (QAP m/3)

Hill, Clement; age ca 54; 23 Feb 1724 (PGLR I.624); age ca 56; 22 Jun 1727 (PGLR M.217); age ca 57; 20 May 1728 (PGLR M.291); age 63; 1734 (PGLR T.202); Clement, Sr.; age ca 66; 2 Apr 1736 (CCR-MSA 6.159)

Hill, James; m. Elizabeth; children: Margaret, b. 6 Jun 1726; William D., b. 14 Jul 1728 (PGP p. 247-8)

Hill, Clement; son Henry; 6 Feb 1728/9 (PGLR M.433)

Hill, Thomas; 14 Feb 1732 (I 17.66); heirs none; 21 Jan 1734 (AA 13.2b)

Hill, Richard, Dr. [AA]; wife Deborah; 16 May 1737 (PGLR T.476)

Hill, Clement; 10 Jan 1742; 25 Aug 1743; wife Ann; sons John, Henry, Clement; daus. Elinor Holliday; grandson Clement [s/o Henry]; granddaus. Sarah, Millicent, Elinor & Mary Bradley; tracts *Baltimore, The Forrest, Hills Camp, Barrett's Purchase, Bread and Cheese, Spy Park* (MCW VIII.227); 28 Dec 1743 (I 29.37)

Hill, John; wife Margret; child: Thomas, bapt. 12 Dec 1762 (KGP p. 329)

HILLEARY

Hillary, Thomas [dec'd] [CA]; widow Elinor; son Thomas; tract *Three Sisters*; 17 Nov 1707 (PGLR C.206)

Hilleary, Thomas; wife Ellinor; children: Elizabeth, b. 7 9ber 1716; Henry, b. 15 Feb 1726/7 (QAP b/12, 20)

Hilleary, Thomas, Jr.; m. 9 Nov 1727 Sarah Odill; children: Ellinor, b. 20 7ber 1728; Thomas, b. 16 or 19 Feb 1729/30; Thomas, b. 9 Aug 1731; Sarah, b. 10 Nov 1733; Verlinda, b. 4 Mar 1735 (QAP m/4; b/21, 27, 29)

Hilleary [Hillary, Hilleray], Thomas; ___ 1728; 14 Feb 1728/9; wife Elianor; sons Thomas, John, William, Henry; nephew Thomas Williams; daus. Sarah, Elizabeth, Elianor; tracts *The Three Sisters* (MCW VI.93); extx. Eleanor; 5 Aug 1729 (I 14.257); extx. Elianor; 5 Aug 1729 (AA 9.425); extx. Elinor; 6 children: John, Sarah, William, Elisabeth, Elinor, Henry; 16 Jul 1730 (AA 10.362); [unnamed]; widow Ellenor; heirs Sarah, Elizabeth, Elenor, Henry, John, William; 27 Aug 1730 (GB 54)

Hilleary, John; m. 18 Dec 1735 Margret King (QAP m/6)

Hilleary, Eleanor; 26 Jan 1747 (I 35.375)

Hilleary, Thomas, Jr.; 29 May 1772 (I 109.233)

Hillery, John; wife Mary; child: Eleanor, 2 Sep 1772 Broad Creek (KGP p. 378)

Hillary, Thomas, Jr.; 30 Aug 1775 (I 123236)

HILLYARD

Hillyard, Benjamin; wife Sarah [the widow Sarah Bradford]; tract *Darby Island*; 3 Mar 1729/30 (PGLR M.571)

HILTON

Hilton, Andrew; wife Judith; child: Trueman, bapt. 4 Feb 1753 (KGP p. 298)

Hilton, James; wife Monakey; children: William Cavinet, b. 8 Mar 1756; Trueman, b. 7 Mar 1758; Sarah, bapt. 23 May 1762; James, bapt. 6 May 1764 Broad Creek; Luke, bapt. 15 Jun 1766 Broad Creek (KGP p. 317, 330, 348, 357)

Hilton, John; wife Margret; child: Samuel, bapt. 26 Jan 1766 Broad Creek (KGP p. 352)

Hilton, Samuel; m. Elisabeth Tyler; child: Joanna Edger, b. 3 Jun 1770 Broad Creek; Elizabeth Mary, b. 12 Nov 1774 Lower Chapel (KGP p. 374, 380)

HINE

Hine, Hannah; dau. Mary, age 6 years in Oct next; Sep 1698 Ct. (PGCR A.343)

HINSTON

Hinston, Dorman, b. 2 Oct 1723; John Hinston, b. 16 Apr 1728; [parents unnamed] (KGP p. 280)

Hinton, John; wife Mary; children: John, b. 27 Nov 1730; Francis, b. 21 Feb 17__ (QAP b/24/26)

Hinton, Thomas; wife Mary; 29 Jul 1735 (PGLR T.300)

Hinston, William; [relations VA & Baltimore Co.]; 24 Nov 1749 (I 41.377)

Hinson, John; wife Margaret; child: Elizabeth, b. 13 Apr 1754 (KGP p. 306)

HITCH

Hitch, Christopher, Jr.; wife Rebecca; child: Nathan, bapt. 10 Apr 1768 Upper Chapel (KGP p. 370)

Hitch, Christopher; wife Sushanna; children: Bartholomew, b. 18 Jul 1753; Barton, bapt. 10 Apr 1768 Upper Chapel (KGP p. 300, 369)

HOBBS

Hobbs; Anne [age 10 on 28 Feb last]; Orson and Valentine [twins age 8 years on 10 Sep next]; ch/o Joyce Hobbs; f-i-l James Shields; bound out; 28 Aug 1734 (PGCR V.95)

Hobbs, Thomas; wife Ann; children: Susannah, b. 11 Sep ____; Ann, b. 2 Dec ____; John, b. 1 Nov 174_; ____(f), b. 2 Feb 1756 (QAP b/33, 34, 35, 37)

Hobbs, Vallentine; admx. Rebecca; 7 Sep 1776 (I 124.9)

HOCKER

Hocker, Nicholas; wife Sophia; children: Mary, b. 19 Feb 1713/4; Phillip, b. 15 Jul 1716 (QAP b/9, 13)

HODGES

Hodges, Thomas; wife Charity; children: Thomas, b. 3 9ber 1697; Presotia (f), b. 13 May 1700; John, b. 30 Sep 1702; Charles Ramsey, b. 18 Feb 1704; Charity, b. 5 Aug 1707; Elizabeth, b. 7 May 1710; Sarah, b. 22 Mar 1713 (QAP b/2, 3, 9)

Hoges, Thomas; wife Charrity; son Thomas, age 6 on 3 Nov next; bound out; Nov 1703 (PGCR B.263)

Hodges, Thomas; wife Charity; children: Presosia, Charles Ramsey, Charity; bound out; Aug 1711 Ct. (PGCR G.77, 78)

Hodges, Sarah; age 2 this month; bound out; Mar 1715 (PGCR G.719)

Hodges, Elizabeth; age 5 on 7 May last past; bound out to Thomas and Ann Brasheers; Aug 1715 (PGCR G.785)

Hodges, Benjamin; 11 Feb 1770; 3 Aug 1772; wife Deborah; children: Charles, Thomas, Benjamin, Lucy, Mary, Elizabeth, Walter; unborn child; bro. Charles Ramsey Hodges; tracts *Thropland, Lunda, Coleberts Lott* (MCW XIV.227); extx. Deborah; 1 Dec 1772 (I 112.131, 143)

Hodges, Benjamin Ramsay; heir Charles Clagett Hodges; 30 Nov 1775 (GB 328)

HODGKIN

Hodgkin, Thomas; age 32; 7 Jul 1731 (PGLR Q.525)

Hodgskins, Thomas; son Philip; dau. Lucy; 1756 (I 74.170)

Hodgkin, Ralph; wife Mary; children: Perry Green, b. 10 Oct 1773 Broad Creek; Walter, b. 30 Oct 1775 Broad Creek (KGP p. 385, 387)

Hodgkins, Philip; admx. Rachel; 9 Jun 1774 (I 117.454)

HODGEN

Hogen, Mary; d/o Mary; bound out; Jun 1706 (PGCR C.74)

HOGGARD

Hoggard, Andrew; tailor; 16 Apr 1740; 24 Jun 1740; [no relations] (MCW VIII.95); Andrew; [Scotland]; 11 Aug 1740 (I 25.182); 9 May 1744 (AA 20.165)

HOGGINS

Hoggins, Peter; age ca 55; immigrant; 7 May 1747 (CCR MSA 8.296)

Hoggins, Peter; 30 Jul 1774; 28 Jun 1775; wife Elizabeth; children: Richard, Peter (MCW XVI.72)

HOLDEN

Holden, Richard; 12 May 1731 (I 16.154)

HOLING

Holing, William; m. 3 Aug 1709 Mary ____; children: John, b. 23 Jan 1711; William, b. 11 Oct 1713 (KGP p. 260)

HOLLAND

Holland, Otho; child: Prudence, b. 7 Sep 1719 (QAP b/15)

Holland, James; m. 9 8ber 1729 Amy Simmons; children: Elizabeth, b. 25 Aug 1730; John, b. 23 Dec 1731; Josias, b. 23 Jan 1733/4 (QAP m/5; b/24, 25, 27)

Holland, Thomas; admx. Margrett; 22 Nov 1735 (I 21.190)

Holland, Thomas; admx. Mary; 21 Jan 1735 (I 21.501)

Holland, Margaret; 5 Mar 1745; 1 Dec 1745; sons Richard, Thomas; daus. Elizabeth England, Casandra, Margaret, Isbale (MCW IX.59); _Feb 1745 (I 32.64); 12 Nov 1747 (AA 24.182); 6 children [unnamed]; 16 Nov 1749 (AA 27.183)

Holland, Thomas; widow Margaret [dec'd]; 15 Nov 1749 (AA 27. 181)

Holland, Abraham; wife Asenah; children: Thomas, b. 2 Feb 1762; Reason, b. 24 Apr 1764 (PGP p. 267, 272)

HOLLANDHEAD

Hollandhead, John; wife Hannah; children: Thomas and Jane, b. 30 Aug 1759 (KGP p. 318)

Holinshead, John; wife Sushannah; child: Benjamin, bapt. 4 Jul 1762 (KGP p. 331)

HOLLEY

Holly, John; m. 4 Mar 1712 Hester Birch; both of this parish; child: Thomas, b. 17 Dec 1713 (KGP p. 269)

Holly, William; age 8 on last day of Feb next; bound out; Aug 1729 (PGCR P.133)

Holley, Nathaniel; wife Mary; child: Mary Elinor, b. 21 Nov 1753 (KGP p. 304)

Holly, Thomas; wife Elisabeth; child: Elisabeth, bapt. May-Jul 1761 (KGP p. 323)

Holey, Nathaniel; wife Mary; children: Thomas, b. 23 Aug 1762; Sushannah, bapt. 23 Jun 1765 Lower Chapel (KGP p. 328, 351)

Holley, John; wife Maria; child: Thomas, b. 1 Feb 1763 (PGP p. 269)
Holey, John; wife Elizabeth; child: Thomas, bapt. 9 Feb 1766 Lower
    Chapel; John, bapt. 17 Apr 1768 Lower Chapel (KGP p. 352, 369)
Holley [Halley], Thomas; ex. Elisabeth; 16 Jun 1769 (I 102.32)

HOLLIFIELD
Hollyfield, Joseph; blacksmith; 4 Feb 1763; 30 Aug 1764; wife Alice;
    grandfather Thomas Hollyfield; son Joseph Wyatt; daus. Ann, Elizabeth,
    Mary (MCW XIII.53); admx. Alice Shuback [w/o Richard]; 24 Jun [with 1764]
    (I 87.123)

HOLLOWAY
Holloway, Charles; 18 Mar 1729 (I 15.505

HOLLYDAY
Hollyday, Thomas; wife Mary; Sep 1696 Ct. (PGCR A.44)
Hollyday, Thomas; 20 Feb 1703; sons James, Leonard; dau. Margery; cous.
    William Holliday; mother Ann Skinner; bro. & sis. Thomas and Martha
    Greenfield; tract Billingsley Point, Holliday's Choice (MCW III.1); 12 May
    1703 (I&A 3.577)
Hollyday, James; age 19 years; choses Leonard Hollyday as guardian; Mar
    1716 (PGCR H.32)
Hollyday, Thomas, Col.; 25 Apr 1716 (I&A 37a.4); 28 Apr 1718 (I&A 39a.49)
Hollyday, Leonard; wife Sarah [d/o Thomas Smith of CA]; tract
    Brookefield; 25 Mar 1720 (PGLR F.305/881)
Hollyday, Leonard, Col.; age near 40; 1731 (PGLR Q.523)
Hollyday, Leonard, gent.; 7 Nov 1739; 26 Jun 1741; sons Thomas, Leonard,
    Clement; daus. Elizabeth, Mary; nephew Leonard Covington; bro. James;
    sister Marjory Gantt [w/o Thomas]; b--i-l John Smith; tracts Holydays Will
    Goose Meadow, Crews Meadow, Burnt House, True Man's Acquaintance,
    Buzzard Island, Newells Adventure, Indian Creek, Nottingham (MCW VIII.135);
    30 Jul 1741 (I 26.356); ex. Mrs. Eleanor; 23 Nov 1742 (I 27.268); extx. Mrs.
    Elioner and Mr. Thomas; children: Thomas [accountant], Elisabeth, Mary,
    Leonard, Clement; 25 Nov 1742 (AA 19.315); extx. Eleanor; daus. Elisabeth,
    Mary Waring [w/o Francis]; 23 Sep 1743 (AA 19.475); exs. Eleanor Murray
    [w/o Dr. William of Dorchester Co.]; 22 Aug 1745 (AA 21.399); heir
    Leonard; 29 Aug 1745 (GB 143); heirs Leonard Holliday, Thomas Bradley,
    Thomas Holliday; 28 Nov 1753 (GB 190)
Hollyday, James; wife Sarah; tract Billingsley; 18 May 1741 (PGLR Y.307)

Hollyday, Leonard; chooses guardian; Nov 1744 (PGCR CC.590)

Holliday, Clement; age 16 on 18 Sep next; choses Leonard Holliday as guardian; Nov 1753 (PGCR MM509)

Hollyday, Thomas, gent.; 3 Jan 1767; 28 Jan 1767; wife Anne; bros. Leonard, Clement; sisters Mary Waringe, Elizabeth; nephew Lancelot Richard Thomas Lee; niece Amelia Lee; tracts *Holyday's Wildgoose Meadow, Chew's Meadow, Burnt House, Retaliation Muzoonscoon, Newton* (MCW XIII.172-3); extx. Ann; 6 Apr 1767 (I 91.317); extx. Ann Cook [w/o John]; 27 Oct 1767 (I 100.14)

HOLMEARD

Holmeard, James; wife Elizabeth; 26 Mar 1729 (PGLR M.390)

Holmeard, James, Sr.; wife Elizabeth; son James, Jr.; tract *The Addition*; 22 Jun 1741 (PGLR Y.314)

HOLMES

Holmes, William; wife Mary; child: Edward, b. 21 Jul 1713 (QAP b/9

Holmes, Mary; son John; tract *Troubles*; 5 Mar 1719 (PGLR F.293/872)

Holmes, Edward; age ca 73; 20 Jun 1729 (PGLR M.438)

Holmes, William; wife Mary; tract *Hill's Choice*; 7 Mar 1733 (PGLR T.79)

Holmes, Edward, Sr.; 19 Sep 1736; 1 May 1739; wife Martha; son William; grandson Edward; grandaus. Mary, Sary, Jemima, Varlinday, Rachel & Elizabeth Holmes, Clara Mackeen; tract *Plummer's Pleasure* (MCW VIII.29); 17 Jun 1739 (I 24.193)

Holmes [Holms], William; 27 Oct 1740; 27 Mar 1741; wife Mary; sons Edward, John, William; daus. Mary Brasshear, Clara Mekean, Sarah, Jemima, Vorlinda, Rachel, Elizabeth, Febe; tracts *William and Mary, Wolfes Harbour, Addition of Wolfes Harbour* (MCW VIII.132); 5 Aug 1741 (I 26.201); 11 Nov 1742 (AA 19.204); 6 Jun 1744 (AA 247)

Holmes, John; wife Iszabel; tract *Newfound Land*; 7 Jul 1742 (PGLR Y.503)

HOLT

Holt, Ralph; wife Ann; child: Elizabeth Stimpson, b. 16 Jan 1765 (PGP p. 274)

HOLTON

Holton, John; admx. Elisabeth; 2 Oct 1711 (I&A 32c.151)

HOOK

Hook, Nathanaell; wife [unnamed]; son John [infant]; Jun 1696 Ct. (PGCR A.9)

Hook, Thomas; wife Annabell; Jul 1696 Ct. (PGCR A.11)

Hook, James; wife Margaret; child: Mary, b. 17 7ber 1708 (QAP b/3)

Hook, William; planter; 26 Jan 1732/3; 29 Aug 1733; wife Sarah; d-i-l Elizabeth Harges; tract *Good Will* (MCW VII.32)

Hook, James; admx. Margarett; 26 Jul 1738 (I 24.111); admx. Margaret; children [unnamed]; 27 May 1739 (AA 17.170)

Hook, James; bro. John; tract *Kittocton Bottom*; 26 Nov 1740 (PGLR Y.244)

HOOKER

Hooker, Robert; 25 May 1711 (I&A 32b.186)

Hooker, Samuel [Dorchester]; wife Margrett; tract *Twyford*; 15 Mar 1720 (PGLR I.102)

Hooker, Robert; planter; 2 Apr 1751; 26 Jun 1751; wife Elizabeth; daus. Mary Sadler, Elizabeth, Amy, Rebecca, Ann, Alles, Tabitha; son Robert Deakins (MCW X.158); extx. Elisabeth; 28 Aug 1751 (I 47.287); admx. Elisabeth; 24 Jun 1752 (I 51.59); extx. Elisabeth; children: Mary Sadler, Elisabeth, Amy, Rebecca, Anne, Ales, Tablitha; 24 Jun 1752 (AA 32.363)

HOOPS

Hoops, Andrew; 4 Feb 1729 (I 15.430)

Hoops, John; 28 Sep 1743; 23 Nov 1743; [no relations] (MCW VIII.243); 22 Feb 1743 (I 28.385)

HOPKINS

Hopkins, John; m. 19 Nov 1717 Elizabeth Dunning; children: James, b. 28 Sep 1718; John, b. 26 Dec 1719; Joseph, b. 2 Jan 1721 (KGP p. 268)

Hopkins, Andrew; age ca 34; 13 Sep 1725 (CCR CL.1057-1063)

Hopkins, Sam.; wife Linney; child: William Pritchet, b. 7 Nov 1759 (PGP p. 281)

Hopkins, James; wife Linney; child: Silas, b. 15 Jun 1761 (PGP p. 261)

HOPKINTON

Hopkinton, Thomas; m. 25 Mar 1740 Ann _____ (PGP p. 229)

HOPPER

Hopper, John, Sr.; children: Susanna, John Jr., Mary, Samuel; 11 Feb 1729 (PGLR M.533)

HORTON

Horton, Robert [SM]; wife Margery [relict of Richard Gardiner]; tract *The Margery*; 1 Nov 1703 (PGLR C.87a)

HOSKINSON

Hoskinson; Eliner & Mary; cous. James Moore, Sr.; 10 May 1717 (PGLR F.623)
Hoskinson, Thomas; wife Ann; children: Priscilla, 5 Mar 1741; John, b. 9
  Mar 1742/3; Jesse, b. 29 Oct 1745; Ningg (m), b. 7 Nov 1747; Josiah, b.
  16 Dec 1749; Ann, b. 8 Apr 1753 (PGP p. 254)

HOULT

Hoult, Ralph; wife Ann; child: William, b. 6 Mar 1763 (PGP p. 269)

HOW

How, Thomas; child: Mary, bapt. 5 Jun 1768 Broad Creek (KGP p. 363)

HOWARD

Howard, John; wife Rebecca [d/o Thomas Brooke]; son Thomas Howard;
  tract *Brooke Chance*; 16 Feb 1729 (PGLR M.538)
Howard, Sarah; age 4 on 31 Oct next; bound out; Aug 1729 (PGCR P.133)
Howard, Cornelius [dec'd]; wife Elizabeth; 26 Jun 1729 (PGLR M.446)
Howard, Charles; wife Ann; child: John Walker, b. 19 Aug 1760 (PGP p. 259)
Howard, Penelope; 15 Jan 1763; 17 Oct 1763; daus. Susannah Frasher,
  Mary Edelin; d-i-l Mary Dyer; grandson Annocletus Dyer; s-i-l Philip
  Edelen (MCW XII.207); widow; 1 Dec 1763 (I 83.142)

HOWELL

Howell, William; 30 Dec 1718; 27 Jan 1718; wife Christian [who ran away]
  (MCW IV.186); 30 Jan 1718 (I 2.62); 5 Aug 1719 (AA 2.235)
Howell, Samuel; 29 Jan 1725 (I 11.361); 25 Jun 1726 (AA 7.387)
Howell, John; planter; 15 Apr 1734; 3 Jun 1734; wife Martha; tract *Swansey*
  (MCW VII.92); extx. Martha Person [w/o Edward]; heirs none; 23 Feb 1735
  (AA 14.171); extx. Martha Pearson [w/o Edward]; 27 Mar 1735 (I 20.418)

HOWEN

Howen, Elias; wife Mary; child: John, b. 24 Jan 1776 Lower Chapel (KGP p.
  381)

HOWERTON

Howerton, William; 8 Oct 1722 (I 8.228); 19 Jul 1723 (AA 5.188); 19 Jul 1723
  (AA 8.237)
Howerton, William; m. 24 7ber 1724 Alice Henniss (QAP m/3)
Howerton, Jane [alias Overton]; age 7 in middle of Dec last; Jun 1725 (PGCR
  L.638)

HOWES

Howes, Henry; age ca 16; servant; Aug 1698 Ct. (PGCR A.333)

HOXTON

Hoxton, Hyde; 24 Feb 1741; 2 Apr 1754; wife Susannah; son Walter (MCW XI.20)

HOYE

Hoy, Paul; 4 Jan 1727/8; 20 Feb 1727; wife [unnamed]; sons James, Dorset and Isaac; daus. Mary, Margrett, Anne, Martha (MCW VI.56); 31 May 1728 (I 13.149); children: Mary Ann, Martha, Dorsett, Isaac, Margaret; 3 May 1729 (AA 9.341); widow Frances; heirs Mary [Bevan], Anne, Martha, Dorsett, Isaac, Margaret Hoye; 29 Aug 1729 (GB 50)

Hoye [Hay], Frances; 8 Dec 1732; 2 Jun 1733; husband Paul Hoye, dec'd; sons Dorset, Isaac; daus. Margaret, Mary, Ann, Martha; niece Ann Buchannan; s-i-l Charles Bevan (MCW VII.26); heirs Mary, Anne, Martha, Dorsett, Margaret; 27 Aug 1736 (GB 85)

Hoye, Mary; age 14 Mar last; choses guardian; Jun 1736 (PGCR W.56)

Hoye, James; 30 Nov 1739 (I 24.329)

HUCKER

Hucker, Robert; 20 Apr 1711; 5 May 1711; wife Amy, dec'd [d/o William Selby & bro. of William]; sons Samuel [b. 11 Oct 1699], Robert [b. 11 Sep 1706]; daus. Elizabeth [b. 14 Dec 1701], Amy [b. 27 Jul 1708] (MCW III.206); 29 May 1712 (I&A 33b.181); 29 Jul 1712 (I&A 33b.27)

HUDSON

Houdsin, Richard; 19 Feb 1733 (AA 12.167)

Hudson, Peter; wife Judith; child: Mary, bapt. 14 Jan 1753 (KGP p. 297)

HUGGINS

Huggins, John; wife Ann; tract *Draughton*; 6 Apr 1716 (PGLR F.534)

HUGHES

Hughes, Timothy; age ca 12; servant; Jun 1698 Ct. (PGCR A.317)

Hughes, John; m. 20 9ber 1710 Sarah Holland; child: Elizabeth, b. 13 Feb 1711/2 (QAP m/1; b/8)

Hews, Richard; 2 Feb 1716 (I&A 37c.131); 23 Apr 1716 (I&A 37a.49)

Hughs, William; s/o Richard [dec'd]; bound out; Mar 1721 (PGCR K.89)

Heugh, Andrew; m. 14 Oct 1751 Sarah Needham [by Moses Tabbe, curate]; children: Elizabeth, b. 27 Oct 1754; Sarah, b. 30 Jun 1756; Anna, b. 28 Jun 1758; Margret, b. 16 Jun 1760 (PGP p. 280, 281)

Huse, William; wife Mary; children: William, bapt. 3 Dec 1752; John, b. 30 Jan 1755 (KGP p. 297, 307)

Hughes, James; wife Mary; child: George White, b. 13 Nov 1762 (PGP p. 269)

Hughes, Thomas; wife Ann; child: Lloyd, bapt. 8 Jun 1766 Lower Chapel (KGP p. 346)

HUGOE

Hugoe, Israel; 31 Mar 1743; 3 May 1743; son William; daus. Mary, Ann; bro. Jacob; b-i-l Leonard Pile (MCW VIII.214); admx. Ann; 24 Aug 1743 (I 28.228); admx. Anne; heirs William, Anne; 27 Jun 1744 (AA 20.329); extx. Anne; 26 Mar 1745 (AA 21.213)

HULSE

Hulse, William; b. King & Queen Parish, St. Mary's Co., age ca 6 on 12 Aug 1732 (PGLR Q.532)

HUMPHREY

Humfrey, Henry; wife Sarah; children: Henry, b. 11 Feb 1747; Elizabeth, bapt. 3 May 1752; Deborah, b. 21 Feb 1755; John, b. 23 Jan 1757; Thomas Talbot, b. 22 Feb 1759 (KGP p. 296, 302, 308, 314, 321)

Humphrey, Joseph; m. 25 Sep 1748 Anne Jenkins by Rev. Henry Addison (KGP p. 288)

Humphrys, Susannah; 15 Sep 1757 (I 65.194)

Humphrey, Henry; 30 Jan 1760; 28 Nov 1760; wife [unnamed]; "her" 7 children; sons Henry, John, Thomas Talburt; daus. Eleaner, Sarah Ann, Elizabeth, Deborah (MCW XII.21); extx. Sarah [widow]; 19 Feb 1761 (I 75.3); 11 Jun 1761; extx. Sarah Humphreys; children: Henry, John, Thomas Talburt, Eleanor, Sarah Ann, Elisabeth, Deborah; 2nd distribution names Marian and omits Sarah Ann (ABB 3.74, 81); widow Sarah; heirs Henry, John, Thomas, Talbutt, Eleanor, Sarah, Ann, Elizabeth, Diana; 23 Jun 1762 (GB 218)

Humfrey, Henry; wife Elizabeth; child: John, b. 14 Jan 1774 Broad Creek (KGP p. 385)

HUNT

Hunt, Jonathan; wife Sushannah; child: Ann, bapt. 4 Jul 1762 (KGP p. 331)

HUNTER

Hunter, William; to marry Rebecca Dillum, widow; 22 Nov 1711 (PGLR F.155)

Hunter, Thomas; 24 May 1718 (I 1.4); 13 Apr 1719 (AA 2.8)

Hunter, William; son Hunter, Jr.; dau. Mary Piles [wife of John]; tract *Hunter's Folly*; 5 Aug 1723 (PGLR I.480)

Hunter, William, Sr.; 6 May 1728; 25 Jun 1728; wife Rebecca; son William; dau. Mary Pile [w/o John]; grandchildren: Hunter, William, John & Mary Piles, Thomas Hunter; tract *Huntersfield* (MCW VI.67); 5 Jul 1728 (I 13.191); 4 Dec 1729 (AA 10.99)

Hunter, Thomas; wife Isabell; child: Elizabeth, bapt. May-Jul 1761 (KGP p. 323)

Hunter, William; age ca 60; 6 Oct 1724 (PGLR I.600); age ca 65; 8 Jun 1725 (PGLR I.645)

HURLEY

Hurley, Daniel; wife Elizabeth; Nov 1704 (PGCR B.338a)

Hurley, Daniel; 11 Jul 1706 (I&A 25.385); admx. Elisabeth; 3 May 1707 (I&A 26.290)

Hurley, John; wife Precious; child: Zachariah, b. 22 May 1760 (PGP p. 258)

Hurley, William; wife Rachel; children: Daniel, b. 15 Aug 1760 Broad Creek; John, bapt. 16 May 1762; William, b. 5. Feb 1765 Broad Creek; ____, b. 12 Dec ____ Upper Chapel; Nathan, b. 12 Jan 1766 Upper Chapel; Mary, b. 30 Aug 1769 Upper Chapel (KGP p. 327, 347, 354, 356, 370, 374)

Hurley, Harison; m. Sarah ____; child: William, b. 16 Jun 1761 (PGP p. 261)

Hurley, Cornelius; wife Mary; children: Bathsheba, bapt. 6 Jun 1762; William, bapt. 26 May 1765 Upper Chapel; Rodey, bapt. 15 Nov 1767 Upper Chapel (KGP p. 330, 358, 366)

Hurley, Thomas; wife Jane; children: Daniel, b. 9 Jun 1762; William, bapt. 28 Apr 1765 Broad Creek (KGP p. 331, 346)

Hurley, Edmond; wife Rachel; children: Alena, bapt. 17 Oct 1762; Joshua, bapt. 15 Jul 1764 Upper Chapel or Broad Creek; Sushanna Beane, bapt. 10 Aug 1766 Upper Chapel (KGP p. 328, 342, 355)

Hurley, Cornelius; wife Mary; children: Rachel, b. 9 Mar 1772 Upper Chapel, Joel, b. 8 Apr 1773 Upper Chapel (KGP p. 388, 389)

Hurley, Thomas; wife Jane; children: Joshua, b. 4 Mar 1773 Upper Chapel; Esekiel, b. 5 Feb 1776 Broad Creek (KGP p. 382, 390)

Hurley, William; wife Rachel; child: Arnold, b. 23 Mar 1773 Broad Creek (KGP p. 378)

Hurley, Isaac; wife Tamar; child: Isaac, b. 24 Sep 1775 Upper Chapel (KGP p. 392)

HURST
Hurst, Mary, age 5 this month; d/o Ann Hurst; bound out; Jun 1711 Ct. (PGCR G.69a)

HUSBAND
Husband, David; 17 Jan 1761 (I 73.47)

HUSK
Husk [Hust], Edward; wife Elizabeth; children: John Randel, bapt. 2 Oct 1768 Lower Chapel; Susanna Barrot, b. 6 Jul 1770 Broad Creek; Lucy Barret, b. 6 May 1774 Lower Chapel (KGP p. 371, 374, 379)

HUSWEL
Huswel, William; wife Rebecca; child: Benoni, b. 27 May 1759 (KGP p. 321)

HUTCHINS
Howchin [Houthins], Jno.; planter; 24 Apr 1709; 23 Aug 1711; wife Jane; son William (MCW III.210); ex. Jane; 2 Jun 1712 (I&A 33a.211)

Hutching, Richard; [with 1716] (I&A 38a.117); 25 Jan 1717 (I&A 39c.124)

HUTCHISON
Hutcheson, Ruth; bore a bastard child; Jun 1699 Ct. (PGCR A.429)

Hutchison, William; wife Sarah [d/o Robert Doyne]; tract *Saturday's Work*; 9 Jan 1702/3 (PGLR C.39)

Hutchison, William; wife Sarah; son John; tract [unnamed]; 25 Oct 1703 (PGLR C.84)

Hutchison, William; 13 Dec 1708; 23 Apr 1711; wife Sarah; sons John, William; daus. Ann, Mary, Elizabeth; father John; bro. George; tracts; *Sangwhaire, Jessimund, Piscataway Forest, Friendship, Hazard, Little Worth, White Haven, Carlyle, The Vineyard, Saturday Work, Speedwell, Carick Fergus, Want Water, Rottendam, The Indian Town, Wheeler's Purchase, Joint Interest, Wheeler's Adventure, The Chance, Hickory Hills, The Hogg Penn* (MCW III.211); mentions Mrs. Hutchison [dec'd]; 5 children [unnamed]; 12 Oct 1713 (I&A 35b.33)

Hutchison, Sarah; 16 Apr 1711; 23 Apr 1711; son George; others; late husband William Hutchison (MCW III.212)

Hutchinson, Thomas; m. 7 8ber 1723 Ann Bennet (QAP m/3)

Hutchinson, William; children: Mary Abington [w/o John], William; d-i-l
Ann [now w/o Gabriel Parker, Calvert Co.], Elizabeth [now w/o
William Piles]; 3 Feb 1728 (CCR-MSA 5.449)

Hutcheson, William; 12 Jul 1729 (I 14.297)

Hutchinson, William; wife Rachel; 1735/6 (MCW VII.162)

HUTTON

Hutton, Richard; wife Margarett; 1761 (MCWXII.102)

Hutton, Richard; 13 Apr 1772; 27 Aug 1772; wife Mary; dau. Mary; tract
The Hatchel (MCW XIV.239)

HYATT

Hyatt, Charles; wife Sarah; children: Ann, b. 11 Mar 1706; Peter, b. 30 Jan
1707; Ann, b. 10 Mar 1711/2; Elizabeth, b. 22 Mar 1714; Penelope, b. 20
Apr 1716; William, b. 18 Feb 1717 (QAP b/2,3, 6, 9, 11, 13)

Hyatt, Charles; admx. Sarah; 25 Jun 1726 (I 11.433); widow Sarah; 20 Nov
1729; (AA 10.42)

Hyatt, Peter, m. 1728 Alice Howerchild (QAP m/5)

Hyatt, Seth; wife Alice; children: Seth, b. 5 8ber 1718; Shadrack, b. 25 Feb
1720/1 (QAP b/17)

HYDE

Hide, Ruth; 30 Sep 1696 (I&A 14.53)

Hyde, Hannah; d-i-l Elizabeth Hyde; Jun 1698 Ct. (PGCR A.318)

Hyde [Hide], Thomas [dec'd]; widow m/2 Bartholomew Goff; daus. Mary
Hide, Elizabeth Hide [m. Robert Johnson]; 14 Aug 1703 (PGLR C.64)

Hide, John; 26 Mar 1729 (AA 9.331)

Hyde, Isaac; wife Mary; children: Sarah, b. 29 7ber 1725; Elizabeth, b. 24
Mar 1731; Ann, b. 14 May 1733 (QAP b/19, 24, 26)

Hyde, Isaack [Isaac]; 5 Aug 1734 (I 20.282); widow [unnamed, dec'd]; 21 Jun
1735 (AA 13.142); 23 Mar 1736 (AA 15.302); 29 Mar 1739 (AA 17.156)

Hyde, Thomas; orphan; age 15, 26 Jan next; bound out; Aug 1734 (PGCR V.102)

Hyde, Thomas; orphan; age ca 14; 28 Sep 1734 (PGLR T.184)

Hyde, Ann; orphan; d/o Isaac; Aug 1735 (PGCR V.535)

HYNES

Hynes, Elisabeth [age 11]; Eleanor [age 6 last Aug]; ch/o Jane; bound out;
Jun 1723 (PGCR L.78)

HYTEN

Hyten, Joseph; wife Sarah; child: Cloe, b. 28 Sep 1773 Lower Chapel (KGP
p. 384)

INEL
Inel, George; wife Amy; 1743/4 (MCW VIII.244)

INGLEHART
Igleheart, John; wife Mary; children: ___ha (f), b. 21 Jul 1764, John, b. 23 Jun 1770; Richard, b. 11 Sep 1772; Jacob, b. 30 Mar 1774; Jemima, b. 31 May 1776 (QAP m/8, 38)

Inglehart, ____; ch/o Sarah; b. 28 Aug 1765 (QAP b/39)

Ingleheart, Jeremiah; wife Mary; child: Elizabeth, b. 18 Apr 1775 Upper Chapel (KGP p. 391)

INGRAM
Ingram, Thomas; 30 May 1718 (AA 1.5)

INNIS
Innes [Innis], Robert, Dr.; admx. Elisabeth; 26 Feb 1739 (I 25.31); widow Elisabeth; 10 Mar 1743 (AA 20.59)

IRELAND
Ireland, Elizabeth; lately Elizabeth Berry; age ca 50; 13 Sep 1725 (CCR CL.1057-1063)

Ireland, John; admx. Elisabeth; 31 Jan 1726 (I 11.910); John [London]; admx. Elisabeth; heirs [London]; 9 Dec 1727 (AA 8.510)

Ireland, Alexander; age ca 11 years; bound out; Mar 1750 (PGCR LL.134)

IRVIN
Irvin, Alexander; wife Esther; child: Alexander, b. 7 Jul 1764 (PGP p. 272)

ISAAC
Isaack, Joseph; son Joseph, age 16 Feb last; Mar 1697 Ct. (PGCR A.296)

Issack, Joseph; son Richard; [with 1703] (I&A 24.221)

Isaac, Richard; wife Sarah; children: Mary, b. 4 May 1712; Rachel, b. 2 Jul 1716; Kezia, b. 5 Feb 1719; Richard, b. 21 Jan 1720/1; Drusilla, b. 5 Apr 1723; Jemima, b. 21 May 1727? (QAP b/12, 16,18, 20)

Isaack, Richard; age ca 36; 28 Apr 1716 (CCR CL.285)

Isaac, Richard; wife Sarah; s-i-l Joseph Peach; tract *Isaac's Discovery*; 20 Sep 1726 (PGLR M.98)

Isaac, Richard; age ca 62; 18 Nov 1740 (PGLR Y.233); age ca 65; 26 Mar 1741 (PGLR Y.266)

Isaac, Richard, Sr.; 10 Mar 1759; 28 Jun 1759; sons Richard, Joseph; daus. Sarah Ridgley, Rachel Jones, Kesiah Fowler, Drusilla Fowler, Jemima Jacobs; s-i-l Wishall Ridgley; tracts *Isaac Park, Beall's Park, Mary's*

Delight, Stony Plains, Isaac's Discovery (MCW XI.238); 10 May 1762; exs. Richard & Joseph Isaac (ABB 3.143); 11 Feb 1760 (I 69.289, 327)

Isaac, Joseph; 4 Jul 1771; 24 Oct 1774; wife Hannah; children: Richard, Joseph, Sutton, Sarah; tracts *Stony Plains, Martha's Choice* (MCW XVI.8); extx. Hannah; 13 Apr 1775 (I 123.115)

IVINGTON

Ivington, John; wife Elizabeth; child: Ann, bapt. 1 Mar 1752 (KGP p. 295)

JACKOE

Jackcoe, Thomas; age ca 30; 1737 (PGLR T.504)

JACKSON

Jackson, John; wife Ruth; tract *Addition to Jackson's Necessity*; 1 Aug 1719 (PGLR F.201/788)

Jackson, William John; wife Agnes; children: Elliner, b. 18 Feb 1725/6; Ann, b. 14 Jul 1729; Nicholas, b. 24 Jan 1731/2 (PGP p. 247-8, 250)

Jackson, William; 3 Jan 1734 (I 20.339); heirs none; 3 Feb 1734 (AA 12.2b)

Jackson, John; age ca 13; bound out; Aug 1743 (PGCR CC.314)

JACO

Jaco, Thomas; 25 Sep 1749 (AA 27.69)

Jaco, John; 6 Sep 1764; 6 Dec 1764; wife Ann; grandchildren: Ann, John, Joseph & Priscilla Ryon (MCW XIII.66); 30 Nov 1770; admx. Ann Jacoe (ABB 6.18)

JACOB

Jacob, Joseph; wife Elizabeth; children: Benjamin, b. 10 Dec 1710; Elizabeth, b. 13 Jn 1712; Shadrack, b. 13 Apr 1716; Rebecca, b. 22 Aug 1718; Joshua, b. 17 Jan 1720/1; John, b. 19 May 1723; Joshua, b. 17 Sep 1725 (QAP b/5, 9, 12, 14, 16, 18, 19)

Jacob, John; wife Ann; children: Joseph, Benjamin; tract *Jacob's Hope*; 29 Feb 1712/3 (PGLR F.261)

Jacob, Benjamin; wife Alice; children: Mordecai, b. 24 May 1714; Sarah, b. 17 May 1719; Benjamin, b. 29 Aug 1724 (QAP b/10, 15, 19)

Jacob, Mordicai; m. 10 Sep 1741 Ruth Tyler; children: Ruth, b. ____; (QAP m/7; b/33)

Jacob, Mordicai; m. 7 Dec 1745 Jemima Isaac; children: Mordecai, b. 9 Sep 1748; Sarah, b. 30 Apr 1750; Alice, b. 31 May 1752; ____ (m), b. 1 May 1755; ____ (m), b. 13 Oct 1757; ___ma, b. 1 Dec 1759; ____ (f), b. 2 Oct 1762 (QAP m/7; b/33, 38)

Jacob, Mordicai; 11 Oct 1770; 8 May 1771; wife Jemima; father Benjamin; children: Benjamin, Moridcai, Sarah, George, Jemima, Eleanor; tracts *Evans Range, Widows Purchase, Bowies Addition* (MCW XIV.177); 4 May 1772; widow [unnamed]; legatees Sarah, Alice, Isaac, George, Jemima & Eleanor Jacob (ABB 6.123); heir Mordecai; 25 Aug 1775 (GB 313)

Jacob, Benjamin; m. 21 Apr 1771 Elenor Odell (QAP m/7)

JACTINUS
Jactinus [Jacktinns], Orlander Ultra; 1 Dec 1711 (I&A 33a.37); 20 Feb 1712 (I&A 33b.155)

JAMES
James, Thomas; wife Elizabeth; tract *Little Deane*; 12 Aug 1702 (PGLR C.9)

James, Thomas, Jr.; wife Mary; child: Thomas, b. 4 May 1716 (QAP b/11)

James, John; wife Mary [d/o John Soper, Sr.; granddau. of Damaris James]; 9 Feb 1725 (PGLR I.707)

James, Thomas, Sr.; dau. Elinor Eckly [w/o John]; tract *Vale of Benjamin*; 14 Feb 1734 (PGLR T.228)

James, Thomas; m. 13 Jan 1735 Elizabeth Lashle (QAP m/6)

James; mulatto child of Jane Normans, servant; sold to age 21; Aug 1737 (PGCR W.497)

James, John; age 3 on 23 Nov instant; bound out; Nov 1739 (PGCR X.496)

James, John; planter; 17 Apr 1747; 13 Apr 1748; wife Margaret; mgr. of estate Peter Becraft; son Daniel James [minor]; tract *Allaway* (MCW IX.148)

James, John; wife Elizabeth; child: Mary, b. 26 Oct 1761 (KGP p. 324)

James, Thomas; wife Nancy; child: Anna Statia, b. 30 Dec 1771 Upper Chapel; Elizabeth, b. 11 Feb 1774 Upper Chapel (KGP p. 388, 390)

James, William; wife Elizabeth; child: Charles, b. 7 Oct 1772 Upper Chapel (KGP p. 389)

JANE
Jane, mulatto d/o mulatto Beck; age 1 year on 1 Mar next; Jun 1742 (PGCR AA.3)

JANES
Jeanes [Janes], Joseph; 14 Jan 1719/20; 19 Feb 1719; wife Elizabeth; sons Joseph, Edward, William; daus. Mary, Ann (MCW IV.224); 21 Mar 1720 (I 4.102); widow Elizabeth; heirs Joseph, Edward, Mary, William, Anne; 29 Nov 1722 (GB 16)

Janes [Jeanes], William; wife Martha; children: Henry, b. 13 Sep 1750; Wm. Paine, b. 10 Dec 1752; John, b. 17 Nov 1754; Elinor, b. _ Jun 1757; Samuel, bapt. 7 Mar 1762; Martha Ann, bapt. 9 Sep 1764 Broad Creek (ICR; KGP p. 302, 307, 320, 325, 357)

Janes, Edward; wife Ann; child: Edward, bapt. 19 Apr 1752 (KGP p. 295)

Janes, John; m. 2 Jan 1760 Elizabeth Welling by Rev. Eversfield (KGP p. 316)

Jenes, William; wife Jane; child: William, b. 30 Oct 1767 Upper Chapel (KGP p. 366)

JARBER

Jarber, James; wife Martha; children [twins]: Thomas Jason Lanham and Mary Ann Randy, b. 4 Dec 1775 Broad Creek (KGP p. 382)

JARBOE

Jarboe, Stephen; wife Elizabeth; child: Cassandrah, b. 20 Mar 1764 (PGP p. 272)

JARO

Jaro, Thomas; 3 May 1745 (I 31.35)

JAW

Jaw, John; admx. Ann; 31 Dec 1764 (I 104.257)

JEARELL

Jearell [Garrell], Richard; wife Alce; tract part of *Denn*; 14 Oct 1704 (PGLR C.122a)

JEFFERSON

Jefferson, Weldon; wife Ann; tract *Brook Grove*; 6 May 1724 (PGLR I.548)

JEFFREY

Jeffrey, Alexander; wife Ann; child: Benjamin Berrey, bapt. 10 Aug 1766 Upper Chapel (KGP p. 364)

Jefferys, William; wife Elizabeth; child: William, bapt. 12 Jun 1768 Upper Chapel (KGP p. 370)

Jeffry, Alexander; son Benjamin; 1768 (MCW XIV.95)

Jeffress, Alexander; wife Ann; child: Lucy Sprigg, b. 27 Sep 1772 Upper Chapel (KGP p. 389)

JENKINS

Jenkings, John; wife Elizabeth; children: Priscilla, b. 16 7ber 1710; Elizabeth, b. 19 Aug 1712; Mary, b. 22 Oct 1713 (QAP b/11)

Jenkins, Thomas; age ca 17 years; servant; Mar 1716 (PGCR H.32)

Jenkins, Thomas [CH]; wife Ann; dau. Elizabeth Edelen [w/o Edward]; 15 Feb 1719; tract *Pinnar* (PGLR F.287/867)

Jenkins, Enoch; m. 26 Jan 1718 Anne Clarvo; child: Francis (m), b. 21 Apr 1721 (KGP p. 268)

Jenkins George; admx. Susannah; 11 Nov 1727 (I 12.389); admx. Susanna; heirs Henerita, Thomas, John, George, William; 1 Feb 1728 (AA 9.257)

Jenkins [Jenckins], Enoch; 19 Feb 1733/4; 23 Mar 1733/4; wife Ann; sons Francis, John, Daniel, Bartholomew, Zachariah, Josias; dau. Ann; tracts

God's Gift, Rome, Pearsimmon Tree Branch (MCW VII.70); admx. Ann Philips [w/o John]; 26 Oct 1734 (I 20.62); admx. Anne Phillips [w/o John]; children: Francis, John, Daniel, Zachariah, Bartholomew, Josias, Anne; 1 Dec 1735 (AA 14.81); heirs Frances, John, Daniel, Zachariah, Bartholomew, Josiah, Anne; 25 Aug 1736 (GB 83); heirs Francis, John, Daniel, Zachariah, Bartholomew, Zachariah, Anne; 25 Jun 1743 (GB 125)

Jenkins, Daniel; wife Ruth [d/o John Peerce]; tract *Port Royal*; 11 Jan 1734 (PGLR T.255)

Jenkins, Josias; chooses John Jenkins as guardian; Aug 1749 (PGCR LL.6)

Jenkins, John; wife Rachel; child: Lucy, bapt. 9 Jun 1751 (KGP p. 294)

Jenkins, Bartholemew; wife Mary; child: Catherine, bapt. 23 Aug 1752; Daniel, b. 26 Aug 1761, bapt. 25 Oct 1761; Enock, bapt. 24 Jun 1764 Upper Chapel; Batholemew, bapt. 12 Oct 1766 Upper Chapel; Margaret, b. 13 Feb 1772 Upper Chapel; Amelia, b. 20 Jul 1774 Upper Chapel (KGP p. 297, 323, 341, 354, 389, 391)

Jenkins, John; wife Frances; child: Joseph, b. 22 May 1755; James, b. 29 Oct 1761; Ann, b. 14 Oct 1764 Broad Creek; William, bapt. 10 Apr 1768 Upper Chapel (KGP p. 309, 324, 342)

Jenkins, Zachariah; wife Sarah; child: Mary, b. 23 May 1755; Susanah, bapt. 7 Feb 1762 (KGP p. 309, 325)

Jenkins, Francis; daus. Priscilla & Catherine Jenkins; 1767 (MCW XIV.35)

Jenkins, Zachariah; wife Martha; child: Sarah Ann, bapt. 13 Oct 1765 Broad Creek (KGP p. 349)

Jenkins, William; 4 Feb 1767 (I 91.310)

JENKINSON

Jenkinson, Daniell; admx. Elisabeth Chisick [w/o Thomas]; 12 Aug 1706 (I&A 25.386)

JENNINGS

Jennings, William; 23 May 1711; 15 Aug 1711; daus. Ann, Sarah; sons Thomas, James (MCW III.211)

Jennings, William; wife Mary; children: William, Anne, Sarah, Thomas, James; bound out; Aug 1711 Ct. (PGCR G.77)

Jenning, William; extx. Mary; 26 Sep 1712 (I&A 33b.77, 80)

Jennings, John; age 6 on 26 Apr last past; Jun 1718; s/o Mary (PGCR H.669)

Jennings, Thomas; wife Elizabeth; child: Frances, b. 15 Dec 1737 (KGP p. 288, 301)

Jennings, Thomas; 6 Oct 1738; wife Elizabeth; dau. Frances; tract *Jacob* (MCW VIII.106); extx. Elisabeth; 18 Mar 1740 (I 26.29); extx. Elisabeth Batts [w/o

Humphrey]; dau. Frances [age 5]; 21 Jan 1742 (AA 19.307); extx. Eliza; 23 Jun 1742 (I 27.25); extx. Elisabeth Batt [w/o Humphry]; 10 Jun 1743 (AA 25.96); extx. Elisabeth Batt; 17 Apr 1747 (I 35.47)

Jennings, Joseph, Rev.; 20 May 1748 (I 37.121)

Jenning, Thomas; wife 13 Jan 1754 Christy Partee (KGP p. 301)

Jennings, John; wife Sarah; child: Ann, b. 23 Oct 1764 (PGP p. 274)

Jennings, Thomas; wife Sarah; child: Lucy, b. 27 Nov 1772 (PGP p. 279)

Jennins, Charles; wife Elizabeth; child: Mary, b. 19 Mar 1775 Upper Chapel (KGP p. 391)

JERVIS

Jervis, William; 10 Jun 1719; 30 Apr 1720; wife Magdalen; step-son William Wilcoxon; tract *Warwick* (MCW V.5); extx. Magdalen; 3 Jul 1721 (AA 3.363)

JEWEL

Jewel, George; wife Amey; son William; tract *Brightwell's Hunting Quarter*; 2 Feb 1742 (PGLR Y.591)

JOHNSON

Johnson, Thomas; wife Mary; tract *Green's Purchase*; 30 Mar 1704 (PGLR C.144)

Johnson, Robert; wife Elizabeth; children: Elizabeth, b. 23 Mar 1709; Joseph & Benjamin, b. 5 Dec 1715; Francis, b. 19 Feb 1718 (KGP p. 281)

Johnson, John; [with 1710] (I&A 31.136); 20 Oct 1711 (I&A 33a.39)

Johnson, Bernard; children: Mary Willery [w/o Philip], Elizabeth Williams [w/o Hugh], Catherine Rawlins [w/o Paul], Martha Nelson [w/o Thomas]; tracts *Dove's Nest, Dove's Peirch*; 10 Oct 1711 (PGLR F.156)

Johnson, Nathaniell; age ca 6; s/o Richard; bound to Evan Jones and Ann [his now wife]; Jun 1716 (PGCR H.85)

Johnston, Robert; planter; 14 May 1717; 6 Jul 1717; wife Elizabeth; sons Joseph, Benjamin, James; dau. Elizabeth; tracts *Poor Man's Industry* (MCW IV.113); 17 Aug 1717 (I&A 37b.185)

Johnson, John; s/o Mary; bound to Jonathan Wadhams & wife Joan; Nov 1717 (PGCR H.310)

Johnson [Johnston], Stephen; 30 Apr 1719 (I 2.127); extx. Elisabeth; 27 Jan 1719 (AA 2.490); heirs Jacob, Michael, Eleanor; 28 Aug 1720 (GB 13); extx. Elisabeth Wildman [w/o William, a runaway]; 19 Aug 1721 (AA 3.517); widow Elizabeth; heir Michael; 27 Nov 1728 (GB 42)

Johnson, Nathaniel; bound out to learn art of a shipwright; Nov 1720 (PGCR K.12)

Johnson [Johnston], Thomas; age ca 50 odd years; 20 May 1725 (PGLR I.675); age ca 60; 1727-28 (PGLR M.269)

Johnston, Thomas; age ca 42; 17 Aug 1725 (PGLR I.676)

Johnson, Randolph; wife Mary; children: Rebecca, b. 3 10ber 1728; Randolph, b. 17 May 173_ (QAP b/22, 28)

Johnson, Michael; age ca 14 last Sep; choses mother Elizabeth Wildman as guardian; Nov 1728 (PGCR O.335)

Johnson, Thomas; age ca 24; 17 Jun 1730 (PGLR Q.11)

Johnson, Jacob; admx. Sarah; dau. Elisabeth [age ca 3]; 27 Feb 1732 (AA 11.648); _ Apr 1732 (I 16.500); heir Elizabeth; 28 Nov 1733 (GB 61)

Johnson, John; wife Susanna; tract *Penny's Choice*; 24 Apr 1740 (PGLR Y.165)

Johnson, Samuel, Capt.; mariner, Capt. of *The Charles*; 14 Jun 1741; 14 Sep 1741; [no relations] (MCW VIII.149)

Johnson, Hannah; 23 Mar 1742/3; 1 Jun 1743; sons: Robert, Stephen, Thomas; granddau. Anne (MCW VIII.233)

Johnson, Peter; adm. Mary; 19 Jun 1747 (I 35.378)

Johnson, William; wife Ann; children: Elisabeth, b. 16 Jan 1762; Sarah, b. __ Nov 1764 (PGP p. 263, 273)

Johnson, Thomas; 9 Apr 1748; 17 Nov 1750; [no relations]; tract *Peter's Point* (MCW X.115)

Johnson, Mary; child: Nathaniel, b. 4 Apr 1752 (KGP p. 305)

Johnson, Joseph; wife Elizabeth; child: Isaac, bapt. 3 May 1752 (KGP p. 296)

Johnson, John; [age 3] on 9 Apr 1754 when he & his bro. Nathaniel [age 1] were bound to Leonard Day (KGP p. 311)

Johnson, John; wife Elizabeth; child: Sarah, b. 7 Oct 1756 (KGP p. 314)

Johnson, Joseph; wife Elisabeth; child: Anne Morris, b. 6 Jan 1760 (PGP p. 280)

Johnson, Benjamin; wife Sarah; child: Sarah, bapt. 12 Dec 1762 (KGP p. 329)

Johnson, John; wife Jamina; child: James, bapt. 14 Jun 1767 Broad Creek (KGP p. 361)

Johnson [Johnston], John; 15 May 1766 (I 89.306); 22 Sep 1769; adm. James Johnson (ABB 5.389); 15 Nov 1771; 6 children [unnamed] (ABB 6.143); heirs Monica, John, Joseph, Ignatius Sim, Mary Ann; 26 Nov 1771 (GB 301)

Johnson, Matthew; wife Jane; child: Zachariah, b. 18 Mar 1772 Broad Creek (KGP p. 378)

Johnson, Thomas; wife Margery; child: Masse, b. 11 Jul 1773 Upper Chapel; Sarah, b. 12 Jun 1775 Upper Chapel (KGP p. 390, 391)

Johnson, James; wife Martha; child: William Womsley, b. 8 Apr 1776 Broad Creek (KGP p. 382)

JONES

Jones, Henry; 7 May 1698 (I&A 16.106)

Jones, William; wife Dorathy; tract Cuckholds Delight; 29 Jan 1700 (PGLR A.415)

Jones, Richard; wife Anne; tract Bealington; 18 Apr 1702 (PGLR A.437)

Jones, George; wife Johanna; tract Gedling; 16 Apr 1703 (PGLR C.137)

Jones, William; orphan; age ca 15; uncle William Hill; 22 Jun 1703 (PGCR B.239a)

Jones, Moses; 4 Jul 1704; 22 Mar 1704/5; wife Elizabeth; sons John, Thomas, Notley; daus. Jone, Anne, Eliza.; tracts Thomases Chance, Pinner (MCW III.61); 16 Mar 1705 (I&A 25.226); extx. Elisabeth Edlin [w/o Edward]; Jul 1708 (I&A 28.259); extx. Elisabeth Edlin [w/o Edward]; 14 Feb 1714 (I&A 36b.28); extx. Elisabeth Edelen [w/o Edward]; 12 Jul 1725 (AA 7.29); widow Elisabeth Edlin [w/o Edward]; 7 Mar 1727 (AA 8.167)

Jones, Hugh; 11 Jan 1705/6; 28 Jan 1705/6; [no relationships] (MVW III.72); 28 Jan 1705 (I&A 25.218)

Jones, Richard; age ca 50; 6 Oct 1712 (CCR CL.42)

Jones, Evan of Annapolis, batchelor; m. 28 May 1713 Mary Bradford, spinster of Prince George's Co.; m. by Rev. John Fraiser (KGP p. 259)

Jones, Edward; wife Elizabeth; children: John, b. 2 Oct 1713; William, b. 17 Apr 1716; Philip, b. 16 Oct 1719 (KGP p. 281, 282)

Jones, Sophia; age 4 on 17 Jan last; f-i-l [?step-father] Evan Thomas; bound out to Robert Oram and wife Ruth; Jun 1714 (PGCR G.610)

Jones, Richard; m. 18 Feb 1717 Jane Sweringen (QAP m/1)

Jones, Evan; 12 Feb 1718 (I 2.63)

Jones, Richard; wife Elizabeth; children: Abraham, b. 8 May 1719; Elizabeth, b. 12 10ber 1720; Joseph, b. 4 8ber 1722; Richard, b. 27 Jul 1724; Benjamin, b. 14 May 1726; Samuel, b. 29 Mar 1728; Isaac, b. 19 Jan 1729; Jacob, b. 30 Nov 1731; Henry, b. 14 Aug 1733 (QAP b/14, 16, 17, 19, 21, 23, 27)

Jones, Joseph; extx. Elisabeth; widow, 3 sons & 2 daus [unnamed]; 27 Aug 1720 (AA 3.210)

Jones, David; widow Margarett Markland; 2 Jun 1721 (I 11.37)

Jones, Edward; carpenter; 18 Apr 1722; 29 May 1722; wife [unnamed]; sons Lewin, James, Edward, John, William, Philip (latter 4 minors) (MCW V.106); extx. Elisabeth Barnes; 15 Jun 1722 (I 9.154); extx. Elisabeth Barnes [w/o Henry]; 21 May 1723 (AA 5.173); extx. Elisabeth Barnes [w/o Henry]; 21 Mar 1725 (AA 7.302); heirs Lewin, James, Edward, John, William, Philip; 24 Nov 1725 (GB 26)

Jones, Hannah; child: William, b. 1 Apr 1723 (KGP p. 278)

Jones, Richard; m. 26 Nov 1724 Ann Bivin (QAP m/6)

Jones, Moses [dec'd]; children: Thomas [dec'd, no heirs], Notley [dec'd, no heirs], Elizabeth; tract *Thomas' Chance*; 27 Jul 1727 (PGLR M.226)

Jones, James; age 18 yrs. and 6 mos.; 24 Aug 1727 (PGCR N.491)

Jones, George, Capt.; widow Johanna; daus. Anne Nailor [w/o James], Mary Magruder [w/o Nathaniel, Sr.]; 13 Jan 1729 (AA 10.185); George, Sr.; 22 Mar 1729 (I 14.1); 6 Aug 1730 (AA 10.384)

Jones, Richard; wife Rachel; child: Thomas, b. 16 May 1731 (QAP b/24)

Jones, Thomas; son Richard; tracts *Clark's Purchase, Reiley's Neglect*; 28 Nov 1733 (PGLR T.29)

Jones, John; planter; 31 Dec 1736; 7 Feb 1736/7; wife Ann; sons Henry, John; daus. Ann, Cathern; tracts *Lyon's Hole, Partnership, Hazard* (MCW VII.203); widow Ann; children: Henry, John, Ann, Catherine; 1 Feb 1737 (AA 16.64); extx. Anne Decregar [w/o William]; children [unnamed]; 26 Mar 1739 (AA 17.153)

Jones, William; m. 31 Jan 1737/8 Mary Pammer; children: William, b. 23 Jan 1738/9; Thomas, b. 23 Oct 1743; Notley, b. 6 Sep 1746; Mary, b. 23 Mar 1749; John, b. 12 Feb 1753; Sarah, b. 9 Jul 1755; Butler, b. 6 Nov 1758; Henry, b. 3 Apr 1761 (KGP p. 282, 299)

Jones, David; 3 Dec 1737 (I 23.432)

Jones, Johannah; 13 May 1738; 17 Feb 1742/3; son George; daus. Alling, Mary Bright, Ann Neill; grandsons, John & Lisha Harben [ss/o Johannah], Alexander; granddaus. Susanna & Elizabeth Magruder, Johannah Birkhead, Rebecca Miller (MCW VIII.197)

Jones, Richard, Sr.; 28 Jan 1740; 25 Mar 1741; wife Ann; granddau. Ann Simmonds; tracts *Joanes Field, Addition to Bacon* (MCW VIII.132); extx. Ann; 29 Apr 1741 (I 26.55)

Jones, John; wife Sarah; children: Charles, b. 12 Aug 1740; Nathan, b. 4 Nov 1742; Dorothy, b. 2 May 1745; Edward, b. 19 Mar 1746/7; Lydda, b. 13 Mar 1750/1; Mary, b. 22 Jun 1753 (PGP p. 255)

Jones, Michael; wife Elizabeth; step-son Samuel Freeman [s/o Elizabeth]; 2 Feb 1742 (PGLR Y.596)

Jones, David; heirs of age; 22 Feb 1742 (AA 19.311)

Jones, Ann; b-i-l Robert Brashear, Jr.; tract *Brashear's Meadows*; 22 Jun 1742 (PGLR Y.494)

Jones, Henry; admx. Ann; 31 Nov 1742 (I 27.275); admx. Ann Norton [w/o Alexander]; 17 Nov 1743 (AA 20.60); admx. Anne Norton [w/o Alexander]; children: Notley, Frances, John, Henry, Silvester; 25 Nov 1744 (AA 20.535);

admx. Ann Norton [w/o Alexander]; 10 Nov 1746 (AA 23.90); heirs Notley, Francis, John, Henry, Sylvester; 25 Aug 1748 (GB 163)

Jones, Edward; extx. Elianor; 10 Aug 1744 (I 30.80); extx. Elianor; 4 children: Josias, Eliza, William, Charles; 25 Jun 1746 (AA 22.197); heirs Josiah, Elizabeth, William, Charles; 27 Aug 1747 (GB 159)

Jones, William; wife Mary; children: Lewin, b. 24 Sep 1746; Ann, b. 17 Aug 1748; William, b. 12 Aug 1751, bapt. 1 Dec 1751; Samuel, b. 17 Nov 1753; Sarah, b. 9 Jul 1755; Charity, b. 8 Jun 1756; Vialetta, b. 12 Mar 1763; Clement, b. 7 Mar 1766 Broad Creek (KGP p. 294, 304, 309, 311, 313, 320, 330)

Joanes [Jones], William; 9 Feb 1751 (I 49.45); 20 Mar 1753 (AA 33.388); children: Ignatious, Elisabeth, Catherine, Luranat; 29 Aug 1754 (AA 36.386)

Jones, Edward; wife Mary; child: John, bapt. 15 Dec 1751; Leonard, b. 17 Nov 1753; [d. 24 Nov 1753]; Violinder, b. 3 Nov 1754; Rebecca, b. 10 May 1755; Zachariah, b. 28 Aug 1757 (KGP p. 294, 301, 307, 308; 321)

Jones, Charles; wife Elizabeth; children: Mary Ann, b. 12 Aug 1752; John Courts, b. 11 Sep 1754; Sarah, b. 11 Sep 1756; Nelly Coats, b. 4 Nov 1760 (PGP p. 253, 256,280)

Jones, Philip; wife Penelopy; child: Elinor, b. 11 Jan 1755; Thomas, b. 23 Jan 1757; Ann, b. 17 Apr 1763 at Broad Creek; Linney, bapt. 24 Oct 1765 Broad Creek; John, bapt. 24 May 1768 Lower Chapel; Hatton Middleton, b. 1 Mar 1774 Lower Chapel (KGP p. 307, 314, 337, 359, 368, 379)

Jones, John; wife Elizabeth; child: Rebecca, b. 3 Jan 1759 (KGP p. 321)

Jones, Evan; wife Ann; child: Sarah, b. 26 Sep 1760 (PGP p. 259)

Jones, Evan; child: John, d. 7 Oct 1760 (PGP p. 285)

Jones, John; wife Casander; child: Benit, b. 15 Sep 1761, bapt. 25 Oct 1761; Kesander, b. 8 Oct 1765 Lower Chapel (KGP p. 323, 345)

Jones, William; m. 1 Mar 1762 Sarah Lanham (KGP p. 320); children: Ann, b. 30 Sep 1762; Sarah, bapt. 9 Sep 1764 at Broad Creek (KGP p. 320, 328, 339)

Jones, Edward; child: Basell, bapt. 18 Apr 1762 (KGP p. 326)

Jones, Edward; wife Elizabeth; children: Edward, b. 27 May 1762; William, b. 11 Oct 1765 Broad Creek (KGP p. 330, 360)

Jones, Benjamin; wife Elizabeth; child: Thomas, bapt. 6 Feb 1763 at Broad Creek; John Bowles, bapt. 14 Jun 1767 Broad Creek (KGP p. 336, 361)

Jones, William; wife Judith; children: Hezekiah, b. 18 May 1763; Jane, b. 25 Jul 1764 (PGP p. 270, 274)

Jones, John; wife Kasey; child: John Wheeler, b. 24 Nov 1764, bapt. 29 Jan 1764 at Upper Chapel (KGP p. 340)

Jones, Edward; wife Elenor; children: Altheaw, b. 2 Dec 1764 Broad Creek; Shalota Brookes, bapt. 8 Feb 1767 Broad Creek (KGP p. 346, 360)

Jones, Knotley; wife Elenor; child: Henry Swan, b. 16 Jul 1765 Broad Creek (KGP p. 349)

Jones, Charles; wife Marian; child: John Lanham, b. 13 Nov 1765 (PGP p. 277)

Jones, Henry; wife Ann; children: Elizabeth, bapt. 24 Nov 1765 Broad Creek; Lucey, bapt. 6 Dec 1767 Upper Chapel; Charles Becket, b. 30 Aug 1769 Broad Creek; Colmore, b. 23 Sep 1773 Broad Creek (KGP p. 349-50, 366, 373, 385)

Jones, Elizabeth; child: Mary Ann Lewin, bapt. 22 Jun 1766 Broad Creek (KGP p. 353-4)

Jones, Edward; wife Monaca [Monakey]; children: Moses, bapt. 29 Nov 1767 Lower Chapel; Edward, b. 31 Oct 1773 Broad Creek (ICR; KGP p. 368, 385)

Jones, John; child: Moses, bapt. 28 Aug 1768 Broad Creek (KGP p. 364)

Jones, Benjamin; child: Joseph Walker, b. 17 Apr 1770 Broad Creek (KGP p. 374)

Jones, Philip Luin; wife Rebecca; child: Bayne, b. 21 Jun 1770 Broad Creek (KGP p. 374)

Jones, Thomas; wife Susanna; child: Thomas, b. 7 Mar 1772 Upper Chapel (KGP p. 388)

Jones, Philip Luin; wife Charity; child: Henry, b. 4 Oct 1772 Broad Creek; Sarah, b. 14 Sep 1775 Broad Creek (KGP p. 382)

Jones, Abraham; admx. Ann; 2 Nov 1773 (I 117.347); 19 Mar 1773; admx. Ann Clark [w/o Joshua]; child Mary (ABB 7.24); admx. Ann Clark [w/o Joshua]; 6 Mar 1775 (I 121.336); heir Mary; 28 Mar 1775 (GB 334)

Jones, Edward; wife Elizabeth; child: John Luin, b. 2 Apr 1773 Broad Creek (KGP p. 379)

Jones, John; wife Eleanor; child: Sarah Ann, b. 9 Dec 1774 Broad Creek (KGP p. 386)

Jones, Benjamin; wife Elizabeth; child: Ezzable, b. 21 Sep 1775 Broad Creek (KGP p. 387)

Jones, Notly; wife Ann; child: John, b. 9 Oct 1775 Broad Creek (KGP p. 382)

Jones, Edward; 11 Nov 1767; 31 Mar 1777; wife Monica; 9 children: John, Virlinder, Zachariah, James, Basil, Elisah Kea [I ack. this is my child], Moses, Electius, Edward (MCW XVI.185)

JORDAN

Jordan, Thomas [VA]; wife Elizabeth; tract *Billingsly's Point*; 22 Apr 1725 (PGLR I.627)

Jordan, John; wife Ruth; children: Elizabeth, b. 9 May 1763; Samuell, b. 19 Jun 1765 (PGP p. 271, 276)

Jordan, Samuell; m. Elliner; child: John, b. 25 Jul 1765 (PGP p. 277)

JOSEPH

Joseph, William; admx. widow Elisabeth; 9 Nov 1714 (I&A 36a.140)

Joseph; age 3 months; s/o mulatto Jane; Nov 1745 (PGCR DD.279)

JOSLING

Josling, Elisabeth; 29 Oct 1712 (I&A 33b.78)

JOWLES

Jowles, Henry, Col. [SM]; wife Sible; tract *Grove Hurst*; 10 Jun 1700 (PGLR A.320)

JOY

Joy [Joye], Peter [SM]; wife Anne; tract *Kingstone*; 28 Apr 1701 (PGLR A.451)

JOYCE

Joyce, John; 28 Nov 1699 (I&A 19-1/2b.3)

Joice, John; wife Sarah; tract *Nicholls Hunting Quarter*; 1 Dec 1721 (PGLR I.195)

Joyce, John; m. 3 Jul 1721 Sarah Brooks; children: John, b. 13 Dec 1731; James b. __ Jul 1734 (?) (QAP m/2; b/25, 34)

Joyce, Thomas; m. 22 Apr 1716 Elizabeth Cheeny; children: Thomas, b. 1 Feb 1718; John, b. 29 10ber 1720; Elizabeth, b. 27 Sep 1722; Cheeny, b. 7 Jul 1724 (QAP m/1; b/17, 18)

Joyce, Elizah; age 11 on 22 April next; bound out; Mar 1750 (PGCR LL.136)

JULIEN

Julien, Jacob; 25 Mar 1747; 30 Aug 1751; wife Catharine; child Rachell; bros. Isaac, John, Stephen (MCW X.169)

JUNIS

Junis, Robert, Dr.; admx. Elisabeth; 8 Jan 1741 (AA 18.231)

JURES

Jures, James; wife Alice; June 1698 Ct. (PGCR A.319)

Jures, James; age 5 on last of Jun; bound out to learn carpentry; Jan 1700 (PGCR B.93)

KANADY

Kanady, Daniell; age ca 11; servant; Jun 1698 Ct. (PGCR A.316)

KEATON

Keaton, John; wife Elizabeth; children: Mary, b. 30 Jan 1729; Elizabeth, b. 28 Oct 1731; Charles, b. 20 Aug 1733; John, b. 1 Jun 1735; Lidia, b. 30 Aug 1737 (KGP p. 272)

KEDELL

Kedell, John; admx. Abigail Moody [w/o Roger]; 8 May 1744 (AA 20.153)

KEECH

Keech, James [SM]; wife Elizabeth; tract *Thorpland*; 5 Dec 1705 (PGLR C.151a)

KEENE

Keen, Richard; binds himself as servant; Mar 1706 (PGCR C.39)

Keene, Richard; age ca 37; 4 Oct 1726 (PGLR M.221); age ca 55; Feb 1745 (CCR MSA 8.63); age ca 59; 31 Oct 1748 (CCR MSA 8.787)

Keene, Richard; merchant; 25 May 1751; 27 Aug 1754; wife Margaret; son Henry; daus. Sarah, Mary, Lucy Clagett, Sarah, Martha; tracts *The Seller House, Little Addition to George Greevs Land, Keene's Purchase, Charles Hill* (MCW XI.46); extx. Mrs. Margarett; 1 Oct 1754 (I 60.156)

Keene Richard; extx. Mrs. Mary; 24 Jun 1755 (I 61.46)

Keene, Margaret; widow; 13 Sep 1755; 26 Nov 1755; dau. Margarett Hilleary [widow]; sons Francis King, Cave Williams; grandson Thomas Hilleary [s/o Margaret], Francis King; granddau. Barbara Magruder (MCW XI.108); 2 Aug 1763; ex. Capt. Francis Keene (ABB 4.33)

Keen, Mary; 3 Aug 1763; 26 Jul 1764; sister Sarah Hance (MCW XIII.31)

Keene, Martha; 1 Feb 1772; 31 Jul 1775; sister Sarah Beny [?Berry] (MCW XVI.72)

KEHONE

Kehone, James; age ca 22; servant; Jun 1698 Ct. (PGCR A.317)

KEIRSEY

Keirsey, Thomas; age ca 16; servant; Jun 1698 Ct. (PGCR A.317)

KELLY

Kelly, Bryan; age ca 14; servant; Aug 1698 Ct. (PGCR A.333)

Kelly, John; age ca 14; servant; Aug 1698 Ct. (PGCR A.333)

Kelly, Mary; age 3 on 29 May next; d/o Elizabeth Taylor; Nov 1711 Ct. (PGCR G.124)

Kelly, James; age 8 on 15 Apr next; s/o Jarvis and Elizabeth Winson; bound out; Nov 1714 (PGCR G.692)

Kelly, Brian; 5 Jan 1742; 3 May 1745; wife Mary; children: Joseph, Benjamin, Thomas; tracts *Dispute, Advantage, Two Brothers* (MCW IX.32); extx. Mary; 23 May 1745 (I 32.259)

Kelly, Daniel; age ca 14 on 29 instant; bound out; Mar 1744 (PGCR CC.276)

Kelly, Barnaby; m. 25 Dec 1753 Henewrittta Athey (KGP p. 301)

Kelly, Thomas; wife Hanah; child: Elisabeth, b. 9 May 1763 (PGP p. 269)

Kelly, Edward; wife Margret; child: James, bapt. 29 Nov 1767 Broad Creek (KGP p. 361)

KEMPTON

Kempton, William; age ca 15; servant; Jun 1698 Ct. (PGCR A.316)

KENDLE

Kendle, John; admx. Abigail; 28 Aug 1740 (I 25.180)

KENDRICK

Kindeck, Thoms; children: Rebecca; b. 12 Oct 1715; Ann, b. 11 Jan 1717; Mary, b. 25 Feb 1719; Sarah, b. 25 Mar 1722 (KGP p. 263)

Kendrick, Thomas; wife Sarah; children: Ruth, bapt. 19 Apr 1752; John, b. 27 May 1756; Rebeckah, b. 22 Dec 1761; Charles, bapt. 15 May 1764 at Broad Creek (KGP p. 314, 325, 339)

Kindrick, John; wife Ellinor; child: Nathan Offutt, b. 4 Jul 1762 (PGP p. 267)

KENESTON

Kinningston [Keneston], Thomas; 4 May 1699 (I&A 19.55); admx. Deborah; 6 Dec 1700 (I&A 20.51)

Kennerson, Deborrer; 20 Apr 1703; 1 May 1703; [no relationship noted] (MCW III.14); 3 May 1703 (I&A 22.149); 13 Jun 1705 (I&A 3.389)

KENNEDY

Kennedy, James; 28 Sep 1773 (I 118.167)

KENNETT

Kennett, John Boyce; bound to Robert Wheeler, Sr. and his son Daniel; Nov 1739 (PGCR X.501)

KENNICK

Kennick, William; age 15 next April; chooses guardian; Jun 1733 (PGCR S.333)

KERBY

Kerby, John; wife Ann; children: Charles, b. 4 Nov 1773 Broad Creek; William, b. 9 May 1776 Upper Chapel (KGP p. 385, 392)

KERMEY

Kerney, Jeremy; alias Macknew; age 2 on 11 May last; bound out; Mar 1711 Ct. (PGCR G.43a)

KERRY

Kerry, Michaell; 21 Nov 1698 (I&A 18.56)

KERSEY

Kersey, Michael; 15 May 1699 (I&A 19-1/2b.7)

KERSNER

Kersner, George; admx. Ann; 3 Nov 1748 (I 37.164)

KERWOOD

Kerwood, Benjamin; wife Mary; child: Elizabeth Phillops, bapt. 9 Mar 1766 Broad Creek (KGP p. 353)

KEY

Key, James; age ca 16; servant; Aug 1698 Ct. (PGCR A.333)

Key, Elizabeth; age ca 12 May last; bound out; Jun 1728 (PGCR O.135)

Key, James; age 5 on 7 Apr next; s/o Mary Collier; bound out; Aug 1736 (PGCR V.150)

KEYTON

Keyton, John; wife Elizabeth; children: Mary, bapt. 16 Dec 1764 Upper Chapel; Moses, bapt. 30 Nov 1766; Aron, bapt. 30 Nov 1766 Broad Creek (KGP p. 348, 355)

KIDWELL

Kidwell, Thomas; wife Ann; child: Benjamin Branson, bapt. 5 Jun 1768 Broad Creek (KGP p. 363)

KING

King, Edmond; wife Elizabeth; son John; bound out; Aug 1711 Ct. (PGCR G.77)

King, Elizabeth; age 5 this Mar; d/o Elizabeth; Mar 1713/4 (PGCR G.539)

King, Henry; admx. Mary; 2 Apr 1714 (I&A 35a.152); adms. John Milles & wife Mary; 6 Oct 1714 (I&A 36a.188)

King, Francis; m. 26 Sep 1717 Margaret Sprigg [d/o Col. Thomas]; children: Margaret, b. 28 Aug 1718; Thomas, b. 5 9ber 1720; Cave, b. 1 Jun 1722; Francis, b. 19 Jan 1724/5 (QAP m/2; b/14, 16, 17, 19)

King, Walter; 28 Apr 1722 (I 8.87)

King, Charles; age 9 mos. this date; bound out; Jun 1726 (PGCR L.631)

King, Francis; admx. Margrett; 13 Aug 1726 (I 11.568); admx. Margret; 20 Sep 1727 (I 12.286); extx. Margrett; heirs 2 boys, 2 girls [unnamed]; 30 Sep 1727 (AA 9.124); widow Margaret; 13 Aug 1728 (AA 9.41, 102)

King, William [dec'd]; widow Eleanor; children: Constance, Ann, Mary, Elizabeth; 7 Feb 1727 (PGLR M.256)

King, William; age ca 64; 4 Apr 1732 (PGLR Q.575)

King, William; admx. Francis; son Thomas; daus. w/o Robert Walmsley, w/o Alexander Crutch; 26 Mar 1734 (AA 12.220); heirs of age; 23 Mar 1735 (AA 14.218); son Thomas; dau. [w/o Alexander Crutch]; 25 Aug 1736 (AA 15.183)

King, Margaret; son Thomas; 24 Dec 1741 (PGLR Y.429)

King, Mary; age 4 mos.; bound out; Nov 1742 (PGCR AA.215)

King, Francis; 29 Apr 1751 (I 48.176)

King, Francis; wife Sarah; child: Mary, b. 11 Oct 1759 (KGP p. 318)

King, Richard, Jr.; wife Eleanor; children: William, b. 24 May 1762, Richard, bapt. 26 Aug 1764 Broad Creek; David, b. 19 May 1775 Upper Chapel (KGP p. 331, 343, 391)

King, John; wife Elenor; children: Ruth, bapt. 4 Jul 1762; Elenor, bapt. 19 Feb 1764 at Upper Chapel; Elizabeth, bapt. 26 Jan 1766 Broad Creek (KGP p. 331, 352, 340)

King, James; wife Sarah; children: Charles, bapt. _ Oct 1763 at Lower Chapel; Mary, bapt. 19 Jan 1766 Lower Chapel; Amealea, bapt. 10 Jul 1768 Lower Chapel (KGP p. 335, 352, 371)

King, Edward; wife Ann; children: Susannah, b. 8 Jan 1764 Lower Chapel, Ann, bapt. 28 Dec 1766 Broad Creek (KGP p. 344, 348)

King, Thomas; wife Elenor; children: Ann, bapt. 29 Dec 1765 Lower Chapel; Susanna, b. 26 Oct 1769 Broad Creek; Precilla, b. 23 Feb 1772 Lower Chapel (KGP p. 352, 373)

King, Henry; admx. Mary; 13 Nov 1770 (I 104.252); admx. Mary; 29 Nov 1770 (I 104.253, 262)

King, Francis; admx. Frances; 11 Dec 1771 (I 112.92, 119)

King, William; wife Latitia; child: John Duckett, b. 28 Jan 1772 Upper Chapel (KGP p. 389)

King, Edward; wife. Ann; children: Mary, b. 23 Dec 1773 Lower Chapel; James, b. 23 Apr 1776 Broad Creek (KGP p. 379, 383)

King, James; wife Sarah; child: Sebra (f), b. 1 Jul 1774 Lower Chapel (KGP p. 380)

King, Thomas; admx. Elisabeth; 9 May 1774 (I 117.442)

King, John; wife Eleanor; child: Mary, b. 13 Sep 1774 Broad Creek (KGP p. 386)

King, Elisha; m. 11 Dec 1775 Lydia Webster Upper Chapel; children: Ann, b. 31 Sep 1776; others b. after 1776 (KGP p. 392)

King, Henry; 11 Jul 1776; admx. Mary Crackells [w/o Thomas]; 2 daus. [unnamed] (ABB 7.31)

King, James; wife Eleanor; child: Anne, b. 30 Nov 1776 Lower Chapel (KGP p. 381)

KINGSBERRY

Kingsbury, Elizabeth [late of Calvert Co.]; 6 Mar 1743; 3 Mar 1743; sons James, Samuel Evans; daus. Priscilla Groom, Elizabeth Lucas, Ann Pottenger (MCW VIII.214); 14 Jul 1743 (I 28.315); rep. of age [unnamed]; 16 Nov 1744 (AA 20.521); 22 Aug 1746 (AA 22.285)

Kingsberry, Demilon; wife Elizabeth; children: Margret, b. 11 Jan 1762; Elizabeth, bapt. 8 Jul 1764 at Broad Creek (KGP p. 330, 339)

KIRKWOOD

Kirkwood, John; surgeon; St. Paul's Parish; 9 Jun 1740; 22 Jul 1740; wife Elizabeth; son Richard; bro. William; b-i-l Bradford Bevin (MCW VIII.95); 16 Aug 1740 (I 26.17); 30 Jun 1748 (AA 25.101)

KISTON

Kiston, Edward; age ca 45; 1738 (PGLR T.635)

KITCHEN

Kitchen, William; m. 22 Dec 1722 Ann Evans (QAP m/3)

Kitchin, William; age 9 on 9 Oct last; bound out; Mar 1735 (PGCR V.292)

KNEEGLE

Kneegle, James; child: Loy'd Carlton Tawney Hilton, b. 20 Oct 1771 Upper Chapel (KGP p. 388)

KNEWSTUB

Knewstubb [Newstubb], Robert; wife Hannah; children: Elizabeth, b. 21 10ber 1707; Mary, b. 15 Jul 1708; Martha, b. 1 Jan 1712; Robert, b. __ ____ 1715; Sarah, b. 10 Jul 1721 (QAP b/10, 11, 17)

Newstubb [Newshib], Robert, Sr.; 10 May 1745 (I 32.293); 26 Jun 1746 (AA 22.213)

KNIGHT
Knight, Peter; age ca 15; servant; Jun 1710 (PGCR D.316)
Night, Sarah; age ca 61; 1734 (PGLR T.124)
Knight, Peter; 30 Sep 1735 (I 21.502); 26 Aug 1736 (AA 15.185)
Knight, Edward; wife Mary; 14 Apr 1737 (PGLR T.454)
Knite, Mary; child: Heneritta, bapt 9 Mar 1766 Broad Creek (KGP p. 352-3)

KNOTT
Knott, James; admx. Sarah; 12 Aug 1773 (I 114.300); admx. Sarah; 28 Feb 1774 (I 114.308); admx. Sarah Boyd [w/o Abraham]; 13 Nov 1776 (I 124.7); 18 Nov 1776; admx. Sarah Boyd [w/o Abraham]; 8 children [unnamed] (ABB 7.67)

KNOWLAND
Knowland, Tracy [s/o Alexander]; wife Aphin; child: Allison, b. 9 Jan 1765 (PGP p. 272)

KUNHOLT
Kunholt, John; d. 1 Sep 1696; Jun 1698 Ct. (PGCR A.318)

KYLOW
Kylow?, John; age ca 17; servant; Jan 1699 Ct. (PGCR B.12)

LACCOUNT

Laccount, John; 8 Jun 1708 (I&A 28.253)

LAKEY

Lakey, Christopher; m. 15 7ber 1724 Mary Huntly (QAP m/3)

LAKING

Laking, Abraham; m. 10 Oct 1717 Martin [?Martha] Lee (QAP m/1)

Laking, Abraham; 25 Nov 1744; 16 Dec 1743; wife Martha; sons Abraham, Joseph, Benjamin; tracts *Joseph and Margaret's Rest* (MCW VIII.237); extx. Martha; 13 May 1745 (I 30.376); extx.; Martha; 4 young children [unnamed]; 14 May 1745 (AA 21.245); widow Martha; heirs Sarah Lyeth, Abraham, Martha Plummer, Joseph, Deborah, Elizabeth, Mary, Rachel, Benjamin, Ruth; 28 Aug 1745 (GB 142)

LAMAR

Lamar, Thomas, Sr.; 4 Oct 1712; 29 May 1714; wife Ann; sons Thomas, John; (MCW IV.11); 18 Aug 1714 (I&A 36a.189); extx. Ann; son John; 4 May 1715 (I&A 36b.225)

Lemar, Thomas, Jr.; wife Martha; child: John, b. 22 Apr 1713 (QAP b/8)

Lemarr, John; m. 21 Jan 1714 Susanna Tyler (QAP m/1)

Lamar, Thomas; 11 May 1747; 31 Jan 1749; sons Robert, Thomas, John, Samuel, James, Alexander; ss-i-l William Williams, Clementious Davis; tracts *Joseph and James, The Conclusion, My Son Thomases Marsh, Two Brothers, The Pines, Hunting Hill* (MCW X.74)

Lamar, John, Jr.; 2 Nov 1756; 24 Mar 1757; wife Sarah; 6 children; sons William Bishop, Mark, Jacob, John; daus. Rebecca, Susanna; tract *Major's Lot* (MCW XI.258-9); 4 Jun 1757 (I 63.408); 20 Nov 1762; extx. Sarah Lamar; children: William Bishup, Mark, Jacob, Rebecca, Susanna, John (ABB 3.164)

Lamar, John; 28 Feb 1758 (?); 1 Nov 1774; wife Susanna; sons Mureane, Richard, Robert, Jacob, John, Thomas; daus. Susanna, Anne, Mary, Elizabeth, Rachel, Priscilla; tract *Mayor's [Major's] Lot* (MCW XVI.6-7); extx. Suanna; 19 Jan 1775 (I 123.423); 6 Nov 1776; extx. Susanna Lamar; 10 children: legatees Susanna, Ann, Mary, Elisabeth, Rachel, Marcus & Richard Lamar (ABB 7.72)

LAMBETH

Lambeth, Richard; planter; 4 May 1721 (I 6.4); 15 Jul 1721 (AA 3.517)

LANCASTER

Lancaster, Richard; 18 Jun 1724 (I 11.140); 10 Nov 1725 (AA 7.163)

Lancaster, Thomas; age ca 48; 20 Feb 1744 (CCR JK#4.565)

Lancaster, Henry; age ca 11 on 25 Dec next; bound out; Jun 1744 (PGCR CC.403)

Lancaster, Thomas; 1 Apr 1772; [no relations]; tract *Easy Purchase* (MCW XIV.224)

LANDERS

Landers, Robert; wife Mary; tract *The Forrest*; 10 Jul 1722 (PGLR I.299)

LANDSBERRY

Landsberry, Thomas; wife Ruth; son Thomas; tract *Soe Soe*; 16 Dec 1736 (PGLR T.431, 432))

LANSDALE

Landsdale, Isaac; 20 Nov 1733 (I 17.581)

LANE

Lane, John; 13 Sep 1712; 17 Dec 1715; [no relation] (MCW IV.41); 5 Nov 1716 (I&A 37a.142); 8 May 1717 (I&A 38a.115)

Lane, John; wife Ann; child: John, b. 1723 (QAP b/18)

LANGDON

Langdon, Abel; wife Margrette; child: Elisabeth, b. 27 Sep 1762 (PGP p. 267)

LANGLEY

Langley, William; wife Sarah; child: John Noble, b. 28 Sep 1773 Lower Chapel (KGP p. 384)

LANGWORTH

Langworth, William [CH]; [s/o John]; daus. Elizabeth Hagan [w/o James], Mary Routhorn [w/o Joseph]; tract *Widow's Mite*; 9 Aug 1714 (PGLR F.415)

LANHAM

Lanham, John; sons John, Richard, Thomas; Nov 1697 Ct. (PGCR A.260)

Lanham, John, Jr.; m. 14 Feb 1708 Mary Dickinson; children: Thomas, b. 7 Mar 1709; John, b. 14 Aug 1712; Mary, b. 3 Jan 1714; William, b. 21 Sep 1717; Elizabeth, b. 22 Sep 1721; Eliazar, b. 3 Jan 1723; Elisha, b. 23 Jun 1725, Elizabeth, b. 21 Dec 1727 (KGP p. 266)

Lanum, John; son Thomas 'having but one hand'; Nov 1711 Ct. (PGCR G.128)

Lanham, John, Sr.; son John, Jr., Richard; tract *Lanham's Addition*; 22 Sep 1713 (PGLR F.277)

Lanham, John, Sr.; wife Dorothy; son John, Jr.; tract *Lanham's Addition*; 16 Nov 1717 (PGLR F.14/541)

Lanham, William; m. 15 Jan 1720 Alce Tolburt; children: Joseph and Benjamin, b. 18 Oct 1721; John, b. 12 Dec 1723; Sarah, b. 9 May 1735 (KGP p. 280)

Lanham, Ralph, m. 21 Feb 1720 Ellenor Jones; child: Elizabeth, b. 14 Oct 1722 (KGP p. 270)

Lanham, Edward; children: John, b. 30 Dec 1722; Notley, b. 11 Oct 1724; Mary, b. 29 Jan 1726; Josias, b. 2 Sep 1728; Susana, b. 7 May 1731; Edward, b. 28 Feb 1732; Sarah, b. 9 May 1735 (KGP p. 280, 281)

Lanham, Edward; wife Asenath; tract *Lannum's Delight*; 23 Oct 1723 (PGLR I.490)

Lanham, Edward; wife Essina; son John; tract *Stone's Delight*; 29 Apr 1724 (PGLR I.544)

Lanham, Thomas; wife Sarah; children: Elianor, b. 10 Apr 1724; Stephen, b. 28 May 1726; Mary, b. 3 Jul 1728 (KGP p. 271, 272)

Lanham, John; age ca 65; 8 Jun 1725 (PGLR I.647); age ca 70; 1729 (PGLR M.445); John, Sr.; age ca 74; 1732 (PGLR Q.480)

Lanham, Thomas; wife Margaret; children: Elizabeth, b. 10 Apr 1732; Jesse (m), b. 2 Jan 1733; Mary, b. 17 Feb 1736; Henry, b. 30 Mar 1739; Rennie (f), b. 3 Apr 1742; Martha, b. 3 Nov 1745; John Dickinson, b. 25 Dec 1748 (KGP p. 298)

Lenham, John, Jr.; wife Mary; son Thomas; tract *Lenham Folley*; 10 Oct 1734 (PGLR T.194)

Lanham, Edward; wife Susane; children: Richard, b. 16 Jul 1737; Rachel, b. 10 May 1739 (KGP p. 286)

Lanham, John, Jr; son John; 19 Sep 1738 (PGLR T.651)

Lanham, Richard; wife Winnefred; dau. Rachel Mitchell [w/o Ignatius] [CH]; tracts *Remains, Addition to Remains*; 26 Feb 1738/9 (PGLR T.699); wife Winnefred; dau. Elizabeth Hardey [w/o William] tracts *The Remains, Attition to The Remains*; 13 Jul 1743 (PGLR Y.716)

Lanham, John, III; m. 16 Jan 1738/9 Mary Piles; child: Hunter, b. 15 Mar 1739/40 (KGP p. 287)

Lanham, James; wife Elinor; children: Abraham, b. 13 Apr 1740; Jacob, b. 22 Aug 1745; Sarah, b. 24 Jul 1748; Isaac, b. 27 Jun 1752, bapt. 23 Aug 1752 (KGP p. 297, 298, 299)

Lanham, John; wife Mary; son Thomas, Jr.; tract *Two Johns*; 2 May 1741 (PGLR Y.278, 279)

Lanham, Ralph; admx. Elinor Leach [w/o John]; 9 Dec 1743 (AA 20.98, 137); heirs, Zachariah, Nathan Mary, Aaron; 29 Aug 1744 (GB 135)

Lanham, John III; admx. Sarah; 8 Jun 1750 (I 43.307); admx. Sarah; children: Hunter, Basil, Allen, Hezeriah; 16 Feb 1750 (AA 29.220)

Lanham, Josias; wife Mary; children: Henry Wilder, bapt. 28 Apr 1751; Solomon, b. 2 Jan 1753; Solomon, b. 2 Jan 1754 [Solomon recorded twice same page] (KGP p. 293, 304)

Lanham, Edward; child: Lenor (f), rec'd rites of church 29 Mar 1752 (KGP p. 295)

Lanham, John; wife Catherine; children: William, bapt. 4 Feb 1753; Drusilla, b. 10 Mar 1757 (KGP p. 298, 320)

Lanham, Edward; wife Catherine; child: Aldred (f), b. 8 Sep 1753 (KGP p. 301)

Lanham, Benjamin; wife Sarah; child: Joseph, b. 18 Nov 1754 (KGP p. 307)

Lanham, Elizabeth; child: Bathsheba Virgin, b. 26 Apr 1755 (KGP p. 308)

Lanham, Shadrack; wife Sarah; children: Sarah, b. 9 Apr 1755; Henry, bapt. 28 May 1761; Mary Ann, b. 13 Apr 1763 at Upper Chapel; Thomas, bapt. 16 Mar 1766 Upper Chapel; Tabitha, bapt. 4 Sep 1768 Upper Chapel; Elisabeth, b. 20 Jun 1770 Upper Chapel (KGP p. 308, 322, 332-3, 354, 371, 375)

Lenham [Lanham], Moses; 10 Nov 1756 (I 62.179)

Lanham, William; wife Cassindra; child: Thomas, b. 25 Jan 1757 (KGP p. 314)

Lanham, Josias; wife Elizabeth; child: John Downs, b. 13 Aug 1758 (KGP p. 321)

Lanham, Ely; wife Christean; children: George, bapt. 7 Feb 1762 (KGP p. 325) [mother unnamed]; Mary, bapt. 3 Oct 1763 at Broad Creek (KGP p. 338)

Lanham, Jesey; wife Elizabeth; children: Henry Dickerson, b. 25 Jul 1760; Margret Lee, bapt. 7 Feb 1762 [mother not named]; Jesey Brookes (m), b. 16 Sep 1764 at Broad Creek; Thomas Hunter Piles, bapt. 24 Nov 1765 Broad Creek; Jessey Brookes (m), bapt. 17 Jun 1764 Broad Creek (KGP p. 259, 325, 339, 350, 356)

Lanham, Edward; 9 Dec 1762; 19 May 1766; wife Catharine; children: Jonah, Mary, Asonan (f), Mildred, Henry, Bursheba, Edward, Susannah, Rachel, Sarah; grandchild Sarah Bias Wilder Lanham; tract *Stones Delight* (MCW XIII.120); admx. Catharine; 6 Aug 1766 (I 89.313); 1767; extx. Catharine McKinnon [w/o Daniel]; legatees Josiah, Mary, Arsenah, Mildred, Henry, Bersheba, Edward, Susannah, Rachel, Sarah, Sarah Bias Wilder Lanham (ABB 5.17); heirs [unnamed]; 24 Aug 1768 (GB 267)

Lanham, Edward; wife Catharine; children: Edward, b. 18 Aug 1762; Robert Poore, bapt. 14 Jul 1765 Lower Chapel (KGP p. 327, 351)

Lanam, Jacob; wife Elizabeth; child: James Boswell, bapt. 26 Jun 1763 Broad Creek (KGP p. 363)

Lanham, Josias; wife Elizabeth; child: Josias Wilder, bapt. 11 Feb 1765 Lower Chapel (KGP p. 350)

Lanham, Zachariah; admx. Mary; 14 May 1767 (I 94.69); 20 Jul 1769; admx. Mary Lanham (ABB 5.242); widow Mary; heirs Richard, Mary, Eleanor, Winefred, Ann, Mealey, Edward; 27 Jun 1775 (GB 281)

Lanham, Elizer; admx. Christian; 23 Jun 1767 (I 95.15); 8 Nov 1770; admx. Christian Fry [w/o Leonard] (ABB 6.22); heirs [unnamed]; 26 Aug 1772 (GB 307)

Lanham, Martha; 28 Dec 1767; 4 Apr 1768; husband Thomas (MCW XIV.35)

Lanham, Ralph; wife Charity; children: Zachariah, b. 15 Mar 1768, bapt. 15 May 1768 Broad Creek; Notley, b. 27 Mar 1770; Ann Wheat, b. 28 Apr 1777 (KGP p. 272, 362)

Lanham, Winnifred; 2 Jan 1770; 27 Nov 1771; children: Edward, Rachel Mitchell, Mary, Benedict Hardey, Cushman Burch, Ann Clements; grandsons Richard, John, William & Josias Jenkins; granddaus. Mary Fry, Winifred Jenkins (MCW XIV.195); 26 Feb 1772 (I 117.135)

Lanham, Allin [Allen]; 8 Feb 1770; 4 Jan 1777 (I 125.342); 4 Jan 1777; ex. Hazariah Lanham; reps. Elisha, Cate & Price Lanham [no relationships noted] (ABB 7.72)

Lanham, Josias; wife Elizabeth; children: Anna Roby, b. 20 Jan 1772 Broad Creek; Mary, b. 9 Oct 1773 Lower Chapel (KGP p. 377, 379)

Lanham, Allen; wife Sene; child: Katharine, b. 5 Apr 1772 Broad Creek (KGP p. 378)

Lanham, Elias; wife Ann; children: John, b. 3 Dec 1772 Broad Creek; Violetta Spick, b. 8 May 1775 Lower Chapel (KGP p. 378, 381)

Lanham, Jesse; wife Elizabeth; child: Terressha, b. 28 Sep 1773 Broad Creek (KGP p. 385)

Lanham, Samuel; wife Charity; child: Thomas, b. 2 Jul 1774; John, b. 6 Apr 1776 (KGP p. 386, 392)

LANKTON

Lankton, Mary; son James, age 7 on 10 Dec next; 27 Mar 1741 (PGLR Y.394)

Lankton, James; wife Elizabeth; child: James, b. 19 Apr 1765 (PGP p. 275)

LANSDALE

Lansdale, Isaac; wife Margaret; child: Thomas Lancaster, b. 14 Aug 1727 (QAP b/21)

Lansdale, Isaac; 14 Oct 1737 (AA 14.414)

Lansdale, Charles; m. 19 or 20 Apr 1767 Catherine Wheeler, d/o Clement Wheeler; children: Elizabeth Ann, b. 12 Nov 1769; Henry, b. 18 Jul 1771;

Susannah, b. 12 Jun 1776; Charles Gates, b. 9 Apr 1778 Lower Chapel
(KGP p. 287, 376)

LARGE

Large, Philip; 11 Jul 1747 (I 35.219); admx. Solony; 28 Jun 1748 (AA 25.98)

Large, Salome [Solomy]; 17 Feb 1749 (I 41.384); heirs Elisabeth [age 12],
Philip [age 4]; 10 Feb 1749 (AA 27.273); children: Elisabeth, Philip; 27 Jun
1750 (AA 28.243); 28 Nov 1751 (AA 31.254); 28 Nov 1751; children: Eliza &
Philip Large (ABB 1.20); heirs Elizabeth, Philip; 1 Dec 1752 (GB 181)

LARKIN

Larkin, Thomas [AA]; wife Margaret; tract part of Essington; 29 Mar 1705
(PGLR C.128a)

Larkin, Benjamin; wife Rachel; children: Thomas, b. 26 Mar 1763; John, b.
21 Feb 1765 (PGP p. 268, 276)

LASHLEY

Lashly, John; wife Alice; children: Robert, b. 25 Sep 1705; John, b. 7 Apr
1708; Mary, b. 25 Mar 1711; Joseph, b. 5 Jan 1713/4; Elizabeth, b. 26
Mar 1716 (QAP b/2, 9, 11)

Lashly, John; 21 Nov 1717; 11 Dec 1717; wife Eals; 6 [unnamed] children
under 21 (MCW IV.122); 12 Dec 1717 (I 1.10); 8 Sep 1719 (AA 2.233)

Lashle, Robert; m. 16 Jan 1735 Elizabeth Soper (QAP m/6)

LATIMORE

Latemore, Mark; wife Mary; child: Elizabeth, bapt. 14 Oct 1764 Lower
Chapel (KGP p. 345)

Latimore, Samuel; wife Lydda; child: Mary Pen, b. 11 Mar 1775 Lower
Chapel (KGP p. 380)

LAWRANCE

Larrance, Philip; 30 Sep 1696 (I&A 14.62)

Lawrance, John; late of Liverpool, Lancashire, England; m. 28 Aug 1749
Miss Mary Plafay of Piscataway; children: Margarett, b. 12 Jul 1750; on
the 13th christened by Rev. Theophilius Swift, rector of Portobacco
Parish, Charles Co. (KGP p. 288-9)

LAWS

Laws, Michael; wife Aine; child: Cassandria, bapt. 29 Aug 1751; [ICR lists her
as Cassandria Cotts] (KGP p. 294)

LAWSON

Lawson, John; 4 Apr 1749; 26 Mar 1749; father, mother & grandmother [unnamed]; sisters Martha Baden, Lettice Naylor; nephews Thomas & Robert Baden; tract *Lawsons* (MCW X.24-5); admx. Elisabeth; 10 Oct 1749 (I 42.43); admx. Elisabeth; 11 Jun 1750 (AA 28.158); admx. Elisabeth; 28 Mar 1750 (AA 29.236); widow Elizabeth; heirs [surviving]; 23 Nov 1757 (GB 206); 10 Jun 1761; admx. Elisabeth Lawson; father [unnamed]; nephew Thomas & Robert Baden; sisters Martha Baden, Lettice Naylor (ABB 3.82); 30 Jun 1762; admx. Elisabeth Lawson; children: Martha Baden, Lettice Naylor; father & grandfather [unnamed]; grandchildren of daus. [unnamed] (ABB 3.144) widow Elizabeth; heirs Martha Baden, Lettice Naylor; 29 Aug 1764 (GB 240)

Lawson, Elisabeth; 3 May 1766 (I 123.102)

Lawson, James; wife Amela; child: Elizabeth, b. 28 Dec 1773 Lower Chapel (KGP p. 379)

Lawson, Thomas; 30 Sep 1756; 25 Mar 1761; dau. Lettis Naylor [w/o George]; grandson John Lawson Naylor; tract *Stoke* (MCW XII.47); 8 Apr 1761 (I 74.168)

Lawson, Thomas; wife Elizabeth; child: Elizabeth, bapt. 19 Jun 1768 Lower Chapel (KGP p. 369)

Lawson, Elisabeth; 17 Apr 1775; [no relations] (ABB 7.38)

LAXSON

Laxon, Thomas; 22 Jan 1713 (I&A 35a.340, 341); 9 Feb 1714 (I&A 36b.14)

LAYYEAR

Layyear, John; wife Elizabeth; child: Jacob, b. 22 Sep 1763 (PGP p. 276)

LAZENBY

Lazenby, Robert; wife. Lucy; child: Elisabeth, b. 12 Feb 1763 (PGP p. 269)

Lazenbee, Henry; wife Margreet; child: Mary, b. 24 Dec 1764 (PGP p. 273)

LEACHMAN

Leachman, Andrew; m. 8 May 1712 Ellinor Burk; child: Samuel, b. 19 May 1714 (QAP m/1; b/10)

LEAVETT

Leavett, Robert; 15 Aug 1735 (I 21.31)

LECOUNT

Lecount, John; 8 Apr 1707 (I&A 27.87)

LEE

Lee, William, wife Ann; children: Mellona, b. 1 Jun 1689; John, b. 19 Jun 1691; Elizabeth, b. 3 Mar 1693/4; Margaret, b. 14 Jan 1695/6; Martha, b. 20 Jun 1699 (QAP b/1)

Lee, William; son John; Nov 1697 Ct. (PGCR A.260)

Lee, William; wife Jane; children: John, b. 8 Jun 1710; Margratt, b. 1 Oct 1712; Mary, b. 26 Jan 1714; William, b. 1 May 1718; James, b. 12 Feb 1719/20; Anna, b. 7 Feb 1721/2; Clemant, b. 21 Aug 1725; Christopher, b. 1 Jan 1725/6 (KGP p. 264)

Lee, Philip; wife Sarah [d/o Thomas and Barbary Brooke]; son Thomas; tract *Brookefield;* 29 Dec 1713 (PGLR F.312)

Lee, John; wife Ellinor; child: Ann, b. 11 Jul 1717 (QAP b/12)

Lee, Philip; m. widow of Maj. Dent ca 11 yrs. ago; 20 Apr 1719 (CCR CL.548)

Lee, Sarah, w/o Philip Lee, gent.; 16 Nov 1724; 28 Nov 1724; son Arthur; father Thomas Brooke; bro. Thomas Brooke, gent. (MCW V.190)

Lee, William; 30 Oct 1727 (I 12.530); children: John, Margaret, Mary, William, James; 4 Apr 1729 (AA 9.335)

Lee, James; wife Mary; tract *Deep Creek;* 24 Nov 1733 (PGLR T.16)

Lee, Richard, Capt.; age ca 30; 6 Mar 1735 (CCR-MSA 6.256); age ca 37; 17 Jan 1743 (CCR MSA 8.45)

Lee, Philip; son Philip; grandson Philip; 5 Dec 1735 (PGLR T.338)

Lee, Philip, gent.; 20 Mar 1743/4; 1 May 1744; current wife Elizabeth; father Col. Richard of VA; wife Sarah [dec'd]; sons Richard [wife Grace], Arthur [s/o 1st wife Sarah, dec'd], Hancock, Corbin, John, George, Francis, Thomas, Philip [dec'd]; daus. Letitia, Eleanor, Elizabeth, Alice, Hannah, Margaret, Ann Russell, _____ Patts [w/o William]; grandson Philip [wife Grace]; tracts *Rehoboth, Bart's Hope, The Addition, Lee's Purchase, Paradise* (MCW VIII.264); 11 Dec 1744 (I 30.125); 20 Dec 1748 (I 37.413, 415); widow Elisabeth; Sarah, Elisabeth & Lettice [daus. of Philip, Jr.], Philip Thomas, Sarah, Eleanor & Hannah [child. of Richard]; dau. Hannah; others [named but not identified]; 6 Feb 1748 (AA 26.21)

Lee, Anna Maria; 8 Sep 1746; 1 Sep 1747; [no relations] (MCW IX.124)

Lee, Thomas, gent.; [with 1749 probates]; son Thomas Sim; dau. Sarah Brooke Lee; nephews Philip [s/o Philip], Archer [s/o Arthur]; tracts *Paradice, Lee's Purchase, Stump Dale* (MCW X.62)

Lee, James; planter; 10 Oct 1748; 25 Mar 1752; wife [unnamed] (MCW X.107)

Lee, John; wife Ann; child: William, b. 26 Jan 1755 (KGP p. 307)

Lee, John; 8 Aug 1758 (I 65.190)

Lee, Hancock; 13 Oct 1759; 5 Nov 1759; bros. Corbin, John, George; sisters Ann Russell, Alice Clark, Margaret Lymer, Letitia Wardrop, Hanna Bowie; nephews, Daniel Bowie, Hancock Lee [s/o John of VA] (MCW XI.246); 28 Dec 1759 (I 74.155)

Lee, Elizabeth; child: Elizabeth, b. 6 Sep 1761 (PGP p. 261)

Lee, John; heirs [unnamed]; 24 Aug 1768 (GB 268)

LEECH

Leech [Leach], William; wife Mary; children: Sarah, b. 18 Jan 1762; Elizabeth, b. 28 Nov 1765 (PGP p. 264, 277)

Leech, John; wife Mary; children: Martha and Sarah [twins], b. 20 Feb 1763; William, b. 31 Oct 1764 (PGP p. 268, 273)

LEECHMAN

Leechman, Eleanor; age 8 on 15 Jun inst.; Samuel, age 8 on 15 Jun inst.; bound out; Jun 1725 (PGCR K.452)

LEEK

Leek, Henry; wife Elizabeth; child: Obed, b. 1 May 1765 (PGP p. 276)

LEIPER

Leiper, James; surgeon residing in Philadelphia about to embark for Lisbon; wife Elizabeth; children: George, Robert, Lucy Ann Hebbard; mother Helen Scott; bro. Thomas; nieces Nancy, Junet; tracts *Wheelers Hope, Appledore* (MCW XIV.220); 10 Aug 1772 (I 109.230); 17 Aug 1772 (I 109.235)

LEISY

Leisy, Joseph; age 65; 1 Mar 1731/2 (PGLR Q.602)

LEMAN

Leman, Hickford; 29 Aug 1733 (AA 12.56)

LEMASTER

Lemaster, Abraham; wife Anne; child: Catherine, b. 20 Nov 1754 (KGP p. 308)

Lemasters, Thomas; wife Elizabeth; child: Thomas, b. 12 Apr 1760 (PGP p. 281)

Lemaster, Thomas; wife Letis; child: Jacob, bapt. 13 Feb 1763 at Upper Chapel (KGP p. 332)

LEMMON

Lemon, Hickford; age ca 51; 8 Oct 1724 (PGLR I.600); age ca 56; 1728 (PGLR M.347)

Lemmon, Hickford; 22 May 1732; [no relationships] (MCW VI.220); 17 Aug 1732 (I 16.579); 24 Jan 1735 (AA 14.144)

LENTHALL

Lenthall, William; wife Elizabeth; children: Samuel, b. 15 Jul 1715; Mary, b. 5 Jan 1719/20 (QAP 11, 16)

LETCHWORTH

Letchworth, Joseph, 25 Jun 1700 (I&A 20.89); 3 Aug 1703 (I&A 24.35)

Letchworth, Thomas; 14 Mar 1721; 21 Jun 1722; wife Elizabeth; sons Thomas, Joseph; daus. Anne, Mary, Elizabeth; tracts *Joseph and Mary, Brook Court Mannor, Two Friends* in Charles Co. (MCW V.123); f-i-l Alexander Magruder; 15 Mar 1722 (I 8.87); extx. Elisabeth; f-i-l Alexander Magruder; 26 Nov 1722 (I 9.150); extx. Elisabeth; widow & 4 child. [unnamed]; 2 Dec (AA 5.295) widow [m/2 Edward Truman]; sons Thomas, Joseph Letchworth; tract *Brook Court*; 8 May 1725 (PGLR I.633); heirs Anne, Mary, Thomas, Joseph; 24 Nov 1725 (GB 25)

LETHCOE

Lethcoe, Thomas; wife Mary; child: Winsor Flandagen, b. 25 Mar 1775 Broad Creek (KGP p. 387)

LEVLET

Levelet, John Michal; 20 Mar 1717 (AA 1.6); 22 Jan 1718 (AA 1.357)

LEVETT

Levett, Robert [England]; to marry Elizabeth Clarke, widow; b-i-l Benjamin Lawrence [AA]; 12 Aug 1713 (PGLR F.368)

Levett, Robert; [mentions Robert & John's pictures drawn by their father's order]; 29 Jan 1722 (I 9.155)

Levett, Elizabeth; widow; 22 Sep 1725; 25 Nov 1725; husband Robert [dec'd]; sons Robert, John; daus. Elizabeth Duskin, Margaret & Ruth Clark; bro. Daniel Mariartee; sister Margaret Sprigg (MCW V.204); 12 Dec 1726 (I 13.354); widow; 4 Jan 1728 (AA 9.235); widow of Thomas; 23 Oct 1731 (AA 11.193); former admx. Elisabeth; 21 Oct 1732 (AA 11.500); son John; 16 Aug 1735 (AA 13.247)

Levett, Robert; adm. Margret Clarke; 10 Sep 1727 (I 12.253)

Levett, Robert [dec'd]; widow Elizabeth; 16 Jan 1729 (CCR-MSA 5.34)

Levett, John [age ca 17] and Robert [age ca 19]; choose guardian; Aug 1733 (PGCR S.402)

Levett, Robert; minor; siblings John, Margaret Buchana [w/o George], Ruth
    Rawlings [w/o Moses], Elisabeth Diskin [w/o John]; 16 Aug 1735 (AA
    13.248)
Levit, William; age 8; bound out; Mar 1742 (PGCR AA.341)

LEVISTON
Leviston, James; age 12 on 7 May last; bound out; Jun 1745 (PGCR DD.91)

LEWIN
Lewin, Philip; planter; 20 Jul 1722; 15 Aug 1722; dau. Elizabeth Jones,
    Mary Gibbs [w/o James] also Mary Gilbert, dec'd [w/o James];
    grandsons Phillip & James Gibbs [s/o Mary], James Jones [s/o
    Elizabeth]; granddaus. Mary Anne & Jane Gibbs [ds/o Mary], Mary
    Gilbert [d/o James & Mary]; tracts *Stone Hill, Philip' Folley, Dickinson's
    Delight* (MCW V.114); extx. Elisabeth Barnes; 15 Oct 1722 (I 9.153); extx.
    Elisabeth Barnes [w/o Henry]; 21 May 1723 (AA 5.173); extx. Elisabeth
    Barnes [w/o Henry]; 21 Mar 1725 (AA 7.303); heirs Philip, James, Mary
    Ann, Mary & Jane Gibbs; 24 Nov 1725 (GB 27)

LEWIS
Lewis, Thomas; 22 Mar 1695; 3 Jun 1696; wife Catharine; children: Richard,
    Thomas, John (MCW II.102); 16 Jan 1696 (I&A 14.42); widow Katherine Watkins
    [w/o John]; 3 Jul 1699 (I&A 19.67)
Lewis, Sarah; orphan; age 9 on 25 Mar next; bound out; Aug 1701 (PGCR
    B.122)
Lewis, Patience; age 4 in Mar next; bound out by mother and step-father
    John Underwood; Nov 1703 Ct. (PGCR B.262a)
Lewis, Jonathan; wife Mary; children: Thomas, b. 11 7ber 1706; William,
    b. 13 8ber 1708; Jonathan, b. 29 Aug 1711; John, 30 Nov 1713; Daniel, b. 6
    8ber 1715; David & Jonathan [twins], b. 7 8ber 1718; Mary, b. 28 7ber
    1720 (QAP b/2, 3, 5, 8, 11, 14, 16)
Lewis, John; 5 Mar 1710/1; 20 Apr 1711; wife Elizabeth (MCW III.206); extx.
    Elisabeth; 6 Jun 1711 (I&A 32b.178); extx. Elisabeth Pearson [w/o Francis]; 5
    Feb 1712 (I&A 33b.168); widow Elisabeth Pearson; 13 Mar 1713 (I&A 35a.298)
Lewis, Elisabeth; widow; children: Thomas, John, Stephen, Sarah, Priscilla,
    Samuel, Jane; grandson John Davis [s/o Jane]; [undated - ca 1711] (PGLR
    F.154)
Lewis, Thomas; sons John, Thomas Jr.; tract *Buttersy*; 20 Aug 1711 (PGLR F.101)
Lewis, John; age 13 in Jan next; bound out; Jun 1715 (PGCR G.764)
Lewis, Davis & Jonathan; age 5 on 7 Oct last; twin ss/o Mary Beckett
    bound out; Mar 1723 (PGCR L.243)

Lewis, Jonathon; 13 Feb 1724 (I 11.222); 29 Jun 1726 (AA 7.443)

Lewis, Jonas; wife Elizabeth; tract *Ketakin Bottoms*; 22 Feb 1734 (PGLR T.239)

Lewis, John; admx. Winifred; 13 Jun 1748 (I 37.45); admx. Winferd; children: Mary, John, Anne, Priscilla; [undated with 1749] (AA 26.113); widow Winefred; heirs Mary, John, Anne, Priscilla, Thomas; 29 Aug 1750 (GB 168)

Lewis, John; wife Sarah; child: Kezia Pigman, b. 30 Dec 1755 (KGP p. 312)

Lewis, Abner; 15 Feb 1757 (I 63.102)

Lewis, Charity; child: Sarah, b. 20 Aug 1759 (KGP p. 318)

Lewis, John; wife Elizabeth; child: Absalam, b. 2 Mar 1760 (PGP p. 259)

Lewis, John; child: Elizabeth Thomas, bapt. 18 Apr 1762 (KGP p. 326)

Lewis, John; wife Sarah; children: Thomas, b. 25 Jan 1764; bapt. 11 Mar 1764 Broad Creek; Sarah, bapt. 10 Aug 1766 Upper Chapel (KGP p. 356, 364)

Lewis, Thomas; wife Elizabeth; child: Daniel, bapt. 18 Jan 1767 Broad Creek (KGP p. 360)

LEY

Ley, James; m. Susanna; child: Thomas, bapt. 24 Nov 1751 (KGP p. 294)

LIDDELL

Liddell, William; dau. Jane; tract *Cuckold's Point*; 27 Nov 1711 (PGLR F.132)

LINDOCE

Lindoce, Alexander [dec'd]; dau. Alice; tract *Allison's Adventure*; 25 May 1728 (PGLR M.280)

LINDSEY

Linzee, Eliz.; age ca 21; servant; Jun 1706 (PGCR C.61)

Lindsey, Samuel; wife Sarah; child: John, b. 15 Mar 1758; Thomas Pannell, bapt. 12 Jun 1761; George, bapt. 1 Jan 1764 at Broad Creek; Elizabith Elener, b. 20 Mar 1766 Broad Creek; Sushanna, b. 22 Mar 1768, bapt. 26 Jun 1768 Broad Creek (KGP p. 320, 322, 338, 353, 363)

LINGAN

Lingan, George [AA]; wife Ann; dau. Martha Willson [w/o Josiah]; tract *Buttington*; 8 Apr 1699 (PGLR A.299)

LINTHORNE

Linthorne, William; wife Elizabeth; tract *Ramsely's Delight*; 6 year lease; 12 Oct 1702 (PGLR C.118c)

LINTON

Lenton, William; wife Elizabeth; children: Rebecca, b. 14 Jan 1698; William, b. 29 Apr 1701; George, b. 14 Dec 1703 (QAP b/1)

Linton, William; 9 Jan 1731 (I 16.133); 8 Apr 1732 (AA 11.364); [with 1732] (I 17.3); 29 Nov 1732 (AA 11.706)

Linton, George; wife Mary; child: Margery, b. 16 May 173_ (QAP b/28)

LISBEY

Lisby, Aaron; admx. Mary; 28 Nov 1749 (I 42.52)

Lisbey, Samuel; wife Sushannah; children: Thomas, bapt. 18 Apr 1762 [mother unnamed] (KGP p. 326); Sushannah, bapt. 17 Jun 1764 at Broad Creek; Elenor, bapt. 22 Mar 1767 Broad Creek (KGP p. 339, 360)

LITHGO

Lithgo, James; wife Mary; child: Elizabeth, b. 24 Oct 1764 Broad Creek (KGP p. 342)

LITTLEJOHN

Littlejohn, Mercilius; 3 Nov 1740; 18 Mar 1740; wife Elizabeth; father Oliver; sons Charles, Samuel, Henry; dau. [unnamed] (MCW VIII.142)

LITTON

Litton, Michael; wife Mary; child: Tabitha, b. 14 Jan 1763 (PGP p. 270)

Litton, Michael; wife Tabitha; child: Burton, b. 9 Sep 1764 (PGP p. 272)

LIVERS

Livers, Arnold; 11 Jun 1750/1; 28 Aug 1751; wife Helena; sons Anthony, James, Arnold, Robert; daus. Mary, Rachel, Jacoba Clementina; grandson Arnold Elder; granddaus. Ann Livers [d/o James], Eliza. Elder; bro. John Hawkins, Sr.; tracts *Duke's Wood, Arnold's Chance, Arnold's Delight, Cole's Good Will* (MCW X.177-8); extx. ?Thelma; 26 Feb 1752 (I 48.371); 7 Sep 1753; extx. Helena Collard [w/o Samuel] (ABB 1.94, 112, 113); extx. Helena Collard [w/o Samuel]; 7 Sep 1753 (AA 35.59, 99; 36.97, 276, 350)

Livers, Anthony; age 18 on 13 Jan next; choses Thomas Sandsbury, Jr. as guardian; Jun 1753 (PGCR MM.415)

Livers, Arnold; age 16 on 24 Oct next; choses Samuel Collard as guardian; Jun 1753 (PGCR MM.415)

LLOYD

Lloyd, William; m. 9 Apr 1707 Grisell Johnston; children: Thomas, b. 10 Feb 1709; Anne, b. 23 Oct 17[09]?; Mary, b. 12 Dec 1714; Jane, 16 Mar 1718 (ICR; KGP p. 261, 262)

Loyd [Loyde], Thomas; 27 Feb 1726/7; 28 Mar 1728; sons Ben, John; dau. Sarah (MCW VI.60)

Loyd, Benjamin; wife Teresa; tract The Taylertown; 5 Feb 1728 (PGLR M.460)

Lloyd, John; orphan; age ca 13; bound out; Sarah, orphan; age ca 3 put under guardianship of kinsman James Pelley; Mar 1729 (PGCR O.411)

Lloyd, Thomas; extx. Anne Cockshutt; 9 Sep 1729 (AA 9.472, 476)

Lloyd, Thomas; legatee Benjamin; 15 Jun 1730 (AA 10.308)

Lloyd, [father's & sister's estates - unnamed]; heir John; 23 Jun 1730 (GB 53)

Loyde, Benjamin; wife Tensha; tract Taylorton; 6 Jun 1741 (PGLR Y.329)

Lloyd, John; wife Margret child: Benjamin, bapt. 14 Jul 1765 Lower Chapel (KGP p. 352)

Lloyd, Denis; child: James, b. 30 Dec 1766 Broad Creek (KGP p. 360)

LOCK

Lock, Allen; 26 Oct 1733; admx. Mary; 26 Oct 1733 (I 17.497); admx. Mary Johnson [w/o Thomas]; 26 Mar 1734 (AA 12.218, 12.341)

LOCKER

Lockyer, Thomas, Jr.; wife Elinor; children: Ann, b. 1 Sep 1707; Mary, b. 28 Mar 1708[/9]; Abigell, b. 25 Apr 1710; Thomas, b. 24 Sep 1712 (KGP p. 259)

Locker, John; m. 31 Aug 1713 Magdlen Ray; children: John, b. 5 Dec 1714; William, b. 22 Jun 1717; Thomas, b. 11 Mar 1719 (KGP p. 277)

Locker, Thomas; m. 13 Jan 1716 Elliner Evans; children: Walter, b. 4 Jun 1714, Grissel, b. 28 Feb 1715 [m. 26 Sep 1732 Samuel Smith]; John, b. 26 Feb 1717; Phillip, b. 10 Dec 1719 (KGP p. 259, 267); [This marriage clearly dated 1716 with the births of the 4 children following]

Lockar, Thomas; d. 1722; wife Elizabeth [widow of Robert Johnson] (KGP p. 281)

Lockyer, John; wife Magdalen; tract Gleaning, Pasture; 21 May 1723 (PGLR I.488)

Locker, Thomas; 15 Jun 1722 (I 7.309); exs. Thomas Charter & wife Elisabeth; 6 May 1723 (AA 5.186); heir Frances (f); 24 Mar 1725 (GB 28)

Locker, Thomas; wife Elizabeth; dau. Anne Talbott [w/o Benjamin]; tract Gleanings; 26 Nov 1728 (PGLR M.332)

Locker, John; age ca 40; 1730 (PGLR M.556)

Lockyer, Walter; grandson of Walter Evans; tracts Gleanings, Pasture; 26 Nov 1737 (PGLR T.579)

Lockyer, Thomas, Sr.; wife Elizabeth; son Thomas; tracts Gleanings, Pasture; 26 Nov 1737 (PGLR T.579)

Locker, Thomas; wife Elizabeth; son Walter; 7 Nov 1738 (PGLR T.670)

Locker, Philip; m. 9 Jun 1750 Elizabeth Evans by Rev. Henry Addison; children: Isaac, b. 3 Jan 1752, bapt. 23 Feb 1752; Phillip, b. 29 Jun 1753; James, b. 11 Mar 1755; David, b. 12 Mar 1757; Elizabeth, b. 31 May 1759; Thomas, bapt. 12 Jun 1761; Demeleon (f), bapt. 11 Dec 1763 at Broad Creek; Ann, bapt. 18 Jan 1767 Broad Creek (KGP p. 289, 291, 294, 300, 308, 314, 318, 322, 338, 360)

Locker, John; wife Ann; child: Abigail, bapt. 25 Dec 1752 (KGP p. 297)

Locker, Buttler; 1 Dec 1756 (I 63.8)

Locker, William; wife Elizabeth; children: Mary, b. 13 Jan 1760; Sarah Ann, bapt. 4 Jul 1762; Butler, bapt. 19 May 1765 Broad Creek (KGP p. 318, 331, 347)

Locker, Thomas; wife Rebecca; child: Walter, b. 4 Jul 1765 (PGP p. 274)

LOCKLIN

Locklen, John; wife Susan; children: Jane, b. 16 Dec 1722; John, b. 16 Apr 1725; Jeremiah & Mary [twins]; b. 27 Sep 1727 (QAP p.27)

Locklin, Margret; 10 Jan 1735/6; 18 Feb 1735/6; [no relations] (MCW VII.162); 14 Mar 1735 (I 21.268); children: Piscilla, John; 1 Jun 1737 (AA 14.317)

Locklin, John; age ca 2 mos.; bound out; Mar 1735 (PGCR W.1)

LOCKWORTH

Lockworth, Joseph; 14 Dec 1699 (I&A 19-1/2b.8)

LOGAN

Logan, John; wife Elizabeth; children: Sarah, b. 30 May 1745; John Vinson, b. 13 Aug 1748; Rebecca, b. 30 Jul 1752; Walter, b. 4 May 1756 (KGP p. 322)

LOMAN

Loman, Michael; wife Mary; child: John, b. 14 May 1764 (PGP p. 276)

LOMAX

Lomax, Amon; 9 Oct 1724 (I 11.23)

LONG

Long, Benja.; 15 Dec 1715; 19 Jan 1715; wife Eliza., sons Thomas age 12, Benjamin [s/o Elizabeth]; daus. Jane [to be of age at decease of testator],

Anne age 10, Mary age 8, Susanna age 7 (MCW IV.41); 15 Mar 1715 (I&A 36c.230); [with 1716] (I&A 37c.124)

Long, Susannah; age 7; d/o Benjamin; service; Mar 1716 (PGCR H.32)

Long, Robert; 3 Oct 1727 (I 12.287); 3 Oct 1727 (AA 8.382)

Long, Locker; wife Elenor; children: Antoney, bapt. 15 Jan 1764 Lower Chapel; bapt. 15 Jun 1766 Broad Creek (KGP p. 344, 348)

Long, Mary; child: Lenard, bapt. 15 Jun 1766 Broad Creek (KGP p. 348)

LONGDON

Longdon, Edward; wife Loruhama; child: Alphamore, b. 27 Aug 1775 Broad Creek (KGP p. 387)

Longdon, James; wife Elisabeth; child: Elisabeth, b. 28 Mar 1763 (PGP p. 270)

LORD

Lord, Ruth; age ca 41; 1730 (PGLR Q.10)

Lord, Joseph; age ca 40; 1730 (PGLR Q.14)

Lord, Joseph; wife Ruth; tract *Barbadoes*; 10 Apr 1734 (PGLR T.108)

LOUGHLAN

Loughlan, Henry; age 6 mos; s/o Priscilla Loughlan; bound to William and Rachel Hitchinson; Jun 1748 (PGCR HH.169)

LOVE

Love, Aaron; wife Elizabeth; children: Anne, b. 1 Aug 1769; Sophia, b. 4 Sep 1773 (QAP m/8)

LOVEJOY

Lovejoy, Samuel; age 2 on May next; bound out; Jan 1703 (PGCR B.275)

Lovejoy, Samuel; wife Jane; tract *Poplar Hills*; 26 Jun 1728 (PGLR M.288)

Lovejoy, Joseph; age ca 78; 1738 (PGLR T.604)

Lovejoy, John; admx. Margaret; 16 Oct 1741 (I 27.266); widow Margaret; heirs Alexander, Precious, Edward, John; 30 Aug 1744 (GB 137)

Lovejoy, Joseph; parish of St. Pauls; 20 Feb 1743; 6 May 1748; wife Ann; sons Samuel, Joseph; dau. Ann Berry [w/o Humphrey] (MCW IX.141-2); 22 Feb 1749 (AA 27.275)

Lovejoy, Samuel; 23 Feb 1761; 23 Jun 1762; wife Jeane; [no relationships] (MCW XII.143); 7 Aug 1766 (I 89.310)

LOVELESS

Loveless, Fauslin; wife Mary; tract *Turrell Green*; 19 Nov 1714 (PGLR F.421)

Lovelace, Thomas; orphan; age 12 Jun next; bound out; Mar 1721 (PGCR K.83)

Loveless, Benjamin; wife Sarah; children: Zadock, b. 12 May 1760; Reason, b. 2 Aug 1764 (PGP p. 260, 272)

Loveless, Jno. Baptist; wife Eliner; child: Arch, b. 25 Jul 1761 (PGP p. 261)

Lovelace, Joseph; wife Sarah; child: Hazel (m), b. 31 Mar 1766 (PGP p. 278)

Loveless, Luke; wife Mary Ann; child: Una, b. 2 Sep 1774 Broad Creek (KGP p. 386)

LOWE

Lowe, Anne late of St. Mary's Co.; 14 Jun 1718; 23 May 1718; bro. Nicholas Lowe, sisters Jane Bowles [w/o James], Dorothy, Susanna Maria Diggs, Elizabeth, Mary; bros. Henry, Bennett and Nicho.; nephew Henry Diggs [s/o of sister Susanna]; tract *Golden Grove* in Dorset Co. (MCW IV.204)

Low, William; age ca 70; 10 Jun 1725 (PGLR I.649)

Lowe, William, Sr.; son John, William Lowe, Sr.; tract *Beale's Benevolence*; 2 Jul 1727 (PGLR M.270); dau. Susanna Gardiner [widow of John]; grandson Clement Gardiner; 4 May 1731 (PGLR Q.262, 263)

Lowe, William, Jr.; wife Phillice; tract *Beall's Benevolence*; 5 Aug 1738 (PGLR T.622)

Lowe, William; son William [wife Easter]; 5 Apr 1740 (PGLR Y.156)

Lowe, John; admx. Hester; 1 Dec 1740 (I 26.26); admx. Hester Devall [w/o Mareen]; 27 Nov 1741 (AA 18.410)

Lowe, Henry, Jr.; wife Ann; children: Sam, b. 2 Sep 1751, bapt. 1 Dec 1751; Mary Ann, b. 7 Sep 1753; John Tolson, b. 30 Sep 1754; Ann, b. _ Mar 1755; Elizabeth, b. 18 Apr 1756; Bassil, b. 21 Mar 1759; Ann, b. 30 May 1761; Rebeccah, bapt. 18 Apr 1762; Mary, bapt. 15 May 1764 at Broad Creek; Dennis, bapt. 24 Aug 1766 Broad Creek; Nicholas, b. 6 Apr 1768, bapt. 5 Jun 1768 Broad Creek (KGP p. 290, 294, 300, 306, 307, 313, 320, 322, 326, 329, 359, 363)

Lowe, John; wife Mary; child: John, bapt. 16 Apr 1752 (KGP p. 295)

Lowe, Henry; m. 20 Dec 1753 Nancy Lindsey (KGP p. 301)

Low, Nathan; wife Mary; child: Reason (m), bapt. 11 Apr 1762 (KGP p. 326)

Low, William; m. Elenor; child: Kesiah, bapt. 4 Jul 1762 (KGP p. 330)

Low, James; 15 Mar 1765; 25 Jun 1765; sister Catherine in Scotland; cousin David Low (MCW XIII.76); 5 Jul 1765 (I 90.142)

Lowe, Thomas; wife Verlinda; children: Charles Fendley, bapt. 8 Feb 1767 Broad Creek; Walter Stonestreat, b. 3 Sep 1769 Broad Creek; Thomas, b. 21 Apr 1772 Broad Creek (KGP p. 360, 373, 378)

Lowe, John; 11 Nov 1767; 13 Jun 1773; children: John, Henry, Eleanor Dawson, Rebecca Beane (MCW XV.177-8); 12 Jul 1774 (I 117.450, 452)

Low, Zadock; wife Sarah; children: Neamiah, bapt. 6 Nov 1768 Upper
Chapel; Samuel, b. 31 Oct 1772 Upper Chapel (KGP p. 372, 389)

Low, Richard; wife Sarah; child Mary (MCW XVI.168)

Low, Samuel; 24 Sep 1770; 19 Dec 1771; wife Sophonah; children:
Sapphaniah, Boston, Amey, Rachel, Easter, Barsheba, Marcey (MCW
XIV.202); 21 Mar 1774; extx. Sophano Lowe; 7 children [unnamed] (ABB
6.275)

Lowe, Henry, Jr.; wife Ann; child: Francis, b. 9 Mar 1772 Upper Chapel
(KGP p. 389)

Lowe, Samuel; wife Sephina; child: Zeophaniah, b. 12 Mar 1772 (KGP p. 305)

Lowe, Nicholas; wife Sarah; children: Lethe, b. 8 Mar 1773 Broad Creek;
Winifred, b. _ Oct 1775 Broad Creek (KGP p. 378, 382)

Lowe, Nathan; wife Mary; children: Nathan, b. 27 Jul 1773 Upper Chapel;
Nathaniel, b. 22 Jan 1776 Broad Creek (KGP p. 382, 390)

Lowe, Thomas; 19 Mar 1773; 24 Nov 1773; wife Virlinda; sons Charles,
Walter; father John (MCW XV.124); extx. Verlinda; 3 Jan 1774 (I 114.304); 28
Aug 1775; exs. Oliver Birch & wife Virlinda; sons Charles, Walter (ABB
7.58)

Lowe, Richard; wife Sarah; children: Mary, b. 12 Mar 1774 Upper
Chapel; George, b. 6 Nov 1775 Upper Chapel (KGP p. 390, 392)

Lowe, Henry, Sr.; 16 Jun 1773; 24 Mar 1774; wife Ann; children: John,
Mical, Mary Ann, Henry, Harry; mentions James Low [s/o John, Jr.] (MCW
XV.136)

Lowe, Henry; wife Ann; child: Anthony, b. 1776 Broad Creek (KGP p. 382)

LOWDEN
Lowden, Thomas; m. Eliza. Walker; children: Rachel, b. 4 Oct 1721 or
1722 (KGP p. 263, 284)

LOWNDES
Lowndes, Christopher; wife Elizabeth; children: Ann Margaret, b. 15 Jun
1748, bapt. 7 Aug 1748; Benjamin, b. 30 Dec 1749; Francis, b. 19 Oct
1751; Samuel, b. 20 Jul 1753; Elizabeth, b. 7 Apr 1755 (KGP p. 288, 302)

Lowndes, Christopher; wife Sarah; child: Sarah, b. 7 Apr 1755 (KGP p. 308)

LUCAS
Lucas, Thos.; wife Dorothy; children: Charles, b. 20 Apr 1692; Susannah, b.
3 Dec 1703; Sarah, b. 18 9ber 1705; Jane, b. 4 7ber 1707; Mary, b. 12
7ber 1712 (sic); James, b. 27 Feb 1712/3 (sic) (QAP b/1, 2, 3, 6, 8)

Lucas, Thos., Jr.; wife Ann; children: Thomas, b. 30 Mar 1712; William, b.
15 Mar 1713/4; Sarah, b. 1715 (QAP b/6, 9, 11)

Lucas, Charles; m. 20 Nov 1718 Elizabeth Evans; children: Charles, b. 1 July 1721; Elizabeth, b. 1 Mar 172_; Thomas, b. 12 Apr 172_; Mary, b. 13 Jun 17__; Ann, b. ____; ____ (m), b. 19 Jul 1730; Richard, b. 29 Jul 1732; ____ (f), b. 17 Oct 1734; Samuel, b. 23 Nov 1736 (QAP m/2; b/26, 30, 31)

Lucas, Thomas; planter; 18 Oct 1721; 26 Feb 1721/2; wife Dorothy; sons Thomas, Charles, John (age 12 on 12 Jun last), James (age 8 last Feb), Samuel (age 4 last Sep), daus. Mary Scott [w/o Wm.], Eliza. Moore [w/o George], Susana, Sarah, Jane (MCW V.91); 26 Mar 1722 (I 7.208); extx. Dorothy; widow, 7 child. [unnamed]; 20 Apr 1724 (AA 5.409); extx. Dorothy; 20 Feb 1724 (AA 6.322); widow Dorothy; heirs Jane, John, Mary, James, Samuel, Susan, Sarah; 24 Mar 1724 (GB 20)

Lucas, Thomas; wife Ann; children: Charles, b. 1 Mar 1726; Barton, b. 29 Jan 1729/30 (PGP p. 260, 272)

Lucas, Charles; planter; 8 Jun 1740; 28 May 1741; sons Thomas, Charles, William, Richard, Samuel; daus. Elizabeth, Mary, Ann, Sarah; wife Elizabeth (MCW VIII.128); extx. Elisabeth; 21 Aug 1741 (I 26.154)

Lucas, Thomas, Sr.; 31 May 1756; 24 Jun 1756; sons Barton, Basil, Thomas; daus. Margaret Hamilton, Sarah (MCW XI.136)

Lucas, William; wife Johanah; child: Jonathan, b. 2 Dec 1761 (PGP p. 261)

Lucas, William; wife Sarah; child: William, b. 17 Jan 1765 (PGP p. 276)

LUCK

Luck, Andrew; wife Rebecca; child: Benjamin, bapt. 18 May 1766 Upper Chapel (KGP p. 354)

LUDWELL

Ludwell, Jane; age 10 on 2 Feb past; orphan of William [dec'd]; guardian appointed; Jun 1710 (PGCR D.318)

LUKE

Luke, John; wife Jane; children: William Fraser, b. 15 Apr 1762; John, b. 16 Jul 1764; bapt. 9 Sep 1764 at Broad Creek (KGP p. 339)

LUKETT

Lukett, William; age 6 mos.; s/o Mary; bound out; Mar 1719 (PGCR H.973)

LUSBY

Lusby, John [dec'd] [AA]; wife Eleanor [m/2 Thomas Wells of AA Co.]; children: Jacob, John, Aaron [PG], Thomas, Samuel, Rachel [dec'd], Mary [dec'd], Eleanor [dec'd]; 30 Apr 1746 (CCR MSA 8.221)

Lusby, Thomas; 21 Jul 1750 (I 43.497; 44.103); 27 Mar 1753; admn. Jacob Lusby (ABB 1.76)

Lusby; Susanah; 28 Dec 1750 (I 47.323)

Lusbey, Samuel; wife Susannah; child: Susannah, bapt. 17 Jun 1764 Broad Creek (KGP p. 356)

LUTTERMILS

Luttermils, John [dec'd]; extx. Margaret; Jun 1703 (PGCR B.239)

LUTTON

Lutton, Caleb; wife Grace; children: Caleb, b. 27 Jan 1724; John, b. 4 Jul 1726; Sarah, b. 22 Jun 1728; Elizabeth, b. 13 Jun 1730; Johanna, b. 7 Jul 1732; Grace, b. 31 Dec 1742 (PGP p. 250, 251)

LUX

Lux, John; mariner; 29 Jan 1727 (I 13.64); John, Capt.; 12 Jun 1728 (AA 9.200; 10.442)

LUXON

Luxon, John; admx. Elisabeth; 1 Dec 1762 (I 80.276)

LYLES

Lyle, Darby; age ca 12; servant; Jun 1698 Ct. (PGCR A.3167)

Lyle, Robert [CA] [s/o William]; wife Elizabeth; tract *Waughton*; 29 Nov 1699 (PGLR A.332)

Liles, Robert; m. 12 10ber 1723 Priscilla Nutwell (QAP m/3)

Lyles, Barberry; husb. dec'd; children: William, Robert, Henry, Eleanor, Elizabeth, Mary; 28 Apr 1735 (PGLR T.256)

Lyles, George; 1 May 1760 (I 70.236)

Lyles, Hilliary; 26 Apr 1769; 28 Jun 1769; children: Priscilla, Zachariah, James (MCW XIV.101); 7 Jun 1769 (I 102.30); 6 Oct 1770 (I 105.265); 27 Feb 1772; 3 children: Priscilla, Zachariah, James (ABB 6.192); Priscilla, Zachariah, James; 23 Mar 1774 (GB 318)

Lyles, Zachariah; wife Margery; children: Robert (twin), b. __ Sep ____; Thomas (twin), b. __ Sep ____; [poss. 1750s] (QAP b/36)

Lyles, Zachariah; 20 Apr 1768 (I 96.339)

LYNCH

Lynch, Bryan; age ca 9; servant; Nov 1703 Ct. (PGCR B.263)

Linch, Thomas; admx. Mary Boyde; 30 Apr 1724 (AA 5.411)

LYNES

Lynes, Phillip [CH]; wife Margarett; tract *Batchelors Harbour*; 31 Aug 1700 (PGLR A.385)

Lynes, Philip [CH]; wife Ann; tract *Clarke's Inheritance*; 2 Jan 1706 (PGLR C.178)

LYNN

Lynn, David; wife Elizabeth; children: Jane, b. 16 Jul 1747; Sarah, b. 13 Apr 1749; David, b. 15 Jul 1750; Rose, b. 30 May 1753; Catherian, b. 17 Jul 1756; John, b. 29 Aug 1760 (PGP p. 260, 261)

Lynn, Davie; wife Elizabeth; child: Elizabeth, b. 25 Feb 1750 (PGP p. 260)

LYON

Lyon, Samuel; wife Susannah; child: Elizabeth, b. 26 Mar 1759 (PGP p. 257)

Lyon, Michael; wife Eleanor; son John Leonard; 1761 (MCWXII.143)

LYSBA

Lysba, Samuel; wife Susanna; child: Robert, b. 14 Mar 1772 Broad Creek (KGP p. 378)

MABURTON
Maburton, William; wife Lucrease; child: ____, b. __ Mar 17__ (pg. torn) (QAP 28)

MACATEE
Macatee, John; wife Charity; child: Colmore Wade, b. 14 Feb 1775 Lower Chapel (KGP p. 380)

MACCA
Macca, Ann; child: Elizabeth Ann, b. 17 Jan 1774 Broad Creek (KGP p. 385)

MACCARTEE
Maccartee, Daniel; 21 Mar 1710 (I&A 31.137); admx. Jane; 12 Apr 1710 (I&A 31.141)

MACCLASH
McClash [MackClash], William; admx. Jane; 6 Jul 1745 (I 32.181); admx. Jane; 22 Jul 1746 (AA 22.284)

Machelash, Robert; wife Sarah; child: William, bapt. 2 Feb 1752 (KGP p. 294)

McLish, Robert; admx. Sarah; 14 Mar 1760 (I 70.225)

MACOLLOUGH
Macollough, Thomas; tailor; admx. Mary Mackuler; no kin in Md.; 11 Mar 1733 (I 17.728)

MACCOLLUM
Maccollum [Maccolms], John; 6 Jul 1726 (I 11.884); widow [unnamed, North Brittain]; 18 Apr 1727 (AA 8.196); 25 Oct 1727 (AA 8.445)

MACCONNELL
McConnell, John; 10 Feb 1742 (I 27.363), John; 26 Jun 1744 (AA 20.327)

MACCOW
Maccow, Rodman; age ca 15; servant; Jun 1698 Ct. (PGCR A.316)

MACCOY
Maccoy, Henry; age ca 11 years; Elizabeth, age ca 7 years; bound out; Aug 1744 (PGCR CC.517)

MACUBBIN
Mackubin, John; wife Anne; tract Mother's Gift; tract 17 Oct 1728 (PGLR M.337)
Macubbin, [unnamed]; heir Zachariah; 27 Nov 1771 (GB 299)

MACDANIEL

Mackdaniell, Owen; age ca 12; servant; Jun 1698 Ct. (PGCR A.317)

MacDaniel, David; m. 1715 Sarah Jones (QAP m/1)

MackDaniel, David; dau. Ann; tract *Plaine Dealing*; 13 Mar 1720 (PGLR I.121)

McDaniell [Makdanniell], David; 16 Jul 1720 (I 4.102); 26 Aug 1720 (AA 3.213)

Mcdaniel, Mary; child: Mary, b. 7 Jul 1761 (PGP p. 264)

MacDanol, Alexander; wife Stacey; child: James Steward, bapt. 11 Aug 1765 Broad Creek (KGP p. 349)

McDanall, Jarrard; child: John Atchinson, bapt. 31 Aug 1766 Upper Chapel (KGP p. 355)

McDaniel, Edward; 14 Oct 1771; 16 Dec 1771; children: John, Walter, Edward, William; ?dau. Margaret Roberts (MCW XIV.194)

McDaniel, John; wife Sarah; children: Elizabeth Gibbs, b. 12 Oct 1772 Lower Chapel; William Gibbs, b. 3 Feb 1775 Lower Chapel (KGP p. 380, 383)

McDaniel, Reuben; wife Katharine; children: William, b. 6 Feb 1774 Broad Creek; Reuben, b. 28 Mar 1776 Broad Creek (KGP p. 382, 385)

McDaniel, William; wife Mary; child: William, b. 18 Sep 1775 Lower Chapel (KGP p. 381)

McDaniel, John; wife Mary; child: Mary, b. 21 Feb 1776 Lower Chapel (KGP p. 381)

MACDONALD

Mackdonald, Robert; age 5 next Christmas; Susannah; age 12 mos. this day; bound out; Jun 1717 (PGCR H.243)

Macdonald, Groves; age 2 on 26 May last; s/o Grace; bound out; Aug 1736 (PGCR W.150)

McDonald, Dunkin; wife Elinor; children: John, b. 19 Oct 1750; Elizabeth Dennis, b. 9 Jan 1754; Mary Elinor Webster, b. 24 Dec 1755 (KGP p. 292, 305)

Macdonald [Mackdaniel], Duncan; admx. Eleanor; 18 Oct 1762 (I 79.225)

McDonald, Edward; 30 Dec 1771 (I 108.336)

MACDUGAL

Macdugle, Hugh; wife Elizabeth; child: Alexander, b. 6 8ber 1727 (QAP b/21)

Mackdoggie [Mackdugall, McDoggle], Hugh; 18 Jun 1735; 11 Jul 1735; wife Elizabeth; son John; daus. Mary and Elizabeth (MCW VII.142); 18 Jun 1736 (I 21.349); heirs John, Mary; 26 Nov 1745 (GB 146); 6 Aug 1753; extx. Eliza Ricketts [w/o Benjamin] (ABB 1.76)

Macdugle [Mcdugil], John; m. 20 Feb 1757 Charity Duvall; child: Samuel, b. _____ (QAP m/7; b/36)

MACE
Mace, Henry; age ca 20; servant; Aug 1698 Ct. (PGCR A.333)

MACFULL
McFull [McFoall], James; widow Elisabeth; 24 Jun 1743 (I 28.366); 27 Dec 1744 (AA 21.64)

MACGILL
Macgill, John; m. 4 Dec 1759 Elizabeth Duvall; children: b. ____; Ann, b. 15 Nov 17__; James Hilleory, b. 8 Sep 1773 (QAP m/7; b/38, 46)

Macgill, Thomas; wife Ellinor; children: child, b. ____; Thomas, b. 15 Jan 1767 (QAP b/38)

MACHTEE
Machtee, Elizabeth [widow]; children: John, b. 3 Mar 1744; William, b. 23 Jan 1746 (KGP p. 293)

MACKALL
Mackall, James [CA]; wife Anne; tract Brooke's Reserve; 17 Jun 1713 (PGLR F.250)

MACKANY
Mackany, John; 20 Nov 1733 (I 20.451)

MACKAY
MacKay [McKay], William; 23 Nov 1758; 30 Nov 1758; sons John, James; dau. Priscilla (MCW XI.222); 22 Dec 1758 (I 67.111)

MACKELLY
Mackelly, Brayan; wife Mary; child: Rebecca, b. 11 Jun 1716 (QAP b/12)

MACKERMIT
Mackermit, Anguish; 15 Sep 1725; 3 Nov 1725; wife Jennet (MCW V.202); 13 Apr 1726 (I 11.432); heirs [North Brittain]; 22 Oct 1726 (AA 8.105); 2 Jun 1727 (AA 8.239)

MACKERRY
McKerry, John; 11 Jun 1735 (AA 13.146)

MACKEY
Mackey, John; 21 Feb 1774 (I 115.281)

Mackey, William; heir John Mackey; tracts *Twyver, Tann Yard*; 29 Jun 1768 (GB 259, 266)

MCKINNON
Mckinnon, Daniel; wife Ruth; child: ___h, b. 10 Mar 1752 (QAP b/37)
Mekinnon, Daniel; wife Catharine; child: Daniel, bapt. 7 Jun 1767 Lower Chapel (KGP p. 367)

MACKLAND
Mackland, Anguis; 6 May 1717 (I&A 39c.83)

MACKLEAN
Maclan [Macklan], John; wife Margaret; children: John, b. 3 Aug 1712; Katherine, b. 6 Mar 1714; James, b. 6 9ber 1717 (QAP b/8, 11, 13)
Mackean, Peter; m. 5 Aug 1736 Clara Holmes (QAP m/7)
Macklean, John; wife Elizabeth; child: Margeret, bapt. 22 Jul 1750 (PGP p. 253)
McClean, William; wife Mary; children: Mary, bapt. 12 May 1751; Susanna, b. 29 Mar 1753 (KGP p. 293, 300)
Macklane [McLane], John, Sr.; 22 Mar 1759; 13 Oct 1766; wife Margaret; children: William, John, James, Cathrine Nicholls (MCW XIII.130); extx. Margaret; 17 Nov 1766 (I 91.317)
McClain, Phillip; wife Mary B.; child: William Casey, b. 5 Aug 1765 (PGP p. 273)

MACKLEFISH
Macklefish, Thomas; wife Susannah; child: Susannah, b. 13 Nov 1734 (QAP b/29)

MACKLENANE
Macklenane, Brice; wife Hester; children: Rebeccah, b. 3 Dec 1718; Mary, b. 10 Feb 1720 (KGP p. 269)

MACKNAMARRA
Macnamarra, Abbigale, b. 11 Nov 1759 [no parents listed] (PGP p. 280)
Macnamarra, Patrick; wife Mary; child: William Cook, b. 25 Feb 1763 (PGP p. 269)

MACKNEW
Mackew, Jeremie [d. by 1716]; wife Sarah; children: Lucey, b. 8 Feb 1709; Anne, b. 8 Nov 1711; Edward Marley, b. 14 Aug 1713; William, b. 14 Aug 1715 (KGP p. 268, 269)

Macknew, Jeremiah; 26 Mar 1716 (I&A 36c.161); adms. widow Sarah Mahall [w/o Timothy]; 6 Aug 1717 (I&A 37b. 190)

Macknew, Jeremiah; wife Martha; child: Elizabeth, b. 20 Jul 1765 (PGP p. 275)

MACKUNE

Mackune, Edward; orphan; age ca 15; chooses guardian; Mar 1728 (PGCR O.13)

Mackune, Williams; age ca 12; chooses Uncle Edward Marler as guardian; Mar 1728 (PGCR O.13)

MACKUTER

Mackuter, Thomas; admx. Mary Burgess [w/o John]; [heirs ?England]; 27 Aug 1735 (AA 13.277)

MACKMILLION

Mackmillion, John; age 3 on 31 Oct last; bound out; Nov 1724 (PGCR L.376)

MACPHERSON

Mcferson [Macferson], Markham; 10 Aug 1725 (I 11.28); 10 Aug 1725 (AA 7.80)

McPherson, Walter; wife Mary; children: Letty Dent, b. 22 Jun 1774 Lower Chapel; Samuel, b. 1 Apr 1776 Lower Chapel (KGP p. 380, 381)

MACQUEEN

Macqueen, Timithy; child: William, b. 18 Aug 1716 (KGP p. 263)

Macqueen, Timithy; wife Jane; child: John, b. 9 Oct 1719 (KGP p. 263)

McQueen [Mcqueen], Timothy; admx. Jane; 21 Jul 1725 (I 11.26); admx. Jane Fisher [w/o Ralph]; admx. wife [unnamed] of Ralph Fisher; 15 Mar 1726 (AA 8.238); admx. Jane; 28 Mar 1726 (I 11.433); 25 Apr 1726 (AA 7.339); heirs William, John; 28 Mar 1727 (GB 30)

MADING

Maddin, Dennis; wife Mary; children: Sophia, b. 7 Feb 1689; John, b. 6 Feb 1791 (QAP b/1)

Mading, Joseph; wife Mary; child: Benjamin, b. 3 Jul 1760 (PGP p. 259)

Mading, Mordica; wife Ann; child: Sarah, b. 15 Jun 1760 (PGP p. 258)

Mading, Denniss; wife Stacy; child: Elener, b. 11 Aug 1761 (PGP p. 261)

MAGATEE

Magatee, Edmond; admx. Hester; 1 Nov 1734 (I 20.172); [as Edmund, Jr.]; admx. Hester; children: Elisabeth, Sarah; 1 Aug 1735 (AA 13.269); heirs Elizabeth, Sarah; 27 Mar 1739 (GB 101)

Maggatee, John; son Henry; tract Maggatees; 1741 (PGLR Y.385)

MAGEE

Magee, John; joyner; 22 May 1745 (I 32.259)

MAGILL

Magill, James, Rev.; m. 8 Oct 1730 Mrs. Sarah Hilleary (QAP m/5)

MAGNUS

Magnus, Petegree; wife Mary; child: Benjamin, b. 6 Apr 1754 (PGP p. 256)

MAGRIGER

Magriger, Alexander; wife Ellenor; children: Ellenor, b. 28 Dec ____;
Mary, b. 20 May [Aug] ____; Catherine, b. 20 Aug ____; John, b. 3 Dec
____; Daniel, b. 22 Aug ____; Eliza, b. 29 Mar ____(KGP p. 285)

Magrigger, Eleanor; son John; tract His Lordship's Kindness; 30 Jul 1730
(PGLR Q.81)

MAGRUDER

Magruder, Alexander; son Samuel; 26 Apr 1700 (PGLR A.427)

Magruder, Alexander; wife Ann; tract Charightigth now Magruder's Delight;
21 Jun 1701 (PGLR A.379)

Magruder, Nathaniell; wife [heir of Giles Blizard]; tract Bero Plains; 20
Apr 1703 (PGLR C.95)

Magruder, Nathaniell; wife Susan; tract Bero Plains [Bewplaine]; 30 Aug
1707 (PGLR C.198a)

Magruder, Ninian; wife Elizabeth; children: Samuel, b. 24 Feb 1708; John,
b. 11 10ber 1709; Ninian, b. Apr 1711; Sarah, b. 19 Mar 1713/4;
Elizabeth, b. 4 9ber 1717; Nathaniel, b. 30 9ber 1721; Rebecca, b. 7 Feb
1725; Rachel, b. 23 Jan 1726/7 (QAP b/6, 9, 13, 17, 21)

Magruder, Samuell; 23 Nov 1710; 16 Apr 1711; wife Sarah; sons Samuel,
Ninian, John, James, William, Alexander, Nathaniel; daus. Verlinda,
Mary, Elizabeth, Sarah; bros. Alexander, Nathaniell; "brother" John
Pottinger; tracts Good Luck, Magruder's Delight, Alexandria, Dunblean,
Turkey Cock (MCW III.194); Samuel, Sr.; extx. Sarah; 5 Jun 1711 (I&A 32b.168);
extx. Sarah; 31 Dec 1711 (I&A 33a.38); extx. Sarah; 9 Aug 1712 (I&A 33b.30);
extx. Sarah; 6 Apr 1715 (I&A 36b.136, 154)

Magruder, Samuel; wife Ellinor; children: Robert, b. 11 8ber 1711;
Zachariah, b. 24 Jul 1714 (QAP b/510)

Magruder, Samuel; wife Elinor; sons Samuell and Robert; dau. Sarah;
will of John Lane, written 1712 (MCW IV.41)

Magruder, John; m. 1 Dec 1715 Susanna Smith (QAP m/1)

Magruder, Sarah; son Nathaniel; 26 Nov 1716 (PGLR F.563)

Magruder, Ninian; wife Elizabeth; tract *Beall's Gift*; 3 Sep 1720 (PGLR I.14)

Magruder, Samuel, Sr.; wife Eleanor; dau. Sarah Tubman [w/o Richard]; tract *Forrest Green*; 23 Nov 1726 (PGLR M.154)

Magruder, Samuel; age ca 44; 20 May 1728 (PGLR M.292)

Magruder, Samuel, Jr.; wife Jane; children: Margaret, b. 20 Apr 1729 (QAP b/23)

Magruder, Sarah; dau. Eleanor Wade [w/o Nehemiah]; 6 Feb 1730 (PGLR Q.210)

Maugruder, Samuel III; wife Margreat; children: Elizabeth, b. __ Nov 1730; Ruth, b. 8 Jul 1732; Sarah, b. 11 Apr 1734; Ninian Beall, b. 22 Nov 1735; Ann, b. 8 Jul 1738; Margreat, b. 20 Sep 1740; Joseph, b. 16 Oct 1742; Samuel Bruce, b. 14 Oct 1744 (PGP p. 252)

Magruder, Nathaniel; planter; 13 Mar 1731; 27 Mar 1734; wife Mary; daus. Ann, Mary, Susannah, Elizabeth; son: George; tracts *Anchovie Hills*, *The Venture*, *The Levels* (MCW VII.69); admx. Mary; 1 Jul 1734 (I 18.271); 3 Sep 1734 (I 20.54); extx. Mary; children: Anne, George, Elisabeth, Mary, Susanna, Alexander; 24 Jun 1735 (AA 13.264)

Magruder, Alexander; age ca 60; 7 Jul 1731 (PGLR Q.525); age ca 70; 24 Aug 1741 (PGLR Y.360)

Magruder, Sarah; widow; 16 Jan 1731; 9 May 1734; sons Samuel, Ninian, John, James, William, Alexander; daus. Eleanor Wade [w/o Nehemiah], Elizabeth Bell [w/o William], Virlinder Bell [w/o John]; Mary Clagett, dec'd [w/o George]; granddau. Sarah Clagett, Sarah [d/o Ninian]; grandsons John [s/o Ninian]; tract *Headake* (MCW VII.113); heirs Samuel, Ninian, James, William and Alexander Magruder; also William Beall, Sr., Nehemiah Wade, Sarah Clagett; 22 Mar 1736 (GB 89); 22 Jun 1736 grandson John Magruder; granddau. Mary Edmonson [d/o James] (AA 15.38)

Magruder, Samuel; wife Eleanor; son Robert, tract *T* and *Lanham's Delight*; son Zachariah, tract *Friendship*; 29 Nov 1734 (PGLR T.207, 208)

Magruder, Robert; m. 5 Dec 1734 Sarah Crabb (QAP m/6)

Magruder, John; age ca 42; bro. Samuel; 22 Mar 1735 (CCR-MSA 6.27)

Magruder, Robert; planter; 3 Mar 1735/6; 23 Jun 1736; wife Sarah; dau. Eleanor; bro. Elias; nephew Samuel (MCW VII.182); admx. Sarah; 30 Sep 1736 (I 22.26); extx. Sarah; 29 Jun 1737 (AA 14.320); widow Sarah; dau. Eleanor; 3 Sep 1740 (AA 18.45); heir Eleanor; 28 Nov 1740 (GB 116)

Magruder, George; age ca 15; chooses guardian; Jun 1737 (PGCR W.417)

Magruder, Alexander, Sr.; age ca 63; 1737 (PGLR T.504)

Magruder, Ninian, Sr.; son Ninian; 28 Mar 1738 (PGLR T.570)

Magruder, Ninian; wife Mary; children: Elizabeth, b. 2 Nov 1738; William, b. 6 Aug 1740 (PGP p. 251)

Magruder, James; wife Barbary; sons James, Enoch; tract Norway; 30 Nov 1739 (PGLR Y.116)

Magruder, Elias; father [Samuel, Sr.] appointed guardian; Jun 1743 (PGCR AA.478)

Magruder, Alexander; 4 Feb 1739/40; 20 May 1746; wife Susannah; daus. Elizabeth Whitaker [w/o Robert], Sarah Butler; sons Hezekiah, Alexander; grandaus. Priscilla & Ann Magruder [ds/o Alexander]; bro. Nathaniel Magruder [dec'd]; nephews George, Alexander [ss/o Nathaniel]; tracts Jordan, Quicksale (MCW IX.67); extx. Susanna [widow]; 20 Feb 1746 (AA 23.277); extx. Susanna; 31 Mar 1746 (I 35.41)

Magruder, Nathaniel; heirs Mary, Elizabeth, Susannah; 29 Aug 1741 (GB 118); extx. Mary Bright [w/o William]; 5 children unnamed]; 28 Aug 1745 (AA 22.47)

Magruder, Susanah; chooses George Magruder as guardian; Mar 1745 (PGCR DD.9)

Magruder, John; age ca 51; 29 May 1745 (CCR JK#4.590)

Magruder, Samuel, Jr.; son Haswell; 1746 (MCW X.87)

Magruder, James, Jr.; admx. Cave; 10 Dec 1747 (I 37.48)

Magruder, Robert; heir Eleanor; 2 Jul 1748 (GB 161)

Magruder, John; 15 Aug 1750; 14 Sep 1750; wife Susanne; sons Nathan, Zadock, Nathaniel; daus. Cassandra, Rebeckah, Elizabeth Burgis; tracts Bealsfast, Alexander, Beals Benevolence, Greenwood, Beals Purchase, The Saplin Thickett, Dispute, The Ridge, Charles and Benjamin, Knaves Dispute, Turkey Thickett, Robert and Sarah, Chance, Three Brothers, Good Luck (MCW X.103); 29 Jan 1750 (I 47.103); 13 Dec 1752 (AA 33.228); 13 Dec 1752 (I 51.120); 13 Dec 1752; ex. Nathaniel Magruder (ABB 1.62); children: Nathan, Zadock, Elisabeth Burgess [w/o Richard], Cassandra Hillary [w/o Henry]; 23 Aug 1753 (AA 35.50); 23 Aug 1753; ex. Nathaniel Magruder (ABB 1.87); heirs Rebecca; 28 Mar 1754 (GB 193)

Magruder, James; admx. Cave [widow]; 26 Jun 1751 (AA 30.110); heirs Barbara, Francis, Margaret; 26 Jun 1752 (GB 177)

Magruder, Ninian; 6 May 1751; 26 Jun 1751; 11 children; sons Samuel, John, Ninian, Nathaniel, James; daus. Sarah Beall, Elizabeth Perry, Ann Clagett, Rebecca Offutt, Rachel Clagett, Verlenda Magruder; tracts Magruder's Purchase, Addition to Magruder's Purchase, Honesty, Alexandra, Grubby Thickett (MCW X.158-9); 4 Feb 1752 (I 48.425); 23 Feb 1753;

ex. James Magruder (ABB 1.62); children: Virlinda Williams [w/o Walter], Rachel Clagett [w/o Thomas, Jr.], Rebecca Offutt [w/o James], Elisabeth Perry [w/o Benjamin], Sarah Beall [w/o William], John, Nathaniel, Ann Clagett [w/o Thomas, Sr.]; 23 Feb 1753 (AA 33.333; 35.49)

Magruder, Hezekiah; wife Susana; child: Rebecca, b. 19 Sep 1759 (PGP p. 257)

Magruder, Nathaniel; wife Elizabeth; child: Walter, b. 15 Jun 1760 (PGP p. 258)

Magruder, Samuel Wade; wife Lucy; children: Charles, b. 26 Apr 1761; Sarah, b. 15 Jan 1763 (PGP p. 261, 270)

Magruder, Nathaniel; wife Mary; child: Nathaniel Jones, b. 22 Nov 1761 (PGP p. 263)

Magruder, Jeremiah; wife Mary; will of Mary Henderson; written 1761; (MCWXII.102)

Magruder, Nathan; wife Rebecca; child: Jeffery, b. 20 Apr 1762 (PGP p. 263)

Magruder, Haswell; wife Charity; child: Jane Sprigg, bapt. 6 Jun 1763 at Upper Chapel (KGP p. 332)

Magruder, Zadoc; child: Elisabeth, b. 10 Feb 1764 (PGP p. 271)

Magruder, Haswell; child: Easter Beall, bapt. 9 Dec 1764 Broad Creek (KGP p. 342)

Magruder, William; 14 Mar 1765; 22 Jul 1765; wife Mary; children: Susannah, Thomas, Jemima, Barbara, Elizabeth, Vilendar, Basil, George Frazer, Ann Young; tracts *Turkey Cock Branch, Vale of Benjamin* (MCW XIII.93)

Magruder, Joseph; wife Mary; child: Samuel Jackson, b. 2 Mar 1765 (PGP p. 273)

Magruder, Hezekiah; admx. Martha; 17 Jul 1768 (I 98.45); 14 Sep 1770; admx. Martha Magruder (ABB 6.18); heirs Alexander Wilson, James Wilson & Josiah Wilson Magruder; 27 Mar 1772 (GB 302)

Magruder, Haswell; wife Charity; children: Sophia, b. 29 Feb 1771 Upper Chapel; William, b. 3 Jul 1773 Upper Chapel (KGP p. 388, 390)

Magruder, Mary; 23 Feb 1772; 13 Jul 1774; sons Thomas, George Fraser & Basil Magruder; daus. Barbara, Elizabeth, Vilender, Susannah Warfield, Jemima Perry; ss-i-l Peter Young, Azel Warfield, Joseph Perry (MCW XV.178)

Magruder, James; admx. Mary; 18 Mar 1773 (I 114.52)

MAHALL

Mahall, Timothy; wife Jane; 3 Aug 1697 (PGLR F.190)

Mahall, Timothy; extx. Mary Adkee [w/o Thomas]; 22 Oct 1734 (I 20.338); exs. Thomas Adkins and wife Mary; heirs under age Timothy, Sarah,

Elisabeth; most [unnamed] are of age; 30 Jun 1735 (AA 13.146); extx. Mary Atkins [w/o Thomas]; 22 Mar 1745 (I 20.455)

Mahall, Timothy; m. 17 ___ 1745 Mary Stephens; child: Edward, b. 24 Sep 1746 (KGP p. 288)

MAHUE

Mahue, James; wife Frances; child: Harrison:, b. 9 Nov 1734 (QAP b/28)

MAID

Maid, Thomas; m. 13 7ber 1724 Jane Pope; children: Thomas, b. 14 Jun 1726; Ann, b. 11 Jun 1728 (QAP m/3; b/19, 22)

MAJOR

Major, Edmond; wife Elizabeth; tract *Stoke*; 26 Aug 1718 PGLR F.105/663)

MAKFIELD

Makfield, Robert; age ca 17; servant; Mar 1713 (PGCR G.292)

MALLAR

Mallar, Thomas; 15 Sep 1711 (I&A 32c. 151)

MANDER

Mander, Elizabeth; child: Basill, b. 10 Apr 1762 (KGP p. 330)

MANDUIT

Manduit, Jasper; age 17 in July next; chooses guardian; Mar 1750 (PGCR LL.134)

Mauduit, William; admx. Mercy; 5 May 1750 (I 43.217); [with 1752] (I 49.109); adms. Joseph Chew and wife Mary; 21 Sep 1752 (ABB 1,.60); admx. Mercy Chew [w/o Joseph]; children: Jasper, Deborah Jackson [w/o Alexander]; 21 Sep 1752 (AA 33.5); admx. Mary Chew [w/o Joseph]; 13 Nov 1754 (AA 36.481); admx. Mary Chew [w/o Joseph]; children: William, Ann, Deborah, Jaspar; 4 Jul 1761 (ABB 3.82)

Manduit, Jasper; 11 May 1775; 11 Sep 1775; wife Hannah; sister Deborah Jackson; cous. William Jackson, Jasper Manduit Jackson (MCW XVI.80)

MANSELL

Mansell, George, m. 4 Mar 1714 Sarah Norwood, gentleman and gentlewoman of Anne Arundel Co. (KGP p. 260)

Mansell, Robert; 26 Oct 1717 (I 1.421)

MANY

Many, Richard; wife Ann; child: William, b. 12 7ber 1716 (QAP b/16)

Maney, Jemima; age ca 16 mos.; bound out; Nov 1748 (PGCR KK.34)

MARBURY

Marbury, Francis; wife Mary; tracts Thomasses Chance, Little Ease; 19 Feb 1699 (PGLR A.307)

Marbury, Francis; wife Mary [d. 11 Feb 1713]; children: Leonard, b. 31 Jan 1708; Luke, b. 10 Mar 1710; Mary, b. 8 Feb 1713 (KGP p. 267)

Marbury, Francis; m/2 14 Sep 1714 Frances Heard; both of this parish; children: Martha Ann, b. 11 Sep 1715; William, b. 24 Feb 1716; Henry, b. ____, d. 23 Nov 1720; Sushanah, b. 5 Feb 1721 (KGP p. 267)

Marbury, Francis, age ca 62; 6 Oct 1724 (PGLR I.600); age 64; 2 Mar 1725 (PGLR I.645); age ca 66; 1728 (PGLR M.346)

Marbury, Francis; 1 Jan 1734; 22 Jan 1734/5; sons: Eusebius, Leonard, Eli, Luke, William; daus. Mary Ann, Susannah, Barbara Frazer, Lucy Hatton, Elizabeth Davidson, Tabitha Hoye; s-i-l John Davison; tracts Littleworth, School House, Mistake, Appledore, Tewksbury, Applehill (MCW VII.124); 15 Mar 1734 (I 20.353); ss-i-l Joseph Hatton, John Dawson, James Smallwood, James Hoy; dau. Susanna Marbury; 25 May 1738 (AA 16.236)

Marbury, Leonard; wife Penelopy; tracts Marbury's Chance, Carroll's Kindness, Little Troy; 1 Jan 1736/7 (PGLR T.437)

Marbury, Luke; age ca 32; s/o Francis; 1743 (PGLR Y.657); age ca 33; 17 Jan 1743 (CCR MSA 8.50)

Marbury, William; wife Martha; children: Ann, b. 15 Dec 1738; Ellender, b. 17 Oct 1740; Elizabeth, b. 9 Oct 1742; Joseph, b. 22 Nov 1744; Francis Heard, b. 3 Jan 1746; William, b. 6 Dec 1748; Martha, b. 16 Jul 1751; Henry, b. 3 Mar 1753; Susanna, b. 4 Apr 1757; Sarah, b. 18 Jun 1760; William, b. 7 Nov 1762 (KGP p. 301, 302)

Mardurt, William [merchant]; m. 12 Dec 1727 Bridgett Coghlan (KGP p. 272)

Marbury [Marberry], Luke; admx. Elisabeth; 30 Nov 1759 (I 66.198); 21 Aug 1760; admx. Elisabeth Marberry; 3 children [unnamed] (ABB 3.36, 74); widow Elizabeth; heir Luke; 30 May 1764 (GB 238)

MARGURY

Margury, Francis; children: William, Susanna; 7 Jan 1735 (AA 14.142)

MARIARTE

Mariarte, Daniel; wife Eleanor; tract Maiden's Dowry; 27 Feb 1713 (PGLR F.332)

Mariarte, Edward; 8 Sep 1721 (AA 3.524)

Mariarte, Ninian; m. 8 May 1735 Jane Griffin (QAP m/6)

Mariartee, Ninian; age ca 44; 14 Jun 1745 (CCR JK#4.596)

Mariarte, Ninian; 10 Dec 1748; 3 Feb 1748/9; [no relations]; tracts *Darnalls Grove* now *Charlesses Folly* (MCW IX.194)

Mariarte, Ninian; mother Eleanor; 9 Jun 1752 (PGLR Q.513)

MARKLAND

Markland, Matthew; admx. Margaret; 18 Jun 1744 (I 30.83)

Markland, Jonathan; wife Prisilah; child: Richard, b. 29 ___ 1762 (PGP p. 264)

MARLBOROUGH

Marlborough, Francis; age ca 70; 17 Aug 1732 (PGLR Q.528)

MARLEY

Marley, Griffin; wife Elizabeth [d/o Robert Lyle]; children: Thomas, Griffin; tract *Waughtown*; 20 Dec 1715 (PGLR F.531)

MARLOW

Marloe, Edward; wife Mary; tract half of *Westmoreland*; 8 Nov 1700 (PGLR C.116c)

Marloy, Ralph; m. 22 May 1717 Anne Middleton; children: Elizabeth, b. 28 Feb 1717/8; Martha, b. 22 Jul 1719; Middleton, b. 18 Jun 1721; Mary, b. 26 Feb 1724; John, b. 27 Dec 1726; Sarah, b. 5 Sep 1729; Ann, b. 19 Aug 1731; Ellenor, b. 12 Aug 1733; Susanah, b. 13 Dec 1736; Rebecca, b. 3 Apr 1739; Samuel Middleton, b. 20 Oct 1741 (KGP p. 276)

Marloe, Ralph; wife Ann; cous. Richard; 8 Mar 1733 (PGLR T.91)

....

The following recorded as they appear in both sets of records; duplications included; it appears that children b. prior to 1755 belong to Lydia; 1755 and later to Eleanor.

Marlowe, John; wife Lidea or Elener; children: Middleton, b. 21 Sep 1746; Smallwood Cogill, b. 14 Oct 1749; Ann, b. 1 Jul 1752; Thomas Dorset, b. 24 Jun 1755; John, b. 3 Jun 1757; William, b. 15 May 1759; Amey Ann, b. 21 Feb 1761 Broad Creek (KGP p. 362)

Marloe, John; wife Lydia; children: Smallwood Cogill, b. 14 Oct 1749 (ICR); Ann, bapt. 29 Oct 1752 (ICR; KGP p. 297)

Marloe, John; wife Elinor; child: Thomas Dorsett, b. 21 Jun 1755 (ICR; KGP p. 311); Amey Ann, bapt. May-Jul 1761 (ICR; p. 323)

Marloe, John; wife Mary; child: Ann, b. 21 Feb 1756 (KGP p. 312)

....

Marlow, Edward; 4 Nov 1761; 30 Nov 1761; wife Sarah; daus. Eleanor Stevens, Mary, Ann; sons Richard, William, George, Samuel, Abel;

grandson Butler Marlow; bro. William Marlow; tract *Timothy and Sarah* (MCW XII.102); extx. Sarah; 9 Feb 1762 (I 77.93); extx. Sarah Marlow; children: Eleanor, Mary, Richard, William, George, Samuel, Abel; 4 Jan 1763 (ABB 3.180)

Marlow, James; wife Mary; child: John, b. 14 Jun 1762 (KGP p. 331)

Marlow, Joseph; wife. Mary; child: Mary, b. 17 Aug 1762 (KGP p. 328)

Marlow, Richard; wife Lidea; child: William Berrey, bapt. 5 Apr 1767 Lower Chapel (KGP p. 367)

Marlow, Ralph; 13 Jun 1770; 23 Oct 1770; wife Ann; children: Elizabeth Baynes, Martha Marbury, Sarah Ward, John, Ann Smallwood, Susannah Dorset, Sarah Roe, Dorothy, Rebecka (MCW XIV.150-1); admx. Rebecca; 14 May 1771 (I 108.336); 21 May 1772; extx. Ann, Rebecca Marlow; children [unnamed] (ABB 6.122); heirs Ann, Rebecca; 26 Aug 1774 (GB 321)

Marlow, Samuel Middleton; admx. Dorothy; 18 Apr 1770 (I 102.274)

MARONEY

Maroney, James; age ca 17; servant; Aug 1698 Ct. (PGCR A.333)

MARSH

Marsh, Richard; age ca 79; 9 Apr 1713 (CCR PC.877)

Marsh, Gilbert; 11 Feb 1724/5; 19 Feb 1724/5; grandson John (MCW V.184); 1 Mar 1724 (I 11.221); widow [dec'd, unnamed]; 16 Feb 1725 (AA 7.274)

MARSHALL

Marshall, Joshuah [Joshua]; 7 May 1702 (I&A 22.147); 11 Apr 1712 (I&A 33a.153)

Marshall, John; age ca 17; servant; Aug 1710 (PGCR G.2)

Marshall, Thomas; wife Elizabeth [widow of James Stoddert]; tract *Southampton*; 23 May 1727 (PGLR M.245)

Marshall, William; age ca 15; chooses his bro. Thomas Marshall as guardian; Nov 1735 (PGCR V.620)

Marshall, Thomas; guardian of Sarah, Rebecca; 16 Nov 1736 (PGLR T.421)

Marshall, Josias; wife Mary; child: John, bapt. 3 Jul 1763 at Upper Chapel (KGP p. 333)

Marshall, Thomas Henson; wife Rebecca; children: Elizabeth, bapt. 11 Feb 1765 Lower Chapel; Mary, bapt. 7 Jun 1767 Lower Chapel (KGP p. 350, 367)

Marshall, Josias; 29 May 1775; 15 Aug 1775; wife Mary; sons Benjamin Hanson, Richard, Thomas, John; dau. Letty; tract *Marshall's Adventure* (MCW XVI.72); [as Josiah]; extx. Mary; 31 Aug 1775 (I 123.226)

Marshall, Thomas; wife Mary; children: Elizabeth Fendall, bapt. 13 Apr 1766 Broad Creek; Josias, bapt. 8 May 1768 Lower Chapel (KGP p. 347, 369)

Marshall, William; age ca 40; 1731 (PGLR Q.374)

Marshall, William; 23 Apr 1734; 29 Jul 1734; sons Thomas, John, William; dau. Sarah, Rebekah; tracts *Carrick, Charles, Pesquasco* (MCW VII.102); 8 Oct 1734 (I 20.65); 28 Dec 1734 (I 20.343); 14 Feb 1735 (I 21.440); family [unnamed]; 14 Feb 1735 (AA 14.148); heir William; 24 Mar 1736 (GB 92); 9 Aug 1736 (I 22.216); 2 Feb 1737 (AA 16.183); heirs Sarah, John, Rebecca; 1 Apr 1738 (GB 99)

MARSHAM

Marsham, Richard [CA]; wife Ann [widow of Henry Brent]; Nov 1696 Ct. (PGCR A.68182)

Marsham, Richard; 14 Apr 1713; 7 May 1713; dau. Sarah Haddock; grandchildren: Basil Waring [wife Martha]; Leonard, Richard & ?Clement Brooke, Mary Bourman, Marsham Waring [wife Henrietta]; great-grandchildren: Thomas Waring [s/o Basil]; Samuel, Marsham, William, Catherine, & Margrett Queen [ch/o Samuel]; Richard Marsham, Basil, Sarah Waring [ch/o Marsham]; kinsman William Murdock; tracts *Strife, Troublesome, Childrens Loss, Walnutt Thickett, Content, St. Katherines, Inclosure, Mt. Pleasant, The Exchange, Marsham's Rest, Barron Point, Trundle Bed Cuckold* (MCW III.240); 22 Dec 1713 (I&A 35a.299)

MARTIN

Martin, James; 25 Aug 1706; 8 Nov 1706; [no relationships] (MCW III.82); 10 Nov 1707 (I&A 27.262)

Martain, Stephen; admx. Jane; 26 Mar 1745 (AA 21-212); admx. Joyce; 26 Mar 1745 (I 30.357)

Martin, Henry; wife Elisabeth; children: Mary, bapt. 2 Oct 1768 Lower Chapel; Michael, b. 22 Jan 1771 Lower Chapel; Zephaniah, b. 2 Mar 1773 Lower Chapel; Ann, b. 17 Feb 1775 Lower Chapel (KGP p. 371, 376, 380, 384)

Martin, Thomas; wife Rosamond; children: George, bapt. 15 Jan 1764 Lower Chapel; James, bapt. 14 Jul 1765 Lower Chapel; Smithey (m), bapt. 1 Nov 1767 Lower Chapel; Elizabeth, b. 9 Jan 1772 Broad Creek; James, b. 14 Jan 1774 Lower Chapel; Susanna, b. 30 Mar 1776 Lower Chapel (KGP p. 344, 351, 368, 377, 379, 381)

Martin, Michill; wife Mary; child: Josias Lanham, b. 13 Oct 1767, bapt. 1 Nov 1767 Lower Chapel (KGP p. 368)

Martin, Thos.; child: Mildred, b. 22 Nov 1769 Upper Chapel (KGP p. 372)
Martin, Michael; wife Mary; child: Clo Tilder (f), b. 17 Feb 1772 Lower
Chapel (KGP p. 383)

MARTINDALE
Martindale, John, Capt.; [Liverpool]; 25 Apr 1737 (I 22.264)

MASEY
Masey, Henry; admx. Elisabeth; family [unnamed]; 28 Jul 1748 (AA 25.103)

MASON
Mason, Robert; son John; tract *Grimes Ditch*; 2 Jun 1703 (PGLR C.72a)
Mason, Phillip; 27 Apr 1705 (I&A 25.132)
Mason, John; wife Elizabeth; children: James, b. 1 Aug 1705; Elizabeth, b.
15 Jun 1708; John, b. 7 Mar 1710 (QAP b/5)
Mayson, Phil; m. 10 Jan 1713 Elizabeth Dunning; children: Richard, b. 14
Dec 1714; Frances, b. 10 Mar 1715; Phill, b. 12 Jul 1718 (KGP p. 275)
Mason, Matthew [SM]; wife Mary; tract *Salup*; 24 Oct 1719 (PGLR F.250/835)
Mason, John; blacksmith; 2 Mar 1725; 10 May 1726; wife Elisabeth; sons
James, John; dau. Elizabeth (MCW V.224); extx. Elisabeth; 28 May 1726 (I
11.502); extx. Elisabeth; 8 Apr 1727 (AA 8.179)
Mason, James; m. 22 or 9ber 1727 Susanna Tucker (QAP m/4)
Mason, Robert; wife Susanna; 14 Jun 1732 (PGLR Q.460)
Mason, William; 18 May 1747 (I 35.48)
Mason, Samuel; d. 28 Sep 1763; wife Sarah; children: John, b. 2 Nov 1749,
bapt. 14 Apr 1750; Virlender Fair, b. 25 Dec 1753; Elizabeth, b. 9 Mar
1756; Philop, b. 8 Apr 1759; Mary Ann, b. 30 Jun 1760; Thomas, b. 1 Aug
1761; Sarah, b. 14 Jul 1763 at Lower Chapel and Broad Creek (KGP p. 336,
338)
Mason, Samuel, Jr.; 10 Nov 1763 (I 83.156); 30 Jul 1765 (I 90.141)
Mason, John; admx. Sarah; 15 Aug 1775 (I 123.229)

MASSEY
Massey, Elizabeth; 15 Jan 1757; 15 Mar 1757; daus. Mary Hanson, Mary
Batts, Elizabeth Hanson; granddaus. Elizabeth Greenfield, Mary Barnes,
Sarah Barnes; s-i-l John Hanson (MCW XI.157); 17 Mar 1757 (I 63.99); 26 Nov
1758; ex. John Hanson, Sr. (ABB 2.105, 118)
Massey, Henry; admx. Elisabeth; 17 Jun 1747 (I 35.120); admx. Elisabeth; 28
Jul 1747 (I 35.213); admx. Elisabeth; 8 Dec 1748 (AA 25.244)

MASTERS

Master, Robert; 14 Apr 1716; ex. Wm. Norris who m. the deceased's ____;
(I&A 37a.68); 6 Apr 1717 (I&A 38a.121)

Masters, William; son Nathan; 22 Aug 1720 (PGLR I.124)

Masters, William; wife Mary; tract *Gum Spring*; 13 Mar 1721 (PGLR I.307)

Masters, William; wife Ann; traxt *The Discord*; 26 Aug 1729 (PGLR M.540)

Masters, Martha; child: Elizabeth, b. 9 May 174_ (KGP p. 292)

Masters, Nathan; wife Frances; 16 Jul 1744 (I 29.437); admx. Priscilla
    Willson; 3 children: Priscilla, Elisabeth, Mary; 1 Oct 1745 (AA 22.48)

Masters, William; child: Ezekill, bapt. 12 Dec 1762 (KGP p. 329)

MATNE

Matne, Anthony; son John; dau. Hannah; 12 Dec 1724 (PGLR I.601, 602)

Mattu, Anthony; wife Hester; child: John, b. 14 10ber 1706 (QAP b/14)

MATTHEWS

Mathews, William; 12 Nov 1739; 22 Mar 1739; wife Mary; daus.
    Elizabeth, Mary, Hannah; son William; d-i-l Sarah Ancram (MCW VIII.84);
    widow Mary; heirs Elizabeth, William, Mary, Hannah, Margaret; 27
    Aug 1741 (GB 121)

Matthews, Roger; 27 Mar 1739 (I 24.92); widow is d/o admn. Francis Piles;
    29 Nov 1739 (AA 17.320)

Matthews, Thomas; 24 Jun 1757; 6 Feb 1762; nephew Thomas Matthews
    [s/o William]; bros. John, Maximilliam; sisters Mary, Theodosia Short;
    tract *O'Neil's Desert* (MCW XII.158)

MATTLAINE

Mattlaine, John, Sr.; son John, Jr.; 24 Mar 1717 (PGLR F.29/553)

MAUHANE

Mauhane, Thimithy; m. 7 Apr 1716 Sarah [widow of Jeremie Macknew];
    children: Mary, b. 10 Jul 1717; Ellenor, b. 7 Mar 1718; Timithy, b. 26
    Sep 1720 (KGP p. 268)

MAUNDER

Maunder, Ann; age 5 on 8 Sep next; d/o William; Jun 1718 (PGCR H.670)

MAWDESLY

Mawdesley [Mandesley, Maudesly, Moddelly], John; planter; 7 Dec 1743;
    19 Jan 1743/4; wife Sarah; sons John, Clemond & John Garland
    Mawdesley; dau. Mary Jones; tracts *Claget's Purchase*, *Green Spring* (MCW

VIII.244); admx. Sarah; 1 May 1744 (I 29.140); extx. Sarah Redding [w/o Patrick]; 12 May 1746 (AA 22.212); John; extx. Sarah Redding [w/o Patrick]; 20 Mar 1748 (AA 26.40); extx. Sarah Redding [late Mandesly]; children: Clement, Monica [both of age]; Mordecai, Ann, John Garlanat [these 3 under age]; 3 Feb 1753 (AA 33.291); 3 Feb 1753; extx. Sarah, w/o Patrick Redding; formerly Sarah Mawdesly (ABB 1.59)

Maudesly, Sarah; heirs Monica, Mordecai, Ann, John; 26 Jun 1753 (GB 182)

MAYEY
Mayey, Zachariah; wife Susannah; child: Kesander, bapt. 24 Jul 1763 at Upper Chapel (KGP p. 333)

MAYHEW
Mayhew, James; 28 Sep 1735; 25 Aug 1742; wife [unnamed]; sons James, John, William, Harrison; tracts *The Advantage, The Incloser* (MCW VIII.178)

Mayhew, William; wife Sarah Ann; children: Henry, b. 6 Mar 1760; Ann, b. 27 Mar 1762; Mary, bapt. _ Mar 1765 Upper Chapel (KGP p. 328, 358)

Mayhew [Mayhue], James; wife Jamima; children: Aron, bapt. May-Jul 1761; James Constantine, b. _ Dec 1763 at Upper Chapel; Moses, b. 11 Sep 1765 Lower Chapel; Reason Luckus, bapt. 6 Dec 1767 Upper Chapel; Leven, b. 13 May 1774 Upper Chapel (KGP p. 323, 340, 345, 366, 391)

Mayhew, William; bro. Aaron; 1761 (MCW XIV.94)

Mayhew, John; wife Mary Ann; children: Elizabeth, b. 15 Aug 1763 Upper Chapel; John, b. 14 Oct 1764 Upper Chapel or Broad Creek; Francis, bapt. 18 May 1766 Upper Chapel; Mildred, b. 9 Aug 1774 Upper Chapel (KGP p. 342, 354, 391)

Mayhew, Samuel; wife Lydda; child: Henry, b. 10 Nov 1775 Broad Creek (KGP p. 382)

MEARS
Mears, James; wife Marg.; child: Mary, b. 2 Jul 1734 (QAP b/28)

Meares, Isaac [age ca 5]; William [age ca 8]; James [age ca 12]; ch/o Martha; bound out; Jun 1721 (PGCR K.245)

MECONIA
Meconia, Daniel; wife Jane; child: Mary, b. 16 Mar 1709/10 (QAP b/4)

MEEKINS
Meekins, John; wife Mary; child: Elizabeth, bapt. 26 Apr 1751 (KGP p. 295)

MEHONY

Mehony, Denis; wife Mildred; 1718 (MCW IV.204)

MENRIS

Menris [Menus], John; wife Dorothy; children: John, b. 22 Mar 1774 Upper Chapel; William, b. 3 Feb 1776 Broad Creek (KGP p. 382, 390)

MERRETT

Merrett, Mary; age 11 next Oct; s/o Sarah; bound out; Mar 1738 (PGCR W.652)

MESSENGER

Messenger, Rev. Joseph, late Minister to the Episcopal Congregation at Dumfried, North Britain, now Rector of St. John's Parish, Prince George's Co.; wife Mary; children: Mary, b. 11:50 p.m. 14 Jan 1776, bapt. Easter Sunday, 7 Apr 1776 (KGP p. 415); other children b. after 1776

MESSMAN

Messman, James; widow & children [unnamed]; 1 Sep 1726 (AA 7.492)

METCALFE

Metcalfe, Mary; children: Susan, George, Vachell; grandchildren: Archiball & Lidia Butt; 5 Aug 1741 (PGLR Y.379)

MIDDLETON

Middleton, Robert; wife Mary; tract *Apple Hill*; 8 Jan 1699 (PGLR A.295)

Middleton, Thomas; wife ____ Penelipeo; children: Hatton, b. 9 Dec 1705; Thomas, b. 29 Jan 1707; Mary, b. 24 Feb 1709; Penelepeo Weston, b. 29 Mar 1712 (KGP p. 265)

Middleton, John; wife Mary; tract *Wheeler's Purchase*; 20 Nov 1706 (PGLR C.176)

Middleton, William [CH]; wife Elizabeth; tract *Godfather's Gift*; 18 Jun 1719 (PGLR F.199/786)

Middleton, John, Capt.; age 52; 5 Oct 1725 (PGLR I.696); age ca 55; 1728 (PGLR M.346)

Middleton, Thomas; age 47; 5 Oct 1725; 25 Nov 1725 (PGLR I.696); age ca 50; 1729 (PGLR M.445); Thomas, Sr.; age ca 55; 1732 f-i-l Thomas Dickinson, Sr. (PGLR Q.480)

Middleton, Hatton; admx. Jane; 11 Aug 1733 (I 17.280); admx. Jane Goddart [w/o John]; heirs Martha, Penelope; 8 Jul 1734 (AA 12.341); heirs Martha, Penelope; 27 Aug 1735 (GB 70)

Middleton, John; wife Mary; dau. Charity Luckett [w/o William]; tract *Thomas & Mary, Willett's Enlargement*; 10 May 1740 (PGLR Y.168)

Middleton, Holland [CH]; wife Sarah; tract *Long Point*; 14 Oct 1740 (PGLR Y.220)

Middleton, Thomas, Sr.; 4 Jan 1745 (I 32.291)

Middleton, Hugh; wife Rachael; children: Ignatius, b. 10 Dec 1772 Lower Chapel; Hutchinson, b. 8 Dec 1775 Lower Chapel (KGP p. 380, 384)

Middleton, Horatio; m. 23 May 1775 Susanna Stoddert; child: Samuel, b. 31 Mar 1776 Lower Chapel (KGP p. 377)

MILES

Miles, Maurice [Morrice]; wife Mary; children: Sabrina, b. 7 Jan 1702; Mary, b. 7 7ber 1704; Martha, b. 27 Jan 1706; Sarah, b. 25 Dec 1708; Elizabeth, b. 3 8ber 1710; Ellinor, b. 26 Jun 1714; Ann, b. 6 Apr 1721; Maurice, b. 24 7ber 1723 (QAP b/3, 5, 10, 17, 18, 25)

Miles, Mary; orphan of Thomas Barnett [lately dec'd]; Aug 1703 (PGCR B.251)

Miles, Morris; wife Mary; tract *Chipping Cambden House*; 6 Oct 1715 (PGLR F.495)

Miles, Thomas & Elisabeth; she is also called Elisabeth White; [with 1717] (I&A 38a.121)

Miles, Thomas; wife Mary; dau. Elizabeth; 18 Jul 1718 PGLR F.81/628)

Miles, Thomas; wife Mary; children: Maurice, b. 6 May 1719; Jonathan, b. 6 Jan 1722/3; Joseph, b. 26 Mar 1726; Margery, b. 31 Dec 1731/2 (QAP b/10, 15, 18, 19)

Miles, Thomas; admx. Elisa; 6 Feb 1726 (I 11.902)

Miles, Thomas; 2 d./6 mo./1725; 23 Nov 1726; wife Elizabeth; sons Thomas, John [mother Elizabeth]; daus. Sarah Plummer [w/o Samuel], Elizabeth, Rachel [mother Elizabeth] (MCW VI.10); widow Elizabeth; heirs John, Rachell; 26 Mar 1727 [?8] (GB 44); extx. Elisabeth [Quaker]; children: Sarah Plummer [w/o Samuel], Thomas, Elisabeth Roberts [w/o Samuel]; 13 May 1728 (AA 9.152)

Miles, Morris; age ca 50; 22 Sep 1730 (PGLR Q.157); age ca 60; 5 Jun 1740 (PGLR Y.185)

Miles, William, Sr.; age ca 63; 1734 (PGLR T.504)

Miles, Thomas; planter; 16 Feb 1750/1; 26 Nov 1751; wife Mary; daus. Elizabeth, Mary, Sarah, Margaret, Ann, Rebecca, Margery; sons Jonathan, Joseph, Thomas, Richard, Isaac (MCW X.194-5); extx. Mary; 23 Mar 1752 (I 48.377); extx. Mary Higgins [w/o William]; 28 Mar 1753 (AA 34.46); 28 Mar 1753; extx. Mary Higgins [w/o William]; minor children:

Thomas, Richard, Isaac Miles; Margery Faulkner [w/o Gilbert]; [1.63 does not mention Margery] (ABB 1.63, 112, 113); extx. Mary Higgins [w/o William]; 3 Apr 1754 (AA 36.287, 346); heirs Thomas, Isaac; 27 Aug 1754 (GB 195)

Miles, Elizabeth, 18 Jan 1751; 16 Jun 1752; daus. Sarah Cole [w/o William], Elizabeth Price [w/o Mordica]; sons Samuel White [s/o Guy], Benjamin White, John Miles (MCW X.218); 29 Jun 1752 (I 51.36); 10 Jun 1753; exs. Samuel White, John Miles (ABB 1.63, 76); 10 Jun 1753 (AA 34.137)

Miles, Richard; age 15 on 19 Apr next; choses John Orme (carpenter) as gurdian; Mar 1753 (PGCR MM.371)

Miles, Thomas; age 17 on 17 Jul last; choses William Higgins as guardian; Mar 1753 (PGCR MM.371)

Miles, Thomas; 24 Apr 1760; 24 Apr 1760; sister Sarah Plummer (MCW XI1.232)

Miles, John; wife Mary; child: Nicholas, b. 15 Mar 1765 (PGP p. 275)

Miles, William; admx. Mary; 11 Feb 1768 (I 97.122)

Miles, Marget; 25 Jul 1775; 28 Nov 1776; children: Monaca Webb, Priscillah & Susannah Miles; granddaus. Margett Webb, Routh Truman Winser (MCW XVI.168)

MILLER

Miller, John; wife Ann; tract Hazard; 27 Mar 1703 (PGLR C.89a)

Miller, Thomas; admx. Sarah; 18 May 1712 (I&A 33a.230)

Milles, William; 20 Aug 1718 (I 1.456)

Miller, George; 15 Nov 1718; wife Ruth; son Adam; dau. Ruth Holsill; granddau. Mary Miller; grandsons George & John Holsill, Jr.; (MCW IV.194-5)

Miller, Adam; wife Phillis; tract Monduit's Beginning; 18 May 1725 (PGLR I.665)

Miller, John; age ca 60; 1729 (PGLR M.485); age ca 63; 4 Apr 1732 (PGLR Q.575); age ca 66; 6 Aug 1735 (PGLR T.359); age ca 68; 24 Dec 1736 (PGLR Y.84)

Miller, Adam; age ca 38; 11 May 1733 (PGLR T.25)

Miller, John; wife Ann, age ca 48; 29 Oct 1736 (CCR-MSA 6.21)

Miller, Robert; age ca 8; bound out; Jun 1745 (PGCR DD.89)

Miller, Ann; 29 Nov 1746 (I 34.210); 29 Jun 1748 (AA 25.99)

Miller, Charles; wife Mary; child: John Jacob, bapt. 29 Aug 1762 (KGP p. 332)

Miller, Adam; 28 Dec 1763 (I 84.199)

MILLS

Mills, William [b. 11 Oct 1695]; Tabitha [b. 26 Oct 1697]; Verlinda [b. 7 Jan 1699]; ch/o William; Mar 1708 (PGCR C.221a)

Mills, William; bro. John; Nov 1696 Ct. (PGCR A.60)

Mills, William; wife Elizabeth; tract part of *Trenant*; 16 Apr 1701 (PGLR A.384)

Mills, William; 8 Jan 1705 (I&A 25.223); 29 Oct 1706 (I&A 26.136); [with 1708] (I&A 29.174)

Mills, Catherine; d/o William; bound out; Aug 1714 (PGCR G.633)

Mills, Alexander; wife Elizabeth; children: Sushannah, b. 20 Jun 1716; Alexander, b. 11 Nov 1718; Anne, b. 19 Nov 1719; William, b. 1 or 30 Sep 1720; Alexander, b. 11 Nov 1723 (KGP p. 272, 278)

Mills, John; 21 Oct 1717; 25 Jan 1717; sons William, Robert, Richard, John; daus. Ellinor, Seliner, Mary Travis; granddau. Elizabeth Travis; grandsons John and William Mills Travis (MCW IV.176); 13 May 1716(?) (I&A 39b.75); 6 Feb 1717 (I&A 39b.77)

Mills, John; wife Mary; tract *Diamond*; 4 Jun 1726 (PGLR M.43)

Mills, Alexander; wife Mary; child: John, b. 14 Apr 1755; Alexander, b. 2 Sep 1762 (KGP p. 308, 327)

Mills, John; wife Rebecca; children: Charles, b. 11 Nov 1760; Anne, b. 3 May 1763 (PGP p. 269)

Mills, John; wife Sarah; children: Rachel, b. 1 May 1714; Ann, b. 12 Mar 1717; Sarah, b. 18 7ber 1720 (QAP b/10, 16)

MILLSTEAD

Millsteed, Thomas; planter; 6 Sep 1737; 31 Dec 1737; wife [unnamed]; bros. Edward, William, John; tracts *Bachelor's Park, Milsteed Range, Winter Imployment, Mountin* (MCW VII.229); admx. Johanna; 8 Mar 1737 (I 23.421); extx. Johannah Acton [w/o Henry]; dau. Elisabeth; 26 Mar 1739 (AA 17.151); heir Elizabeth; 28 Nov 1739 (GB 105)

MILNER

Milner, Isaac [dec'd] [London]; widow Anne; 5 Dec 1713 (PGLR F.371)

MINER

Minner, John; wife Dorathy; child: Mary Jean, b. 5 Jul 1769 Broad Creek (KGP p. 373)

Miner, Daniel; 14 Sep 1773; 21 Sep 1773; wife Ann (MCW XV.97)

MIRA

Mira, Anna Christianna [age 7 next Aug]; Alicia [age 5 next May]; Hans Peter [age 3 next April]; servants; Mar 1723 (PGCR L.4)

MIRTH

Mirth, John [dec'd] [CA]; son John; tract part of *Woods Joy*; 13 Nov 1696 (PGLR A.12)

MISKELL

Miskell, Thomas; 5 Nov 1709 (I&A 31.408); 20 Jun 1712 (I&A 33b.33)

Miskell, William; wife Anne; tract *Forrest*; 16 Jul 1720 (PGLR I.36)

MITCHELL

Mitchell [Mitchel], John; wife Elizabeth; children: John, b. 28 Feb 1717; Sarah, b. 31 Aug 1720; David, b. 14 Feb 1722/3; Michael, b. 12 Aug 1726; George, b. 7 Feb 1728/9; Elizabeth, b. 10 Jan 1731/2 (QAP b/13, 16, 18, 20, 22, 25)

Mitchell, John [dec'd]; wife Susanna [?d/o Margery Sprigg]; *Greenwood*; 2 Feb 1725 (PGLR I.712, 714)

Mitchell, Mordacai; wife Martha; tract *Fortune*; 28 Jan 1726 (PGLR M.110)

Mitchell, John; wife Elizabeth; dau. Mary Callander [w/o William]; 26 Apr 1726 (PGLR I.729)

Mitchell, Robert; wife Mary; tract *?Her Park*; 25 Nov 1740 (PGLR Y.250)

Mitchell, David; wife Mary; children: Mary, b. ____; Elizabeth, b. 9 Dec 1744; John, b. __ Jun ____; Sarah, b. ____; James, b. _ Feb ____; Keziah, b. __ Mar ____ (QAP b/33, 34, 36)

Mitchell, John; wife Elizabeth; children: Hugh, b. 12 Apr 1746; Elizabeth, b. 6 Jun 1749; David, b. 9 Feb 1752; Margaret, b. 29 Jan 1754; Sarah, b. 5 Jun 1756 (QAP b/36)

Mitchel, Lydia; age ca 9; bound out; Jun 1748 (PGCR HH.176)

Mitchell, John, Sr.; 4 Jun 1748; 25 Aug 1752; wife Elizabeth; sons John Jr, David, Mary Lee, Sarah Atterbary; granddau. Elizabeth Yaxley (MCW X.235)

Mitchell, Mary; 26 Oct 1759; 30 Dec 1767; children: John, Thomas, Henry; grandchildren: Denwood, John & Watkins Cramphin [ss/o John]; Thomas Cramphin [s/o Thomas]; Robert Henry & Basil Richard Cramphin; Batson Cramphin [s/o John, dec'd]; Elizabeth & Alice Cramphin [ds/o Henry, dec'd]; Jean Cramphin [d/o John], Ruth Cramphin [d/o Henry]; d-i-l Jane [widow of John]; tract *Aaron* (MCW XIV.36)

Mitchel, David; wife Mary; child: Elias, b. 12 Mar 1761 (PGP p. 260)

Mitchell, John; wife Mary; child: Benjamin, b. 20 May 1761 (KGP p. 324)

Mitchell, William; wife Sarah; child: Enock, b. 25 Mar 1762 (KGP p. 330)

Mitchill, Joseph; wife Elizabeth; child: Elizabeth Marbury, b. 8 Jun 1762 (KGP p. 331)

Mitchel, James; wife Charity; child: Thomas, b. 6 Aug 1762 (PGP p. 267)

Mitchell, James; wife Kesiah; children: William, b. 15 Jul 1772 Upper Chapel; Mordeca, b. 7 Mar 1775 Upper Chapel (KGP p. 389, 391)

Mitchel, Benjamin; wife Priscilla; child: Eleanor, b. 15 Apr 1773 Upper Chapel (KGP p. 390)

Mitchell, Alvin; wife Katherine; child: Walter, b. 21 Nov 1774 Upper Chapel (KGP p. 390)

Mitchell, Benjamin; wife Ossilla [?Priscilla]; child: Benjamin, b. 19 Mar 1775 Upper Chapel (KGP p. 391)

MITCHISON

Mitchison, John; wife Constant; children: Constant, b. 1 May 1707; Ann, b. 23 Jun 1712; Elizabeth, b. 25 Apr 1715; John, b. 15 Feb 1721 (KGP p. 279)

MOBBERLY

Moberly, John, Sr.; sons John, James, William, Edward, Thomas; ca 1707 (PGLR C.208a)

Mobberly, John; wife Elizabeth; 1 Jun 1708 (PGLR C.212)

Moberly [Mobberly, Mobborly], John, Jr.; m. 12 Feb 1711/2 Rachel Pindell; children: Edward, b. 8 8ber 1716; John, b. 2 May 1720 (QAP m/1; b/11, 12, 16)

Moberly, John, Sr.; m. 28 Feb 1716 Susanna Scraggs, widow of Aaron Scraggs; children: John & Samuel [twins], b. 31 Jan 1717; Ann, b. 5 Feb 1718/9 (QAP m/2; b/13, 14)

Moberly, John, Sr.; wife: widow of _____ Robinson; 8 Dec 1719 (CCR CL.551)

Mobberly, Edward; school master; 14 Apr 1721(?); 24 Aug 1761; children: Rebecca, Edward, Francis, Rebecca; tracts *Rencher's Adventure* (MCW XII.81)

Mobberly, John; wife Anne; 18 Jan 1727 (PGLR M.279)

Mobberly, John; admx. Susanna Boulton; 12 Feb 1728 (I 14.290); widow Susannah Bolton [w/o Henry]; 21 Mar 1731 (AA 11.7)

Mobely, Thomas; wife Mary; child: Mary, b. 2 Nov 1733 (QAP b/27)

MOCKBEE

Mackeboy, Williams; age ca 14; servant; Nov 1698 (PGCR A.355)

Mockbee, Matthew; wife Jane; children: James, b. 20 10ber 1702; William, b. 22 10ber 1704 (QAP b/6)

Mockbee, Matthew; 16 May 1709 (I&A 30.447)

Mockbee, Brock; m. 22 Dec 1715 Eliza. Beckett; children: Edward, 23 May 1716; Sarah, b. 8 8ber 1718; Brock, b. 12 9ber 1720; Elizabeth, b. 9 Aug 1723; James Offert, b. 11 Aug 1725; Lucy, b. 5 Jan 1727/8; William, b. 22 Apr 1730; Mary, b. 22 Dec 1732 (QAP m/1; b/11, 14, 16, 18, 19, 21, 23, 26)

Mogbee, Matthew [dec'd]; widow Jane [age ca 53]; 8 Dec 1719 (CCR CL.551)

Mackaboy, Patrick; daus. Elizabeth, Sarah; 26 Aug 1724 (PGLR I.580)

Mockibey, Brock; age ca 35; 31 May 1731 (PGLR Q.608)

Maccabe [Macaby], Lacy; wife Ann; child: Elizabeth Ann, b. 9 Apr 1731; Lacy (m), b. 26 Jan 1732/3 (QAP b/24, 26)

Mockbee, William; mother Jane; 12 Aug 1736 (I 22.25)

Mockbee, Jane; 2 Mar 1743/4; 27 Nov 1746; husband Matthew Mockbee [dec'd]; step-son Matthew Mockbee; dau. Jane Doull; son Thomas Joice; d-i-l Sarah Joice; s-i-l Dr. James Doull (MCW IX.90-1); 3 Mar 1746 (AA 23.163)

Mockbee, Ed.; wife Sarah; children: William Nicholls, b. 16 Sep 1759; Dorcas, b. 13 Mar 1762 (PGP p. 257. 263)

Mockbee, Brock; m. Margrette; child: Richard, b. 5 Dec 1764 (PGP p. 274)

Mocaboy, Zachariah; wife Ann; child: John Speek, b. 10 Sep 1773 Upper Chapel (KGP p. 390)

MOLAND

Moland [Molen], Samuell; wife Virlinder; children: Hazel, b. 23 Nov 1763; Vincent, b. 2 Jul 1765 (PGP p. 274)

Moland, Sameull; wife Mary; child: Mary, b. 26 Jun 1760 (PGP p. 259)

MONROW

Monrow, John; wife Mary; child: Sarah, bapt. 14 Oct 1764 Lower Chapel; Ann, bapt. 30 Nov 1766 Broad Creek; Mary, b. 1 Feb 1774 Lower Chapel (KGP p. 345, 348, 379)

MOORE

Moore, James; wife Mary; tract *Beales Hunting Quarter*; 23 Jun 1697 (PGLR A.52)

Moor, William; wife Rachel; children: Ann, b. 12 Jul 1700; Ryley & John [twins], b. 8 Feb 1702/3; Samuel, b. 15 Feb 1704/5; William, b. 10 Apr 1707; Rachell, b. 18 May 1710; George, b. 16 7ber 1712 (QAP b/7)

Moore, Mordicay; m. widow Ursula Burges; tract *Westfalia*; 10 Aug 1704 (PGLR C.165a)

Moor, John; m. 7 Nov 1706 Elizabeth Danielson; children: John, b. 29 Mar 1708; Mary, b. 22 Mar 1710; John, b. 4 10ber 1712; Margaret, b. 4 Aug 1715; Priscilla, b. 3 Jul 1720; Mordecai, b. 17 10ber 1722; Thomas, b. 20

Aug 1724; Phillip, b. 3 Mar 1727/8; Dorcas, b. 22 Jul 1734 (QAP m/1; b/6, 7, 11, 17, 18, 19, 21, 28)

Moore, James, Jr.; children: James, b. 1 Aug 1715 (?); Alice, b. 1 Jan 1715 (?); Ruth, b. 30 Jul 1720; Priscilla, b. 21 Feb 1725; Elizabeth, b. 6 Dec 1727 (PGP p. 247-8)

Moor, George; wife Elizabeth; child: Mary, b. 11 May 1716; George, b. 7 Jul 1717 (QAP b/12, 13)

Moore, James, Sr.; son James, Jr.; grandson James; tract *Barbadoes*; 1 Jan 1718/9 (PGLR F.205/792)

Moore, William; wife Mary; tract *Piney Hedge*; 8 Sep 1718 PGLR F.95/648)

Moore, Thomas; wife Mary; tract *Margery*; 5 Feb 1720 (PGLR I.94)

Moore, Ryley [s/o William]; m. 16 Aug 1726 Sarah Holland; child: William, b. 15 May 1727 (QAP m/4; b/21)

Moore, Richard [AA]; wife Margaret; 25 Oct 1726 (PGLR M.106)

Moore, James; wife Barbara; tract *Gleaning*; 25 May 1723 (PGLR I.444)

Moore, Henry; age ca 64;1728 (PGLR M.344); age ca 72; 10 Mar 1734 (PGLR T.280)

Moore [Morl, Moorle], James; carpenter, St. George's Parish; 29 Oct 1728; 27 Nov 1728; wife [unnamed]; sons Archibald, James, Robert; daus. Euphen, Barbara; tracts *The Gleanings, Archibald's Lott, Allisons Park* (MCW VI.85); admx. Barbra Hardy; 15 Feb 1729 (I 13.442); extx. Barbery Hardy [w/o John]; heirs Archibald, James, Upham, Barbary; 5 Dec 1729 (AA 10.103); extx. Barbara Hardy [w/o John]; heirs Archibald, James, Uphain, Barbary; 24 Mar 1730 (AA 10.694)

Moore, James, Sr.; age ca 105; 22 Jul 1729 (PGLR M.481)

Moor, Henry; 17 Mar 1732/3; 17 Feb 1735/6; wife Sarah; daus. Sarah, Esther, Charity, Ann Davis, Benedicto, Elizabeth; sons William, Henry; tract *Moor's Chance, Wheller's Choice, Moor's Rest* (MCW VII.161); admx. Sarah; 9 Apr 1736 (I 21.341); ex. Sarah; son Henry [minor]; 2 Sep 1737 (AA 14.408)

Moore, John, Jr.; wife Elizabeth; tract *Moore's Industry*; 18 Nov 1733 (PGLR T.19)

Moore, James, Sr.; age 110; wife Mary; grandson James Hoskinson; tract *The Gift*; sons George Moore [tract *?Sliger Lofe*], Benjamin [tract *Child's Portion*], Peter; 9 May 1735 (PGLR T.270 - 273)

Moore, John; wife Catherine; tract *Spriggen Lott*; 16 Apr 1741 (PGLR Y.299)

Moore, John; carpenter; 17 Oct 1749; 25 Sep 1754; wife Elizabeth; sons Mordecai, Thomas, Philip; dau. Darkis Moore; tract *Moore's Industry* (MCW XI.45-6)

Moore, James; wife Sarah; child: Thomas, b. 24 Feb 1754 (KGP p. 311)

Moore, James; wife Ann; children: Prisillah, b. 17 Nov 1760; Elisabeth, b. 25 Mar 1762; Martha, b. 2 Oct 1765 (PGP p. 259, 263, 277)

Moore, Peter; wife Easter; children: Alexander Clayland, b. 3 Apr 1763 at Upper Chapel; Easey, b. 19 May 1765 Broad Creek (KGP p. 332, 347)

Moore, Mordecai; wife Sophia; child: Elizabeth, b. 27 Jul 1764 (PGP p. 276)

Moore, Benjamin & son James; wit. will; 1770 (MCW XIV.221)

Moore, Peter; 18 Feb 1770; 15 Jun 1772; children: Rhoda, Dorcas, Jesse, Josiah, Zadock, Mary Osbourn [w/o William], James, Nathan, Samuel (MCW XIV.221); 7 Aug 1772 (I 109.231); heirs grandsons Robert Moore, Alexander Cleland Moore; 29 Mar 177_ (GB 278, 279); heir Alexander Cleland Moore; 6 Dec 1773 (GB 314, 316)

Moore, James; wife Ann; child: James Draden, b. 12 Oct 1773 Upper Chapel (KGP p. 390)

MORDANT

Mordant, William; m. 22 10ber 1715 in Anne Arundel Co. Ann Watts; [no marriage recorded found AA Co.] (QAP m/2)

Mordant, William; wife Anne; tract *Margery*; 29 Jan 1724 (PGLR I.640)

Mordant, William; 31 Mar 1741; 20 Apr 1741; granddau. Elizabeth Burgess (MCW VIII.132); 24 Apr 1741 (I 26.79)

MORDESLEY

Mordesley, John; wife Sarah; 25 Jan 1738 (PGLR T.676)

Mordesly, John; 15 Oct 1752 (I 51.39)

MORGAN

Morgan, Law.; wife Sarah; child: Robert, b. 4 May 1728 (PGP p. 247-8)

Morgan, Richard; wife Esther; child: Luritta, b. 23 May 1765 (PGP p. 276)

MORIAN

Morian, John; age ca 18; servant; Jan 1699 Ct. (PGCR B.12)

MORIARTE

Moriarte, Daniel; wife Eleanor; tract *Maiden's Dowry*; 19 Jul 1720 (PGLR F.282/863)

MORRIS

Morris, Richard; age ca 12; Nov 1703 Ct. (PGCR B.262a)

Morriss, James; wife Ann; child: John, b. 20 10ber 1717 (QAP b/13)

Morriss, Mary; infant age 2 yrs.; d/o Hannah; bound out; Mar 1721 (PGCR K.83)

Morriss [Morrice], James; m. 7 Jul 1728 Katherine Shaun; child: Thomas, b. 1 Jan 1729 (QAP m/5; b/23)

Morris, Mauris; age ca 55; 29 May 1730 (PGLR Q.153); age ca 56; 7 Jul 1731 (PGLR Q.526)

Morris, Maurice [Morris]; wife Elizabeth; son Thomas; tract *His Lordship's Kindness*; 30 Jul 1730 (PGLR Q.78)

Morriss, John; wife Elizabeth; children: Susanna Page, b. 11 Nov 1754; Elizabeth Page, b. 21 Nov 1756; Martha Ann, b. 24 Nov 1758 (KGP p. 308, 314, 321)

Morriss, Morriss; wife Ann; child: Owen, b. 12 Feb 1757 (KGP p. 314)

Morris, John; wife Elizabeth; child: George, b. 27 Jan 1763 at Broad Creek (KGP p. 337)

Morris, Daniel; wife Mary; child: Ann, bapt. 22 Jun 1766 Broad Creek; Mary Dent, bapt. 15 May 1768 Broad Creek (KGP p. 353; 362)

MORRISON

Morrison, James; wife Ann; tract *Inclosure*; 29 Aug 1723 (PGLR I.477)

MORROW

Morrow, John; wife Mary; child: Mary, b. 1 Feb 1774 (KGP p. 379)

MORS

Mors, Ebenezar; m. 28 Apr 1735 Sarah Fox; ?children: Debrah, b. 18 Jun ____; Obidiah, b. 5 Feb ____; Hannah, b. 6 Aug ____ (KGP p. 284)

MOSMAN

Mosman, James; nok [none in county]; 25 Jul 1726 (I 11.474)

MOULDER

Moulder, Griffith [dec'd]; ?wife Margaret; 17 Mar 1716 (PGLR F.515)

MUDD

Mudd, John; wife Mary; children: Ann Telting, b. 22 May 1763 at Broad Creek; John, b. 9 Jun 1769 Broad Creek (KGP p. 337, 373)

MULLIKEN

Mullikin, James; wife Jane; son Thomas, James; others; tract *Chelsey*; f-i-l [step-father] James Williams; mother Mary Williams [w/o James]; 28 Aug 1697 (PGLR A.94, 95)

Mullikin, James; daus. Mary, Ellen; 1707 (MCW III.91)

Mulliken, James; wife Charity; children: James, b. 5 Mar 1709; Elizabeth, b. 25 7ber 1711; Mary, b. 27 Jan 1714; John, b. 29 Mar 1716; Margaret, b.

30 Nov 1719; Jeremy, b. 30 Jan 1722; Belt, b. 8 Feb 1725; Charity, b. 6 Feb 1727; Thomas, b. 24 May 1729 (QAP b/4, 8, 11, 22, 23)

Mullakin, James; age ca 51; 14 Jun 1714 (CCR CL.27)

Mulliken, Thomas; m. 25 8ber 1714 Eliza. Wilson; children: John, b. 29 Jul 1715; Rachel, b. 25 Apr 1718; Mary, b. 25 Jan 1723/4; Elizabeth, b. 20 Jan 1728/9 (QAP m/1; b/11, 13, 18, 23)

Mullikin, James, Sr.; 22 May 1718 (I 2.212); 10 Oct 1719 (AA 2.350); 4 Jul 1720 (AA 3.55n)

Mullikin, James, Sr.; wife Charity; child: Benjamin, b. 12 Nov 1721 (QAP b/25)

Mulliken, James; age ca 55; 3 Oct 1724 (PGLR I.595)

Mulliken, John; wife Katherine; children: Lewis, b. 6 Feb 1723; Katherine, b. 24 Aug 1727; John, b. 2 Mar 1730/1 (QAP b/18, 21, 24)

Mullikin, Frances; wife Charity; tract *Woodjoy*; 28 Feb 1726 (PGLR M.137)

Mullikin, James [dec'd]; wife Mary; son James; dau. Elizabeth; tract *Woods Joy*; 24 Mar 1726 (PGLR M.222)

Mulliken, William; m. 6 Jun 1727 Margaret Turner; children: Margaret, b. 1 Mar 1728/9; Mary, b. 22 Jan 1728; Basil, b. 2 Dec 17__ (QAP m/4; b/13, 21, 23, 29)

Mulliken, James; m. 31 Oct 1734 Mary Pottinger (QAP m/6)

Mullikin, James, Jr.; wife Mary [d/o Samuel Pottenger]; tract *Felloeship*; 30 Apr 1736 (PGLR T.374)

Mullikin, James; 4 Mar 1739; 25 Apr 1740; wife Charity; sons Jeremiah, Thomas, Benjamin, James; grandson James Duvall; daus. Elizabeth Duvall, Mary Norwood (MCW VIII.83); extx. Charity; 16 Jun 1740 (I 25.88); widow Charaty; children: Jeremiah, Elisabeth Duval, James, Mary Norwood; 10 May 1746 (AA 20.180)

Mullikin, Thomas; 15 Jul 1745; 23 Nov 1746; wife Elizabeth; sons William, Thomas; daus. Eleanor, Elizabeth, Charity Mulliken, Rachel Goodman, Mary Harper (MCW IX.177); extx. Elisabeth; 17 Jan 1748 (I 40.188); extx. Elisabeth; children: William, Thomas, Rachel, Mary, Elinor, Elisabeth, Charity; 26 Jan 1750 (AA 29.219); widow Elizabeth; orphans, William, Thomas, Charity; 28 Nov 1751 (GB 175)

Mullikin, James, Jr.; admx. Mary; 10 Oct 1749 (I 41.178); admx. Mary Brashers [w/o John, III]; children: James, Mary, Charity, Samuel; 4 Jun 1751 (AA 30.77)

Mullikin, William; 15 Feb 1750/1; 28 Aug 1751; bro. Thomas; mother Eliza (MCW X.177); 25 Nov 1751 (I 48.375)

Mulliken [Mullakin, Mullikin], Lewis; wife Mary; children: John & Elizabeth [twins], b. 23 Jan 1752; bapt. 15 Mar 1752; Archabald [Achippa], b. 13 Dec 1753; Mary, b. 13 Feb 1755; Lewis, b. 6 Mar 1757; Esther, b. 7 Jun 1759; Humphrey Becket, b. 23 Aug 1763; Catherin, b. 30 Aug 1765 (PGP p. 271, 277, 295, 304)

Mulliken, James, Jr.; admx. Mary Brashears [w/o John, III]; 4 children [minors] James, Mary, Charity, Samuel; 30 Mar 1752 (AA 32.325); admx. Mary Brashears [w/o John III]; children: James, Mary, Charity & Samuel Mulliken; 30 Mar 1752 (ABB 1.42) heirs James, Mary, Charity, Samuel; 27 Jun 1753 (GB 183)

Mullekin, William; bro. [unnamed]; 20 Aug 1752 (AA 33.150)

Mullikin, James; widow Charity; heir James; 20 Dec 1759 (GB 213)

Mulliken, Thomas; m. 4 Feb 1761 Elizabeth Williams (QAP m/7)

Mullican, Thomas; planter; admx. Mary; 10 Oct 1763 (I 83.155)

Mullakin, Samuel; wife Katherine; child: James, 7 Jan 1772 Broad Creek (KGP p. 386)

Mullikin; Samuel; children: James, b. 17 Jan 1772; Joseph and Mary, b. 29 Dec 1773 Lower Chapel (KGP p. 380)

Mullikin, Samuel; wife Ruthania; children: Joseph and Mary, b. 29 Dec 1774 Broad Creek (KGP p. 386)

MULVAINE

Mulvaine, Eleanor; age 4 on 31 Dec 1715; bound out; Mar 1723 (PGCR L.241)

MURDOCK

Murdock, John; wife Katharine; tract *Londee*; 22 Jul 1710; (PGLR F.182)

Murdock, George; wife Eleanor; dau. Mary Nuthall; tract *Sprigg's Request*; 6 Feb 1728/9 (PGLR M.368)

Murdock, William; wife Ann; children: John, b. 10 Feb 1729; Addison:, b. 31 Jul 1731; John, b. 16 May 1733 (QAP b/24, 27)

Murdock, William; wife Ann; tracts *The Exchange, Marsham's Rest*; 27 Aug 1740 (PGLR Y.255)

Murdock, William; age ca 34; 20 Feb 1744 (CCR JK#4.564)

Murdock, George; 14 May 1760; 9 Mar 1761; son William; dau. Ann Beall; grandchildren: George, William, Precialla, Elianor & Martha Murdock; Anne, George, Elizabeth, William Murdock Beall, Elisha & Mary Beall (MCW XII.47)

Murdock, William; 23 Mar 1766; 2 Dec 1769; children: Rebecca, Margaret, John, Mary, Eleanor Hall, Catherine Sim, Addison; tracts *Bowles Choice* (MCW XIV.105)

MURPHEY

Murphey, Michall; age ca 15; servant; Sep 1698 Ct. (PGCR A.343)

Murfey, Zachariah; child: Elizabeth, b. 10 Oct 1761 (KGP p. 324)

Murfey [Murphy], Zachariah; wife Sushanna [Susanna]; children: Mary, bapt. 13 Apr 1766 Broad Creek; Sushanna Attaway, bapt. 10 Jun 1768 Lower Chapel; Sharlotte, b. 12 Jul 1775 Lower Chapel (KGP p. 347, 371, 381)

MURRY

Murry, Edward; wife Mary; child: Joshua, b. 9 Sep 1765 (PGP p. 276)

MUSGROVE

Musgrove, Benj'm; wife Mary; child: Lydia Margaret, bapt. 22 Oct 1752 (KGP p. 297)

MUSLEBROOK

Musslebrook [Muslebrook], James; 13 Apr 1714; 29 May 1714; [no relations]; estate left to Geo. Nailer, Jr. & dau. Martha (MCW IV.11); 16 Jul 1714 (I&A 36a.102); 12 Apr 1715 (I&A 36b.163)

NALLEY

Nalley, Samuel; wife Sarah; child: Mary, b. 19 Oct 1774 Lower Chapel
(KGP p. 380)

NASH

Nash, John; age 6 on 4 May next; bound to Robert Coots and Mary his
wife; Mar 1723 (PGCR L.2)

NATION

Nation, George; wife Ann; children: John, b. 7 Feb 1703/4; Nathaniel, b. 27
Apr 1706 (QAP b/1, 2)

NAVANE

Navane, James; orphan age ca 11 next June; bound out; Mar 1733 (PGCR S.249)

NAYLOR

Nailer, George, Jr.; dau. Martha; 1714; heirs of James Musslebrook (MCW
IV.11)

Nailor, George, Jr.; age ca 48; 13 Sep 1729 (PGLR M.519)

Nailor, George, Sr.; age ca 78; 1732 (PGLR Q.449)

Naylor, George; 31 Jan 1739/40; 24 Mar 1740; sons George, Battson; daus.
Sarah, Dorcus, Ann Graham [w/o Thomas]; tract *Forest of Fancy* (MCW
VIII.132)

Naylor, Samuel; child: Benjamin Turner, b. 25 Sep 1761 (KGP p. 327)

Naylor, George; wife Verlinder; child: Rebeccah, bapt. 16 Oct 1763 at
Broad Creek (KGP p. 338)

Naylor, Batson; 26 Jun 1769; 28 Jun 1769; wife Margit; children: Batson,
Benman, George, Anne, Matthew, Elizabeth, Lettice; tracts *Wood Brig*
(MCW XIV.101); extx. Margaret; 10 Aug 1769 (I 102.25); extx. Margaret; 10
Aug 1769 (I 102.25); 30 Nov 1770; exs. Margaret & George Naylor;
children [unnamed] (ABB 6.41); widow Margaret; heirs George, Ann,
Barton, Benjamin, Martha, Elizabeth, Lettice; 26 Aug 1772 (GB 309)

NEALE

Neale, Arther; age ca 15; servant; Jun 1698 Ct. (PGCR A.316)

Neale, James [CH]; wife Elizabeth Calvert [d/o William]; mentions dau.
Mary's marriage to Charles Egarton [s/o Charles]; 10 Apr 1702 (PGLR
A.449)

Neale, John Moss; age ca 10; servant; Jun 1712 Ct. (PGCR G.211)

Neale, James, Sr. [CH]; wife Elizabeth; dau. Ann Cole [w/o Edward]; tracts
St. Anthony, *St. Dorothies*; 25 May 1716 (PGLR F.529)

Neall, Jane; age 2 on 18 Mar instant; bound out; Mar 1740 (PGCR X.571)

Neale, Charles [CH]; wife Mary; tract *Three Sisters*; 9 Sep 1741 (PGLR Y.395)

Neale, Richard; choses guardian; Mar 1746 (PGCR DD.403)

Neal, Richard; wife Sarah; children: John, bapt. 12 Oct 1762; Zachariah, b. _ Jul 1763 at Lower Chapel; Samuel, bapt. 23 Jun 1765 Lower Chapel (KGP p. 327, 335, 351)

Neale, Thomas; wife Elizabeth; child: Mary, bapt. 8 Apr 1764 Upper Chapel (KGP p. 341)

Neel, Richard; child: Richard, bapt. 3 May 1767 Broad Creek (KGP p. 360)

Neal, Richard; wife Sushanna; child: Nathaniel, bapt. 5 Jun 1768 Broad Creek (KGP p. 363)

Neal, Thomas; wife Elizabeth; child: Thomas Richard, b. 5 Nov 1772 Upper Chapel (KGP p. 389)

Neal, Richard; wife Sarah; children: William Arter Sasser, b. 14 Feb 1773 Broad Creek; Elizabeth, b. 27 Sep 1775 Broad Creek (KGP p. 379, 387)

NEEDAM

Needam, William; m. 17 May 1736 Martha Throne; child: William, b. _ Mar 1736[/7] (KGP p. 271)

NELSON

Nelson, Arthur; wife Valentine; son John; 10 Sep 1715 (PGLR F.465)

Nelson, John [dec'd]; wife Mary [m/2 Edward Rockwood of Charles Co.]; m/3 John Gosling [VA]; tract *Gelhard*; 22 Feb 1724 (PGLR I.617)

Nelson, John; wife Jane; tract *Buck's Lodge*; 19 Aug 1729 (PGLR M.474)

Nelson, William; age ca 34; 6 Jun 1735 (PGLR T.280)

Nelson, Robert; wife Elizabeth; child: Basil, b. 27 Jul 1762 (PGP p.270)

NEWCOMB

Newcomb, William; widow Elisabeth Roberts [widow of Reuben]; 7 Apr 1752 (AA 32.97)

NEWMAN

Newman, Butler; wife Verlinda; children: George, b. 23 Oct 1760 (with 1765) Broad Creek; Butler Stonestreet, b. 29 Mar 1763 at Broad Creek; Mary Elenor, bapt. 19 May 1765 Broad Creek; Elizabeth, bapt. 27 Nov 1767 Lower Chapel; Jane, b. 28 Apr 1773 Broad Creek (KGP p. 337, 347, 349, 368, 384)

NEWTON

Newton, Joseph; wife Ann Odall; children: Sarah, b. 28 Aug 1721; Mary, b. 12 Jul 1723; Ann, b. 9 Feb 1727; Elizabeth, b. 19 Apr 1730; Nathaniel, b. 1 Aug 1736 (KGP p. 285)

Newton, Robert; wife Ann; child: Elizabeth, b. 1732 (QAP b/26)

Newton Robert; m. 28 Aug 1735 Elizh. Smith (QAP m/6)

Newton, Joseph; 20 Jan 1748/9; 23 Feb 1748/9; daus. Sarah, Mary Ann, Elizabeth, Rebecca, Rachell, Margaret, Susannah; son Nathaniel; b-i-l Thomas Hillery (MCW IX.194); extx. Ann; 12 Jun 1749 (I 39.65); admx. Anne; children: Anne, Mary, Elisabeth, Nathaniel, Rebecca, Rachel, Margrett, Susannah; 26 May 1750 (AA 28.156); extx. Ann; children: Mary, Ann, Elisabeth, Nathaniel, Rebecca, Rachel, Margaret, Susannah; 27 May 1751; 27 May 1751 (AA 30.109); widow Ann; heirs Mary, Ann, Elizabeth, Nathaniel, Rebecca, Rachel, Margaret, Susannah; 27 Nov 1751 (GB 173)

Newton, John; wife Dinnah; child: John, b. 28 Jan 1763 at Upper Chapel (KGP p. 332)

Newton, Anne; 13 Oct 1771; 20 Dec 1771; children: Sarah, Nathaniel, Margaret, Susannah, Mary, Ann, Elizabeth, Margaret, Rachael, Rebecca (MCW XIV.202); 19 May 1772 (I 108.330); heirs Mary, Ann, Elizabeth, Rebecca, Rachil, Margaret, Susanna, Nathaniel; 24 Nov 1776 (GB 338)

NICHOLAS

Nicholas, John; wife Martha; child: Joseph, b. 24 Dec 1753 (KGP p. 305)

NICHOLLS

Nicholls, Symon; wife Jane; child: James, b. 28 Jun 1705 (QAP b/2)

Nicholls, William; m. 9 7ber 1711 Mary Mockby; children: William, b. 21 Mar 1713/4; Sarah, b. 10 Feb 1718/9 (QAP m/1; b/9, 14)

Nicholls, William; wife Mary; tract *Green Clift*; 3 Nov 1711 (PGLR F.176)

Nicholls, William; m. 13 Feb 1715 Ann Burrows; child: William, b. 24 Mar 1718 (QAP m/1, b/13)

Nicholls, Thomas; m. 8 Oct 1717 Ann Davis; children: William, b. 24 Mar 1718; John, b. 21 Jan 1720; Thomas, b. 12 Nov 1724; William, b. 17 Jan 1727 (QAP m/1; b/13, 247-8)

Nicholls, Simon; son John; 16 Mar 1721 (PGLR I.125)

Nicholls, Simon; wife Jane; tract *Simon's Lott*; 28 Aug 1723 (PGLR I.485)

Nicholls, ____; age ca 6; s/o William and Anne [now wife of William Clarke]; Jun 1724 (PGCR L.312)

Nicholls, Simon, Sr.; age ca 67; 17 Aug 1725 (PGLR I.676); age 70 & upwards; 1731 (PGLR Q.397)

Nicholls, Simon, Sr.; dau. Janse Hurst; 1727/8 (PGLR M.270)

Nicholls, Williams; orphan age ca 15; chooses Uncle Brock Mockboy as guardian; Mar 1728 (PGCR O.14)

Nicholls, William; wife Mary; child: Ann, b. 24 Dec 1731 (QAP b/30)

Nicholls, Simon; dau. Rachel; 29 Nov 1735 (PGLR T.336)

Nichols, William; m. 10 Nov 1737 Sarah Green (QAP m/7)

Nicholls, Mary; d/o Grace; bound to Mary White; Nov 1738 (PGCR X.192)

Nichols, Edward; wife Sarah; tract Nichols' Contrivance; 10 Aug 1742 (PGLR Y.543)

Nichols, Catherine; child: Christopher, b. 24 Nov 1753 (KGP p. 305)

Nicholls, Simon, wife Ann; children; John Haymond, b. 10 Apr 1756; Thomas, b. 22 Sep 1758 (PGP p. 257)

Nicholls [Nichols], Thomas; wife Cassandra; children: William, b. 18 Sep 1759; Rebecca, b. 20 May 1761; Daniel, b. 23 Apr 1763; Thomas, b. 22 Nov 1765 (PGP p. 257, 262, 268, 278)

Nicholls, Thomas; wife Elizabeth; children: William, b. 11 Apr 1761; Erasmus, b. 1 Apr 1765; Thomas Case, b. 15 Apr 1774; John, b. 18 Oct 1776 (PGP p. 261, 273, 279)

Nichols, Basill; wife Margery; children: Massey (f), b. 21 Dec 1761; Easter, bapt. _ Aug 1763 at Upper Chapel; Gilbert, bapt. 19 Apr 1767 Upper Chapel (KGP p. 305, 333, 365)

Nicholls, John; wife Elizabeth; child; John, b. 27 Sep 1772 (PGP p. 279)

NILANDIHAM

Nilandiham, George; wife Elizabeth; child: Martha Dent, b. 17 Jan 1774 Lower Chapel (KGP p. 379)

NIXON

Nixon, Jonathan; m. 29 Jul 1738 Mary Scaritt late of Leek, Staffordshire, England; children: Hugh, b. 8 May 1745; Joshua, b. 1 Sep 1747; Mary, b. 17 May 1750; Richard, b. 6 Mar 1752; Jonathan, b. 6 May 1754, bapt. 16 May 1756; Elizabeth, b. 10 Apr 1756; Amey, b. 9 May 1763 Broad Creek (KGP p. 269, 313, 357)

NOBLE

Noble, Joseph, b. 17 Apr 1689 Cockmouth, Cumberland; d. 14 Dec 1749; s/o Joseph and Cathrine; m. 2 Dec 1708 Mary Wheeler; both of this parish; children: Sarah, b. 8 Nov 1709; Elizabeth, b. 3 May 1712; Joseph,

b. 15 Apr 1715; Francis, b. 27 Dec 1719; Catherine, b. 14 Nov 1721; Salome, b. 23 Apr 1724; Mary, b. 31 May 1727; John, b. 5 Feb 1732; William Fraser, b. 8 Nov 1735 (KGP p. 272, 273)

Noble, John, Jr. [SM]; sister Mary [dec'd; no heirs]; cous. William Spinke; tract *Sugar Lands*; 12 Jun 1727 (PGLR M.257)

Noble, Joseph; age ca 42; 19 Oct 1730 (CCR-MSA 5.464)

Noble, George; age ca 40; f-i-l John Sheppard; 19 Oct 1730 (CCR-MSA 5.449)

Noble, George; d. 14 Sep 173_; m. 27 Jan ____ Charity Wheeler; d. 3 Sep 1735; gentleman and gentlewoman of Piscataway Parish; children: Elizabeth, b. 23 Jan 1722, d. 17 Sep 1735; Anne, b. 16 Feb 1725/6; Thomas, b. 19 Apr 1728; George, b. 16 Jan 1729[/30]; John, b. 3 Sep ____, d. 26 Oct 1735 (ICR; KGP p. 270)

Noble, Joseph; dau. Mary; 1735 (MCW VII.162)

Noble, George; 6 Sep 1735; 24 Nov 1735; sons Thomas, George, John; daus. Elizabeth, Anne; tracts *Piscataway Mannor, Wett Work, Spring Garden, Addition, Dry Work, Chance* (MCW VII.156); 29 Feb 1735 (I 21.393); 27 May 1737 (I 23.176)

Noble, Joseph; m. 5 Mar 1738 Martha Tarvin [d/o Richard]; children: William Dent, b. 10 Mar 1739/40; Elisabeth, b. 11 Jan 1743/4; Clement, b. 24 Feb 1748/9; Richard, bapt. 21 Jul 1751 (KGP p. 273, 294)

Noble, Francis; children: Ann, b. 14 May 1747; Mark, b. 5 Sep 1749 (KGP p. 288)

Noble, Joseph, Sr.; 6 Dec 1747; 15 Jan 1749/50; wife Mary; sons Joseph, Francis, John, William; daus. Elizabeth, Catharine, Solome, Mary; granddau. Mary Elinor Hawkins; tract *Littleworth* (MCW X.63); extx. Mary; 26 May 1750 (I 43.105); extx. Mary; children: Joseph, Francis, John, William, Elisabeth Stockett, Catherine, Solome, Mary Baynes; 9 Mar 1750 (AA 29.222); widow Mary; heirs, Joseph, Francis, John, William, Elizabeth, Catherine, Solomy, Mary Noble, Mary Elinor Hawkins; __ Nov 1751 (GB 174)

Noble, George; wife Elizabeth; child: Charity Fendall, b. 1 Mar 1752 (KGP p. 316)

Noble, Charles; 22 Jun 1756; probate Liber TD, folio 483 (MCW XI.124)

Noble, Thomas; wife Mary; child: Thomas, b. 5 Mar 1756 (KGP p. 312)

Nobel, George; 31 Mar 1760; ex. John Addison (ABB 3.11); admx. Elisabeth; 4 May 1761 (I 74.162)

Noble, Thomas; admx. Mary Ann [widow]; 11 Jun 1762 (I 78.324); 1764; ex. Mary Ann Gilbert [w/o Francis] (ABB 4.89); admx. Mary Ann Gilbert [w/o Francis]; 31 Jan 1765 (I 102.237); widow Mary Ann Gilbert [w/o Francis];

heir George Noble; 28 Mar 1765 (GB 242); 1764 &18 Mar 1769; admx.
Mary Ann Gilbert [w/o Francis] (ABB 4.89, 5.234)

Noble, Mary; 31 May 1765; 14 Apr 1765; children: Cathrine, John,
William, Francis, Joseph, Elizabeth, Salome, Mary (MCW XIII.120)

Noble, George; 27 Aug 1770; admx. Elisabeth Hawkins [w/o James] (ABB
5.388); heirs Charity Fendall Noble; 25 Mar 1772 (GB 303)

NOE

Noe, Samuel; admx. Sarah; dau. Rachel [age 4]; 8 Jul 1741 (AA 18.296)

NOLAND

Noland, William; wife Esther; child: James Smith, b. 2 Sep 1764 (PGP p. 276)

Noland, Stephen; wife Mary; child: Ann Marllor, b. 14 Jul 1765 (PGP p. 276)

NORMAN

Norman, Rebecka; age ca 4 in Nov next; bound out; d/o Elizabeth Norman,
now Elizabeth Taylor; Mar 1711 Ct. (PGCR G.42)

Norman, Ann; age 5 on 25 Jan last; d/o Mary Taylor; bound to Michael
and Elizabeth Wellman; Jun 1716 (PGCR H.85)

NORRIS

Norris, Caleb; wife Mary; tract *Cheney*; 26 Mar 1729 (PGLR M.396)

Norris, Caleb; age ca 54; 28 Feb 1731 (PGLR Q.430); age ca 54; 4 Apr 1732
(PGLR Q.573); age ca 61; 24 Dec 1736 (PGLR Y.84); age ca 54; 4 Apr 1732 (PGLR
Q.573); age ca 64; 1737 (PGLR T.509)

Norris, John; age ca 52; 1731 (PGLR Q.389)

Norris, John; 24 Jan 1733; 15 Apr 1735; wife Mary; sons William,
Benjamin, John [dec'd]; grandson John [s/o John]; tract *Hopewell* (MCW
VII.168); admx. Mary; 19 Jul 1736 (I 21.435); Dr.; extx. Mary; 17 Mar 1737
(AA 15.335); heirs William, John; 28 Jun 1738 (GB 100)

Norris, Mary; 31 Aug 1738; 15 Apr 1745; son Benjamin; grandchildren:
William, John, Anne Norris [ch/o Benjamin] (MCW IX.22)

Norris, William; schoolmaster of All Saint's Parish; 1 Jan 1746/7; 27 Jan
1748; wife Elizabeth; son William Sierrs; dau. Elizabeth Sierra; tract
Serras Love (MCW X.9)

NORTHEN

Northen, William; wife Hanah; child: Jane, b. 15 Sep 1728 (PGP p. 247-8)

NORTON

Norton, Alexander; 28 Oct 1774 (I 119.55); 13 Nov 1775; widow [unnamed]; 4 children [unnamed] (ABB 7.36)

Norton, Henry; age ca 20; servant; Aug 1698 Ct. (PGCR A.332)

Norton, Jacob; wife Mary; child: Nehemiah, b. 12 Oct 1774 Upper Chapel (KGP p. 390)

Norton, John; wife Elizabeth; child: Henry Willson, bapt. 10 Aug 1766 Upper Chapel; Jane, 1 Jul 1773 Upper Chapel (KGP p. 355, 390)

Norton, John; wife Jane; children: Katherine, b. 14 Jan 1730/1; Nehemiah, b. 2 May 173_; Margery, b. 2 Jan 1735 (?) (QAP b/25, 28, 30)

Norton, Nimeah; wife Elizabeth; child: Mary, b. 27 Jan 1774 Upper Chapel (KGP p. 390)

Norton, Robert; m. Cloe _____; children: Elizabeth, b. 29 Jan 1772 Broad Creek; Mille Ann, b. 27 Jun 1773 Broad Creek; Alexander, b. 23 Apr 1775 Broad Creek (KGP p. 377, 384, 387)

Norton, Thomas; age ca 54; 1732 (PGLR Q.473)

Norton, Thomas; m. Katherine; children: Margery, b. 31 Oct 1774 Upper Chapel; Eleanor, b. 2 May 1776 (KGP p. 392)

Norton, William; m. Elinor; children: Sarah, b. 20 Jan 1759; Alexander, b. 16 Mar 1760; Martha, bapt. 18 Apr 1762; Frances (f), bapt. 6 May 1764 Broad Creek; Nathaniel, b. 18 Mar 1766 Broad Creek; James, bapt. 15 May 1768 Broad Creek; Mary, b. 5 Aug 1772 Broad Creek; Norman, b. 21 Jan 1775 Broad Creek (KGP p. 318, 326, 353, 357, 362-3, 378, 386)

NOW

Now, Samuel; admx. Sarah; 20 Aug 1740 (I 25.286)

NUGENT

Nugent, William; 16 Oct 1724 (AA 6.172)

NUTTER

Nutter, Edward; planter; 1 Oct 1722 (I 8.101); admx. Frances Nutter; now w/o Christopher Beanes; 4 Dec 1723 (AA 6.87); heirs Francis, Margaret, Elizabeth; 24 Mar 1725 (GB 21)

NUTTHALL

Nutthall, John [SM]; wife Eliner [widow of Thomas Hillary]; tract part of *Three Sisters*; 25 Jun 1700 (PGLR A.218)

Nuthall, James; wife Margaret; tract *Hatchett*; 12 Aug 1702 (PGLR C.14a)

Nutthall, Eleanor; widow; daus. Eleanor Pratt, Mary Nutthall; tract *Sprigg's Request*; 9 Feb 1727/8 (PGLR M.263, 264)

O'BRYAN

O'bryan, Terrance; m. 4 May 1720 Mary Tewill; children: Edward, b. 12 Sep 172_; Ellinor, b. 13 Apr 172_; Katherine Brian, b. 6 Jan 172_; Rebecca, b. 11 Jun 1729 (KGP p. 277)

O'CONNER

O'Conner, Patrick; wife Jane; child: William, bapt. 4 Dec 1763 (ICR)

ODANIEL

Odaniel [Odaniell], Michael; wife Mary; children: Sarah, b. 11 Jan 1764; Walter, b. 5 Aug 1765 (PGP p. 272, 277)

ODELL

Odell, Thomas; wife Sarah; children: Ann, b. 18 Nov 1703; Regnall, b. 24 Oct 1705; Sarah, b. 10 Apr 1709 (QAP b/4)

Odell, Thomas; 29 Apr 1717; 11 Apr 1721; wife Sarah; sons Thomas, Henry, Rignell; daus. Ann, Sarah; s-i-l Ninian Magruder (MCW V.92); extx. Sarah; widow & 3 sons; 9 May 1722 (AA 5.147)

Odell, Sarah; 28 Jun 1727 (I 12.129)

Odell, Rignall; wife Sarah; children: James, b. 12 Jul 1731; Rignall, b. __ May 17__ (QAP b/24, 29)

Odell, Henry; wife Ann; children: Thomas, b. 28 Jul 17__; Elizabeth, b. 11 Jan 17__ (QAP b/23, 24)

Odell, Henry; 19 May 1738; 10 Jul 1738; wife Ann; sons Thomas, Regnall; daus. Elizabeth, Ellenor (MCW VII.250)

Odell, Rignal; m. 25 Aug 1754 Martha Duckett (QAP m/7)

Odell, Rignall; admx. Sarah Prather [late Odell]; 8 Apr 1754 (I 57.430)

ODEN

Oden, Jonathan; wife Elizabeth; child: ____ (f), b. __ M__ ____ (QAP b/39)

Oden [Oate, Ogle], Thomas; wife Sarah; child: Francis Ann (f), b. 12 May 1751; Elinor, b. 19 Apr 1753 (ICR; KGP p. 293, 301)

Oden, Jonathon; admx. Elisabeth; 8 Sep 1772 (I 112.123)

OFFUTT

Offutt, William, Sr.; son William, Jr. [wife Jane]; tract *Clewerwell* and *The Enlargement*; son James [wife Rachel]; tract *William & James*, 25 Nov 1725 (PGLR I.692)

Offutt, William; planter; 10 Nov 1732; 10 Jun 1734; wife Mary; sons Edward, William, James, John, Nathaniel, Samuel, Thomas; daus. Sarah Harris [w/o Thomas], Mary Bowie [w/o John, Jr.], Jane; tracts

Neighbourhood, Gleaning, Gleaning"s Addition, The Outlett, Calverton Edge, Offutt's Pasture, The Younger Brother, Offutt's Adventure, Addition, Covert (MCW VII.85) admx. Mary Offutt; 13 Sep 1734 (I 20.45); admx. Mary; sons Thomas [minor], William, James; ss-i-l Thomas Waring, John Bowie; 30 Apr 1735 (AA 13.84); extx. Mary; 4 children Samuel, Nathaniel, Jane Waring, Thomas; 28 Jun 1737 (AA 14.318); admx. Mary; sons Nathaniell, Samuel; Thomas Waireing for his wife; 28 Mar 1739 (AA 17.154); orphan Thomas; /s/ Mary, Matthew & John Offutt; 23 Jun 1739 (GB 103)

Offutt, Edward; wife Eleanor [d/o Archibald Edmonson, Sr.]; son Archibald; dau. Jane; 30 Jan 1733 (PGLR T.58)

Offutt, William, Jr.; admx. Jane; 8 Sep 1737 (I 23.422, 424), admx. Jane [widow]; 7 children James, Jane, William, Sarah, Priscilla, Kezia, Alexander; 27 Mar 1739 (AA 17.168); heirs James Offutt, Mary Magruder, Jane, Sarah, William, Priscilla, Kezia and Alexander; 6 Mar 1740 (GB 108)

Offutt, James; wife Sarah; tract *Brock Hall*; 2 May 1743 (PGLR Y.664)

Offutt, John; 10 Sep 1743; 22 Nov 1743; wife Esther (MCW VIII.243)

Offutt, Nathaniel; age ca 29; 29 May 1745 (CCR JK#4.593)

Offutt, Mary; 9 Mar 1747/8; 11 Sep 1748; sons Edward, James, Samuel, Nathaniel; dau. Sarah Harris; dec'd sons William, John; dec'd daus. Jane Warring, Mary Bowey (MCW IX.164); 1 Mar 1748 (I 41.225); Mary [widow]; children Edward Offutt, Sarah Harris; 13 Dec 1749 (AA 27.209); 23 Jul 1750 (AA 28.183)

Offutt, Ninian; wife Mary; child: Benjamin Magruder, b. 4 Dec 1765 (PGP p. 278)

OGDON

Ogdon, Nehemiah; m. 21 Nov 1733 Mary Cooper (PGP p. 229)

Ogdon, Gordon; wife Christian; child: Josias, b. 7 Jan 1754 (KGP p. 306)

OGLE

Ogle, Samuel; 1 Mar 1753 (AA 33.338)

OLIVER

Oliver, John; m. 9 Apr 1716 Mary Isaac (QAP m/1)

Oliver, John; age ca 40; 19 Mar 1724/5 (PGLR I.624); age ca 50; 22 Sep 1730 (PGLR Q.160)

Oliver, John; wife Bridget; tract *Hope*; 6 Nov 1736 (PGLR T.427)

Oliver, William; age ca 60; 1738 (PGLR T.607)

ONEAL

Onealis, Anthony; wife Elizabeth; child: Elliner, b. 1 Dec 1726 (KGP p. 271)

ONeal, Arthur; admx. Deborough; 17 Jan 1739 (I 25.28); admx. Deborah; heirs Charles, James, Margrett, Richard; dau. w/o Joseph Selby, dau. w/o William Finch; 28 Nov 1740 (AA 18.137)

ONEBY

Oneby, Stephen; son Thomas; chooses f-i-l [?step-father] James Watts as guardian; Nov 1700 (PGCR B.81)

ORCHARD

Orchard, John; 1 Aug 1745; ss-i-l, Joseph & Nathaniel Ryon (MCW IX.47); 25 Oct 1745 (I 32.289); 20 Jul 1747 (AA 23.341)

ORME

Orme [Orm], Robert, Sr.; 17 Jan 1713; 22 Apr 1722; sons Robert, Jr., John, Moses, Aaron; dau. Sarah Tanyhill; grandsons John Tanyhill, Robert Orme; bro. Geo Ransome (MCW IV.28); [with 1715] (I&A 36b.166); [with 1715] (I&A 36c.110); 27 Apr 1716 (I&A 36c.293, 296)

Oram, Robert; admx. Jane; 25 Jun 1728 (I 13.147); admx. Jane; heirs James, Anne, Martha; 25 Mar 1729 (AA 9.328); heirs James, Jane, Martha; 24 Jun 1730 (GB 56); widow Jane Pelly [w/o James]; children: James, Ann, Martha; 19 Jun 1731 (AA 11.104)

Orme, John; wife Cibby; tract Mt. Calvert Manor; 10 Mar 1732 (PGLR Q.615)

Orme, John; 28 Oct 1757; 24 Aug 1758; wife Ruth; sons John, James, Archibald, Ebenezer Edmonston; daus. Jane, Elizabeth, Septima, Octava; granddau. Nancy (MCW XI.213)

Orme, John; 17 Aug 1765; 5 Nov 1766; children: Jesse, Richard, John, Sibbel, Robert, William, Mary; grandchild Hezekiah (MCW XIII.131); 27 Jan 1766 (I 91.308)

Orme, Moses; 19 Jun 1770; 17 Dec 1772; wife Ann; children: Moses, Elley, Sarah Mitchell, Ann Reynolds, Rebeccah Miles, Nathan, Jeremiah, Mary Selby, Philip; grandchild. Samuel Taylor Orme [s/o Moses], Eleanor Reynolds [d/o Ann]; tract Towgood (MCW XV.97); extx. Ann; 20 Nov 1773 (I 118.174)

Orme, Ruth; 27 Jun 1774; 29 Mar 1775; children: Elizabeth White, Octavio Smith, Septuma Allen, James & Archibald Orme, Jane Threlkield; grandchildren: Ruth & Eleanor Orme, Nancy Beall [w/o Thomas]; tracts Leathe, Collington (MCW XVI.39-40)

Orme, Jesse; 3 Apr 1775 (I 123.122)

ORRICK

Orrick, William; wife Hannah; children: James Grinniff, b. 24 Jun 1709; John Griniff, b. 22 Jul 1712 (QAP b/8)

ORSBORN

Orsborn, William; child: Sharlota, b. 19 Dec 1762 (KGP p. 329)

Orsborn, John; child: Stephen, bapt. 10 Aug 1766 Upper Chapel (KGP p. 364)

ORTON

Orton, Thomas; wife Jane; Aug 1697 Ct. (PGCR A.222)

OSBORN

Osborn, Benjamin; admx. Mary; 21 Apr 1744 (I 29.306); admx. Mary; children Thomas, Benjamin, William, Mary; 28 Apr 1745 (AA 21.222); extx. Mary; 6 Aug 1745 (AA 21.398)

Osborn, John; planter; 26 Aug 1745; 5 Apr 1751; sons William, John; tract *Trundlebed Cuckold* (MCW X.138)

Osborn, Robert; planter; 25 Nov 1768; 19 Feb 1769; wife Elizabeth (MCW XIV.95); extx. Elisabeth; 6 Mar 1769 (I 100.12); admx. Elisabeth; 24 Jun 1772 (I 109.167)

Osborn, Elisabeth; niece Tomsoline Alen; 10 Dec 1772 (I 112.128)

OSTIN

Ostin, John; 11 Jul 1753; admx. Elizabeth Ostin; John and Jones [of full age], Michall [age 13 yrs.] (ABB 1.76); admx. Elisabeth; children John, Jonas, Michael [age 13]; 11 Jul 1753 (AA 34.253)

OTHAHAM

Othaham, Hugh; 16 May 1713 (I&A 35a.161)

OUCHTERLONG

Ouchterlong, John; wife Priscilla; child: Margaret, b. 30 Jan 1731/2 (QAP b/25)

Ouchterlong, John; wife Mary; child: Patrick, b. 3 Feb 1752; bapt. 22 Mar (PGP p. 253)

OWDEN

Owden, David; wife Rachel; child: Gerrerd, b. 9 Jul 1762 (PGP p. 264)

Owden, Johnathon; admx. Elisabeth; 9 May 1774 (I 117.420)

OWEN

Owen, John; wife Elizabeth; children: John, b. 18 Dec 1706; Spicer, b. 14 Jan 1708; Henry, b. 10 Dec 1710 (KGP p. 260)

Owen, John; 14 Aug 1711 (I&A 32c.59, 60)

Owen, Robert; wife Mary; 30 Jul 1714 (PGLR F.400)

Owen, Robert; 25 Jan 1715 (I&A 37b.37)

Owen, Edward; wife Elizabeth; child: Robert, b. 1 Feb 1729 (QAP b/24)

Owen, Robert; m. 25 Feb 1731 Rachel Hook (PGP p. 229)

Owen, Thomas; wife Elizabeth [widow of John Cade]; her son Robert Cade; tract *Plymouth*; 8 Jun 1731 (PGLR Q.351)

Owen [Oweing], William; 23 Feb 1733 (I 18.268); 10 Jun 1735 (AA 13.131)

Owen, Thomas; wife Sarah; children: Sabina, bapt. 28 Mar 1762; Sauley, bapt. 26 Feb 1764 Lower Chapel; Martha, bapt. 15 Mar 1767 Lower Chapel (KGP p. 326, 344)

Owen, John; wife Susannah; child: John Neal, b. 15 May 1762 (PGP p. 267)

Owen, Robert; wife Kiziah; child: Edward, b. 23 Nov 1763 (PGP p. 270)

Owen, John; wife Esther; child: Hezekiah, b. 16 Sep 1764 (PGP p. 272)

PACK

Pack, Thomas; wife Elizabeth; children: Rachel, b. 17 Jun 1761; Elizabeth, b. 4 Feb 1766 (PGP p. 261, 278)

Pack, Richard; wife Johanah; children: Benjamin, b. 18 Nov 1764; Hezekiah, b. 24 Feb 1766 (PGP p. 272, 278)

PAGE

Page, Daniel; wife Mary; child: Mary, b. 13 Jul 1727 (QAP b/20); children: ___y (f), b. 20 Aug 1729; Sushanah, b. 16 Jan 1732; ___hall (f), b. 31 Dec 1733 (ICR; KGP p. 283)

Page, Bingley; extx. Martha; 5 Mar 1746 (I 35.49); admx. Martha; children Alexander, James, Jess, Martha, Hester, Elisabeth; 7 Oct 1747 (AA 24.154); widow Martha; heirs Alexander, James, Martha, Jesse, Esther, Jane; 29 Mar 1749 (GB 166)

Page, Daniel; 19 Jun 1762; 28 Feb 1768; wife Mary; children Daniel, George & Anthony Drane Page, Elizabeth Morris, Lucy Hodgkin, Mary Boone, Susannah Lanham, Rachel Hodgkin, Mildred Berry (MCW XIV.35); 1 Mar 1768 (I 98.7); 23 Aug 1769; daus. Elisabeth Morris, Lucy Hodgkin, Mary Boone, Susannah Lanham, Rachel Hodgkin, Mildred Berry, sons Daniel, George & Anthony Deane Page (ABB 5.230); heirs Mary, Anthony, Elizabeth; 29 Aug 1771 (GB 295)

Page, George; 7 Jan 1769; _ Feb 1769; wife Elizabeth; bro. Daniel (MCW XIV.95); 23 Aug 1769 (I 102.23)

PAGETT

Paggett, Thomas [CA], wife Sarah; tract [unnamed]; 31 May 1696 (PGLR A.16)

Padgett, Thomas; s-i-l Richard Hill; Mar 1705 (PGCR B.377a)

Paggett, William; chooses Thomas Paggett as guardian; Nov 1716 (PGCR H.138)

Paggett, Thomas, Sr.; wife Elizabeth; son Thomas, Jr.; 31 Jul 1722 (PGLR I.339)

Pagett (Paggett), Thomas; planter; 17 Jul 1728; 26 Nov 1728; wife [unnamed]; granddau. Elizabeth (MCW VI.86); admx. Elisabeth; 25 Mar 1729 (I 14.3); 24 Nov 1729 (I 15.425), widow Elisabeth; 8 Oct 1731 (AA 11.183)

Padgett, John; admx. Elisabeth; 18 Dec 1770 (I 106.159)

PAINE

Paine, James; age ca 7; s/o John; bound out; Nov 1696 (PGCR A.57)

Paine, James; s/o James; bound out; Sept 1702 (PGCR B.193)

Paine, Robert; wife Ann; servants of Thomas Roper; 16 May 1704 (PGLR C.114a)

Pain, Robert; wife Ann; children: Mary, b. 17 9ber 1704; Susanna, b. 3 8ber 1708; Rachel, b. 5 7ber 1711 (QAP b/7)

Pain, Robert; admx. Ann; 20 Jul 1727 (I 12.265); admx. Ann; 25 Jun 1728 (AA 9.17); admx. Anne; heirs Mary, Susanna, Rachell, Elisabeth, Penolope, Uphen, Anne; 26 Mar 1729 (AA 9.330)

Pain, Francis; age ca 29; 1730 (PGLR Q.68)

Pain, John; age ca 66; 6 Jun 1735 (PGLR T.280)

Payne, Moses; age 2 Nov last; s/o Rachel; bound out; Jun 1737 (PGCR W.419)

Paine, Elizabeth; child: Ann, b. _ Feb 1746 (KGP p. 289)

Pane, Thomas; wife Annonias; child: Thomas, bapt. Mar 1765 Lower Chapel (KGP p. 350)

Pain [Pane, Payn], John; wife Mary; children: Silvanous, bapt. 27 Sep 1767 Broad Creek Elisabeth, b. 24 Oct 1769 Broad Creek; Mary Prince, b. 31 Mar 1772 Broad Creek; Sarah, b. 12 Apr 1774 Broad Creek (KGP p. 361, 373, 378, 385)

PALLE

Palle, Anna; age 12 ca 25 Dec; d/o Reba [?Rebecca] Taylor; bound out to William & Jane Vinicum; Nov 1721 (PGCR K.421)

Pally, James, age ca 6 on 31 Mar last; Nov 1721 (PGCR K.417)

PALMER

Palmer, Thomas; planter; [with 1709] (I&A 30.437); widow Elisabeth Lumas [w/o Aarom]; 3 Mar 1711 (I&A 33a.115); adms. Aaron Lomax and wife [unnamed]; 18 May 1711 (I&A 32c.153); widow Elisabeth Lumos [w/o Aaron]; 26 Aug 1710 (I&A 32b.30)

Palmer, William; m. 24 Nov 1734 Elizabeth Vernon (QAP m/6)

Palmer, John; m. 22 Feb 1735 Mary Lanham; children: Rachel, b. 30 Nov 1736 or 7; Sarah, b. 27 Jun 1745; John, b. 17 Feb 1749; William, b. 23 Jan 1752 (KGP p. 282, 292, 298) [found on p. 298 as ___mer, John; wife Mary; 4 children named as theirs]

Palmer, John; 17 Nov 1764 (I 86.183)

PARKER

Parker, Peter; wife Susanna; child: Margaret, b. 8 10ber 1713 (QAP b/9)

Parker, Richard; wife Sarah; child: Sarah, b. 14 Feb 1722 (QAP b/17)

Parker, Gabriel; wife Ann [d/o William Hutchison]; 17 Sep 1725 (PGLR I.682)

Parker, Gabriel; wife Ann; son Hutcheson; tract *Sangkar*; 17 Apr 1731 (PGLR Q.257)

Parker, Richard; 25 Jun 1733 (I 17.362); heirs son & 3 more children [unnamed]; 13 May 1734 (AA 12.291)

Parker, Gabriel; wife Elizabeth, dec'd [d/o Thomas Greenfield]; 16 Aug 1738 (PGLR T.653)

Parker, Peter; age ca 60; 17 Apr 1739 (PGLR Y.58)

Parker, John; admx. Jane; 2 children under age; 24 Jun 1741 (I 26.54); widow Jane; heirs Elizabeth, John; 29 Jun 1743 (GB 127)

Parker, Gabril [CA]; wife Anne; son Gabril, Jr.; tract *Piscataway Forrest*; 21 Aug 1741 (PGLR Y.359)

Parker, George; wife Elizabeth; tracts *Archer's Pasture, Gidland*; 24 Nov 1742 (PGLR Y.552)

Parker, Samuel; 29 Jun 1744 (I 29.308); 29 Jun 1744 (AA 20.332)

Parker, Elizabeth; age ca 27; 14 Jun 1745 (CCR JK#4.594)

Parker, Gabriel, Jr.; 27 Nov 1745; 16 Dec 1745; wife Sarah; father Gabriel (MCW IX.60)

Parker, Peter; 21 Apr 1751; 27 May 1751; grandson William Tyler; tract *The Hour Glass* (MCW X.154)

Parker, John; wife Mary; child: Zachariah, b. 23 Sep 1761 (PGP p. 263)

Parker, William; 11 Sep 1773; 25 Aug 1775; wife Hannah; daus. Ann Weaver [dec'd], Sarah Sullivan, Mary, Martha, Rachel, Hannah; sons Derrick, Thomas; tract *The Adventure* (MCW XVI.73)

PARLETT

Parlett, Martin; m. 16 Apr 1723 Mary Burrows; child: William, b. 4 Jan 1723/4 (QAP m/3; b/18)

PARMER

Parmer, James; wife Jane; child: Anne, b. 23 Jan 1776 Lower Chapel (KGP p. 381)

Parmer, John; wife Mary; child, Ann, b. 30 Apr 1772 Broad Creek (KGP p. 378)

Parmer; John; child: Eliakin, b. 16 Aug 1773 Broad Creek (KGP p. 385)

PARR

Parr, John; 27 Apr 1745; 13 Nov 1746; wife Mary; sons Mark, John, Arthur, Matthew; daus. Thame Ward, Elizabeth (MCW IX.86); 9 Jun 1748 (I 36.23)

PARRIS

Parris, William; sons John, Daniel; d-i-l Elizabeth Magriger; 25 Aug 1729 (PGLR M.468)

PARROCK

Parrock, James; admx. Jeane; 26 Jun 1734 (I 18.269); admx. Jane; 28 Sep 1734 (AA 12.627); admx. Jane Currey [w/o John]; children Hannah, Thomas, Elisabeth; 24 Jun 1735 (AA 13.264)

PARROTT

Parrott, Gabriel [AA]; dau. Susannah Parker [w/o George]; grandson George Parker [wife Ann]; tract *Eglington*; 9 Dec 1718 (PGLR F.113/675)

PARSHFIELD

Parshfield, Margaret; child: Sophia, b. 30 7ber 1714 (QAP b/11)

PATRICK

Patrick, John; wife Mary; child: William, bapt. 22 Mar 1752 (ICR)

Patrick, Richard; age ca 17; servant; Jun 1698 Ct. (PGCR A.317)

PATTEN

Patten [Pattan], David; 24 Apr 1721 (I 5.57; 6.40); 15 Nov 1722 (AA 5.64)

PAUL

Paul, William; wife Honor; s-i-l William Price; 19 Oct 1736 (PGLR T.441)

Pawl, William; 30 May 1743; [no relations] (MCW VIII.214); 5 Dec 1743 (I 28.367); 26 Jun 1744 (AA 20.328)

PEACH

Peach, Joseph; m. 17 Feb 1725/6 Mary Isaac, d/o Richard; children: Isaac, b. 2 Jan 1728/9; Joseph, b. 5 May 1731; Elizabeth, b. 27 Apr 173_; William, b. 25 Aug 173_; Richard, b. 25 Dec 1738; ____ (f), b. 8 Jul 1740 (QAP m/4, b/21, 27, 28, 30, 32)

Peach, Joseph, Sr., schoolmaster; 26 Jan 1760; 30 Oct 1764; children Richard, Isaac, John, William, Joseph; daus. Elizabeth Hill, Sarah, Mary, Martha; tracts *Farmer's Reserve, Isaac's Discovery, Peaches Plains, Strip, Balance, Search, Peaches Lot* (MCW XIII.48); 29 Oct 1765 (I 88.270)

Peach, John; 31 Oct 1769 (I 104.264); 18 May 1772; adm. Joseph Peach (ABB 6.144); heir John Peach; 23 Aug 1773 (GB 311)

Peach, Joseph; planter; 6 Nov 1774; 16 Jan 1775; wife Lucy; sons Joseph, Samuel; bros. Isaac, Richard; tracts *Isaac's Discovery, Farmer's Reserve, Peach's Plains, Beaver Dam Neck, Peaches Addition, Bear Bacon* (MCW XVI.59); extx. Lucy; 29 May 1775 (I 123.119)

PEACOCK

Peacock, John; wife Mary; children: Joshua, bapt. 29 Mar 1752; Cloe, b. 30 May 1754 (KGP p. 295, 306)

Peacock, Benjamin; wife Kesander [Casandria]; children: John, bapt. 28 Sep 1766 Lower Chapel; Hezekiah, b. 18 Dec 1773 Lower Chapel (KGP p. 367, 379)

Peacock, John Holden; wife Jane_; child: Selah, b. 24 Jan 1772 Lower Chapel (KGP p. 383)

Peacock, Benjamin; wife Casandria (KGP p. 379)

PEAK

Peek, Ann; dau. Jane, b. 15 Feb 1723 (PGLR I.682)

Peak, Richard; children: Mary, b. 14 Jun 1729; Thomas, b. 10 Jun 1731 (PGP p. 249, 250)

Peak, Joseph; wife Margrette; children: Thomas, b. 25 Jun 1760; Hezekiah, b. 8 Jan 1762 (PGP p. 258, 262)

Peak, Thomas; wife. Mary; child, Samuel, b. 22 Oct 1761 (PGP p. 260)

Peek, Priscilla; age 8 mos.; d/o Jane Peek; bound to Robert Richards and wife Edith; Jun 1747 (PGCR FF.620)

PEARCE

Pearce, Sarah [eld. d/o Thomas Sprigg, Sr.]; son John Pearce; tract *Northampton, Kettering*; 16 Mar 1700 (PGLR A.361)

Pearse, John; wife Mary; children: John, b. 8 Nov 1730; Peter, b. 8 Apr 1732 (KGP p. 278)

Pearce, John; son Edward; also 3 sons [unnamed]; 26 Aug 1740? (PGLR Y.210)

Peerce, Edward; wife Lydia; children: John Waters, b. 22 Dec 1745; Sarah, b. 1 May 1747; Elizabeth, b. 18 Nov 1749 (PGP p. 253)

Peerce [Pearce], Edward; planter; 16 Jan 1750/1; 3 May 1751; wife Lydia; son John Waters; daus. Sara, Elizabeth Childs (MCW X.146); 27 Mar 1754; extx. Lydia (ABB 1.112); extx. Lidia; 11 May 1751 (I 47.297); extx. Lydia; 27 Mar 1754 (AA 36.291); widow Lydia; heirs John Waters, Sarah, Elizabeth; 29 Nov 1754 (GB 196)

Peerce, William; wife Rachel; children: James Riley, b. 14 Jan 1763; Ruth, b. 18 May 1765; William, b. 28 Feb 1768 (PGP p. 269, 271, 275)

Pearce, John; 7 Aug 1766 (I 89.312); 10 May 1768; admn. John Pearce (ABB 5.97)

PEARLE

Pearle, Robert; wife Anne; tract *Archer's Pasture*; 26 Nov 1736 (PGLR T.423)

PEARSON

Parsons, Thomas; 1 Jun 1712; 24 Jun 1712; wife Joan; dau. Margrett; son Samuel (MCW III.227); 12 Sep 1713 (I&A 34.98)

Pearson [Person], Francis; 16 Jul 1713; 26 Sep 1713; wife Eliza.; tract Collington (MCW IV.11); extx. Elisabeth; 7 Mar 1714 (I&A 36b.117); exs. Samuel Warner & wife Elisabeth; 8 Mar 1716 (I&A 36c.296)

Pearson, Robert; 5 Feb 1727/8; 5 Mar 1727/8 (MCW VI.57); 11 Jul 1728 (I 13.152)

Pearson, Edward; contract to marry Martha Howell; 27 Agu 1734 (PGLR T.180)

Parsons, George; m. 14 Nov 1736 Sarah Venson (QAP m/7)

Pearson [Parson, Person], Edward; planter; 6 Mar 1747; wife Martha; tract Littleworth (MCW X.37); extx. Martha; 18 Mar 1749 (AA 28.20); extx. Martha; 9 Sep 1749 (I 41.166)

Persons, John; 13 May 1757 (I 63.97)

PECK

Peck, Joseph; s/o mulatto Jane; Nov 1744; Nov 1744 (PGCR CC.585)

Peck, John; age ca 15 mos.; s/o Jane; bound out; Nov 1749 (PGCR LL.80)

PEDDYCOAT

Peddycoart, Nathan; wife Sarah; children: William Barton, b. 5 Apr 1739; Basil, b. 2 Jul 1740; Elianor, b. 27 Apr 1744; Thomas, b. 4 Feb 1745/6 (PGP p. 252)

Peeley, Calver; wife Mary; child: Benjamin, b. 30 Oct 1764 (PGP p. 272)

Peeley, James; wife Jane; child: Antsey (f), b. 30 Oct 1764 (PGP p. 272)

Peeley, Harrison; wife Sarah; child: Jane, b. 24 Dec 1764 (PGP p. 272)

PEIRPOINT

Parpoint, Mahitable; age ca 52; 8 Dec 1719 (CCR CL.550)

Peirpoint [Pierpont], Larkin [Larking]; m. 18 9ber 1725 Charity Duckett; children: Larkin, b. 24 7ber 1726; Jonathan, b. 3 Aug 1732 (QAP m/4; b/20, 26)

Peirpoint, Larkin; m. Sarah Simmons; 1730 (QAP m/5)

PELLEY

Pelley [Pilley], James; Mt. Calvert; 19 Mar 1746/7; 25 Jun 1747; wife Jane; sons James, Jr., Richard, Calvert, Harrison; daus. Sarah Leitch, Elizabeth Mills, Margaret Launge, Jemima, Kezie; tract Bells Wiln (MCW IX.112); extx. Jayn; 20 Aug 1747 (I 35.328); extx. Jayne [widow]; 26 Nov 1748 (AA 25.212); extx. Jane; ss-i-l John Mills, Baker Long, Josiah Leach; children [under age] James, Richard, Harrison, Calvert, Jemima, Kesiah; 23 Aug 1749 (AA 27.70)

PELMORE

Pelmore, James; wife Jane; child: Ann Harrison, b. 4 Mar 1774 Lower Chapel (KGP p. 379)

PENN

Penn, Charles; wife Elizabeth; children: Lucian (f), b. 14 Mar 1763; John Winn, b. 31 Mar 1765 (PGP p. 269, 277)

PENSON

Penson, William; age ca 54; 1731 (PGLR Q.297)

Penson, William; planter; 3 May 1741; 1741; niece Mary; bro. Thomas; tracts *Elizabeth, Partnership, Part of Dann* (MCW VIII.149)

PERDEE

Perdue, Jeremiah; wife Sarah; tract *Casteel*; 17 Feb 1739 (PGLR Y.5)

Perdee, Jeremiah; 5 Jun 1758; 1 Jan 1759; wife Sarah; tract *Casteel* (MCW XI.231)

PERKINS

Perkin, John; wife Dorothy; son Thomas; tract *His Lordship's Kindness*; 5 Mar 1725 (PGLR I.721)

Perkins, John; child: Sarah Perkins, b. 1 Apr 1750 (KGP p. 293)

Perkins, Thomas; admx. Mary; 25 May 1750 (I 43.308); heir Thomas Perkins; 27 Mar 1754 (GB 191)

Perkins, John; wife Elinor; child: Susanna, bapt. 23 Aug 1752 (KGP p. 297)

Perkins, John; wife Ann; children: Thomas, b. 14 Jan 1755; Rachill, b. 5 Nov 1763 at Broad Creek (KGP p. 307, 338)

Perkins, John; wife Mary; child: Andrew, b. 19 Sep 1755 (KGP p. 311)

Perkins, John; 24 Sep 1763; 20 Nov 1763; wife Mary; son Richard [by 1st wife]; ch/o Mary: Henry, Dorothy, Elizabeth, Mary, Eleazar (MCW XII.212); extx. Mary; 6 Feb 1764 (I 83.150)

Perkins, Mary; child: Elizabeth, bapt. 23 Oct 1763 at Upper Chapel (KGP p. 334)

Perkins, James; child: John Gibbs, bapt. 1 Jan 1764 at Broad Creek (KGP p. 338)

Perkins, John; 21 May 1769; admx. Ann Perkins (ABB 5.142); heirs [unnamed]; 27 Jun 1775 (GB 282)

PERRIE

Perry, John, age 4 yrs. next August; s/o Susannah; bound out; Mar 1697/8 Ct. (PGCR A.296)

Perry, John; wife Ann; children: John, b. 19 Aug 1711; Robert, b. 24 Aug 1713; Mary, b. 2 Jun 1715; Jennet, b. 24 10ber 1722 (QAP b/5, 8, 10, 17)

Perry, Joseph, 30 Jul 1716 (I&A 37a.146); admx. Elisabeth [widow]; 16 Dec 1717 (I&A 39c.86)

Perry, Hannah; child: Mary, b. 2 Jun 1719 (QAP b/10)

Perrie, Samuel; wife Sarah; tract *Barton's Hope*; 6 Aug 1720 (PGLR I.26)

Perry, Elizabeth; widow; children: Charles, Ignatius, Mary, Easter, James, Elizabeth, Benjamin; 26 Nov 1724 (PGLR I.588)

Perry, James; age 16 on 1 Mar last; s/o Joseph Perry and Elizabeth, now w/o John Anderson, tailor; chooses bro. Charles as guardian; Jun 1725 (PGCR L.453)

Perry, Benjamin; age 15 on 10 May next; chooses bro. Charles as guardian; Nov 1725 (PGCR L.511)

Perry, John; m. 11 Jul 1727 Elizabeth Millman; child: Richard, b. 6 Mar 1732/3 (QAP m/4; b/27)

Perrie [Perry], Samuel, Maj.; admx. Sarah; 16 Dec 1729 (I 15, 289, 296); widow Sarah Andrew [w/o Patrick]; 31 Jul 1731 (AA 11.130); admx. Sarah Haddock; 18 Jan 1733 (I 18.250); admx. Sarah; heirs Samuel, Sarah, Ann; 28 Sep 1734 (AA 12.633); admx. Sarah; son Samuel; 24 Jun 1735 (AA 13.260); 4 Jun 1736 (I 21.502); admx. [confusing]; dau. Anne, son Samuel; 4 Jan 1739 (AA 17.489, 515); 16 Sep 1741 (AA 18.301)

Perry, James; age ca 50; 1731 (PGLR Q.396)

Perry, James; wife Rebecca; child: Ruth, b. 30 Oct 1732 (PGP p. 250)

Perrie, Samuel; minor; guardian Col. Somerset Smith; 26 Mar 1734 (PGLR T.89)

Perrie [Pearre], James; children: Alexander, Ann, James, Mary; 28 Mar 1734 (PGLR T.102)

Perry, Ignatius; age ca 34; 6 May 1736 (CCR-MSA 6.31)

Perry, John; m. 9 Jan 1735 Priscilla Ray; children: John, b. 19 Sep 1737; Sarah, b. 21 Aug 1740; Robert, b. 29 May 1742; Catherine, b. 17 Feb 1744; Priscilla, b. 12 Mar 1746; James, b. 10 Jun 1747; Esther, b. 27 Jan 1748; Zasock, b. 10 Nov 1750; Ann, b. 27 Apr 1752; Rachel, b. 17 Oct 1753; ___ah (m), b. 5 Apr 1755; ___ah (f), b. 27 Mar 1757 (QAP m/7; b/37)

Perry, Edward; wife Elizabeth; children: ____m (m), b. 20 Dec 1740; Ann, b. 9 Apr 1743; Sarah, b. 12 Mar 1746; Edward, b. 19 Jun 1751 (QAP b/37)

Perrey, Charles; wife Rachel; child: Ignatius, b. 25 Dec 1740 (PGP p. 251)

Perry, Charles; planter; 8 Apr 1741; 24 May 1741; wife Rachel; son Ignatius; bros. James, Benjamin; sister Easther [Hester] (MCW VIII.142); extx. widow Rachel Pottinger [w/o Robert]; 15 Sep 1741 (I 30.360); extx. Rachel Pottenger [w/o Robert]; son Ignatius; sister Easter; 8 Aug 1745 (AA 21.385)

Perry [Perrie], John; tailor; 9 May 1753; 28 Jun 1753; wife Elizabeth; sons John, Edward, Joseph; daus. Jane Inglehearst [w/o Jacob], Mary Harrison [w/o George], Ann Watson [w/o James], Elizabeth Basil [w/o John] (MCW X.271); 28 Aug 1754; extx. Elizabeth Perry (ABB 1.118); extx. Elisabeth; 28 Aug 1754 (AA 36.388); extx. Elisabeth; 14 Sep [1754] (I 57.289)

Perry, James; 19 Jul 1762; 18 Aug 1764; wife Mary; sons John, James, Alexander; daus. Anne Makelay, Mary Buhan (MCW XIII.53)

Perry, Benjamin; wife Elizabeth; child: Charlte (f), b. 14 May 1765 (PGP p. 276)

Perry, John; wife Sebe; child: Constatia, b. 4 Jun 1773 Lower Chapel (KGP p. 384)

Perry, John; wife Tabitha; child: William, b. 24 Sep 1775 Lower Chapel (KGP p. 381)

PETERS

Peters, John Samuel; admx. Mary; 9 Jul 1764 (I 84.157)

PHELPS

Phelps, Josiah; age 16 on 20 Nov next; bound to Zekiel Bazil to be shoemaker; Mar 1753 (PGCR MM.371)

Phelpes, Robert; wife Sarah; children: Walter, bapt. 9 Mar 1766 Broad Creek; Jessey, bapt. 28 Aug 1768 Broad Creek; Robert Watts, b. 6 Feb 1775 Broad Creek (KGP p. 353, 364, 386)

PHILLIPS

Philips, Thomas; wife Ann; child: Abigail, b. 13 Feb 1753 (KGP p. 300)

Philips, Samuel, b. 1764 (ICR)

Philpes, Robert; wife Sarah; child: Benjamin, bapt. Apr 1765 Broad Creek (KGP p. 346)

Phillips, John; wife Sabra; child: Bettsy, b. 22 Jul 1765 (PGP p. 277)

Phillops, Bedder; wife Virlender; child: John Dawson, b. 30 Sep 1765 Broad Creek (KGP p. 349)

Philipes [Phillops], Phillop; wife Lurana [Lewranca]; children: Amoss, b. 9 Jan 1766 Lower Chapel; Elizabeth, b. 12 Dec 1767 Broad Creek (KGP p. 346, 364)

Phillops, Bedder; wife Lurana; child: Vialinder, bapt. 6 Nov 1768 Upper Chapel (KGP p. 372)

PHILMORE
Philmore, William; 24 Dec 1726 (I 11767)

PHILPOTT
Philpot, Henry; wife Mary; child: Thomas, b. 27 Jul 1761 (PGP p. 261)

Philpott [Filpot], Barton; wife Martha; children: Mary Barton, b. 1 Nov 1762; Martha Keech, b. 12 Jan 1764 Broad Creek; Benjamin, b. 21 Feb 1766 Broad Creek; Elizabeth Waring, b. 15 Dec 1767, bapt. 24 Jan 1768 Lower Chapel; Charles, b. Oct 1769 Broad Creek (KGP p. 348, 356, 368, 373)

Philpott, [unnamed]; heirs Charles Thomas, Zachariah; 25 Mar 1767 (GB 251)

PHIPPARD
Phippard, William; 18 Aug 1709 (I&A 30.218); 4 Sep 1710 (I&A 32.32)

PHIPPS
Phipps, Solomon; mariner; 7 Sep 1738 (I 23.454)

PHOENIX
Phoenix [Pharix], Edward; 8 Apr 1713; 25 May 1714; wife Dinah; dau. Jane Hynde [w/o Thomas] (MCW IV.10); 31 May 1714 (I&A 35a.356); extx. Dinah; 16 May 1715 (I&A 36b.228)

PICKERING
Pickrin [Pickerine, Pickrum], Thomas; 6 May 1741; 25 Mar 1741; sons, Ralph, Joseph, Thomas, Benjamin, Samuel; dau. Elizabeth (MCW VIII.133); 1 Jun 1741 (I 26.361)

Pickering, Ralph; wife Elizabeth; child: Lewranah (f), b. 19 Feb 1763 at Broad Creek (KGP p. 337)

Pickering, Thomas; child: Samuel, bapt. 18 Apr 1762 (KGP p. 326)

Pickrin, Thomas; 25 Jan 1742 (AA 19.310)

PICKETTS
Picketts, Amy; age 1 on 7 Mar last; bound out; Nov 1738 (PGCR X.189)

PICKRELL
Pickrell, Ralph; wife Elizabeth; child: Ellender, b. 20 Feb 1754 (KGP p. 305)

Pickrell, Thomas; m. 15 Oct 1712 Elizabeth Marloy; children: Sarah, b. 7 May 1715; Ralph, b. 3 May 1719; Joseph and Mary, b. 1721 (KGP p. 276)

PICKTON
Pickton, Richard; wife Elizabeth; 3 Oct 1733 (PGLR Q.704)

PIGMAN

Pigman, John; 10 Oct 1712; 27 Oct 1712; wife Sarah; sons John, Mason; daus. Mary, Elizabeth, Grace, Catherine, Ann (MCW IV.200); 10 Dec 1712 (I&A 33b.192); extx. Sarah; 30 Mar 1712 (I&A 34.137); extx. Sarah; 20 Oct 1713 (I&A 34.231)

Pigman, John; [s/o John]; wife Vickderany; tract *Parndon*; 29 Mar 1732 (PGLR Q.424)

Piggman, John; age ca 45; 1743 (PGLR Y.701)

Pigman, Nathaniel; wife Ann; child: Joseph Waters, b. 4 Feb 1765 (PGP p. 276)

PILBORN

Piborn [Pilburns], John, Sr.; 23 Sep 1747; 25 Nov 1747; sons John, Benjamin; daus. Ruth, Mary, Rachel Calvin, Sarah Prather (MCW IX.124); 15 Jan 1747 (I 37.232)

PILE

Pile, Richard, Dr. and Frances Duvall [w/o Mareen]; convicted of unlawful cohabitation; Jun 1700 Ct. (PGCR B.51a)

Piles, Francis, Jr.; wife Sarah; 27 Apr 1721 (PGLR I.140)

Piles, John; wife Mary; children: Hunter, b. 30 May 1721; Mary, b. 18 Jan 1722; William, b. 24 Dec 1724; John, b. 11 Mar 1728; Thomas Richard, b. 17 Jun 1729 (KGP p. 281)

Pile, William; m. 29 Apr 1723 Eliza. Hutchinson; children: Richard, b. 9 Feb 1726/7; William, b. 3 Apr 1729 (QAP m/3; b/20, 23)

Piles, Francis, Sr.; 23 May 1726; 24 Apr 1727; sons James, John, Francis, Richard, Leonard; daus. Elizabeth, Anne, Jane; s-i-l Robert Orme; tracts *Cuckolds Point, Come Unto Him* (MCW VI.26); 10 Jun 1727 (I 12.275); heir Leonard; 25 Jun 1728 (AA 9.15)

Piles, Leonard; age ca 25; 1729 (PGLR M.484); age ca 34; 24 Dec 1736 (PGLR Y.84); age ca 40; 1743 (PGLR Y.703)

Pile, Francis; age ca 36; 1729 (PGLR M.484); age ca 47; 17 Apr 1739 (PGLR Y.58); age ca 50; 1743 (PGLR Y.703)

Pile, Richard; d. 24 May 1731; widow Mary [d. ca Jan 1732]; son William; dau. Elizabeth [m. Edward Sprigg]; 27 May 1746 (CCR JK#4.4.571)

Pile, Richard; physician; 24 May 1731; 10 Jul 1731; wife Mary; son William; dau. Elizabeth Sprigg [w/o Edward]; grandsons Richard & William [ss/o William], Richard Sprigg [s/o Elizabeth]; tracts *Joices Plantation, Major's Lott, Bells Purchase, Copes Hill, Expedition, Rantom, Mistake, Piles Gift* (MCW VI.194); 4 Oct 1731 (I 16.349); 8 Dec 1732 (I 16.630,

17.196); widow [unnamed]; 2 Aug 1733 (AA 11.728); son William; dau.
Elisabeth Sprigg [w/o Edward]; George Parker [husband of widow]; 12
Aug 1743 (AA 19.447)

Pile, William; d. 5 Nov 1732; widow Elizabeth; d. by 1746 [m/2 George
Parker]; 27 May 1746 (CCR JK#4.4.571, 591)

Pile, William; 18 Mar 1732; 27 Feb 1732/3; wife Eliza.; sons Richard,
William; dau. Mary; tracts The Addition, The Mistake, Pile's Discovery
(MCW VII.3); extx. Elisabeth Parker [w/o George]; heirs Richard, William;
30 Sep 1738 (AA 17.9); heirs Richard, William, Mary; 12 Apr 1740 (GB 111)

Pile, Mary; 25 May 1734 (AA 12.238); 18 Aug 1741 (I 26.365); [as widow];
children: Jane Griffin, Elisabeth Parker [w/o George and widow of
William Pile], Elisabeth; ch/o William [Richard, William, Mary]; 7
Feb 1743 (AA 20.50); heirs William, John, Richard, Francis, Sarah; 27 Jun
1744 (GB 132)

Piles, John; planter; 19 Apr 1735; 27 May 1735; wife Mary; sons Hunter,
William, John, Richard, Francis; daus. Mary, Sarah; tracts Hunter's Field,
Hunter's Folley, Lamesly (MCW VII.135); 16 Oct 1735 (I 21.164); extx. Mary;
children: Hunter, William, John, Richard, Francis, Mary, Sarah; 14 Oct
1736 (AA 15.215)

Piles, Hunter; age ca 16; chooses Leonard Piles as guardian; Nov 1735
(PGCR V.617)

Piles, James; wife Mary; tract The Golden Rod; 25 Mar 1742 (PGLR Y.450)

Piles, Richard, age 16 in Feb last; and William, age 14 in Apr last; choose
guardian; Jun 1743 (PGCR AA.676)

Pile, Richard; s-i-l Edward Sprigg; son Richard; 14 Jun 1745 (CCR JK#4.594)

Piles, William; wife Margaret; child: Elinor, bapt. 8 Dec 1751 (KGP p. 294)

Piles, Francis; wife Dorothy; children: Lucy, b. 7 Nov 1753; Mary
Dickinson, b. 28 May 1755; Sarah, b. 24 Aug 1757; Frances (f), bapt. 7
Feb 1762; Henry Humphry, bapt. 3 Oct 1763 at Broad Creek (KGP p. 304,
309, 320, 325, 338)

Pile William; admx. Margaret; 24 Dec 1755 (I 60.442); 26 Mar 1757; admx.
Margaret (ABB 2.57); widow Margaret; heirs [surviving]; 23 Nov 1757 (GB
205)

Piles, Francis; 20 Mar 1761; 22 Mar 1763; wife Sarah; sons Francis, Josiah,
Leonard, Bazil, Osburn, Henry; daus. Naomia Willet, Sarah Beall (MCW
XII.180-1); extx. Sarah; 12 May 1763 (I 81.357)

Piles, William; carpenter; 28 Sep 1761; 20 Aug 1761; son Jonathan Hunter;
daus. Elenor, Mary Ann; tracts Lambsbey's, Hudson's and Birches Race
(MCW XII.96); 4 Mar 1762 (I 77.83)

Piles, Richard, Dr.; wife Elizabeth; child: William, b. 14 Dec 1761 (KGP p. 324)

Piles, Francis; admx. Dorothy; 16 Feb 1764 (I 83.148)

Piles, Dorathey; child: Elizabeth, bapt. 3 Aug 1766 Broad Creek (KGP p. 359)

Piles, Leonard; 19 Mar 1773; 21 Feb 1774; wife [unnamed]; children: Francis, Ann Townsend, Elizabeth Drane, Martha Haney, Eleanor Berry, Lucy Smith, Leonard, Rebecca, Elizabeth [the younger]; grandchild Leonard [s/o Francis]; tracts *Cuckolds Point*, *Brooke Hill* (MCW XV.137); extx. Elisabeth; 19 May 1774 (I 115.277); 14 Jan 1775; admx. Mrs. Elisabeth Piles (ABB 7.3)

Piles, Osburn; wife Mary; child: Sarah, b. 2 Aug 1774 Upper Chapel (KGP p. 391)

PINDALL

Pindell, Phillip; wife Elizabeth; children: Elizabeth, b. 17 Jan 1709/10; Philip, b. 7 Mar 1712/3; Mary, b. 8 Jul 1715; John, b. 8 10ber 1718; Priscilla, b. 7 Aug 1722; Thomas, b. 15 Mar 1723/4; Mary, b. 8 9ber 1728; Elianor, b. 22 Apr 1732 (QAP b/4, 8, 11, 14, 18, 21, 25)

Pindall, Thomas; 12 Jun 1710; 5 Aug 1710; wife Mary; sons Thomas; Philip, Abraham, Isaac; daus. Joice Gladston, Mary, Rachell (MCW III.178); 18 Dec 1710 (I&A 32a.97); admx. Mary; 7 Jul 1711 (I&A 32b.198); extx. Mary [widow]; 3 Dec 1714 (I&A 36a.1919)

Pindle, Mary; sons Philip, Abraham, Isaac; dau. Joyce Gladland; 27 Dec 1714 (PGLR F.429)

Pindel [Pindell], Thomas; wife Jane; children: Edward, b. 29 7ber 1724; Jacob, b. 6 8ber 1726; Thomas, b. 28 7ber 1728; Phillip & Rachel [twins], b. 20 Nov 1731 (QAP b/4, 19, 20, 25)

Pindle, Thomas; admx. Jayne; 9 Aug 1734 (I 20.41); extx. Jane; children: Edward, Jacob, Thomas, Phillip, Rachel; 24 Jul 1740 (AA 18.25)

Pindle, Philip; age ca 52; 1736 (PGLR T.444); [see Anne Arundel Co. records]

Pindall, Thomas; heirs Edward, Jacob, Thomas, Philip, Rachell; 26 Mar 1741 (GB 117)

Pindall, Elisabeth; 23 Oct 1747 (I 40.185)

Piddle, Philip; wife Elizabeth; 1761 (MCWXII.102)

PINSON

Pinson, James; 30 Mar 1714 (I&A 35a.308); [with 1714] (I&A 36b.243)

PIRKINS

Pirkin, John; wife Doraty; children: John, b. 19 Jan 1728; ____ (f), b. 10 Feb 1729; ____ (m), b. 2 Dec ____ [no mother's name]; ?Elizabeth, b. __?Jun 1736; ?Dorothy, b. 4 Jan 1740/1 (KGP p. 284)

Pirkins, James; wife Elizabeth; child: James, bapt. 11 Aug 1765 Broad Creek (KGP p. 349)

Pirkins, John; wife Ann; child: Ann, b. 5 Oct 1765 Broad Creek (KGP p. 349)

Pirkins, Richard; wife Lucey; child: Rebecca, bapt. 28 Apr 1765 Broad Creek; Zilfa, bapt. 7 Aug 1768 Broad Creek (KGP p. 347, 363)

Purkins [Perkins]; admx. Ann; 8 Apr 1767 (I 94.67)

PLATER

Plater, George [SM]; wife Rebecca; tract *Strife*; 27 Jan 1738 (PGLR T.693)

PLAYFAY

Playfay, Philip; admx. Catherine; 1 Jun 1734 (I 30.43); widow Catherine; dau. Mary; 3 Jun 1739 (AA 17.212); widow Catherine; heir Mary; 26 Mar 1740 (GB 209)

Plasay, Mary; age ca 16; chooses mother Catherine as guardian; Nov 1748 (PGCR KK.26)

PLOWDEN

Plowden, George [SM]; wife Margrett; tracts *Thorpland* and *Perry Hills* now called *St. David*; 2 Dec 1696 (PGLR A.161)

PLUMMER

Plummer, Thomas, Jr.; m. 6 Feb 1715 Sarah Wilson (QAP m/1)

Plummer, Thomas; 29 Jan 1726; 26 Jun 1728; wife Elizabeth; sons Thomas, Samuel, James, Philimon, Jerom, George, John, Micajah, Yate, Abezar; daus. Priscilla, Phebe; tracts *Seaman's Delight, Swanson's Lott, Dundee, Part of Dundee* (MCW VI.65); admx. Elisabeth [Quaker]; 29 Jul 1728 (I 13.223); widow Elisabeth [Quaker]; children: Thomas, Samuel, Philemon, James, Priscilla, Phebe; 8 Jul 1730 (AA 10.334); extx. Elisabeth; 18 Nov 1734 (I 19.166)

Plummer, Philemon; wife Elizabeth; children: Kezia, b. 4 Jan 1728/9; Sarah, b. 28 9ber 1730 (QAP b/22, 24)

Plummer, Thomas; son George [Quaker]; 1731 (PGLR Q.235); wife Elizabeth [Quaker]; 1731 (PGLR Q.234)

Plummer, Philemon; bro. Jerome; 14 Jul 1732 (PGLR Q.515)

Plummer, Elizabeth; 27 Mar 1736; 8 Jul 1736; sons Thomas, Samuel, George, James, John, Jerome, Phillimon, Micajah, Yate, Abiezer; daus.

Priscilla Ouchtclony, Phoebe Williams; tracts *Liford* (MCW VII.182); 24 Nov 1736 (I 22.161); children: Thomas, Samuel, George, James, John, Jerom, Philemon, Priscilla Ouchterlong, Phebe Williams; 8 Aug 1737 (AA 14.310)

Plummer [Plommer], John; 17 Jan 1739; 2 Feb 1739/40; bros. Samuel, Thomas, George, James, Jerum, Philimon, Yate, Cager, Bezor; sisters Prisila, Phebee (MCW VIII.74); 8 Feb 1739 (I 25.30)

Plummer, Philemon; 11 Oct 1744 (I 30.66); widow [unnamed]; son John; 8 other [under age]; 31 Aug 1747 (AA 24.57); widow Elizabeth; heirs Ashach, Elizabeth, Philemon, Jeram, George, Dorcas; 24 Aug 1748 (GB 162)

Plummer, George; 8 Jul 1753; 14 Jan 1754; [no relationships noted] (MCW XI.16)

Plummer, Samuel; 13 Jan 1754; 2 Feb 1760; wife Sarah; sons Thomas, Joseph, Samuel, Abraham; daus. Cassandra Ballenger, Sarah Plummer; s-i-l Richard Holland; tracts *Roses Purchase, Upper Getting, Hunting Lott, Food Plenty, Rocky Hill, Hickory Plains, Help, Rich Hill* (MCW XII.231)

Plummer, Edward; wife Jane; child: Kissiah, b. 26 May 1761 (PGP p. 261)

Plummer, John; wife Elizabeth; child: Rebecca, b. 26 Dec 1763 (PGP p. 269)

Plummer, Phillimon; wife Sarah; child: Phillimon, b. 7 Aug 1764 (PGP p. 276)

Plummer, James; 23 Nov 1770; 13 Apr 1772; wife [unnamed]; children: Jemima Hodges, Sarah Wells, Anne; tracts *Batchelors Choice, Wickhams Good Will* (MCW XIV.215)

PLUNKET

Plunket [Plinket], Thos.; 5 Oct 1716; 17 Jul 1717; [no relations] (MCW IV.138)

POLE

Pole [Paul], Elizabeth; had bastard child; Jun 1697 Ct. (PGCR A.169)

POLSON

Polson, Thomas; 8 Oct 1720 (I 5.56)

POMFREY

Pomfrey, William; wife Elizabeth; children: Mary, b. 22 Aug 1772 Upper Chapel; Sarah, b. 14 Aug 1774 Broad Creek (KGP p. 386, 389)

POORE

Pooer, Robt.; m. 27 Jun 1710 Anne Lewis; children: Mary, b. 4 Oct 1711; Elizabeth, b. 18 Feb 1714; Ellinor, b. 10 Dec 1722 (KGP p. 268)

Poor, Robert; wife Mary; child: Rachel, b. 8 Jan 1759 (KGP p. 321)

Poor, Robert; 8 Nov 1762; 24 Mar 1762; wife Mary; her 4 children (MCW
XII.119); admx. Mary; 31 Mar 1762 (I 78.319); 14 Dec 1762; extx. Mary
Poore; 4 children [unnamed] (ABB 3.181)

Poors, Mathew; 30 Mar 1717 (I&A 38a.32)

POPE

Pope, Jane; child: William, b. 18 Jan 1723/4 (QAP b/18)

Pore, Robert; wife Mary; child: Elizabeth, b. 15 May 1762 (KGP p. 330)

Pope, Nathaniel; wife Elizabeth; children: Amealea, bapt. 3 Jul 1763 at
Upper Chapel; Priscilla, bapt. 2 Feb 1766 Lower Chapel; Nathaniel,
bapt. 3 Jul 1768 Upper Chapel; Elizabeth, b. 18 Apr 1773 Upper
Chapel; Ann, b. 31 Aug 1775 Upper Chapel (KGP p. 333, 346, 370, 390, 391)

Pope, Joseph; wife Elizabeth; child: Elizabeth, b. 6 Nov 1773 Upper
Chapel (KGP p. 390)

POSEY

Posey, [unnamed]; heir Ignatius Posey; 3 Apr 1747 (GB 157)

POTTENGER

Pottinger, John; wife Mary; children: Sarah, b. 20 Jul 1688; Mary, b. 22
8ber 1689; John, b. 20 Aug 1691; Samuel, b. 11 Apr 1693; Robert, b. 25
Feb 1694/5; Rachel, b. 20 Jun 1700; Jemima, b. 2 8ber 1702; William, b.
3 May 1704; Verlinda, b. 18 8ber 1706 (QAP b/3)

Pottinger, Samuel; m. 11 Jul 1717 Eliza. Tyler [d/o Robert] (QAP m/2)

Pottinger, Robert; m. 2 Dec 1718 Ann Evans (QAP m/2)

Pottenger [Pottinger], John, Jr.; 18 Mar 1719/20; 24 Mar 1719; wife Sarah;
father John Pottenger, bros. Samuel and Robert Pottenger; "bro."
Richard Purnal (MCW V.2); bros. Samuell, Robert; [with 1720] (I 4.49);
widow & 1 dau. [unnamed]; 28 Oct 1720 (AA 3.156); heir Sarah; 27 Jun 1720
(GB 10, 72)

Pottinger, William; widow Rachel [w/o Joseph Milburn Semmes of
Charles Co.]; 2 children [unnamed]; 21 Jul 1722 [?1732] (AA 11.435)

Pottinger, John; age ca 67; 22 May 1729 (PGLR M.440)

Pottinger, John; son Robert; tract *Pottinger's Desire*; 18 Sep 1729 (PGLR M.497)

Pottenger, John; 2 Aug 1734; 7 Apr 1735; sons, Samuel, Robert, William
[dec'd]; daus. Rachel Purnell, Verlinder Wade, Sarah Isaac, Mary
Holmes; grandsons Samuel & Robert [ss/o Samuel], Robert [s/o
Robert], William [s/o William, dec'd], John & Richard Purnell [s/o
Rachel]; granddau. Sarah [d/o John, dec'd]; tracts *Newbury, The
Remainder, As Good as We Could Get* (MCW VII.128); 11 Apr 1735 (I 20.481);

legatees Samuel, Robert, Sarah Pottenger; payments to ss-i-l Richard
Isaac, Richard Purnell, Zephaniah Wade; 8 Mar 1736 (AA 15.269); son
Samuel; grandsons Samuel, Robert; 31 Mar 1736 (AA 14.209); admx. Sarah;
17 Mar 1739 (I 25.121)

Pottenger, Robert; 20 Mar 1735/6; 5 Jun 1738; wife Ann; sons John, Richard,
Robert; daus. Mary, Elizabeth Bowie, Ann, Rachel, Sarah, Ellenor; tract
Green's Delight (MCW VII.240); extx. Ann; 19 Jul 1738 (I 23.433); extx. Ann; 27
Jun 1739; son John; dau. w/o John Bowie; 27 Jun 1739 (AA 17.215)

Pottinger, John; heirs Martha Pottinger [d/o William]; children of Mary
Holmes [w/o William]; 12 Apr 1740 (GB 110)

Pottenger, Samuel; 13 Jan 1735; 25 Mar 1742; wife Elizabeth; father Tyler;
sons Robert, John; daus. Susannah, Elizabeth, Jemima, Mary Mullikin,
Priscilla; tracts Wickhams and Pottengers Discovery, Addition to First
Purchase, Fellowship (MCW VIII.163); extx. Eliza; 8 Apr 1742 (I 27.51); exs.
Elisabeth and James Drane; 28 Jul 1743 (AA 19.436); adms. Elisabeth and
James Drane; daus. Susannah Simmonds [w/o Richard], Jemima Child
[w/o Henry], Elisabeth Baldin; 27 Aug 1744 (AA 20.324); extx. Elisabeth
Drane [w/o James]; father John; grandchild. of John Pottinger: Pricilla,
Rachel Holmes, John Pottinger; 10 Nov 1746 (AA 22.413); heirs Samuel,
Robert, Susannah, Jemima, Priscilla, Mary; 28 Nov 1746 (GB 154)

Pottinger, Sarah; age ca 15 on 8 May last; chooses guardian; Jun 1735 (PGCR
V.401)

Pottinger, Prisella; age ca 15; chooses guardian; Aug 1743 (PGCR CC.4)

Pottinger, Samuel; chooses James Draine as guardian; Mar 1745 (PGCR
DD.19)

Pottinger, Robert; age ca 14; choses James Draine as guardian; Aug 1747
(PGCR GG.97)

Pottinger, Robert; planter; 20 Apr 1748; 29 Mar 1753; wife Rachel; dau.
Ann; sisters or children Elizabeth, Mary, Ann, Rachel, Sarah, Elinor;
tract Green's Delight (MCW X.254); extx. Rachel; 12 Apr 1753 (I 54.139); extx.
Rachel; 22 Jan 1754 (I 60.30); 27 Mar 1757; extx. Rachel Pottinger; children
Ann Pottinger, unborn child (ABB 2.59); widow Rachel; heirs Ann, "child
Rachel was big with"; 23 Nov 1757 (GB 204)

Pottenger, John; age 17 on 14 Dec last; chooses Samuel Pottenger as
guardian; Jun 1752 (PGCR MM.241)

Pottenger, Ann; widow; 18 May 1767; 3 Feb 1768; children: Elizabeth
Cramphin, Ann Beall [w/o James], Rachel Magruder [w/o Zadock],
Eleanor MacGill [w/o Thomas], Mary Congrove; grandchildren: Robert
Pottenger [s/o Robert], Allen & John Bowie, Robert Cramphin, Ann &

Rachel Pottenger [ch/o Robert], Basil & Richard Pottinger Cramphin [ss/o Elizabeth], Elizabeth & Sarah Smith [ds/o Mary]; bro. Samuel Evans; sister Priscilla MacClain (MCW XIV.35-6); 24 Aug 1768 (I 96.331)

POTTER

Potter, William; wife Mary; child: _____ (m), b. _____ (QAP b/38)

POWELL

Powell, William; planter; 3 May 1714; 1 Oct 1726; wife Mary Ann; son John (MCW V.231); admx. Mary Ann; 14 Nov 1727 (I 12.385); admx. Mary Anne; 14 Nov 1727 (AA 8.447); extx. Mary Ann Smith [w/o James] son John; 5 Dec 1729 (AA 10.101)

Powell [Powel], John, Jr.; m. 8 Oct 1731 Mary Knewstub; [d/o Robert]; children: Mary, b. 8 Oct 1732; Hannah, b. 9 Jun 1736 (QAP m/5; b/30)

Powel, John; wife Sarah; children: John Burrous, bapt. 12 Feb 1764 Broad Creek; William Palmer, b. 9 May 1766 Broad Creek; Ann, bapt. 1 Jan 1769 Broad Creek (KGP p. 353, 356, 372)

Powell, Samuel; wife Mary; child: Hennewritta, bapt. 29 Mar 1752 (KGP p. 295)

POWER

Powers, Mathew; 30 Dec 1717 (I&A 39c.125)

Power, Robert; m. 5 Oct 1752 Mary Barker (KGP p. 293)

Power, John; wife Jane; child: William, bapt. 4 Feb 1753 (KGP p. 298)

Power, John; wife Elizabeth; child: George, b. 16 Mar 1775 Lower Chapel; Charlotte, b. 6 Apr 1772 Lower Chapel (KGP p. 380, 383)

PRAGG

Pragg, William; age ca 13; servant; Jun 1712 Ct. (PGCR G.211)

PRATHER

Prater [Prather], George; 23 May 1698; 29 Jul 1698; wife Mary; bros. William, Thomas and John; sister Jane Molikine; tract Orphan's Gift (MCW II.150)

Prather, William; wife Ann; children: William, b. 8 Mar 1700; Jane, b. 12 ber 1703; Priscilla, b. 21 7ber 1707; Margaret, b. 8 7ber 1709; Joseph, b. 11 Jul 1711; John, b. 12 Jun 1715; Sarah, 23 Mar 1716 (QAP b/7, 11, 13)

Prather, John; wife Katherine; children: Mary, b. 28 7ber 1705; John, b. last day Feb 1707/8; Lucy, b. 29 May 1710 (QAP b/7)

Prather, Jonathan; son John; 1707 (MCW III.91)

Prather, Jonathan; wife Elizabeth; tract *Toogood*; 26 Aug 1707 (PGLR C.191a); Jonathan, Sr.; wife Elizabeth; children: Susanna, b. 1 8ber 1708; Rachel, b. 11 7ber 1711 (QAP b/7)

Smith, Jane; [widow of John]; 27 Jul 1710; 7 Dec 1713; sons William, Thomas, John, Jonathan Prater; grandchildren Elizabeth, Mary, John, other [ch/o John Prater], Priscilla [d/o William Prater], Ann, Martha, Jane, Susannah [ds/o Jonathan Prater]; Thomas, John, Philip, Eleanor, Rachel [ch/o Thomas Prater], William, Priscilla, Margarett [ch/o William Prater] (MCW III.258)

Prather, Thomas; 13 Dec 1711; 15 Mar 1711/2; wife Martha; sons Aaron, Thomas, John Smith Prather; daus. Elinor, Rachel; tracts *Orphan's Gift, Andrew, Sprigg's Request* (MCW III.221); bros. William, John; 7 Jun 1712 (I&A 33b.32); extx. Martha; 6 children [unnamed]; 12 May 1713 (I&A 33b.147)

Prather, Jonathan, Jr.; wife Jane; children: William, b. 12 7ber 1712; Mary, b. 14 Apr 1716; Elizabeth, b. 27 Jul 1718 (QAP b/7, 11, 14)

Prather, John; widow Katherine; bro. William; 7 Jan 1718 (I 2.136); widow Catherine; [with 1720] (I 4.251); widow Katherine; 2 sons & 4 daus. [unnamed]; 12 Nov 1720 (AA 3.157); nok John, Sr., John; 13 Dec 1720 (I 4.287); [as Jonathan]; widow Katherine; heirs John, Lucy, Edward, Jane, Elizabeth; 28 Jun 1720 (GB 11)

Prather, Thomas [dec'd]; widow Martha [w/o Stephen Yoakely]; children John Smith, Rachel, Philip, Aaron; 25 Mar 1723 (PGLR I.525)

Prater, William; age ca 40; bro. Thomas; f-i-l John Smith; 6 Feb 1717 (PGLR I.593)

Prather, John Smith, m. 17 Feb 1725/6 Elizabeth Nutwell; children: Josiah, b. 21 10ber 1727; Martha, b. 20 Apr 1730; Jeremiah, b. 7 Jul 173_; Aaron, b. 173_; Elinor, b. 2 Apr 173_; Elizabeth, b. 23 Sep 1740 (QAP m/4; b/21, 23, 24, 27, 32)

Prather, Thomas; wife Elizabeth; children: Thomas Clagett, b. 9 May 1726; Richard, b. 1 Aug 1727; Margaret, b. 14 8ber 1728; Mary, b. 6 Jan 1729; Basil, b. 1731; Henry, b. Sep 1732; James, b. 27 Jan 1735; Sarah, b. 2 Feb 1739 (QAP b/19, 21, 22, 23, 24, 27, 30, 32)

Prather, Aaron; age ca 15; chooses guardian; Aug 1726 (PGCR N.8)

Prather, John; wife Mary Ann; tract *Elizabeth & Samuel's Delight*; 1 Jun 1727 (PGLR M.243)

Prather, Jonathan; wife Mary; child: Mary, b. 20 Sep 1729 (QAP b/23)

Prather, Philemon; wife Katherine; children: Margaret, b. 14 7ber 1730; Martha, b. 17 Jan 1732/3 (QAP b/24, 27)

Prather, John; wife. Mary; child: Sarah, b. 31 Oct 1731 (QAP b/25)

Prather, William, Sr.; wife Ann; son William, Jr.; mother Jane Smith; tract *Turkie Flight*; ?dau. Priscilla Prather, tract *Orphan's Gift*; dau. Margaret Prather; dau. Jane Turner [w/o Solomon]; 13 Mar 1733 (PGLR T.81 - 84)

Prather, Johnathon, Jr.; admx. Jane Ward [w/o William]; 21 Aug 1734 (AA 12.404)

Prather [Prayther], Jonathan, Sr.; 4 Dec 1734; 23 Mar 1735/6; sons Jonathan [dec'd], John, Thomas; daus. Elizabeth, Ann, Martha, Jean, Susannah, Rachel, Sarah; wife Elizabeth; grandsons William [of Jonathan], John Dorsett; granddau. Rachel Dorsett (MCW VII.168); heirs Thomas, Elizabeth, Mary, Jonathan; 22 Nov 1737 (GB 96

Prather, Thomas, Jr.; wife Elizabeth; children: Ellinor, b. 15 Mar 173_; Charles, b. 18 Sep 1735 (QAP b/28, 29)

Prather, William, Sr.; wife Ann [d/o George Yate]; tract *Cheney*; 15 Dec 1735 (PGLR T.342)

Prather, Jonathan [dec'd]; widow Elizabeth; dau. Rachel; 21 Apr 1737 (PGLR T.455)

Prather, Cathrine; son John; 1740 (MCW VIII.98); 27 Mar 1741 (I 26.28)

Prather, Thomas; wife Elizabeth; tract *Beall's Gift*; 28 Nov 1741 (PGLR Y.414)

Prather, Thomas; admx. Joyce Coleman [w/o Thomas]; 24 Jun 1742 (I 27.28); [as Thomas, Sr.]; widow Joyce Coleman [w/o Thomas]; 3 children Elinor, Sarah, James; 11 Jun 1744 (AA 20.243)

Prather, John; wife Elinor; tract *Orphan's Gift*; 9 Jul 1742 (PGLR Y.523)

Prather, John; admx. Elinor Lacklin [w/o Jeremiah]; 6 Mar 1750 (AA 29.184); admx. Elinor Larklin [late Prather]; 16 Jun 1750 (I 44.414); admx. Elinor Lacklin [w/o Jeremiah]; 10 Mar 1752 (AA 32.63)

Prather, Samuell; wife Susannah_; child: Eliner Aldrige, b. 20 Jul 1761 (PGP p. 262)

Prather, Aron; wife Mary; child: Basil, b. 1 Feb 1762 (PGP p. 262)

Prather, John Smith; 14 Jul 1763; 3 Sep 1763; wife Elizabeth; sons Jeremiah, Josiah; Zachariah; daus. Eleanor Beall, Rachel, Martha Odell; grandson John Smith Prather [s/o Josiah]; tracts *Bear Garden Enlarged, Deer Park* (MCW XII.206); extx. Elisabeth; 2 Mar 1764 (I 83.151); 4 Dec 1767; extx. Elisabeth Deakins [w/o William]; dist. to Jeremiah Prather and his 2 daus. Martha Odell & Rachel Prather (ABB 5.49); widow Joyce Coleman [w/o Thomas]; 3 children Elinor, Sarah, James; 11 Jun 1744 (AA 20.243)

Prater, Zefaniah; wife Rachel_; child: Thomas, bapt 10 Apr 1768 Upper Chapel (KGP p. 370)

Prather, Baruck; m. 16 Nov 1775 Sarah Higgins [see original records for children] (PGP p. 283)

PRATT

Pratt, John; m. 28 Jul 1724 Ellinor Williams; children: John, b. 19 Jul 1725; Elizabeth, b. 10 Oct 1726; Elianor, b. 13 Oct 17__; Thomas, b. 8 Mar 1730 (QAP m/3; b/19, 23, 24)

Pratt, Thomas; m. 2 Feb 1755 Eleanor Magruder; children: _____ (f), b. _____; _____ (m), b. _____ (QAP m/7; b/38, 39)

PREECE

Preece, Henry; wife Elizabeth; children: William, b. 19 Mar 1762; Thomas, b. 22 Feb 1763; Margrett, b. 23 Aug 1765 (PGP p. 268, 277)

PRICE

Price, Thomas; admx. Elisabeth [widow]; 8 Aug 1711 (I&A 32c.149); admx. Elisabeth; 9 May 1712 (I&A 33a.179)

Price, John; 7 May 1712 (I&A 33a.175)

Prise, Edward; planter; 29 Apr 1717; 18 May 1717; wife [unnamed]; *Litchfield, Planter's Delight* (MCW IV.94)

Price, Honour; son William; dau. Sarah Pearson [w/o John]; 6 Jul 1725 (PGLR I.655)

Price, Thomas; admx. Elisabeth; 15 May 1727 (I 12.205); heirs Mary, Thomas, Anne, Sarah, Richard, Benjamin; 24 Jun 1728 (GB 45)

Price, Elisabeth; 11 Dec 1727 (I 13.47); heirs Thomas, Richard, Benjamin, Mary, Ann, Sarah [eldest son age ca 14]; 27 Aug 1728 (AA 9.65); heirs Thomas, Richard, Benjamin, Mary, Anne, Sarah; 26 Mar 1729 (AA 9.330, 341)

Price, Thomas; wife Martha; tract *Clement Hill*; 5 Sep 1741 (PGLR Y.390)

Price, Benoney; wife Mary; children: Ignatius, b. 15 Sep 1754; Reason (m), bapt. May-Jul 1761; Loyd Beall, bapt. 23 Oct 1763 at Upper Chapel; Fredrick, bapt. 18 Aug 1765 Upper Chapel; Benedict Beall, bapt. 10 May 1767 Upper Chapel (KGP p. 306, 323, 334, 359, 365)

Price, John; child: William, bapt. 3 Apr 1768 Broad Creek (KGP p. 362)

PRICHARD

Prichard, John, gent.; 10 Oct 1741; 30 Oct 1741; wife Katherine; kinsman Anthony Donne (MCW VIII.147)

Prichard, Richard, Capt.; extx. Rebecca Tilley; 4 Feb 1740 (I 26.411); 21 Mar 1742 (I 27.430); extx. Rebecca Tilley; 11 May 1744 (AA 20.196); widow Rebecca Tilly; 30 Oct 1742 (AA 19.179)

Pritchard, John [dec'd]; widow Catherine; 25 Feb 1745 (CCR JK#4.530)

Pritchard, John; widow Rebeccah [now Rebeccah Tilley]; 21 Feb 1752 (CCR MSA 8.1125)

PRIGG

Priggs, John Frederick Augustus; child: Fredrick Augustus, b. 27 Oct 1749; bapt. 10 Mar 1749/50 (PGP p. 253)

Prigg, Josias; wife Mary; child: Margaret, b. 2 May 1775 Upper Chapel (KGP p. 391)

PRINCE

Prince, Mary; age 2 on 7 Apr; bound out; Mar 1742 (PGCR AA.351)

PRINDWELL

Prindwell, John; age 14 on 29 Sep next; request sister's husband, Benjamin Attien; bound out; Jun 1726 (PGCR L.638)

PRITCHETT

Pritchett, John, b. in _herbury Parrish in Stafordshire; s/o Michll. Pritchett; m. 2 Mar 1701 Eliza. Bener, b. in Stepney Parrish in Middlesex [d. 22 Feb 1712, bur. parrish churchyard]; children: William, b. 2 Oct 1703; John, b. 11 Sep 1707; Marey, b. 12 Mar 1708; Thomas, b. 15 Mar 1710 (KGP p. 259)

Pritchett, John; wife Margaret; children: Elizabeth, b. 22 Mar 1735/6; Elliner, b. 10 Aug 1740; Joseph, b. 29 Mar 1734; Margaret, b. 23 Mar 1737/8 (PGP p. 250, 251)

Pritchett, Thomas; wife Elizabeth; child: William, b. 4 Dec 1759 (PGP p. 281)

Pritchett [Pritchet], William; wife Kisiah; children: William, b. 16 Oct 1761; Jane, b. 25 Sep 1765 (PGP p. 262, 277)

PROCTOR

Proctor, William; m. 12 Apr 1726 Jane Partridge (QAP m/4)

PROSON

Proson, James; wife Rachel; child: Sarah, b. 2 May 1765 (PGP p. 274)

PUMFREY

Pumfrey, William; age 4 on 10 Jan last; bound out; Aug 1737 (PGCR W.400)

PUNCH

Punch, Page; age 10 on 13 Dec last; s/o Mary; bound out; Mar 1703 (PGCR B.232)

PUNNETT

Punnett, Joseph; age ca 51; 1730 (PGLR M.556)

PURDEY

Purdey, Henry; wife Sarah; children: Henry, b. 23 Apr 1762; John Hosey, b. 9 May 1764, bapt. 5 Aug 1764 Upper Chapel; Sarah Ann, bapt. 10 Apr 1768 Upper Chapel (KGP p. 330, 341, 370)

PURDUM

Purdum, John; wife Kizia; children: James, b. 3 May 1763; Walter, b. 12 May 1765 (PGP p. 268, 276)

PYBORN

Pyborn, John; wife Sarah; tract *John & Sarah*; 29 Dec 1729 or 30 (PGLR M.562)

PYE

Pye, Edward; m. 25 Feb 1735 Sarah Queen; child: Elizabeth, b. 15 Dec _____ (KGP p. 278)

Pye, Charles; bro. Walter [CH]; 8 Oct 1737 (PGLR T.563)

Pye, Walter, Jr.; 6 Nov 1742 (I 27.274); 23 Nov 1744 (AA 20.534)

QUANDO

Quando [Quondo], Henry; 16 Apr 1743 (I 29.139); 1 May 1744 (AA 20.247)

QUEEN

Queen, Samuel; m. 17 Feb 1723 Sarah Edelen; children: Samuell, b. 13 Jan 1724; Edward, b. 15 Jan 1726; Henry, b. 14 Oct 1729; Katherine, b. 2 Oct 1731; Sarah, b. 9 Oct 1734 (KGP p. 277, 278)

Queen, Marsham; wife Mary; tract *Hudson's Range*; 23 Nov 1723 (PGLR I.508)

Queen, John; age ca 45; wife [unnamed] widow of Henry Robins; 19 Oct 1730 (CCR-MSA 5.461)

Queen, John; age ca 40; 1731 (PGLR Q.372)

Queen, Samuel; 27 Dec 1733; 21 Mar 1733/4; wife Sarah; sons Samuel, Edward; unborn child; dau. Catherine; bro. Marsham; b-i-l James Edelin; tracts *The Inclosure, Underwood, The New Design* (MCW VII.70)

Queen, Samuel; admx. Sarah; _ Jun 1734 (I 20.340); extx. Sarah; children: Samuel, Henry, Katherine, Sarah; 6 Dec 1735 (AA 14.83); heirs Samuel, Henry, Catherine, Sarah; 24 Nov 1736 (GB 87)

Queen, James; age ca 16 in Jan last; choses guardian; Jun 1745 (PGCR DD.89)

Queen, Samuel; 9 Feb 1758; 18 Mar 1758; wife Henrietta; sons Edward, Walter, Henry; daus. Catherine, Henrietta, Mary Ann; bro. Henry; tracts *Inclosed, Underwood* (MCW XI.198); ex. Henrietta; 29 Jun 1758 (I 64.434); 1763; exs. Henrietta Jameson [w/o Henry], Henry Queen; children: Walter, Henry, Catharine, Henrietta, Mary Ann (ABB 4.10); heirs Walter, Henry, Catherine, Henrietta, Mary Ann; 21 Dec 1763 (GB 232, 287); heirs Walter, Henry, Henrietta, Mary Ann; 24 Jun 1767 (GB 253)

Queen, Edward; 6 Apr 1768 (I 96.343)

RABBLIN

Rablin, John; 6 Dec 1704; wife Elizabeth; sons John Rablin, Sr. [b. 27 Jul 1691]; John Rablin, Jr. [b. 26 May 1702]; William [b. 5 Jun 1689]; Katharine [b. 16 Jan 1694]; unborn child (MCW III.80); 13 Feb 1704 (I&A 3.685); 13 Feb 1704 (I&A 3.685); extx. widow Elisabeth Norris [w/o Caleb]; 14 Dec 1706 (I&A 26.145)

RADFORD

Radford, John; carpenter; *Sinnicar Landing*; 16 Jan 1728; 10 Mar 1728; wife Sarah; sons Henry, John, Thomas; tracts *Sinnicar Landing, Ocbrook, Radford's Chance, Newton, Darby Island, Melborne, Three Islands United, The Henry, Long Acre, Samariea, Olbias* (?) *Choyce* (MCW VI.99); extx. Sarah; 12 Mar 1729 (I 15.264)

RAMSEY

Ramsey, Thomas; 5 Jun 1708 (I&A 28.258)

Ramsey, Grace; widow; granchildren: Phebe, Patience & Asenath [ds/o William and Mary Spires]; 30 Sep 1735 (PGLR T.328)

RAMSFORD

Ramsford, Giles; wife Susanna; tract *The Gores*; 24 May 1728 (PGLR M.274)

RANGER

Ranger, Samuell; wife Ann; ?bro. John; tract *Londonderry*; 15 Dec 1707 (PGLR C.219)

RANKIN

Rankin, James; 12 Jul 1709 (I&A 29.405)

RANSOM

Ransom, George; 5 Dec 1717; 18 Jan 1717; sons George, Jr., William, Richard, Ignatius and Joseph; dau. Elizabeth Harris; tracts *The Wedge*; legatees Sarah Taneyhill and her son James (MCW IV.175-6); 6 Feb 1717 (AA 1.9); 9 Nov 1719 (AA 2.369)

Ransom, William; 15 Jul 1718; 9 Aug 1718; sister Elizabeth Harris; bros. George, Richard, Ignatius, Joseph (MCW IV.182); s/o George [dec'd]; 26 Jul 1720 (AA 3.210)

Ransom, George; bro. William; tract *The Wedge*; 31 Oct 1718 (PGLR F.139/709)

Ransom, Richard [CA]; wife Elizabeth; tract *Land Above*; 11 Sep 1735 (PGLR T.314)

Ransom, George; dau. Elizabeth; granddau. Amy Selby; tract *The Wedge*; 23 Jun 1740 (PGLR Y.189)

Ransom, Ignatius; wife Priscilla; dau. Elizabeth; Elizabeth Kirkwood [grandmother of Elizabeth Ransom]; 2 Oct 1740 (PGLR Y.257)

Ransom, Richard; wife Abigail; child: ____ (f), b. 25 Dec 1753 (KGP p. 304)

RANTER

Ranter, Nathaniel; admx. Mary; 9 Apr 1761 (I 74.169)

Ranter, James; admx. Johnannah; 21 Aug 1765 (I 90.134)

RANTOU

Rantou, James; wife Frances; tract *Beall's Reserve*; 3 Aug 1737 (PGLR T.538)

RATCLIFF

Ratcliff, Robert; admx. Mary; ss-i-l James Hyett, William Gooden; 21 Jun 1740 (I 25.24); admx. Mary; 21 Jun 1740 (AA 17.487)

RATTERFORD

Ratterford, John; 9 Jul 1726 (AA 7.445)

RAWDRY

Rawdry, Elizabeth; dau. Sarah; bound out; Jun 1711 PGCR H.6)

RAWLINGS

Rawlings, John; age ca 7 years; s/o William Rawlings; Nov 1699 (PGCR B.1a)

Rawlings, Moses; wife Ruth [d/o Elizabeth Lovett]; 12 Jan 1731/2 (PGLR Q.570)

Rawlings, William [AA]; wife Elizabeth; tract *Roper's Range*; 26 Jan 1741/2 (PGLR Y.434)

Rawlings, Paul; admx. Ann; 21 Aug 1767 (I 95.19); 24 Aug 1767; admx. Ann Rawlings (ABB 5.42)

RAY

Ray, William, Jr.; wife Elizabeth; children: William, b. 31 8ber 1705; John, b. 10 Aug 1707; Luke, b. 15 Jun 1709; Margaret, b. 29 Jan 1711/2; Elizabeth, b. 25 Dec 1713; Ellinor, b. 16 10ber 1715; Mary, b. 14 7ber 1718; Rebecca, b. 13 8ber 1720; Thomas, b. 27 10ber 1722/3 (QAP b/6, 9, 12, 16, 17)

Ray, Joseph; wife Alice; children: Katherine, b. 26 Apr 1713; Priscilla, b. 16 Mar 1714; Mary, b. 5 9ber 1716; Cranby, b. 14 7ber 1718 (QAP b/8, 10, 12, 14)

Ray, Luke; wife Susannah; children: Rebecca, b. 19 Jul 1717; Rachel, b. 19 Jul 1717 (QAP b/13)

Ray, John; 24 Mar 1718; 12 Apr 1718; [no relations named] (MCW IV.141); Duke [?Luke]; 12 Dec 1718 (I 4.250); 12 Sep 1720 (AA 3.207)

Ray, John; 4 Jul 1730 (I 15.518)

Ray, Joseph; age ca 42; 31 May 1731 (PGLR Q.608)

Ray, William, Sr.; s-i-l Benjamin Norris; grandson William Norris; tract *The Forrest*; 30 Apr 1731 (PGLR Q.259)

Ray, William; granddaus. Mary Swearingen, Elizabeth Swearingen; 28 Jun 1732 (PGLR Q.493)

Ray, William; wife Ann; child: John, b. 6 Aug 173_ (QAP b/28)

Ray, William; 25 Jul 1732; 12 Jan 1737/8; sons William, Joseph; daus. Elizabeth Boyd, Jane Ward, Magdalen Locker, Mary Swearingan, Francis Whittner, Anne Norris; granddau. Francis Boyd; grandsons William & John [ss/o Joseph]; tracts *Charles and Thomas, Beal's Hunting Quarter* (MCW VII.236); 18 May 1738 (I 23.178)

Ray, John; wife Sarah; children: John, b. 23 Jun 1732; Elizabeth, b. 20 Jan 1734; Sarah, b. 7 Oct 1735; Mary, b. 20 Nov 1737; Benjamin, b. 7 Nov 1739; William, b. 19 Sep 1741; Phillis, b. 8 Aug 1743; James, b. 12 Jun 1745; Lucy, b. 28 Jun 1747; Anne, b. 4 Nov 1749; Samuel, b. 5 May 1753; Josias, b. 4 Jan 1757 (PGP p. 255, 256)

Ray, William; widow Elizabeth Warner; heirs William Jr., Samuel; 29 Nov 1733 (GB 62)

Ray, George; admx. Susanna; [children under age]; 11 Jun 1735 (I 20.452); admx. Susanna; son George; 30 Jan 1738 (AA 16.181)

Ray, William; granddau. Priscilla Perree; 7 Apr 1735 (PGLR T.260)

Ray, William; son John; tract *Turkey Thickett*; 23 Mar 1736/7 (PGLR T.449)

Ray, Joseph; wife Alice; will of Mary Duvall; 1739 (MCW VIII.95)

Ray, James; b. 1 Oct 1725; bound out; Mar 1739 (PGCR X.277)

Ray, William; wife Sarah; child: Nathaniel, b. 24 May 1753 (PGP p. 256)

Ray, David; age 5 months on 4 Jul next; bound to Francis Early to age 21; Jun 1753 (PGCR MM.415)

Ray, Luke; wife Elisebeth; children: Elisabeth, b. 7 Sep 1759; Milley, b. 1 May 1761; Sarah, b. 25 Feb 1763; Rignal, b. 9 Jan 1765 (PGP p. 257, 260, 268, 273)

Ray, William; wife Mary; child: George, b. 19 Nov 1759 (PGP p. 281)

Ray, Sarah; child: Elisabeth, b. 22 Apr 1759 (PGP p. 257)

Ray, John; wife Mary; children: Racheal, 10 Nov 1760; Darcas, b. 9 Jan 1766 (PGP p. 255, 260)

Ray, Benjamin; wife Elizabeth; child: Elliner, b. 31 May 1765 (PGP p. 274)

Ray, Sarah; son Thomas; 1768 (MCW XIV.59)

RAYLEY

Rayley, Tarence; admx. Mary; 2 Apr 1745 (AA 21.214)

READ

Read, Charles; planter; 19 Mar 1713 (I&A 35a.297)

Read, Richard, Capt.; son Richard; 24 Feb 1730 (I 17.498); Richard, Capt.; unadministered by Mary; 18 Oct 1734 (AA 12.493)

Read, Mary; 9 May 1732; 29 Nov 1732; sons Richard, Joseph More; tract *Mare and Colt* (MCW VII.2); 3 Nov 1733 (I 18.132); only heir of age in MD son Richard; 26 Aug 1736 (AA 15.184)

Read, John; age ca 50; 16 Jul 1734 (PGLR T.154); age ca 50; 17 Apr 1739 (PGLR Y.58)

Read, James; 5 Mar 1735 (I 21.267); heirs ?[GB]; 11 Apr 1737 (AA 15.303); heirs unknown; 24 Jul 1740 (AA 18.24)

Read, Elizabeth; age ca 40; Nov 1740 (PGLR Y.235)

Read, John; 27 Apr 1741 (I 26.353); adms. Robert Ridle & his wife Frances; 9 May 1744 (AA 20.241)

Reed, John; wife Elizabeth; tract *Reed's Delight*; 5 Feb 1743 (PGLR Y.647)

READY

Ready, John; wife Ester; child: Daniel, bapt. 19 Jun 1763 at Lower Chapel; Eleanor, bapt. 6 Oct 1765 Lower Chapel (KGP p. 335, 351)

REALY

Realy, Phillip; 24 Feb 1726 (I 11.914)

REASLING

Reasling, Mathias; 25 Mar 1747; 13 Jun 1747; wife Barbara; son John; dau. Rachel (MCW IX.113); 11 May 1748 (I 35.519)

REAVES

Reaves [Reeves], John; wife Ellinor; children: Ellinor, b. 1 Mar 1708; John, b. 19 Jun 1710; Thomas, b. 29 May 1713 (QAP b/6, 9)

Reaves, John; planter; 2 Apr 1718; 5 Apr 1718; dau. Ellinor, not yet 16; 3 sons John, Thomas and Daniel, not yet 18 (MCW IV.141); 23 Apr 1718 (I 2.238); 10 Oct 1719 (AA 2.360); 4 Jul 1720 (AA 3.55b)

Reaves, Thomas; 5 Dec 1729 (I 16.12)

Reeves, William; wife Ann; children: Josias, 15 Feb 1757; Elizabeth, b. 22 Oct 1759 (KGP p. 318)

REDDING

Redden [Reden, Redding], John; wife Ruth; children: John, bapt. 10 Apr 1768 Upper Chapel; Harriat, b. 21 Nov 1772 Broad Creek; Katherine, b. 14 Jan 1775 Broad Creek (KGP p. 370, 378, 386)

REDMAN

Redman, John; wife Sarah; children: Francis (m), bapt. 19 Jul 1752; Joseph, b. 6 Jun 1755; Charles, b. 24 May 1757, Jesey King, b. 31 Oct 1760; Lewey, b. 12 Aug 1763 Lower Chapel (KGP p. 297, 308, 350)

Redman, John; wife Clo; child: Charles King, b. 7 Aug 1774 Broad Creek (KGP p. 386)

Redman, John; admx. Sarah; 4 Feb 1777 (I 125.353)

REGLEY

Regley, Samuell; 17 Jan 1712 (I&A 33b.156)

RENOLDS

Renolds, Charles; wife Ann; child: Nathan Orme, bapt. 17 Sep 1766 Broad Creek (KGP p. 359)

RENSHAW

Renshaw, William; wife Ann [widow of Thomas Fletchall]; tract *Fletchall's Garden*; 19 May 1718 (PGLR F.76/620)

Renshaw [Rainshaw], William; 14 Jan 1741/2; 12 May 1742; wife Anne; tracts *Cuckold's Delight* (MCW VIII.234); 2 Sep 1742 (I 27.264); 25 Nov 1743 (AA 20.61)

RESENER

Resener, Michael; wife Catherine; tract *Cattail Marsh*; 13 Mar 1741 (PGLR Y.446)

RESTING

Resting, Elizabeth; child: Ann, b. 4 Mar 1714 (QAP b/11)

Resting, Edward; m. 18 Mar 1715/6 Mary Chaffey (QAP m/1)

Reston, Edward; age ca 42; 22 Apr 1736 (CCR-MSA 6.161); age ca 46; 17 Apr 1740 (PGLR Y.176)

REYNER

Reyner, James; age 13 mos.; s/o Sarah Reyner; bound out; Aug 1730 PGCR P.454)

RHODES

Roads, Nicholas; extx. Alice Williams [w/o John]; 2 Feb 1712 (I&A 33b.173)

Rhodes, Richard [dec'd]; son Nicholas; 27 Apr 1712 (PGLR F.181)

Rhodes, Nicholas; son John [wife Elizabeth]; tract *Beall's Pasture*; 28 Mar 1723 (PGLR I.396)

Rhodes, John; admx. Elisabeth; 16 Nov 1734 (I 20.384); admx. Elisabeth; 24 Jun 1735 (AA 13.266); widow Elizabeth; heirs Nicholas, John, Mary, Elizabeth, Anne; 24 Aug 1736 (GB 80)

RICE

Rice, Roger; wife Susanna; child: Roger, b. 14 Aug 1708 (QAP b/7)

Rice, Hugh; wife Sarah; bro. James; tract *Brightwell's Hunting Quarter*; 2 Feb 1742 (PGLR Y.602)

Rice, George; wife Sarah; children: George, b. 1 Oct 1763; Joseph, b. 28 Nov 1765 (PGP p. 271, 277)

RICH

Rich, Eliza; 7 Mar 1726 (I 11.782)

RICHARDS

Richards, Samuel; planter; 9 Dec 1752; 18 Dec 1752; wife Mary; sons Samuel, John, George Prietter; daus. Mary, Sarah (MCW X.242); 27 Dec 1752 (I 52.95); extx. Mary Seaborn [w/o Edward]; 20 Dec 1753 (AA 36.7)

RICHARDSON

Richardson, Richard [AA]; wife Anne; tract *Bear Bacon*; 26 Mar 1739 (PGLR Y.158)

Richardson, Susanna; 2 Feb 1764 (I 82.254); 11 May 1768; admn. Henry Howard (ABB 5.97)

Richardson, Thomas; 5 Mar 1758; 15 May 1758; wife Susannah; dau. Mary Culver; son Thomas; granddau. Susannah Culver [d/o Henry]; tracts *Rachel's Hope* (MCW XI.213); extx. Susannah; 6 Jun 1758 (I 65.493); 24 Aug 1759; legatees Thomas, Mary; acting ex. Susanna Richardson (ABB 4.21)

RICKETTS

Ricketts, Thomas; wife Rebecca; children: Thomas, b. 20 Mar 1703; John, b. 11 Jul 1705; Edward, b. 15 7ber 1706; Benjamin, b. 7 May 1708; Rebecca, b. 17 Aug 1712; Richard, b. 28 Jan 1714/5; Margaret, b. 27 Feb 1716; Susanna, b. 15 Apr 1720; Nicholson, b. 15 May 1721 (QAP b/2, 3. 8. 10, 12, 15, 17)

Ricketts, Thomas [AA]; wife Sarah; tract *Ridgly & Tyler's Chance*; 24 Feb 1706 (PGLR C.183a)

Ricketts, Anthony; wife Mary; child: Anthony, b. 9 Feb 1760 (PGP p. 281)

Ricketts, William; wife Sarah; child: Basil, b. 31 Mar 1761 (PGP p. 261)

Richetts, William; wife Drusillah; child: Edward, b. 21 Mar 1762 (PGP p. 263)

Richett, Merchant; wife Martha; child: Elizabeth, b. 11 Aug 1765 (PGP p. 274)

RIDDLE

Riddle, John; wife Elizabeth; children: John, b. 25 Jul 1708; George, b. 10 7ber 1710 (QAP b/3, 5)

Riddell, John; son George; 1718 (MCW IV.141)

Riddle, John; wife Margaret; child: Elizabeth, b. 13 10ber 1721 (QAP b/16)

Riddle, John, Jr.; m. 9 Feb 1729 Elizabeth Lentall; children: John, b. 16 Nov 1734; George, b. ___ Jan ____; Samuel, b. ____; ____, b. 15 Aug 1739; ____, b. 10 Dec 1740; Basil, b. ____ 36; Jeremiah, b. ____; Elizabeth, b. ____; ___nah (f), b. ____ (QAP m/5; b/28, 30, 31, 32, 36, 37)

Riddle, John; m. 31 May 1735 Eleanor Lee (QAP m/6)

Riddle, John; d-i-l Rachel Lee; s-i-l Aaron Lee; [?step-children]; 19 Nov 1737 (PGLR T.552, 553)

Rydle, John; age ca 70; 26 Nov 1739 (PGLR Y.107)

Riddle, John; 19 Aug 1745; 20 May 1746; wife Elenor; son John; dau. Elizabeth Linten (MCW IX.71)

Riddle, Samuel; wife Sarah; child: Linney, bapt. _ Sep 1763 at Upper Chapel (KGP p. 334)

Riddle, Jacob; wife Sarah; children: Jacob, b. 26 May 1764, bapt. 5 Aug 1764 Upper Chapel; Elizabeth Lunn, bapt. 31 May 1767 Upper Chapel (KGP p. 341, 365)

Riddle, Andrew; wife Jane; child: Andrew, bapt. 27 May 1764 Upper Chapel (KGP p. 341)

Riddle, Mary; child: Charles Duvall, b. 13 Mar 1765 (QAP b/39)

Riddle, Francis; daus. Sarah, Susannah; 1768 (MCW XIV.63)

Riddle, Samuel; 15 Oct 1773 (I 114.50)

RIDGEWAY

Ridgeway, John; children: Robert, b. 25 Mar 1713; Elizabeth, b. 9 Oct 1714; John, b. 1 Sep 1716; Jonathan, b. 23 Mar 1717; Rebacca, b. 5 Feb 1721 (KGP p. 279)

Ridgway, John; wife Elizabeth; child: Jonathan, b. 16 Mar 1717 (QAP b/13)

Ridgeway, John; wife Elizabeth; tract Clarkson's Purchase; 12 Jul 1718 (PGLR F.125/690)

Ridgeway, John; son Roger; 10 Sep 1733 (PGLR Q.690)

Rigway, William; wife Sarah; child: Mary Ann, bapt. 15 Nov 1767 Upper Chapel (KGP p. 366)

Ridgeway, Robert; wife Martha; children: Jesse, b. 3 Nov 1772 Upper Chapel; Mary, b. 9 Jul 1774 Upper Chapel; Zachariah, b. 5 Jan 1776 Upper Chapel (KGP p. 389, 391, 392)

Ridgeway, Richard; wife Charity; children: Mordeca (m), b. 5 Oct 1772 Broad Creek; James, b. 29 Nov 1774 Broad Creek (KGP p. 382, 386)

RIDGLEY

Ridgely, Charles; heir of Robert, dec'd; tracts *Timberly*, *Generals Guift*; Nov 1698 (PGLR A.291, 292)

Ridgley, Charles [AA]; wife Deborah; tract *Croome*; 20 Apr 1701 (PGLR C.54)

Ridgley, Charles; 29 Jun 1705 (I&A 3.703); admx. Deborah; [d/o Capt. John Dorsey]; 4 Oct 1705 (I&A 25.48)

Ridgely, Henry, merchant; 30 Apr 1705; 13 Jul 1710; wife Mary; unborn child; son Charles; bro. Wm. Ridgley; dau. Sarah [w/o Thomas Odall]; grandsons Henry & Nicholas Ridgley [ss/o Henry], Henry Ridgley [s/o Charles], Henry & Thomas Odall; tracts *Catton*, *Larkin's Forrest*, *Mary's Delight*; *Hogg Neck*, *Waldridge*, *Ridgeley's Lot* at Huntington, Anne Arundel Co. (MCW III.175-6); [as Henry, Col.]; 16 Oct 1710 (I&A 32a.68) [with 1712] (I&A 33b.187)

Ridgley, Henry, Col. [dec'd]; grandsons John Brewer [wife Dinah], Joseph Brewer, Thomas Odell, Jr.; tract *Mary's Delight*; 30 Nov 1715 (PGLR F.503)

Ridgley, Henry, Col. [dec'd]; grandson Henry Ridgley; tract *Enfield's Chase*; 13 Mar 1717 (PGLR F.34/560)

Ridgley, Westal; wife Sarah; child: William, b. __ ___ 17__ (QAP b/29)

RIGBY

Rigby, Mary; son. Thomas; 1744 (MCW X.109)

Rigby, Thomas; age 8 years; guardians Henry Wilsford and wife Mary; Nov 1750 (PGCR LL.244)

RIGDON

Rigden, John; 16 Dec 1706; 3 Feb 1706; son John [b. 6 Apr 1701]; dau. Elizabeth [b. ca last of Aug 1699]; tracts *Gromes Lott*, *Ladd's Designe* (MCW III.87); 17 Dec 1707 (I&A 28.3); 17 Nov [with 1709] (I&A 30.222); 9 Aug 1712 (I&A 33b.35, 76)n; 2 Aug 1717 (I&A 38a.38)

RIGGS

Riggs, James, Sr.; 21 Aug 1744; 4 Mar 1744; wife Elizabeth; sons James, John, Edmond; daus. Sarah Riggs, Jane Cramphin (MCW IX.14); extx. Elisabeth; 22 Apr 1745 (I 31.199); extx. Elisabeth; 29 Jan 1746 (AA 23.41)

Riggs, Edward [Edmond]; wife Ruth; children: John Summers, b. 5 Oct 1760; Samuell, b. 20 Jan 1765 (PGP p. 259, 273)

RIGHT

Right, Philbert; m. 3 10ber 1712 Ester Bycraft; children: Ann, b. 11 8ber 1713; Peter, b. 31 Mar 1717; Philibert, b. 4 7ber 1719; Rebecca, b. 1722 (QAP m/1; b/9, 12, 25, 27)

Right, Thomas; wife Elizabeth; child: Thomas, b. 6 Apr 1773 Broad Creek (KGP p. 378)

RILEY

Riley, Hugh; wife Mary; tract *Second Lott*, part of *The Beginning* and *Rileys Folly*; also *First Late*; 28 May 1698 (PGLR A.115, 117)

Ryley, Samuel; wife Elizabeth; child: Margaret, b. 24 Nov 1706 (QAP b/2)

Ryler [Riley], Hugh; age ca 60; 10 Aug 1710 (CCR PC.844); age ca 61; 14 Jun 1714 (CCR CL.27); age ca 63; 12 Apr 1716 (CCR CL.285); age ca 66; 8 Dec 1719 (CCR CL.550)

Reyley, Samuell; 12 Apr 1712 (I&A 33b.202)

Ryley, Hugh; wife Rebecca; tract *Ryley's Range*; 20 Dec 1712 (PGLR F.219)

Ryley, Eliphar; wife Elizabeth; child: Ellinor, b. 5 Jan 1714/5 (QAP b/10)

Ryley, Hugh; dau. Elizabeth Chapplin [w/o William]; tract *Ryley's Gift*; [undated, with 1716] (PGLR F.579)

Reley, Phillip; 2 bros. on my mother's side Mason Pigman, David Cole; 15 Jan 1727 (AA 8.514, 515); heirs Mason & David Cole; 26 Jun 1729 (GB 49)

Reily, Bryan [Bryant]; 21 Jun 1734; [no relations] (MCW VII.92); admx. Mary; 27 Sep 1734 (I 20.38); [as Benjamin]; extx. Mary; heirs none; 24 Jun 1735 (AA 13.262); extx. Mary; 7 Oct 1737 (AA 14.467); 22 Aug 1738 (AA 16.348); admx. Mrs. Bryant Reyley; 22 Aug 1738 (I 23.366); widow Mary Reily; heirs Robert Daves Cook, Lawrence Debutts, Anne Cooke, Alice Cook, William Rawlings; 28 Nov 1739 (GB 106)

Riley, Mary; age ca 58; Nov 1740 (PGLR Y.235)

Riley, Eliphaz; age ca 54; 1743 (PGLR Y.701)

Reyley, Terence; admx. Mary; 1 Nov 1744 (I 30.214)

Riley, John; wife Elizabeth; child: William, b. 20 Dec 1745 (PGP p. 252)

Rhily, Rebecca; 24 Sep 1747; 21 Jan 1747/8; sons Hugh, Pharo; daus. Elizabeth, Hannah (MCW IX.138); _ Jun 1748 (I 36.80)

Riley, Ninian; wife Elizabeth; children: Rachel, b. 31 Dec 1750; Ann, b. 8 Feb 1760; Ninian, b. 10 Apr 1762 (PGP p. 253, 2632, 281)

Riley, Eliphaz, member of the Protestant Reformed Church of England; 8 Dec 1759; 30 May 1760; children: Mary Douglas, Rachel, Ann, John,

Jeremiah; s-i-l Capt. Robert Douglas; grandchildren: James Riley [s/o Jeremiah], James Riley [s/o John]; tract *Hop-Yard* (MCW XII.230)

Riley, Hugh; wife Sarah; children: Elliner, b. 3 Jun 1761; James, b. 8 Jun 1763 (PGP p. 261, 268)

Riley, Jeremiah; wife Tabathia; child: Jeremiah, b. 14 Sep 1761 (PGP p. 262)

Reyley [Rayley], Mary; 22 Nov 1748; 27 Aug 1763; sons John Johnson, Robert Dove Cook; daus. Ann Hugoe, Elizabeth Piles [w/o Leonard], Else Estep [w/o Philemon]; grandsons William Johnson Rawlings, William Hugoe; granddaus. Ann Hugoe, Mary Rawlings (MCW XII.212), Mary; widow; 21 Nov 1763 (I 82.147)

Riley, ____; wife Sarah; child: Esther, b. 26 Jul 1765 (PGP p. 274)

RINE

Rine, Darby; admx. Ann Orchard [w/o John]; 27 Sep 1734 (AA 12.624); heirs William, John, James, Joseph, Nathaniel; 28 Jun 1736 (GB 77)

Rine, John; wife Mary; child: Elizabeth, b. 20 Sep 1765 (PGP p. 277)

RISTON

Riston, Edward; age 3 years; s/o Abigall Clifford; bound out; Jun 1697 (PGCR A.170)

Riston, Edward; wife Mary; tract *Crayfield's Delight*; 28 Nov 1739 (PGLR Y.114)

Ristow, Edward; age ca 35; 18 Mar 1728/9 (PGLR M.480)

ROACH

Roach, Richard; wife Deborah; children: Mac Micajah, b. 22 Mar 1712; Mary, b. 8 8ber 1714; Katherine, b. 23 8ber 1716; Richard, b. 2 Apr 1719 (QAP b/9, 10, 15)

ROBERTS

Roberts, John; m. 9 Jan 1734 Ann Swift (QAP m/6)

Roberts, Elizabeth; age 2 yrs. & 3 mos. 25 Mar inst.; bound out; Mar 1735 (PGCR V.302)

Roberts, Reuben; wife Elizabeth; tract *Ryley's Lott*; 15 Apr 1740 (PGLR Y.164)

Roberts, Aaron; age ca 47; 1737 (PGLR T.504); age ca 50; 24 Aug 1741 (PGLR Y.360)

Roberts, Aaron; 22 Dec 1743; 23 Jan 1743/4; wife Ann; dau. Anne Smith [w/o Abraham]; granddaus. Anne & Margaret Cunningham; tracts *Aaron's Deprieve* (MCW VIII.244)

Roberts, Reuben; admx. Elisabeth; 10 Feb 1749 (I 41.374); admx. Elisabeth [widow]; 7 Apr 1752 (AA 32.96)

Roberts, Robert; child: Elizabeth, bapt. 18 Apr 1762 (KGP p. 326)

Roberts, Billingly; wife Margreet; child: Elliner, b. 9 Aug 1765 (PGP p. 277)

Roberts, Sushanna; child: Henry Evans, bapt. 30 Mar 1766 Broad Creek (KGP p. 353)

ROBEY

Robey, Thomas; wife Dorathey_; child: Velinder, b. 7 Dec 1761 (KGP p. 324)

Robey, Pryer; wife Susannah; child: Ann, b. 21 Jul 1764 (PGP p. 176)

Robey, Ignatious; wife Willallamina; child: Loyd, b. 3 Jan 1766 (PGP p. 278)

ROBINCE

Robince, Henry; extx. Margrett Queen; w/o John [accountants are very aged]; 25 Apr 1713 (I&A 34.207); extx. Margrett Queen [w/o John]; 26 Dec 1713 (I&A 35a.5); exs. John Queen & wife Margaret; 2 Sep 1715 (I&A 36c.43)

ROBINS

Robins, Henry; 20 Feb 1710/1; 2 Apr 1712; wife [unnamed]; sons Henry, James, Thomas; daus. Margrett, Mary; tracts *Harner's Pie Patch, Robin's Delight* (MCW III.219); extx. Margrett Robins; 23 Jun 1712 (I&A 33b.3)

Robins, Henry; 29 Jul 1717; 5 Oct 1717; sister Margaret; bro. James (MCW IV.113)

Robins, Thomas, carpenter; 22 Feb 1718; 4 Apr 1719; wife [unnamed]; dau. Elizabeth; bro. James (MCW IV.205); 18 Jan 1720 (AA 3.216)

Robins, John [age 9] and William [age 8]; bound out; Nov 1719 (PGCR H.929)

Robins, William, wife Anne; child: Thomas, b. 27 May 1740 (KGP p. 288)

Robins, William; admx. Anne; 12 Aug 1755 (I 59.170)

ROBINSON

Robson, Richard; wife Martha; children: Mathew, b. 6 Mar 1702; Ann, b. 28 Apr 1704; Richard, b. 14 9ber 1708 (QAP b/5)

Robinson, John; 21 Jul 1703 (I&A 24.4); widow Ann Jones; [with 1703-4] (I&A 3.73)

Robinson, Andrew; 11 Aug 1708; 2 Oct 1709; wife Katharine; sons Charles [b. 11 Jan 1699], Andrew (b. May 1704) (MCW III.156)

Robinson, William; age ca 11; servant; Jun 1710 (PGCR D.316a)

Robeson, Andrew; wife Catherine; children: Charles, Andrew; bound out; Aug 1711 Ct. (PGCR G.78)

Robinson, James; wife Solyma; 24 Mar 1713/4 (PGLR F.388)

Robinson, James; 21 Jan 1716 (I&A 38a.13); widow & 1 sis. [England] [unnamed]; adms. John Docwra and wife Salome; 15 Nov 1720 (AA 3.160)

Robson, Richard; wife Elizabeth; children: John, b. 5 7ber 1712; Mary, b. 26 Aug 1714 (QAP b/6, 10)

Robinson, Richard; wife Elizabeth; child: William Robinson, b. 27 Jan 1716 (QAP b/12)

Robson, Richard; planter; 23 Oct 1716; 15 Dec 1716; wife Eliza.; 4 children: Mathew, Richard, John, Mary (MCW IV.62); wife [unnamed]; 4 children [unnamed]; 16 Oct 1717 (I&A 39c.123)

Robinson, Robert; 24 Dec 1716 (I&A 38a.31)

Roberson, James; admx. Solome Dockerry [w/o John]; 11 Nov 1717 (I&A 37b.208)

Robenson, Andrew; s/o Catherine; bound out; Mar 1721 (PGCR K.102)

Robinson, John; m. Jun 1721 Hester Maclenane; [widow of Brice] (KGP p. 269)

Robinson, Charles; m. 26 May 1728 Ann Gentle; children: Charity, b. 5 Mar 1728; Charles, b. 15 Apr 1731; James, b. 6 Jul 1733; Catherine, b. 6 Nov 1735; Elenor, b. 20 Jun 1738; Mary, b. 5 Dec 1740 (KGP p. 280, 287)

Robinson, Peter; m. Dec 1740 Anne Athey; children: Elizabeth, b. 13 Apr 1741; James, b. 5 Jul 1742 (KGP p. 287)

Robetson, Mathew; age ca 38; 28 Mar 1741 (PGLR Y.267)

Robinson, James, Sr.; child: Thomas Sedgwick, b. 22 Sep 1747 (KGP p. 292)

Robinson, Robert; admx. Rachel; 26 Mar 1753 (I 54.148)

Robinson, James, Jr.; wife Mary; child: Virlinder, b. 10 Apr 1753 (KGP p. 300)

Robinson, Isaac; wife Elizabeth; children: Elinor, b. 9 or 10 Dec 1753; John, b. 30 Oct 1756; Leonard, b. 17 Feb 1759 (KGP p. 304, 322)

Robinson, Charles; wife Ann; child: Charity, b. 23 May 1754 (KGP p. 306)

Robinson, James; wife Mary; children: Elizabeth Lewin, b. 23 Jan 1756; Mary, b. 4 Feb 1759; Sarah, b. 22 Aug 1761; bapt. 18 Oct 1761 (KGP p. 312, 321, 323)

Robinson, John; wife Penalopey; children: William Foord, b. 26 Oct 1756; James, b. 27 Aug 1762 (KGP p. 314, 328)

Robertson, James; admx. Sarah; 4 May 1759 (I 67.108)

Robinson, Robert; wife Rachell; children: Zachariah, bapt. 6 Jun 1762; Mary, b. 6 Aug 1764 Upper Chapel (KGP p. 330, 341)

Roberson, Joseph; wife Elizabeth; child: Arthur, b. 31 Aug 1764 (PGP p. 274)

Robinson, Isaac; child: James, bapt. 30 Jan 1763 at Lower Chapel (KGP p. 334)

Robinson, Charles; admx. Sarah; 19 Oct 1763 (I 89.315)

Roberson, Sarah; widow; 17 Apr 1765 (I 90.135)

Robinson, Benjamin; wife Priscilla; child: William, bapt. 30 Jun 1765 Broad Creek; Henry, b. 20 Jul 1772 Upper Chapel; Sarah Elizabeth Ford, b. 2 Mar 1775 Broad Creek (KGP p. 347, 387, 389)

Robinson, Charles; 22 Mar 1767; admx. Ann Robinson (ABB 5.21)s; heirs Charles, James, Catherine, Eleanor, Mary, John, Keziah, Andrew Greer, Charity; 23 Nov 1768 (GB 269)

Robinson, John; wife Druscilla; child: Elizabeth Johnson, b. 1 Apr 1772 Lower Chapel (KGP p. 383)

Robinson, Nathan; wife Elizabeth; child: Robert, b. 18 Aug 1772 Upper Chapel (KGP p. 389)

Robinson, James; wife Mary; children: Sarah, b. 18 Oct 1772 Upper Chapel; Rachel, b. 24 Feb 1774 Upper Chapel; Amelea, b. 22 Nov 1775 Upper Chapel (KGP p. 389, 390, 392)

Robinson, John Crown; wife Verlinder; children: Mary, b. 24 Oct 1772 Broad Creek; Arther Samuel, b. 18 Feb 1775 Broad Creek (KGP p. 378, 386)

Robinson, Basil; wife Patty; child: Nancy, b. 9 Mar 1773 Upper Chapel (KGP p. 389)

Robinson, Basil; wife Martha; children: Elizabeth, b. 20 Sep 1774 Upper Chapel; William Calvert, b. 9 Jan 1776 Broad Creek (KGP p. 382, 91)

RODRY

Roddery, Sarah [AA]; widow or spinster; 9 Sep 1699 (PGLR A.179)

Rodry, Sarah; 29 Jun 1714 (I&A 36a.145)

Rodry, John; wife Mary; children: Elizabeth, b. 10 10ber 1712; John, b. 7 Dec 1714; Sarah, b. 19 Jan 1716; Solomon, b. 12 Mar 1720/1 (QAP b/7, 10, 12, 16)

ROE

Roe, William; admx. Elisabeth; 21 Aug 1735 (I 21.263); admx. Elisabeth; heirs ?GB; 25 May 1736 (AA 14.259)

ROGERS

Rodgers, Matthew; age ca 14; servant; Mar 1700 Ct. (PGCR B.26)

Rogers, Elizabeth; age 5 weeks; bound out to John Brent and wife Elizabeth; Jun 1717 (PGCR H.240)

Rogers, Mary [2-1/2 yrs] and William [age 8 years; bound out; Jun 1717 (PGCR H.241)

Rogers, Hugh; m. 9 Jun 1720 Jane Anderson (QAP m/2)

Rogers, John; wife Joan; tract Three Beale's Manor; 29 Jan 1727 (PGLR M.254)

Rogers, John; 10 Feb 1735; 5 May 1740; wife Joan; sons John, Samuel; dau. Agness tracts Rogers Chance, John and Joans Choice (MCW VIII.75); John, Sr.; 15 Dec 1740 (I 25.318); John, Sr.; widow [unnamed] & 3 children Agnes [w/o John Williams], John, Samuel; exs. Joan & Samuel [accountant]; 29 Jun 1741 (AA 18.228)

Rogers, John; 19 Apr 1740; 22 May 1740; wife Dorothy; dau. Lucy (MCW VIII.82); John, Jr.; extx. Dorothy Pelt [?Belt]; 1 Sep 1740 (I 28.30, 31); John, Jr.; extx. Dorothy Belt [w/o Higginson]; 22 Aug 1743 (AA 19.450); heir Lucy; 27 Jun 1744 (GB 131)

Rogers, Nicholas; wife Margret; children: Abraham, b. 18 Oct 1760; Prudence, b. 3 Sep 1762; Mary, b. 20 Oct 1764 (PGP p. 275)

ROLLINGS

Rollings, Richard; wife Mary; 15 May 1725 (PGLR I.625)

Rollings, Paul. Sr.; age ca 71; 26 Jun 1734 (PGLR T.124)

ROOK

Rook, John; bastard child by Deborah Woodfield; Feb 1698/9 (PGCR A.385)

Rook, John; binds son Rooke Dance (?); age 1-1/2; Jun 1700 Ct. (PGCR B.55a)

Rook, John; age ca 47; 20 Oct 1711 (CCR PC.766)

Rooke, John; 16 Jan 1712 (I&A 33b.187); 7 Mar 1712 (I&A 33b.159); 20 Feb 1713 (I&A 35a.1)

Rook, John; wife Jane; mother Alice; tract *Gedling, Archer's Pasture*; 17 Aug 1720 (PGLR I.45)

Rook, John [NC]; wife Jane; s/o John Rook; 23 Sep 1725 (PGLR M.461)

ROSE

Rose, John [dec'd]; sons Francis, Samuel; 27 Mar 1716 (PGLR F.521)

Rose, Richard; 30 Apr 1716; 29 Jun 1717; [no relations]; tract *Rose's Purchase* (MCW IV.109); 8 Feb 1717 (I&A 39c.89); 2 Aug 1717 (I&A 37b.184)

Rose, Andrew; nok [an infant]; 11 May 1724 (I 10.356); [as Ross, Andrew]; 11 Jul 1726 (AA 7.446)

Rose, Thomas; wife Susan; children: William, b. 23 10ber 1724; Sarah, b. 25 Jan 1726/7 (QAP b/21)

Rose, Richard; 27 Mar 1754; extx. Eleanor Rose (ABB 1.113); extx. Elianor; 27 Mar 1754 (AA 36.292); widow Eleanor; heirs George, John; 26 Nov 1755 (GB 199)

ROSS

Ross, Alexander; age ca 15; servant; Nov 1696 (PGCR A.57)

Ross, Reuben; wife Elizabeth; children: Elizabeth, b. 24 Aug 1715; John, b. 19 10ber 1718; Thomas, b. 15 Jun 1721 (QAP b/11, 14, 17)

Ross, Reuben; carpenter; 12 Aug 1722; 21 Jan 1722; wife Elizabeth; daus. Mary, Elizabeth; sons, Reuben, John and Thomas; b-i-l Thomas Harwood (MCW V.120); 4 Mar 1722 (I 8.99); admx. Elisabeth; 25 Mar 1724 (AA 5.365); admx. Elisabeth; 9 Aug 1726 (AA 7.447)

ROTHERY

Rothery, William; wife Elizabeth; tract [unnamed]; 7 Mar 1710 (PGLR F.62)
Rothery, Sarah; 10 Nov 1714 (I&A 36a.174)

ROUGHT

Rought, William [CA]; dau. Ann Austin [w/o William]; formerly Ann
Walker; 1 Aug 1707 (PGLR C.210)

ROUSBEY

Rousbey, Christopher [England]; bro. William; "natural son" Charles
Butler; tract Croome; 6 May 1698 (PGLR A.112)

ROWE

Rowe, John; wife Christian; child: William, b. 18 July 1752, bapt. 16 Aug
1752 (KGP p. 293, 297)
Rowe, Eleanor; heirs George, John; 2 Dec 1761 (GB 217)
Row, Thomas; wife Elizabeth; child: Daniel, bapt. _ Mar 1765 Lower
Chapel (KGP p. 350)
Rowe, Anthony; wife Sarah; child: William, b. 15 Jun 1773 Lower Chapel
(KGP p. 384)

ROWLAND

Rowland [Roland], George; wife Rebecca; children: Gordon, bapt. 14 Jan
1753; Rhoderick, b. 13 Nov 1754; John, bapt. _ Sep 1763 at Lower
Chapel; Priscilla, bapt. 23 May 1766 Broad Creek (KGP p. 297, 307, 335, 348)
Rowling [Roland], Thomas; wife Ann; children: Priscilla, bapt. 23 May
1766 Broad Creek; Elizabeth Martin, bapt. 17 Apr 1768 Lower Chapel;
Robert, b. 1 Sep 1772 Lower Chapel; Rebeccah, b. 1 May 1774 Lower
Chapel (KGP p. 369, 379, 383)
Rowlings, Robert; wife Martha; child: Drucilla, b. 7 May 1773 Lower
Chapel (KGP p. 384)

ROYNE

Royne, James, Jr.; admx. Sarah; 5 Dec 1770 (I 106.164)

ROZER

Rozer, Notley; 6 Apr 1727; 5 Aug 1727; wife Elizabeth; son Henry; dau.
Ann; unborn child; tracts Admirathoree, Dunnington Manor (MCW VI.36);
admx. widow Elisabeth; 31 Aug 1727 (I 12.394); admx. Elisabeth; 28 May
1728 (I 13.153); ex. Elisabeth; heirs Catherine, Henry, Elisabeth [eldest age

ca 6]; 6 Sep 1728 (AA 9.68); extx. Elisabeth; 11 Oct 1732 (AA 11. 523); heirs Henry, Elizabeth; 28 Aug 1735 (GB 74)

Rozer, Anne; age ca 16; d/o Notley, dec'd; chooses guardian; Jun 1727 (PGCR N.350)

Rozer, Elizabeth; widow; 10 Oct 1732; 3 May 1733; daus. Catharine, Elizabeth; son Henry [Harry]; bro. Dr. John Whetenhall; mentions Mr. Rozer, dec'd (MCW VII.18); 21 Dec 1733 (I 17.722)

Rozer, Henry; dau. Mary; 1749/50 (MCW X.97)

RUDD
Rudd, Charles; 16 Nov 1752 (I 54.136)

RUDDERFORD
Rudderford, John; 28 May 1724 (I 10.92)

RUSSELL
Russell, Abraham; wife Ann; child: Elizabeth, b. 9 Apr 1776 Broad Creek (KGP p. 382)

RYAN
Ryan, James; widow Sarah; heir Cloritta; 24 Mar 1774 (GB 317)

RYNE
Ryne, Richard; motherless boy age 8 on 20 June last; bound to Joanna Edgar, widow; Aug 1724 (PGCR L.333)

SACKLAND
Sackland, Jeremiah; wife Eliner; child: Ruth, b. 29 Dec 1761 (PGP p. 262)

SAFFORNE
Safforne [Safforns], Mary; age 5 years; d/o James and Mary; bound out; Nov 1707 (PGCR C.180)

SALTER
Salter, Thomas; wife Margaret; child: Thomas, b. 30 Sep 1775 Upper Chapel (KGP p. 392)

SALTERMETE
Saltermete [Saltemet], John; 28 Nov 1699; 6 Nov 1700; wife Margaret; her children: Samuel, Joseph and Hannah Copeling (MCW II.214); extx. Margret; 22 Nov 1701 (I&A 21.155)

SANDERS
Sanders, Mary, spinster; 2 Mar 1723/4; 23 Mar 1723; dau. Diana; husband [not named] (MCW V.163)
Sanders, Mathew; age ca 60; 6 Jun 1735 (PGLR T.280)

SANKEY
Sankey, Thomas; m. 21 May 1723 Martha Marshall (QAP m/3)

SANSBURY
Sandsbury, Francis; age ca 70; in Maryland almost 53 years; 9 Jul 1731 (PGLR Q.522)
Sansbury, Richard; 21 Dec 1752; 28 Mar 1753; wife Sarah; sons Gabriel, William, Francis, Richard, John, Thomas; daus. Lettice, Ann Dew, Ruth (MCW X.255); extx. Sarah Michall [w/o John]; 14 Apr 1753 (I 55.103); extx. Sarah Mitchall [w/o John]; 27 Mar 1754 (AA 36.288); 27 Mar 1754; extx. Sarah Mitchell [w/o John] (ABB 1.112); heirs Gabriel, Anne, William, Ruth, Francis, Richard, John, Violetta, Thomas; 6 Dec 1755 (GB 201)
Sansbury, John; wife Eleanor; child: Arnold Middleton, b. 21 Feb 1776 Broad Creek (KGP p. 382)

SAPCOTT
Sapcott, Elizabeth; had mulatto bastard child; Aug 1698 Ct. (PGCR A.339)

SARGANT
Sargant, William; wife Sarah; child: Mary, b. 30 Jul 1765 (PGP p. 277)

SASSER

Sasser, John, Jr.; wife Christian [late Chrisian Gibbons]; tract *Barton's Hope*; 6 Jan 1731 (PGLR Q.405)

Sasser, William; admx. Elisabeth; 7 Feb 1735 (I 21.27)

Sasser, Roger John; age ca 67; 1738 (PGLR T.604)

Sasser, Roger John; 7 May 1751; 25 Mar 1752; wife Elizabeth; child John [wife Christian]; grandsons William, Roger John; tracts *Little Grove, Smith's Pasture, Long Look* (MCW X.208); widow Elisabeth; 14 May 1752 (I 51.17); extx. Elisabeth; 7 Sep 1753 (AA 35.166)

Sasser, Roger John; 26 May 1770 (I 104.263)

SAUSBURG

Sausburg, Francis; age ca 75; 6 Aug 1735 (PGLR T.359)

SAVAGE

Savage, John; wife Rachel; child: James Morris, bapt. 28 Dec 1766 Lower Chapel (KGP p. 367)

SAWYER

Sawyers, Humphrey; planter; [no relations] (MCW VIII.2); 13 Nov 1738 (I 24.93)

SCAGGS

Scaggs, Aaron; m. Susanna; children: Charles, b. 9 10ber 1709; Moses, b. 10 Jul 1714; Susanna, b. 11 Aug 1716 (QAP b/11, 12)

Scaggs, Richard; m. Dec 1727 Mary Brushier; children: Thomas, b. 22 8ber 1728; Susanna, b. 21 Oct 1730 (QAP m/4; b/21, 24)

SCAINS

Scains, Christopher; heirs [England]; 16 Dec 1727 (AA 8.512)

SCAMPER

Scamper [Scamport, Scampord], Peter; 27 Feb 1715; 15 Mar 1715/6; wife Jane (MCW IV.41); 17 Apr 1716 (I&A 36c.184); extx. Jane [dec'd]; 22 Apr 1716 (I&A 37a.121, 125)

Scamper [Scamport], Jane; 1 Mar 1715; 15 Mar 1715/6 (MCW IV.41)

SCANDELL

Scandell, Ann; age ca 48; 1 Jul 1726 (PGLR M.28)

Scandell, Michael; age ca 30; 1 Jul 1726 (PGLR M.28)

SCHOMATER

Schomater, Conrad; wife Susana; child: Elizabeth, b. 22 Feb 1736 (QAP b/30)

SCOTT

Scott, Thomas; wife Elizabeth; child: Mary, b. 4 9ber 1698 [or 1699] (QAP b/2)

Scott, Elizabeth; widow; dau. Mary; Sep 1699 Ct (PGCR A.469)

Scott, William; wife Mary; children: Thomas, b. 14 Feb 1702; William, b. 10 Dec 1704 (QAP b/1)

Scott, Thomas; age ca 26; 15 Jul 1729 (PGLR M.487)

Scott, William; age ca 57; 15 Jul 1729 (PGLR M.487)

Scott, Thomas; admx. Elisabeth; 6 Nov 1739 (I 24.295)

Scott, Andrew; wife Mary; tract *Bacon Hall*; 10 Apr 1741 (PGLR Y.264)

Scott, Charles; heirs John Griffith, William Lyle; 3 Dec 1745 (GB 148)

Scott, Andrew; heir [?Lord Proprietary]; 26 Jun 1746 (GB 149)

Scott, William; 25 Feb 1749/50; 25 Aug 1752; wife Mary; sons Henry, Zachariah; daus. Henereta Shaw, Rachel, Ruth Hamilton; granddau. Ruth Hamilton (MCW X.233-4); admx. Mary; 25 Mar 1752 (I 48.381); extx. Mary; 27 Mar 1753 (AA 34.51); 27 Mar 1753; extx. Mary Scott (ABB I.63); widow Mary; heirs Henry Scott, Zachariah Scott, Henrietta Shaw, John Jenkins, Ruth Hamilton; 29 Aug 1753 (GB 186)

Scott, Henry; wife Mary; children: Rachel, b. 26 Mar 1755; Amma (f), b. 1759 (KGP p. 308, 318)

Scott, John; wife Mary; children: Elenor, bapt. 4 Jul 1762; Zachariah, b. 14 Jan 1763 at Broad Creek; Sushanna, bapt. 24 Nov 1765 Broad Creek (KGP p. 331, 338, 350)

Scott, Zachariah; wife Elizabeth; children: Thomas, b. 17 Jul 1763; Elizabeth, b. 25 Sep 1764 Broad Creek; James Wood, bapt. 16 Sep 1766 Broad Creek; William, bapt. 15 May 1768 Broad Creek; Henry, b. Nov 1771 Broad Creek; Quila Ann, b. 17 Feb 1774 Broad Creek (KGP p. 342, 359, 362, 377, 385)

Scott, John; children: Sarah, b. 2 Feb 1764, bapt. 4 Mar 1764 Broad Creek; John Simpson, bapt. 12 Apr 1767 Broad Creek (KGP p. 356, 360)

Scott, Zachariah; child: Ruth, bapt. 28 Oct 1764 Upper Chapel or Broad Creek (KGP p. 342)

Scott, Henry; wife Mary; child: John Smith, bapt. 31 Aug 1766 Upper Chapel (KGP p. 355)

Scott, Catherine; widow; 14 Mar 1776; 26 Mar 1776; s-i-l John Scott; husband John Scott (MCW XVI.130); 6 Apr 1776 (I 122.207.210)

Scott, George; 29 Aug 1771; 25 Sep 1771; wife Elizabeth; children Margaret, Ann, Isabella, Ariana, George; unnamed children; m-i-l Margaret Dick; s-i-l Robert Peter; tracts *Fortune Enlarged, Norway* (MCW XIV.184)

Scott, John; wife Mary; child: Mary Ann, b. 19 Mar 1773 Lower Chapel
(KGP p. 384)

Scott, Sabritt [Sabret]; 22 Jul 1774; 17 Oct 1774; wife [unnamed]; children
Richard Keene, John, Judson & Edward Scott; tracts *Croome, Timberly,
Additions* (MCW XVI.8); extx. Martha; 6 Feb 1775 (I 121.367, 369)

Scott, Henry; 16 Nov 1776; 20 May 1776; wife Mary Benit; dau. Ann, others
[unnamed] (MCW XVI.188)

Scott, William; wife Mary; s-i-l Thomas Hamilton; tract *William & Mary
Increased*; 1 Sep 1742 (PGLR Y.603)

Scott, Zachariah; 19 Apr 1775; 8 May 1775; children: Charles, Amy,
Jemima, William, James; niece Ruth [w/o Roger Brooke Beall]; great-
niece Ann Beall [d/o Ruth] (MCW XVI.71-2)

Scott, Zachariah; 27 May 1775 (I 123.122); heirs Charles, Amelia, James,
William; 13 Dec 1775 (GB 329, 330, 331); 19 Apr 1776 (I 123.405, 406); 26 Mar
1777; children: Charles, Amy, Jemima, William, James (ABB 7.63)

SCRIVENER

Scrivener [Screvener], John; wife Rebecca; children: Mary, b. 30 Dec 1763;
Delilah, b. 1 Sep 1765 (PGP p. 269, 277)

SCUDMORE

Scudamore, Baldwin; wife Elizabeth; child: Virlinder, b. 4 Aug 1757 (KGP p.
320)

SEARCE

Searce, Nathan; wife Sushannah; child: Malinda Ann, bapt. 18 May 1766
Upper Chapel (KGP p. 354)

Searce [Sarce, Scarce, Searse], David; wife Casander; children: Robert,
bapt. 10 Aug 1766 Upper Chapel; James, bapt. 4 Sep 1768 Upper
Chapel; Elizabeth, b. 17 May 1774 Upper Chapel (KGP p. 371, 391)

Scarse, Catharine; 18 Aug 1773 (I 114.47); 24 Mar 1774; admx. Shadrack
Scarce (ABB 6.270)

Searce, Shadrack; wife Eleanor; child: James Norton, b. 26 Sep 1774 (KGP p.
391)

Searse, David; wife Kesander; child: Robert, bapt. 10 Aug 1766 (KGP p. 364)

SEIPER

Seiper?, James; widow Elizabeth; heir Lucy Ann Herbert Seiper; 26 Aug
1772 (GB 307)

SELBY

Selby, William; 5 Nov 1698; 25 Feb 1698/9; wife Mary; daus. Mary Sollers [w/o Robert], Susanna, Ann; sons William, Charles, Samuel; tracts *Good Luck, Pack's Meadow, Leeth, Groome's Lodge, Towgood, Twyfort, The Farm* (MCW II.169); extx. Mary Cecill [w/o Joshua]; 30 Jul 1701 (I&A 20.237)

Selby, William; dau. Ann Tucker; 7 Mar 1710 (PGLR F.62)

Selby, Samuel; m. 12 Dec 1717 Sarah Smith [d/o Nathan Smith in Ann Arundel Co.] (QAP m/2)

Selby, William; wife Elizabeth; tract *Toogood*; 22 Jan 1725 (PGLR I.710)

Selby, William; planter; 18 Oct 1732; 1 Aug 1733; sons William Magruder Selby, Samuel, Joseph, Thomas, John, Nathan; wife Elizabeth; bro. Samuel; daus. Sarah, Susannah; mother Elizabeth; tracts *Chew's Folly, Leith, Essex Lodge, Toogood* (MCW VII.26); 13 Oct 1733 (I 17.496); 3 Aug 1734 (I 20.70); children: Thomas, Joseph, John, Sarah, Susannah; 14 Nov 1734 (AA 12.644); heirs Joseph, John, Sarah, Susannah; 24 Mar 1736 (GB 93)

Selby, Samuel; wife Amy [granddau. of George Ransom]; tract *The Wedge*; 23 Jun 1740 (PGLR Y.189)

Selby, Nathan; 28 Feb 1744; 4 Apr 1745; wife Easter; children: William, Nathan, John; tract *Toogood* (MCW IX.15); 11 Apr 1745 (I 31.208); 10 Mar 1747 (I 35.437)

Selby, John & Sarah; choose Samuel Selby as guardian; Mar 1745 (PGCR DD.16)

Selby, Susannah; choses Thomas Selby as guardian; Mar 1745 (PGCR DD.20)

Selby, Joseph; admx. Sarah; 9 Apr 1752 (I 51.21); admx. Sarah; 27 Aug 1752 (I 54.143); admx. Sarah; 30 Nov 1753 (AA 35.322); 30 Nov 1753; admx. Sarah Selby (ABB 1.87)

Selby, Nathaniel; heir John; 25 Jun 1760 (GB 215)

Selby, John, planter; 15 Feb 1763; 26 Mar 1767; wife Sarah; children Kenelm Groom, John Smith, Henrietta; tract *Discovery Adjoining Same* (MCW XIII.175); extx. Sarah; 13 May 1767 (I 94.65); 24 Nov 1767; extx. Sarah Selby, widow; children Kenelm Groom, John Smith & Henrietta Selby (ABB 5.59); admx. Sarah; 24 Aug 1768 (GB 264)

Selby, Samuell; wife Ann; child: Martha, b. 27 Mar 1765 (PGP p. 277)

SERJANT

Serjant, James; wife Elliner; child: Elliner, b. 3 Dec 1763 (PGP p. 269)

SEWALL

Sewell, Nicholas; dau. Jane Brooke [w/o Clement]; part of *Brookefield*; 27 Nov 1703 (PGLR C.106a)

Sewall, Nicholas [SM]; wife Susanna; tract *Brookfield*; 27 Sep 1697 (PGLR A.83)

Sewell, Nicholas [SM]; sons Clement, Nicholas, Jr.; tract *Sewall's Addition*; 1 Jun 1730 (PGLR M.601)

Sewall, Robert; heir Robert; 28 Jun 1732 (GB 59); heir John; 28 Aug 1735 (GB 73)

Sewall, Clement [SM]; wife Mary; tract *Hacthornheath*; 23 May 1735 (PGLR T.303)

Suell, Leonard; wife Tracy; child: Elizabeth, b. 14 Sep 1772 Lower Chapel (KGP p. 383)

SEYMOUR

Seymour, Elizabeth; age 3-1/2 on 1 Mar instant; d/o Elizabeth Baley; bound out; Mar 1713/4 (PGCR G.539)

SHANKS

Shanks, Thomas; wife Susana; child: William, b. 18 Sep 1775 Lower Chapel (KGP p. 381)

SHARDENATTE

Shardenatte, John; 24 Apr 1701 (I&A 20.169)

SHARKEY

Sharkey, William; extx. Penelope Howard [w/o Ignatius]; 22 May 1740 (I 25.401)

SHARPE

Sharp, Elizabeth; age ca 11; servant; Jun 1698 Ct. (PGCR A.316)

Sharpe, John; wife Mary; children: John Oliver, b. 8 Jul 1763, bapt. 11 Mar 1764; Mary, bapt. 26 Feb 1764 Lower Chapel (KGP p. 344)

SHAW

Shaw, Mary; d/o John age 3; bound out; Jun 1696 Ct. (PGCR A.9)

Shaw, John; wife Elizabeth; Nov 1697 Ct. (PGCR A.258)

Shaw, James; cooper; 13 Apr 1718; 27 Jun 1718; wife Margaret; sons William, Christopher, James; uncle Christopher Thompson (MCW IV.162); 3 Jun 1719 (I 2.212); widow Margaret; heirs Christopher, William, James; 20 Feb 1722 (GB 17)

Shaw, John; m/1 Elizabeth; children: Joseph, b. 28 May 1737 (KGP p. 289); m/2 Sarah; children: Elizabeth, b. 26 Oct 1743; Mary, b. 1 Dec 1747; Billy, b. 7 Dec 1749; Sarah, b. 28 Oct 1751, bapt. 8 Dec 1751; John, b. 17 Sep 1755 (KGP p. 289, 290, 294, 315)

Shaw, Henrietta; widow; 6 Jul 1765; 10 Aug 1765; children: Henrietta, Rebecca, Zachariah, Josiah; m-i-l Mary Scott (MCW XIII.93); 24 Aug 1765 (I 89.311) 10 Sep 1766; ex. Joseph Shaw; children: Josiah, Rebecah, Henrietta, Zachariah (ABB 5.1); heirs Rebecca, Heneritah, Zachariah; 28 Aug 1767 (GB 254)

Shaw, [unnamed]; heir Zachariah; 25 Jun 1766 (GB 243)

Shaw, Josias; wife Mary; child: William, b. 8 Sep 1767 Upper Chapel; James Shaw, b. 22 Dec 1769; Elizabeth, b. 19 Sep 1771 (KGP p. 391)

Shaw, Bille; wife Sarah; child: Mary, b. 30 Nov 1775 Lower Chapel (KGP p. 381)

Shaw, John; wife Jane; child: Joseph, b. 1 Mar 1776 Lower Chapel (KGP p. 381)

Shaw, Rebecca; binds her son [ye son of Wm. Bradfoard]; age 4 last Mar; Jun 1700 Ct. (PGCR B.53)

Shaw, William, Jr.; 28 Oct 1759; 26 Dec 1759; wife Henrietta; sons Josiah, William, Zachariah; tracts Brother's Choice (MCW XI.267-8); extx. Henrietta; 29 Feb 1760 (I 69.333); 28 Sep 1761; extx. Henrietta Shaw; children [unnamed] (ABB 3.117); widow Henrietta; heirs Josias, William, Rebecca, Henretta, Zachariah; 25 Aug 1762 (GB 221)

Shaw, William; planter; 16 Aug 1773; 16 Nov 1775; wife Elizabeth; children: Charles, Mary, Charity, Angus; grandchild William Shaw [s/o Angus]; tract William and Elizabeth, Forest Put (MCW XVI.79-80); 12 Dec 1775 (I 123.420); 6 Nov 1776; widow [unnamed]; 13 children; daus. Mary, Charity (ABB 7.73)

SHEARWOOD

Shearwood, Thomas; wife Ann; child: Rodey Swann, bapt. 12 Feb 1764 Broad Creek (KGP p. 356)

SHECKELLS

Sheckells, Abraham; wife Ann; child: Frances, b. 20 Sep 1764 (PGP p. 276)

Shekle, Hezekiah; wife Hanna; child: Elizabeth, b. 23 Oct 1774 Broad Creek (KGP p. 386)

SHEHAN

Shehan [Shehorn, James; wife Susanah; children: Mary Ellender, b. 18 Sep 1760; Ann, b. 23 Jul 1764 (PGP p. 274)

SHEIRCLIFF

Sheircliff, William; planter; 5 Apr 1740; wife Penelope; sons Lenard, Thomas, John; dau. Mary (MCW VIII.84)

Shircliff, Leonard; 1 May 1752 (I 49.43); 16 May 1753 (I 55.164); 1 Oct 1753 (AA 35.256)

Sheircliff, John; admx. Mary; 11 Apr 1758 (I 65.263)

SHELBY

Shelby, Evans; wife Catran; tract *Maiden's Choice*; 14 Jun 1740 (PGLR Y.179, 180)

SHELTON

Shelston, William; m. 25 Nov 1739 Katherine Neall; children: William Neall, b. 25 Dec 1739; M___ (f), b. 16 Jul 1742 (KGP p. 288)

Shelton, Francis; wife Elizabeth; children: Elizabeth, b. 23 May 1760 (PGP p. 258); Alice Coston, bapt. 19 Dec 1762 (KGP p. 329)

SHEPARD

Shepard, Thomas; 16 Mar 1698 (I&A 19.139); 26 Mar 1700 (I&A 20.64)

Sheppard, Ann; age 2 on 10 Jun inst; d/o Ruth; bound out; Jun 1725 (PGCR L.452)

Shepard, John; 23 Mar 1726 (I 11.900)

Shepard, Richard; extx. Elisabeth; 21 Nov 1729 (I 15.399)

Shepherd, Sarah; 26 Mar 1764 (I 87.128)

SHEREDINE

Sheredine, Thomas [BA]; wife Tabitha; tract *Haddington*; 30 Oct 1739 (PGLR Y.100)

SHERIFF

Sheriff, Thomas; wife Frances; child: Jeremiah, b. 31 Jul 1740 (QAP b/32)

Sheriff, Samuel; wife Sarah; children: Elizabeth, b. 5 Oct 1753 (?); Martha, b. 16 Sep 1757 (QAP b/39)

Shriff, John; wife Elizabeth; child: John, bapt. 12 Dec 1762 (KGP p. 329)

SHERWOOD

Sherwood, John; m. 19 8ber 1724 Jemima Ryley; child: Elizabeth, b. 20 9ber 1728 (QAP m/4, b. 21)

Sherwood, Thomas; wife Ann; children: Job, bapt. 15 Dec 1751; Thomas, b. 14 Dec 1755 (KGP p. 294, 312)

Sheskley, William; wife Mary; children: Thomas, b. 12 Oct 1724; John, b. 5 Oct 1727 (KGP p. 271)

SHILLINGSWORTH

Shillingsworth [Chillingsworth], William; plasterer; 8 Sep 1725; 24 Mar 1725; mother Jane; bro. Richard Karter; sisters [unnamed], bro. Francis' wife (MCW V.220); 26 Jan 1726 (I 11.779)

SHILLITOES

Shillitoes, William; 4 Aug 1704; 22 Nov 1704; [no relations] (MCW III.48)

SHIRLY

Shirly, George; wife Mary; children: Edward, b. 28 10ber 1719; Ann, b. 15 Feb 1721/2 (QAP b/16/17)

Sherley, George; admx. Mary; 11 Feb 1726 (I 11.883); admx. Mary; 15 Feb 1727 (AA 8.508)

Shirly, Ann; age 10 on 25 Feb last; d/o Mary Oram [w/o James]; Mar 1747 (PGCR GG.458)

SHOEMAKER

Shoemaker, Conrad; admx. Susanna; 16 Apr 1764 (I 86.182)

SHORE

Shore, Richard; age ca 32; 23 Aug 1732 (PGLR Q.532)

SHREVE

Shreve [Shrieve], Thomas; wife Frances; children: Samuel, b. 14 May 1731; Thomas, b. 8 Jan 1732/3; Benjamin, b. 6 Jul 1734; Martha, b. 2 Jun 17__ (QAP b/26, 28, 31)

SHREWSBURY

Shrewsbury, Ann; age ca 20; servant; Feb 1698/9 Ct. (PGCR A.386)

SHUNNAM

Shunnam, John; age ca 15; servant; Sep 1701 (PGCR B.137)

SHUTT

Shutt, John; wife Judith; child: Mary, 14 Mar 1754 (KGP p. 305)

SIBROE

Sibroe, Samuel; wife Elizabeth; child: Sarah, b. 16 Jun 1754 (KGP p. 308)

SILKWOOD

Silkwood, [male]; b. 1 Apr 1729; bastard s/o Margaret Silkwoods; bound out; Aug 1729 (PGCR P.135)

SIMMONS

Simmons [Simons], Jonathan; wife Elizabeth; son Joseph; tract *Western Branch Manor*; 13 Jul 1701 (PGLR C.55)

Simmons, Jonathan; wife Elizabeth; child: Isaac, b. 3 Oct 1705; Ann, b. 3 Jul 1712 (QAP b/2, 8)

Simmons, John; extx. Rebecca Mackie [w/o Henry]; 11 Apr 1709 (I&A 31.140)

Symmons, Jonathan; wife Elizabeth; child: Sarah, b. 3 Mar 1714/5 (QAP b/10)

Simmons, Joseph; wife Jane; children: Joseph, b. 5 Feb 1717/8; Samuel Jones, b. 3 May 1716 (QAP b/11, 14)

Simmons, Jonathan; 9 Jan 1724; 1 Dec 1726; wife Elizabeth; sons Jonathan, Joseph, Richard; daus. Eliza., Mary, Ann, Rebecca, Ainie, Sarah, Marjory (MCW VI.2); extx. Elisabeth; 25 Feb 1726 (I 11.708); widow Elisabeth; children: Elisabeth Ridgway, Ann Madden, Joseph Simmons; 11 Jan 1728 (AA 9.242, 289); widow Elizabeth; heirs Richard, Rebecca [late wife of Joseph Brown, Jr.], Amy, Sarah, Margery; 25 Jun 1729 (GB 47)

Simmons, Jonathan; m. 20 Jun 1734 Elizabeth Swearingen; child: Jonathan, b. 9 Aug 1735 (QAP m/6; b/29)

Simmons, Richard; wife Susanah; tract *Amy*; 24 Aug 1742 (PGLR Y.546)

Simmons, Elizabeth; 10 Mar 1757; 23 Nov 1757; sons Johnathan, Richard; daus. Rebecca Machcally, Mary Higgins, Amy Holland, Sarah Pierpoint; grandson Jonathan Simmons [s/o Jonathan] (MCW XI.182); 8 Dec 1757 (I 65.491)

Simmons, Jonathan; 25 May 1761; 26 Aug 1761; wife Elizabeth; sons Jonathan, Joseph, William, Richard, Isaac, Van, Jesse, Jacob; dau. Ruth; tract *Conogochique Manor* (MCW XII.82); extx. Elisabeth; 20 Nov 1761 (I 77.96; 78.317); 4 Jan 1763; extx. Elisabeth Simmons; children: Jonathon, Joseph, William, Ruth, Richard, Isaac, Van, Jesse, Jacob (ABB 3.181); widow Elizabeth; heirs Jonathan, Ruth, Isaac, Richard, Van, Jesse, Jacob; 26 Jul 1764 (GB 235)

Simmons, Samuel; wife Linney; child: Martha, bapt. 10 May 1767 Upper Chapel (KGP p. 365)

Simmons, Jonathan; wife Elizabeth; child: Susanna, b. 7 Sep 1775 Upper Chapel (KGP p. 392)

Simmons, Johnathan; wife Mary; child: ____, b. __ Mar ____ (QAP b/38)

SIMMS

Simms, Richard; age ca 15; servant; Aug 1699 Ct. (PGCR A.446)

Sims, Alexander; wife Ruth; child: Elizabeth, b. 12 Sep 1725 (KGP p. 272)

Simms, Elizabeth; d/o William Clarkson; heir Francis Simms; tract *Stony Hill*; 21 Jun 1736 (PGLR T.384)

Sim, Patrick, Dr.; extx. Mary; 17 Feb 1741 (I 26.41, 45); admx. Mary; dau. [w/o Clement Smith], dau. [w/o Thomas Lee]; 10 May 1744 (AA 20.189); widow Mary; heir Joseph; 30 Mar 1747 (GB 156)

Simms, Cleyburn; age 13 on 8 Apr last; choses father Cleyburn Simm as guardian; Jun 1743 (PGCR AA.476)

Sim, Patrick, Dr.; d. 24 Oct 1740; widow Mary; 21 Jan 1745 (CCR MSA 8.257)

Simm, William; 1 Apr 1751 (I 47.282)

Simms, Anthony; admx. Elisabeth; 1 Nov 1756 (I 62.102); widow Elizabeth; heir Mary; 28 Mar 1758 (GB 212); 11 Sep 1758; admx. Elisabeth Simmes; orphan Mary (ABB 2.94)

Sim, Mary; Upper Marlborough Town; 16 Feb 1758; 21 Mar 1758; daus. Barbara and Christian Smith; son Joseph Walter Sim; grandchildren Thomas Sim Lee and Barbara Brook Lee [ch/o Christian Smith], Patrick & Mary Sim [ch/o Joseph Walter] (MCW XI.198); 15 Sep 1760 (I 77.88)

Sim, Joseph; wife Catherine; infant dau. Mary Brooke Sim; 1768 (MCW XIV.59)

Sim, Lettice [previously Lettice Thomson]; w/o Col. Joseph Sim; 23 Feb 1776; 2 Apr 1776; children: Alice Corbin & Mary Lee Thomson; nephew Alexander Symmer, Jr., Hancock Lee [s/o John]; step-dau. Mary Brook Sim; bros. John & George Lee; sister ___ Symmer (MCW XVI.130)

SIMNER

Simner, Mary; child: Murrier (f), b. 8 Oct 1769 Broad Creek (KGP p. 373)

SIMPSON

Simpson, James; age ca 50; 1730 (PGLR M.567)

Simpson, Joseph Green; admx. Elisabeth; 22 Jun 1750 (I 43.310); admx. Elisabeth; children [eldest age 10]: Thomas, John, Sarah, Andrew; 23 Dec 1751 (AA 32.64); 23 Dec 1751; admn. Elizabeth; children: Thomas, John, Sarah & Andrew Simpson (ABB 1.26); widow Elizabeth; heirs Thomas, John, Sarah, Andrew; 28 Nov 1752 (GB 180)

Simpson, John; wife Sarah; children: Ann, bapt. 26 Jan 1752; Hezekiah, b. 10 Sep 1753; Ellender, b. 23 Feb 1755; John, b. 18 Mar 1760; Josias, bapt. _ Aug 1763 at Broad Creek (KGP p. 294, 301, 307, 318, 337)

Simpson, Andrew; wife Alice; children: Jane, bapt. 2 Aug 1752; Andrew, b. 11 Mar 1754 (KGP p. 297, 305)

Simpson, Gilbert; wife Mary; children: Libby, b. 14 Aug 1757; Mary Ann, bapt. 18 Apr 1762; Sarah, bapt. 30 Sep 1764 at Broad Creek; Verlinder, b. 7 Apr 1772 Broad Creek (KGP p. 320, 325, 339, 370)

Simpson, James; wife Priscilla; children: Thomas, b. 5 Oct 1763; bapt. 13 Nov 1763 at Broad Creek, John, b. 4 Jun 1765 Broad Creek; Lewin, b. 3 Sep 1767 Lower Chapel; Priscilla, b. 28 Apr 1773 Broad Creek; Sarah, b. 6 Nov 1775 Broad Creek (KGP p. 349, 368, 382, 384)

Simpson, Joseph; wife Charity; children: Phillop Tenaley, b. 1 Oct 1764 Broad Creek; Thomas, b. 5 Oct 1768 Broad Creek; Mildred, b. 13 Sep 1775 Broad Creek (KGP p. 342, 364, 387)

Simpson, Thomas; child: Thomas, bapt. 3 Apr 1768 Broad Creek (KGP p. 362)

Simpson, John; wife Sarah; children: Mary Ann, b. 26 Oct 1769 Upper Chapel; Susanna, b. 24 Jun 1772 Broad Creek (KGP p. 372, 378)

SINCLAIR
Sincler [Sinkler], William; wife Elizabeth; children: Isabell, b. 4 Apr 1702; Elizabeth, b. 18 Aug 1704; Nathaniel & William [twins], b. 31 Jan 1707; James, b. 19 Aug 1715 (QAP b/1, 12, 30)

Sinkler, William; wife Elizabeth; tract *William & Elizabeth*; 22 Nov 1726 (PGLR M.108)

Sinclair [Sinclare], William; wife Lydda [Lidea]; child: James, bapt. 3 Jul 1763 at Upper Chapel; Elizabeth, b. 3 Jan 1765 Broad Creek; John, bapt. 21 Dec 1766 Broad Creek; Archibald, b. 20 Jun 1774 Lower Chapel (KGP p. 333, 346, 348, 379)

SITTON
Sitton, John; m. 9 Jun 1729 Elizabeth Pindel; children: Elizabeth, b. 15 May 173_ [Friday, 9 am]; Benjamin, b. 17 Apr 1732 [Monday]; Philip [eldest] & John [twins], b. 15 Aug 1733 [Wednesday] (QAP m/5; b/24, 25, 27)

Sitton; John; wife Elizabeth [d/o Philip Pindell, Sr.]; granddau. Elizabeth Sitton; 12 Sep 1730 (PGLR Q.95)

SKIDMORE
Skidmore, Bauldin; wife Elizabeth; child: Samuel, b. 12 Oct 1763 at Broad Creek (KGP p. 338)

SKINNER
Skinner, William [CA]; wife Elizabeth; tract *Hatchett*; 12 Aug 1702 (PGLR C.1)

Skinner, William [CA]; [s/o Robert]; bro. Clarke; tract *Hatchett*; 12 Aug 1702 (PGLR C.14a)

Skinner, Clarke [CA]; wife Ruth; tract *Ladsford's Guift*; 11 Aug 1707 (PGLR C.189)

Skinner, Mackall; age ca 20 last Jan; chooses bro. Robert as guardian; Aug 1728 (PGCR O.234)

Skinner, Nathaniel; age 17 last Apr; choses bro. Robert as guardian; Aug 1728

Skinner, Robert, gent.; 25 Aug 1736; 1 Oct 1736; bros. Nathaniel, Mackall; mother Mrs. Ann Bruse (MCW VII.193); 27 Jun 1738 (I 23.365); 10 Apr 1740 (AA 17.463)

Skinner, Nathaniel; admx. Elisabeth Letchworth [w/o Thomas]; 16 Jun 1743 (I 28.499); 8 Nov 1753; Thomas Letchworth intermarried with Elizabeth Skinner, admx. (ABB 1.82, 134); admx. Elisabeth Letchworth [w/o Thomas]; 8 Nov 1753 (AA 35.272); heir Elizabeth Skinner; 28 Nov 1753 (GB 188)

Skinner, Elizabeth; under age 14; court appointed Thomas Holliday as guardian; Nov 1753 (PGCR MM.509)

Skinner, Mackall; admx. Ann Cox; 3 Jun 1754 (I 57.287)

Skinner, Alexander; s/o Ann Skinner; 1767 (MCW XIV.49)

SLATER

Slater, Richard; wife Jane; children: Jane, b. 24 Mar 1773 Broad Creek; Mary, b. 3 Mar 1776 Lower Chapel (KGP p. 378, 381)

SLOE

Sloe, Alexander; wife Lidea; child: Sarah, bapt. 7 Jun 1767 Lower Chapel (KGP p. 367)

SLOYWOOD

Sloywood, Robert; wife Kesander; child: Sarah, bapt. 4 Jul 1762 (KGP p. 331)

SMALL

Small, Jer.; exs. Richard Rolings and his wife Mary; 16 Apr 1724 (AA 6.28)

SMALLWOOD

Smallwood, Benjamin; 24 Jun 1737 (I 22.266)

Smallwood, Mathew [CH]; wife Mary; tract *School House*; 19 Feb 1739 (PGLR Y.127)

Smallwood, Thomas; wife Mary; child: Bayne, bapt. 1 Mar 1752 (KGP p. 294)

Smallwood, John; wife Ann; child: Ann Middleton, b. 25 Jun 1755 (KGP p. 308)

Smallwood, James; wife Jemima; child: Hepburn, b. 1 Mar 1760 (PGCR p.260)

Smallwood, Eliga; wife Sarah; child: John, b. 2 Jan 1763 at Broad Creek (KGP p. 337)

Smallwood, John, Sr.; 17 May 1765 (I 87.124)

Smallwood, James; wife Sushanna; child: Francis Heard, bapt. 25 May 1766 Broad Creek (KGP p. 348)

Smallwood, Thomas; wife Elizabeth; 1772 (MCW XIV.220)

SMART

Smart, Anthony; wife Sarah [formerly Sarah Summers; her male child, age 11 next Nov, raised by Hannah Edwards]; Sep 1697 Ct. (PGCR A.233)

Smart, Batholomew; age 12 next Jan; bound out; Nov 1725 (PGCR L.507)

SMITH

Smith, Thomas [CA]; wife Mary; tract Strife; 26 Aug 1695 (PGLR !.26)

Smith, John [PG]; wife Ann; tract Long Looked For; 27 Nov 1700 (PGLR A.343) [CH]; wife Ann; tract Smith's Green; 23 Mar 1704 (PGLR C.83a)

Smith, Daniell; age 9 on 10 Jun next; s/o Daniel Smith; mother Dorothy Owen; bound out; Mar 1705 (PGCR B352c)

Smith, John; planter; Mattapany Landing; 3 Sep 1707; 23 Sep 1707; wife Jane; nephew John Bowie; "brother Thomas Prather"; tracts Thropland, Hope Yard, Hope's Addition, Brooke Wood, Brook Field (MCW III.91); [with 1707] (I&A 28.115); exs. Jane; 3 Nov 1709 (I&A 30.235)

Smith, George, Dr.; 21 Apr 1711 (I&A 32c.34)

Smith, Daniell; 13 Jun 1711 (I&A 32b.187)

Smith, John [CH]; age ca 73; 20 Oct 1711 (CCR PC.766)

Smith, Nicholas; wife Mellona; children: Joanna, b. 3 Aug 1712; William, b. 14 Mar 1715; Sarah, b. 18 Apr 1717 (QAP b/8; 15)

Smith, John [CA]; son John; [undated, with 1712] (PGLR F.189)

Smith, Jane; 7 Jan 1713 (I&A 35a.383); 6 Sep 1715 (I&A 36c.41); 14 grandchildren [unnamed]; 2 Feb 1716 (I&A 37c.126, 127)

Smith, William; wife Jane; child: Nathan, b. 9 Mar 1714 (QAP b/12)

Smith, Thomas; m. 2 Feb 1715 Elizabeth Rigden; child: Cassandra, b. 3 Jan 1716 (QAP m/1; b/13)

Smith, William; wife Hannah; tract Seaman's Delight; 29 Sep 1716 (PGLR F.572)

Smith, Thomas; [with 1716] (I&A 37a.182)

Smith, William the elder [CH]; nephew William and his bro. Adam [England]; 28 Jun 1718 (PGLR F.73/615)

Smith, Henry; wife Mary; tract Beall's Pleasure; 6 Aug 1718 (PGLR F.89/639)

Smith, John; blacksmith; 8 Jul 1718; 10 Aug 1719; wife Elizabeth; son John; daus. Margaret Smith, Mary Townley [w/o John] (MCW IV.214); blacksmith; 24 Oct 1720 (I 4.250)

Smith, John; m. 25 Apr 1721 Mary Rand; both of this parish (KGP p. 266)

Smith, Nicholas; children: Annestia, b. 28 Dec 1721; John, b. 8 Jan 1723; Thomas, b. 14 Dec 1725; Elizabeth, b. 6 Dec 1727 (PGP p. 247-8)

Smith, William; 13 Feb 1723 (I 9.372)

Smith, John; widow Elisabeth; 2 Jan 1724 (I 10.355); 24 Mar 1724 (AA 6.325); 28 Mar 1726 (I 11.266); 1 Aug 1726 (AA 7.493); heirs Ann, Mary; 31 Mar 1727 (GB 32)

Smith, John, Col. [CA]; wife Sarah; tract Brook Wood; 24 Dec 1726 (PGLR M.128)

Smith, William; m. 3 Aug 1727 Elizabeth Mason; children: Richard, b. 15 Jul 1728; William, b. 20 Feb 1729 (?); John, b. 3 Jun 1732 (QAP m/4; b/21, 26)

Smith, Samuel; wife Elizabeth; tract Smithfield; 20 Jun 1730 (PGLR Q.136)

Smith, Nicholas; wife Mary; child: Jemima, b. 3 May 1731 (PGP p. 250)

Smith, Samuel; m. 26 Sep 1732 Grissel Locker; children: John, b. 15 Dec 1735; Elinor, b. 15 Oct 1737 (KGP p. 286)

Smith, Eleanor [CA]; son John Addison Smith; tracts Batchelor's Harbour, Swan Harbour; 18 Aug 1733 (PGLR Q.684)

Smith, John; admx. Mary Offutt; 13 Sep 1734 (I 20.44); heirs ?England; admx. Mary Offutt; 27 Aug 1735 (AA 13.276)

Smith, James; wife Mary; tract Knaves Disappointment; 30 Dec 1734 (PGLR T.215)

Smith, William; 4 Mar 1739; 28 Nov 1750; wife Lucy; daus. Jane Cleland [w/o Thomas], Elizabeth White [w/o Benjamin], Alice, Anna; sons Archibald, James, Philip, Benoni, Anthony, Nathan; unborn child; s-i-l Joseph Belt [s/o Benjamin]; tracts Moors Plains, One of Smith Folly, Edmondston's Pasture (MCW X.123); 24 Dec 1750 (I 47.294)

Smith, William, Sr.; wife Lucy; tract Cool Spring Level; 26 Oct 1739 (PGLR Y.103)

Smith, Rees; admx. Anne [Quaker]; 19 Jul 1740 (I 25.429); widow Anne [Quaker]; 22 Apr 1741 (AA 18.160)

Smith, Walter; heir Richard Smith; 24 Mar 1741/2 (GB 123)

Smith, Nicholas; age ca 55; 28 Mar 1741 (PGLR Y.267)

Smith, Thomas; 6 Nov 1745 (I 31.373); tailer; b. Ireland; 28 Jan 1745 (AA 22.112)

Smith, Jonas; 18 Mar 1750 (I 47.13); 29 Nov 1751 (AA 31.255); heir James [age 6]; 28 Aug 1751 (AA 31.78); 24 Mar 1752; [no relations] (ABB 1.33, 60); 24 May 1752 (AA 32.166) 8 Nov 1752; James Smith, age ca 10 years; bound to Abraham Wood at Nottingham (ABB 1.62); 8 Nov 1752 (AA 33.199)

Smith, Samuel; wife Grissel; child, Zadoc [Sadoe] bapt. 12 May 1751; Samuel, b. 8 Apr 1755 (KGP p. 293, 308)

Smith, Joseph; 29 Nov 1751; [no relations] (ABB 1.20)

Smith, John, Capt.; admx. Mary; 11 May 1752 (I 48.488); admnx. Mary; 7 May 1753 (AA 34.67)

Smith, James; m. 27 Jan 1756 Mary Welling; children: Henry, b. 4 Feb 1757; James, b. 5 Sep 1759; Violender, b. 28 Dec 1760; John Welling, bapt. 9 Mar 1766 Broad Creek; Ann, b. 2 Sep 1768 Broad Creek; William, b. 20 Jan 1771 Broad Creek (KGP p. 302, 315, 353, 364, 374)

Smith, John [s/o Samuel Smith] supposed to be father of Elizabeth Smith, b. _Dec 1759 [bapt. at James Sommers 30 Sep 1759] by Elizabeth Eastern; given to John Johnson (KGP p. 318); [see Elizabeth Johnson]

Smith, John; 14 Feb [?1759]; admx. Mary Smith; children: Sarah, Mary & Henrietta (ABB 3.29)

Smith, Nicholas; wife Susannah; children: James, b. 29 May 1760; Garard, b. 9 Jan 1762 (PGP p. 258, 260)

Smith, Nathan; wife Rebecca; children: Orlando, b. 16 Feb 1761; Precious, b. 10 Jan 1763 (PGP p. 260, 270)

Smith, John; wife Ann; children: William, b. 11 Sep 1761 (PGP p. 261); John, bapt. 18 Aug 1765 Lower Chapel; Henry, b. 2 Feb 1768 Upper Chapel (KGP p. 345, 370)

Smith, Christian; 12 Feb 1762; 24 Mar 1762; son Thomas Sim Lee; daus. Sarah Brooke Lee, Eleanor Addison Smith; bro.-in-law Clement Smith; s-i-l Mrs. Catherine Sin [Sim], sister Barbara Smith; bro. Joseph Walter Sim (MCW XII.119); widow; 24 May 1763 (I 80.278); 31 Aug 1767; ex. Maj. Joseph Simm; children: Thomas Lee, Sarah Brooke Lee, Elisabeth Contee [w/o Theodore], Eleanor Addison Smith; b-i-l Clement Smith; s-i-l Catharine Simm; sis. Barbara Smith; bro. Joseph Walter Simm (ABB 5.61); heir [unnamed]; 29 Jun 1769 (GB 272) heir Eleanor [now of age]; 7 Apr 1770? (GB 279)

Smith, Lander; wife Martha; children: Kesandera, b. 6 May 1762; Elener, bapt. 22 Apr 1764 at Upper Chapel; Whitfield, bapt, 10 Apr 1768 Upper Chapel (KGP p. 330, 340, 370)

Smith, Nathan; adm. Margaret & James Smith; 10 Apr 1762 (I 78.322)

Smith, John; wife Charity; child: Elenor, b. 22 Nov 1762 at Broad Creek; Mary Ann, bapt. 9 Jun 1765 Broad Creek (KGP p. 336, 347)

Smith, John; wife Elliner; children: Melender, b. 28 Mar 1763; Zadock, b. 7 Apr 1765; William, b. 27 Aug 1772 (PGP p. 268, 275, 278)

Smith, John; wife Mary; child: Elizabeth, bapt. 11 Oct 1763 at Lower Chapel (KGP p. 335)

Smith, Nathan; 15 Feb 1765; admn. James Smith (ABB 4.94)

Smith, David; wife Sarah; child: Elizabeth, bapt. 7 Jul 1765 Upper Chapel (KGP p. 358)

Smith, John; wife Elizabeth; child: Martha, bapt. 4 Feb 1766 Lower Chapel (KGP p. 352)

Smith, Orlando; wife Martha; child: Orlando, b. 17 Feb 1766 Upper Chapel (KGP p. 354)

Smith, Archibald; 2 Apr 1765 (I 87.120); 18 Aug 1766; admn. Zachariah Lyles (ABB 4.174)

Smith, John; wife Sarah; child: Robert, b. 29 Jun 1768 Broad Creek (KGP p. 363)

Smith, Matthew; wife Verlinder; child: Sally, b. 5 Mar 1772 Upper Chapel (KGP p. 389)

Smith, Nathan; minor; 15 Dec 1772 (GB 310)

Smith, Orlander; wife Martha; child: Neomi, b. 1 Apr 1774 Upper Chapel (KGP p. 390)

SMOOT

Smoote, Thomas; sons John Nathan, William, Thomas, Charles; 1703 (MCW III.62)

Smoot, John; planter; 20 Oct 1747; 25 Nov 1747; wife Mary; sons John, Edward; dau. Mary; tracts *Sealls Desire, Crumford* (MCW IX.125); extx. Mary; 12 Apr 1748 (I 36.140);15 Apr 1752; extx. Mary Fletchell [w/o Thomas] (ABB 1.31)

Smoot, John; age 16; choses guardian; Jun 1748 (PGCR HH.178)

SNALL

Snall, Jeremiah; 29 Nov 1720; 13 Jul 1723; wife Mary (MCW V.138); extx. Mary; 20 Jul 1723 (I 9.4)

Snell, Jeremiah; admx. Martha; 11 May 1753 (I 57.103)

SNOW

Snow, John; 12 Mar 1739; 25 Nov 1740; wife Mary (MCW VIII.106); admx. Mary; 11 May 1741 (I 26.355)

SNOWDEN

Snowden, Richard; wife Elizabeth; tracts *Snowden & Welch, Joseph's Neglect; Happy Choice;* 27 May 1727 (PGLR M.229)

Snowden, Richard; wife Ann; tract *Shepherds Hard Fortune;* 25 Mar 1742 (PGLR Y.456)

Snowden, Thomas; son Henry; 1748 (MCW X.115)

Snowden, Richard, Jr.; 16 Mar 1753; 11 Apr 1753; wife Elizabeth; sister Elizabeth; bros. Samuel, John; nephews Richard Crabb, Samuel Thomas, Richard Snowden [s/o Thomas]; tract *Addition to Charley Forrest* (MCW X.267)

Snowden, Thomas; 1 Jul 1765; 24 May 1770; wife Mary; children Henry, Richard, Thomas; father Richard [dec'd]; tracts *Davis Ford, Peter Point, Brook Grove, Bacon Hall, Diamond, Snowden Darling* (MCW XIV.136); 18 May 1772 (I 108.283)

Snowden, Henry; 19 Feb 1775; 22 Apr 1775; bro. Thomas; father Thomas; tract *The Forge* (MCW XVI.48)

SOLLARS

Sollars, Robert [CA]; wife Mary [d/o William Sellby]; tract *Bealington, Good Luck*; 26 Apr 1700 (PGLR A.427)

Sollars, Robert [AA]; wife Mary; son Robert; 20 Feb 1711/2 (PGLR F.107)

Sallers, John; wife Mary; child: Sarah, b. 2 Feb 1729/30 (QAP b/23)

SOMMERS

Sommer, James; wife Mary; children: Sirvina (f), b. 24 Oct 1746; John, b. 2 Oct 1748; Mary, b. 11 Jan 1751; Virlinder, b. 11 Jul 1753 (KGP p. 309)

Sommers, George; wife Elizabeth; child: Virlinder, b. 2 Jun 1754 (KGP p. 306)

Sommers, Thomas; wife Rachel; child: John Dent, b. 13 Jul 1754 (KGP p. 306)

Sommers, Dent; wife Maryan; child: Sarah, b. 23 Sep 1754 (KGP p. 306)

SOPER

Soaper, John; cooper; wife Mary; tract *Marborrow Plains*; 30 Jul 1703 (PGLR C.71a)

Soaper, John; wife Mary; tract *Good Luck*; 27 Sep 1711 (PGLR F.143)

Soper, Jane; child: Mary, b. 26 8ber 1717 (QAP b/13)

Soaper, John, Sr.; daus. Lucy, Sarah; 5 Sep 1726 (PGLR M.102)

Soper, John; wife Leah; child: Jemima, b. 28 Aug 1734 (QAP b/29)

Soper [Soaper], John; planter; 29 Nov 1742; 11 Apr 1742; sons John, Robert; daus: Esther Duvall, Mary James, Phillice Lowe, Acquilla Shaw, Lucy Lashley, Priscilla, Leah, Jamima; s-i-l Mareen Duvall, Jr.; grandsons, John and Robert; tract *Barton's Vinyard* (MCW VIII.205); 2 May 1743 (I 28.164); children Sarah [dec'd], John, Robert, Mary James, Phillis Lowe, Lucy Lashley [w/o Robert], Aqquilla Shaw [w/o John], Esther Duvall [w/o Mareen, Jr.]; 21 Nov 1746 (AA 22.440)

Soaper, John; wife Martha; children: Elizabeth, b. 23 Jan 1747; Zadock, b. 15 Feb 1749; Susanna, b. 23 Mar 1752, bapt. 10 May 1752; Mary, b. 31 Dec 1753 or 1754; Sarah, b. 12 Mar 1756 (KGP p. 296, 305, 313)

Soper, Thomas; wife Sarah; children: William Fredrick, bapt. 11 Apr 1762; Charles Bleadon, bapt. 23 Oct 1763 at Upper Chapel; Thomas, bapt. 18 Aug 1765 Upper Chapel (KGP p. 326, 334 359)

Soper, John; wife Martha; children: Nathan, bapt. 11 Apr 1762; Rebeccak, b. 20 Apr 1764; bapt. 24 Jun 1764 Upper Chapel; Bassil, bapt. 19 Apr 1767 Upper Chapel (KGP p. 326, 341, 365)

Soper, Alexander; wife Mary; children: Robert, bapt. _ Aug 1763 at Broad Creek; Phillop Evens, bapt. 30 Jun 1765 Broad Creek (KGP p. 337, 347)

Soaper, Thomas; 15 Jan 1765 (I 91.313); 26 Mar 1767; admx. John Cooke (ABB 5.18)

Soper, Leonard; wife Elizabeth; child: Mary, bapt. 19 Apr 1767 Upper Chapel; Alexander, b. 7 Mar 1772 Upper Chapel; John, b. 2 Sep 1773 Upper Chapel; Eleanor, b. 24 Oct 1775 Upper Chapel (KGP p. 389, 390, 392)

Soper, Charles; wife Mary; child: Joseph Belt, bapt. 26 Jul 1767 Broad Creek (KGP p. 361)

Soper [Soaper], John, Sr.; 23 Apr 1758; 28 Mar 1768; wife Susannah; children: Mary Ellis, Susannah Darnal, Sarah Talbut, Charles, Basil, Rachel, John, Thomas, James & Nathan Soper (MCW XIV.35); 1 Apr 1768 (I 96.337); 10 Dec 1768; widow [unnamed]; children Susannah, Sarah, John, Charles, Thomas, James, Nathan, Basil, Rachel Soper (ABB 5.178)

Soper, John; wife Ann; child: James, bapt. 24 Jul 1768 Upper Chapel (KGP p. 370)

Soper, Bassil; wife Massey; child: Samuel, bapt. 1 Jan 1769 Broad Creek (KGP p. 372)

Soaper, Thomas; heirs Frederick, Charles, Thomas [?sons of John]; 29 Mar 1771 (GB 291)

Soper, Robert; wife Sarah; child: Benoni, b. 6 Nov 1774 Upper Chapel (KGP p. 391)

Soper, Thomas; heirs Charles Bladen Soper, Thomas Soper, William Frederick Soper; 28 Mar 1775 (GB 334, 336); heirs William Bladen, Charles Bladen & Thomas Soaper; 30 Mar 1775 (GB 277)

SOUTH

South, Thomas; 5 Jun 1742 (I 27.124); 9 Aug 1743 (AA 19.443)

SOUTHER

Souther, Christopher; age ca 49; 27 Oct 1773 (CCR MSA 13.97)

SPALDING

Spalding, Thomas [SM]; wife Cathran; tract *St. Thomas*; 13 Jan 1740 (PGLR Y.253)

SPANGLER

Spangler, John; admx. 10 Jun 1773 (I 117.355)

SPARKES

Sparkes, Mathew; wife Elenor; children: Sarah, b. 23 May 1753; Josiah, b. 26 Aug 1761; True Love, b. 21 Jul 1764 Upper Chapel (KGP p. 300, 323, 358)

Sparkes, Mathew; wife Margrey; child: Elizabeth, bapt. 2 Nov 1766 Upper Chapel; Jane, bapt. 6 Nov 1768 Upper Chapel (KGP p. 354, 372)

SPARROW

Sparrow, Mary; age 2 on 12 Mar last; d/o William; Aug 1714 (PGCR G.633)

Sparrow, William; 3 Feb 1729 (I 15.400); heirs Mary, Matthew, Eleanor; 24 Aug 1730 (GB 57); 26 Nov 1730 (AA 10.566)

SPAUL

Spaul, John; 25 Jun 1761; 31 Oct 1761; wife Alice (MCW XII.97); extx. Alice; 16 Feb 1762 (I 78.316)

SPEAKE

Speake, John; wife Winifred; son John, Jr. [wife Elizabeth]; tract *Plimouth*; 24 Nov 1718 (PGLR F.166/748)

Speake, John, Jr. [CH]; wife Elizabeth; tract *Plymouth*; 11 Jan 1728 (PGLR M.356)

Speake, John, Sr.; wife Winifred [d/o John Wheeler]; son John, Jr.; tract *Plymouth*; 8 Jun 1731 (PGLR Q.346)

Speak, Robert; wife Luckresha; child: Sarah, b. 10 Aug 1761, bapt. 6 Sep 1761 (KGP p. 323)

SPENSER

Spenser, Jas.; wife Elliner; child: John, b. 5 Mar 1761 (PGP p. 261)

Spencer, Joseph; age 11 on 1 Oct next; bound out; Jun 1736 (PGCR W.51)

SPICER

Spicer, George; planter; 11 May 1711; 21 May 1711; wife Mary; daus. Ann Miskill, Sophia Spicer; tract *The Forrest* (MCW III.204); 5 Jun 1711 (I&A 32c.149); extx. Mary; 24 May 1712 (I&A 33a.190, 209); extx. Mary [widow]; 21 Nov 1713 (I&A 35b.17)

SPIERS

Spiers [Spires], William; wife Mary; children: Phebe, b. 3 Apr 1726; Patience, b. 13 Jun 1728; Asenath, b. 7 Jun 1730 (PGP p. 247-8, 249)

Spiers, Zachariah; wife Dianah; child: Hezekiah Gaither, b. 8 Feb 1765 (PGP p. 276)

SPOLLUXFIELD

Spolluxfield, James; wife Israel; child: Eliphelet, b. 8 Jan 1757 (KGP p. 314)

SPRADOSE

Spradose, William; wife Elizabeth; tract *Spradose Forrest*; 2 Jan 1721 (PGLR I.91)

SPRIGG

Sprigg, Thomas, Sr.; 9 May 1704; 29 Dec 1704; son Thomas; daus. Elizabeth Wade & children, Ann Gittens & children; Oliver Nutthall & children; Martha Prather & children; ss-i-l _____ Wade, Phillip Gittens, Thomas Prater; grandson Thomas Stockett [s/o Thomas], ?Oliver Stockett; tracts *Northamton, Kellering*; *Manor of Collington*; grandsons Thomas, Oliver (MCW III.48); 28 Jan 1704 (I&A 3.571)

Sprig, John; 17 Dec 1705 (I&A 25.107, 115)

Sprigg, Thomas; cous. Charles Calvert [VA], Richard Calvert [SM]; 31 Oct 1707 (PGLR C.206a)

Sprigg, Edward; m. 26 Apr 1720 Elizabeth Pile [d/o Dr. Robert]; children: Richard, b. 28 Apr 1721; Edward, b. 12 Jun 1723; Elizabeth, b. 21 Jul 1723 (?); James, b. 27 Jan 1724/5; Thomas, b. 21 Feb 1726/7; Gilbert, b. 11 Aug 1730; Mary, b. 17 Aug 1742 (QAP m/2; b/17, 19, 20, 26)

Sprigg, Thomas; son Thomas; 15 Feb 1722 (PGLR I.367)

Sprigg, Thomas, Jr.; wife Margery; children: John, b. 26 9ber 1716; Mary, b. 15 10ber 1723 (QAP b/14, 18)

Sprigg, Osborn; wife Elizabeth; child: Margaret, b. 20 Mar 1726 (QAP b/22)

Sprigg, Thomas; admx. Margery; 28 May 1726 (I 11.405); admx. Margery; 29 Nov 1726 (AA 8.98); [as Thomas, Maj.]; admx. Margery; 14 Jun 1727 (AA 8.231); 7 Nov 1728 (AA 9.103) admx. Margery; 29 Jul 1730 (I 15.555); widow Margery; 29 Jul 1730 (AA 10.375); widow Margery; heirs Thomas, John, Ann, Edward, Mary; 28 Mar 1734 (GB 63); admx. Margery Belt [w/o Joseph]; 30 Jun 1737 (AA 15.341)

Sprigg, Osborn, m. 11 Jul 1727 Rachel Belt; d/o Col. Joseph; children: Lucy, b. 9 Jan 1728/9; Ester, b. 16 Feb 1730/1; Rachel, b. 1 Jun 1733; Priscilla, b. 26 Sep 1735 (QAP m/4; b/22, 24, 29)

Sprigg, Thomas, Maj. [dec'd]; widow Margery; 8 Oct 1731 (CCR-MSA 5.427)

Sprigg, John; age ca 20; choses bro. Thomas as guardian; Nov 1736 (PGCR W.266)

Sprigg, Edward; age ca 16; choses bro. Thomas as guardian; Jun 1737 (PGCR W.423)

Sprigg, Margarett; 14 Apr 1740 (I 25.93)

Sprigg, Osborn; age ca 38; 29 May 1745 (CCR JK#4.591)

Sprigg, Edward; wife Ellinar; child; Edward, b. 1 Nov 1746 (PGP p. 252)

Sprigg, Osborn; 6 Jan 1749/50; wife Rachel; daus. Rachel, Priscilla, Elizabeth, Ann; sons Joseph, Osborn, Thomas; ss-i-l Thomas Bowie, Baruch Williams; tracts *Darnall's Grove*, *Abell's Lott*, *Stock Quarter* (MCW X.61-2); extx. Rachel; 1750 (I 48.190); extx. Rachel; 8 Aug 1753 (AA 35.1)

Sprigg, Osborn; d. ca 8 Jan 1749 (CCR MSA 8.644)

Sprigg, Edward; 30 Nov 1751; 21 Feb 1752; wife Mary; children: Edward, Frederick, Margaret, Gilbert, James, Jacob; unborn child; tracts *Happy Choice*, *Addition to Pile's Dlight*, *Three Pastures*, *Little Cove*, *North Hampton*, *Catharine*, *Addition to Catharine*, *Sprigg's Meadow*, *The Gore*, *The Lane* (MCW X.194-5); extx. Mary; 22 May 1752 (I 54.213, 217); [as Col.]; extx. Mary; dau. Lucy, b. after death of dec'd; 13 Jul 1753 (AA 35.28)

Sprigg, James; wife Elizabeth; children: Leven, bapt. 14 Mar 1762; Reason, bapt. 31 Aug 1766 Upper Chapel (KGP p. 325, 355)

Sprigg, Gilbert; 5 Apr 1765 (I 87.144); heir John; 10 Nov 1766 (GB 249)

Sprigg, James; wife Elenor; child: Mary, bapt. 4 Sep 1768 Upper Chapel (KGP p. 371)

Sprigg, Jacob; 21 Mar 1770; 13 Apr 1770; bro. Frederick; sister Lucy; father Edward [dec'd]; mother Mary; f-i-l Thomas Pindle; s-i-l Mary Pindle; tracts *Addition to Happy Choice*; relative Wm. Turner Wooton (MCW XIV.124)

Sprigg, Priscilla; 27 Jun 1776; 17 Aug 1776; sisters Mary, Amy & Elizabeth Sprigg; bro. John Clark Sprigg (MCW XVI.166)

SPRY

Spry, Francis; wife Elizabeth; tract [unnamed]; 25 Jan 1699 (PGLR A.189)

SPURER

Spurer [Spurier], Green; wife Aves; children: Thomas, b. 25 Dec 1763; Joseph, b. 10 Jul 1764 (PGP p. 269, 276)

SPYVEY

Spyvey, John; wife Rosanah; child: Ann, b. 4 Aug 1772 (PGP p. 278)

ST. CLARE

St. Clare, Robert; wife Rebecca; child: Dorothy, b. 4 Feb 1761; George, b. 14 Apr 1763 at Upper Chapel (KGP p. 330, 333)

STAFFORD

Stafford, Richard; age ca 15; servant; Feb 1698/9 Ct. (PGCR A.386)

Stafford, Thomas; wife Isabell; tract *Swanson's Lot*; 27 Feb 1728 (PGLR M.375)

STALLINGS

Stalings, Benjamin; admx. Sarah; 27 Jun 1753 (I 55.104)

Stallings, Joseph; wife Elisabeth; child: Martha, b. 12 Oct 1772 (PGP p. 279)

STALLYONS

Stallyons, Joseph; wife Elizabeth; child: Jacob, bapt. 4 Aug 1751 (KGP p. 294)

STAMP

Stamp, Thomas; 4 Feb 1756 (I 62.167); heirs Joseph, Elizabeth, Mary; 29 Mar 1758 (GB 210)

STAMPER

Stamper, Robert, Capt.; 30 Apr 1744 (I 29.156); 28 Jun 1744 (AA 20.330)

STANLEY

Stanley, John; bro. Edward; uncle Hugh Stanley; tract *Willard's Purchase*; 3 Oct 1701 (PGLR C.16a)

Stanley, John; 9 Mar 1702/3; 3 Aug 1705; cous. John Edwards (MVW III.75)

STANSBURY

Stansbury, Edmund; 18 Feb 1748; 29 Mar 1749; ss-i-l Michael Covlisall, Michaell Coots; tract *Chance* (MCW IX.196)

STARKEY

Starkey, Lawrence; 26 Mar 1729 (I 14.17); 25 Nov 1729 (AA 10.95)

STEEL

Steel, John; wife Elizabeth; child: Lydia, bapt. 22 Oct 1752 (KGP p. 297)

Steal, Alexander; wife Lydda; child: Mildred, b. 5 Nov 1773 Lower Chapel (KGP p. 379)

STEUART

Steuart, William; 21 Sep 1763 (I 82.150)

STEVENS

Stevens, Edward; age 7 Dec last; orphan; Mar 1697/8 Ct. (PGCR A.298)

Stephens, Richard; wife Sarah; son Benjamin; 3 Aug 1697 (PGLR F.190)

Stephens, William; wife Rebacca; child: Thomas, b. 1 Aug 1745 (KGP p. 288)

Stephens [Stevens], Richard; wife Elizabeth; children: Mary Annis, b. 27 Nov 1751; Edward Briggs, b. 24 May 1754; John, b. 6 Mar 1757; Rebecca, b. 23 Feb 1759; Ruth Johnson, b. 11 Mar 1761; Elizabeth, b. 9 Jan 1765 (PGP p. 257, 259, 275)

Stevens, Edward; wife Frances; child: Martha, bapt. 1 Mar 1752 (KGP p. 295)

Stevens, Henry; 21 Jul 1752; 13 Sep 1752; wife Blanch; sons Gabrel, John, Solomon, Absolom, Benjamin; daus. Lucy, Keziah, Susanna, Soloman; tract *Widow's Trouble* (MCW X.233); wife Blanch; 14 Feb 1753 (I 53.1)

Stevens, Henry; wife Blanch; child: Lowey (f), b. 25 Mar 1753 (KGP p. 300)

Stephens, Robert; child: Robert, bapt. 28 Mar 1762 (KGP p. 326)

Stevens, John; admx. Eleanor; 9 Aug 1764 (I 87.121); 10 Sep 1765; admx. Eleanor (ABB 4.151)

Stevens, William; wife Elizabeth; child: George Gardner, b. 11 Feb 1773 Lower Chapel; William Darnall, b. 13 Jan 1775 Lower Chapel (KGP p. 380, 384)

Stevens, Thomas; wife Eleanor; child: Elizabeth, b. 15 Apr 1773 Lower Chapel; Mary Darnall, b. 1774 Lower Chapel (KGP p. 380. 384)

STEWARD

Steward, Elinor; age 3 on 25 Jan next; orphan of Margery Steward; bound out; Jun 1711 Ct. (PGCR G.69)

Steward, Edward; wife Charity; child: John, bapt. 18 Jan 1767 Broad Creek (KGP p. 360)

STILES

Stiles, William; wife Vialender; child: John, bapt. 3 Oct 1762 (KGP p. 332); Thomas, b. 18 Apr 1765 (PGP p. 275) Mary, b. 22 Sep 1771 (PGP p. 279)

STIMPSON

Stimton [Stimson], Solomon; planter; 9 Jan 1726/7; 26 Jan 1726/7; wife Elizabeth; sons Solomon, Benjamin, Jeremiah; daus. Sarah, Mary; ss-i-l William & Thomas Elder (MCW VI.10); admx. Elisabeth; 5 Apr 1727 (I 11.906); extx. Elisabeth; legatess Solomon Stimson, Benjamin Stimson, Ann Hardy [w/o William]; 20 May 1728 (AA 9.157); exs. Peter Hoggins and wife Elisabeth; 16 Oct 1728 (AA 9.75); exs. Peter Hoggins and wife Elisabeth; 23 Oct 1729 (AA 9.480); heirs Jeremiah, Mary, Sarah; 29 May 1730 (GB 55)

Stimson, Thomas; age ca 75; 19 Mar 1728/9 (PGLR M.480)

Stympson, Jereamiah; age 15 on 8 Jan next; choses guardian; Aug 1730
(PGCR P.459)

Stimton [Stimpson], Benjamin; planter; 23 Sep 1734; 11 Nov 1734; wife
[unnamed]; son Benjamin; tract *Solomon Purchis* (MCW VII.114); admx. Mary;
extx. Mary Smith [w/o Benjamin]; children: Benjamin, Mary, _____; 26
Jan 1735 (AA 14.145); 25 Mar 1735 (I 21.51); extx. Mary Smith [w/o
Benjamin]; 21 Jun 1737 (AA 15.335); admx. Mary Smith [w/o Benjamin];
heirs [unnamed]; 9 Aug 1740 (AA 18.26); heirs Benjamin, Mary, Anne; 26
Nov 1740 (GB 113)

Stimpton, Solomon; wife Hester; tract *Solomon's Purchase*; 18 Jan 1734 (PGLR
T.276)

Stimpson, Benjamin; choses guardian; Nov 1744 (PGCR CC.585)

Stimpson, Jeremiah; wife Rachel; children: Erasmus, b. 14 Apr 1762;
Solomon, b. 4 Mar 1765 (PGP p. 263, 272)

Stimpson, Benjamin; wife Cassandrah; child: Loyd, b. 25 Dec 1764 (PGP p.
272)

Stimpson, Joseph; wife Lucy; child: Solomin, b. 8 Apr 1765 (PGP p. 277)

STOCKETT

Stockett, Thomas; dau. Mary Sollers [w/o John]; 5 Mar 1728 (PGLR M.379);
Thomas [AA]; dau. Elizabeth Beall; 26 Nov 1728 (PGLR M.331)

STODDERT

Stoddart, James; wife Mary; tract *Yarrow*; 28 Jan 1700 (PGLR A.343)

Stoddert, James; wife Elizabeth; tract *Clyde*; 21 Oct 1715 (PGLR F.517)

Stoddert, James; age 57; 23 Feb 1724 (PGLR I.622); age ca 58; 9 Aug 1725
(PGLR I.676)

Stoddert [Stoddart], James; 29 Mar 1726; 31 Mar 1726; wife Elizabeth;
sons James, William, John, Benjamin, Thomas; tracts *Southampton,
Daniell's, The Pasture, Addition, Friendship, Rocky* Creek (MCW VI.9-10)

Stoddert, James; d. ca 1726-7; wife Elizabeth; sons James [d. a few mos.
later], John; 3 Feb 1728 (CCR-MSA 5.449)

Stoddert, James, Jr.; admx. Sarah Weems; 14 Dec 1726 (I 11.911); widow
Sarah Weems [w/o James]; 3 Feb 1726 (I 11.836); 30 Apr 1728 (AA 9.134); 30
Apr 1728 (AA 9.137); 31 Jan 1729 (AA 10.140); heirs Benjamin, Thomas; 25
Mar 1730 (GB 52)

Stoddart, John; m. Marianne Truman; children: James, b. 19 Oct 1728; John
Truman, b. 18 Jul 1732; Thomas Truman, b. 8 Feb 1733/4; William
Truman, b. 15 Mar 1736/7; Kenhelm Truman, b. 11 Sep 1739; Richard

Truman, b. 5 Mar 1741/2; Mary Truman, b. 28 Nov 1744; Walter Truman, b. 30 Apr 1747 (KGP p. 260, 261)

Stoddert, John; wife Mary Amny Truman Stoddert; 9 Sep 1729 (PGLR M.501)

Stoddart, James; 22 Jul 1736 (AA 15.39)

Stoddert, William; 31 Mar 1737 (I 22.215); 29 Dec 1737 (AA 14.518); heirs Benjamin, Thomas; 24 Jun 1740 (GB 112)

Stoddert, James; children: John, Elizabeth, James, William; tract *Beall's Gift*; 28 Nov 1739 (PGLR Y.122)

Stoddert, Thomas; age 19; choses Benjamin Stoddert as guardian; Aug 1743 (PGCR CC.7)

Stoddert, William Trueman; wife Elizabeth; children: Susanna Trueman, b. 4 Dec 1759, Tuesday ca 10 p.m.; Thomas James John, b. 19 Feb 1763, Saturday ca 3 p.m.; Johana Truman, b. 30 Aug 1765, Friday ca 12 midnight (KGP p. 316)

Stodart, Kenalam Truman; children: Ann Truman, b. 25 Nov 1761; Mary Anney Truman, b. 12 Jan 1764 at Lower Chapel (KGP p. 324, 336)

STONE

Stone, William [CH]; wife Theadosia [d/o Zacharia Wade]; tract *Good Luck*; 10 Mar 1698 (PGLR A.163)

Stone, Thomas; extx. Catherine; 28 Sep 1728 (AA 9.71)

Stone, Joseph; wife Elizabeth; children: Ann, b. 25 Aug 1761; Elenor, b. 6 Jul 1764 Upper Chapel; Thomas, bapt. 16 Sep 1766 Broad Creek; Henry, b. 19 Oct 1768 Broad Creek (KGP p. 325, 341, 359, 364)

Stone, David; wife Susanna; child: Eleanor, b. 21 Aug 1772 Upper Chapel (KGP p. 389)

Stone, James; wife Martha; child: Anne, b. 31 Mar 1774 Broad Creek (KGP p. 386)

Stone, Joseph; wife Elizabeth; children: Mary Calvert, b. 9 Mar 1774 Broad Creek; Joseph, b. 15 Feb 1776 Broad Creek (KGP p. 382, 386)

Stone, John; wife Jemimah; child: Henry Evins, b. 19 Apr 1775 Broad Creek (KGP p. 387)

STONESTREET

Stonestreet, Thomas; wife Christian; children: Butler, b. 26 Aug 1703; Edward, b. 23 Dec 1705; Thomas, b. 7 Jun 1708; Anne, b. 23 Mar 1710; Elizabeth, b. 6 Jun 1714 (KGP p. 270)

Stonestreet, Butler; children: Virlinder, b. 12 Apr 1744; Catharine, b. 8 Apr 1747; Ellender, b. 4 Apr 1749; Richard, b. 26 May 1751; Butler Edelen, b. 8 Feb 1756 (KGP p.291)

Stonestreet, Butler; wife Jane; child: Henry, b. 11 Sep 1752; bapt. 29 Feb 1756 (KGP p. 291)

Stonestreet, Edward; wife Elinor; children; Edward, bapt. 14 Jan 1753; Basil Williams, b. 18 Mar 1755 (KGP p. 297, 308)

Stonestreet, Butler; 3 Dec 1755; 29 Dec 1755; wife Jane; sons Henry, Richard; unborn child; daus. Sarah, Mary, Charity, Catharine, Eleanor, Verlinda, Sarah Edelen; nephews John Tolson, Luke Marberry, Henry Low; tracts *Athey's Folly, Littleworth, Wade's Adventure* (MCW XI.121); extx. Jane; 17 May 1756 (I 60.708); 16 Sep 1757; dist. to Richard, Verlinda, Catharine, Elinor, "child wife is pregnant with"; ext. Jayne (ABB 2.85); 26 Jul 1758; extx. Jane Stonestreet; children: Henry, Richard, Butler, Edlin, Mary, Virlinda, Catherine, Elinor (ABB 2.95); heirs Henry, Richard, Butler, Catharine, Eleanor; 3 Dec 1760 (GB 216)

Stonestreet, Catherine; d/o Eleanor; 1770 (MCW XIV.202)

Stonestreet, Edward; 14 Sep 1771; 28 Nov 1771; wife Eleanor; children: Thomas, Joseph, Christian Frey, John, Edward, Basil, Butler (MCW XIV.195); extx. Eleanor; 16 Dec 1771 (I 110.234); 24 Aug 1773; extx. Mrs. Eleanor Stonestreet; 7 children; legatees Thomas & Joseph Stonestreet, Christian Tray [dau.]; others (ABB 6.279); widow Eleanor; heirs Christian, Joseph, John, Edward, Basil, Buttler, Thomas; 29 Mar 1775 (GB 325); heir Richard; 27 Nov 1771 (GB 300), Butler Edelen; minor; 26 Aug 1772 (GB 306)

Stonestreet, John; wife Ann; child: Elizabeth, b. 27 Mar 1773 Broad Creek (KGP p. 378)

Stonestreet, Basil; wife Elizabeth; child: Anna Williams, b. 20 Oct 1775 Lower Chapel (KGP p. 381)

Stonestreet, Joseph; wife Alse; child: Mary Ann, b. 16 Apr 1776 Broad Creek (KGP p. 382)

Stonestreet, Thomas, Sr.; 2 Apr 1771; 1 Nov 1771; children: Edward, Anne Lowe, Elizabeth Ashford; grandchildren John, Basil, Butter, Edward, Verlinder Newman [w/o Butter], Verlinder Lanham; grandsons John, Basil, Butler & Edward Stonestreet, Verlinder Lanham; tract *Battacy* (MCW XIV.195); 18 Dec 1771 (I 110.230); 27 Apr 1773; daus. Ann Lowe, Elisabeth; son Edward; grandchildren, John, Basil, Edward, Verlinda Newman [w/o Butler], Verlinda Lanham; John [s/o Edward] (ABB 6.203); heir [unnamed]; 6 Dec 1773 (GB 315)

Stonestreet, Thomas; age ca 49; 19 Oct 1730 (CCR-MSA 5.452); age ca 57; 24 Nov 1740 (PGLR Y.235)

STORY

Story, Joseph; wife Ann; children: Francis, b. 6 May 1711; Elizabeth, b. 24 7ber 1713; Jane, b. 12 May 1715 (QAP b/10)

Story, Joseph; m. 22 Jan 1717 Jane Soper (QAP m/1)

Story, Joseph; m. 17 Nov 1738 Mary ____; child: William Marmaduke, b. 30 8ber 1721 (QAP m/7; b/17)

STOWETON

Stourton, Robert; extx. Margery; 28 Apr 1717 (I&A 38b.1)

Stoweton, Robert [dec'd] [SM]; widow Margery; tract *Margery*; [undated, with 1720] (PGLR I.48)

STRAWHOW

Strawhow, Adam; wife Easter; granddau. Mary Thickpenny; 27 Nov 1727 (PGLR M.250)

STREET

Street, John; 26 Jun 1733; son Francis (MCW VII.31)

Street, Francis; age 10 on 20 Feb next; s/o Mary Street [widow]; Jun 1733 (PGCR S.286)

Street, Francis; wife Mary; children: Priscilla, b. 3 Apr 1760 [no mother named]; William Beel, b. 10 Apr 1763; Jonan Lewis, b. 31 Dec 1764 (PGP p. 268, 275)

Street, Elisabeth; 10 Apr 1776 (I 122.226)

STRONG

Strong, Nathaniel; wife Mary; child: Nathaniel, b. 21 Sep 1738 (QAP b/32)

Strong, John; wife Ann; child: Susanna, b. 16 Mar 1774 Broad Creek (KGP p. 385)

STUMP

Stump, Thomas; 29 Apr 1723; 10 May 1723; wife Eliza.; 3 sons Thomas, John, William; tract *Stump's Valles* (MCW V.130); 20 Aug 1723 (I 9.6); 6 May 1724 (AA 6.4); orphan [unnamed]; 29 Jun 1726 (AA 7.444)

Stump, Elizabeth; widow; sons Thomas, John, William; 1 May 1730 (PGLR M.585)

SUIT

Suit, Nathaniel; m. 24 Jun 1752 Mary Burch; children: Jessee Burch, b. 27 Sep 1753; Nathaniel, b. 10 Mar 1756; Elisabeth, b. 25 Mar 1758; Edward, b. 15 Aug 1760; Ann, b. 13 Aug 1762; John Smith, b. 4 Sep 1764;

Mary, b. 15 Mar 1767; Susanna, b. 26 Dec 1770 Lower Chapel; Oliver Burch, b. 1 Aug 1773 Upper Chapel (KGP p. 376, 390)

Suit, Nathaniel; admx. Mary; 6 Dec 1775 (I 123.224)

SULLAVIN

Swillivan [Sulavin], Thomas; wife Judey; children: Mary, b. 7 Jan 1752; Ann, b. 17 Aug 1754; Adkey (m), b. 23 Dec 1755; Thomas, b. 15 Aug 1757; Rebecker, b. 29 Apr 1759; Daniel, b. 19 Nov 1760; Judey, b. 4 Mar 1762; bapt. 18 Apr 1762; Isaac, b. 4 Jan 1764; Isaac, bapt. 26 Feb 1764 Lower Chapel; Lidea, b. 3 Apr 1766 (KGP p. 319, 326, 344)

Sulavin, Daniel; wife Ann; child: Charlotte, bapt. 6 Nov 1768 Upper Chapel (KGP p. 372)

SUMMERS

Sumers, [male]; age 11 next Nov; s/o Sarah Summers [now Sarah Smart, w/o Anthony]; raised by Hannah Edwards; bound out; Sep 1697 (PGCR A.233)

Sumers, John; 1 Mar 1703; 27 Nov 1705; wife Rebecca; dau. Sary Westly; grandson Samuel Westly; sons William and John Sumers (MCW III.86); widow [unnamed]; 30 Oct 1707 (I&A 27.244); extx. Rebecca Mackee [w/o Henry]; 20 Jul 1708 (I&A 28.263); 25 Feb 1711 (I&A 33a.115)

Summers, John; wife Mary; tract Pitchcroft; 10 Jul 1713 (PGLR F.269)

Sumers, James; wife Mary; children: Survine (f), b. 24 Oct 1746; John Smith, b. 2 Oct 1748; Mary, b. 7 Jan 1750 (KGP p. 291)

Summers [Sumers], George; wife Elizabeth; children: Ann, bapt. 17 May 1752 (KGP p. 296); George, b. 26 Aug 1759; Ann, b. 16 Mar 1761 (KGP p. 327)

Summers, James; 8 Jan 1761; 14 Feb 1761; wife Mary; daus. Sebina, Mary, Velinda, Rebecca, Ann; unborn child (MCW XII.49); [as planter]; extx. Mary; 14 Apr 1761 (I 74.160); 20 Nov 1762; extx. Mary Summers; children Sabina, Mary, Virlinda, Rebecca, Ann, James (ABB 3.164); widow Mary; heirs Sebina, Mary, Verlinda, Rebecca, Ann, James; 26 Aug 1763 (GB 230, 273, 280)

Summers, Dent; wife Mary Ann; child: James Dent, bapt. 21 May 1761 (KGP p. 322)

Summers, George; wife Elizabeth; child: Ann, bapt. 21 May 1761; Paul, b. 30 Aug 1763 at Broad Creek (KGP p. 322, 338)

Summers, James; wife Mary; child: James, b. 18 Jul 1761 (KGP p. 323)

Summers, Benjamin; wife Grace; child: Mary, b. 20 Jan 1762 (PGP p. 262) wife Grace; child: John Litten, bapt. 4 Apr 1764 at Upper Chapel; Grace, bapt. 20 Jul 1766 Upper Chapel (KGP p. 340, 365)

Summers, Thomas; wife Rachel; child: Paul Talbutt, b. Jan 1762 (PGP p.262)

Summers, Joseph; wife Ellener; child: Ruth, b. 6 Dec 1765 (PGP p. 277)

Summers, Nathan; wife Mary; child: John, bapt. 10 May 1767 Upper Chapel (KGP p. 365)

Summers, John, Sr.; Aug 1763; 9 Oct 1769; wife Mary; children: Dent, Benjamin, Rebecca King, John, George, William, Thomas, Joseph, Mary Wheat, Rachel Johnson, Ruth Riggs, Jemima Caton (MCW XIV.100)

Summers, Josias; wife Jeremiah; child: Nathaniel, b. 27 Dec 1772 Upper Chapel (KGP p. 389)

Summers, John, Jr.; admx. Dorcas; 10 Sep 1774 (I 118.264)

Summers, John; 3 Apr 1775; admx. Mrs. Lydia Summers (ABB 7.4)

Summers, James; heir Ann; 29 Nov 1775 (GB 288)

SUMMERSET

Summerset, Thomas; 4 Jul 1736 (I 22.33); widow [unnamed]; 14 Dec 1736 (AA 15.260)

SURATT

Suratt [Saratt], Joseph; 24 Feb 1715 (I&A 36c.110); adms. William Lewis & wife Katherine; 16 Oct 1716 (I&A 38a.117,118)

SURBELY

Surbely, William; m. Elizabeth; child: William, bapt. 30 Aug 1752 (KGP p. 297)

SUTAR

Sutar [Sutus], Thomas; wife Easter; children: George, b. 3 Dec 1763 Broad Creek, bapt. 19 Feb 1764 at Upper Chapel; John, bapt. 1 Dec 1765 Lower Chapel (KGP p. 340, 343, 346)

SUTTON

Sutton, John; m. 3 Oct 1746 Mary Beanes; children: Mary Elisabeth, b. 19 Dec 174_; William, b. 8 May 175_; Sarah Ann, b. 24 Sep 175_ (KGP p. 291)

Sutton, John; admx. Mary; son William; 15 Sep 1769 (I 101.235)

Sutton, William; wife Elizabeth; children: Heneretta, b. 29 Mar 1773; John, b. 5 Mar 1775 Broad Creek (KGP p. 387)

SWAIN

Swain, Joshua [Josua]; wife Alse [Ayls]; child: Elija, b. 10 Sep 1769 Upper Chapel; Eleanor, b. 4 Sep 1772 Upper Chapel (KGP p. 375, 389)

SWAN

Swann, John; m. 24 Jan 1720/1 Elizabeth Foster; child: Comfort (f), b. 5 Jul 1725 (QAP m/2; b/19)

Swan, John; wife Elizabeth; tract *Swan's Delight*; 16 Jan 1724 (PGLR I.604)

Swan, John; admx. Elisabeth; 5 Jun 1727 (I 12.169)

Swan, Thomas, Jr.; age ca 31; 1737 (PGLR T.504)

Swann, Thomas, Sr.; age ca 63; 1737 (PGLR T.504); age ca 65; 1738 (PGLR T.607)

Swann, Edward; age ca 37; 1737 (PGLR T.504)

Swan, Thomas; 15 Apr 1762; 14 Sep 1763; wife Catharine; sons Edward, Samuel; grandchildren Thomas Swann [s/o Samuel], Eleanor Swann (MCW XI1.211)

SWANSTONE

Swanstone, Francis [CA]; wife Susanna; tract *Swanson's Lott*; 14 Apr 1713 (PGLR F.254)

SWEARINGEN

Swaringen, Thomas; wife Jane; tract part of *Basingthorp Hall*; 10 Jan 1704 (PGLR C.120b)

Sweringen, Thomas; wife Lydia; children: Thomas, b. 8 Apr 1708; Mary, b. 11 Aug 1710; Laurana, b. 15 8ber 1713; Margaret, b. 17 Feb 1716; Van, b. 22 May 1719 (QAP b/7, 10, 15)

Swearingen, Thomas; 29 Jul 1708; 9 Mar 1711; wife Jane; sons Thomas, Van, Samuel, John (MCW III..203); [as Sr.]; 13 Apr 1711 (I&A 32b.94); extx. Jane; 14 Jul 1713 (I&A 34.63)

Swearingen, John; m. 9 Feb 1715 Mary Ray; children: Mary, b. 29 8ber 1720; Lydia, b. 7 7ber 1726; Thomas, b. 23 9ber 1728; John, b. 6 Aug 1735 (QAP m/1; b/16, 20, 21, 29)

Sweringen, Samuel; m. 14 Feb 1715 Eliza Farmer (QAP m/1)

Swearingen [Sweringen], Van; wife Elizabeth; children: Elizabeth, b. 4 Jul 1715; Rebecca, b. 22 10ber 1716; Mary, b. 17 9ber 1718; Joseph, b. 9 Mar 1720/1; Samuel, b. 6 7ber 1728; ____(f), b. __ May 1732 (QAP b/14, 17, 25)

Sweringen, Jane [widow]; sons John, Samuel; 1 Jun 1716 (PGLR F.553)

Sweringen, Samuel; wife Elizabeth; tract *Clark's Purchase*; 15 Jul 1723 (PGLR I.483)

Sweringen, John; wife Mary; tract *Ryley's Neglect*; 25 Nov 1725 (PGLR I.693)

Swearingen, Thomas; 12 Apr 1726; 12 May 1726; sons Thomas, Van; daus. Mary, Margarit, Lurana; f-i-l Hugh Riley; tracts *The Forrest, Hills Choys, Swearengen's Pasture* (MCW V.224)s; admx. Lidea; 16 Jun 1726 (I 11.434); extx. Lydia; 10 Apr 1727 (AA 8.196)

Sweringen, Van; wife Elizabeth; tract *Hill's Choice*; 7 Mar 1733 (PGLR T.78)

Swearingen, Thomas; wife Sarah; tract *The Forrest*; 15 Jun 1734 (PGLR T.131)

Swaringen, John; wife Mary; children: John, Jr., Ann, Keziah; tract *Bradford's Rest*; 30 Oct 1738 (PGLR T.689)

Swearingein, Thomas; wife Ruth; children: Mary, b. 19 Aug 1760; Abed, b. 28 May 1762; Samuell, b. 22 Nov 1765 (PGP p. 259, 262, 277)

Swearingen, Samuell; wife Mary; child: Merciam, b. 20 Dec 1760 (PGP p. 259)

SWEENY

Sweany, James; wife Frances; children: George Wells, b. 31 Jul 1735; Susannah, b. 8 Mary 1737 (QAP b/29, 30)

Sweeny [Swenie], Derby [Darby]; 8 May 1722; 5 Jun 1722; wife Mary; sons John, Derby, James (MCW V.122) ; 26 Dec 1722 (I 10.194); 10 Sep 1724 (AA 6.170)

Sweaney, Zachariah; wife Darkus; child Drewsila, b. 8 Mar 1761; bapt. 6 Sep 1761 (KGP p. 323)

SWINFORD

Swinford, James; wife Elizabeth; children: Josias, b. 14 May 1761; Lidia, b. 8 Apr 1766 (PGP p. 260, 278)

SWINK

Swink, William; wife Mary; child: George, b. 28 Mar 1772 Upper Chapel; John, b. 6 Feb 1774 Broad Creek; Mary, b. 28 Feb 1776 Broad Creek (KGP p. 382, 385, 388)

SYMMER

Symmer, Alexander; 20 Jan ____; 22 Jan 1766; "relations" John, William Newman & Thomas Dorset (MCW XIII.119)

TALBOT

Talburt, John; s/o Paul Talburt of Pocklinlot, Yorkshire; m. 2 Feb 1696 Sarah Lockyer; d/o Thos. Lockyer of this parish; children: Paul, b. 18 Dec 1697; Thomas, b. 3 Sep 1699; John, b. 23 Feb 1700; Alice, b. 31 Aug 1703; Benja., b. 8 Apr 1705; Osburn, b. 8 Jul 1708; Ann, b. 3 May 1712; William, b. 13 Jan 1715; Sarah, b. 28 Jan 1718; Thomas, b. 20 Dec 1720 (KGP p. 264, 265, 275)

Talbutt, Paull; s/o John Talbutt; m/1 30 Mar 1719 Ann Johnston, d/o Robert Johnson; children: Sarah, b. 25 Jan 1719; Elizabeth, b. 13 Feb 1721 (KGP p. 261, 281); m/2 15 Aug 1722 Mary Rigges (KGP p. 261)

Talbert, John; wife Mary; sons John, Nathaniel; tract His Lordships Kindness; 5 Jun 1727 (PGLR M.237)

Talbott, John; age ca 64; 1730 (PGLR M.556)

Talburt, Paul; wife Ann; son John; tract His Lordship's Kindness; 29 Jul 1730 (PGLR Q.118)

Talbot [Talbutt], John; planter; 12 Apr 1735; 30 May 1735; wife Sarah; sons Thomas, Paul, John, Benjamin, Thomas; daus. Alice, Elizabeth (MCW VII.136); extx. Sarah; son [under age] Thomas; 6 Mar 1735 (AA 14.196); extx. Sarah; 20 Aug 1735 (I 21.50); admx. Sarah; _ Oct 1735 (I 21.216); widow Sarah; heirs Paul, John, Alice, Benjamin, Thomas, Elizabeth; 23 Nov 1736 (GB 86)

Talbot, Thomas; wife Mary; children: Selomi, bapt. 19 May 1751; J____, b. 1 Mar 1757 (KGP p. 293)

Talbott, William; wife Sarah; children: Rachel, bapt. 15 Mar 1752; Henry, b. 29 Jun 1753 (KGP p. 295, 300)

Talbot, Benjamin; wife Elizabeth; child: Joseph, b. 7 Mar 1754 (KGP p. 305)

Talbot, Thomas; wife Elinor; child: Bassil, b. 29 Dec 1754; Notley, b. 13 Sep 1757 (KGP p. 304, 320)

Talbot, Thomas; wife Margaret; child: Osborne, b. 3 Mar 1755 (KGP p. 307, 314)

Talbot [Talbut, Talburt, Talbert], Paul; wife Martha; children: Susanah, b. 9 Jan 1759; Charles, b. 15 Feb 1761; Elizabeth, b. 3 Aug 1763 at Broad Creek; Paul, b. 18 Feb 1766 Broad Creek; Casandrew, b. 22 Jun 1768 Broad Creek; Ann, b. 14 Apr 1773 Broad Creek; Benjamin, b. 13 Sep 1775 Broad Creek (KGP p. 327, 338, 353, 364, 379, 387)

Talbart [Talburt], Thomas; 4 Apr 1759 (I 69.298)

Talbut, William; wife Sarah; children: Mary, bapt. 12 Jun 1761; Nathan, b. 4 Apr 1763 at Broad Creek; Charles, b. 26 May 1765 Broad Creek (KGP p. 322, 337, 347)

Talbot, Sarah; widow; 1762 (I 79.233)

Talbot, Basill; wife Sarah; children: Thomas Athey, b. 4 Feb 1763 at Broad Creek; Bassill, bapt. 28 Apr 1765 Broad Creek; Elizabet Fendley, bapt. 26 Jul 1767 Broad Creek (KGP p. 336, 361)

Talbut, Tabitah; child: Mary Ann Walker, bapt. 22 Jan 1764 Broad Creek (KGP p. 356)

Talbut, Thomas; wife Elizabeth; children: Catherine, b. 8 Nov 1764 Broad Creek; James, bapt. 3 May 1767 Broad Creek (KGP p. 342, 347, 360)

Talbutt, Josiah; wife Mary; child: Elliner, b. 15 Mar 1765 (PGP p. 273)

Talbutt, Thomas; wife Elliner; children: Lewis, b. 26 Mar 1765; Nancey, bapt. 6 Dec 1767 Upper Chapel (PGP p. 273, 275, 366)

Talbot, Tobias; wife Sarah; child: Solomey, bapt. 28 Aug 1768 Broad Creek (KGP p. 364)

Talbert, Josias; wife Mary; child: Elizabeth, b. 7 Oct 1775 Broad Creek (KGP p. 387)

TANEY

Taney, Thomas; wife Jane [admnx. of Henry Trueman]; June 1697 Ct. (PGCR A.165)

Taney, Thomas [CH]; wife Jane; s-i-l Edward Trueman [s/o Henry]; Thomas Trueman [youngest s/o Henry]; tracts *Woods Joy, Timber Neck*; 10 Dec 1697 (PGLR A.81)

Taney, Michael; ex. Thomas Taney; Oct 1699 Ct. (PGCR A.484)

Taney, Jane; son Edward Truman; 2 Jun 1729 (PGLR M.425)

Tanie, William; wife Elizabeth; child: Walter, b. 3 Apr 1762 (PGP p. 263)

TANNEHILL

Tanehill, John; wife Sarah [widow of Robert Bowen, s/o Robert]; 15 Nov 1710 (PGLR F.45)

Tanyhill, William; sons Ninian, Andrew; Mar 1713 (PGCR G.292)

Taneyhill, Sarah; son James; 1717 (MCW IV.175-6)

Tannehill, William, Sr.; wife Ruth; son William, Jr.; tract *Killarnock*; 29 Nov 1722 (PGLR I.346)

Tunnihill, John; age almost 16; nephew of Elizabeth Bowen; chooses guardian; Mar 1725 (PGCR L.559)

Tanihill [Tannihill, Tawnihill], Sarah; 8 Aug 1725; 3 Sep 1725; sons John, James; bro. Moses Orme (MCW V.198); 16 Feb 1725 (I 11.224)

Tanyhill, William; age ca 73; 17 Aug 1725 (PGLR I.676); age ca 76; 15 Jul 1729 (PGLR M.486)

Tanyhill, John; age 15 on 16 Sep last; chooses uncle Moses Orme as guardian; Jun 1726 (PGCR L.639)

Tannehill, William; 15 Sep 1729; 28 Mar 1732; wife [unnamed]; sons James, William (MCW VI.212); extx. Euphan; 12 Apr 1732 (I 16.450); widow Euphan; 21 Jun 1732 (AA 11.415)

Tannihill, William; age ca 70; 27 Aug 1730 (PGLR Q.161)

Tanyhill, William; age ca 36; 1730 (PGLR Q.15)

Tanihill, Andrew; wife Sarah; tract Hamilton's Addition; 2 Jun 1731 (PGLR Q.278)

Tannehill, Ninian; wife Christian; bro. James Tannehill; 7 Apr 1732 (PGLR Q.510)

Tannyhill, Ninian; age ca 52; 29 May 1745 (CCR JK#4.591)

Tanehill, William; wife Sarah; child: William Harriss, b. 2 ___ 1762 (PGP p. 261)

Tannehill, William; wife Elizabeth; child: Jemimah, b. 12 Nov 1775 Upper Chapel (KGP p. 392)

TASKER

Tasker, George; wife Margaaret; children: Elenor, bapt. 4 Dec 1763 at Lower Chapel; George, bapt. 30 Nov 1766 Broad Creek (KGP p. 335, 348)

TATTERSHELL

Tattershell, Philip; wife Terisa; tract Ludford's Gift; 17 Nov 1710 (PGLR F.25)

TAYLOR

Taylor, Edward [England]; wife Margaret; tract Moores Plains; 31 Jul 1699 (PGLR A.390)

Taylor, Samuell; 20 Nov 1705; 10 Oct 1706; wife Verlinder; son Samuel; tract Taylorton (MCW III.87); extx. Virlinda; [with 1708] (I&A 29.185); admx. Verlinda Browne [w/o John]; 7 Jun 1710 (I&A 31.132)

Taylor, Nathaniell, Rev.; 10 Feb 1709 (I&A 32c.159)

Taylor, Ann; age 7 in Jan last; d/o Bethia; bound out; Jun 1709 (PGCR D.173)

Taylor, Roger; wife Mary; children: Ann, b. 23 Feb 1710/1; William, b. 12 Jan 1723/4 (QAP b/6, 9)

Taylor, Sarah; age 5 mos.; mulatto d/o Elizabeth; bound out; Nov 1711 (PGCR G.125)

Taler, Robert; age ca 50; 13 Jan 1714 (CCR CL.107)

Tailor [Taylor], Joseph; merchant; 14 Mar 1717 (I&A 39c.126); merchant; 8 Apr 1717 (I&A 38a.85)

Taylor, Joseph [dec'd]; bro. Benjamin [England]; 15 Nov 1714 (PGLR F.443)

Taylor, Robert; age ca 51; 20 Apr 1719 (CCR CL.548)

Tailor, William; age 11 in Feb next; s/o Mary; bound out; Mar 1723 (PGCR L.239)

Taylor, James; wife Hannah; 20 Oct 1725 (PGLR Q.707)

Taylor, Samuel; age 6 on 10 Oct last; s/o Mary; bound out to Allen Lock and Mary his wife; Nov 1727 (PGCR N.612)

Tayler, William; sister Elizabeth; 1727/8 (MCW VI.57)

Taylor, Robert; age ca 65; 19 Oct 1730 (CCR-MSA 5.452)

Taylor, Robert; nok in Charles Co.; 25 Nov 1733 (I 17631); 26 Jun 1734 (AA 12.339)

Taylor, Samuel; age ca 36; 1737 (PGLR T.504); age ca 38; 29 Jan 1738 (CCR JK#4.45)

Taylor, John; planter; 17 Jan 1736; 29 Nov 1738; sons John, James, Thomas (youngest); daus. Mary, Ann; wife Unice (MCW VIII.29)

Taylor, John; admx. Sarah; 28 Aug 1741 (I 26.480) admx. Sarah Field [w/o Bartholomew]; 23 Jan 1743 (I 29.302); admx. Sarah Fields [w/o Bartholomue]; 3 children William, Matthew, John; 18 Jun 1744 (AA 20. 326); heirs William, Martha, John; 27 Jun 1745 (GB 140); [Skinner names the middle child as Matthew and the guardian bond says Martha]

Taylor, James; 13 Jan 1740 (I 25.402); 10 Dec 1741 (AA 19.58)

Taylor, Robert; extx. Mary Henderson [w/o Rev. Jacob]; granddau. Ruth Tyler [w/o Mordecai Jacob]; 11 May 1744 (AA 20.193)

Taylor, William; age ca 7 months; s/o Thomas and Mary Taylor; bound to William and Anne Price; Aug 1746 (PGCR FF.9)

Taylor, Margaret; age ca 42; 31 Oct 1748 (CCR MSA 8.744)

Taylor, Hugh; admx. Elisabeth; 26 May 1749 (I 40.185); admx. Elisabeth; children: Richard George & Elisabeth Gordon Taylor; 2 Oct 1749 (AA 27.189)

Tayler, Thomas; wife Rose; child: Henry, bapt. 8 Sep 1751 (ICR)

Taylor, Samuel; admx. Mary Throne [w/o Jonathon]; 25 Jun 1752 (AA 32.364)

Taylor, Thomas; wife Jane; child: Virlinda, bapt. 31 May 1767 Upper Chapel (KGP p. 366)

Taylor, Francis; wife Ann; child: Richard, b. 14 Jan 1775 Upper Chapel (KGP p. 391)

TENLEY

Tinnally, Phillip; age ca 12; servant; Nov 1705 (PGCR B.440)

Tenanly, Philip; m. 2 Jul 1720 Grace Thomas; children: William, b. 29 Jun 1721 (KGP p. 267)

Tenaley, Benjamin; wife Sushannah; child: Vialinda, bapt. 10 Jan 1768 Broad Creek (KGP p. 362)

Teneley, Philip, Sr.; 13 Nov 1772; 25 Nov 1772; wife Grace; children: Joseph, Benjamin, Charity Simpson, Mary Ridgaway, Sarah Williams,

Anne Murphey, Josiah; granddau. Vinaford Wornall; tracts *Tenely Chance, Hunters Kindness, Radford Chance* (MCW XV.96)

Tenley [Tennely], Philip, Jr.; admx. Hannah; 11 Sep 1773 (I 117.340)

Tenley, William; wife Lydda; child: Tracy Ann, b. 9 Jul 1774 Broad Creek (KGP p. 386)

Tennely, Josias; wife Monacha; child: Philip, b. 6 Jun 1775 Broad Creek (KGP p. 387)

Tenley, Benjamin; wife Susanna; child: Cloe, b. 22 Sep 1775 Broad Creek (KGP p. 387)

Tennley, Grace; 14 Nov 1775; children Ann Murphy, Mary Ridgway, Charity Simpson, Benjamin, Josias; grandchildren Phillip & Grace [ch/o Josias] (MCW XVI.82)

TENANT

Tenant, Thomas; wife Charity; children: Sarah, b. 11 Jul 1762; Elenor, bapt. 12 Aug 1764 Lower Chapel; Amey, bapt. 19 Jul 1767 Lower Chapel (KGP p. 331, 345, 367)

TENT

Tent, John; admx. Abigall; 2 Jun 1716 (I&A 37a.90)

Tent, Abigail; widow; age ca 63; 18 Mar 1728/9 (PGLR M.480)

Tent, Abigail; free Mulatto; age ca 67; 2 Apr 1736 (CCR-MSA 6.162)

TERRETT

Terrett, Nicholas; wife Jane; tract part of *Mawburnes Plaines*; 15 Sep 1694 (PGLR A.440)

TEWELL

Tewell, Charles; child: William, b. 23 Aug 1711; Charles, b. 15 Feb 1717 (ICR; KGP p. 277)

THICKPENNY

Thickpenny, John; bound out his sons John age 14 ye 17th this instant, Henry age 12 on 14 Oct last; Thomas, age 5 on 27 Oct last; Jan 1699 Ct. (PGCR B.15a)

Thickpenny, Hannah; age 2; servant; Sept 1699 Ct. (PGCR A.464)

Thickpenny, Henry; m. 5 Jan 1715 Rachel Dowden; child: Mary, b. 14 8ber 1716 (QAP m/1; b/12)

Thickpenny, Henry; wife Rachel; son John; tract *Senicar Landing*; 7 Mar 1722 (PGLR I.717-1/2)

Thickpenny, Henry; 27 Nov 1728 (I 13.323)

THISICK

Thisick, Thomas [CE]; wife Elizabeth [alias Elizabeth Blandford]; son Charles; dau. Margaret Pressley; 3 Aug 1741 (PGLR Y.354)

Thisick, Thomas [alias Blanford]; son Charles; 25 Aug 1742 (PGLR Y.514)

THOMAS

Thomas, Danell; wife Anne; children: Elizabeth, b. 6 Dec 1709; John, b. 1 Mar 1712; Winfrett, b. 4 Apr 1714; Anne, b. 1 Mar 1716; Mary, b. 1 May 1719 (KGP p. 267)

Thomas, Daniel, Sr.; sons William, Daniel; tract *Friendship*; 18 Feb 1713 (PGLR F.313)

Thomas, John; 14 Dec 1713 (I&A 35a.27, 36); 14 Dec 1713 (I&A 35a.389)

Thomas, William; m. 7 Dec 1721 Anne Jenkins (KGP p. 268)

Thomas, Daniel; dau. Ann Berry; 1 Jul 1734 (PGLR T.137)

Thomas, William; wife Elizabeth_; children: John, b. 7 Jun 1736; Edward, b. 2 Oct 1740; Benjamin, b. 29 Aug 1745; Francis, b. 23 Jul 1748; Sarah Ann, b. 27 Feb 1750; William, bapt. 28 Jun 1752 (KGP p. 292, 296)

Thomas, Daniel, Sr.; s-i-l William Berry; 12 Nov 1736 (PGLR T.418)

Thomas, John; age ca 57; Nov 1740 (PGLR Y.235)

Thomas, Daniel, Sr.; 2 Jun 1741; 21 Sep 1742; wife Ann; sons William, Daniel, John; daus. Grace Turnely, Winifred Lewis, Anne Berry [dec'd], Elizabeth Clancy (MCW VIII.183)

Thomas, Ann; 9 Jul 1746; 21 Jul 1746; daus. Wenefred Lois, Elizabeth Clensey; sons William, Daniel, John; grandsons William & Philip Tenaly, Jr. [also Fendly]; granddaus. Sarah & Ann Berry (MCW IX.89); 31 Jan 1746 (I 34.211)

Thomas, Jesse; age 6 mos & 22 days; mulatto s/o Catharine; sold to highest bidder; Aug 1747 (PGCR GG.91)

Thomas, Gabriel; age 3 mos.; bound out; Jun 1750 (PGCR LL.176)

Thomas, Henry; wife Lucey [Lusifer]; child: John, b. 17 Jul 1762; Drusilla, bapt. 26 Feb 1764 Lower Chapel (KGP p. 331, 344)

Tomas, Thomas; wife Ann; child: Ann Willson, b. 19 Apr 1767 Upper Chapel (KGP p. 365)

Thomas, Thomas; _ Oct 1772; 5 Sep 1774; wife Eleanor; sons Thomas, William, James; daus. Jane, Elizabeth, Mary Siscle, Sophania Maenus & Jesse Thomas; tract *After Stamp* (MCW XVI.24)

Thomas, Thomas; wife Ann; child: Eleanor, b. 7 Oct 1773 Broad Creek; Susanna, b. 21 Nov 1775 Broad Creek (KGP p. 382, 385)

THOMPSON

Thompson, Christopher; wife Grace [admx. of Lawrence Rowland]; mentions Rowland orphans; Nov 1696; Nov 1697 Ct.(PGCR A.59, 265)

Thompson, Christopher; wife Grace; Jan 1699 Ct. (PGCR B.20)

Thompson, Christopher; bro. William; tract *White Lackington*; 26 Jan 1699 (PGLR A.199)

Thompson, Christopher; wife Grace [widow of James Williams, Sr.]; tract *Chelsey*; 18 Oct 1703 (PGLR C.96)

Thompson, Margaret; child: Sarah, b. 24 Jul 1709 (QAP b/4)

Thomson, Walter; age ca 21; servant; Mar 1713 (PGCR G.292)

Thompson, John; 23 Feb 1714 (I&A 36b.248)

Thompson, John; age 9 on 14 Nov last; s/o John; bound out; Mar 1717 (PGCR H.181)

Thompson, William; wife Sarah; children: William, b. 4 10ber 1720; Rachel, b. 14 Jan 1722/3 (QAP b/16, 17)

Thompson, Charistopher; age ca 62; 17 Aug 1725 (PGLR I.676); age ca 60; 1727-28 (PGLR M.269); age ca 60; 19 Oct 1730 (CCR-MSA 470); age ca 65; 2 Aug 1732 (PGLR Q.670)

Thompson, Walter; widow Catherine; 27 Jan 1726 (I 11.778); widow Catharine [now w/o Phillip Plafay]; 26 Feb 1727 (AA 8.524)

Thompson, Walter [dec'd] [Scotland]; wife Margaret; son William [England]; bro. William [Scotland]; 19 Dec 1726 (PGLR M.209)

Thompson, William; age ca 80; 22 Aug 1729 (PGLR M.269, 488)

Thomson, William; age ca 70; 16 Jun 1730 (PGLR Q.12)

Thompson, Christopher; planter; 20 Nov 1731; 21 Jan 1733/4; wife Grace; nephew Robert Ridell, John; cous. William Shaw; tracts *Chelsy, Asdell, White Lackington* (MCW VII.51); admx. Grace; 7 Feb 1733 (I 17.729); extx. Grace; 27 Sep 1734 (AA 12.626)

Thompson, Grace; widow; 13 Apr 1739; 7 Jul 1741; (?) son William; (?) grandchildren: John Thompson, Margaret Shaw, Mary Perry (MCW VIII.189);15 Jul 1741 (I 27.161); 8 Oct 1742 (AA 19.164); 27 Sep 1743 (AA 19.482)

Thompson, William; wife Mary; children: John, b. 3 Sep 1753; Sarah, b. 3 Sep 1755; Zachariah, b. 1 May 1762 (KGP p. 301, 312, 330)

Thompson, John; wife Sarah; child: Elizabeth, b. 26 May 1754 (KGP p. 306)

Thompson, John; 4 Apr 1754; 16 Oct 1754; [no relations] (MCW XI.54)

Thompson, Thomas; planter; 15 Jan 1755; 20 May 1755; sons Thomas, James, Henry, Joseph Green, John; daus. Elizabeth, Anne (MCW XI.88-9); 7 Jul 1755 (I 59.166)

Thompson, John; wife Agnes; child: Robert, b. 13 Apr 1756 (KGP p. 313)

Thompson, Mungo; wife Ann; child: Magrett, b. 17 Feb 1762 (PGP p. 264)

Tompson, William; wife Mary; child: Zachariah, b. 1 May 1762 (PGLR p. 331)

Tompson, James; wife Catharina; children: John, bapt. 25 Jun 1762; Thomas, bapt. 16 Dec 1764 Upper Chapel; James, bapt. 23 Oct 1768 Lower Chapel (KGP p. 331, 355, 372)

Tompson, John; wife Sarah; children: Arminta, bapt. 3 Oct 1762; Samuel, bapt. 9 Sep 1764 at Broad Creek; Randel, bapt. 10 Jul 1768 Lower Chapel (KGP p. 332, 339, 371)

Thompson, William; wife Penalopy; children: Lenord, bapt. 12 Dec 1762; Elizabeth, bapt. 19 May 1765 Broad Creek (KGP p. 329, 347)

Thompson, Adam, Dr.; John Lee, Jr. of VA appt. trustee of marriage articles between Dr. Thompson and Mrs. Lettice Wardrop; 1762 (MCWXII.158)

Thompson, Thomas; 29 Jan 1763; 8 May 1763; wife Cloe; sons Charles, Thomas (MCWXII.206); ex. Chloe Thomas (sic); 1762 (ABB 4.95); 13 Jun 1763 (I 82.13); admx. Chloe; 26 Aug 1768 (GB 265)

Tompson, John; wife Mary; child: Rachill, bapt. 10 Jul 1763 at Broad Creek (KGP p. 337)

Thomson, Henry; 22 Sep 1763 (I 83.144)

Tompson, William; wife Mary; children: Clement, bapt. 4 Nov 1764 Lower Chapel; Elener, bapt. 10 Jul 1768 Lower Chapel (KGP p. 345, 371)

Tompson, John; wife Mary Ann; child: Margret, bapt. 17 Nov 1765 Lower Chapel (KGP p. 351)

Tompson, William; child: Elenor Marbury, bapt. 8 Feb 1767 Broad Creek (KGP p. 360)

Thompson, Adam, Dr.; Upper Marlborough; 16 Sep 1767; 26 Sep 1767; wife Lettice [in New York City at present]; children: Alice Corbet & Mary Lee Thompson; grandchildren: James Thompson [s/o Rosana Riley]; Thompson, Andrew [s/o Themesina Furns] (MCW XIV.49); extx. Lettice; 24 Nov 1768 (I 98.47); heirs Alice, Mary; 27 Aug 1771 (GB 294)

Thompson, Jos.; wife Catherin; child: Joseph Benton, b. 19 Sep 1769 (PGP p. 263)

Thompson [Tompson], Mary; 29 Apr 1771 (I 105.297)

Thompson, William; wife Peneleper; child: Anne, b. 8 Mar 1773 Broad Creek (KGP p. 378)

Thompson, William; wife Penelope; child: Ozsah (m), b. 18 Dec 1773 Broad Creek (KGP p. 385)

Thompson, Arthur; wife Comfort; children: Elizabeth, b. ____, John, b. ____; ____, b. ____ (QAP b/34)

THORN

Thorn, James; wife Susanna; children: Susanna, b. 30 Mar 1752, bapt. 3 May 1752; Henry, b. 16 Sep 1755 (KGP p. 296, 306, 311)

Thorn, William; nok "in the Jerseys"; 9 Feb 1756 (I 60.712)

Thorn [Thorne], Thomas; wife Rachill; children: Hesekiah, bapt. 3 Jul 1763 at Upper Chapel; Thomas, b. 3 Feb 1766 Upper Chapel (KGP p. 333, 354)

Thorn, James; 22 Jan 1767; 6 Mar 1767; wife Susannah; children: Thomas, Ephraim, Benjamin, Zachariah, James, Henry, Clocey, Susanna; grandchildren: Bennet, John Wheller, & Catharine Jones (MCW XIII.176); 15 Jul 1767 (I 95.223)

Thorn, Zachariah; wife Martha; children: Henry Burch, bapt. 3 Apr 1768 Broad Creek; Zachariah, b. 25 Dec 1775 Broad Creek (KGP p. 362)

Thorn, Thomas; wife Casandra; children: Joshua, b. 9 Dec 1771; Rachel, b. 10 Apr 1773 Upper Chapel; William, b. 20 Oct 1774; Eleanor, b. 20 Jan 1776 Broad Creek (KGP p. 382, 388, 389, 391)

Thorn, Zachariah; child: Walter, b. 14 Aug 1773 Broad Creek (KGP p. 385)

Thorn, Benjamin; wife Alelea; child: John, b. 10 Nov 1773 Broad Creek (KGP p. 385)

Thorn, William; 18 Jul 1774; 22 Aug 1774; sister Dorothy; bros. Absolom, Peregrine, Barton; mother [unnamed] (MCW XV.179); 30 Aug 1774 (I 118.265); 8 Nov 1774 (I 119.113, 122)

Thorn, Benjamin; wife Mildred; child: Casandra, b. 24 Dec 1775 Broad Creek (KGP p. 382)

THRALLS

Thralls [Thrawles], Richard; wife Rebecca; children: Casa (f), b. 14 Aug 1763; Isaac, b. 4 Oct 1765 (PGP p. 271, 277)

THRASHER

Thresher, Benjamin; wife Mary; child: James, b. 22 Sep 1727 (PGP p. 247-8)

Threshor [Threshir], Benjamin; 19 Nov 1740; 3 Mar 1740; wife Mary (MCW VIII.114); extx. Mary; 16 May 1741 (I 25.456)

Thrasher, Mary; widow; children: Thomas, Mary, John, William, Sarah, Margaret, Benjamin; tract The Benjamin; 22 Mar 1742 (PGLR Y.626)

Thrasher, William; wife. Margaret; child: Elisabeth, b. 3 Mar 1763 (PGP p. 268)

THRONE

Throne, Martha; child: Nottley, b. 29 ___ 1735 (KGP p. 271)

Throne [Thrown], Jonathon; admx. Mary; 21 Aug 1753 (I 55.161); 16 Dec 1754; admx. Mary Throne; only dau. Mary Throne [age 3 next Oct] (ABB 1.128); widow Mary; heir Mary, Jr.; 26 Nov 1755 (GB 200)

Throne, Mary; 6 Jan 1757; 28 Jun 1759; daus. Varlinda Orme [w/o Moses], Priscilla Taylor, Ann Taylor, Susanna Taylor, Mary Throne; bro. Richard White (MCW XI.238)

Throne, Mary; 21 & 24 Aug 1760; ex. Moses Orme, Jr.; legatees Casandra Orme, Priscilla Taylor, Ann Taylor, Susanna Taylor, Mary Throne (ABB 3.35, 7.51)

Throne, Mary; heir Mary; 23 Jun 1762 (GB 219)

TILER
Tiler, John; wife Elizabeth; child: John, bapt. 11 Feb 1765 Lower Chapel (KGP p. 350)

TILLEY
Tilly, Francis; age 4 on 1 Jan last; Jane, age 2 on 4 Mar last; ch/o Elizabeth; bound out; Jun 1706 (PGCR C.74)

Tilley, Thomas; m. 3 Nov 1726 Rebecca Bateman (QAP m/4)

Tilley, Thomas [dec'd]; wife Rebecca; son Thomas; dau. Mary; 1741 (MCW VIII.147)

Tilley, Thomas; wife Mary; child: Ann, b. 4 Apr 1762 (KGP p. 330)

Tilley, Rebecca; widow; 11 May 1762; 19 Jun 1770; children: Thomas, Mary; grandau. Elizabeth [d/o Mary Tilley]; tract *Black Ash* (MCW XIV.158)

TIMSON
Timson, Thomas; wife Catherine; 1723 (PGCR L.132)

TINGLE
Tingle, James; wife Jane; servants; 14 Feb 1727/8 (PGLR M.333)

TINNEY
Tinney, John; parish of Rev. Geo. Murdock; 3 May 1748; 18 Jun 1756; wife Ann (MCW XI.137)

TIPIN
Tipin, Anne; age 10 mos.; bound out; Nov 1728 (PGCR O.334)

TOLBERT
Tolbert, William; wife Sarah; child: Susanna, b. 16 Feb 1775 Broad Creek (KGP p. 386)

TOLLOWELL

Tollowell, Richard; wife Mary; 16 Feb 1729/30 (PGLR M.543)

TOLSON

Tolson, Francis, b. Wood Hall, Cumberland, Bright Church Parish [s/o Henry Tolson, Esq.]; m. 22 Sep 1707 Mary Clark [d/o Robert Clark of this parish]; children: Henry, b. 8 Jul 1708; Francis, b. 28 Aug 1710; Gilbert, b. 4 Nov 1712 (KGP p. 265, 266)

Tolson, Francis; 23 Apr 1730; 11 Mar 1730/1; wife Ann; sons Henry [s/o 1st wife], John; dau. Frances; d-i-l Alice Lindsay [w/o Anthony]; Samuel Lindsey [s/o Alice] (MCW VI.181); 20 Mar 1730 (I 16.234); admx. Frances [?widow]; 28 Oct 1731 (I 16.397); admx. Frances; 21 Dec 1732 (AA 11.570); admx. Frances; 21 Dec 1732 (AA 11.567); admx. Francis Stonestreet [w/o Butler]; heirs none by admx.; 26 Feb 1733 (AA 12.212)

Tolson, Henry; extx. Mrs. Frances; 10 Jan 1731 (I 16.396, 470)

Tolson, John; 17 Aug 1768; 31 Oct 1768; children: Henry, John, Francis, Ann, Elizabeth; tracts *Tolson's Purchase, Stokes, Staurday's Work, Hutton Lockrice, Manchester, Friendship, Hunter's Field, Hunter's Folly, Radford's Chance, Tolson's Delight, Godfrey's Chance, Pardon* (MCW XIV.63-4)

Tolson, John; heirs [unnamed]; tracts *Steak, Saturday's Work, Hutoon Lockery, Vigo, Tolson's Purchase*; 10 Nov 1769 (GB 273)

TOMLINSON

Tomlinson, Grove; wife Mary; her son Thomas Gore; tract *Good Luck*; 18 Jan 1720 (PGLR I.47)

TOMS

Toms, Robert; wife Sarah; children: Thomas, b. 14 Feb 1729; Thomas, b. 24 Jun 1732 (QAP b/25, 26)

Toms, Thomas; choses guardian; Nov 1744 (PGCR CC.579)

TORFIELD

Torfield, Thomas; adjudged age ca 15-1/2; Aug 1734 (PGCR V.99)

TOULSON

Toulson, Francis; son Jon.; 1724/5 (MCW VI.1)

TOWERS

Towers, Thomas; admx. Catherine Council Towers; 2 Sep 1732 (I 16.626); admx. Catherine Council Towers; 26 Jun 1733 (AA 12.20)

TOWGOOD

Towgood, Josias; 9 Dec 1752; 28 Mar 1753; son Josias; daus. Mary, Martha Anne, Elizabeth; b-i-l William Beames, Jr. (MCW X.254); 14 May 1753 (I 55.106); 28 Aug 1754; exs. William & Colemore Beans (ABB 1.117); orphans [unnamed]; 28 Aug 1754 (AA 36.387); heirs Josias, Elizabeth; 27 Mar 1755 (GB 197)

Towgood, Eleanor [Elisabeth]; 9 Aug 1775 (I 123.125)

TOWNLEY

Townley, John [or William]; admx. Mary; dau. Elisabeth; 27 Aug 1740 (I 25.177)

Townley, John; admx. Mary; 2 daus. Elisabeth, Mary; 30 Jun 1744 (AA 20.333)

TRACY

Tracey, Charles; 30 May 1698 (I&A 16.140); 9 Jul 1699 (I&A 19.106); 26 Jun 1700 (I&A 19-1/2b.141)

Tracey, Teague; wife Mary; tract *Cucholds Poynt*; 30 Mar 1699 (PGLR A.167)

Tracy, Jacob; wife Jeremiah; children: William Willit, b. 20 Oct 1759; Sarah, b. 11 Mar 1762 (PGP p. 263, 281)

Tracy, Perarce; wife Tobisa; child: Peerce, b. 6 Jun 1762 (PGP p. 264)

Tracy, Alear.; wife Uphin; child: Reason, b. 3 Jul 1762 (PGP p. 264)

Tracy, Timothy; wife Ellener; children: Priscilah, b. 30 Jan 1762; Melender, b. 16 Feb 1764 (PGP p. 263, 272)

Tracy, William; wife Mary; child: Virlinder, b. 20 Aug 1765 (PGP p. 277)

TRADANE

Tradane, John; wife Ann; tract *Killfadda*; 25 Aug 1734 (PGLR T.197)

TRAIL

Trail, David; wife Margrett; child: Darcass, b. 14 Dec 1759 (PGP p. 280)

Trail, Charles; wife Susanah; child: Becca Neighbourghs, b. 17 Oct 1764 (PGP p. 273)

TRAVERS

Travers, James; wife Mary; children: John, b. 15 Jan 1710/1; William Mills, b. 16 Apr 1713; Elizabeth, b. 28 Aug 1715 (QAP b/5, 9, 11)

TRAYHERN

Trayhern [Trahern], Nehemiah; wife Amelia; children: John, b. 2 Aug 1772 Broad Creek; Samuel, b. 31 Jul 1775 Broad Creek (KGP p. 378, 387)

TRAYL

Trayl, William; wife Frances; child: Elizabeth, b. 3 Jun 1765 (PGP p. 274)

TREE

Tree, John; 4 May 1772; admx. Eleanor Tree (ABB 6.116)

TRIGG

Trigg, Clement; wife Sarah; child: _____ miah (m), b. 13 Nov 1727 (?) (QAP b/20)

Trigg, Samuel; child: Margery, bapt. 21 May 1761 (KGP p. 322)

Trigg, Clemant; wife Mary; children: William, bapt. 3 Jul 1763 at Upper Chapel; Joshua, bapt. 10 Apr 1768 Upper Chapel (KGP p. 333, 369)

Trigg, Jeremiah; wife Ealse; child: Jeremiah, bapt. 21 Jun 1767 Upper Chapel (KGP p. 365)

Trigg, Clement; wife Mary; child: Simeon, b. 5 Mar 1773 Broad Creek (KGP p. 378)

TRUDELL

Trudell, John; wife Hannah; son Thomas; 25 Sep 1713 (PGLR F.275)

TRUELOVE

Truelove [Trulove], Thomas; dau. Eleanor; 26 Aug 1728 (PGLR M.309)

Trulove, Thomas; 28 Jun 1728 (I 13.146); posthumous dau. [unnamed]; 26 Mar 1729 (AA 9.334)

TRUMAN

Truman, James; wife Ann [her 2nd husband Robert Skinner]; daus. Martha, Mary Elizabeth; bros. Nathaniel Truman, Thomas Truman; tracts *Truman Hills, Trumans Choyce Deminished, Retalliation, Addition, Maxoonscon, Barrens, The Goores, Newton, Prevention, Purcxhase, Trumans Lott, Trumans Chance, Trumans Hope, Wolves Den, Nottingham, Trumans Acquaintance*; 17 Sep 1698 (PGLR A.97)

Truman, Henry [dec'd]; children: Edward, Thomas, Jane Taney [w/o Thomas]; 14 Apr 1710 (PGLR I.321)

Truman, Mary [SM]; son Leonard Hollyday; [undated, with 1713] (PGLR F.253)

Truman, Thomas; 15 Sep 1717; 14 Jan 1717; wife Sarah; mother Mrs. Jane Taney; sons Henry, James; bro. Edward; dau. Jane; unborn child; nephew Thomas Truman; tracts *Thomas and Anthony's Choice* (MCW IV.172); 19 May 1718 (I 1.1, 3); 6 Dec 1718 (I 3.80); widow Sarah; children: Henry, Jane, James, Thomas Greenfield; mother Jane Taney 23 Oct 1719 (AA 2.364); widow Sarah; heirs Henry, James, Thomas, Jane; 28 Jun 1720 (GB 6)

Truman, Edward; admx. Elisabeth; 26 Nov 1729 (I 15.270); admx. Elisabeth; children 2 daus., 1 son; 7 Jan 1730 (AA 10.603); admx. Elisabeth; 29 Aug

1733 (AA 12.54); admx. Elisabeth; 29 Aug 1733 (I 17.361); heirs Ann, Benjamin, Mary; 20 Mar 1735 (GB 67)

Truman, Elisabeth; children: Thomas, Joseph & Ann Letchworth; also Mary Trueman; tract *Two Friends*; 4 Mar 1733/4 (PGLR T.64)

Truman, James, gent.; 26 May 1744; 30 Aug 1744; bros. William, Henry; sisters Elizabeth, Sarah; nephew Henry Smoot, Thomas, James; niece Susanna (MCW VIII.280-1)

Truman, Henry; 30 Sep 1755; 23 Mar 1756; wife Ann; sons Thomas, James, Henry, Alexander, Edward; tracts *Brittington, Dawson's Purchase, Buttington, Thomas and Anthony's Chance* (MCW XI.126)

Truman, Ann; 8 Apr 1760; 24 Jun 1760; children: Thomas, James, Sarah, Henry, Jane, Alexandre, Edward (MCW XII.230); 24 Aug 1768; children: Thomas, James, Leonard, Cloe, Clara, Sarah, Henry, Jane, Alexander, Edward (ABB 5.188)

Trueman, Henry; heirs [unnamed[; 28 Jun 1775 (GB 283)

TUBMAN

Tubman, Richard; age ca 30; 1730 (PGLR M.568)

Tubman, George; wife Mary; child: Sarah Martha, b. 19 Jul 1764 Lower Chapel (KGP p. 345)

Tubman, George; child: Richard, bapt. 28 Jun 1767 Lower Chapel (KGP p. 367)

TUCKER

Tucker, William; wife Katherine; child: Mary, b. 12 Mar 1704 (QAP b/2)

Tucker, William; 25 Nov 1718 (I 1.77)

Tucker, William; wife Jane; tract *Tucker's Cultivation*; 20 Jul 1723 (PGLR I.492)

Tucker, William; wife Jane; children: Elizabeth, b. 21 May 172_; Lucretia, b. 3 10ber 172_; Jemima, b. 28 Feb 1728; William, b. 11 Jul 1730 (QAP b/25)

Tucker, Thomas; age ca 60; 1738 (PGLR T.604)

Tucker, John; age ca 32; 1738 (PGLR T.604)

Tucker, Thomas; 17 May 1749 (I 40.54); 16 Apr 1750 (I 43.104); 20 Apr 1750 (AA 28.156)

Tucker, Thomas; wife Dianah; child: Ann, bapt. May-Jul 1761; Verlinder, b. 20 Oct 1763 at Upper Chapel; George, b. 13 May 1764 Upper Chapel or Broad Creek (KGP p. 323, 333, 342)

Tucker, Thomas; wife Sarah_; child: Sushanna, bapt. 9 Dec 1764 Broad Creek (KGP p. 342)

Tucker, John; wife Ann; child: Samuel, b. 21 Jul 1765 (PGP p. 275)

Tucker, William; wife Elizabeth; child: Sebina, bapt. 18 Aug 1765 Lower Chapel (KGP p. 345)

Tucker, George; wife Mary; child: William, bapt. 5 Jun 1768 Broad Creek (KGP p. 363)

Tucker, Thomas; child: Bassil, b. _ Nov 1769 Upper Chapel (KGP p. 375)

Tucker, William; wife Margery; child: Levi, b. 16 Jan 1774 Upper Chapel (KGP p. 390)

Tucker, Randolph; wife Christian; child: Zachariah, b. 8 Apr 1775 Upper Chapel (KGP p. 391)

TUGWELL

Tugwell, Mary; d/o William; bound out; Jul 1696 Ct. (PGCR A.11)

TULL

Tuell, Charles; admx. Mary Tull [w/o Terrence Byron]; 6 Dec 1720 (AA 2.149)

Tuel, William; wife Rachell; child: Jonathan, b. 31 Oct 1762 (PGP p. 267)

Tuill, William; wife Rachel; child: Althea, b. 19 Aug 1771 Broad Creek (KGP p. 377)

TUMLISON

Tumlison, James; wife Patience; children: Margery, b. 8 Jun 1738; Easter, b. 30 Aug 1740; Jesse, b. 13 Oct 1744; James, b. 2 Mar 1749; Thomas, b. 17 Apr 1752; Elizabeth, b. 25 Feb 175_ (PGP p. 253, 254)

TURKE

Turke, James; age ca 14; servant; Jun 1711 Ct. (PGCR G.69)

TURLEY

Turley, James; wife Elizabeth; tract *Turley's Choice*; 14 Aug 1742 (PGLR Y.517)

Turley, John; wife Mary; child: James, b. 25 May 1760 (PGP p. 258)

Turley, Thomas; wife Elizabeth; children: Ruth, b. 1 Jun 1760; Benjamin, b. 29 Apr 1762 (PGP p. 258, 264)

Turley, James; wife Marian; John, b. 25 Jan 1761; James, b. 20 Jan 1763 (PGP p. 260, 268)

TURNER

Turner, William [CA]; wife Joyce; tract *Acquascat*; 22 Oct 1696 (PGLR A.44)

Turner, John; wife Sarah; children: Margaret, b. 4 Mar 1699; Sarah, b. 1 9ber 1702; Ann, b. 16 May 1705; Mathew, b. 1 Jan 1706; Dorcas, b. 1 Mar 1708 (QAP b/12)

Turner, Edward; wife Mary [d/o Alexander Smith]; son Arthur; 21 Feb 1707 (PGLR C.204)

Turner, Abraham; age ca 18; servant; Aug 1710 Ct. (PGCR G.3)

Turner, John; age ca 44; 20 Mar 1715 (CCR CL.273)

Turner, Edward; wife Susanna; children: John, b. 29 Mar 1715; Elizabeth, b. 16 Jun 1717; Edward, b. 9 8ber 1719 (QAP b/11, 16)

Turner, William; wife 27 Jan 1718 Ann Mancy [Maney?]; child: Susanna, b. 2 8ber 1719 (QAP m/2; b/16)

Turner, John, Jr.; m. 1 [or 10] Jul 1718 Elizabeth Brushier, d/o Samuel Bruchier; children: Sarah, b. 13 May 1719; John, b. 3 Mar 1720/1; Elizabeth, b. 17 Mar 1723; Ann, b. 15 Oct 1725; ___rnett, b. 10 Jun 1728; Rachel, b. 30 Dec 1730; Shadrac, b. 28 Dec 1732/3; Dorcas, b. __ May 17__; (QAP m/2; b/16, 25, 27, 29)

Turner, John, Sr.; 2 Dec 1720; 9 Dec 1723; wife Sarah; sons John, Solomon, Philip; 5 daus. Margaret, Sarah, Elizabeth, Anne, Darcelt; tract *Ralphs* (MCW V.152); extx. Sarah; 13 Feb 1723 (I 9.371)

Turner, Joseph; 2 Aug 1722 (I 8.19)

Turner, John; age 9 on 29 Mar inst.; s/o Susannah; bound out; Mar 1723 (PGCR L.239)

Turner, Edward; mother Catherine Stimpson; 18 Dec 1723 (I 10.252); 24 Mar 1724 (AA 6.324)

Turner, Philip; 11 Apr 1726 (I 11.361); 23 Aug 1727 (AA 8.310); heirs Solomon, Margrett, Sarah, Elizabeth, Ann, Darcas; 28 Mar 1728 (GB 34)

Turner, John; admx. Sarah; 29 Jun 1726 (AA 7.444) heirs Margaret, Elizabeth, Sarah, Ann, Darcus; 26 Nov 1726 (GB 29)

Turner, John; age 5 mos.; s/o Mary; Jun 1730 (PGCR P.411)

Turner, Solomon; wife Jane; child: Lydia, b. 28 May 1732 (QAP b/26)

Turner, Sarah; 14 Oct 1729; 26 Nov 1739; sons Soloman, John [dec'd]; daus. Sarah, Elizabeth, Margarett, Ann (MCW VIII.52); 19 Feb 1739 (I 27.357)

Turner, John, Jr.; wife Frances_; children: Frances, b. 17 Nov 173_; Frances, b. 17 Nov 1736 (QAP b/30)

Turnur, John; 8 Jul 1738; 29 Nov 1738; wife Elizabeth; sons John, Samuel, Shadrick, Philip; daus. Sarah, Elizabeth, Ann, Rachell, Dorkcus; father John; tracts *The Addition, Ralphoe* (MCW VIII.2); extx. Eliza; 27 Feb 1738 (I 24.93); extx. Elisabeth; 27 Feb 1739 (AA 17.395)

Turner, John; heirs Rachel, Dorcas; 25 Nov 1743 (GB 129)

Turner, Solomon; 5 Feb 1757; 22 Nov 1757; wife Jane; sons John, Josias, Jeremiah; tract *Polpho [Ralpho]* (MCW XI.182)

Turner, Thomas; 27 Jan 1758; 13 Apr 1769; wife Mary; dau. Mary (MCW XIV.87)

Turner, John; child: Zachariah, bapt. 2 May 1762; Elizabeth, bapt. 12 Aug 1764 Lower Chapel (KGP p. 327, 345)

Turner, Samuell; wife Mary; child: Mary, b. 19 Oct 1762 (PGP p. 267)

Turner, Shedrick; wife Sarah, children: Thomas, b. 14 Jul 1764 Upper Chapel; Ann, bapt. 2 Nov 1766 Upper Chapel (KGP p. 341, 354)

Turner, Jonathan; wife Mary; children: Elizabeth, bapt. 15 Mar 1767 Lower Chapel; Jonathan, b. 1 Apr 1773 Lower Chapel (KGP p. 367, 384)

Turner, Benjamin; wife Partison; dau. Sarah, bapt. 18 Sep 1768 Broad Creek (KGP p. 364)

Turner, John; wife Mercy; children: Edward, b. 6 Apr 1773 Broad Creek; George Burress, b. 10 Oct 1775 Lower Chapel (KGP p. 378, 381)

Turner, John; 5 Aug 1775; 16 Mar 1777; mother Elizabeth Turner; sisters Sarah, Rachel; child John (MCW XVI.187)

TURTON

Turton, John; wife Equila [Quilla]; children: Jose Harrison, b. 22 May 1774 Lower Chapel; Fielder Henderson, b. 14 Apr 1776 Lower Chapel (KGP p. 379, 381)

TYLER

Tyler, Robert; wife Susanna; children: Edward, b. 2 7ber 1696; Mary, b. 1 Feb 1697; Susanna, b. 14 Jul 1700; Elizabeth, b. 22 9ber 1701; Priscilla, b. 12 Jun 1703; Robert, b. 9 Aug 1704; Maren, b. 20 Feb 1707; Jane, b. 20 May 1709 (QAP b/1, 4)

Tyler, Robert; age ca 42; 14 Jun 1714 (CCR CL.26)t; age ca 44; 20 Mar 1715 (CCR CL.272); age ca 53; 19 Mar 1724/5 (PGLR I.624); age ca 55; 4 Oct 1726 (PGLR M.216); age ca 60; 31 May 1731 (PGLR Q.608); age ca 65; 6 Feb 1732/3 (PGLR T.285)

Tyler, Edward; wife Elizabeth; children: Samuel, b. 18 9ber 1714; Susanna, b. 24 Feb 1717; Edward, b. 18 Jan 1719/20; Robert, b. 8 10ber 1723; Priscilla, b. 26 9ber 1725 (QAP b/10, 15, 18, 19)

Tyler [Tylor], William, carpenter; 18 Apr 1718; 25 Jan 1721; wife Eliza.; son William; daus. Mary, Eliza.; tracts Mattersey's [?Battersey], Clarkson's Purchase (MCW V.92); extx. Elisabeth Massey [w/o Henry]; 17 Feb 1722 (AA 5.175)

Tyler, Robert, Mr.; m. 10 Jun 1718 Madam Mary Dodd (QAP m/2)

Tyler, Robert; wife Mary; tract Howerton's Range; 9 Mar 1720 (PGLR I.99)

Tyler, John Baptist; 20 Mar 1721/2; 13 Aug 1722; wife Ann; 2 daus. Eliza., Mary; tract *Dutchman's Employment* (MCW V.110) [also see Baptistyler]

Tyler, William; [d. __ Dec 1722]; wife Elizabeth; children: William, b. 9 Jun 1706; Mary, b. 9 Aug 1709; Elizabeth, b. 7 Jul 1713 (KGP p. 275)

Tyler, Robert, Jr.; m. 7 Jan 1724/5 Mary Wade; children: Ruth, b. 15 Feb 1725/6; Robert, b. 5 9ber 1727; Mary, b. 28 Jan 1729; Susanna, b. 12 Aug 172_; William, b. 20 Aug 1733 (QAP m/4; b/19, 21, 23, 25, 27)

Tylor, Edward; 21 Sep 1726 (I 11.656); admx. Elisabeth; 6 Jun 1727 (AA 8.209); widow Elizabeth; heirs Samuel, Susannah, Edward, Elizabeth, Robert, Priscilla; 23 Aug 1727 (GB 33)

Tyler, Samuel; m. 11 Jul 1734 Susanna Duvall; children: Edward, b. 23 Feb 1734; Samuel b. 22 Jan 1737 [?1739]; William, b. ____ (QAP m/6; b/28, 33, 34)

Tyler, Robert, Sr., gent.; 29 Dec 1735; 24 Aug 1738; wife Mary; sons Edward [dec'd], Robert, Mareen; daus. Mary Whitehead, Susannah Lamar, Elizabeth Pottenger, Priscilla Wickam; d-i-l Elizabeth [widow of Edward Tyler & James Baldwin]; granddaus. Mary [d/o Robert], Ruth; grandsons Edward & Robert Tyler [ss/o Edward], John, Tyler, Robert Tyler [s/o Robert], Thomas and James Baldwin [ss/o Mary Baldwin Whitehead], William Tyler [s/o Robert], Robert Pottenger [s/o Samuel]; s-i-l Samuel Pottenger; tracts *Darnall's Grove, Brough, Bodwell's Choice, Basin Thorp Hall, Riley's Lott, Tyler's Chance, Howerton's Range, Ridgely's & Tyler's Chance, Tyler's Range* (MCW VII.257); extx. Mary Henderson [w/o Jacob]; children: Elisabeth Pottinger [w/o Samuel], Priscille Wickham [w/o Nathaniel], Susannah Lemarr [w/o John], Manson, Robert; grandchildren: Robert [s/o Mary], William, Mary; 29 Aug 1741 (AA 18.290)

Tyler, Robert; wife Mary; children: Thomas, b. 3 Oct 1749; Robert, b. 20 Jan 1751; Edward, b. 2 Mar 175_; Elizabeth, b. 5 Jan 1755; Mary, b. 15 Oct 1757; John, b. 19 Aug 1759; Easther, b. 5 Apr 1761; Samuel, b. 4 Jul 1763; Sarah, b. 4 Apr 1767 (QAP b/39)

Tyler, Mereen; 9 Aug 1750; 29 Nov 1752; [no relations] (MCW X.244)

Tylor, William; 25 Dec 1753; 27 Mar 1754; sisters Susannah, Sarah; bro. Robert (MCW XI.34)

Tyler, William; wife Sarah; child: Elinor Robinson, b. 23 Jan 1755 (KGP p. 307)

Tyler, Robert; wife Elinor; child: Millicent, b. 13 Oct 17_; Robert Bradly, b. 1 Jul 1759 (QAP b/36, 39)

Tyler, Samuel; m. 21 Feb 1762 Susanna Duvall; children: Christain (f), b. 28 Nov 1767; Trueman, b. 9 Sep 1771; Millisent, b. 15 Sep 1777 (QAP m/7; m/8; b/39, 46)

Tyler, John; heirs [unnamed]; 13 Mar 1769 (GB 270)

UNGLES

Ungles, John; age 4 on 9 May last; s/o Mary; bound out; Nov 1733 (PGCR S.473)

UNDERWOOD

Underwood, William; wife Charety; child: Josias, bapt. 7 Aug 1768 Lower Chapel (KGP p. 371)

Underwood, John; wife Mary; child: Tracy, b. 21 Oct 1773 Lower Chapel (KGP p. 384)

Underwood, William; admx. Charity; 29 Jun 1776 (I 124.8)

UPTON

Upton, Thomas; children: Thomas, b. 5 Sep 1730; Mary, b. 4 Feb 1738 (QAP 28)

Upton, Thomas; wife Martha: children: John, b. 27 Apr 1752, bapt. 7 Jun 1752; Elizabeth, bapt. 14 Feb 1762; Archabald, bapt. 26 May 1765 Upper Chapel; Samuel, bapt. 10 Apr 1768 Upper Chapel (KGP p. 296, 299, 324, 358, 370)

Upton, George; wife Elizabeth; children: Sarah, b. 1 May 1762; Ann, bapt. 19 Feb 1764 at Upper Chapel (KGP p. 330, 340)

Upton, Thomas; 26 Sep 1773; 24 Nov 1773; wife Martha [2nd wife]; children: Sarah [d/o ?former wife], Elizabeth, Archibald, Samuel, Eleanor, [others unnamed] (MCW XV.168); extx. Martha; 24 Mar 1774 (I 114.297)

URIS

Uris [Urie], Michael; age ca 48; 1730 (PGLR Q.14); age ca 54; 8 Jun 1732 (PGLR Y.327)

Uris [Youri], Michel; 3 Nov 1730; 28 Sep 1751; wife Margaritt; tracts *Smyrna, Yannon* (MCW X.179); extx. Margaret Youric; 12 Dec 1751 (I 49.47)

Ury, Margaret; 11 Feb 1760; 31 Oct 1768; [no relations] (MCW XIV.63)

VERNALL

Vernall, Sarah; age ca 5; bound out; Jun 1726 (PGCR L.631)

VAN

Van [Vawn], William; 1 Feb 1739 (I 27.137)

VANDIKE

Vandike, Andrew; admx. Mary; 25 Jul 1763 (I 84.200)

VANDIVER

Vandiver, George; wife Ann; child: Edward, b. 29 Jan 1753 (PGP p. 255)

VANMETRE

Vanmetre, John [VA]; wife Margaret; tract Metre; 5 Aug 1741 (PGLR Y.348)

VEARS

Vears, Nehemiah; wife Susanah; children: Sarah, b. 16 Sep 1759; Elizabeth, b. 15 Mar 1761; Ann, b. 12 Dec 1762; Elliner, b. 29 Aug 1764 (PGP p. 260, 267, 272, 280)

Vears, Daniell; m. Susannah; children: John, b. 10 Mar 1760; Susanah, b. 12 Jan 1762; Mary, b. 20 May 1763; Elisha, b. 11 Dec 1765 (PGP p. 262, 268, 277, 281)

VEITCH

Veitch, Nathan; admx. Ann; 3 Nov 1705 (I&A 25.114); extx. Anne Weaver; 17 Dec 1707 (I&A 28.6)

Veach, John; m. 29 Sep 1731 Sarah Hodges; child: John, b. 21 Jun 1732 (QAP m/5; b/26)

VENDER

Vender, Robert; age ca 13; servant; Jun 1699 Ct. (PGCR A.424)

VENMAN

Venman, John; 6 Apr 1711; 24 Jul 1711; wife Ann (MCW III.209); 2 Aug 1711 (I&A 32c.151); extx. Ann Brashiers [w/o Thomas]; 29 Mar 1712 (I&A 33a.161)

VERMILLION

Vermulian, Giles; wife Jane; children: Giles, b. 10 Sep 1708; James, b. 10 May 1710; John, b. 4 Feb 1712; Martha, b. 6 Jun 1714; Jane, b. 6 Apr 1716; Thomas, b. 25 Apr 1718; Jane, b. 29 Sep 1720; William, b. 27 Jul 1723 (KGP p. 283, 284)

Vermulen, Giles; age ca 45; 19 Oct 1730 (CCR-MSA 5.470)

Vermillion, William; wife Ann; child: Jesse (m), b. 25 Oct 1753 (KGP p. 301)

Vermillion, Robert; wife Elizabeth; child: Robert, b. 26 Jan 1755 (KGP p. 307)

Virmillon, Thomas; wife Sarah; children: Mary, bapt. 31 Jul 1763 at Upper Chapel; Thomas, bapt. 7 Jul 1765 Upper Chapel; Sarah, bapt. 31 May 1767 Upper Chapel (KGP p. 333, 358-9); Caleb, b. 27 Dec 1771 Upper Chapel (KGP p. 388)

Virmillon, Robert; wife Elizabeth; children: John, bapt. _ Sep 1763 at Lower Chapel; Sarah, bapt. 31 May 1767 Upper Chapel (KGP p. 335, 365);; Nickadamas, b. 22 Nov 1767, bapt. 24 Jan 1768 Lower Chapel (KGP p. 368)

Vemillion, Edward; wife Mildred; child: Sarah, b. 18 Nov 1772 Lower Chapel (ICR; KGP p. 383)

Vermillion; Benjamin; wife Esther; child: Elizabeth, b. 29 Sep 1773 Upper Chapel (KGP p. 390)

Vermillion, James; wife Rachel; child: Abraham, b. 8 Oct 1773 Lower Chapel (KGP p. 379)

Vermillion; Giles; wife Mary; child: Leonard, b. 19 Nov 1773 Upper Chapel (KGP p. 390)

VERNOY

Vernoy, Cornelius; wife Senar; tract *Walnut Tree Island*; 2 Apr 1740 (PGLR Y.184)

VINCENT

Vincent, Benjamin; wife Mary; child: Ann, b. 6 Mar 1772 (PGP p. 278)

VINSON

Vinson, Mary; servant; had bastard child; Jun 1698 Ct. (PGCR A.319)

VIRGIN

Virgin, John; wife Elizabeth; tract *Fox Hole*; 22 Aug 1727 (PGLR M.227)

WADDAM

Waddam, Jonathan; 7 Dec 1737; wife Elizabeth; tracts *Nelson's Purchase, Valentine Garden, Hickory Hill* (MCW VIII.205)

Waddams [Widams], Elizabeth; 16 Dec 1756; 23 Mar 1757; only son Orlando Smith (MCW XI.158); 6 Jul 1757 (I 65.188)

WADE

Wade, Robert; 4 Nov 1713; 2 Feb 1713; wife Eliza.; sons Zachary, Robert, Nehemiah, Zephaniah, Richard; daus. Elinor Magruder, Ann Wade; tracts *Stony Harbour, Margaret Overton, Forrest Green, Friendship* (MCW III.255-6); [as Capt.]; 3 Feb 1713 (I&A 35a.312); exs. William Penson & wife Elisabeth; 28 Oct 1714 (I&A 36b.113)

Wade, Richard [CH]; wife Mary; tract *Wade's Adventure*; 23 Feb 1714 (PGLR F.438)

Wade, Richard; m. 19 Feb 1728 Elizabeth Edgar [d. 2 Jul 1737]; children: Sarah Edgar, b. 29 Dec 1732; John, b. 16 Nov 1735 (KGP p. 286)

Wade, Robert; wife Ann [now w/o Alexander Magruder]; daus. Eleanor, Ann; father Zachariah; tract *Forrest Green*; 25 Mar 1731 (PGLR Q.242)

Wade, Zephaniah; wife Virlinda; tract *Market Overton*; 27 Jul 1731 (PGLR Q.323)

Wade, Zachariah; s/o Robert; tract *Stony Harbour*; 15 Apr 1734 (PGLR T.115)

Wade, Richard; dau. Sarah Edgar Wade; 26 Feb 1738/9 (PGLR T.697)

Wade, Robert, Jr.; wife Elizabeth; tract *Wade's Adventure*; 3 May 1738 (PGLR T.581)

Wade, Nehemiah; wife Eleanor; tract *Market Overton*; 27 Oct 1738 (PGLR T.661)

Wade, Zachariah; m. 3 Nov 17__ Nancy Noble; children: George, b. 22 May 1744; Zachariah Meeks, b. 4 Apr 1748; Charity Mary, b. 11 Jul 1753; Lancelet, b. 11 Nov 1757 (KGP p. 312, 313)

Wade, Zachariah; 13 Dec 1744; 8 Apr 1745; wife Mary; father Robert; son Zachariah; daus. Meek, Ann, Mary Ann, Elizabeth, dec'd [w/o Richard Harrison, dec'd]; grandchildren: Joseph & Virlinder Harrison, George Wade; nephew & niece John & Sarah Wade; tracts *Stoney Harbour, Wade's Adventure* (MCW IX.22); admx. Mary; 29 Apr 1745 (I 31.37); extx. Mary; heirs [unnamed]; 10 Nov 1746 (AA 23.86)

Wade, Richard; [wife Hester] child: Zacharia Playfy, b. 25 Feb 1754 (KGP p. 305); [wife Easter] children: Elizabeth Hameton, bapt. 19 Jun 1763 at Lower Chapel; Mary, bapt. 2 Jun 1765 Lower Chapel (KGP p. 335, 351); [wife Esther]; child: Bethlem, b. 31 Oct 1772 Lower Chapel (KGP p. 383)

Wade, Mary; 1 Mar 1756; 18 Jul 1766; children: Meek Wagner (f), Ann
  Price, Mary Noble, Zachariah Wade; s-i-l Richard Harrison; grandson
  Josep Harrison; tract *Lanham's Folly* (MCW XIII.119); 24 Jul 1766 (I 95.18)
Wade, Robert; wife Mary; child: Francis (m), bapt. 7 Mar 1762 (KGP p. 325)
Wade, Doshe; child: Verlinder, bapt. 12 Dec 1762 (KGP p. 329)
Wade, Mary, Mrs.; d. 9 Apr 1766, age 74; Broad Creek (KGP p. 343)
Wade, John; wife Charity; child: Zachariah, bapt. 24 May 1768 Lower
  Chapel (KGP p. 368)

WADGE
Wadge, James; wife Mary; child: Archabald, b. _ Mar 1775 Broad Creek
  (KGP p. 386)

WAGER
Wager, Thomas; child: Alee, bapt. 1 May 1768 Upper Chapel (KGP p. 370)

WAILES
Wailes, Benjamin; 10 Dec 1726; 7 Apr 1729; wife Elizabeth; sons Joseph,
  Levin; tracts *Tossitter, Fortune, Might Have Had More, Joseph's Lott* (MCW
  VI.92); 24 Feb 1729 (I 15.426); widow Elisabeth [dec'd]; son [unnamed]; 7 Jan
  1730 (AA 10.595)
Wailes, Levin; admx. Ann; 3 Aug 1757 (I 65.260); 5 May 1762; admx. Ann
  Wales; children [unnamed] (ABB 3.143); 4 Jan 1763; extx. Ann Wales; 7
  children: Benjamin, Sarah, Samuel Perry, Elisabeth, Levin Covington,
  John, Ann (ABB 3.181); widow Ann; heirs Benjamin Wailes, Sarah
  Ladyman, Samuel Perry Wales, Elizabeth Wales, Leven Covington,
  Wales, John Perry Wales, Ann Wales; 24 Mar 1763 (GB 226)

WAKEFIELD
Wakefield, Abil; wife Mary Ann; child: Samuel, bapt. 23 Mar 1766
  Broad Creek (KGP p. 348)

WALKER
Walker, Charles; wife Rebecca; children: Elizabeth, b. 22 10ber 1695;
  Charles, b. 9 May 1698; Rebecca, b. 11 Apr 1700; Mary, b. 11 May 1702;
  Ruth, b. 11 Apr 1704; Isaac, b. 5 Mar 1706; Ann, b. 10 Apr 1708;
  Richard, b. 4 Mar 1709/10; Crecy (f), b. 26 8ber 1713; Joseph, b. 24
  10ber 1715; Rachel, b. 6 Feb 1717 (QAP b/4, 9, 15)
Walker, Dormand; wife Sarah; children: John, b. 18 Feb 1709; Thomas, b.
  24 Aug 1712 (KGP p. 266)

Walker, Charles; age ca 46; 14 Jun 1714 (CCR CL.27); age ca 48; 20 Mar 1715 (CCR CL.274); age ca 60; 18 Mar 1728/9 (PGLR M.477); age ca 55; 19 Mar 1724/5 (PGLR I.624)

Walker, Thomas [runaway]; children: Elizabeth, Jane & John; children bound out; their aunt Rebecca, w/o Thomas Gatwood; Aug 1722 (PGCR K.617)

Walker, Charles, Sr.; age ca 50; 20 May 1725 (PGLR I.675)

Walker, Perman; age ca 60; 1 Jul 1726 (PGLR M.27)

Walker, Charles, Sr.; planter; 28 May 1730; 30 Oct 1730; wife Rebecca; sons Charles, Joseph; daus. Elizabeth, Rebecca, Mary, Ruth, Ann, Creecy, Rachel; b-i-l Richard Isaac; tracts Bacon Hall, Cut Short (MCW VI.169); widow Rebecca; 9 Mar 1731 (AA 11.310)

Walker, Dorman; age ca 66; 1731 (PGLR Q.296)

Walker, Mary; age 13 Feb last; chooses guardian (PGCR X.277)

Walker, John; admx. Elisabeth; 26 Nov 1740 (AA 18.136)

Walker, Charles; son Charles [wife Rebecca]; grandson Joseph; tract Bacon Hall; 26 Mar 1741 (PGLR Y.266)

Walker, Francis; wife Catherine; children: Francis, b. 30 Nov 1744; John, b. 13 Dec 1746; Elizabeth, b. 11 Jun 1748; Mary, b. 29 Oct 1750; Ann, b. 3 Aug 1752; Ellender, b. 3 Mar 1755; Benjamin, b. 8 Jan 1757; John, b. 17 Oct 1758; Elisha, b. 20 Mar 1763 Broad Creek; Violinda, bapt. 28 Apr 1765 Broad Creek; Rebecca, bapt. 14 Jun 1767 Broad Creek (KGP p. 299, 300, 346, 356, 361)

Walker, Thomas; wife Elizabeth; child: Benjamin, bapt. 17 May 1752 (KGP p. 296)

Walker, Isaac; wife Elizabeth; children: Charles, bapt. 10 May 1752, Catherine, b. 12 Jan 1755 (KGP p. 296, 307)

Walker, Thomas; wife Sarah; child: Mary, b. 11 Jan 1756 (KGP p. 312)

Walker, John; wife Elizabeth; child: Mary, b. 21 Oct 1759 (PGP p. 281)

Walker, Jacob; wife Elizabeth; child: Elizabeth, bapt. _ Sep 1763 at Upper Chapel (KGP p. 334)

Walker, Richard; wife Elliner; child: Margrette, b. 21 Jun 1765 (?) (PGP p. 273)

Walker, John; wife Rachel; children: Edward Lanham, b. 1769 Broad Creek; Richard Lewis, b. 17 Feb 1772 Lower Chapel; John, b. 14 May 1774 Broad Creek (KGP p. 364, 386, 383)

Walker, Richard; admx. Chloe; 11 Dec 1769 (I 104.272)

Walker, Benjamin; wife Elizabeth; children: Thomas, b. 3 Dec 1772 Broad Creek; Benjamin, b. 27 Apr 1774 Broad Creek; Susa., b. 15 Mar 1776 Broad Creek (KGP p. 382, 3 86)

Walker, Henry; wife Eleanor; children: Mary, b. 5 Jun 1772 Lower Chapel; Thomas, b. 23 Oct 1773 Broad Creek (KGP p. 383, 385)

Walker, Benjamin; wife Elizabeth; child: William, b. 18 Sep 1774 Lower Chapel (KGP p. 380)

Walker, Frances; wife Sarah; child: Mary, b. 30 Nov 1774 Broad Creek (KGP p. 386)

Walker, John; wife Elizabeth; child: Sarah, b. 31 Mar 1775 Broad Creek (KGP p. 386)

Walker, Charles; wife Jane; child: James Short, b. 17 Nov 1775 Broad Creek (KGP p. 382)

WALL

Wall, Thomas; wife Mary; tract part of *Brookefield*; 15 Jun 1704 (PGLR C.111)

Wall, John; wife Elizabeth; 1716 (PGCR H.141)

Wall, Thomas; age 67; free 46 yrs.; 2 Jun 1732 (PGLR Q.522)

Wall, William [Dorchester Co.]; wife Katherine; tract *Smith's Pasture*; 28 Mar 1737 (PGLR T.496)

Wall, Thomas; admx. Mary; 12 Jul 1756 (I 63.36); 20 Jun 1757; admx. Mary Wall (ABB 2.66)

WALLACE

Wallis, Richard; 18 Dec 1697 (I&A 15.336)

Wallis, Richard; widow Mary Hill [w/o John]; 15 Jul 1704 (I&A 3.377)

Wallace, James; orphan age 9; f-i-l [step-father] John Hill; bound out; Nov 1705 (PGCR B.439)

Wallace, James; wife Mary; tract *Brother's Industry*; 21 Nov 1726 (PGLR M.100)

Walliss, Thomas; m. Susana; child: Thomas, bapt. 2 Jun 1751 (KGP p. 294)

Wallace, William; wife Susanah; child: Mary, b. 21 Oct 1759 (PGP p. 281)

Wallace, John; wife Eliner; child: Christain, b. 21 Jul 1761 (PGP p. 262)

Walis, Elizabeth; child: Henry, bapt. 1 Jan 1764 at Broad Creek (KGP p. 338)

WALLINGSFORD

Wallingsford, Benjamin; m. Elizabeth; children: Sarah, b. 24 Oct 1714; James, b. 29 May 1717 (QAP b/13)

Wallingford, John; bro. Benjamin; 30 Oct 1739 (CCR JK#4.84)

Wallingsford, Elizabeth; 11 Apr 1741; 24 Jun 1741; sons John, James, Nicholas, Benjamin; daus. Joseph, Elizabeth Dove, Sarah Brasshears; grandson Benjamin (MCW VIII.143); 17 Jul 1741 (I 26.362); children of

Benjamin: Nicholas, Benjamin, Sarah Brashear [w/o William], Joseph, Elisabeth Dove [w/o John]; 29 Jun 1743 (AA 19.524)

Wallingsford, Benjamin; wife Mary; tract *Perry Wood*; 7 Apr 1742 (PGLR Y.467)

Wallingsford, John; 9 Mar 1761; 25 Mar 1761; bro. James; nephew James Wallingsford (MCW XII.48); 20 Apr 1761 (I 78.321); 23 Jun 1762; ex. James Wallingsford [s/o James] (ABB 3.143); heir James, Jr.; 27 Mar 1764 (GB 241)

WALTERS

Walters, Joseph; 27 Jun 1744 (AA 20.330)

Walters, Thomas; 19 Aug 1754 (I 58.244)

WAPLE

Waple, James; 1 May 1717 (I&A 38a.114)

WARD

Warde, Murphy; 20 Mar 1706/7; 6 Feb 1707; wife Mary; son Murphy; daus. Sarah Warde, Mary Allen; granddau. Mary Backer; tracts *Woodbridge, Stocke, Burges Chance, Wee Stocke* (MCW III.103); widow Mary Dellahunt [w/o John]; 20 Aug 1709 (I&A 29.424)

Ward, Murphey [s/o Murphy, dec'd]; wife Elizabeth; tract *Woodbridge*; 26 Jun 1708 (PGLR C.1229-231)

Ward, John; m. 6 Nov 1711 Elizabeth Smith (QAP m/1)

Ward, James; wife Susanna; children: Nathan, b. 12 Feb 1713; Frances, b. 17 Jan 1716 (QAP b/22)

Ward, James; wife Susannah [formerly Susannah Swanson]; tract *Swanson's Lott*; 10 Dec 1714 (PGLR F.428)

Ward, William; m. 27 Dec 1723 Jane Prather; children: Nathan, b. 29 Feb 1723/4; Catharine, b. _____ (QAP m/3; b/19, 28)

Ward, Murphy [dec'd]; widow Mary [m. _____ Dellahunt]; son Murphy; 27 Jul 1726 (PGLR M.68)

Ward, Thomas; f-i-l George Wells; 8 Dec 1726 (PGLR M.103)

Ward, John; age ca 65; 1730 (PGLR M.567)

Ward, Henry; age ca 54; 1730 (PGLR Q.68); age ca 59; 6 Jun 1735 (PGLR T.280)

Ward, Murphy; age ca 46; 1731 (PGLR Q.396)

Ward, Nathan; age 8 last day of Feb; bound out; Jun 1734 (PGCR R.89)

Ward, Nathan; wife Margret; child: Wells, b. 30 Jun 1735 (QAP b/29)

Ward, Henry; 13 Apr 1738; 4 Jun 1739; wife Margaret; sons Benjamin, John; daus. Elizabeth, Ann; kinsman William Denson; tracts *Saunderses*

Pleasure, Saunderses Neglect (MCW VIII.31); extx. Margaret; _ Nov 1739 (I 24.293); extxs. Mrs. Margrett, Elisabeth; 21 Aug 1740 (AA 18.27)

Ward, John; wife Innocent; children: Jonathan, b. 23 May 1751; by mistake bapt. Jonathan by Rev. Jones; John Jonathan, bapt. 18 Aug 1751; Priscilla, b. 1 Apr 1753 (KGP p. 292, 294)

Ward, Benjamin; wife Sarah; child: Elender, b. 12 Sep 1754 (KGP p. 306)

Ward, Benjamin; wife Sarah; children: Elizabeth, bapt. 20 May 1764; Ralph Marlow, bapt. 25 May 1766 Broad Creek; George, b. 25 May 1768, bapt. 10 Jul 1768 Lower Chapel (KGP p. 341, 347-8, 371)

Ward, Thomas; 18 Feb 1758; 19 May 1770; wife Lucretia; children: Lucretia, John; grandchild Lucretia Ward (MCW XIV.158-9)

WARDROP

Wardrop, James of Upper Marlborough, now in New York City; 11 Dec 1759; 2 Aug 1760; wife Lettice; nephew Robert Bull [s/o Robert of Leith, Scotland]; b-i-l Alexander Symour, merchant (MCW XII.231-2); ex. Lettice; 29 Nov 1760 (I 72.34)

WARING

Waring, Basil; m. 31 Jan 1709 Martha Greenfield; children: Thomas, b. 30 9ber 1710; James Haddock, b. 5 May 1713; Sarah Haddock, b. 11 Apr 1721; Samuel, b. 11 Mar 1722/3 (QAP m/1; b/9, 16, 18)

Waring, Basill; wife Martha [d/o Thomas Greenfield]; tract *Masonscon*; 12 Feb 1714/5 (PGLR F.455)

Waring, Marsham, gent.; 12 Mar 1730; 20 Oct 1732; wife Eleanor; daus. Sarah, Ann; sons Basil, Richard Marsham; tracts *Mount Pleasant, Hearts Delight, Brooke Land, Indian Field, Bryan Dayley* (MCW VI.233); 10 Mar 1732 (I 17.6); widow Elianor; children: Sarah, Basil, Ann; 23 Sep 1734 (AA 12.443); 20 Jan 1735 (AA 14.143); 26 Sep 1741 (AA 18.46); family [unnamed]; 30 Jun 1737 (AA 14.408, 434)

Waring, Basil; admx. Mrs. Martha; 25 Jul 1733 (I 17.363); admx. Martha; heirs Francis, Martha, Bazill, Sarah, Samuel; 30 Sep 1734 (AA 12.637); 23 Jun 1737 (AA 15.330); heirs Basil, Sarah, Samuel; 29 Nov 1737 (GB 95)

Waring, Thomas; m. 12 Dec 1734 [or 1735] Jane Orford; children: Martha, b. 20 Jan 1735; Mary, b. 24 Jul 1738; Basil, b. 15 Nov 1740 (QAP m/6; b/29, 33)

Waring, Basil; minor age ca 19; chooses grandmother Sarah Haddock as guardian; Aug 1736 (PGCR W.235)

Waring, Richard Marsham; 17 Aug 1743; 1 Sep 1743; wife Elizabeth; sons Richard Marsham, Henry, John, Basil; bro. Basle; sisters: Sarah, Anne

Holliday, Martha Hawkins, and Francis; "bro." Henry Hawkins; tracts *Marsham's Rest, The Exchange, His Lordship's Favor, Barren Point, Mt. Pleasant, Jamaica* (MCW VIII.227); extx. Elisabeth; 22 Dec 1743 (I 29.145); extx. Elisabeth; heirs Richard Marsham, Henry, John & Basil Waring; 30 Nov 1744 (AA 21.65); extx. widow Elisabeth Owing [w/o Thomas]; 11 Jaun 1749 (AA 27.244); widow Elisabeth Owen [w/o Thomas]; 6 Jun 1750 (AA 28.122); heirs Richard Marsham, Thomas, John, Basil; 30 Aug 1750 (GB 169)

Waring, Samuel; 1 Jun 1744; 23 May 1746; bros. Basil, Thomas; tract *Warring's Lott* (MCW IX.71); 24 Aug 1747 (I 35.218)

Waring, James Haddock; 13 Sep 1746; 14 Dec 1747; wife Elizabeth (MCW X.133)

Waring, Martha; 8 Dec 1752; 6 Jan 1758; daus. Sarah Duckett [w/o John], sons Francis, Basil, Thomas; granddau. Ursula Burgess; d-i-l Elizabeth Waring (MCW XI.189)

Warring, Samuel; 10 Jan 1761 (I 73.49)

Waring, Thomas; admx. Lucy [widow]; 30 Apr 1761 (I 74.144)

Warron, Basill; wife Elizabeth; child: Thomas, b. 7 Aug 1761 (KGP p. 323)

Waring, Richard Marsham; 3 Apr 1765; 9 Jun 1765; bros. Henry, John; tracts *Jamaica, Mt. Pleasant* (MCW XIII.120); 7 Jul 1766 (I 89.308)

Waring, Francis; 15 Dec 1765; 7 Feb 1769; wife Mary; children: Leonard, Thomas, James Maddock, Clement Hollyday, Basil, Ann Hawkins, Martha, Elizabeth, Mary; tracts *Magoon Mansion, The Gore, Warington, Warington Park, Terra, Truman's Hills* (MCW XIV.94); [as Maj.]; 6 Jun 1769 (I 102.18); 14 Sep 1770 (I 107.297)

Warrin, Bassil; wife Ann; child: Thomas, bapt. 19 Apr 1767 Upper Chapel (KGP p. 365)

Waring, Basil, Jr.; 26 Mar 1776; 16 May 1776; wife [unnamed]; children: James, Thomas, Elizabeth, Eleanor, Easter & Martha Waring; cous. Basil Waring; nephew Basil Waring (MCW XVI.167)

WARINGFORD

Waringford [Warinford], Benajmin; wife Elizabeth; children: Nicholas, b. 22 Aug 1703; Benjamin, b. 6 May 1706; Elizabeth, b. 2 Jan 1708/9 (QAP b/3)

Waringford, Benjamin; wife Mary; child: Mary, b. 26 Mar 1732 (QAP b/26)

WARMAN

Warman, Francis; wife Catherine; children: Thomas Jenkins, b. 10 Dec 1770 Upper Chapel; Joshua, b. 30 Aug 1774 Upper Chapel (KGP p. 375, 391)

WARNER

Warner, Samuel; m. 15 Aug 1715 Elizabeth Person; children: Sarah, b. 29 Mar 1717; Samuel, b. 17 7ber 1719 (QAP m/1; b/15)

Warner, Samuel; planter; 21 Nov 1731; 29 Mar 1732; wife Elizabeth; son Samuel; dau. Sarah (MCW VI.213); admx. Elisabeth; 18 Jun 1732 (I 16.503); 28 Nov 1732 (I 17.61); extx. Elisabeth; 14 Mar 1732 (AA 11.589)

Warner, Elizabeth; son Stephen Lewis of Virginia; tract Collington; 29 Nov 1733 (PGLR T.49)

WARREN

Warren, Samuell, Sr.; son Samuell, Jr.; 25 Nov 1718 (PGLR F.130/697)

Warren, Hugh; wife Margaret; child: Richard, b. 6 Aug 1732 (QAP b/26)

Warren, Samuel; 25 Sep 1742; 27 Aug 1743; wife Rose; son Samuel; dau. Elizabeth (MCW IX.47)

WATERS

Waters, Samuel; wife Jane; children: John, b. 10 10ber 1698; Susanna, b. 7 Aug 1705; Samuel, b. 15 Sep 1707; Mary, b. 1 Apr 1709; Elizabeth, b. 30 Sep 1710; Joseph, b. 27 Jan 1711; Deborah, b. 4 Mar 1713; Richard, b. 2 Mar 1715; William, b. 7 May 1716; Margaret, b. 14 Mar 1718; Rachel, b. 16 Mar 1720; Mordecai, b. 7 Mar 1722 (QAP b/6,7, 22)

Waters, Jane; child: William Ellurburton Waters, b. 26 Dec 1705 (QAP b/6)

Waters, Samuel; wife Jane; tract Jerico; 15 Dec 1716 (PGLR F.596)

Waters, John; wife Charity; children: Samuel, b. 28 Jan 1726; Elizabeth, b. 12 Feb 1729; John, b. 11 Dec 1734; Mary, b. 15 Jan ____; William, b. 25 Sep ____ (QAP b/22, 24, 30)

Waters, William; wife Isabell; tract Dorman's Folly; 24 Mar 1730 (PGLR M.551)

Waters, Samuel; wife Francis; tract Water's Lot; 25 Jun 1730 (PGLR Q.39)

Waters, Samuel, Jr.; wife Artridge; father Samuel, Sr.; tract Cheney; 21 Jan 1733 (PGLR T.71)

Waters, Joseph; 8 Feb 1743 (I 29.303)

Waters, Elizabeth; 7 Jan 1745; 15 Apr 1747; sons Joseph, John, William [dec'd]; daus Mary Webster, Margaret Holland [dec'd]; grandson Thomas Holland (MCW IX.100); 24 Jul 1747 (I 35.123)

Waters, Samuel; 10 Oct 1747; 16 Sep 1749; wife Jane; sons John, Mordecai, Samuel, Richard, William; daus. Margret Mullikin, Susannah, Mary, Elizabeth, Deborah, Rachel; tracts Jericho, Cumberstone, Hogyard, Charles and Benjamin, The Cherry Walk (MCW X.42)

Waters, Thomas; 29 Jun 1765; admx. Sarah Watters; children: Richard, Rachel, John, Ann, Thomas, Mathew, Casandra (ABB 4.99); admx. Sarah; 18 Oct 1765 (I 87.125); heirs Richard, Rachel, John, Anne, Thomas, Nathan, Kassandra; 25 Nov 1767 (GB 256)

Waters, John, Jr.; planter; 17 Nov 1768; 27 Oct 1774; children: Samuel, William, Thomas, Elizabeth, Arnold, Mary Williams, Sarah Norris, Ann, Susannah, Charity; grandson John Williams [s/o Stockitt]; tracts *Madens Fancy, Indian Town Land, Resurvey, Waters Purchase, Jemeco and Cherry Walk* (MCW XVI.21-2); [as John (Quaker)]; 27 Nov 1775 (I 123.220)

Waters, Samuel; planter; 10 Mar 1769; 17 May 1773; wife Artridge; sons Samuel, Robert, Edward, Stephen, Henry; daus. Margaret, Artridge, Gulialmariah; grandson Samuel Peach [s/o Sarah]; tracts *Cleming, Waters' Loss, Addition to Hogyard, The Core of Cherry Walk, Cherry Walk, Addition to Cherry Walk, Common Warrant, Jericho, Addition to Jericho, The Spring* (MCW XV.124)

WATKINS

Wattkins, Cornelius [dec'd]; widow Elizabeth; Oct 1699 Ct. (PGCR A.476)

Wattkins, Katherine; 7 Nov 1698 (I&A 17.137)

Watkins, John; 19 Jun 1703; 18 Jul 1703; wife Mary; d-i-l Ann Lewis, ss-i-l Thomas and John Lewis and Edward Eanis; s-i-l Richard Lewis (MCW III.22)

Wattkins, John; ex. Mary; 14 Mar 1705 (I&A 25.274)

Watkins, John; 11 Nov 1743; 7 Dec 1743; wife Mary; sons John, Stephen, Nicholas; daus. Sarah Gassaway, Anne, Frances, Mary, Hester, Jean (MCW VIII.235)

WATSON

Watson, William; planter; 22 Jan 1722; 30 Nov 1726; wife Jane; sons Williams, James; s-i-l John Thomas (MCW VI.2); 7 Feb 1726 (I 11.775); extx. Jane Lovejoy [w/o Samuell]; 25 Aug 1727 (AA 8.530)

Watson, James; age ca 32; 13 Sep 1729 (PGLR M.519); age ca 41; 1734 (PGLR T.504)

Watson, Henry; wife Lucy; children: Nancy Ann, b. 8 Oct 1732; John, b. 22 Mar 1734; Henry, b. 24 Feb 1735/6; Mary, b. 28 Jun 1742 (?) (PGP p. 250, 251)

Watson, James; wife Elizabeth; tract *Poplar Hills*; 27 Mar 1739 (PGLR T.701)

Watson, William; wife Elizabeth; tract *Wattson's Luck*; 26 Jun 1739 (PGLR Y.71)

Watson, David; wife Sarah; children: Mary, b. 24 Feb 1730; George, b. 27 Jul 1739 (QAP b/24, 32)

Watson, William; 20 Jan 1743; 20 Jul 1743; wife Elizabeth; sons William, James, Benjamin (MCW VIII.226); extx. Elisabeth; 22 Nov 1743 (I 28.385); extx. Elisabeth Brightwell [w/o Richard]; heirs Mary, Elisabeth, Martha, Jayne, Jemima, Catherine; 3 Aug 1744 (AA 20.335); heir [?Lord Proprietary]; 14 Jul 1746 (GB 151)

Watson, David; dau. Mary; 1751 (MCW X.184)

Watson, Francis; wife Osley; child: Robert, bapt. 31 Jul 1763 at Upper Chapel (KGP p. 333)

Watson, Samuel; wife Sarah; children: Sarah, b. 28 Jun 1763; Peregreen, b. 16 Sep 1765 (PGP p. 268, 275)

Watson, James; 15 Jul 1769; 17 Mar 1777; sons William, James, John, Isack; daus. Elizabeth, Jane, Sarah; grandson Alexander Oliver; tracts *Wood Come*, *Watson's Forest*, *Colbork*, *Bood Come by Chance*, *Standles Chance*, *Trenant*, *Woodburn*, *Colebrook*, *Horse Head* (MCW XVI.186)

WATTS

Watts, James; 3 Jul 1703; 2 Aug 1703; s-i-l Thomas Oneby; Ann Greenfield [d/o Thomas]; Matthew Greenfield (MCW III.14); 5 Aug 1703 (I&A 3.274)

Watts, James; wife [unnamed, dec'd]; 12 Nov 1712 (I&A 33b.68)

Watts, William [England]; 15 Jun 1714 (I&A 35a.371)

Watts, Ja.; 3 Aug 1716 (I&A 37a.129)

Watts, Samuell; wife Mary; child: James, b. 8 Nov 1761 (PGP p. 263)

WAUGH

Waugh, James; wife Mary; children: Ann, b. 16 Jan 1763 at Broad Creek; John, bapt. 22 Mar 1767 Broad Creek (KGP p. 338, 360)

Waugh, James; wife Mary; children: Mary, b. 7 Jan 1773 Broad Creek; Archibald, b. 10 Mar 1775 Broad Creek (KGP p. 378, 387)

WAUGHOP

Waughop, Thomas [SM]; wife Mary [granddau. of John Evans]; 5 Sep 1719 (PGLR F.248/834)

WEATHERBORNE

Weatherborne, Peter; age 4 mos. on 9th day of this month; s/o Jane; bound out; Mar 1712 (PGCR G.175)

WEATHERS

Weathers, Charles; m. 1 Sep 1724 Margarett Peake; child: Mary, b. 25 Apr 1725 (KGP p. 282)

WEAVER

Weaver, Richard; wife Ann; tract *Weaver's Delight*; 14 Sep 1720 (PGLR I.49)

Weaver, Richard; age ca 45; 10 Jun 1728 (PGLR M.292)

Weaver, Richard; wife Rachel; child: Ann, b. 12 Sep 1730 (QAP b/28)

Weaver, Ann; 15 Jul 1746; 27 Aug 1746; sons James Veath, Richard Weaver; daus. Ann Davis, Mary Master (MCW IX.90)

WEBB

Webb, Elizabeth; orphan age 13; bound out; Jan 1706 (PGCR C.110A)

Webb, Deborah [age 8], John [age 10], and Mary [age ca 5]; ch/o Humphry; bound out; Nov 1706 (PGCR C.95a, 96a)

Webb, Thomas; m. 19 Nov 1734 Elizabeth Child; child: Thomas, b. 18 Sep 1736 (QAP m/6; b/31)

Webb, Thomas; wife Rebecca; children: Bankes, bapt. 24 Jun 1764 Upper Chapel Thomas, bapt. 2 Nov 1766 Upper Chapel (KGP p. 341, 354)

Webb, John; wife Kesiah; child: William, bapt. 19 Jun 1768 Lower Chapel (KGP p. 369)

WEBSTER

Webster, Ann; age ca 9 Christmas next; servant; Sep 1699 Ct. (PGCR A.464)

Webster, John; age ca 13; servant; Aug 1707 (PGCR C.154a)

Webster, William; age ca 14; servant; Jun 1712 Ct. (PGCR G.211)

Webster, William; wife Elizabeth; children: Mary, b. 2 Sep 1724; Thomas, b. 14 Nov 1726; Elizabeth, b. 16 Aug 1728; William, b. 15 Jun 1731; Ellenor, b. 22 Jun 1733; John, b. 4 Sep 1735; James, b. _ Mar 1737/8; Sarah, b. _ ___ 1740/1; Mary Ann, b. 14 Feb 1742/3; Philip, b. _ Feb 1744, Jane, b. _ Oct 1745 (KGP p. 278, 296)

Webster, Eliz., Jr.; child: Mary Elinor, b. 31 Mar 1749 (KGP p. 291)

Webster, Thomas; m. 5 Jan 1752 Mary Guy by Rev. Addison; children: George, b. 29 Sep 1752, bapt. 22 Oct 1752; Monokey Guy (f), b. 30 Nov 1753; Mary, b. 1 Mar 1755; William, b. 31 Aug 1757; Thomas, bapt. 2 May 1762, Elizabeth, bapt. 20 Sep 1767 Lower Chapel (KGP p. 295, 297, 304, 315, 316, 327, 368)

Webster, William, Jr.; m. 12 Sep 1756 Ann Turner; children: Elizabeth Lidia, b. 31 Oct 1757; John, b. 7 Nov 1759; Ann, b. 23 Jan 1762; William, b. 27 Sep 1764, bapt. 14 Oct 1764 Lower Chapel; Sarah, b. 16 Oct 1767, bapt. 1 Nov 1767 Lower Chapel; Jonathan, b. 23 Aug 1770; Philip, b. 17 Mar 1773 Lower Chapel; Zaphaniah, b. 2 Feb 1776 (KGP p. 313, 315, 345, 368, 381, 384)

Webster, John; m. 13 Oct 1764 Joanner C. Stevens; children: John Stone, b. 7 Aug 1765 Lower Chapel; William Rosamond, b. 4 May 1769 [d. 28 Nov 1775, age 7]; Rezin, b. 22 Feb 1772; Susanna Darnel, b. 21 Apr 1774; Elizabeth Rebecah, b. 12 Dec 1777; William R., b. 12 Dec 1779, Leven, b. 23 May 1783 Upper Chapel (KGP p. 375); [John Webster d. 10 Nov 1783]

Webster, James; wife Mary Ann Phebe; children: William Brewis, bapt. 2 Jun 1765 Lower Chapel; James Gibbs, bapt. 17 Apr 1768 Lower Chapel; Elizabeth, b. 30 Mar 1772 Lower Chapel; Lucy Ann, b. 4 Dec 1774 Lower Chapel; Hezekiah, b. 20 Apr 1776 Lower Chapel (KGP p. 351, 367, 380, 384)

Webster, John; wife Catharine; children: John Stone, b. 7 Aug 1765; William Rosemend (m), bapt. 5 Jun 1768 Broad Creek (KGP p. 351, 363)

Webster, John Stone; s/o John; 1772 (MCW XV.4)

WEDDING

Wedding, Thomas; wife Elenor; child: Nickademus, b. 1 Sep 1762 (ICR; KGP p. 327)

WEDGES

Wedges, Samuel; mulatto s/o Mary; b. 31 Oct last; bound out; Nov 1738 (PGCR X.192)

WEEMS

Weene, Elizabeth [w/o John]; transported for 14 years; 14 Apr 1742 (PGLR Y.560)

Weems, Thomas; wife Mary; children: John Scot, b. 20 May 1766; Walter, b. 11 Nov 1767 (QAP b/39)

WELLING

Welling, John; wife Mary Ann; children: Mary, b. 6 Aug 1736; Elizabeth, b. 31 May 1738; William, b. 21 Dec 1741; Jane, b. 30 Mar 1744; Thomas, b. 28 Nov 1748; Jemima, b. 29 Oct 1750; Zachariah, b. 15 Jun 1752, bapt. 28 Jul 1752; Keziah, b. 2 Aug 1755 (KGP p. 289, 290, 297, 315)

Welling, Jane; children: George, b. 11 Jun 1769; Hesiah [not Kesiah] (f), b. 13 Jun 1769 Broad Creek (KGP p. 373)

Welling, Thomas; wife Ann; child: John Perkins, b. [with 1773] Broad Creek (KGP p. 385)

WELLS

Wells, Thomas, Sr.; wife Frances; children: Robert, b. 5 Aug 1693; Joseph & Sarah [twins], b. 30 7ber 1697; Elizabeth, b. 11 May 1699 (QAP b/5)

Wells, Thomas, Jr.; wife Martha; children: Thomas, b. 28 Jan 1710/11; John, b. 26 8ber 1712; Mary, b. 12 Aug 1715 (QAP b/5, 8, 11)

Wells, Thomas; age ca 61; 14 Jun 1714 (CCR CL.27)

Wells, John; m. 12 8ber 1715 Margaret Parsfeild [Parshfield] (QAP m/1)

Wells, Nathan; m. 13 Dec 1716 Mary Duckett; children: Elizabeth, b. 14 9ber 1717; Mary, b. 27 Aug 1719; Sarah, b. 13 Apr 1721; Nathan, b. 8 Apr 1723; Jemima, b. 3 Feb 1724/5; Richard, b. 26 Jan 1726/7; George, b. 11 Jan 1728/9; Susanna, b. 9 Dec 1730 (?); Kezia, b. 1 Nov 1732; John Ducket, b. 2 Jan 1733; Jacob, b. 21 Sep 1735 (QAP m/4; b/14, 15, 19, 20, 21, 24, 26, 28, 31)

Wells, Thomas, Sr.; planter; 26 Sep 1718; 5 Jan 1718; wife Frances; sons, Thomas, Robert, Nathan, Joseph; daus. Frances, Mary, Sarah, Elizabeth; tracts *Strife, Something* (MCW IV.186); widow Frances; 6 Sep 1720 (AA 3.214)

Wells, Robert; wife Ann; children: Thomas, b. 2 Dec 1717; Mary, b. 29 Jan 1718/9; Sarah, b. 15 May 1720; Nathan, b. 27 10ber 1722; Eliabeth, b. 27 Mar 1727; Robert, b. 7 Feb 1728/9; William, b. 7 Jan 1730; Jemimah, b. 20 Jul 1732; Margret, b. 13 Aug 1734 (QAP b/5, 14, 15, 18, 20, 21, 24, 34)

Wells, George; m. 16 Jun 1725 Susanna Ward (QAP m/4)

Wells, Thomas; wife Martha; 1739 (MCW VIII.51)

Wells, Isaac; 10 Mar 1746; 10 Apr 1747; wife [unnamed]; sons John, Isaac Edwards, Samuel, Benjamin; daus. Mary, Elizabeth, Ann; tracts *Low Lands, Children's Chance, Wells' Invention* (MCW IX.106); 5 Mar 1747 (I 35.436); widow Ann; 24 Aug 1748 (AA 25.110)

Wells, Thomas; planter; 7 Oct 1748; 25 Jun 1751; sons John, Thomas; dau. Mary Duvall (MCW X.158); 3 Jul 1751 (I 51.25)

Wells, George; 16 Feb 1764; 20 Apr 1771; wife Sarah; sons George, Joseph (MCW XIV.169)

Wells, William; admx. Mary Wells [alias Mary Smith]; 6 Nov 1772 (I 110.216, 236)

WELSH

Welsh, John [AA]; wife Rachel; son John, Jr.; 2 Nov 1730 (PGLR Q.165)

Welch, Barbara; age 3 on 15 Oct next; d/o Elizabeth; bound out; Aug 1732 (PGCR S.11)

Welch, William; admx. Martha; 2 Jul 1734 (I 18.273)

Welsh, John; 24 Feb 1748; 20 May 1749; wife Mary (MCW X.10)

WEST

West, Benjamin; m. 16 May 1728 Susanna Stockett, d/o Thomas Stockett of Anne Arundel Co.; children: Joseph, b. 28 Nov 1731; Benjamin, b. 17 Feb 1734 (QAP m/5; b/25, 28)

West, Joseph; planter; 25 Aug 1731; 23 Nov 1731; wife Rebeccah; sons William, John, Benjamin; dau. Mary Kelly; grandson Joseph Kelley; tracts *Two Brothers, The Joseph, Blakeburn* (MCW VI.198); extx. Rebecca; 9 Feb 1731 (I 16.610)

West, Benjamin; 9 Nov 1744; 27 Jun 1745; son Joseph; dau. Sarah; bro. John (MCW IX.41); 16 Aug 1746 (I 33.306); mother Rebecca; 23 Nov 1747 (AA 24.203)

West, Joseph; wife Mary; children: Edward Owen, b. 26 ___ 1760; Lawrence Owen, b. 14 Dec 1762 (PGP p. 260, 270)

West, John; wife Rachel; children: Reason, b. 31 May 1760; Rebecca, b. 23 Sep 1762; Simeon, b. 23 Dec 1764; William, b. 29 May 1765 (PGP p. 259, 267, 272, 274)

West, William; wife Elizabeth; child: Thomas, b. 19 Oct 1762 (PGP p. 267)

West, Benjamin; wife Virlinder; child: Hilleary, b. 12 Oct 1765 (PGP p. 277)

WESTLY

Westly, Samuell; 29 Oct 1700 (I&A 20.138)

Westly, Samuell; age ca 10; sevant; Aug 1710 (PGCR G.3)

Westly, Humphry; age ca 10 mos.; bound out; Mar 1742 (PGCR AA.341)

WHARTON

Wharton, Thomas; age 18; 24 Jan 1725 (PGLR I.715)

Wharton, Elizabeth [widow]; son by her 2nd marriage John Digges; tract *Barbadoes*; 2 Apr 1728 (PGLR M.313)

WHAW

Whaw, James; wife Mary; child: Singleton, b. _ Sept 1765; bapt. 30 Jun 1765 Broad Creek (KGP p. 347)

WHEAT

Wheate, John; admx. Jeremiah Perdue & wife Sarah; 1 Aug 1712 (I&A 33a.216); admx. Sarah Perdue [w/o Jeremiah]; 4 children [unnamed]; 22 Dec 1712 (I&A 33b.177)

Wheat, William; wife Ann [d/o Thomas Wall]; tract *Smith's Pasture*; 25 Jul 1729 (PGLR M.457)

Wheat, Francis; wife Sarah; children: ____, b. 4 May 172_; ____, b. 18 Nov 173_; ____, b. 7 Jan 173_; ____, b. ____ (m), b. 21 Feb 173_; ____(f), b. 3 Nov 174_; Elizabeth, b. 11 Sep 174_ (KGP p. 304) [recorded 10 ___ 1755]

Wheat, John; children: Sarah, b. 4 May 1728; John, b. 18 Nov 1730 (KGP p. 281)

Wheat, John; wife Ann; children: Amey, b. 23 Feb 1738; Josias, b. 31 Oct 1740; Benjamin, b. 27 Nov 1742; Notley, b. 27 Mar 1745; Tabitha, b. 15 Feb 1746; Charity, b. 2 Sep 1749; Stacy, b. 30 Nov 1751 (KGP p. 298)

Wheat, Francis; wife Elizabeth; children: Zachariah, bapt. 8 May 1764 at Broad Creek; Vialinda, bapt. 30 Mar 1766 Broad Creek (KGP p. 339, 353)

Wheat, John; wife Mary; children: Sarah, b. 24 Oct 1765 Broad Creek; Joseph, bapt. 7 Aug 1768 Broad Creek (KGP p. 359, 363)

Wheat, Francis, Sr.; 24 Jan 1767; 24 Oct 1774; wife Sarah; children: Francis, John; tract *Coole Spring* (MCW XVI.7-8); 21 Jan 1775 (I 121.330)

Wheat, Benjamin; wife Elizabeth; child: John, bapt. 6 Nov 1768 Upper Chapel (KGP p. 372)

Wheat, Frances, Jr.; wife Elizabeth; child: Elizabeth, b. 25 Apr 1773 Broad Creek (KGP p. 384)

Wheat, John; wife Mary; child: Thomas, b. 15 Feb 1774 Broad Creek (KGP p. 385)

WHEELER

Wheeler, Francis; wife Winefritt; children: Leonard, b. 3 Jun 1691; Mary, b. 14 Nov 1693; Charity, b. 19 May 1699; Francis and Winnifrett [twins], b. 25 Jan 1701; William, b. 14 Sep 1704; Clement, b. 3 Jun 1706; Ignatius, b. 14 Oct 1709; Anne, b. 13 Oct 1712 (KGP p. 260)

Wheeler, Ignatius [CH]; wife Francis; tract *Indian Field*; 22 Feb 1696 (PGLR A.63)

Wheeler, Charles; wife Mary; Mar 1700 Ct. (PGCR B.27a)

Wheeler, John [CH]; wife Dorathy; tract *Wheelers Purchase*; 19 Sep 1700 (PGLR A.411)

Wheeler, John [dec'd]; bro. James; grandson James; tract *Wheeler's Purchase*; 2 Feb 1705 (PGLR C.156)

Wheeler, Benja.; wife Eliza.; children: Jane, b. 13 Apr 1705; Thomas, b. 19 May 1708; Mary, b. 5 Nov 1710; Benj., b. 4 Oct 1712 (KGP p. 265)

Wheeler, Robert; wife Grace; children: Thomas, b. 5 9ber 1706; Robert, b. 23 Dec 1708; John, b. 22 10ber 1710; Mary, b. 16 Jul 1713; Daniel, b. 18 9ber 1714; Samuel b. 9 Jan ____ (?1718) (QAP b/5, 8, 10, 22)

Wheeler, Francis; wife Winifred; dau. Mary Noble [w/o Joseph]; tract part of *Major's Choice*; 14 Oct 1718 (PGLR F.110/671)

Wheeler, Francis, age ca 50; 1 Jul 1726 (PGLR M.27); age ca 55; 1728 (PGLR M.346); [as Francis, Sr.]; age ca 50-60; 19 Oct 1730 (CCR-MSA 5.468); age ca 60; 1731 (PGLR Q.372)

Wheeler, James; age ca 40; 1 Jul 1726 (PGLR M.27)

Wheeler, Luke [SM]; wife Prothania; tract *Red Bird Thickett*; 1 Jun 1727 (PGLR M.305)

Wheeler, Thomas; m. 6 Mar 1732/3 Susanna Duckett (QAP m/6)

Wheeler, Robert, Jr.; m. 23 9ber1732 Ann Duckett; child: Sarah, b. __ __ 17__ (QAP m/6; b/29)

Wheeler, Clemant; m. 5 Feb 1732/3 Elizabeth Edelen; children: Catharine, b. 25 Jul 1734 [m. 20 Apr 1767 Charles Lansdale]; __usana (f), b. 2 Jan 1735; Clemant, b. 13 Mar 1737/8 (KGP p. 283; ICR)

Wheeler, Ignatius [SM]; wife Charity; tract *Wheeler's Purchase*; 5 Jun 1734 (PGLR T.288)

Wheeler, Thomas; age ca 77; 26 Apr 1735 (PGLR T.253)

Wheeler, Francis; planter; 3 Nov 1735; 18 Feb 1735/6; sons William, Leonard, Francis, Clement, Ignatius; dau. Ann Jones; grandsons John, Ignatius [ss/o Leonard]; tract *Major's Chance, Major's Choice* (MCW VII.161); Francis, Sr.; 21 May 1736 (I 21.340); 15 Feb 1736 (?) (AA 15.302)

Wheeler, Leonard; wife Elizabeth; children: Ignatius, b. 23 Jan 173_; Samuel, b. 4 Feb 173_; George, b. 3 Dec 173_; Edward, b. 10 Oct 1738 (KGP p. 285, 287)

Wheeler, Robert; carpenter; 7 Oct 1740; 23 Nov 1748; wife Grace; sons Robert [wife Ann], Daniel, Thomas, Samuel; dau. Mary; granddau. Sarah Wheeler [d/o Robert]; grandson Robert [s/o Robert]; tracts *Farmers Marsh, Addition to Farmers Marsh* (MCW IX.176-7); [as Robert, Capt.]; extx. Grace; _ Dec 1748 (I 43.498); 29 Sep 1750; extx. Grace; son Samuel; 29 Sep 1750 (AA 29.2)

Wheeler, Francis; wife Elizabeth; child: Samuel, b. 9 Apr 1742 (KGP p. 269)

Wheeler, James; age ca 58; 1743 (PGLR Y.657)

Wheeler, Clement; admx. Elisabeth; children: Catherine, Henry, Clement, Susannah; 9 Mar 1750 (AA 29.221); admx. Elisabeth; 19 Nov 1750 (I 44.443); widow Elizabeth; orphans Mary, Clement, Catherine, Susannah, Jane; 24 Mar 1752 (GB 176)

Wheeler, Robert; 3 Sep 1751; 25 Mar 1752; wife Ann; children: Sarah, Sarah-Ann, Mary, Lydiah, Elizabeth, Ruth (MCW X.208); extx. Anne; 3 Apr 1752 (I 51.56); heirs Sarah, Ann, Mary, Lydia, Elizabeth, Ruth, Thomas, Robert, Richard; 29 Aug 1752 (GB 185); 4 Apr 1753; exs. Matthew

Roberson & Ann his wife (ABB 1.63); extx. Ann Roberson [w/o Matthew]; 11 May 1753 (AA 33.423)

Wheeler, Ignatius; m. 29 Jul 1753 Elizabeth Marbury; children: Luke Marbury (1st son), b. 25 Jul 1754; Elenor (1st dau.), b. 28 Dec 1756; Elisabeth (2nd dau.), b. 28 Dec 1759; Ignatius (2nd son), b. 9 Sep 1763; George (3rd son), b. 1 Aug 1768; Broad Creek (KGP p. 306, 314, 373)

Wheeler, Clement; m. 25 Feb 1759 Jane Stonestreet (KGP p. 322)

Wheeler, Leonard; admx. Elisabeth; 5 Jan 1764 (I 83.145)

Wheeler, Leonard; admn. Susannah; 7 Sep 1765 (GB 261)

Wheeler, Clement; admx. Jane; 28 Oct 1768 (I 98.44)

Wheeler, Ignatius; 4 Jan 1771 (I 106.165); 23 Mar 1774; admx. Hezekiah Wheeler (ABB 6.270); heirs [unnamed]; 25 Nov 1774 (GB 323)

Wheeler, Ignatius; wife Nancy; child: John Noble, b. 5 Mar 1773 Lower Chapel (KGP p. 384)

Wheeler, Samuel; admx. Elisabeth; 15 Jan 1774 (I 118.169)

WHITAKER

Whitaker, Robert; 27 Jun 1753; sons William, Robert, Henry, Alexander; daus. Susannah, Elizabeth, Susan, Sarah, Priscilla (MCW X.271); 30 Jan 1756; extx. Elisabeth Whitaker; children: William, Robert, Susannah, Elisabeth, Susan, Henry, Sarah, Alexander Russell (ABB 2.20); widow Elizabeth; heirs Susanna, Elizabeth, Susan, Henry, Alexander, Priscilla; 2 Nov 1756 (GB 202)

Whitaker, William; 28 Nov 1756; 22 Mar 1757; mother Elizabeth; bros. Henry, Alexander, Robert; tract *Pentland Hills* (MCW XI.174)

Whitaker, Henry; 21 Oct 1772 (I 112.126)

WHITE

White, Guy; 3 Aug 1712; 15 Dec 1712; wife Eliza; sons Guy, Samuel, Benjamin, Francis; daus. Sarah, Eliza.; tracts *Cool Spring Manor, Swanton's Lot* (MCW III.234); admx. Elisabeth; 14 Sep 1714 (I&A 36a.85); planter; extx. Elisabeth; 30 Dec 1712 (I&A 33b.160); extx. Elisabeth; 30 Dec 1712 (I&A 34.117)

White, Bernard; wife Ellinor; child: Ann, b. 14 May 1718 (QAP b/13)

White, Jonathon, Rev.; 30 Jun 1718 (I 1.7); 5 May 1719 (AA 1.413); extx. Elinor Eagon [w/o Charles]; 30 Jun 1721 (AA 3.364)

White, James [AA]; daus. Margaret, Elizabeth Brown [w/o John] [CA]; tract *Eglington*; 9 Dec 1718 (PGLR F.113/675)

Whyte, Bernard, gent.; 20 May 1720; 25 Jun 1720; wife Ellinoer; dau. Ann (MCW V.11); [with 1720] (I 5.102)

White, Jonas; wife Elizabeth [d/o James Gambling, dec'd]; tract *Woods*; 12 Dec 1720 (PGLR I.74)

White, [female]; age 4 on 25 Apr next; d/o Mary; bound out; Aug 1721 (PGCR K.371)

White, Benjamin; m. 1 Feb 1722/3 Ann Hilliard; children: Rebecca, b. 20 Aug 1723; Lettice, b. 12 Dec 1726; Margaret, b. 29 Jul 1729; Rachel, b. 25 Feb 1730; Mary Ann, b. 24 May 1733; William, b. 29 Jul 1735; John, b. 17 Jan 1739; Sarah, b. 5 Oct 1741; Benjamin, b. 12 Jan 174_ (QAP m/3; b/24, 27, 32, 35)

White, Samuel; wife Elizabeth; child: Cassandra, b. 11 May 1732 (QAP b/26)

White, Robert; age ca 51; 11 May 1733 (PGLR T.25)

White, James; wife Elenar; child: Zachary, b. 13 Nov 1737 (PGP p. 254)

White, Benjamin; age ca 47; 1742 (PGLR Y.654)

White, Benjamin; wife Margery; children: Absalom, b. __ Jun ___; Elisabeth, b. 25 Nov ____; Sabrina Frances, b. 25 Jan 1743; John, b. __ Dec ____ (QAP b/34, 35, 36)

White, Joseph; admx. Elisabeth; 14 Aug 1744 (I 30.150); admx. Elisabeth; children: Altheia, Elisabeth, Sarah, Jos.; 2 May 1745 (AA 21.285); widow Elizabeth; heirs Althea, Elizabeth, Sarah, Joseph; 28 Nov 1746 (GB 153)

White, Margeary; child: Zephniah, b. 15 Dec 1749 (PGP p. 253)

White, Zachariah; wife Mary_; child: Burges, b. 20 Mar 1758 (PGP p. 257)

White, Robert; 9 Aug 1758; 14 Apr 1768; children: James, Catherine, Burgess, Sarah Hawkes [?Hawkins], Ann Fleming; grandchildren: Robert Hawkins, Zachariah White, Burgess White, Ann Fleming, Robert White Fleming, Catherine Fleming, Catherine Willson; tracts *Mount Pleasure* (MCW XIV.30)

White, Thomas; child: Amealier, b. 22 Feb 1761 (KGP p. 322)

White, Guy; wife Casander; child: Mary Belt, bapt. 10 Oct 1762 (KGP p. 328)

White, Benjamin; wife Mary; child: Sharlot, b. 12 Feb 1774 Upper Chapel (KGP p. 390)

White, Benjamin; wife Mary; child: Ann, b. __ Dec ____ (QAP b/34)

WHITEHEAD

Whitehead, Mary; 2 Feb 1769; 12 May 1769; children: Taylor Baldwin, Samuel Whitehead, Mary Loyon; grandchildren: James Baldwin, Robert Lyon [s/o Mary]; Elizabeth & Mary Baldwin (MCW XIV.84)

WHITMORE

Whitemoore, Humphrey; wife Mary; children: Elizabeth, b. 16 Apr 1708; Margrett, b. 8 Nov 1710; Mary, b. 19 Sep 1713; Humphrey, b. 10 Mar 1718; William, b. 24 Apr 1720 (KGP p. 275)

Whitmore, John; orphan age 12 on 19 Jan next; bound to Humphry Whitmore; Aug 1748 (PGP HH.341)

Whitmore, William; m. 10 May 1753 Mary Beall by Rev. Henry Addison; child: Charles, b. 25 Sep 1753 (KGP p. 299, 301)

Whitmore, Humphry; wife Elinor; children: Elizabeth, b. 2 Jul 1753; Jonathan, b. 20 Jun 1756; Sarah Ann, bapt. 12 Jun 1763 at Broad Creek; [mother unnmaed] Humphry, bapt. 14 Jun 1767 Broad Creek (KGP p. 300, 314, 337, 361)

Whitmore, William; child: Benjamin, bapt. 26 Jul 1767 Broad Creek (KGP p. 361)

WHITNOLL

Whitnoll, William; wife. Frances; children: Mary, b. 19 Jun 1728; Solomon, b. 24 May 1730; Elisabeth, b. 1 Apr 1732; William, b. __ May 1735 (PGP p. 249, 250)

WHITTAKER

Whittaker, Robert; extx. Elisabeth; 12 Sep 1753 (I 56.29)

WHITTON

Whitton, Isaac; child: Isaac, b. 1 May 1759 (PGP p. 257)

WICKHAM

Wickham, Nathaniel, Sr.; wife Lubina; son Nathaniel, Jr.; tract *Wickham's Park*; 10 Feb 1720/1 (PGLR I.117)

Wickam, Nathaniel; m. 19 Dec 1723 Priscilla Tyler (QAP m/3)

Wickham, Nathaniel; age ca 61; 3 Oct 1724 (PGLR I.597)

Wickham, Nathaniel, Sr.; wife Sabina; tract *St. Andrews*; 30 Jul 1726 (PGLR M.45)

Wickham, Nathaniel, Sr.; age ca 71; 22 Sep 1730 (PGLR Q.157)

Wickham, Nathaniel; age ca 82; 26 Nov 1739 (PGLR Y.107)

WIGFIELD

Wigfull, Mathew; wife Mary; son John; tract *New Park*; 10 Jan 1729 (PGLR M.529)

Wigfield, Mathew; wife Elizabeth; children: Mary, b. 17 Jun 1764, bapt. 5 Aug 1764 Upper Chapel; Rachel, b. 19 Jan 1766 Lower Chapel (KGP p. 3421, 346)

Wigfield, Joseph; wife Elizabeth; children: John Summer, b. 16 Nov 1771; Mary, b. 12 Oct 1773 Upper Chapel (KGP p. 388, 390)

Wigfield, Matthew; wife Elizabeth; children: Matthew, b. 23 May 1772 Upper Chapel; Robert, b. 13 Sep 1775 Upper Chapel (KGP p. 389, 1391; ICR)

Wigfield, Thomas; wife Rhoda; child: Martha, b. 16 Oct 1774 Broad Creek (KGP p. 386)

WIGHT

Wight, John [dec'd]; wife Ann [lately Ann Gant]; Mar 1699 Ct. (PGCR A.408)

Wight [White], John; widow Ann; 8 Mar 1708 (I&A 29.182); admx. Anne Wight; 11 Mar 1714 (I&A 36b.44)

Wight, John; wife Ann [d/o Thomas Greenfield]; tract *The Gores*; 13 Jun 1711 (PGLR F.84),

Wight, James; admx. Ann; 16 Sep 1714 (I&A 36a.163)

Wight, Jane; 16 Sep 1714 (I&A 36a.163)

Wightt [Wight], Anne; widow; 15 Sep 1725; 26 May 1726; son Thomas Gantt; daus. Margery Sprigg, Mary Belt [w/o Jeremiah], Fielder Powell [w/o John]; d-i-l Priscilla Gantt; grandson Thomas Sprigg, Edward Gantt, Edward Sprigg; granddaus. Ann Powell, Ann Sprigg and Ann, Priscilla & Elizabeth Gantt (MCW V.228); 2 Feb 1726 (I 11.841); [as AnnWhite]; 2 Jun 1727 (AA 8.240)

Wight [Wightt, White], John; 17 Jun 1728/9; 12 Apr 1729; wife Ann; sons John, Jonathan, Richard; daus. Mary, Innosense, Ann; tracts *Stepmother's Folly, Hopson's Choice, Wights Forrest, Mair and Colt, Taylorton, Cumpass Hills, Anchovie Hills, Pasqueum, The Goare* (MCW VI.97); admx. Ann; 1729 (I 15.397)]; widow Ann; children: Mary Taylor [w/o Samuel], John, Jonathan, Innocine, Richard; 27 Sep 1731 (AA 11.179)

Wightt, Jonathan; 29 Jun 1756; 11 Aug 1760; wife Mary; sons John, Truman; dau. Elizabeth (MCW XII.11); extx. Mary; 15 Dec 1760 (I 73.58); 29 Sep 1762; extx. Mary Wheeler [w/o Clement]; children: John, Truman, Elisabeth (ABB 3.163); heirs John, Elizabeth & Truman White; 24 Aug 1763 (GB 228); heir Truman; 27 Jun 1765 (GB 244)

Wight, John; 20 Jun 1761; ex. Henry Wight; widow [unnamed]; 3 children John, Truman, Elisabeth (ABB 3.83)

WILCOXEN

Willcoxen, John; 6 Mar 1712; 27 Sep 1716; wife Magdalen; 3 sons John, Lewis, Thomas (MCW IV.61); 17 Oct 1716 (I&A 37a.149); son John; [wih 1716] (I&A 37c.127)

Willcoxon, Thomas; wife Ruth; tract *Lanham's Delight*; 22 Mar 1726/7 (PGLR M.161)

Willcoxon, John; wife Agnes; 25 Nov 1731 (PGLR Q.400)

Willcoxon, Thomas; age ca 36; 1732 (PGLR Q.476)

Wilcoxson, Lewis; wife Susanna; tract *Three Brothers*; 25 Apr 1737 (PGLR T.587)

Wilcoxson, Lewis; wife ?Leusn. [probably Susanna]; tract *Charles Beall's Discovery*; 8 Sep 1737 (PGLR T.523)

Willcoxon, Thomas; wife Ruth; dau. Mary Talburt [w/o Thomas]; tract *Deer Park*; 24 Mar 1740 (PGLR Y.265)

Wilcoxon, Thomas; wife Ruth; child: Levin, b. 20 Oct 1749 (KGP p. 299)

Wilcoxon, Thomas, Jr.; 25 May 1775; 15 Jan 1776; wife Elizabeth; sons Thomas, Henry, Cramphim, George, Anthony, John, Jesse; daus. Mary, Elizabeth, Ruth, Ann; bros. John, Jesse Wilcoxon; tracts *Dear Park, Long Lane, Tolberts Lott, Tolberts Rest, White Marshes* (MCW XVI.167); 30 Sep 1776 (I 125.351)

Wilcoxen, Thomas, Sr.; 16 May 1777 (I 125.344)

WILKERSON

Wilkerson, John; m. Elizabeth; child: Dorcas, b. 8 May 1763 (PGP p. 268)

Wilkerson, William; heir William; _ Dec 1775 (GB 290)

WILKINS

Wilkins, John; 1 Mar 1732 (I 17.14)

Wilkins, John; admx. Esther Griffith [w/o Lewis of Calvert Co.]; 21 Feb 1733 (AA 12.168)

WILKINSON

Wilkinson, William; 29 Sep 1754; 24 Apr 1755; wife Barbara; children: Ann, Susanna, Sarah, Mary; son William Mackall Wilkinson (MCW XI.79); admx. Barbara; 15 Dec 1755 (I 60.445)

Wilkinson, Barbara; 18 Mar 1758 (I 68.197)

Wilkinson, George; wife Esther; children: Mary, b. 19 Jul 1772 Upper Chapel; Thomas, b. 11 Mar 1775 Upper Chapel (KGP p. 389, 391)

WILLER

Willer, Thomas; 4 Feb 1705 (I&A 25.405)

WILLETT

Willett, Ninian [b. 30 Nov 1701], Edward [b. 12 Jan 1703], Thomas [b. 9 Aug 1708]; ch/o Edward and Tabitha; bound out; Nov 1708 (PGCR D.96)

Willett, Edward, Sr.; son Edward, Jr.; tract *Balintun*; 10 Sep 1728 (PGLR M.324)

Willett, Edward; wife Mary; children: Tabithar, b. 4 May 1734; Elizabeth, b. 25 May 1736; Sarah, b. 4 May 1738 (PGP p. 251)

Willitt, Charles; 4 Nov 1737; 20 Dec 1737; wife Mary; sons John Caward, Richard, George, Benjamin; daus. Mary, Elizabeth (MCW VII.249); extx. Mary; 2 Mar 1738 (AA 17.79); admx. Mary; 9 May 1738 (I 23.177); widow Mary; heirs Charles, Mary, Elizabeth, Richard, George, Benjamin; 28 Nov 1739 (GB 104)

Willett, Ninian; age ca 37; 1738 (PGLR T.635)

Willett, Edward; 16 Jun 1743; 11 Feb 1744; sons Ninian, Edward, James, William, Thomas; dau. Ann Swan; tracts *Lick Hill, Beal's Craft, Bealington, Ryley's Plains, Little Dear, Horse Race* (MCW IX.14); 7 May 1745 (I 31.36); 24 Apr 1746 (I 32.179); 24 Apr 1746 (AA 22.163)

Willet, Charles; wife Mary; children: Ann, bapt. 28? Jun 1752; James, b. 29 Mar 1754 (KGP p. 296, 306)

Willett, John; wife Judith; child: Rachel, b. 3 Jun 1755 (KGP p. 308)

Willit, Richard; wife Kesiah; children: Beniall (m), bapt. May-Jul 1761; Charles, bapt. 2 Nov 1763 at Lower Chapel; Sushanna Priscilla, bapt. 23 Mar 1766 Broad Creek; Aquilla, bapt. 24 Jan 1768 Lower Chapel; William Wynn, b. 27 Feb 1775 Lower Chapel (KGP p. 323, 335, 348, 368, 380)

Willitt, William; wife Ann; child: Edward, b. 19 Mar 1765 (PGP p. 275)

Willit [Willett], Richard; wife Ann; children: John Wynn, b. 9 Mar 1770 Broad Creek; Esther Verlinder, b. [with 1772 records] Lower Chapel (KGP p. 374, 384)

Willett, Thomas; 18 May 1772 (I 111.209)

Willett, William, Sr.; 10 Jul 1772; 27 Aug 1772; wife Mary; children: Edward, William, Griffin, Samuel, George, John, James, others [unnamed]; tracts *Beall's Craft, Beallington, Restons Addition* (MCW XV.5); extx. Mary; 9 Mar 1773 (I 112.122, 140); 27 Nov 1773; extx. Mrs. Mary Willett; 11 of the children Elisabeth, Verlinder, Jamima, Tabitha, Ann, Samuel, George, John, Rachel, Mary, James (ABB 6.210)

Willett, Ninian, Sr.; 29 Jun 1773; 9 Nov 1773; children Ninian, Charles, Isaac (MCW XV.123-4); 1 Dec 1773 (I 114.294)

WILLIAMS

Williams, James; 14 May 1691; 18 Jul 1698; nephews John and Benjamin Chapman, Richard Wallis, James Wallis, Richard Hartup; b-i-l John

Chapman; tracts *Chelsey, Pentaland Hills* (MCW II.149); 17 Nov 1698 (I&A 17.140)

Williams, Hugh; wife Elizabeth [admx. of William Graves, dec'd]; Sep 1697 Ct. (PGCR A.228)

Williams; Joseph [AA]; son James; *James Lott*; 22 Dec 1706 (PGLR C.148a)

Williams, James; orphan; bound out; Mar 1711 (PGCR G.43a)

Williams, John; wife Susanna; child: Charles, b. 20 7ber 1711 (QAP b/5)

Williams, James; wife Sarah; child: William, b. 4 Jan 1711/2 (QAP b/6)

Williams, Jeremiah; wife Martha; children: Benjamin, b. 18 Jan 1712; William, b. 22 Aug 1714 (QAP b/10)

Williams, John; wife Sarah; Mar 1713 (PGCR G.291)

Williams, John; wife Lucy; children: John, b. 12 Jun 1713; Elizabeth, b. 1 Aug 1717 (QAP b/9, 13)

Williams, John; age ca 38; 20 Xber 1715 (CCR CL.277))

Williams, George; 4 Mar 1716 (I&A 38a.116, 119)

Williams, Thomas; wife Ellinor; children: Thomas, b. 25 Jan 1717; Ellinor, b. 3 May 1721; Walker, __ ___ 1726; Elisha, b. 12 May 1728; Mary, b. 24 Aug 1732; Rachel, b. 20 Apr 173_ (QAP b/13, 16, 17, 20, 21, 28)

Williams, William; age 5 on 5 Jan last; s/o James and Sarah; bound out; Mar 1717 (PGCR H.182)

Williams, Mary; illegitimate child: Elizabeth, b. 31 Jul 1717 (QAP b/13)

Williams, James; m. 24 Jan 1720/1 Mary Webb; children: Mary, b. 24 Aug 1721; James, b. 22 Aug 1723 (QAP m/2; b/17, 18)

Williams, Jeremiah; age 4 on 18 May next; s/o Jeremiah; bound out; Mar 1722 (PGCR K.486)

Williams, William; age 9 on 22 Aug next; s/o Jeremiah; bound out; Mar 1722 (PGCR K.486)

William, John; wife Alice [widow of Nicholas Rhoads, dec'd]; tract *Larkins Desire*; 28 Aug 1723 (PGLR I.475)

Williams, Baruch; wife Elianor; children: Mary, b. 19 Jan 1717; Hillary, b. 27 Dec 1719 [?1729] (QAP b/23)

Williams, Baruch; planter; extx. Eleanor; 15 Mar 1724 (I 10.88)

Williams, David; wife Jane; child: Basil, b. 10 Mar 1734 (QAP b/29)

Williams, John; admx. Lucy; 22 Jan 1728 (I 15.83); widow Lucy; 1 Oct 1729 (AA 9.470); widow Lucy; heirs Charles, John, Dorothy, Elizabeth, Joseph, Anne, Daniel, Basil, Mary; 25 Nov 1729 (GB 51)

Williams, Benjamin; wife Margaret; tract *Bear Neck*; 2 Mar 1729 (PGLR Q.4)

Williams, Henry; orphan age 3 mos. on 25 Mar inst.; bound out to learn blacksmithing; Mar 1729 (PGCR O.411)

Williams, John; orphan age 3; bound out to learn blacksmithing; Mar 1729 (PGCR O.411)

Williams, Mary; age 12; d/o Baruch; chooses guardian; Nov 1729 (PGCR P.272)

Williams, Baruch; admx. Elinor Pratt [w/o John]; 2 son, 1 dau. [unnamed]; 10 Nov 1730 (AA 10.544)

Williams, Elizabeth; b. 4 Sep 1714; d/o Jean; bound out; Mar 1733 (PGCR S.248)

Williams, David; wife Jane; child: Basil, b. 10 Mar 1734 (QAP29)

Williams, Charles [III]; 8 Feb 1736; 8 Feb 1737/8; wife Sarah; sons Lewis, Charles, David; daus. Elizabeth, Margarett James, Mary; grandson David [s/o David] (MCW VII.237); 27 Jun 1738 (I 23.1818); widow Sarah; children Margaret James [w/o Thomas]; David, Mary Torquison, Elisabeth Hardin [w/o John], Lewis; 9 May 1744 (AA 20.166)

Williams, William; mother Sarah; 22 Mar 1737 (PGLR T.566)

Williams, Samuel; 20 Dec 1737; 26 Sep 1738; [no relations]; *Stevens Hope, Norwich* (MCW VII.258); 4 Nov 1738 (I 23.422)

Williams, John; admx. Dianah; 28 Aug 1740 (I 25.180); admx. Dianna Robinson [w/o William]; children, John, Elinor, Thomas & Elisha Williams; 30 Aug 1744 (AA 20.448); admx. Dianna Robinson [w/o William]; 27 Aug 1746 (AA 23.36)

Williams, Baruck; wife Ellinor [now Ellinor Pratt]; son Hilleary; 22 Apr 1741 (PGLR Y.372)

William, John; 30 May 1743 (I 32.287)

Williams, Joseph; 26 Nov 1746; 13 Feb 1746; wife Catharine; sons Joseph, William; daus. Sarah, Mary; grandson Joseph Williams; tract *Machabee* (MCW IX.98-9); extx. Catharine; 15 Apr 1747 (I 35.44); extx. Cathrine; 9 Aug 1748 (AA 25.107); heirs John, Eleanor, Thomas, Elisha; 30 Nov 1748 (GB 165)

Williams, William; wife Barbara; children: Thomas Owen, b. 9 Feb 1747/8; Elizabeth Owen, b. 30 Oct 1749; Elisha, b. 9 May 1752; Elliner Hilleary, b. 5 Apr 1757; Martha, b. 22 Dec 1759; Edward Owen, b. 18 Apr 1761 (PGP p. 251, 264)

Williams, Thomas; 17 Oct 1749; 7 Dec 1749; wife Elinor; sons Thomas, Barrack, William, Walter, Elisha; daus. Elizabeth, Elinor, Martha Odell, Mary; grandson Thomas Duckett; tracts *The Three Sisters, William Range, Addition to the Fork* (MCW X.63); extx. Elenor; 2 Jan 1749 (I 42.36); extx. Eleanor [widow]; 25 Mar 1752 (AA 32.167, 204); 25 Mar 1752; extx. Elinor (ABB 1.34); extx. Eleanor [widow]; 12 Jul 1753 (AA 34.251)

Williams, William; wife Frances; children: Elizabeth, bapt. 2 Feb 1752; Elizabeth, b. 10 Oct 1754; Benjamin, bapt. 26 Feb 1764 Lower Chapel (KGP p. 306, 344)

Williams, Rich'd; wife Christian; child: Elizabeth, bapt. 17 Dec 1752 (KGP p. 294, 306, 297)

Williams, Baruch; 20 Apr 1753; 8 Aug 1753; wife Lucy; tract Addition to Bacon Hall (MCW X.273); [undated; filed with 1758; no information] (MCW XI.213); 8 Apr 1755 (I 60.345)

Williams, [unnamed]; children: William Prather, b. 29 Apr 1754; Rezin, b. 16 Mar 1763 (PGP p. 255, 70)

Williams, Thomas; m. 1 Feb 1755 Elizabeth Gibbs; children: John Fenly, b. 1 Jan 1756; Ann Brown, b. 13 May 1757; James Gibbs, bapt. 18 Apr 1762 (KGP p. 311, 314, 326)

Williams, Elisha; wife Ann; child: Mary, b. 4 Nov 1759 (PGP p. 280)

Williams, Thomas; wife Elizabeth; child: Violinda, bapt. 9 Sep 1764 at Broad Creek (KGP p. 339)

Williams, Jacob; wife Margrett; child: Elizabeth Magruder, b. 10 Jul 1765 (PGP p. 274)

Williams, Lancelot; 26 Mar 1772 (I 109.135)

Williams, Sarah; child: Hanson, b. 6 May 1774 Lower Chapel (KGP p. 379)

Williams, Thomas; 9 May 1771 (I 106.224); 13 May 1774 (I 117.415)

Williams, William; wife Elizabeth; child: Josias, b. 6 Jan 1775 Upper Chapel (KGP p. 391)

WILLICE
Willice, John; wife Mary; child: Victory, b. 29 Jan 1765 (PGP p. 276)

WILLINGTON
Willington, William; wife Francis; child: Sarah, bapt. 21 Dec 1766 Broad Creek (KGP p. 348)

WILLMOTT
Willmott, William; 14 May 1755 (I 59.52)

WILLOCIE
Willocie, Phillip; age ca 68; 1734 (PGLR T.124)
Willoey, Philip; age ca 75; Nov 1740 (PGLR Y.235)

WILLSON
Wilson, Jonathan; 7 May 1698; 24 Aug 1698; wife Catherine (MCW II.148); innholder; extx. Katherine; 14 Jul 1699 (I&A 19.155); ex. Katherine Wilson; 19 Jul 1707 (I&A 27.31); 30 Aug 1709 (I&A 29.432)

Willson, William; 15 Dec 1698 (I&A 18.51); admx. Sarah Hill [w/o William]; 1 Jul 1699 (I&A 19.171)

Wilson, Jonathan [dec'd]; widow Katherine; Mar 1699 Ct. (PGCR A.418)

Willson, Thomas; carpenter; wife Mary; tract *Cold Spring Manor*; 27 Mar 1704 (PGLR C.123a)

Wilson, Ralph; wife Alice; children: Jane, b. 6 9ber 1706; Elizabeth, b. 10 Jan 1709/10; Ann, b. 13 10ber 1712; Mary, b. 17 Jul 1715; Elizabeth, b. 22 Jan 1717; George & William [twins], b. 24 Apr 1720 (QAP b/3, 4, 8, 15)

Willson, William; age ca 15; step-son to William Hill [dec'd]; bound out; Mar 1711 Ct. (PGCR G.42)

Wilson [Willson], James; extx. Margrett Robince; 23 Jun 1712 (I&A 33b.1); extx. Margaret Queen [w/o John]; 25 Apr 1713 (I&A 35b.23); adms. John Queen and wife Margrett; 20 Oct 1713 (I&A 34.97); extx. Margaret Queen [w/o John]; extx. Margrett Queen [w/o John]; 26 Dec 1713 (I&A 35a.5); 10 Sep 1715 (I&A 36c.42)

Wilson, Josiah; wife Martha; tract *Twiver*; 15 May 1714 (PGLR F.361)

Wilson, Eglantine; child: Martha, b. 20 Apr 1716 (QAP b/13)

Wilson, Thomas; wife Priscilla; children: Joseph, b. 22 9ber 1716; Thomas, b. 2 May 1720 (QAP b/12, 16)

Wilson, Thomas, Sr.; wife Mary; son Thomas, Jr.; tract *Wilson's Enlargement*; 26 Nov 1721 (PGLR I.230)

Willson, John [CH]; wife Lydia; tract *Hardship*; 24 Dec 1721 (PGLR I.671)

Wilson, Lingan; cousins Charles, Henry, Katherine, Thomas Boteler; "children to my aunt"; [undated, with 1722] (PGLR I.55)

Wilson, Josiah, gent.; 11 Nov 1717; 5 Dec 1717; sons Josiah, Lingen, Janus, Joseph, Joshua; dau. Martha; "bro." William Kid; tracts *Kid's Levell, Island Plains, Ozburn's Lott, Buttington, Lingan's Adventure, Back Lingan; The Ridge, The Angles, George's Desire, Addition, Cockalds Point, Beams Landing, Brook Hill, Kingsale, Indian Gyant's Sepulcher* in Charles Co. (MCW IV.108) [as Maj.]; 24 Jul 1718 (I 1.222); [as Maj.]; widow Elisabeth; heirs Henry, Martha; sons James, Lingan; s-i-l William Magruder Selby; 22 Apr 1719 (AA 1.432, 5.366, 6.203, 9.221, 11.413); heirs Lingan, James, Joseph, John, Martha; 23 Nov 1725 (GB 24)

Wilson, Josiah; chooses guardian; Jun 1718 (PGCR H.671)

Wilson, Lingan; chooses guardian; Jun 1719 (PGCR H.861)

Wilson, Joseph; of competent age; chooses bro. Lingan as guardian; Nov 1724 (PGCR L.380)

Wilson [Willson], Josiah; 9 Dec 1726; 14 Mar 1726/7; wife Elizabeth; son Henry; daus. Martha, Margret; tracts *Land Over, Buttington, Orphans' Gift* (Baltimore Co.) (MCW VI.16); admx. Elisabeth; 28 Jun 1727 (I 12.122)

Wilson, Thomas; wife Mary; son Thomas; tract *Wilson's Addition*; 29 Feb 1727 (PGLR M.300); son Lancelot; tract *Thomas & Mary*; 29 Feb 1728 (PGLR M.302)

Wilson, Lingan; age ca 23; 1 Jul 1727 (PGLR M.221)

Wilson, Joshua; age ca 15; s/o Maj. Josiah; chooses bro. Lingan as guardian; Aug 1727 (PGCR N.490)

Wilson, Martha; age ca 15; s/o Maj. Josias; s-i-l Elizabeth Wilson; bro. Lingan; Aug 1728 (PGCR O.245)

Willson, Edward; age ca 38; 22 Sep 1730 (PGLR Q.156)

Willson, Josiah [dec'd]; son Josiah; 29 Nov 1732 (CCR-MSA 5.278)

Wilson, William; age ca 38; 1734 (PGLR T.155)

Wilson, Abraham; age ca 32; 1734 (PGLR T.124)

Willson, Lanslett; age ca 35; 12 May 1735 (PGLR T.279)

Wilson, Henry; age 15 Jan next; chooses guardian; Nov 1736 (PGCR W.263)

Willson, Thomas; wife Priscilla; tract *Wilson's Venture*; 18 Aug 1739 (PGLR Y.77)

Wilson, Henry; wife Ann; child: Osborn, bapt. 7 Jun 1752 (KGP p. 296)

Wilson, James, gent.; 13 May 1743; 18 Jan 1753; wife Sophia; sons Josiah [Josiah], William, James, Lingar; dau. Martha; unborn child; bros. Joshua, Lingar; tracts *Cox's Hays, Spring Branch, Rich Neck, Mount Calvert, Deacons, Bordens* (MCW X.244-5); [as Capt.]; 18 Jun 1753 (I 52.36) 14 Jan 1756 (AA 36.28)

Wilson [Willson]; Thomas; 30 Mar 1744; 1 May 1744; wife Priscilla; children: Thomas, Joseph, Wadsworth, Absalom, Josiah, William, Elizabeth, Priscilla, Mary; tracts *Knaves Dispute, St. Thomas, The Forest, Carrolton, London, The Suburbs, Ridges, Prevention* (MCW VIII.266); extx. Priscilla; 1 May 1744 (I 29.434); extx. Pricilla; 2 Dec 1746 (AA 23.37); admx. Priciall; children: Thomas, Jos., Wadsworth, Absalom, Elisabeth, Priscilla, Josiah, William, Mary Willson; 12 May 1747 (AA 23.281)

Wilson, Joshua; 27 Nov 1745; bros. James, Joseph, Lingan; sister Martha Selby; niece Martha Wilson [d/o James]; nephews William Wilson Selby [s/o William Magruder], William Wilkinson Wilson, Josiah Wilson [s/o James], Samuel Selby, Nathaniel Selby; tract *Mt. Calvert Manor* (MCW IX.60)

Willson, Joseph; 13 Jan 1747 (AA 24.231); 8 Sep 1747 (I 35.166)

Wilson, John; age 14 on 11 Jan next; s/o Sarah Hawker; bound to Richard Wells to age 21 to learn to be shoemaker (PGCR MM.413)

Wilson, Sophia; 9 Apr 1755; 23 Mar 1756; dau. Martha Magruder [w/o Hezekiah]; sons Josiah, William, James, Lingan (MCW XI.126)

Wilson, Josiah, gent.; 5 Oct 1756; 17 Feb 1761; sister Martha Magruder [w/o Hezekiaam]; bros. William, James & Lingan Wilson (MCW XII.48); [as Josias, Capt.]; 2 Mar 1761 (I 74.336); 10 May 1762 (I 78.316)

Willson, Joseph; wife Mary; child: Basell, bapt. 11 Apr 1762 (KGP p. 326)

Willson, Joseph; wife Jane; child: Elizabeth, bapt. 10 Oct 1762 (KGP p. 328)

Willson, Joseph; wife Elenor; children: Lewcy Ann, b. 9 May 1763 at Broad Creek; James Smallwood, bapt. _ Mar 1765 Lower Chapel (KGP p. 337, 350)

Willson, Lancelot; wife Rachel; children: Aquilla, bapt. 21 Jul 1763 at Upper Chapel; Are, b. 15 Sep 1765 Lower Chapel; Lancelot, bapt. 10 Apr 1768 Upper Chapel (KGP p. 333, 345, 370)

Willson, Samuel; wife Margret; children: William, bapt. 17 Jun 1764; Sarah, bapt. 17 Jun 1764 at Broad Creek; Ann, bapt. 9 Jun 1765 Broad Creek (KGP p. 339, 347)

Wilson [Willson], Thomas; wife Ruth; children: Elizabeth, b. 30 May 1761; Jacob, b. 24 Apr 1765 (PGP p. 261, 275)

Wilson, Henry; wife Virlinder; child: Thomas, b. 5 Jun 1761; Lancelott, b. 4 Sep 1765 (PGP p. 262, 275)

Wilson, George; wife Mary; child: William, b. 25 Aug 1761 (PGP p. 262)

Wilson, Joseph; wife Elizabeth; children: Sarah, b. 9 Nov 1761; Nancy, b. 11 May 1764 (PGP p. 263, 272)

Wilson [Willson], George; wife Margretta [Margrilla]; children: John Madox, b. _ Nov 1761; James Dickson, b. 24 Feb 1764 (PGP p. 264, 271)

Wilson, Edward; wife Susannah; child: Sarah, b. 26 Apr 1765 (PGP p. 276)

Willson, Benoney; wife Mary; child: Benoney, bapt. 26 May 1765 Upper Chapel (KGP p. 358)

Willson, Alexander; wife Ann; children: William, bapt. 25 Dec 1765 Broad Creek; Alexander, bapt. 1 Jan 1769 Broad Creek (KGP p. 350, 372)

Wilson, Hugh; near Bladensburgh; 14 May 1771; 18 Jun 1771; wife Elizabeth; sons James, Clement, Ignatius; daus. Mary Shaw, Susannah, Sarah, Elizabeth; tracts Whit Lackinston, Hudsons Range (MCW XIV.177); extx. Elisabeth; 14 Aug 1771 (I 108.118); 1 Sep 1773; admx. Mrs. Elisabeth; legatees Susannah, Sarah, Elisabeth (ABB 6.220); widow Elizabeth; heirs Mary Shaw, Susanna ____; Elizabeth Wilson; 23 Nov 1774 (GB 324)

Wilson, Willson; 13 Sep 1770 (I 104.259); 26 Mar 1772 (I 108.336)

Willson, Lancelot; 27 Jun 1771; 13 Nov 1771; wife Elizabeth; children Basil, Lancelot, Lincey, Elender, Henry, Joseph; tract *Hicon Hills* (MCW XIV.194-5)

Wilson, Josiah; wife Mary; child: Fielder, b. 3 Aug 1772 Upper Chapel (KGP p. 389)

Wilson, William; wife Elizabeth; children: Ann, b. 12 Jan 1773 Upper Chapel; John, b. 12 Sep 1775 Upper Chapel (KGP p. 390, 392)

Wilson, Elizabeth; 18 Aug 1775; 16 Oct 1775; children: Henry, Elender, Martha, Lucy, Cassandra, Basil (MCW XVI.80)

Wilson, Lancelot; 1 Jul 1776; legatees Henry, Joseph, Basil, Linsey (dau.), Eleanor (dau.) (ABB 7.56)

WILMOTT
Wilmott, William; 6 May 1755 (I 61.423)

WILSFORD
Wilsford, Henry; wife Winefrud; child: Sarah, b. 17 Aug 1762 (KGP p. 328)

WILSTEAD
Wilstead, Thomas; age ca 34; 26 Apr 1735 (PGLR T.253)

WINDAM
Windon, Thomas; 21 Dec 1717 (I 1.445); widow Susannah Norris [w/o John, Jr.]; sons Thomas, William; 22 Nov 1719 (AA 2.363); heirs Thomas, William; 24 Aug 1720; heirs (GB 7)

Windam [Windham, Windom], William; m. 23 Apr 1747 Elizabeth Moris, b. 17 Sep 1726; children: Rachel, b. 20 Sep 1749; Thomas, b. 12 Sep 1750 or 1751; Sushannah, b. 30 Mar 1754(?); William, b. 5 Oct 1755; George, b. 2 May 1759; Charles, b. 3 May 1763 Broad Creek; Robert Morris, bapt. 3 May 1767 Broad Creek [no mother named] (KGP p. 292, 311, 319, 337, 360)

WINDER
Winder, William; 4 Sep 1714 (I&A 36b.128)

WINKLING
Winkling, Andrew; 1 Mar 1703 (I&A 3.73); [with 1707] (I&A 26.290)

WINN
Winn, John; m. 5 Feb 1717 Anne Smallwood; children: John, b. 27 Jan 17__; Annake (f), b. 10 Jun 17__, d. 26 Sep 17__; Elizabeth, b. 27 Nov 1722;

Colonial Settlers of Prince George's County, Maryland — page 385

Mary Anne, b. 21 Mar 1725; Josiah, b. 1 Feb 1726; William, b. 18 Oct 1728 (KGP p. 270, 271)

Winn, Josia; wife Ann; child: Elizabeth Broad, bapt. 28 Apr 1751 (KGP p. 293)

Winn, John; wife Sarah; Susanna, b. 25 Dec 1753 (KGP p. 304)

WINNICUM

Winnicum, William; wife Jane; child: Rachel, b. 15 7ber 1715 (QAP b/12)

WINSER

Winser, Jarvis; age ca 73; 25 Jun 1724 (PGLR I.592)

Windsor, Jarvis; age ca 30; 21 Jun 1726 (PGLR M.30)

Winser, Luke; wife Martha; children: Samuell Queen, b. 26 Oct 1759; Casah (f), b. 2 Jan 1762 (PGP p. 262, 280)

Winsor, Ignatius; wife Martha; children: Luke (1st), b. 30 Apr 1765; Benjamin (2nd), b. 15 Jul 1776; Nathaniel (3rd), b. 21 Feb 1778; Ignatius (4th), b. 10 Feb 1780; Anna (5th), b. 12 Feb 1782; Martha (6th), b. 11 Dec 1783; Fielder (7th), b. 12 Feb 1786; Drusillah, b. 25 May 1788 Lower Chapel (KGP p. 377)

Winsor, Elizabeth; child: Linder, b. 12 Jan 1774 Lower Chapel (KGP p. 379)

WINTERS

Winters, Thomas; wife Sarah [d/o John Dorsett, dec'd]; tract Greenwood; 1 Mar 1721 (PGLR I.173)

Winters, Walter; age ca 58; 1730 (PGLR M.567)

WIRT

Wirt, Uriah; farmer; 16 May 1762 (I 79.231)

Wirt, Jacob; 16 Jun 1773; 26 Oct 1774; wife Henrietta; children: Jacob, Catharine, Elizabeth, Henrietta, Uriah Jasper, Willliam; bro. Jasper Wirt; tavern, store in Baldensburgh (MCW XVI.7); nok Katharine Whetstone; exs. Henrietta & Jasper Wirt (I 118.272)

WISE

Wise, John; wife Elisabeth; child: Kitty, b. 20 Oct 1772 (PGP p. 279)

Wise, Thomas; wife Sarah; child: George, b. 15 May 1773 Upper Chapel (KGP p. 390)

Wise, Thomas; wife Mary; child: Richard, b. 1 Sep 1775 Upper Chapel (KGP p. 392)

WISEHAM

Wiseham, Thomas; wife Christain; child: John, b. 22 Jun 1761 (PGP p. 262)

WITHAM

Withers, Thomas; wife Margaret; 24 Nov 1729 (PGLR M.517)

Witham, Henry, Dr.; wife Mary; 15 May 1731 (PGLR Q.311)

WITHERS

Withers, Rebecca; age 3 in Jun last; d/o Mary Wood; bound to Richard and Jane King; Aug 1745 (PGCR DD.178)

WOLFORD

Wolford, William, Sr.; wife Ann; tract *William & Ann*; 21 Aug 1725 (PGLR I.698)

WOOD

Wood, Joane; servant; had bastard child; Jan 1696/7 Ct. (PGCR A.117)

Wood, Thomas; wife Eglantine; children: Thomas, b. 5 Feb 1717; Johanna, b. 10 Mar 1720/1 (QAP b/13, 16)

Woods, John; age ca 46; 8 Jun 1732 (PGLR Y.327)

Wood, Thomas; m. 26 8ber 1732 Mary Lashly: children: John, b. 13 Sep 1733; Elizabeth, b. 20 Jul 1735; Johannah, b. 22 Jun 1737 (QAP m/6; b/29, 31)

Wood, John; admx. Barbara; 4 May 1738 (I 23.188); children: James, John, Peter, Joseph, Rachel; 28 Dec 1739 (AA 17.461); widow Barbara; heirs James, John, Peter, Joseph, Rachel; 27 Nov 1740 (GB 115)

Wood, Joseph; age 16 on 18 Sep next; bound to James Wood to learn to be a tailor; Jun 1752 (PGCR MM.237))

Wood, Thomas; wife Annis [Stacy]; child: John, b. 25 Jan 1753 (PGP p. 256)

Wood, Elijah; wife Mary; child: Elijah, b. 14 Dec 1753 (KGP p. 304)

Wood, James; wife Elizabeth; child: Margaret, b. 14 Jun 1756; Frances (f), b. 28 Jul 1758; Francis (f), b. 23 Feb 1763 at Broad Creek (KGP p. 313, 321, 337)

Wood, Isaac; admx. Mary; 18 Apr 1756 (I 61.425); 28 Nov 1758; admx. Mary Wood (ABB 2.99); widow Mary; heirs John, India, James, Charity, Sarah, Lidia, Jacob, Isaac, Chloe; 28 Jun 1759 (GB 212)

Wood, James; wife Mary; children: Leonard Armstrong, b. 13 Jan 1754; Sarah, bapt. 29 Aug 1762 (KGP p. 305, 332)

Wood, Elisha; wife Mary; child: Amealea, bapt. 19 Dec 1762 (KGP p. 329)

Wood, Lasley; wife Mary; children: Mary, bapt. 8 Apr 1764; Lea, bapt. 10 Aug 1766 Upper Chapel (KGP p. 341, 364)

Wood, Peter; 9 Apr 1764 (I 88.271)

Wood, James; admx. Elisabeth; 28 Jul 1765 (I 87.313); heir John Wilder Wood, grandson of John Wilder; 27 Aug 1766 (GB 248); 24 Jul 1769; admx. Elisabeth Hilton [w/o James] (ABB 5.388)

Wood, George; wife Mary; children: George Burton, b. 27 Aug 1769 Upper Chapel; Elizabeth, b. 3 Mar 1772 Upper Chapel (KGP p. 374, 389)

WOODHEAD

Woodhead, George; 16/17 Jan 1745; 12 Feb 1745/6; [no relations] (MCW IX.60); 9 Mar 1746 (I 35.50)

WOODHOUSE

Woodhouse, David; wife Elizabeth; child: Sarah, b. 1 Sep 1763 at Upper Chapel (KGP p. 340)

WOODWARD

Woodward [Woodard], Francis; wife Winiford [Winifred]; children: William, b. 4 Aug 1752; Zachariah, b. 16 Nov 1762 (PGP p. 255, 267)

WOOLHATER

Woolhater, George; 12 Aug 1767; admx. Mrs. Barbara Woolhater; son George Evan Woolhater (ABB 4.165)

WOOTON

Wooton, Turner; wife Agnis; 14 Aug 1726 (PGLR M.120)

Wootton, Turner; wife Elizabeth; child: Mary, b. 6 Nov 1735 (QAP b/29)

Wooten, Turnor; 25 Feb 1761 (I 73.52)

Wootton, John; 27 Dec 1773; 22 Dec 1774; mother Elizabeth; bro. Richard (MCW XVI.30)

WORMEWOOD

Wormewood, William; age ca 16; servant; Nov 1703 Ct. (PGCR B.262a)

WORNALL

Wornall, Ralph; 18 Jun 1713; 16 Jan 1713; wife [unnamed], son Mark (MCW III.256); widow Mary; son Mark; 29 Jan 1713 (I&A 35a.310); extx. Mary; 18 Dec 1714 (I&A 36b.115); extx. widow Mary; 18 Dec 1714 (I&A 36a.168)

Wornall, Richard; wife Mary; children: William, bapt. 16 Sep 1766 Broad Creek; Thomas, b. 7 Feb 1772 Upper Chapel (KGP p. 359, 388)

Wornold, Richard; wife Ann; child: Richard, b. 23 Sep 1769 Upper Chapel (KGP p. 374)

WRIGHT

Wright, Charles; 28 Sep 1700 (I&A 20.212)

Wright, Henry; wife Ellinor; children: Mary, b. 9 10ber 1728; Margaret, b. 25 Apr 1733 (QAP b/21)

Wright [White], Ann; 21 Jun 1742 (I 27.19)

Wright, Henry; age ca 63; 20 Feb 1744 (CCR JK#4.565)

Wright, Henry; 22 Feb 1744; 31 Oct 1750; daus. Mary Snowden, Margaret; tracts Black Walnut Leavell, Diamon (MCW X.107); 26 Nov 1750 (I 44.312); [with 1751] (I 48.175); 15 Jan 1752; daus. Mary Snowden, Margaret Pile (ABB 1.19); 15 Jan 1752 (AA 31.251); 14 Mar 1753 (AA 33.354)

Wright, Richard; admx. Mrs. Wright; 2 Jun 1758 (I 67.220)

WYNN

Wynn, John, Jr. [s/o John]; m. 24 Aug 1738 Sarah Robey; d. 22 May 1777 age 54; children: John, b. 23 Jul 1739; Elizabeth, b. 30 May 1741; Hezekiah, b. 12 Sep 1742; Sarahan, b. 9 Dec 1744; Violender, b. 13 Sep 1746, d. 12 Oct 1748; Easter, b. 15 Apr 1748, d. 8 Apr 1753; Anaka (f), b. 24 Jan 1749/50; Hannah, b. ____; Easter Virlinder, b. 10 Aug 1755, bapt. 24 Aug 1755; William Smallwood, b. 9 Aug 1757; Hezekiah, b. 22 Oct 1759; Ann, b. 22 Apr 1761; Lucy Ann, b. 26 Sep 1762; Priscilla, b. 16 Apr 1764; Eleanor Ann, b. 13 Nov 1767 (KGP p. 309, 310)

Wynn, John, Sr.; 21 Mar 1752; 11 Apr 1752; sons John, Jr., Josiah; daus. Ann, Jemima, Joan, Mary, Martha, Sussanna; tracts The Indian Field, Governor's Gift (MCW X.208); 10 Jul 1752 (I 49.52); 16 Apr 1753 (I 55.102); 25 May 1753 (AA 34.134); 25 May 1753; adm. John Wynn (ABB 1.76)

Wynn, John, Jr.; 21 Mar 1752; 11 Apr 1752; children: Ann, John Jr., Josiah, Jemima, Joan, Mary, Martha, Susanna; tracts The Indian Field, Governor's Gift (MCW X.208)

Wynn, John, Sr.; d. 25 Mar 1752; wife Ann; d. 20 Feb 1752, age 51; child: John, b. 27 Jan 1720/1 (KGP p. 309)

Wynn, Josias; wife Ann; children: Ann, b. 30 Apr 1755; Josias, b. 27 Mar 1762 (KGP p. 308, 327)

Wynn, Josiah [Josias]; planter; 21 Dec 1763; 21 Jan 1764; wife [unnamed]; sons William, Josiah; dau. Chloe (MCW XIII.14); extx. Ann; 2 Apr 1764 (I 84.202); Josias; minor; 25 Aug 1774 (GB 320); 18 Apr 1765; extx. Ann Higdon [w/o Benjamin]; son John Sharpe; dau. Chloe; other daus. (ABB 4.120)

Wynn, John; wife Ann; child: Lucey Ann, bapt. 10 Oct 1762; Priscilla, bapt. 6 May 1764 Broad Creek (KGP p. 328, 357)

Wynn, John; wife Mary; child: Hezekiah, b. 7 Dec 1774 Lower Chapel (KGP
p. 380)

WYVILL

Wyvill, William; m. 14 Feb 1736 Elinor Boyde; children: Edward Hale,
b. ____; Elizabeth, b. __ Nov ____; Jane, b. 26 Dec 174_; Marmaduke, b.
19 May ____; Mary, b. 27 Jul ____; William, b. 17 Sep 17__ (QAP m/6; b/34)

YACKLEY

Yackley, Robert; m. 8 Jun 1735 Sarah Mitchell; child: John, b. 23 Jan 1735
(QAP m/6; b/34))

YATES

Yate, George [dec'd]; widow Mary [AA]; tract *Westfalia*; 10 Aug 1704 (PGLR
C.165a)

Yates, Charles [CH]; wife Jane; tract *Moor's Littleworth*; 24 May 1720 (PGLR
I.1)

YOE

Yoe, William; 22 Nov 1762 (I 79.227)

YOUNG

Young, Richard; wife Judith; children: Jonathan, b. 1 Mar 1686; Jacob, b. 20
Nov 1697; Mary, b. 12 Jan 1698 (QAP b/2)

Young, Jonathan; wife Mary; child: Richard, b. 16 8ber 1707 (QAP b/3)

Young, Johnathan; wife Mary; children: Anne, b. 27 Apr 1712; Rachel, b. 7
Feb 1714; Judeth, b. 19 Feb 1716; Sarah, b. 7 Jan 1715; Izrall (f), b. 25
____ 1719; Thomas, b. 2 Jan 1720; Mary, b. 25 Feb 1721 (KGP p. 273)

Young, William; age ca 10; servant; Jun 1712 Ct. (PGCR G.211)

Young, William; wife Mary; tract *Elizabeth*; 19 Dec 1723 (PGLR I.512)

Young, James; age ca 54; 1728 (PGLR M.346)

Young, Joseph; children: Margrett, b. 12 Oct 1731; Thomas, b. 10 Jan 1733
(KGP p. 262)

Young, Joseph; wife Keziah [d/o Thomas Withers]; 30 Jan 1733 (PGLR T.63)

Young, William; 11 May 1733; 27 Jun 1733; wife Mary; sons William,
James, Peter (MCW VII.26); 17 Jul 1733 (I 17.496); children: Peter, Ann, Jane,
Elisabeth; 27 Sep 1734 (AA 12.621); widow Mary; heir Peter; 25 Nov 1736
(GB 88)

Young, Jacob; age 2 in Mar last; bound out; Jun 1733 (PGCR S.287)

Young, James; 24 Nov 1733 (I 17.506); 28 Sep 1734 (AA 12.631); heir William;
28 Jun 1736 (GB 78)

Young, Benjamin, Esq.; wife Ann; child: Nottley, bapt. 24 Sep 1738 (PGP p.
251)

Young, William [CA]; wife Clare [widow of Thomas Tasker]; tracts *St.
Andrew, The Grange*; 25 Nov 1740 (PGLR Y.251)

Young, Joseph; admx. Kesiah Cogghill [w/o Smawlwood]; 4 Jun 1741 (I
27.133); admx. Keziah Coghill [w/o of Smallwood]; 23 Aug 1742 (AA 19.313);
heirs Margaret, Thomas; 28 Jun 1743 (GB 126)

Young, Mary; 10 Apr 1742; 25 Aug 1742; daus. Jane, Elizabeth, Eleanor,
Sarah Lemar; sons Peter, William; granddau. Mary [d/o William] (MCW

VIII.178); dau. [w/o Charles Cleget]; 28 Aug 1743 (AA 20.97); daus. Jane Clagett [w/o Charles], Sarah Lemar; 26 Oct 1744 (AA 20.457); 8 Oct 1745 (AA 22.5)

Young, Benjamin; wife Ann, age ca 38; 31 Oct 1748 (CCR MSA 8.747)

Young, Benjamin, Esq.; 15 Oct 1750; 15 Apr 1754; wife Ann; sons Notley, Benjamin; tracts *Learnable Manor, Friendship* (MCW XI.34); extx. Anne; 1 Jul 1754 (I 60.163, 167)

Young, William; 22 Sep 1755; 8 Sep 1760; sons William, John, Hugh; dau. Margaret; tracts *Good Luck, Duke's Wood* (MCW XII.11); 6 Dec 1760 (I 73.44); 4 Mar 1762; ex. John Young; children: William, John, Hugh, Margaret (ABB 3.117)

Young, James; 14 May 1757; 28 May 1757; son James Young, Jr.; dau. Elizabeth Foard (MCW XI.171)

Young, James, Sr.; wife Ann; child: William, b. 18 Jan 1763 at Lower Chapel (KGP p. 334)

Young, James, Jr.; wife Elizabeth; child: Ann, b. 23 Feb 1763 at Lower Chapel (KGP p. 325)

Young, Thomas; wife Eleanor; children: Hezekiah, b. 28 Feb 1763 at Lower Chapel; Thomas, b. 12 Sep 1765 Broad Creek; Kesiah, b. 6 Feb 1768 Broad Creek; Anne Margaret, b. 2 Jul 1772 Lower Chapel; William, b. 12 May 1774 Lower Chapel; Lettice and Dorritha [twins], b. 24 Jan 1776 Lower Chapel (KGP p. 335, 349, 362, 379, 381, 383)

Young, John; wife Mary; child: Kesiah, b. 22 May 1763 at Broad Creek (KGP p. 337)

Young, Ann; 6 Jun 1764; 9 Oct 1764; children: Mary Diggs [w/o Ignatius], Eleanor, Charles, Notley; grandchildren: Daniel & Mary Carroll (MCW XIII.76)

Young, James; wife Rebecca; child: Ann, b. 22 Oct 1764 (PGP p. 274)

Young, John; wife Jeane; child: Jane Warren, bapt. 22 Sep 1765 Broad Creek (KGP p. 349)

Young, Margaret; 7 Jan 1775; 17 Feb 1775; bros. John, Hugh, William; tract *Good Luck* (MCW XVI.59)

Young, Hugh; 25 Jun 1775; 31 Jul 1775; bros. John, William; father William; sister Margaret; tracts *Duke Wood, Goodluck* (MCW XVI.73)

Young, Peter; 6 Oct 1775; 17 Jan 1776; sister Jeen Clagett; nephew Charles Clagett [s/o Jeen]; s-i-l Barbara, Elizabeth & Verlinda Magruder; b-i-l Thomas Magruder; tracts *Thorpland, Perys Hills* (MCW XVI.167); 29 Jan 1776 (I 122.301)

CROSS REFERENCE

Names and plantations are referenced under what appeared to be the most prevalent or logical spelling.

Aaron's Deprieve, see Roberts
Aaron, see Coleman, Mitchell
Abell's Lott, see Sprigg
Abington, see Hutchison
Abr___ Choice, see Bradford
Accord, see Cumming,
　Edmondson
Acquascat, see Galwith, Turner
Acton, see Dunning, Gambra,
　Millstead
Addison's Choice, see Addison
Addison, see Bailey, Ball,
　Brooke, Bryan, Christmas,
　Humphrey, Locker, Noble,
　Webster, Whitmore
Addition, The, see Addison,
　Beall, Brightwell, Clarvo,
　Darnall, Lee, Noble, Odell,
　Pile, Stoddert, Scott, Truman,
　Turner, Willson
Adkee, see Mahall
Adkins, see Mahall
Admination, see Addison
Admirathoree, see Rozer
Admirothona, see Clarke
Advantage, The, see Edgar, Kelly,
　Mayhew, Parker
After Stamp, see Thomas
Air, see Greene
Aix la Chappelle, see Carroll
Aldridge, see Crow
Alexandria, see Magruder

Alias Good Luck, see Berry
Aliquahook, see Beall
Allaway, see James
Allcum, see Allingham
Allen & James, see Bowie
Allen, see Edmondson, Osborn,
　Ward
Allison's Adventure, see Allison,
　Lindoce
Allison's Park, see Beall, Moore
Allison, see Bird
Alloy, see Hatton
Allum, see Dawson
Amphill Grange, see Boyd
Amsterdam, see Edmondson
Amy, see Simmons
Anchovie Hills, see Greenfield,
　Magruder, Wight
Ancram, see Matthews
Anderson, see Cook, Crawford,
　Perrie, Rogers
Andrew, see Perrie, Prather
Angles, The, see Willson
Anglice, see Bradford
Apple Hill, see Marbury,
　Middleton
Appledore, see Boteler, Edelen,
　Leiper, Marbury
Aquascott Alias, see Digges
Archer's Pasture, see Parker,
　Pearle, Rook
Archibald's Lott, see Moore

Argile Cowell and Lorn, see
  Bradford
Arnold's Chance, see Livers
Arnold's Delight, see Livers
Arnold, see Contee
As Good as Any, see Bradford
As Good as We Could Get, see
  Pottenger
Asdell, see Thompson
Ashcom, see Brooke
Ashford, see Stonestreet
Askins, see Armstrong
Atcheson, see Conner
Atchison's Pasture, see Atchison
Athelborough, see Blizard,
  Herbert
Athey's Folly, see Clarkson,
  Coghill, Stonestreet
Athey, see Barker, Kelly,
  Robinson
Atkins, see Mahall
Atterbary, see Mitchell
Attien, see Prindwell
Attwood's Purchase, see Hamilton
Austin, see Rought

Back Lingan, see Willson
Backer, see Ward
Backland, see Andrew, Bigger
Bacon Hall, Addition to, see
  Williams
Bacon Hall, see Beall, Bradley,
  Snowden, Walker
Bacon, Addition to, see Jones
Baden, see Brightwell, Lawson
Baker, see Bell
Balard, see Barker
Baldin, see Pottenger

Baldwin, see Boyd, Butt,
  Pottenger, Tyler, Whitehead
Baley, see Seymour
Balintun, see Willett
Ball Christ, see Beall
Ball, see Addison, Baker
Ballenger, see Plummer
Balls Good Luck, see Ball
Baltimore County, see Contee
Baltimore, see Hill
Bangiah Manor, see Digges
Banister, see Brewster
Baptistyler, see Tyler
Barbadoes, see Conn, Digges,
  Lord, Moore, Wharton
Barker, see Power
Barnes, see Batt, Dunhue, Dyar,
  Edgar, Jones, Lewin, Massey
Barnett, see Miles
Barnobie, see Addison
Barnshee, see Cope
Baron Hall, Addition to, see
  Beall
Barren Point, see Waring
Barren Ridge, see Edmondson
Barrens, The, see Dent, Truman
Barrett's Purchase, see Hill
Barrett, see Ball, Barnard
Barron Point, see Marsham
Bart's Hope, see Lee
Barton's Hazard, see Barton
Barton's Hope, see Barton,
  Gibbons, Perrie, Sasser
Barton's Vineyard, see Soper
Barton, see Beatty, Brawner
Barwick upon Tweed,
Basil, see Perrie, Phelphs

Beginning of Samuel Beall, The,
  see Beall
Beginning, The, see Brothers,
  Riley
Bekean, see Holmes
Bell's Tract, see Bell
Bell, see Brooke, Magruder
Bells Purchase, see Pile
Bells Wiln, see Pelley
Belt's Chance, see Belt
Belt's Meddow, see Belt
Belt's Pigpen, see Belt
Belt's Poor Chance, see Belt
Belt's Range, see Belt
Belt's Tomahawk, see Belt
Belt, see Beall, Bowie, Gordon,
  Rogers, Smith, Sprigg, Wight
Bener, see Pritchett
Bengiah, see Digges
Benit, see Scott
Benjamin's Vale, see Cash
Benjamin, The, see Beall,
  Thrasher
Bennett, see Bromfield,
  Darnall, Denes, Hall,
  Hutchison
Beny, see Keene
Beon, see Dorsett
Bero Plains, see Magruder
Berry Lott, see Berry
Berry's Fortune, see Bradley
Berry; see Addison, Fendall,
  Harrison
Berry, see Clagett, Ireland,
  Keene, Lovejoy, Page, Pile,
  Thomas
Bevan, see Bailey, Blanford,
  Brashear, Hoye, Kirkwood

Bewplaine, see Magruder
Bigger, see Andrew
Billingsley's Point, see
  Billingsley, Greenfield,
  Hollyday, Jordan
Birch, see Holley, Lowe
Birkhead, see Jones
Bivin, see Jones
Black Ash, see Beall, Chittam,
  Tilley
Black Walnut Levell, see Wright
Blackwell, see Brightwell
Bladensburgh, see Chittam
Blakeburn, see West
Blanford, see Edelen, Thisick
Bleu Plaine, see Blizard,
  Addison
Blizard, see Herbert, Magruder
Boarman's Manor, see Hardy
Boarman, see Marsham
Bodwell's Choice, see Tyler
Boen, see Dorsett
Boleing Green, see Crabb
Bolton, see Cloyd, Mobberly
Bonifield, see Briscoe, Brooke
Bonner's Camp, see Bonner
Bonnie's Interest, see Bonner
Bonnifcent, see Bonefant
Bood Come by Chance, see
  Watson
Boone, see Bayne, Bevan, Page
Bordens, see Willson
Boren, see Carmack
Boswell, see Beckwith
Boteler, see Drury, Willson
Boucher, see Addison
Boulton, see Mobberly
Bousey, see Beusey

Bowdell's Choice, see Clarke
Bowen, see Dorsett, Tannehill
Bowers, see Dorsett
Bowie, see Brooke, Duckett,
  Eversfield, Finch, Fraser,
  Hawkins, Lee, Offutt,
  Pottenger, Smith, Sprigg
Bowies Addition, see Jacob
Bowles Choice, see Murdock
Bowles, see Addison, Lowe
Bowling, see Dossett, Greene
Boyd's Delay, see Boyd
Boyd, see Duckett, Knott, Lynch,
  Ray, Wyvill
Boyle, see Boyde
Brace, see Flower
Bradcutt, see Elson
Bradent, see Beall
Bradferd, see Digges
Bradford's Rest, see Baker,
  Bradford, Burch, Farrell,
  Swearingen
Bradford, see Butler, Hillyard,
  Jones, Shaw
Bradley, see Anderson, Beall,
  Hill, Hollyday
Bramewood, see Brainwood
Brashear's Industry, see Brashear
Brashear's Meadow, see Brashear,
  Jones
Brashear's Neck, see Belt,
  Brashear
Brashear's Porcorson, see
  Brashear
Brashears, see Belt, Bevan,
  Browne, Eele, Hodges,
  Holmes, Jones, Mulliken,

  Scaggs, Turner, Venman,
  Wallingsford
Bread & Cheese, see Atchison,
  Evans, Hill
Brent, see Marshall, Rogers
Brewer, see Ridgley
Brice, see Henderson
Bright, see Jones, Magruder
Brightwell's Hunting Quarter, see
  Davis, Jewel, Rice
Brightwell's Range, see Cheshire
Brightwell, see Grear, Watson
Brock Hall, see Bowie, Brocke
Broner, see Brawner, Elliott
Brooke Chance, see Blanford,
  Brooke, Howard
Brooke Court Mannor, see Boyce,
  Letchworth
Brooke Grove, see Cook, Head,
  Jefferson, Snowden
Brooke Hill, see Brooke, Pile,
  Willson
Brooke Land, see Waring
Brooke Point, see Brooke
Brooke Refuse, see Brooke
Brooke Ridge, see Bowie, Boyd,
  Brooke
Brooke Wood, see Brooke, Smith
Brooke's Content, see Brooke
Brooke's Reserve, see Brooke,
  Mackall
Brooke, see Addison, Bowie,
  Culver, Digges, Goddart,
  Greenfield, Howard, Joyce,
  Lee, Marsham, Sewall
Brookefield, Addition to, see
  Brooke

Brookefield, see Bowie, Brooke,
Eversfield, Gibbons,
Hollyday Lee, Sewall, Smith,
Wall
Brother's Choice, see Shaw
Brother's Content, see Beall,
Edmondson
Brother's Delight, see Ball
Brother's Industry, see Wallace
Brother's Joint Interest, see
Addison
Brotherhood, The, see Davis,
Hardy, Haswell
Brougdon, see Brooke
Brough, see Tyler
Brown, see Brashear, Burroughs,
Finch, Fowler, Burroughs,
Simmons, Taylor, White
Browner, see Elliott
Brunt, see Bustian
Bruse, see Skinner
Bryan Dayley, see Waring
Buchannan, see Hoye, Levett
Buck Range, see Contee
Buck's Lodge, see Nelson
Buhan, see Perrie
Bull, see Wardrop
Bullen, see Guyther
Burbidg, see Bradford
Burch, see Beckwith, Harlens,
Harris, Suit, Thorn
Burches Adventure, see Burch
Burches Venture, see Downes
Burges Chance, see Ward
Burgess's Delight, see Burgess
Burgess, see Ball, Greenfield,
Mackuter, Magruder, Moore,
Mordant, Waring

Burgh, see Billingsly
Burk, see Leachman
Burnam, see Gamblin
Burningham, see Gibbons
Burnt House, see Hollyday
Burrows, see Burroughs, Greene,
Nicholls, Parlett
Bursey, see Busey, Hays
Burton, see Barnard
Busey, see Evans
Butler, see Beckwith, Boteler,
Magruder, Rousbey,
Stonestreet
Butt, see Duvall, Ford, Metcalfe
Buttersy, see Lewis
Buttington, see Boteler, Lingan,
Truman, Willson
Buzzard Island, see Hollyday
By Chance, see Hawkins
Bycraft, see Right
Byron, see Tull

Cabidge, see Coots
Cade, see Owen
Cage, see Brightwell
Cain's Purchase, see Blizard
Calder, see Haymond
Callander, see Mitchell
Calvert, see Neale, Sprigg
Calverton Edge, see Odell
Calvin, see Pilborn
Canton, see Addison
Capbell, see Campbell
Captain Oulstons Garrison, see
Carroll
Carlyle, see Hutchison
Carnour, see Conner
Carr, see Bowles

Carrick Fergus, see Doyne,
   Hutchison
Carrick, see Duvall
Carrick, see Marshall
Carroll's Kindness, see Marbury
Carroll, see Brooke, Young
Carrolton, see Willson
Carvill, see Butler
Cash, see Dawson, Farquar, Harr
Casteel, see Casteel, Perdee
Catail Marsh, see Resener
Cate, see Lanham
Catherine, Addition to, see Sprigg
Catharine, see Sprigg
Caton, see Summers
Cattaliel Meddows, see Anderson
Catterall, see Edmondson
Catton, see Butler, Henderson,
   Ridgley
Cedar Neck, see Digges
Cernabby Manor, see Condon
Chaffey, see Resting
Chance, The, see Berry, Dickeson,
   Stansbury, Hutchison,
   Magruder, Noble
Chands, see Beall
Chapman, see Williams
Chapplin, see Riley
Charightigth, see Magruder
Charles & Benjamin, see Beall,
   Berry, Magruder, Waters
Charles & William, see Beall
Charles Beall's Discovery, see
   Wilcoxen
Charles Hill, see Busey, Keene
Charles, The, see Johnson,
   Marshall
Charlesses Folly, see Mariarte

Charley Forrest, Addition to, see
   Bradford, Snowden
Charley, see Hanson
Charter, see Locker
Chartes, see Charters
Cheeney's Beginning, see Cheeny
Cheeney's Delight, see Cheeny
Chelsea Hohim, see Belt
Chelsey, see Mulliken, Thompson,
   Williams
Cheney, see Chaplain, Crow,
   Joyce
Cheney, see Waters
Cherry Walk, Addition to, see
   Waters
Cherry Walk, The Core of, see
   Waters
Cherry Walk, The, see Waters
Chestnut Ridge, see Beall
Chevy Chase, see Belt
Chew's Folly, see Selby
Chew's Meadow, see Chew,
   Hollyday
Chew, see Butler, Manduit
Chichester, see Addison
Child's Portion, see Moore
Children's Choice, see Wells
Childrens Loss, see Marsham
Childs, see Demiliane, Pearce,
   Pottenger, Webb
Chipping Cambden House, see
   Miles
Chisick, see Jenkinson
Chittam's Addition, see Beall
Church, see Bladen
Clackson, see Blanford
Clagett's Purchase, see Clagett,
   Fletchall, Mawdesly

Clagett's Purchase, see Mawdesly
Clagett, see Belt, Bowie,
  Eversfield, Keene, Magruder,
  Young
Clark's Fancy, see Clarke
Clark's Purchase, see Swearingen
Clarke's Inheritance, see Clarke,
  Lynes
Clarke's Purchase, see Clarke,
  Jones
Clarke, see Downes, Duvall,
  Hill, Jones, Lee, Levett,
  Nicholls, Tolson
Clarkson's Purchase, see Tyler
Clarkson, see Simms
Clarvo, see Jenkins
Clary, see Devron
Clay, see Chidley, Deavern
Cleland, see Henderson, Smith
Clement Hill, see Price
Clements, see Clemens,
  Craycroft, Lanham
Cleming, see Waters
Clewerwell, see Offutt
Clifford, see Riston
Clinmerelia, see Carroll
Clouin Course, see Carroll
Clyde, see Clyde, Stoddert
Coape, see Cope
Cobreth's Lott, see Belt, Greenup,
  Hodges
Cockalds Point, see Willson
Cockshutt, see Lloyd
Coghill, see Young
Coghlan, see Marbury
Colchester, see Cramphin
Cold Cranford's Adventure, see
  Beall

Cold Spring Manor, see Collier,
  Douglass, Gerrard, Griffith,
  Willson
Cole Brigade, see Digges
Cole's Good Will, see Livers
Cole, see Henley, Miles, Neale,
  Riley
Colebrook, see Watson
Coleman, see Prather
Collard, see Livers
Collier, see Key
Collington, Manor of, see Sprigg
Collington, see Beall, Bordley,
  Clarke, Condon, Docwra,
  Hepburn, Orme, Waring
Collins' Comfort, see Collins
Colonel's Brigade, see Forbes
Colyer, see Collier
Come Unto Him, see Pile
Common Warrant, see Waters
Compass Hills, see Davis, Wight
Comptons Treatment, see Hawkins
Conclusion, The, see Lamar
Concord, see Bradford
Congrove, see Pottenger
Conn, see Burnee
Conogochique Manor, see
  Simmons
Constant Friendship, see Dawson
Constitution, The, see Beall
Containing, see Fletchall
Contee, see Brooke, Smith
Content, see Brooke, Burch,
  Marsham
Contention, see Hawkins
Cooke, see Adgate, Bradcut,
  Brooke, Candle, Coffee, Cope,
  Hollyday, Riley, Soper

Gailwiths, see Craycroft
Gale, see Clarkson, Greenfield
Gambling, see White
Gambra, see Acton
Gantry, see Hardy
Gantt, see Barton, Bradford,
    Brooke, Greenfield, Hollyday,
    Wight
Garden, see Hagan
Gardiner, see Horton, Lowe
Gardner's Meadow, see Gardiner
Garner's Meadows Resurveyed, see
    Coghill
Garner, see Edelen
Garrell, see Jearell
Gassaway, see Watkins
Gatteridge, see Floyd
Gatwood, see Walker
Gedling, see Jones, Rook
Gelhard, see Nelson
General's Gift, see Darnall
Generosity, see Beall, Bradford
Gentle, see Robinson
George Greevs Land, Little
    Addition to, see Keene
George's Delight, see Edmondson
George's Desire, see Willson
George, see Edmondson
Gerrard, see Calvert
Gibbons, see Sasser
Gibbs, see Lewin, Williams
Gibson, see Haddock
Gidland, see Parker
Gift, The, see Moore
Gilbert, see Lewin, Noble
Gilliard, see Gosling
Gilpin, see Greene

Girl's Portion, see Carroll,
    Franceway
Gisborough Manour, see Addison
Gittens, see Sprigg
Gladland, see Pindall
Gladston, see Pindall
Gleaning, The, see Addison,
    Barrett, Head, Locker, Moore,
    Odell
Gleaning"s Addition, see Odell
Gledling Point, see Greenfield
Glover's Hall, see Dyar
Glover, see Duvall
Goar, Addition to The, see
    Edmondson
Goar, The, see Edmondson
God Father's Gift, Addition to, see
    Beall
God's Gift, see Herbert, Jenkins
Goddard, see Beall
Goddart, see Middleton
Godfather's Gift, see Beall, Belt,
    Middleton
Godfrey's Chance, see Tolson
Goe, see Bateman
Goff, see Hill, Hyde
Golden Drove, see Lowe
Golden Race, see Greenfield
Golden Rod, Addition to the, see
    Bramell
Golden Rod, The, see Pile
Good Luck, Addition to, see Belt
Good Luck, see Beall, Belt,
    Boteler, Brashear, Burke,
    Clarke, Cox, Davis, Dorsett,
    Edwards, Gardiner, Gibson,
    Magruder, Selby, Sollars,
    Soper, Stone, Young

Hamilton, see Gordon, Groome,
  Lucas, Scott
Hance, see Keene
Haney, see Pile
Hanove, see Hepburn
Hanson Branch, see Berry
Hanson, see Massey
Hansontown, see Hanson
Happy Choice, Addition To, see
  Sprigg
Happy Choice, see Snowden,
  Sprigg
Haraman, see Clarke
Harben, see Harven, Jones
Harbutt, see Evans
Hardesty, see Browne
Hardin, see Henry, Williams
Hardship, see Willson
Hardy's Purchase, see Hardy
Hardy, see Dent, Lanham,
  Moore, Stimpson
Harges, see Hook
Hargrove, see Baden, Bevan
Harner's Pie Patch, see Robins
Harper, see Browne, Mulliken
Harr, see Cash, Dawson
Harrel, see Bailey
Harris, see Bowen, Butler,
  Fenley, Greenup, Lock, Offutt,
  Ransom
Harrison, see Brooke, Dorsett,
  Hederick, Henderson, Perrie,
  Wade
Harry's Lott, see Boteler
Harsin, see Williams
Hart Park, see Addison
Hartup, see Williams
Harvey, see Groome

Harvin, see Harben
Harwood, see Boyd, Ross
Haswell, see Beall, Combs
Hatchett, The, see Craycroft,
  Digges, Hutton, Nutthall,
  Skinner
Hatton, see Goe, Marbury
Hawkins Clover Bottom, see
  Hawkins
Hawkins Lott, see Hawkins
Hawkins Merry Peep A Day, see
  Hawkins
Hawkins Plains, see Hawkins
Hawkins, see Dent, Fraser,
  Gantt, Greenfield, Livers,
  Noble, Waring, White
Hawks, see Wilson
Hayharbour, see Brashear
Hay, see Hoye
Hays, see Coots, Hughes
Hayward, see Batt
Hazard, see Bell, Brooke,
  Hawkins, Hutchison, Jones,
  Miller
Head, see Bigger
Headake, see Magruder
Heard, see Marbury
Heart's Delight, see Brooke,
  Waring
Hearwe, see Groome
Hebbard, see Leiper
Hedge's Delight, see Hedges
Help, see Plummer
Henderson, see Gray, Magruder,
  Taylor, Tyler
Henniss, see Howerton
Henrietta Maria, see Darnall
Henry, The, see Radford

Hensley, The, see Burnes
Her Grove, see Bevan
Her Park. see Mitchell
Hermitage, The, see Bowie,
   Butler, Edmondson, Hepburn
Hichinson, see Louglan
Hickory Ford, see Gibbons
Hickory Hills, see Hutchison,
   Waddam
Hickory Plaines, see Gatton,
   Plummer
Hickory Thicket, see Bevan
Hicon Hills, see Willson
Hide, see Goff
Higdon, see Wynn
Higgins, see Miles, Prather,
   Simmons
Higham, see Bayne
Hill's Choice, see Holmes,
   Swearingen
Hill, see Bradley, Browne,
   Carroll, Conner, Cope, Digges,
   Peach, Wallace, Willson
Hilleary, see Keene, Magill,
   Magruder, Newton, Nutthall
Hilliard, see White
Hills Camp, see Hill
Hillyard, see Bradford
Hilton, see Cavenough, Wood
Hines, see Box
Hinson, see Batt
Hinson, see Hinston
Hirkley Thickett, see Blanford
His Lordship's Favor, see Waring
His Lordship's Kindness, see
   Charters, Hardy, Magriger,
   Morris, Perkins, Talbot
Hitchinson, see Loughlan

Hodges, see Plummer, Veitch
Hodgkin, see Brooke, Page
Hoey, see Dorsett
Hog's Harbor, see Brashear
Hogg Neck, see Ridgley
Hogg, see Clagett
Hoggins, see Stimpson
Hogpen, see Gentle, Hutchison
Hogyard, Addition to, see Waters
Hogyard, see Waters
Holdsworth, see Hepburn
Holland, see Greene, Hughes,
   Moore, Plummer, Simmons,
   Waters
Holliday's Choice, see Hollyday
Holly, see Barker
Hollyday's Choice, see Covington
Hollyday, see Bradley, Gantt,
   Greenfield, Hill, Truman,
   Waring, SkinnerP
Holmeard, see Hallam
Holmes, see Brashear, Macklean,
   Pottenger
Holsill, see Miller
Holyday's Wildgoose Meadow, see
   Hollyday
Honesty, see Magruder
Hook, see Fee, Hargest, Owen
Hooker, see Deakins
Hop Yard, see Riley, Smith
Hope's Addition, see Smith
Hope, see Oliver
Hopewell, see Norris
Hopkins, see Contee, Herbert
Hopson's Choice, see Wight
Horse Head, see Watson
Horse Pen, see Edgar

Horse Race, see Ayers, Box,
  Willett
Hoskinson, see Moore
Hour Glass, The, see Parker
Howard, see Brooke, Edelen,
  Gatton, Richardson, Sharkey
Howell, see Clarvo, Pearson
Howerchild, see Hyatt
Howerton's Range, see Tyler
Hoxter, see Brooke
Hoye, see Dorsett, Marbury
Hudson's & Birches Race, see Pile
Hudson's Range, see Conn, Queen,
  Willson
Hugh's Labor, see Brogdon
Hugoe, see Riley
Hunchett, see Hanchett
Hunde, see Phoeniz
Hungerford, see Barton
Hunter's Field, see Pile, Tolson
Hunter's Folly, see Hunter, Pile,
  Tolson
Hunter's Kindness, see Addison,
  Brouer, Elliott, Tenley
Hunter, see Dickeson
Huntersfield, see Hunter
Hunting Hill, see Lamar
Hunting Lott, see Plummer
Huntington, see Abington,
  Clagett
Huntly, see Lakey
Hurst, see Nicholls
Hutcheson, see Hutchison
Hutchinson, see Abington,
  Addison, Clagett, Hutchison,
  Pile, Parker
Hutton Lockrice, see Tolson
Hutton, see Goe

Huys, see Hays
Hyatt, see Brashear, Ratcliff
Hygam, see Bradford
Hynde, see Phoenix

Ijam's Choice, see Clarke
Inclosure, The, see Marsham,
  Mayhew, Morrison, Queen
Indian Creek with Addition, see
  Greene
Indian Creek, see Hollyday
Indian Field, The, see Bowling,
  Waring Wheeler, Wynn
Indian Gyant's Sepulche, see
  Willson
Indian Town Land, see Hutchison,
  Waters
Indose, see Henry
Industry, see Beall
Inglehearst, see Perrie
Iron Works, see Carroll
Irving, see Bayne
Isaac Park, see Isaac
Isaac's Discovery, see Isaac, Peach
Isaac, see Fowler, Jacob, Oliver,
  Peach, Pottenger, Walker
Island of Walnut Trees, see
  Bradford
Island Plains, see Willson

Jackson's Improvement, see Beall
Jackson's Necessity, Addition to,
  see Jackson
Jackson, see Beall, Bell,
  Manduit
Jacob's Addition, see Henderson
Jacob's Hope, see Ducker, Jacob

Jacob, see Bradford, Duckett,
  Jennings
Jacobs, see Duckett, Isaac,
  Taylor
Jamaica, see Waring
James & Mary, see Beall
James Crammer, see Beall
James Lott, see Williams
James, see Cotton, Soper,
  Williams
Jameson, see Queen
Jeffries, see Fletcher
Jemeco, see Waters
Jenkins, see Clarvo, Conn,
  Dickeson, Gibbs, Humphrey,
  Lanham, Scott, Thomas
Jericho, see Waters
Jerman, see German
Jessimund, see Hutchison
Jewel, see Groome
Joanes Field, see Jones
John & Ann, see Carroll
John & James Choice, see
  Dickeson, Rogers
John & Mary's Chance, see
  Hepburn
John & Priscilla, see Hawkins
John & Sarah, see Pyborn
Johnson, see Ball, Bevan,
  Bradford, Charters, Cook,
  Hays, Hyde, Lock, Locker,
  Smith, Summers
Johnston, see Ball, Greenup,
  Johnson, Lloyd, Talbot
Joice, see Mockbee
Joices Plantation, see Pile
Joint Interest, see Hutchison

Jones, see Bradford, Brashear,
  Busey, Edelen, Garrell,
  Goddart, Guttridge, Isaac,
  Johnson, Lanham, Lewin,
  Macdaniel, Mawdesly, Thorn,
  Ward, Wheeler, Robinson
Jopson, see Allingham
Jordan, see Billingsly
Joseph & Margaret's Rest, see
  Gold, Laking
Joseph & Mary, see Letchworth
Joseph & James, see Lamar
Joseph Park, see Carroll, Conn
Joseph's Lott, see Wailes
Joseph's Neglect, see Snowden
Joseph's Good Luck, see Bradford
Joseph, The, see West
Josiah Beginning, see Ballenger
Josiah, see Davis
Jowles, see Forbes
Julian, see Hedges
Juxta Stadium Aureolum, see
  Greenfield

Karter, see Shillingsworth
Kea, see Jones
Keadle, see Gibson
Kedrick, see Hederick
Keech, see Alder, Berry
Keene's Purchase, see Keene
Keene, see Clagett
Kellering, see Sprigg
Kelly, see West
Kennedy, see Betteys
Kennett, see Brightwell
Ketakin Bottoms, see Lewis
Kettering, see Pearce
Kid's Levell, see Willson

Kid, see Willson
Kilfadda, see Tradane
Killarnock, see Tannehill
King, see Culver, Hilleary,
  Keene, Summers, Withers
Kingsale, see Willson
Kingston, see Digges, Joy
Kirkwood, see Ransom
Kittocton Bottom, see Hook
Knaves Dispute, see Magruder,
  Willson
Knaves Dissappointment, see Smith
Knewstubb, see Powell
Knight, see Addison

Labyrinth, see Beall, Edmondson
Lacklin, see Prather
Ladd's Designe, see Rigdon
Ladyman, see Wailes
Lamar, see Blanford, Henderson,
  Tyler
Lamesly, see Pile
Lancaster, see Bradford
Lancaster, see Fletchall
Land Above, see Ransom
Land of Ease, see Edmondson
Land Over, see Bayne, Willson
Landsford's Guift, see Skinner
Lane, see Magruder
Lane, The, see Sprigg
Langworth, see Bowling
Lanham's Addition, see Lanham
Lanham's Delight, see Lanham,
  Magruder, Wilcoxen
Lanham's Folly, see Lanham,
  Wade

Lanham, see Blacklock, Bryan,
  Clarvo, Dickeson, Jones, Page,
  Stonestreet
Lansdale, see Hall
Largo, see Beall, Dorsett
Larkin's Desire, see Williams
Larkin's Forrest, see Ridgley
Larklin, see Prather
Lashly, see Chapman, James,
  Soper, Wood
Launge, see Pelley
Lawrence, see Levett
Lawson, see Bowie
Lawsons, see Lawson
Laxston's Delight, see Bowman
Lay Hill, see Beall
Leach, see Lanham, Pelley
Learnable Manor, see Young
Leathe, see Orme
Lee's Purchase, see Lee
Lee, see Candle, Hollyday,
  Laking, Mitchell, Riddle,
  Simms, Smith
Leeke, see Hepburn
Leitch, see Pelley
Leith, see Edmondson, Selby
Lemar, see Lamar, Young
Lenham, see Lanham
Lentall, see Riddle
LeRoy, see Cugnet
Letchworth, see Brightwell,
  Gantt, Skinner, Truman
Levell, The, see Berry, Magruder
Lewces, see Henry
Lewis, see Athey, Poore, Suratt,
  Thomas, Warner, Watkins
Lick Hill, see Willett
Liford, see Plummer

Linde, see Cussens
Lindsey, see Lowe, Tolson
Lingam's Adventure, see Boteler
Lingam, see Boteler
Lingan's Adventure, see Willson
Linten, see Riddle
Lissey, see Ball
Litchfield, see Price
Litterlona, see Carroll
Little Addition, see Craycroft,
  Digges
Little Cove, see Sprigg
Little Deans, see James
Little Dear, see Willett
Little Ease, see Edelen, Marbury
Little Grove, see Sasser
Little Troy, see Marbury
Little Worth, see Coghill, Culver,
  Dorsett, Edelen, Evans,
  Hutchison, Marbury,
  Stonestreet
Littleton, see Bird
Litton, see Sitton
Lock, see Greenup, Taylor
Locker, see Charters, Evans, Ray,
  Smith
Lockyer, see Locker, Talbot
Locust Thicket, see Addison,
  Bayne, Bowen, Bowie
Lomax, see Palmer
Londee, see Murdock
London Pleasure, see Clarvo
London, see Willson
Londonderry, see Boteler, Ranger
Lone Head, see Beall
Long Acre, see Bradford,
  Dulany, Edgar, Radford
Long Green, see Edmondson

Long Lane, see Berry, Wilcoxen
Long Look, see Sasser
Long Looked For, see Cladius,
  Smith
Long Point, see Hawkins,
  Middleton
Long, see Pelley
Lost Breaches, see Davis
Lovejoy, see Watson
Lovelace, see Loveless
Lovett, see Rawlings
Loving Acquaintance, see Beall
Low Lands, see Wells
Lowden, see Ball, Barrett
Lowe, see Addison, Bowles,
  Hagan, Soper, Stonestreet
Loweden, see Ball
Lower Growrey, see Cosden
Lucas, see Deakins, Kingsbury
Luckett, see Middleton
Ludford's Gift, see Tattershell
Lumas, see Palmer
Lumberland, see Edmondson,
  Hepburn
Lunda, see Hodges
Lundee, see Coots, Hayward
Lunder, see Fraser
Lunster, see Ford
Lyeth, see Laking
Lyles, see Belt, Marley,
  ScottSmith
Lymer, see Lee
Lyon's Hole, see Edelen, Jones
Lyon, see Whitehead
Lyonstrole, see Edelen

MacClain, see Pottenger
MacClash, see Athey

Maccolms, see Maccollum
MacFerson, see Acton,
  Macpherson
MacGill, see Pottenger
Machabee, see Williams
Machcally, see Simmons
Machelash, see Macclash
Mackall, see Brooke, Gantt,
  Hawkins
Mackdoggie, see Macdugal
Mackdougall, see Duvall,
  Macdugal
Mackee, see Summers
Mackeen, see Holmes
Mackie, see Simmons
Macklan, see Macklean
Macknew, see Kermy, Mauhane
Mackuler, see Macullough
Maclan, see Macklean
Maclenane, see Robinson
Macqueen, see Queen
Madden, see Simmons, Mading
Maddox Folly, see Addison
Maenus, see Thomas
Maggatees, see Magatee
Magonn Mansion, see Waring
Magriger, see Parris
Magruder's & Beall's Honesty, see
  Beall
Magruder's Delight, see
  Magruder
Magruder's Purchase, Addition to,
  see Magruder
Magruder's Purchase, see
  Magruder
Magruder, see Beall, Bell,
  Bowie, Clagett, Crabb, Fraser,
  Jones, Keene, Letchworth,

Offutt, Odell, Pottenger, Pratt,
  Wade, Willson, Young
Mahall, see Macknew
Maiden Bradley, see Clarvo
Maiden's Choice, see Shelby
Maiden's Dowery, see Andrew,
  Hepburn, Moriarte
Maiden's Fancy, see Waters
Mair & Colt, see Wight
Major's Chance, see Wheeler
Major's Choice, see Wheeler
Major's Lott, see Dawson, Lamar,
  Pile
Makelay, see Perrie
Manackus, see Farquar
Manaquicy, see Hedges
Manchester, see Bonefont, Tolson
Mancy, see Turner
Maney, see Turner
Manokesey, see Carmack
Mansfield, see Collins
Mansonscon, see Waring
Marberry, see Stonestreet
Marborrow Plains, see Soper
Marbury's Chance, see Marbury
Marbury, see Bayne, Dawson,
  Hatton, Marlow, Wheeler
Margery, The, see Horton, Moore,
  Stoweton
Mariartee, see Levett
Market Overton, see Adams,
  Clarvo, Edgar, Wade
Markland, see Jones
Marlboroug Plains, see Berry
Marlborough, see Clarke
Marler, see Mackune, Noland
Marloe, see Marlow
Marlow, see Dorsett

Mockbee, see Brocke, Duvall,
  Nicholls
Moddelly, see Mawdesly
Molikine, see Prather
Monduit's Beginning, see Miller
Moody, see Kedell
Moore's Chance, see Moore
Moore's Field, Addition to, see
  Bradley
Moore's Field, see Berry
Moore's Industry, see Moore
Moore's Littleworth, see Bradley,
  Clagett, Yates
Moore's Plaines, see Durham,
  Smith, Taylor
Moore's Rest, see Moore
Moore, see Egan, Gentle,
  Hoskinson, Lucas
Mordent, see Fleman
Morgan, see Chittam
Morly's Grove, see Duvall
Morly's Lot, see Duvall
Morris, see Page
Morton, see Brightwell
Mother's Gift, see Batswin,
  Macubbin
Mother's Goodwill, see Cramphin
Mountin, see Millstead
Mt. Arrat Enlarged, see Gittings
Mt. Calvert Manor, see Bradley,
  Cunningham, Davis, Orme,
  Pelley
Mt. Calvert, see Beall, Groome,
  Willson
Mt. Pleasant, see Edwards, Eyre,
  Gardiner, Marsham, Waring
Mt. Pleasuire, see White
Mudd, see Gibbs

Mulatto, see Burgess, Calvert,
  Cann, Dick, Harris, James, Jane,
  Joseph, Peck, Sapcott, Taylor,
  Tent, Thomas, Tinney, Wedges
Mullikin, see Barnard, Duvall,
  Pottenger, Waters
Murdock, see Addison,
  Marsham, Tinney
Murphey, see Tenley
Murray, see Hollyday
My Son Thomases Marsh, see
  Lamar

Naylor, see Jones, Lawson,
  Musslebrook
Neale, see Digges, Jones, Shelton
Needham, see Abington, Hughes
Neighborhood, see Beall, Odell
Nelson's Purchase, see Waddam
Nelson, see Gosling, Johnson
Nest Egg, see Brightwell
Never Fear, see Hawkins
New Castle, see Anderson
New Design, The, see Bayne,
  Queen
New Drumfires, see Beal
New Esopus, see Eltinge
New Exchange Enlarged, The, see
  Herbert
New Park, see Davis, Wigfield
New Troy, see Carroll
Newbury, see Pottenger
Newells Adventure, see Hollyday
Newfoundland, see Child, Holmes
Newland, see Haddock
Newman, see Stonestreet,
  Symmer
Newshib, see Knewstubb

Newstubb, see Knewstubb
Newton, see Burch
Newton, see Hollyday, Radford,
     Truman
Nicholas, see Brocke
Nicholls Hunting Quarter, see
     Joyce
Nicholls, see Beckett, Brooke,
     Carnes, Macklean
Nichols' Contrivance, see Nicholls
Night, see Knight
Ninian Beall Chase, see Adamson
Nixon, see Belt
Noble, see Bayne, Dorsett,
     Hawkins, Wade, Wheeler
Nonesuch, see Addison, Coffer
Normans, see James
Normansell, see Boteler
Norris, see Masters, Rabblin,
     Ray, Waters, Windam
North Britain, see Addison
Northampton, see Pearce, Sprigg
Norton, see Jones
Norway, see Belt, Danielson,
     Erickson, Magruder, Scott
Norwich, see Dorsett, Williams
Norwood, see Mansell, Mulliken
Nottingham, see Hollyday,
     Truman
Nush, see Gold
Nuthall, see Murdock, Sprigg
Nutwell's Branches, see Craycroft
Nutwell's Adventure, see
     Greenfield
Nutwell, see Duckett, Lyles,
     Prather

O'Neil's Desert, see Matthews

Oate, see Oden
Ocbrook, see Radford
Ochterloney, see Collard
Odall, see Newton, Ridgley
Odell, see Beall, Combs,
     Duckett, Hall, Haswell,
     Hilleary, Jacob, Prather,
     Ridgley
Oden, see Brightwell
Offutt's Adventure, see Odell
Offutt's Pasture, see Odell
Offutt, see Beall, Brocke,
     Burgess, Edmondson, Kendrick,
     Magruder, Smith
Ogle, see Oden
Olbias (?) Choyce, see Radford
One of Smith Folly, see Smith
Oneby, see Watts
Orchard, see Rine
Orchard, The, see Dorsett
Orford, see Waring
Orme, see Brightwell,
     Edmondson, Fowler, Groome,
     Jones, Miles, Pile, Shirly,
     Tannehill, Throne
Orphan's Gift, see Belt, Brashear,
     Child, Prather, Willson
Orvin, see Burch
Osbourn, see Moore
Ouchtclony, see Plummer
Outlett, The, see Odell
Overton, see Howerton
Owen, see Cade, Harris, Smith,
     Waring
Owings, see Crow
Oxmontown, see Goodrick
Oxon Branch, see Addison
Oxon Hill Manor, see Addison

Ozburn's Lott, see Willson

Pack's Meadow, see Selby
Page, see Hill
Paggett's Rest, see Barry
Palmer, see Franch
Palmer, see Franch
Pammer, see Jones
Paradise, see Lee
Pardon, see Tolson
Parker, see Clarke, Grear,
  Greenfield, Hutchison, Parrott,
  Pile
Parndon, see Pigman
Parpoint, see Peirpoint
Parrot's Thicket, see Hall
Parrott, see Clarke
Parsfield, see Wells
Parsons, see Pearson
Part of Dundee, see Plummer
Partee, see Jennings
Partnership, The, see Digges,
  Harrison, Jones, Penson
Partridge, see Proctor
Pascuum, see Greenfield
Pasqueum, see Wight
Pasture, The, see Addison,
  Burnham, Gamblin, Locker,
  Stoddert
Patts, see Lee
Peach, see Isaac, Waters
Peaches Addition, see Peach
Peaches Lot, see Peach
Peaches Plains, see Peach
Peacock, see Henrietta
Peake, Weathers
Pearce, see Bell, Conn, Goodrick

Pearsimmon Tree Branch, see
  Jenkins
Pearson, see Condon, Howell,
  Lewis, Price
Peckerson, see Downing
Peerce, see Jenkins
Pelley, see Lloyd, Orme
Pelt, see Rogers
Penny's Choice, see Cook, Johnson
Penson, see Wade
Pentland Hills, see Whitaker,
  Williams
Perdue, see Wheat
Perree, see Ray
Perrie's Purchase, see Barry
Perrie, see Andrew
Perry's Hills, see Plowden,
  Young
Perry, see Dawson, Forrest,
  Magruder, Thompson
Perrywood, see Barton,
  Wallingsford
Person, see Clarvo, Pearson,
  Warner
Pesquasco, see Marshall
Peter's Point, see Johnson,
  Snowden
Peter, see Scott
Petty, see Dixon
Pharix, see Phoenix
Pheasant Hills, see Greenfield
Pheasant Tree, see Greenfield
Philip and Jacob, see Addison
Phillip's Folley, see Gibbs, Lewin
Phillips, see Clarvo, Gatton,
  Jenkins
Phippard, see Browne
Pichelton's Rent, see Beall

Pye's Hard Shift, see Bowen
Pye, see Digges, Edelen

Quantico, see Brooke
Quebeck, Addition to, see Church
Queen, see Belt, Edelen, Hicks,
    Macqueen, Marsham, Pye,
    Robince, Willson
Quick Sale, see Collins,
    Magruder

Rachel's Hope, see Richardson
Radford's Chance, see Tenley,
    Tolson, Radford
Railey's Discovery, see Bowie
Rainshaw, see Renshaw
Raitt, see Duckett
Raley, see Hawkins, Riley
Ralpho, see Basill,Turner
Ramsely's Delight, see Linthorne
Ramsey, see Chittam
Rand, see Smith
Ransom, see Orme, Selby
Rantom, see Pile
Rattle Snake Denn, see Hampton
Rawlins, see Crow, Johnson,
    Levett, Riley
Ray, see Baxter, Beusey,
    Birdwhistle, Calvin, Collier,
    Harben, Locker, Perrie,
    Swearingen
Readey, see Ball
Reaves, see Burley
Recovery, The, see Beall
Red Bird Thickett, see Wheeler
Red House, see Head
Redding, see Mawdesly
Reed's Delight, see Read

Reed, see Read
Refuse, The, see Bramell
Rehoboth, see Lee
Reid, see Burch
Reiley's Neglect, see Jones
Reiley, see Cook, Riley
Remainder, The, see Pottenger
Remains, Addition to, see Lanham
Remains, see Lanham
Rencher's Adventure, see Boteler,
    Brooke, Franch, Mobberly
Renshaw, see Fletchall
Reparation, see Brooke, Cook
Reston's Addition, see Willett
Reston, see Resting
Resurvey, see Waters
Retaliation Muzoonscoon, see
    Hollyday
Retaliation, see Brightwell,
    Greenfield, Truman
Reynolds, see Cook, Haddock,
    Orme
Rhoads, see Williams
Rich Hill, see Hatton, Plummer
Rich Levell, see Brent
Richards, see Carmack, Peak
Richardson, see Beusey
Ricketts, see Macdugal
Riddle, see Read
Ridell, see Thompson
Ridgaway, see Tenley
Ridgby, see Henderson
Ridge, The, see Gladstone,
    Harris, Henderson, Magruder,
    Willson
Ridgely's Lot, see Ridgley
Ridges, see Willson

Simson, see Alder, Conner
Sinkler, see Sinclair
Siscle, see Thomas
Sissill, see Cecil
Sister's Delight, see Ball
Skinner, see Bowie,
  Dholohundee, Dick,
  Greenfield, Hollyday, Truman
Sliger Lofe, see Moore
Smallwood, see Blizard,
  Marbury, Marlow, Winn
Smallwoods Meadow, see Edelen
Smart, see Summers
Smith's Green, see Gibbons,
  Smith
Smith's Pasture, see Sasser Wall,
  Wheat
Smith, see Addison, Bradford,
  Brooke, Burgess, Edmondson,
  Erickson, Hollyday, Locker,
  Magruder, Newton, Orme,
  Perrie, Pile, Pottenger, Powell,
  Prather, Noble, Roberts,
  Selby, Simms, Stimpson,
  Turner, Waddam, Ward,
  Wells
Smithfield, see Box, Smith
Smoot, see Athey, Barton,
  Truman
Smyrna, see Uris
Snowden & Welch, see Snowden
Snowden Darling, see Snowden
Snowden, see Croley, Wright
Soe Soe, see Landsberry
Sollers, see Cecil, Selby,
  Stockett
Solomon Purchase, see Stimpson
Something, see Hawkins, Wells

Sommers, see Smith
Soper, see Duvall, James,
  Lashley, Story
Southampton, see Marshall,
  Stoddert
Spalding, see Edelen
Speedwell, see Hutchison
Spinham, see Brightwell
Spires, see Ramsey
Spradose Forrest, see Fowler,
  Spradose
Sprigg's Meadow, see Sprigg
Sprigg's Request, see Murdock,
  Nutthall, Prather
Sprigg, see Belt, Bowie, Clarke,
  Crabb, Hall, King, Levett,
  Mitchell, Pearce, Pile, Wight
Spriggen Lott, see Moore
Spring Banks, see Dawson
Spring Branch, see Willson
Spring Garden, see Abington,
  Noble
Spring Garden, The Addition to,
  see Abington
Spring, The, see Waters
Spinke, see Noble
Spy Park, see Hill
St. Andrew's, see Barnard, Berry,
  Brashear, Hallam, Wickham,
  Young
St. Anthony, see Fenwick, Neale
St. David, see Plowden
St. Dorothy, see Fenwick, Neale
St. Elizabeth, see Addison
St. James, see Blizard, Fraser
St. John's, see Athey
St. Katherines, see Marsham

St. Richard's Mannor, see
  Abington
St. Thomas, see Spalding,
  Willson
Stamp, see Fletcher
Standles Chance, see Watson
Stanton, see Henderson
Steak, see Tolson
Steal, see Harris
Stephen's Hope, see Dorsett
Stephens, see Mahall
Stepmother's Folly, see Wight
Stevens Hope, see Williams
Stevens, see Conner, Marlow,
  Webster
Stimpson, see Turner
Stock Quarter, see Sprigg
Stockett, see Noble, Sprigg,
  West
Stoddert, see Marshall,
  Middleton
Stokebardolph, see Greenfield
Stokes, see Dulany, Lawson,
  Major, Tolson, Ward
Stone Hill, see Edelen, Lewin
Stone's Delight, see Hawkins,
  Lanham
Stone, see Colbron, Gantt,
  Hawkins
Stonestreet, see Tolson,
  Wheeler
Stony Harbour, see Wade
Stony Hill, see Clarkson, Evans,
  Gibbs, Simms
Stony Plains, see Isaac
Stony Purchase, see Barrett
Stony Stratford, see Franceway

Strife, see Addison, Bowling,
  Clagett, Frederick, Greene,
  Plater, Smith, Wells
Strip, Balance, see Peach
Stubb Hill, see Collier
Stump Dale, see Lee
Stump's Valles, see Stump
Stump, see Fidley, Glover
Substraction, see Bradford
Suburbs, The, see Willson
Sugarlands, see Bradford,
  Brightwell, Noble
Sullivan, see Adkey, Parker
Summers, see Smart
Sunderses Pleasure, see Ward
Susannah's Choice, see Falconer
Sutton, see Bayne
Swan Harbour, see Addison,
  Smith
Swan's Delight, see Swan
Swann, see Browne, Foster,
  Willett
Swansey, see Howell
Swanson's Lott, see Plummer,
  Stafford, Swanstone, Ward,
  White
Swanson, see Ward
Sway & Frys Choice, see Boyd
Sway, see Fry
Swearingen's Pasture, see Davis,
  Swearingen
Swearingen, see Butt, Clary,
  Jones, Ray, Simmons
Swift, see Lawrance, Roberts
Sylvanus Grove, see Gantt
Symmer, see Simms
Symour, see Wardrop

T (plantation), see Magruder
Tabbe, see Hughes
Talbott, see Burgess, Locker,
    Soper, Wilcoxen
Taney, see Truman
Taneyhill, see Tannehill
Tann Yard, see Mackey
Tannehill, see Barrett, Beall,
    Bowen, Deakins, Henry, Orme,
    Ransom
Tannyard, see Bradford
Tarvin, see Noble
Tasker, see Addison, Brooke,
    Young
Taylertown, The, see Lloyd
Taylor's Marsh, see Busey
Taylor's Coast, see Greenfield
Taylor, see Browne, Doyne,
    Greenfield, Kelly, Norman,
    Palle, Throne, Wight
Taylorton, see Wight
Tenely Chance, see Tenley
Tennely, see Burgess
Terra, see Waring
Tewill, see Girton, O'Bryan
Thacker, see Hawlin
Thickpenny, see Strawhow
Thomas & Anthony's Choice, see
    Truman
Thomas & Mary, see Middleton,
    Willson
Thomas' Chance, see Jones,
    Edelen
Thomas' Inheritance, see Bayne
Thomas, see Barnes, Dawson,
    Jones, Snowden, Tenley,
    Watson

Thomases Chance, see Hawkins,
    Marbury
Thompson's Choice, see Berry
Thompson's Lot, see Belt
Thompson's Rest, see Hatton
Thompson, see Belt, Elliott,
    Greene, Henderson, Shaw
Thomson, see Chittam, Simms
Thorne, see Graves
Thorpland, see Brashear, Hodges,
    Keech, Plowden, Young
Three Beall's Manor, see Davis,
    Rogers
Three Brothers, see Hardy,
    Magruder, Wilcoxen
Three Friend's Delight, see Beall
Three Islands United, see Radford
Three Pastures, see Sprigg
Three Sisters, The, see Hilleary,
    Neale, Williams
Threlkield, see Orme
Throne, see Needam, Taylor
Thropland, see Smith
Tilley, see Bateman, Prichard
Timber Neck, see Taney
Timberland, see Blanford
Timberly, see Blanford, Darnall,
    Ridgley, Scott
Timothy & Sarah, see Marlow
Tippin, see Hall
Token of Love, see Ball
Tolberts Lott, see Wilcoxen
Tolberts Rest, see Wilcoxen
Tolburt, see Lanham
Tolson's Delight, see Tolson
Tolson's Purchase, see Tolson
Tolson, see Stonestreet
Tomlin, see Burke

Too Good, see Bigger
Torquison, see Williams
Tossiter, see Wailes
Towgood, see Bayne
Towgood, see Prather, Selby
Towloon, see Busey
Town Quarter, see Carroll
Townley, see Smith
Townsend, see Pile
Travis, see Mills
Tray, see Stonestreet
Trenant, see Mills, Watson
Trent Neck, see Greenfield
Trequair, see Cash
Troubles, see Holmes
Troublesome, see Marsham
True Man's Acquaintance, see
 Hollyday
Truitt, see Duvall
Truman's Choice, Remainder of,
 see Davis
Truman's Hills, see Greenfield,
 Truman, Waring
Truman's Place, see Craycroft
Truman's Acquaintance, see
 Greenfield, Truman
Truman, see Culver, Greene,
 Letchworth, Stoddert, Taney
Trumans Chance, see Truman
Trumans Choyce Deminished, see
 Truman
Trumans Hope, see Truman
Trumans Lott, see Truman
Trundle Bed Cuckold, see
 Marsham
Trundlebed Cuckold, see Osborn
Trunker, see Clarke
Tubman, see Magruder

Tucker's Cultivation, see Tucker
Tucker, see Bromfield, Duncan,
 Mason, Selby
Tunnihill, see Tannehill
Turkey Cock Branch, see
 Magruder
Turkey Cock, see Magruder
Turkey Flight Enlarged, see Elson
Turkey Flight, see Prather
Turkey Thickett, see Beall,
 Magruder, Ray
Turnely, see Thomas
Turner, see Athey, Goe,
 Mulliken, Prather, Webster
Turrell Green, see Loveless
Tweksbury, see Marbury
Twifoott, see Bowen
Twiner, see Dorsett
Twiver, see Mackey, Willson
Two Brothers, see Crabb, Kelly,
 Lamar, West
Two Friends, see Letchworth
Two Johns, see Edelen, Lanham
Twyford, see Hooker, Selby
Tyler's Chance, see Tyler
Tyler's Pasture, see Beck
Tyler's Range, see Tyler
Tyler, see Baldwin, Batt, Beck,
 Bradley, Bradford, Duvall,
 Edgar, Henderson, Hilton,
 Jacob, Parker, Pottenger,
 Wickham

Underdown, see Bowles
Underwood, see Lewis
Underwood, see Queen
Union, The, see Addison
Upper Getting, see Plummer

Upper Marlborough, see Hepburn
Usher, see Bladen

Vale of Benjamin, see Duvall,
   James, Magruder
Valentine Garden, see Waddam
Valentine's Garden, see Crabb
Veatch, see Weaver
Veitch, see Conn
Venman, see Brashear
Venson, see Pearson
Venture, The, see Magruder
Vernon, see Palmer
Vigo, see Tolson
Vilandiham, see Nilandiham
Vineyard, Addition to, see
   Abington
Vineyard, The, see Abington,
   Brooke, Hutchison
Vinicum, see Palle
Virgin, see Dickeson

Wade's Adventure, see Fraser,
   Stonestreet
Wade, see Brooke, Edgar, Hardy,
   Magruder, Pottenger, Sprigg,
   Stone, Tyler
Wadhams, see Johnson
Wagner, see Wade
Waldridge, see Ridgley
Walker's Pasture, see Anderson
Walker, see Ball, Beck, Boyd,
   Brashear, Greene, Lowden,
   Rought
Wall, see Hall, Wheat
Wallace, see Downing, Herbert
Walley, see Boyd

Wallis, see Duckett, Hill,
   Williams, Wallace
Walmsley, see King
Walnut Tree Island, see Vernoy
Walnutt Thickett, see Marsham
Walsh, see Gray
Want Water, see Batt, Hutchison
Warbarton Manor, see Barber,
   Digges, Gardiner
Ward's Pasture, see Busby,
   Greenfield
Ward's Wheel, see Benson
Ward, see Marlow, Parr, Prather,
   Ray, Wells
Wardrop, see Lee, Thompson
Warfield, see Magruder
Waring's Lot, see Waring
Waring, see Andrew, Barton,
   Belt, Brooke, Digges, Gantt,
   Greenfield, Haddock,
   Hollyday, Marsham, Offutt
Warington Park, see Waring
Warington, see Waring
Warinton, see Contee
Warminster, see Browne,
   Billinger, Davis
Warner, see Condal, Pearson,
   Ray
Warwick, see Jervis
Was There Nothing, see Beall
Water's Lot, see Waters
Water's Purchase, see Waters
Waters' Loss, see Waters
Watkins, see Belt, Boyd,
   Harwood, Lewis
Watson's Forest, see Watson
Watson's Luck, see Watson
Watson, see Perrie

Wickham, see Barnard, Barnett,
Henderson
Widow's Mite, see Fletchall,
Langworth
Widow's Purchase, see Belt,
Bowman, Jacob
Widow's Troubles, see Blanford,
Brooke, Stevens
Wiggfield, see Barrow
Wight, see Belt, Greenfield,
Gantt, White
Wights Forrest, see Wight
Wilcoxon, see Hardy, Jennings,
Jarvis
Wildman, see Johnson
Wilkinson, see Beall
Will's Good Will, see Bradford
Willard's Purchase, see Stanley
Willery, see Johnson
Willet, see Chamberlain, Pile
Willett's Enlargement, see
Middleton
William & Ann, see Conn, Head,
Wolford
William & Elizabeth, see Couzen,
Shaw, Sinclair
William & James, see Offutt
William & Mary Increased, The,
see Haswell, Scott
William & Mary, see Holmes
William Range, see Williams
Williams, see Boyd, Demall,
Duckett, Edmondson, Evans,
Farguson, Gibbs, Haswell,
Hilleary, Johnson, Keene,
Lamar, Magruder, Mulliken,
Plummer, Pratt, Rhodes,

Sprigg, Tenley, Thompson,
Waters
Willson, see Boteler, Evans,
Farquar, Harris, Hepburn,
Hill, Lingan, Masters,
Mulliken, Plummer, White
Wilsford, see Rigby
Wilson's Addition, see Willson
Wilson's Enlargement, see
Willson
Wilson's Plaine, see Duvall
Wilson's Venture, see Willson
Wilson, see Magruder, Willson
Windsor, see Adkey
Winser, see Dorsett, Miles
Winson, see Kelly
Winter Imployment, see Millstead
Witchaven, see Dent
Witham, see Hall
Withers, see Young
Wolfe's Harbour, Addition of, see
Holmes
Wolfe's Harbour, see Holmes
Wolves Den, see Truman
Wood Brig, see Naylor
Wood Come, see Watson
Wood, see Beall, Camden, Smith,
Withers
Woodbridge, see Culver, Finch,
Ward
Woodburn, see Watson
Woodfield, see Rook
Woods Joy, see Mirth, Mulliken,
Taney
Woods, see White
Wooton, see Sprigg
Wornall, see Tenley
Wright, see Dorsett, Gantt

Other books by Elise Greenup Jourdan:

1840 to 1850 Federal Census: Tazewell County, Virginia
Francis W. McIntosh and Elise Greenup Jourdan

1860 Federal Census: Tazewell County, Virginia
Francis W. McIntosh and Elise Greenup Jourdan

1870 Federal Census: Tazewell County, Virginia
Francis W. McIntosh and Elise Greenup Jourdan

Abstracts of Charles County, Maryland Court and Land Records
Volume 1: 1658-1666
Volume 2: 1665-1695
Volume 3: 1694-1722

Colonial Records of Southern Maryland: Trinity Parish and Court Records,
Charles County; Christ Church Parish and Marriage Records, Calvert County;
St. Andrew's and All Faith's Parishes, St. Mary's County

Colonial Settlers of Prince George's County, Maryland

Early Families of Southern Maryland: Volume 1 (Revised)

Early Families of Southern Maryland: Volumes 2-10

The Land Records of Prince George's County, Maryland, 1702-1709

The Land Records of Prince George's County, Maryland, 1710-1717

The Land Records of Prince George's County, Maryland, 1717-1726

The Land Records of Prince George's County, Maryland, 1726-1733

The Land Records of Prince George's County, Maryland, 1733-1739

The Land Records of Prince George's County, Maryland, 1739-1743